THE OXFORD GUIDE TO
CONTEMPORARY WORLD LITERATURE

John Sturrock is Consulting Editor of the *London
Review of Books*, and former Deputy Editor of the
Times Literary Supplement.

THE OXFORD GUIDE TO
CONTEMPORARY
WORLD LITERATURE

EDITED BY

JOHN STURROCK

Oxford   New York
OXFORD UNIVERSITY PRESS
1997

Oxford University Press, Great Clarendon Street, Oxford OX2 6DP

Oxford New York

Athens Auckland Bangkok Bombay
Calcutta Cape Town Dar es Salaam Delhi
Florence Hong Kong Istanbul Karachi
Kuala Lumpur Madras Madrid Melbourne
Mexico City Nairobi Paris Singapore
Taipei Tokyo Toronto Warsaw

and associated companies in
Berlin Ibadan

Oxford is a trade mark of Oxford University Press

First published 1996 as The Oxford Guide to Contemporary Writing
First issued in paperback as The Oxford Guide to Contemporary World Literature 1997

British Library Cataloguing in Publication Data
Data available

Library of Congress Cataloging in Publication Data
The Oxford guide to contemporary world literature / edited by John Sturrock.
Includes bibliographical references and index.
1. Literature, Modern—20th century—History and criticism.
I. Sturrock, John.
PN771.097 1996 809'.04—dc20 95-36177
ISBN 0-19-283318-9

1 3 5 7 9 10 8 6 4 2

Typeset by Graphicraft Typesetters Ltd, Hong Kong
Printed in Great Britain
Bookcraft Ltd
Midsomer Norton, North Somerset

Contents

Editor's Introduction

WHAT have writers been up to in France in recent years? Or in Israel? Or in Australia? Or, for that matter, in England? These are questions it would be good to have compact, authoritative answers to, if only we knew of somewhere to look for them. Surveys of contemporary writing are a need thinly provided for, however; they come either singly or not at all, and cover at most just one country or one language. This new *Oxford Guide to Contemporary World Literature* does a great deal better than that. It contains twenty-eight chapters and covers the recent literature of significantly more than that number of individual countries. To my knowledge, nothing else of the sort attempts the width and expertise of coverage we have aimed for here.

'Contemporary' and 'literature' are both terms that need to be made more precise. In the context of this *Guide*, 'contemporary' means since about 1960, so that a majority of the writers whose work is discussed will be still alive, and still producing. Each chapter is intended to describe what has been happening in this literature or that over the past thirty-five years. But there can be no rigid starting-date for surveys of this sort; there are a number of chapters in which what had been happening before 1960 is sufficiently important for its future effects to require description, not least in those countries whose recent political history has had profound consequences for their cultural life.

And then 'literature', a term whose meaning has been valuably extended, since the once fiercely patrolled boundary between so-called 'creative' writing and other kinds of writing was opened up. We can now recognize that there is more to literature than simply poetry and fiction, and the contributors to this *Guide* were invited to look beyond those privileged genres when deciding what to include, to take in writing for the theatre, say, or autobiography, or essays, or criticism, where it seemed of a high enough quality locally to merit attention. In the main, however, it is novelists and poets who dominate these pages.

The idea of each chapter is that it should be succinct but thorough, naming the names that were thought most important and picking out the stylistic and ideological trends that have marked the literature in question over the past three decades. The *Guide* has been written by those well placed professionally not simply to describe the literature, but also to evaluate it: the contributors were encouraged to air their opinions about what they thought was especially good or, on occasion, bad in it. If some contributions are adjudged to be opinionated, so be it; I take that to be a virtue when so many attempts at an encyclopaedic coverage of this kind are too bland. This volume is intended to be helpful, but not definitive: the judgements that it contains may invite disagreement; they are offered in a spirit of incitement, not coercion. It is intended in short as a *guide*, so that whoever uses it will end up knowing which previously unknown or obscure authors are worth tracking down, or which whole literatures might repay a closer look. This volume is not designed to be an end in itself.

The *Guide* does not cover all the literatures there are in the world. That would have required more volumes than one, and would have been a quite unmanageable enterprise. It covers the literatures that seemed most likely to be of interest or concern to English-language readers in the 1990s. Its organization by countries, and by language, is not meant to play down the very obvious internationalism of writing today, compared with the past, and the new permeability of cultural frontiers. It might have been tempting to rely on more avant-garde forms of organization, so as to take account of this seeming loss of national and linguistic rootedness. But readers, in my experience, are far more traditionally minded than writers, and the familiar arrangement of the contents that we have settled on will be, I am confident, the most practical for whoever wants to consult the *Guide*. Similarly, its coverage is as wide as it practicably could have been. To those who complain that it is not wide enough, I can only say that to complain of what is missing when so much is present is to look at things from the wrong end.

The *Guide* has been kept clear of apparatus: there are no footnotes or long bibliographies. The chapters simply end with a short Further Reading list, citing a small number of books recommended by the particular author.

NOTE ON TITLES

Books written in languages other than English are referred to under the title of their published English translation; where they have not been translated, the original title is given, followed by a literal translation in parentheses.

List of Contributors

RICHARD ACZEL is a critic and translator currently teaching at the University of Cologne.

ALISON BAILEY has lived and worked in Beijing and now teaches Chinese literature at the School of Oriental and African Studies in London.

KASIA BODDY is a Lecturer in English at University College London.

BRYAN CHEYETTE is a Lecturer in English at Queen Mary and Westfield College in London and the author of *Constructions of 'the Jew' in English Literature and Society*.

PATRICIA CRAIG is a critic and anthologist, and a regular contributor to the *Times Literary Supplement*.

PETER CRAVEN is a critic living in Melbourne. He co-founded the literary periodical *Scripsi*.

AL CREIGHTON teaches at the University of Guyana in Georgetown.

RICHARD CRONIN teaches at the University of Glasgow. He is the author of *Shelley's Poetic Thoughts: Colour and Experience in Nineteenth-Century Poetry* and *Imagining India*.

SANDRA DJWA teaches Canadian Literature at Simon Fraser University in British Columbia.

JANET GARTON is Senior Lecturer in Scandinavian Studies at the University of East Anglia, and the author, among other books, of *Norwegian Women Writers 1850–1990*.

JOHN GLEDSON was formerly Professor of Brazilian Studies at the University of Liverpool. His books include *The Deceptive Realism of Machado de Assis* and *Poesía y poética de Carlos Drummond de Andrade*.

MARIA GUTERRES is a Lecturer in Portuguese at the University of Liverpool.

PETER HAINSWORTH is University Lecturer in Italian at Oxford, and a Fellow of Lady Margaret Hall. With Michael Caesar, he edited *Writers and Society in Contemporary Italy*.

IGOR HÁJEK came to Britain from Prague in 1968 and subsequently taught at the Universities of Lancaster and Glasgow. Sadly, he died while this volume was in press.

JEREMY HARDING has worked in Africa as a journalist and film researcher since 1980. His book on the continent's national liberation struggles, *Small Wars, Small Mercies*, was published in 1993.

GEORGE HYDE taught for four years in Poland. He is Senior Lecturer in English and Comparative Literature at the University of East Anglia, and the author of books on Nabokov and D. H. Lawrence.

ROBERT IRWIN formerly taught Medieval History at the University of St Andrews. He is the author of four novels and of *The Arabian Nights: A Companion*.

WENDY LESSER edits the *Threepenny Review* in San Francisco and is the author of *Pictures at an Execution: An Inquiry into the Subject of Murder*.

PETER MACKRIDGE is University Lecturer in Modern Greek at Oxford, and author of *The Modern Greek Language*.

MARK MORRIS teaches Japanese Literature at the University of Cambridge, and is a Fellow of Trinity College.

ROBERT PORTER is Reader in Russian Studies at the University of Bristol. He is the author of *Russia's Alternative Prose*, and the translator of Yevgeny Popov's novel *The Soul of a Patriot*.

WIESŁAW POWAGA is a freelance translator from Polish living in London.

IAIN SHARP is a journalist working in New Zealand. He has published two volumes of poetry: *The Pierrot Variations* and *She is Trying to Kidnap the Blind Person*.

ABIGAIL LEE SIX is a Lecturer in Hispanic Studies at Queen Mary and Westfield College in London, and the author of *Juan Goytisolo: The Case for Chaos*.

JOHN TAYLOR writes about contemporary French literature for *France Magazine* and the *Times Literary Supplement*. He is the author of a book of stories, *The Presence of Things Past*.

NED THOMAS is Director of the University of Wales Press, and the author of a book, in English, on *The Welsh Extremist: A Culture in Crisis*, and a study, in Welsh, of the poet Waldo Williams.

RHYS WILLIAMS is Professor of German at University College, Swansea.

JAMES WOOD was formerly chief literary critic of the *Guardian* in London and is currently on the staff of the *New Republic* in Washington.

MICHAEL WOOD is a professor in the English Department at Princeton University, and the author of *America at the Movies* and *The Magician's Doubts: Nabokov and the Risks of Fiction*.

1

AFRICAN COUNTRIES

JEREMY HARDING

INTRODUCING a collection of African oral literature in 1988, the Nigerian polemicist and poet Chinweizu warned against any approach to the subject that reinforces 'an Africa which European racism is flattered to imagine'. Instead, he suggests that 'we [Africans] should listen to Africans talking to Africans about the world'. Writers like Chinweizu are concerned that the encounter between Africa and Europe is neither innocent nor symmetrical: slavery and the colonial past tilt this uneasy exchange in favour of non-Africans. As outsiders, Europeans face a central problem when considering contemporary African writing: to think of it *sui generis* is to condescend to it; to compare it with other traditions—English, American, Indian, or French—is to disregard its specificity.

This dilemma coincides with an interlocking set of dichotomies for the writers themselves: between home and exile, tradition ('African') and modernity ('foreign'); between the use of African languages and European ones; between speech and writing; between the idea of origin and the fact (intellectual and historical as much as physical) of discontinuity; between the virtues of political engagement and the fruitful habits of despair.

Many of these tensions are the products of a past and present of extreme adversity. The colonial episode in African history was one of extraordinary disruption and, though it is over, it remains, in the words of the Zaïrean poet and scholar Vumbi Yoka Mudimbe, 'charged and controversial' for most African writers. As for the present, there is no continent in more obvious disarray and none that is poorer. The politicization of writing that was so obvious in apartheid South Africa is common, though often in more complex ways, to the rest of the continent.

Throughout Africa, authors and journalists have paid for their views with their careers, or with exile, with detention, and, in certain cases like that of the Nigerian journalist Dele Giwa, with their lives (he was killed in 1986). The highly politicized environment in which most writers work is reflected in the texts themselves, and in the terms in which literary debate is conducted. African writers may have much in common, but their range of styles and preoccupations is so diverse that the very idea of 'African literature' (or 'literatures') is better approached as a topographical rather than a purely literary classification.

If this sounds too cautionary a note, it is as well to recall the admonitory strain in African writing itself, most evident among the 'market pamphleteers' of Onitsha in Nigeria in the 1950s and early 1960s, whose titles signal the many pitfalls of life: for example, *Trust nobody in time because human being is trickish. Human being is deep, difficult to know and full of disappointments* by 'The Strong Man of the Pen', Olisa 'Sunday' Okenwa. Such homiletic modes may be seen as a reflection of the fact that the moral fable is still a powerful form in many African societies. The introduction of the book in almost all African cultures is associated with religion—in sub-Saharan Africa, more strongly with Christianity than with Islam. In anglophone African countries the Bible and, from the 1820s, John Bunyan were disseminated in English and local languages by the missionary arm of British imperialism. The book is thus a relatively recent phenomenon in most of Africa; it would be odd if it did not still carry a trace of instructive piety.

'Go home this weekend', says Maudé, a literature teacher, to his class of recalcitrant fifth-formers in a novel by 'Biyi Bandele-Thomas (b. 1967), 'and read Soyinka's *Madmen and Specialists* . . . and come back on Monday with a five-hundred word essay on the play.' In setting this homework, Maudé has been too ambitious. Lakemfa, the schoolboy narrator in *The Man Who Came in from the Back of Beyond* (1991), is cowed by the prospect of writing an essay on Wole Soyinka; and his anxiety is shared. His class complains to the principal that Maudé has been 'giving us assignments from books above our level'. Throughout the novel, Bandele-Thomas refers in this way to other Nigerian writers, often in deference, and on the whole unambiguously. Among younger authors like Bandele-Thomas, the sense of tradition, ancestry even, is strong, especially in Nigeria, which saw a flowering of literature on the eve of independence in 1960 and the emergence of two of the continent's most celebrated writers, Wole Soyinka (b. 1934) and Chinua Achebe (b. 1930), who have dominated the Nigerian literary scene for thirty years or more.

Though a number of earlier African writers had published in colonial languages, Achebe and, to a lesser extent, Soyinka are generally regarded as crucial figures in the 'first wave' of the phenomenon known as 'African literature'. In West Africa, this in fact consisted of a heterogeneous group of writers, including Achebe, the popular novelist Cyprian Ekwensi (b. 1921), and the extraordinary Yoruba visionary Amos Tutuola, and lasted until the early 1960s. It was thought of, not always accurately, as anti-colonialist. The second wave consisted of writers who wanted to come to terms with the shortcomings of the post-colonial élites. The identity of the third wave—to which Bandele-Thomas would belong—is less clear-cut, although the younger writers have tried to reach a wider African audience than that of their predecessors, and the characters in their fiction are often less transparent to political and social issues.

The most obvious misfit in this genealogy is Amos Tutuola (b. 1922), one of the first modern African writers, whose most famous book, *The Palm-Wine Drinkard* (1952), tells the story of an 'expert' drinker's visionary journey—and something of a 'Pilgrim's Progress'—to Dead's Town, a world populated by spirits, demons, and protean creatures whose attentions, often hostile, he must try to withstand. Achebe, meanwhile, crossed from the first wave into the second with *A Man of the People* (1966), the last in a linked sequence of four novels. Soyinka is properly a second-wave writer whose most creative period began in the mid-1960s with *The Interpreters* (1965), a novel which charts the disaffection of the young post-colonial intelligentsia in Lagos. It is the extent of his recognition at home and abroad, including a Nobel Prize for literature in 1986, that has endowed him, retrospectively, with the status of a progenitor.

Had he written it, Lakemfa's essay on Soyinka's play *Madmen and Specialists* (1970) would have had to say something general about the force of the spoken, as opposed to the written, word in almost all African cultures; it might then have gone on to argue that drama is an ideal medium for the African writer. Lakemfa could have supported this view with reference to the Kenyan writer Ngugi wa Thiong'o (b. 1938), whose thoroughly politicized dramas, performed and composed in his native language, Gikuyu, landed him in gaol in the late 1970s. The essay would have had to remark the use of choric devices in Soyinka and could reasonably have suggested that his 'roots' in Yoruba tradition predisposed him to this kind of approach.

All of which, Lakemfa's teacher might have replied, was commendable, but dangerously close to a type-casting of African culture. Colonialism may have left modern African writing in the uncomfortable—yet enviable—position of having to devise, rather than constantly reinvent, a history for itself, but it is debatable how far drama—a spoken form—is affected by such a project. *Madmen and Specialists* is in fact a cosmopolitan work, indebted to the European absurdist tradition, and Soyinka is, above all, an eclectic writer—some of the language in the play strongly resembles the 'tirade' by Lucky in Act I of *Waiting for Godot*: Soyinka was briefly associated with the Royal Court Theatre in London, and produced a version of *The Bacchae* (1973) in which Dionysus is replaced by the Yoruba deity Ogun.

The importance of oral tradition is not at issue in a continent where the majority of people cannot read or write, and where the greatest narratives, epics, and, arguably, lyric verses have been transmitted in performance, by non-literate practitioners for the most part. But the relation of these facts to the growing body of post-colonial writing is unclear. Almost all writers of interest in Africa have incorporated elements of oral tradition into their work, often on grounds that this is a moral and aesthetic necessity. Some writers, like Chinweizu, have reacted against the dismissive colonial attitude to oral composition by endowing oral culture with a transcendent status; writing, by inference, is a pale, mimetic practice, too often haunted by old servitudes—in this case, to the values of an alien (colonial) culture. To some exponents of oral tradition, the very idea of the book is a travesty. In 1960 the Malian novelist D. T. Niane produced a textual version of an epic song about the fourteenth-century West African hero Sonjara. Niane's source—a *griot*, or traditional story-teller, by the name of Mamoudou Kouyaté—broke off from his recitation to denounce the practice of writing:

Other peoples use writing to record the past, but this invention has killed the faculty of memory among them. They do not feel the past any more, for writing lacks the warmth of the human voice. With them, everybody thinks he knows, whereas learning should be a secret. The prophets did not write and their words have been all the more vivid as a result. What paltry learning is that which is congealed in dumb books!

I, Djeli Mamoudou Kouyaté, am the result of a long tradition. For generations, we have passed on the history of kings from father to son. The narrative was passed on to me without alteration and I deliver it without alteration, for I received it free from all untruth.

The idea that 'authenticity' obtains in speech as opposed to writing, in the past as opposed to the present, is troubling for African writers. Kouyaté, whose profession has its own coveted skills, sees the democratic potential of the written word in literate societies as an absurdity, however: knowledge is a concentration of power, to be jealously guarded, and it is unitary. The African writers who emerged in the post-colonial era were serving a more complex apprenticeship—with more than one master.

There were none the less ways to resolve this dilemma. In *The Breast of the Earth* (1975), Kofi Awoonor (originally George Awoonor-Williams, b. Ghana, 1935) argued for the central place of 'oral literature' in several cultures, including those of the Zulu, Yoruba (Nigeria), Akan (Ghana), and the Ewe (Ghana and western Togo), to which he himself belonged. Awoonor had already written a novel (*This Earth, my Brother . . .*, 1971) about the pains of exile, and his reputation as a poet, editor, and anthologist was well established when he published *The Breast of the Earth*. In a sense, however, he invented himself with this book, at the same time clearing the ground for other writers who were weighing the possibility of an African literary genealogy against the literary models they inherited from colonialism.

Awoonor's poetry in the 1960s and early 1970s—*Rediscovery and Other Poems* (1964) and *Night of my Blood* (1971)—had an ease of diction that suggested everyday speech. At the same time, he was a modernist, in precisely the European sense—a condition he shared with other writers of his generation, including Achebe, Soyinka, Ngugi, and a number of authors who had clustered around the two landmark journals of the late 1950s and 1960s: *Black Orpheus* (1957–76), edited in Nigeria, and *Transition* (1961–75), which was edited in Uganda.

By the mid-1970s most of these anglophone writers were no longer concerned with the literary (and ideological) quarrels that attended the francophone *négritude* movement pioneered in the 1930s by Léopold Senghor and Aimé Césaire, and nurtured in Paris after the war, with the support of Jean-Paul Sartre. Negritude, which proposed that there were intrinsic virtues in Africanness, and above all in blackness, was on the whole inimical to the anglophone writers. 'A tiger', said Soyinka, 'does not proclaim his tigritude.' Nevertheless, the idea of *recovery* implicit in negritude, of a vigorous, lyrical African culture, suppressed or subdued by colonialism, remained powerfully present to them. The appeal of Awoonor's book lay in its unsentimental emphasis on oral tradition as a corpus of African 'literature' in its own right. 'Orality' was a store of energy that would inform and invigorate contemporary writing. Awoonor urged a 'return to the traditional sources for inspiration'; the results must be 'forged into the contemporary idioms of our times, enriched by our contact with Europe and Islam'. But he opposed the 'dangerous myth' of 'cultural purity' which he saw in negritude: 'Africa has suffered too long from European ethnocentrism to turn around to proclaim her own brand.'

Awoonor's call to the past lent authority to a trend among anglophone writers who had, in some cases, been inhibited by contingent anxieties about negritude. In Nigeria, Soyinka was already drawing on Yoruba materials; in Uganda, the poet Okot p'Bitek (1931–82) had produced a long poem in his native language, Acoli, which he went on to translate into English and published as *Song of Lawino* in 1966. Ngugi, who had achieved international recognition with three novels in English, had begun to argue the merits of writing in his native Gikuyu. *Petals of Blood* (1977), six years in the making, would be the last novel he composed in English before his detention in 1977.

In South Africa, or rather from exile in various countries—he was an active member of the banned African National Congress—Mazisi Kunene (b. 1930) was working on an epic poem in praise of Shaka, the Zulu imperialist of the early nineteenth century (*Emperor Shaka the Great: A Zulu Epic*, the English version he translated from his own Zulu original, appeared in 1979). During the early 1970s, Awoonor had put his own injunctions in *The Breast of the Earth* to advantageous use, and was followed a few years later by a younger poet, Kofi Anyidoho (b. 1947), also an Ewe speaker.

Guardians of the Sacred Word (1974) is a set of translations from the songs of three Ewe composers, including the dirge poet Vinoko Akpalu (d. 1974), with whom Awoonor spent a period of informal fieldwork in 1970. The results, in translation, are extraordinarily successful. Furthermore, a curious process occurred when Awoonor went out into the field to collect the compositions of his elders: 'There was a void within me that I knew must be filled. I was not a researcher, but a son come home.'

The songs, and Awoonor's gloss, provided salutary evidence that 'African culture' was not necessarily a formulaic, sing-along affair that abolished the distinction between composer, performer, and audience—a familiar prejudice in wealthier countries about art-forms in poorer ones. A versatile composer whose work was haunted by the death of his only child, and by his subsequent lack of progeny, Akpalu had conspired with the community in which he lived to construct himself as the *poète maudit*, god-forsaken and estranged, especially from his relatives, whom he suspected of conniving (probably through sorcery) in his boy's death:

> They put an evil firewood in my hearth
> So I am all alone
> No child to carry my sleeping mat
> And yet they say I must be mute.
> I must not say it. I must not proclaim it.
> Vinoko says he is lost in thought
> So all his songs are lamentations.
> It is my own mother's children who placed an evil wood in my fireplace.

Translations like these tell us that the search for origins can constitute a fair exchange between descendants and predecessors, in which the first undertake to carry the name of the second to a wider world, ostensibly for the good of both. But, because the ancestor must be represented in such a way as to make him intelligible, a measure of invention is required of the successors. In the case of the Ewe composers, the process is also one of condensation and metonymy: words alone are taken to stand for the entirety of a performance that consists of song, percussion, and gesture—a problem common to most renderings of 'oral literature', or 'orature', as it is also known.

Yet, in the act of diminishing the original, the translations also enhance it, by giving it the mobility of the written word. Through this paradoxical motion, the modern African writer who returns to 'traditional sources' can begin to reproduce himself, and devise his 'heritage', carrying both beyond the parochial realm on which he draws for inspiration. The oral and the written are inextricably linked in the emergence of contemporary African literature.

The most persuasive written poetry from late and post-colonial Africa has tended to come from Romance languages: French to a great extent, but also Portuguese (Angola, Mozambique). The father of negritude, Léopold Senghor, is one of Africa's most prolific and renowned poets. But there are many other francophone and lusophone poets of distinction, of whom their English-speaking counterparts have been aware: Birago Diop (b. 1906), David Diop (France, 1927–60), Bernard Dadié (Ivory Coast, b. 1916), Tchicaya U Tam'Si (Congo, b. 1931), Agostinho Neto (Angola, 1922–79), José Craveirinha (Mozambique, b. 1922), and Noémia de Sousa (Mozambique, b. 1927).

In *Myth, Literature and the African World* (1976), Soyinka writes of the 'visionary reconstruction of the past for the purposes of social direction'— a project that he recognized was not particular to Africa—and confirms that his own interest lay less with the practical uses of oral tradition than in an overarching commitment to the richness and complexity of this 'African world', which had little in the way of non-colonial historiography or mythography. Soyinka proposed to retrieve an African—by which he meant mostly Yoruba—world-view from the shadow of the literate, monotheist cultures that had prevailed at its expense.

In a general way, his poetry reflects this concern, but at the level of the line it is remarkable, like that of his contemporaries Christopher Okigbo (1932–67), Gabriel Okara (b. 1921), and John Pepper Clark (b. 1935), for its mannerism. Soyinka's use of metaphor is elaborate and his use of symbols reminiscent of Yeats, another lover of mythopoeia and revivalism.

At its least successful, Soyinka's poetry can be obscure—according to the Chinweizu school of African fundamentalist criticism, he, Clark, and the 'early' Okigbo are paddling in an 'obscurantist cesspool' of 'euromodernism'. At its best, it is a condensed, or coded, version of the anger that has made

Soyinka one of the most courageous writers on the continent. 'Relief'
denounces the wedding ceremony of the then Nigerian leader, General
Gowon, which required the diversion of a relief flight to cater for the
celebrations:

> Empty that plane
> Of bread, damn bread! Turn its nose
> To a different wind, to a perfumed wind
> Fill the hold with cake and wine
> And champagne guests—It's time
> For MY wedding . . .
>   ('A Shuttle in the Crypt')

Awoonor, Okot p'Bitek, and Mazisi Kunene have a more specific, instrumental sense of oral tradition than Soyinka, and are easier to read in consequence. 'I have learned how greatly valued are the oral traditions of
telling the story, dramatizing the story and of making it socially relevant,'
Kunene writes in the preface to *Shaka*. His use of oral tradition in the poem
is scrupulously political: Shaka (c.1795–1828) is celebrated as an African
success; his will-to-power and military skill enable him first to subjugate,
and then to recast the identity of, his subject peoples in the form of the
Zulu 'nation'. The poem is a lengthy incantation, summoning up the prowess of pre-colonial Africa. Section by section, oral tradition invests the poet
and reacquaints the reader with the particular skills of naming, telling, and
commemorating—all of which makes *Shaka* one of the most important
contemporary African poems in English.

Yet its subject-matter and idiom are neither contemporary nor obviously
English. It was first composed in Zulu, by the poet himself, who drew on
a tradition of 'songs of excellence', praise poems, and martial narratives that
pre-dates even the compositions of Shaka's own court poet. Shaka's entry
into the arena of the loyal prince Zihlandlo, in book 13, is typical:

> The bodies of children glistened in the sun with beads
> How beautiful were the women of the Mhkize clan!
> How handsome the tall young men of the Mhkize clan!
> The colours of their adornments glowed in the setting sun.
> Trembling over their shoulders,
> The sun thrust its last light of the evening.
> The rivers echoed as they hurtled into the round holes of stone.
> Returning birds headed for the river to drink.
> They sang their last songs of the evening.
> Darkness descended on the crimson earth,
> Covering our mountains, our faces, but not our song.

The great light of the moon broke through the early night,
Revealing large crowds of dancers and singers.
From many regiments came the boom of song and the beat of feet.
Amid the thunderous echoes of dancing
The poets' voices rose like a great chorus.

Shaka is history inflamed and dignified by hyperbole. The invitation to make judgements is wholly absent, and would be improper in terms of the poem's mythic hospitality. Nor is it precisely the point, as Soyinka demonstrates in his own approach to Shaka, whom he assimilates to Ogun, the Yoruba god of iron, in the long poem *Ogun Abibima* (1976)—a celebration of the Emperor's significance for the 'Black World' (Abibima) in its opposition to apartheid, 'the bastion of inhumanity'.

Okot p'Bitek's tone is more modest. The reach, however, is ambitious. A novelist, teacher, and one-time professional footballer, he is best known for his two long poems *Song of Lawino* and *Song of Ocol*, which achieve their stature by means of a stubborn focus on the domestic front, carefully dressed for a lengthy confrontation between man and woman, modernity and tradition, town and village, European and African, as an Acoli wife derides her husband for transferring his affections to a fashionable woman who has adopted the habits of the West:

Ocol is no longer in love with the old type.
He is in love with a modern girl;
The name of the beautiful one is Clementine.

Brother, when you see Clementine!
The beautiful one aspires
To look like a white woman;

Her lips are red hot
Like glowing charcoal,
She resembles the wild cat
That has dipped its mouth in blood.

Song of Ocol, the reply of the husband, is a reluctant lament for the values of the past, embodied in his wife Lawino, but equally a bitter appreciation of the failures of the post-colonial ideal. There is no way forward and no way back; the answer is a kind of despair which flirts with madness.

Okot's easy, demotic manner, which is so adept at expressing sorrow and derision, is to some extent a result of his reliance on Acoli song. *Song of Prisoner* (1971) persists with the device of narrative, or plaintive, voices, which grounds the poetry in the familiar cadences of 'ordinary speech'. But this conscious choice is not simply a function of African oral tradition. The question, more often, has been how poets—or novelists who turn to poetry, as Achebe did in *Beware Soul Brother* (1972)—can express the urgency that circumstances so often impel them to feel. Among these are injustice, poverty, the fraying of post-colonial ideals, and the rise of corrupt or tyrannical government.

In Nigeria, in the decade before the Biafran war (1967–70), the colonial experience had been acknowledged and explored in depth. The major works on the subject are by Achebe (*Things Fall Apart*, 1958, *No Longer at Ease*, 1960, and *Arrow of God*, 1964) and, in East Africa, by Ngugi (*Weep Not, Child*, 1964, *The River Between*, 1965, and *A Grain of Wheat*, 1967). Both writers had shown how the encounter with colonial authority set up inescapable conflicts within African societies. The village or the extended rural community provided the setting for ordeals that test the heroes of the novels to the limit and, with the intrusion of Christianity, erode the ideas, often of the sacred, that gave these societies their moral cohesion. The scope of Achebe's books is tragic, inasmuch as the outcome of decisions made by the central characters—Okonkwo in *Things Fall Apart*, and the chief priest Ezeulu in *Arrow of God*—has repercussions throughout the community. In Ngugi's work (see below) the early encounter with colonialism foreshadows the uprising of the 1950s in Kenya, and is intended to show that resistance has both a history and a continuity.

A strong disaffection with independence is already present in Ngugi and Achebe by the late 1960s. In Achebe's *A Man of the People* a local dignitary is brought to high national office and into conflict with an idealist hero, Odile, whose place in the independence élite gives him something in common with Soyinka's urbane circle of 'interpreters'. Here, however, the fruits of power are closer at hand and one of the achievements of the novel is to show how 'corruption' is not entirely a matter of personal shortcoming or public decadence.

Disillusionment is apparent also in the bleakly comic work of the Ghanaian Ayi Kwei Armah (b. 1939), especially *The Beautyful Ones Are Not Yet Born* (1968)—a moral tale which raises the problem of the 'unspeakably dishonest' habit of refusing 'to take and give what everyone around was busy taking and giving'. Images of dirt and decay recur throughout the novel, yet it is not a work of disgust. Armah's jaded humour is set off by a sense of curiosity and surprise—a tone that has become gradually more serious in a succession of novels (*Fragments*, 1970, *Why Are We So Blest?*, 1972, *The Healers*, 1978) about greed, the search for virtue in adversity, and the rejection of power—establishment or revolutionary—in favour of more modest, practical solutions to the disordered world of *The Beautyful Ones*.

The Biafran war had a profound effect on Nigeria's writers. It created divisions—J. P. Clark, for instance, took a federalist position, while Achebe spoke out for the Biafran secession; it hastened the withering of faith in Nigeria's post-colonial identity by destroying communities that the writers took to be integral to it; it cost Soyinka two years in prison for consorting with the Biafran leadership in an effort to prevent the war, and Okigbo his life: he volunteered for the Biafran army and was killed in the first year of the war.

The most intense reactions to these events include Soyinka's prose text from prison *The Man Died* (1972), best read in conjunction with his difficult collection of poems *A Shuttle in the Crypt*. There was other writing of interest about the war, including *Destination Biafra* (1981), a novel by the expatriate writer Buchi Emecheta (b. 1940); *Soza Boy* by Ken Saro-Wiwa (1941–95); *Survive the Peace* (1976) and *Divided We Stand* (1980), both by the prolific popular writer Cyprian Ekwensi; *The Combat* (1972), an allegorical reflection on the war by Kole Omotoso (b. 1943); *Never Again* (1976), the third novel by Flora Nwapa (b. 1931); and *Beware Soul Brother*, Achebe's book of poems, which includes a section about the war.

Nigeria's recovery was rapid if not thorough. The 1970s saw a surge of novels by established writers like Ekwensi, whose *Jagua Nana* (1961) had already established his reputation as the most obvious populist descendant of the Onitsha pamphleteers, and younger men like Omotoso, informed by a more political sense of the fiction writer's role. In due course an entirely new generation of writers emerged—including the poet and journalist Odia Ofeimun (b. 1950), Ben Okri (b. 1959), Adewale Maja-Pearce (b. 1953), and Bandele-Thomas. Elsewhere in West Africa, Kojo Laing (Ghana, b. 1946) and Syl Cheney-Coker (Sierra Leone, b. 1945) were publishing work of subtlety and eclecticism—particularly Laing's novel *Sing, Sweet Country* (1986)—that suggested there were no longer any prescribed paths for a writer.

In many ways, the narrative ironies of Bandele-Thomas in *The Man Who Came in from the Back of Beyond* capture the mood, and the quandary, of these younger novelists. The story is a work within a work, a manuscript prepared by the fifth-form teacher Maudé, and read at his house by the schoolboy hero Lakemfa, that recounts the life and times of Bozo Macika, the former boyfriend of a bar-girl that he, Maudé, had befriended during his days as a petty criminal in Lagos. 'Everything in there is true,' Maudé assures Lakemfa, 'except of course for a bit of literary licence.' It emerges in the last few pages of the novel that Maudé is not the author of the manuscript, and that it is pure invention. He derides Lakemfa's 'appetite for sensationalism' and, suitably chastened, Lakemfa undergoes an unconvincing transformation, turning against the logic of cynical self-interest that has previously been his best option.

The residue of the moral fable is much less discernible in Ben Okri's mature fiction, which tends more strongly, and sympathetically, to a narrative of hardship, although the abject quality of life in *The Famished Road* (1991) and its sequel *Songs of Enchantment* (1993) is washed through with magic and reverie. Events and characters—especially that of the child-spirit hero Azaro—belong to two worlds, in constant elision and transaction: the recognizable world of the living, to which Azaro wishes to commit himself as a 'mortal', and the spirit world, from which he has come. The strongest ancestor here is Amos Tutuola, who has gone on, since the success of *The Palm-Wine Drinkard*, to publish another seven books, of which the most recent is *The Witch Herbalist of the Remote Town* (1990).

Altogether, literature in anglophone West Africa through the late 1980s and early 1990s confirmed the role of the forefathers. In 1988 Achebe published *Anthills of the Savannah*, a novel set in contemporary Nigeria which explores many of the issues first taken up more than twenty years earlier in *A Man of the People*. At a memorable moment in the later book, a spokesperson from a regional delegation to Lagos praises the power of narrative, of which Achebe's own grasp is rivalled in West Africa only by the francophone Senegalese writer Sembène Ousmane (b. 1923): 'The story is our escort; without it, we are blind. Does the blind man own his escort? No, neither do we the story; rather it is the story that owns and directs us. It is the thing that makes us different from cattle.'

'I don't want to be sold like cattle,' the heroine Ebla remarks in the Somali Nuruddin Farah's first novel, *From a Crooked Rib* (1970). Farah (b. 1945) and Ngugi wa Thiong'o are the major figures in East African writing, although their preoccupations and manners differ markedly. Farah has been praised for his sensitivity to the character and unenviable situation of Somali women. *From a Crooked Rib* follows the fortunes of Ebla as she flees an arranged marriage in the rural areas, visiting a cousin in Mogadishu and taking up with a young teacher who later leaves for Italy. The novel is written in an understated manner in which no intention beyond the telling of the story is clearly signalled. Yet the 20-year-old girl from the country is inevitably an emblematic figure, who stands not only for other Somali women but, in keeping with Somali and Arabic verse tradition, for her nation, in the midst of the transition to independence. At a decisive point in the book Ebla reflects, 'In future I am responsible for whatever I do . . . In future, I will be myself and belong to myself, and my actions will belong to me. And I will in turn belong to them.'

It is perhaps misleading to speak of Farah and Ngugi in the same breath, even if Kenya and Somalia have a common border. Ngugi's work stresses scale and history; his books are genealogies of rural life in the Kikuyu highlands of Kenya: the characters must express the vicissitudes of their own generations and the force of continuity from one period to the next. *The River Between* is the first novel of a sequence (but the second to be published). A politicized tale of rural Montagus and Capulets, it takes place, in Ngugi's words, 'at a time when the Gikuyu have their land, and the colonial presence is little more than one of missionaries and mission schools, a force which divides the people but does not yet dispossess them'. The second novel, *Weep Not, Child*, deals with the situation of 'the dispossessed, tenant farmers, landless labourers, or fighters seeking to regain the land which is home'. *A Grain of Wheat* unfolds as 'the white colonial landlords are going, leaving behind them the traumatised victims of the struggle and the new black landlords who threaten to perpetuate the system of alienation which colonialism set up'.

Ngugi is passionately anti-colonial and anti-neo-colonial, believing like Soyinka that writing is a form of political intervention; in fiction, essays, and, increasingly, drama, he has written about the struggles of 'the peasants and workers who have built Kenya', and of 'the emergent African bourgeoisie and the African masses'. The ruining of rural tradition by colonialism is a theme that has preoccupied both Achebe and Ngugi, but there is a more material sense of the land itself in Ngugi, for whom the story of the highlands is one of physical, then moral, dispossession (his own father was evicted from his land), offering salutary lessons about the virtues of organizing and resisting.

By the end of the 1960s, however, Ngugi was dissatisfied with the position of African intellectuals, and with the linguae francae (English, French, and Portuguese) handed down to them by European colonialism. His decision to write in his native language Gikuyu—in the mid-1980s, he announced that it would be 'Gikuyu and Kiswahili all the way'—was an attempt to return the stories he told to their rightful audience and thereby to reinvest them with the power he felt was lost by working in English. This contentious decision set Ngugi against other writers, including Soyinka, who are alert to the ethnic and political risks of opting for one African language in a country where as many as four or five different ones may be spoken.

Ngugi's Marxism has had a determining role in his development, first

as a universalizing discourse that sanctioned the use of English in the early
novels, and then as a materialist account of literature that justified his
recourse to a restricted vernacular (Gikuyu) and an eastern lingua franca
(Kiswahili). In a purely personal sense, the shift has not been easy. The
licence for his first play in Gikuyu, *I Will Marry When I Want* (English
edition, 1982), was revoked after a month in which it played to packed
audiences in Nairobi, on grounds that it was subversive. In 1977 Ngugi was
detained for a year. By 1994, with President Daniel arap Moi ensconced in
power, Ngugi still felt unable to return to Kenya.

Nuruddin Farah, too, has spent much of his time in exile. He fled persecution by the Siad Barre regime in 1974 and has remained away from
Somalia ever since. He, on the other hand, has never agonized about working
in a colonial language. 'I write in English to continue to be heard,' he said in
1986, 'otherwise I would be easily silenced.' He does, however, draw freely on
Somali oral tradition, especially for the kind of metaphors common in narrative poetry, his knowledge of which provides his novels with a framework
of allusion that sustains their microscopic interest in human relationships.
From a Crooked Rib contains an early reference to the life and poetry of Cali
Maxamed Xasan, who led the revolt against the British between 1900 and
1920. *Maps* (1986), Farah's most painstaking exposition of the incompleteness
of Somalia, and, by implication, of Somali consciousness, is set in the Ogaden,
which the Siad Barre regime tried to recover from Ethiopia in 1977–8.

Farah M. J. Cawl (b. 1937) writes in Somali, in a more obviously traditional style. His novel *Ignorance is the Enemy of Love* (1974, trans. 1982) is set
during Cali Maxamed's war of resistance, and includes several songs and
verse sequences. He, like Farah, is preoccupied with the status of Somali
women. No woman is inferior in the eyes of God, a fellow-traveller tells the
novel's heroine Cawrala, who will die from the distress of a forced marriage: 'All that was made up by men for their own advantage, so that they
can deprive women of their rights . . . This is why I think that women
ought to study religion and all sorts of knowledge, so that they can get back
their rights from men.'

Cawl's use of verse links the novel directly to Somali oral forms, which
have flourished for centuries and which gained even wider audiences with
the advent of radio after the Second World War. When the clan elders of
northern Somalia sought to restore order in the absence of any national
administration after 1991, poets at reconciliation conferences played the central officiating role they had enjoyed in the past, reminding communities
that there were imperatives beyond the obligations of the feud.

*

Outside West Africa, the tendency to privilege 'orature' over writing in the colonial languages has not always proved easy to maintain—above all, when it holds that writing is an activity pursued at the expense, or neglect, of oral tradition. In Somalia the quite recent adoption of an official Somali orthography, in the early 1970s, actually enhanced the status of oral composition and coincided not only with the spread of literacy but with a flurry of scholarly work that gave rise to a broader awareness of the Somali poetic heritage. In Ethiopia the written word has been in use, albeit restricted, for at least 1,500 years and possibly longer; there is little scope in Ethiopian tradition for a fundamentalist defence of 'orature'. One ancient literary formula known as 'wax and gold' survives in the work of the short-story writer Hama Tuma (b. 1950). The expression occurs in one of his courtroom satires of life under Marxism-Leninism. In 'The Case of the Traitorous Alphabet' (from *The Case of the Socialist Witch Doctor and Other Stories*, 1993) the prosecutor and the judge deliberate whether or not to punish a printer for a seditious typesetting error by making him eat newsprint. The discussion turns to the deviousness of all Habeshas (highlanders). The judge: 'We take the roundabout method, that's all. Why, we hear people sing obliquely of a "train speeding into the night taking all the youth away" when what they really want to do is to attack our government's curative terror.' The prosecutor: 'Wax and gold. It has counter-revolutionary connotations for sure.'

Hama is referring to a fifteenth-century form derived from Ethiopian Orthodox hymns: words are seen as a wax integument covering their meaning, which is gold. Hama's own work, on occasion consummately funny, uses the wax-and-gold formula to examine the cruelties of the Ethiopian dictatorship (c.1974–91) in a series of ludicrous trials for crimes against 'the people' ('a sack of potatoes', in the opinion of the judge, until they have been enlightened by the Party). Hama's courtroom debates are bitterly ironic and the wax integument is swiftly ruptured. He none the less draws on an indigenous written tradition that pre-dates European colonialism by four centuries in order to deride a European political construction—Marxism-Leninism—imposed on the one part of Africa that was never successfully colonized.

Without the equivocal comforts of exile, dissenting writers can expect few consolations: outside South Africa Awoonor, Soyinka, Ngugi, and the Malawian poet Jack Mapanje (b. 1945) are the best-known writers to have been detained by inimical regimes. The trend persists: Soyinka was forced out of Nigeria in 1994, and the writer and activist Ken Saro-Wiwa was hanged in 1995 after a dubious murder trial. Yet few regimes have been more severe than South Africa on dissident writers and journalists, a number of whom were censored, banned altogether, or gaoled; apartheid also damaged the literature of its exiles and internees by locking it into a Manichaean struggle—which almost all writers were obliged to conduct—with the doctrine and state apparatus of white minority rule.

Nadine Gordimer (b. 1923) is one of the central figures of the apartheid period. Bullied and censored, but not exiled, she devised her fiction as a bridge to the outside world and a proof that the 'struggle' was not a monolithic enterprise—it drew in people whose personal lives were often at odds with the political imperatives that drove them. This proof was also her defence against a programmatic fiction which would serve as a monument to the fallen, or the triumphant, in the battle with apartheid.

Some of Gordimer's best work, much of it from the 1950s and 1960s, has little if any explicit political engagement. *Six Feet of the Country* (1956) and *Friday's Footprint* (1960) are scrupulously observed records of the space that lies between groups, races, and individuals in South Africa. The stories take an objective interest in the effects of separate development on ordinary people with little choice in the matter. For twenty years or more Gordimer was exploring the collective pursuit of solitude—the enduring Afrikaner ambition, which subjected every other group in the country, including the English, to the logic of isolation. Despite the distinction she draws between 'alienation' and 'solitude', in many of these stories social and geographical space are so elided that it is hard to know whether her characters are lost in apartheid or merely in the great outdoors.

In the 1970s Gordimer started to come indoors and to prefer the novel to the short story. After *A Guest of Honour* (1970), her characters take up their uncomfortable places within the political struggle. *Burger's Daughter* (1979) confirms the tension that existed, among whites especially, between the public and the private spheres. That this novel's heroine should have been very patently based on one of the daughters of the well-known Communist lawyer Bram Fischer signals a paring down of literary camouflage on Gordimer's part, and of her personal scruples: everything, including the lives of friends and acquaintances, can now be made over for public review.

At the same time, her focus began to close in on the disconsolate world of white activism, the milieu she knew best and could describe without affectation. The question is whether the troubled conscience that she went on to examine throughout the 1980s could in fact reveal the enormity of the situation it was faced with. The laurels bestowed on Gordimer, since *The Conservationist* (1974), by prize juries in Europe, including the Nobel Prize that she won in 1991, suggest that it could. Yet *None to Accompany Me*

(1994), published in the wake of the release of Nelson Mandela, seems to reaffirm the gap between the inner life of the activist and external events— a gulf that conviction alone is unable to cross. The heroine of the novel retires into her own life, as her once troubled conscience fades into a thankful solipsism.

There were other ways to tell the story of apartheid, and other vantage-points from which to tell it. During the 1950s and 1960s the periodical *Drum* provided an outlet for several young black writers, including Richard Rive (b. 1931), Can Themba (b. 1924), and Lewis Nkosi (b. 1936). Like Es'kia (Ezekiel) Mphalele (b. 1919), another *Drum* protégé who went on to co-edit two issues of *Black Orpheus* during the 1960s, Nkosi broke away to become a commentator on fiction, poetry, and drama throughout the continent. He writes as both advocate and town-crier, yet his work has always shown a convincing critical detachment. His most ambitious book is *Tasks and Masks* (1981), which performs its critical task with the confidence, and the cold eye, of an exacting reader. In Nkosi's best-known novel, *Mating Birds* (1986), a tale of white–black sexual transgression, he attempts to commit literary suicide by flinging himself into the shallows of apartheid ethics. As a monologue delivered in gaol by the black lover of a white woman, the novel is a *tour de force*, however, and makes Nkosi's gesture seem more disingenuous still.

Under apartheid numerous writers were obliged in varying degrees to sacrifice their literary talents to the cause: the memorial entablature would have to include Oswald Mtshali (b. 1940), Laura Ngcobo, Sipho Sepamla (b. 1932), Miriam Tlali (b. *c.*1930), Wally Serote (b. 1944), Mandla Langa, Keorapetse Kgositsile (b. 1938), Nadine Gordimer, André Brink, and Athol Fugard (b. 1932). Yet nearly all of these writers have produced work whose interest will outlast the apartheid era, while some have found humour a useful way to ease the sclerosis of anti-apartheid writing. In theory, at least, the post-apartheid settlement offers them a new literary dispensation.

The fiction of J. M. Coetzee (b. 1940) steps outside the usual limits of anti-apartheid writing by making use of literary pastiche and of techniques learnt from the French *nouveau roman* (*Dusklands*, 1974, *The Heart of the Country*, 1977). The extraordinary novels of the 1980s—*Waiting for the Barbarians* (1980), *Life and Times of Michael K* (1983), *Foe* (1986)—are meditations on some larger travesty, of which minority rule and the violence of white settlement in Africa are simply examples. Aspects of apartheid appear in all these books: isolation, terror, the real or imminent collapse of State and society, repression. But the narrative unfolds in a kind of exclusionary zone where the names of real places are admitted only on sufferance and so acquire an alarming unfamiliarity, while the social identity of the characters is often tenuous. The story may be set in the past (*Foe*) or the future (*Life and Times*), but there is also a textual present, as the tense in which the novel is being written intrudes on the setting. The play of past, present, and future may also serve a moral purpose, displaying, for example, the pathology of anticipating a calamity that has already happened.

It is clear that Coetzee has absorbed some of the teachings of contemporary critical theory. But, far from being mandarin, his books really represent a dramatic break-out from the confines of a merely oppositional literature. 'There is something tawdry', Coetzee wrote in 1986, on the theme of torture in South African fiction, 'about *following* the state . . . making its vile mysteries the occasion of fantasy. For the writer, the deeper problem is *not* to allow himself to be impaled on the dilemma proposed by the state, namely, either to ignore its obscenities or else to produce representations of them. The true challenge is how not to play by the rules of the state, how to establish one's own authority, how to imagine torture and death on one's own terms.'

Only a few South African writers indeed have chosen the terms on which to address their subject-matter. More often than not, it is either exile or a period of study overseas that has helped them to do so. Among the most distinguished are Bessie Head (1937–86), who sought refuge across the border in Botswana, and wrote with a quietist passion on the pain of tribal discrimination (*Maru*, 1971) and mental illness (*A Question of Power*, 1974); Breyten Breytenbach (b. 1939), one of the 'Sestigers' or 'sixties group' of Afrikaans-language writers, who, after a lengthy stint in detention, renounced his Afrikaner birthright in *Confessions of an Albino Terrorist* (1982); and André Brink (b. 1935), another of the Sestigers who, like Breytenbach, put out literary and intellectual feelers in Paris before returning home to take issue with apartheid in *Looking on Darkness* (1974), *Rumour of Rain* (1978), and *A Dry White Season* (1978). There are also the rare writers who sacrificed nothing by writing polemically and *well* about apartheid. The best of these are Alex La Guma (1925–85), who died in Cuba after an illustrious career as a fiction writer, and the poets Don Mattera (b. 1935), James Matthews, and Dennis Brutus (b. 1924), whose collection *A Simple Lust* (1973) is among the most widely read poetry of the anti-apartheid movement.

There are limits to what the novel can achieve in societies undergoing the kind of prolonged turmoil with which most African writers are familiar. Achebe gave some indication of the problem when he admitted, during the Biafran war, 'I can't write a novel now. I can write poetry—something

short, intense, more in keeping with my mood. I can write essays. I can
even lecture.' Nkosi took a similar position, arguing that the 'very absorbing, violent and immediate nature of experience' was not conducive to the
production of 'long and complex works of literary genius'. The short-story
writer and critic Njabulo Ndebele (b. 1948) put it better still, arguing that
the 'average [South] African writer . . . produces an art of anticipated sur-
faces rather than of processes', because he already knows the moral landscape of apartheid and the range of possible outcomes. Journalism, the
short story, and the poem were the natural forms for this period.

Oral literature, too, can be more responsive than the novel to political
and social upheaval. Where Southern Africa is concerned, Landeg White
and Leroy Vail have argued persuasively that oral tradition opens up 'the
intellectual, emotional and moral life of the region's societies more clearly
and dramatically than any other source'. But the modern South African
writer cannot escape the obligation to write. Ndebele argues against the
privileging of oral literature and insists 'that the greater impact of the
written word in the social contest for power is undeniable. To assert the contrary is to dangerously romanticise the oral tradition.' Once again, contemporary writing is uneasily situated between the agility of a non-literate
tradition—in which even epic can be reinterpreted—and the discursive poise
of the Western novel.

The essay has always been a useful genre for African writers. Both Ngugi
and Soyinka have written books about their detention (*Detained: A Writer's
Prison Diary*, 1981; *The Man Died: Prison Notes*, 1982), and since he won the
Nobel Prize Soyinka has been at work on a serial autobiography that is
rather less elaborate than his fiction. Achebe, too, has written with candour
about Nigerian politics in *The Trouble with Nigeria* (1983), and many younger
writers who might plausibly have taken to fiction find the essay, or the
reflection on 'direct experience', more workable. 'It took me a long time',
says Adewale Maja-Pearce in *How Many Miles to Babylon?* (1990), 'to find out
that I had little or no talent for fiction, and longer again to understand the
possibilities of the essay as a viable form for saying what I wanted to say.'

It is clear that today the novel in Africa is under stress, in terms of
characterization above all. The events and choices entailed by extremity
tend either to reduce protagonists to ciphers, or to diminish them by comparison with the momentous occasions to which the novelist requires them
to rise. Some of the best novels of the last thirty years—*God's Bits of Wood*
(1960) by Sembène Ousmane, for example—constantly edge towards documentary (itself very often the basis of oral tradition), as though a modern
interiority were inappropriate to the overall conception of the work. In

times of adversity, it is a rare talent for whom the faculty of imagination is more admissible than brisk reportage or reasoned recollection.

As fiction intrudes on historical record, so literary criticism spills over into urgent debates about indignity and political oppression, which is why a talented 'trickster' like Chinweizu, who has likened his critical interventions to the inspired hustling of Nigerian passenger-lorry touts, should be acknowledged as a politician no less than a scholar. Chinweizu and his colleagues regard themselves as bush-clearers, ordering 'the havoc wrought by imperialist hegemony over our culture'. They have also cleared a space for themselves in which they can debunk and denounce with a hyperbole that is sadly absent from most Western discussion of African writing.

Chinweizu's use of 'culture' in the singular is none the less unsettling. 'Our culture/their culture'—this is precisely how unenlightened colonialism envisaged Africa: as a homogeneous land-mass where subjugation had abolished all indigenous history and difference. Other writers would disagree with Chinweizu. Travelling in West Africa (*In my Father's Country: A Nigerian Journey*, 1987) or exploring race and identity in Britain (*How Many Miles to Babylon?*), Maja-Pearce, half-Scots, half-Nigerian, is interested in the 'details which finally distinguish a society from any other', and in the recognition of 'a discrete place which is different from any other place'. One must not be 'seduced by the safety of belonging'—itself only an expression 'of the absence of a larger idea of human relations'.

Kwame Anthony Appiah (*In my Father's House: Africa in the Philosophy of Culture*, 1992) regards Chinweizu, Jemie, and Madubuike as 'nativists': their ambition, in Appiah's words, is 'to wrestle the critical ethnocentrism of their Eurocentric opponents to the ground in the name of an Afrocentric particularism'. The tendency of this project to organize 'its vaunted particularities into a "culture"' is none the less an indication that it is 'covertly universalist'. Appiah is one of the editors of a revived, US edition of the journal *Transition* (later *Ch'indaba*), which, when it published Achebe, Soyinka, Awoonor, and many others during the 1960s and 1970s, took a broadly pan-African position on the continent's literary awakening. But Appiah is no more at ease than Maja-Pearce with a general notion of Africanness. He chides Soyinka for conflating *an* African culture—his own, Yoruba—with an undifferentiated idea of African culture as a whole. For Appiah, there is no such thing. 'There are only so many traditions with their complex relationships—and, as often, their lack of any relationship—to each other.'

Appiah's writings have been praised, by Soyinka among others, as a landmark in the understanding of what it is to reflect on the notion of Africanness and African cultures. They are in fact journeys without landmarks, which invite the reader to circumvent the categories—African and non-African, oral and written, sameness and otherness—that have made earlier excursions by critics and commentators too antithetical. Like Maja-Pearce, Appiah (part Ghanaian, part British) is writing, and thinking, from the vantage-point of mixed descent—which is perhaps what enables him to recognize that there is no pure lineage in African literature any more than there is in those who read it. Like most writing, it is never quite at home in its place of origin.

FURTHER READING

Chinweizu; Jemie, Onwuchekwa; and Madubuike, Ihechukwu, *Toward the Decolonization of African Literature*, i: *African Fiction and Poetry and their Critics* (Enugu, 1980).
——(ed.), *Voices from Twentieth-Century Africa: Griots and Towncriers* (London, 1988).
Finnegan, Ruth, *Oral Literature in Africa* (London, 1970).
Goodwin, Ken, *Understanding African Poetry: A Study of Ten Poets* (London, 1982).
Gordimer, Nadine, *The Black Interpreters: Notes on African Writing* (Johannesburg, 1973).
Ndebele, Njabulo, *The Rediscovery of the Ordinary: Essays on South African Literature and Culture* (Johannesburg, 1991).
Owomoyela, Oyekan, *A History of Twentieth Century African Literatures* (Lincoln, Nebr., 1994).
Ngugi wa Thiong'o, *Moving the Centre: The Struggle for Cultural Freedoms* (London, 1993).
Nkosi, Lewis, *Home and Exile* (London, 1965).
Roscoe, Adrian, *Mother is Gold: A Study in West African Literature* (Cambridge, 1971).

2

ARAB COUNTRIES

ROBERT IRWIN

THE Naksa, or Israeli military victory over Egypt, Syria, and Jordan in 1967, was a major event in Arabic literature. The reality of disaster once again exposed the tawdry rhetoric of those who had led the Arabs to defeat and many now questioned the promises of the region's nationalist and socialist leaders.

The aftermath of the defeat produced a vast literature of despair, rage, and self-criticism, which took many forms. The Syrian Marxist intellectual Sadiq Jalal al-Azm (b. 1937) produced a widely read polemic, *Al-Naqd al-dhati ba'd al-hazima* ('Self-Criticism after Defeat', 1968). According to al-Azm the military defeat was the symptom of broader problems in the Arab world. The various Arab regimes which pretended to be socialist were no such thing. Political institutions were inadequate, and fatalistic attitudes sapped people's will to change things. Al-Azm followed this up in 1969 with *Naqd al-fikr al-dini* ('A Critique of Religious Thought'), in which he predicted that the Arabs would be defeated again, unless they adopted more modern ways of thought and social organization and emancipated themselves from feudal, tribal, and quietist religious values.

In the post-war, post-colonial years a literature of commitment (*al-adab al-multazim*) has been in vogue among Arab writers. According to the Iraqi poet Abd al-Wahhab al-Bayyati, the vision of the poet must be infused with 'an objective understanding of the paradoxes of existence, a discovery of the logic of history, and a dynamic involvement with the events of his own time'. Similarly, according to the Iraqi fiction writer Ahmad Salih (1920–82), 'Art without politics is not art.' Many creative writers in the Arab world still remain in thrall to the idea of a literature of commitment and to the idea that literature should seek to change society, as well as registering the changes taking place in it. In the years since the Naksa there has been a tendency in novels, poems, and plays for happy endings to give way to an unhappy one and for committed heroes to be replaced by alienated victims and outsiders. One now reads a lot about *qalaq* (anxiety). Even someone like the novelist Halim Barakat, who remains totally committed to a political and revolutionary literature, shuns Socialist Realist techniques in favour of a more fragmented narrative as better fitted to express a sense of crisis in the Middle East.

Since modern Arab literature is so highly politicized, it is not surprising to find Palestinian writers and themes taking a central role. The novella *Men in the Sun* (1963; trans. 1978) by the Palestinian novelist and short-story writer Ghassan al-Kanafani (1936–72) is one of the most admired and quoted works of modern Arab fiction. Kanafani's story presents the plight of unemployed Palestinians in exile realistically, but with unmistakable allegorical overtones. The Palestinians who are trying to smuggle themselves across the Kuwaiti border in the empty water tank of a lorry are not so much killed by the heat of the desert sun, as doomed by their silence. 'Why didn't you knock on the sides of the tank? Why didn't you say anything? Why?' Evidently Kanafani's story is a call for activism. His later novella *What Remains to You* (1966; trans. 1990), set in a Palestinian refugee camp in the Gaza Strip, expresses Kanafani's continuing commitment to the cause of socialist revolution. His manner of telling this and other tales is complex, however, ceaselessly shifting from viewpoint to viewpoint, place to place, and time to time. Kanafani wrote many fine (if often gloomy) short stories which have been widely translated and anthologized. In 'The Slave Fort' the wasted empty years are compared to oyster-shells without pearls. 'The Little One Goes to Camp' is an evocation of poverty that is simultaneously comic, savage, and profound. A spokesman for the Popular Front for the Liberation of Palestine, Kanafani was murdered by an Israeli car bomb in Beirut in 1972.

Mahmoud Darwish (b. 1941), another spokesman for the Palestinian cause, is one of the Arab world's leading poets—perhaps *the* leading poet. His public readings command audiences of many thousands. He was born in Palestine, but was taken to Lebanon by his fleeing parents in 1948. Subsequently, he crossed secretly back into what had become Israel and he was educated there. After suffering repeated harassment and imprisonment by the Israelis, however, he left for Egypt in 1971. Later he moved to Lebanon, and since the Lebanese troubles began he has lived in Paris. In 1981 he founded the important literary periodical *al-Karmel*. An anthology of his poetry was selected and translated into English by Denys Johnson-Davies as *The Music of Human Flesh* (1980).

Darwish is one of many writers who have resorted to literature in order to preserve the Palestinian heritage. In his poems, Palestine becomes an emblematic country of the mind, a lost Arcadia. Oranges frequently feature in his poems, the reference being to the flourishing state of citrus cultivation in Palestine prior to 1948. The horse, emblem of the Fatah liberation movement, also makes frequent appearances. As the years have gone by there has been a tendency for his poems to become both more complex and more grim. In 'On Poetry' he attacks the imagery and style of traditional poems as being inappropriate to the problems of a new age. 'The hour struck, Khayyam drank on | and under the rhythm of his drugged songs | we remained as poor as ever.'

Darwish has been a consistent advocate both of free verse and of the use of the demotic. For over a century now the Arab literary world has been riven by debate about whether it is better to use the demotic (*amiyya*) or literary Arabic (*fusha*). Those who favour the demotic argue, among other things, that in doing so they are accurately reflecting how people speak, that the colloquial usages make their writings accessible to a wider public than the literary élite. Those who favour literary Arabic point out that its use has helped and does help the unity of the Arabic-speaking world. Literary Arabic is comprehensible to educated readers everywhere, from Iraq to Morocco. This is not necessarily the case with the various forms of the demotic. If literary Arabic is renounced, then so too is the glorious heritage of classical Arabic literature, as well as the Koranic resonances which suffuse so much of it. Feelings on the question have run high and Naguib Mahfouz has described the colloquial as 'a disease of language'. Palestinian writers like Kanafani, Habibi, and Darwish, however, have chosen to write in the demotic, seeking thereby to preserve the specifically regional heritage of Palestine.

A very different solution to the language question has been adopted by the Palestinian novelist, poet, and essayist Anton Shammas (b. 1950). He lives in Israel and writes in Hebrew, using that language to preserve and celebrate the Palestinian experience and, like Caliban, to curse those who taught it to him. His *Arabesques* (1988) is an intricately structured novel in which an account of the fortunes of an extended Palestinian family from 1874 onwards is juxtaposed with what is plainly autobiographical material concerning the writer's experiences in France and the United States. The book's complexity depends not only on the entwined destinies of kinsmen, but on the recurrent invocation of such things as oil presses, cupboards, farmyard implements, and doorways. In this way the vanishing culture of Palestinians is tacitly contrasted with the 'kitsch culture' (as Shammas has described it elsewhere) of the Israelis.

The novelist Emile Habibi (b. 1921) also lives within the borders of Israel, but he writes in Arabic. His *The Secret Life of Saeed the Pessoptimist*

(1972; trans. 1982) is the story of a naïve Arab who seeks to collaborate with the occupying Israelis. In the long run, however, he falls foul of the authorities and is imprisoned several times. In prison he becomes the centre of a Shakespeare study circle—whose sessions seem to involve his lying on the floor and being kicked in the stomach by the guards. In his dealings with the Israelis Saeed is buoyed up by his communications with extra-terrestrials, with whom he has made contact in a secret tunnel dug by the Crusaders under the port of Acre. Habibi's much-acclaimed novel is a picaresque comic fantasy about the psychopathology of the dispossessed. His second novel, *Ikhtayyi* (1985), is similarly a loosely constructed and sarcastic satire about life under Israeli occupation and the quest for a Palestinian identity.

Sahar Khalifa (b. 1941) is another of the leading Palestinian novelists writing under the Israeli occupation. *Wild Thorns* (1976) is her third novel, but so far the only one to have been translated into English. The novel's protagonist Usama returns to Israeli-occupied Nablus some time in the 1970s, with the purpose of organizing resistance there and, more specifically, of preventing Arab labourers going off each day to work in Israel proper. Khalifa presents a nuanced view of the difficult options of armed resistance and collaboration. In this and other writings she suggests that there is more than one form of oppression and that there is no reason for the struggle for the liberation of women to take second place to the struggle for the liberation of Palestine. She also highlights some of the tensions within the liberation struggle—notably between those who have stayed and those who have gone into exile.

Jabra Ibrahim Jabra (b. 1919) is a Palestinian, educated in Britain and the United States, who has spent much of his writing career in Iraq. A leading novelist and poet, he has also written extensively about literature and the visual arts, and has translated many key works of Western literature and criticism. In particular, his translation of the Tammuz section of Frazer's *Golden Bough* has, as we shall see, had important consequences for modern Arabic literature. As a critic, he has drawn attention to the excesses of Arab novels of political commitment and has cautioned against making fictional characters behave like wind-up dolls. His first novel, *Hunters in a Narrow Street* (1960), set in Baghdad in the 1950s, was actually written in English.

He is best known, however, for his Arabic novel *The Ship* (1970; trans. 1985). This is ostentatiously cosmopolitan in its range of cultural reference and has been attacked by some Arab critics for what is perceived to be its excessive pessimism and defeatist harping on the theme of suicide. The ship of the title is cruising from Beirut to Naples and Marseilles. On board are a loosely linked group of intellectual men and women. In the course of the voyage they will debate the grand themes of life, love, and death. But Jabra uses several narrative voices to tell his story and there are feverish interior monologues on the pains of exile and of sexual jealousy and denial. Several of the men are obsessively attracted to Luma, an Iraqi woman who has a voluptuous body and a remarkable (and somewhat implausible) knowledge of the teachings of St Thomas Aquinas. Before the story ends one of the voyagers will commit suicide. Political themes, particularly the loss of Palestine, are certainly not absent, but one is more conscious of a highly cerebral eroticism. In Jabra's critical essays he has emphasized the importance of the *Arabian Nights* as a source of inspiration for modern Arabic literature in general and his own writings in particular. The image of Sindbad, dispossessed and wandering, has appeared again and again in his prose and poetry.

Tawfiq Sayigh (1923–71) spent his boyhood in Palestine but, like his literary ally Jabra, he was educated in England and the United States. Also like Jabra, he was a distinguished translator, having translated Eliot's *Four Quartets* into Arabic. Sayigh was an advocate of free verse and of modernist experiments with prose poetry. His poetry favours modern, urban settings within which the topics of the homeless wanderer and unrequited love are usually treated ironically.

Although the Lebanese civil war began in 1975, for a long time it seemed conceivable that a peace might soon be brokered and many of those who could have fled the country stayed on. But from 1982 onwards, the year of the Israeli invasion, Beirut ceased to be a place where literature could be safely produced. Prior to this, it had been the publishing capital of the Arab world and writers who could not get their books published in their own country often managed to do so in Lebanon. Many avant-garde literary periodicals were founded in Beirut. The American University was an important focus of cultural life and Palestinian writers in exile further enriched Lebanon's cultural life. In the last couple of decades, however, there has been a notable exodus of writers and intellectuals to Paris, London, and the United States.

In the late 1950s and early 1960s Jabra's translation of Frazer, taken in conjunction with translations of *The Waste Land* and the poems of Edith Sitwell, was to influence an entire school of Arab poets in Lebanon and elsewhere. These were the 'Tammuzis', who included in their number Jabra himself, Yusuf al-Khal, Sayyab, Khalil al-Hawi, and Adonis. Their poems deal with the archetypal and mythic themes of death and rebirth, portraying the Middle East as a waste land awaiting an Arab regeneration.

Adonis (b. 1930; the pen-name adopted by Ali Ahmad Said) is the towering presence among these poets. Adonis was born in Syria but has spent the greater part of his life as a writer in the Lebanon. His career has been turbulent and, like so many Arab writers, he has experienced imprisonment and exile. Adonis is one of the Arab world's leading cultural spokesmen. As such he has (paradoxically) been a channel for European influences on poetry, and at the same time a vociferous opponent of Western values. 'We no longer believe in Europe. We no longer have faith in its political system or in its philosophies.' According to Adonis, everything worthwhile has been invented in the East. All the same, as a francophone who now lives in Paris, he has embraced a diverse pantheon of cultural heroes, including Muhammad, Abu Nuwas, Marx, Mao, Baudelaire, Apollinaire, Gramsci, and Malraux.

He has also taken a particular interest in Surrealism and has published a critical study of its links and parallels with Sufism. In *An Introduction to Arab Poetics* (1990) Adonis argues that 'modernism'—a state of mind not tied to any particular century—flourished under the Abbasid caliphs. Only the Crusades caused a set-back to Arab literary experimentation. Adonis has discovered prototypes and sources for an indigenous Arab modernism in certain highly original medieval poets and mystics. In his influential and polemical study of Arab poetry *al-Thabit wa' l-mutahawil* ('The Fixed and the Changing', 1974) he attacks traditional Islamic values for inhibiting progress in the Arab world. In 1968–9 Adonis was one of the prime movers in the launching of the literary periodical *al-Mawaqif* in Beirut, which has not only provided the chief outlet for experimental Arab writing, but has also served as a channel for introducing contemporary French literature and critical theory to the Arab world.

Adonis's own poetic voice is oracular, even apocalyptic at times, for he believes that the rebel poet has a leading role in history as visionary redeemer. The 'Songs of Mihyar the Damascene' cycle of poems, in which the visionary voice is that of Mihyar, an imaginary medieval king, first appeared in 1961, but the full version was only published in 1983. In it Mihyar assumes the identity of various legendary and oracular figures, many of them associated with past catastrophes, and he gives cryptic instruction on the secret nature of the world. 'Hadha huwa ismi' ('This is my name'), a post-1967 poem, set in what is typically an urban landscape in decay, with its apocalyptic imagery of fire and flood, is an eloquent, if somewhat cryptic, howl of grief and rage at the Arab defeat. 'Qabr min ajl New York' ('The Funeral of New York', 1971) is, if anything, even more bitter. The opening image is that of New York as a woman clutching a rag called Liberty in one hand, while with the other she strangles the rest of the world.

Like Darwish, Adonis can command large audiences for his readings. His verses are public in the sense that they are written to be read aloud in public places and that their tone is grandiose and rhetorical, but in another sense his message is intensely private and therefore difficult. His poems are personal in that only he can really be quite sure what they mean, yet also impersonal inasmuch as in these poems he allows the public no window into his private concerns. Despite his commitment to fundamental change in society, one sometimes gets the impression that Adonis does not really believe that the masses are up to the revolution he has in mind for them.

If Adonis's poems furnish an apocalyptic commentary on Lebanon's troubles, Lebanese novelists have tended to represent them more realistically. Halim Barakat (b. 1933) is a sociologist, as one might guess from the content of his novels. His first novel, Six Days (1961; trans. 1991), gives an account of the fighting in 1948 against the Zionists in a fictitious seaside village. The Arabs are defeated by their own backwardness as much as by the external enemy. In his more recent novel Days of Dust (1974), Barakat describes the equally disastrous fighting in 1967. This novel, which makes use of multiple viewpoints, is based in part on the author's sociological surveys and interviews with those who took part. Days of Dust is not mere reportage, however. His central character is a Palestinian academic, Ramzi Safadi, who is having an affair with an American woman, Pamela, and who believes he cannot cease his wanderings or find peace until he meets a woman who can commit herself to him absolutely. Pamela, who doubles as a sounding board for his opinions and as a symbol of Western corruption, is in the end not the person he is looking for and Days of Dust is, perhaps inevitably, a gloomy novel.

Death in Beirut (1976) by Tawfiq Yusuf Awwad (1911–89) covers similar ground in a more old-fashioned and melodramatic manner. In this novel, set in Beirut in 1968, at a time when Lebanon was under repeated attack from Israel, Tamima, a Shiite girl from southern Lebanon, falls in love with a young Maronite student of liberal progressive views, but is then seduced by a nihilist journalist and consequently repudiated by the man she loves. As with Days of Dust, personal themes are interwoven with public ones and the novel ends with Tamima being spurred on by her personal tragedy to vow that 'I shall fight under any sky against all legal codes and traditions sanctioned by society. I shall stab them with my own hand. Because, in their name, under the sky of my own country, society has denied me the right to life.'

Elias Khouri (b. 1948) is a novelist, publisher, and critic, who, despite his Christian background, aligned himself with the Palestinians and Muslims in the Lebanese civil war. 'Palestine is everyone's dream . . . Palestine is a state of mind, every Arab is a Palestinian, every poor person with a gun is a Palestinian.' His novel *Little Mountain* (1977) is an account of the fighting in Lebanon in 1975–6 in which he himself took part. It is a mixture of fact, fiction, folk-tale, autobiography, and fantasy. Its manner can be characterized as gloomy picaresque.

A remarkable feature of Lebanese fiction in the last couple of decades has been the explosion of writing by women. Many of these writers are currently writing in exile, however. Hannan al-Shaykh (b. 1945), one of the leading feminist novelists in Arabic, lives in London. Her *The Story of Zahra* (1986) begins in Beirut before the outbreak of the civil war and ends while that war is still in its early stages. Zahra comes from a poor Shiite family. For her, the enemy is not the Phalangists or the Palestinians, it is men—her father, the wife-beater and braggart, her spoilt and talentless brother, her lascivious and unsentimental first lover, her proprietorial husband, and, finally, the militia sniper she has sex with in the concluding chapters of this exceedingly bleak novel. One of the unusual achievements of the book is to point to the fact that there were many, particularly among the poor and the minorities, who gained rather than lost from the war. A subsequent novel, *Women of Sand and Myrrh* (1989), deals with the plight of four women in a country which bears more than a passing resemblance to Saudi Arabia.

While *The Story of Zahra* is probably the best-known novel written in Arabic to deal with the predicament of women in the Lebanon, a number of others have been written by Lebanese women in French or English, among them Etel Adnan's French novel *Sitt-Marie Rose* (1982), in which the eponymous heroine is raped and tortured by Phalangists; and Andrée Chedid's novel, also in French, *The Return to Beirut* (1989), an elegiac lament for the land that civil strife was about to destroy.

These themes of dispossession and alienation are to be found among Egyptian writers, too, but Egypt's cultural solidity and self-confidence has also encouraged the exploration of other, quite different sorts of experience and the Egyptian writer's tone is often more relaxed. Together with Lebanon, Egypt is the main publishing centre of the Arab world. Magazines (both highbrow and lowbrow) are economically more viable than, for example, British ones, so that short-story writers and poets have access to a wide market. (It is important to note that poetry has always taken precedence over prose in the estimation of cultured Arabs.) It is also extremely common for novelists to publish their works first in serial form in newspapers. The history of the Arab novel is short: *Zaynab*, by the Egyptian writer

Muhammad Husayn Haykal, published in 1913, is commonly regarded as the first proper novel in Arabic. Naguib Mahfouz, who was born in 1911, is therefore two years older than the genre he has practised with such success (he won the Nobel Prize in 1988, the first Arab writer to do so). He was unable to live from his writing, however, and worked as a civil servant until his retirement in 1971.

Mahfouz is astonishingly prolific and has proved himself a master of both old-fashioned narrative and literary experimentation. By the beginning of 1967 he had already published seventeen novels and three collections of short stories. Some of these books are masterpieces of world literature. The *Cairo Trilogy*, consisting of *Palace Walk* (1956; trans. 1990), *Palace of Desire* (1957; trans. 1991), and *Sugar Street* (1957; trans. 1992), follows the fortunes of a shopkeeper and his family in a richly visualized Cairo from 1917 to 1945. At their most profound level, these books explore the processes of personal, historical, and metaphysical change. The *Cairo Trilogy* is an old-fashioned work, and none the worse for that, being old-fashioned in its confidence, richness, and seriousness.

Children of Gebelawi was published in serial form in Cairo in 1959, and in English translation in 1981. Set in a poor quarter of Cairo, very like that in which Mahfouz grew up, it presents, in thinly disguised allegory, the history of the world and the challenges presented to humanity in turn by Moses, Jesus, Muhammad, and Western technology. Mahfouz's treatment of religion in the novel offended Islamic rigorists. *The Thief and the Dogs* (1960; trans. 1984), an existentialist *roman noir*, which combines crime, political polemic, and mysticism, is one of Mahfouz's finest achievements. The thief, Said Mahran, comes out of prison seeking both revenge and answers to the mystery of existence. But Mahran is a confused petty criminal, whose quest is doomed to failure, and the dogs will hunt him down.

Others of Mahfouz's novels which have been translated include *Mirrors* (1977), which contains fifty-five brief character sketches of people whom the narrator has encountered in the course of his life from the 1920s to the present day. Much of it is fairly clearly based on people that Mahfouz has himself known and some of the models for the pen-portraits are only lightly disguised. Some characters, on the other hand, may stand for aspects of the author's own personality. Cumulatively, the sketches build up into a socio-political inquiry into Egypt's loss of direction after the débâcle of 1967 and the death of Nasser in 1970. *Respected Sir* (1975; trans. 1986) is a short novel about a careerist bureaucrat—the subject of so many Egyptian novels—his ambitions, and his naïvely drafted programme of self-improvement. His pathetic story is narrated in the deliberately inappropriate language of hyperbole.

The Fountain and the Tomb (1975; trans. 1988), which is more a series of linked sketches and short stories than a novel in the full sense, draws heavily on Mahfouz's boyhood memories of life in Cairo's crowded and inturned quarters, with their gangsters, shopkeepers, dervishes, porters, donkey-men, water-sellers, and harlots. *The Harafish* (1977; trans. 1994) has much the same setting. It is a splendidly melodramatic saga of ganglords and members of the lumpenproletariat in one of the older quarters of Cairo. This novel, certainly one of Mahfouz's best, has a dual ancestry. In part, it draws on medieval Arab folk-tales which celebrated the exploits of bold and crafty thieves. In part, however, its plotting and ambience reflect the conventions of the popular Egyptian *futuwwa*, or gangster film. To a large degree the novel is a fictional version of 'salvation history', in which the community led by certain heroic individuals is engaged on a quest for social justice and, beyond that, for the meaning of existence. Of all Mahfouz's novels, this is perhaps the freest from European influence.

Although the erotic scenes to be found in some of his novels, particularly *The Cairo Trilogy*, have earned Mahfouz the sobriquet of 'the sex teacher', looking at his work as a whole, what is most striking is its pervasive, stern moralism. The novelist appears to be fiercely committed to a form of socialism that owes more to mysticism than it does to Marx. However, he has been criticized for failing to create positive, revolutionary characters, for not offering enough moral uplift, and for making only oblique criticisms of Sadat's regime. His attitude to religion is less clear. In *The Harafish*, for example, he seems to be suggesting that man needs God to give meaning to life and death, and yet there is no evidence of God's existence. Even as early as *The Cairo Trilogy*, ageing and the approach to death, with no assurance of an afterlife, was a major preoccupation in Mahfouz's novels.

Mahfouz's friend and admirer Ghitani (b. 1945) started out in life as a designer of patterns for carpets, but later turned to journalism. He is also well known as an expert on the architecture of old Cairo. He has written six novels, as well as numerous short stories. His best-known novel, *Zayni Barakat* (1971; trans. 1988), is based on the real-life career of a market-inspector of that name in early sixteenth-century Cairo. But, despite its skilful pastiche of the styles of late medieval chroniclers and chancery hacks, it is hardly a standard historical novel. For one thing, it has unmistakable contemporary resonances, being chiefly concerned with such matters as torture, espionage, corruption, political paranoia, and military defeat. The rise and fall of Zayni Barakat, who, besides being a market-inspector, was also an expert torturer, is chronicled from multiple viewpoints. It becomes clear to the reader that Zayni Barakat was a man born ahead of his time. Another novel, *Incident in Zafrani Alley* (1976; trans. 1988), tells the story of the impact on a quarter of Cairo of a supposedly wonder-working *shaykh*, who claims to be able to cure impotence. Again, it is easy to detect in this contemporary political undertones.

Many of the boldest experiments in modern Arabic literature have involved going back to medieval sources. The *Thousand and One Nights*, for example, plays a crucial initiatory role in *City of Saffron*, the masterpiece of Edwar al-Kharrat (b. 1926). Kharrat, a distinguished translator, short-story writer, and novelist, is very unusual among Arabic novelists in laying stress in his writings on aesthetic values at the expense of political and social problems. In *City of Saffron* (1989) Mikhael (who surely stands for the author in this heavily autobiographical work of fiction) looks back on his boyhood in Alexandria in the 1930s and 1940s, his discovery of the delightful secret that is so carefully guarded by adults, and his sexual maturation. The novel is full of vivid, Proustian memories. Yet despite the intensity of its evocation, the city that is evoked is not entirely of this world. Chapter after chapter drifts into erotico-mystical incantation and Alexandria's beaches become scenes of surrealist hallucination. Mikhael is obsessed with something he cannot name, but which is surely sex. Mikhael's creator, however, is primarily preoccupied with past time and its recovery through memory and literary creation.

An early example of a modernist writer in Egypt was Sonallah Ibrahim (b. 1937), who has been praised by Kharrat for his 'cynical, sophisticated bitterness'. In Ibrahim's long short story 'The Smell of It' (1964), nothing much happens. A man comes out of prison, presumably, like Ibrahim himself, having been imprisoned for political reasons. The story then sets out to evoke—successfully—a mood of disaffection and erotic frustration. It has the gloomy distinction of having been the first literary work to be banned by President Nasser. Some of Ibrahim's work has been translated as *The Smell of It and Other Stories* (1971).

Yusuf Idris (1927–91), recognized in his lifetime as Egypt's leading short-story writer, was more conventional in style and in his choice of themes. His stories, which often have rural settings, tend to be about poor people. Idris was a doctor and some of his stories have medical backgrounds. Two collections have been published in English: *The Cheapest Nights* (1978) and *Rings of Burnished Brass* (1984). One of his novels, with a rural setting, has been translated as *The Sinners* (1984). Idris was also a noted polemicist, wielding his pen against Sadat, America, Israel, bureaucratic corruption, and sexual oppression. Like Ibrahim, he was one of Nasser's political prisoners.

The 1960s was the golden age of Egyptian theatre (since then, Moroccan and Tunisian dramatists have produced the more vital work). Alfred Faraj's celebrated two-part play *Hallaq Baghdad* ('The Barber of Baghdad', 1964) borrowed the meddling and loquacious barber from the *Arabian Nights* and made him work to unite two lovers in the first half of the play and to protect the honour of a widow in the second. Despite its overtly comic and romantic themes, *Hallaq Baghdad* carries within it strident denunciations of the rottenness of the times and the corruption of state power.

More generally, Arabic drama, when not dourly devoted to political education, has tended towards slapstick. When plays are serious, they often give the impression of having been written to be read rather than performed. Abd al-Sabour's (1931–81) free verse drama *Murder in Baghdad* (1972) is very serious, however, an attempt at a politically committed Passion play in verse, retelling the story of the crucifixion of a tenth-century Sufi, al-Hallaj, as if he had died as a martyr for socialism. Others of al-Sabour's plays have also been translated and his poems have appeared in numerous anthologies in English. In what is probably his most famous poem, 'The Tartars Have Invaded', rich in disconnected but vivid images of death and destruction, the Tartars, who invaded the Middle East early in the thirteenth century, become the unmistakable forerunners of the Israelis.

Alifa Rifaat (b. 1930) is a writer who has taken risks of a domestic sort in order to write, for many of her stories were written in the bathroom, so as to keep them secret from a patriarchal and possessive husband. Unlike most Arab women writers, she writes from within a traditional Islamic perspective and has no knowledge of any foreign language. Folklore and Islamic liturgy play a large part in her stories. A collection of these, *Distant View of a Minaret and Other Stories*, was published in English in 1983. Cumulatively, they paint a gloomy picture of women's lot in modern Egypt, being tales of futility, isolation, and unsatisfied desire. Rifaat does not seem to reject men outright, so much as find them unsatisfactory. In 'My World of the Unknown' a frustrated woman abandons conventional values in favour of intercourse with a phallically shaped female djinn. Rifaat's achievement is less strident and more literary than that of Sadawi.

Outside Egypt, Naguib Mahfouz's achievement in fiction is matched, perhaps even exceeded, by the Sudanese novelist al-Tayyib Salih (b. 1929). Salih has written some of the most famous short stories in the Arabic language. Among them, 'The Wedding of Zein' and 'The Doum Tree of Wad Hamid' are satirical yet tender portraits of village life on the banks of the Nile. In 'The Wedding of Zein',

The frogs croak at night, and from the north there blows a humid breeze bringing with it a smell that is a mixture of perfume of the flower of the tall acacia tree and the smell of wet firewood, the smell of thirsting, fertile land when it is given water, and the smell of dead fish thrown up by the waves on to the sands. On moonlit nights, when the moon's face is rounded, the water turns into an enormous illuminated mirror over whose surface move the shadows of date palms and the branches of trees.

In another excellent, but very different, short story, 'Cypriot Man', Salih meditates on the linked vulgarities of Western culture, sexual desire, and death, and a particularly strong relationship is established between the two last.

Salih's beautifully crafted, multi-layered novel *A Season of Migration to the North* (1969) is one of the masterpieces of modern Arabic fiction. It begins, like many of his stories, in a traditional village on the banks of the Nile, but the rural setting is the frame for the story of a sophisticated, highly intelligent young Sudanese, Mustafa, who travels to the heart of darkness in England to study and work there. English women fall for him and for his evocations of an exotic vision of Sudan. Mustafa is a kind of Shahriyar (the King in the frame-story of the *Arabian Nights*) and the women who sleep with him inevitably perish, three of them through suicide. Then, Mustafa has a fateful meeting with a woman whom he murders: 'Everything which happened before my meeting her was a premonition; everything I did after I killed her was an apology, not for killing her, but for the lie that was my life.' After Mustafa's release from prison, he returns to his Nilotic village, where he will encounter a narrator who is perhaps merely another aspect of himself.

The difficulties of compartmentalizing Middle Eastern literature within national frontiers can be illustrated by the example of Abd al-Rahman Munif, who was born in Jordan in 1933, trained as an oil economist in Egypt, and at one time held Saudi citizenship. More recently, he has lived in Paris and in Damascus. The work for which he is best known, the pentalogy of novels *Mudun al-Milh* ('Cities of Salt', 1984–9), deals with affairs in the fictional Sultanate of Mooran, but this sultanate bears more than a passing relationship to the Kingdom of Saudi Arabia. In general, Arab novels have tended to favour urban settings and Munif is unusual in setting his in a (brilliantly evoked) desert environment and in tackling in fictional form the threat to traditional desert ways of the coming of the oil industry and of economic development.

In the English translation, Munif's overall title has been used for that of the first volume. In *Cities of Salt* (1988) the villagers have their first encounter with the Western oil technology that will change their lives irrevocably and for the worse. The second volume, *The Trench* (1993), details the rise to power of a political charlatan, Dr Mahmalji, as the Sultan's chief adviser and his success in siphoning off much of the Sultanate's new wealth. In subsequent volumes, each one of which is narrated in a different manner, Munif continues to explore the corrupting effects of oil wealth on government and society. The pessimistic message is that the grandiose new structures will in time dissolve like salt in water—a message that has not been well received in Saudi Arabia, where Munif has been stripped of his citizenship.

Although Iraq has in the past been host to distinguished writers like Munif and Jabra, neither it nor Syria guarantees freedom to the creative writer. The leading left-wing Iraqi poet Abd al-Wahhab al-Bayyati (b. 1926) spent years in exile in Syria, Lebanon, Egypt, and the Soviet Union, before being recalled to his native land and given a diplomatic posting to Madrid. In his verse messages of hope war with images of despair. The modernist poet and dramatist Muhammad Maghout (b. 1934), one of Syria's leading literary figures, was exiled in Lebanon for a while and spent time also in the Gulf. His poem 'When Words Burn' concerns the horrific destruction of Lebanon, yet the narrator's voice remains characteristically self-deprecating: 'and I am looking for a fat girl | to rub myself against on the tram'. Maghout is a cynical ironist who shuns the oracular style favoured by so many other poets of his generation.

The self-educated, working-class author Zakariyya Tamir (b. 1931) used to be editor of Syria's leading cultural magazine *al-Ma 'arifa* (which is government-sponsored), but in 1975 he was banned and moved to England. One of the foremost short-story writers in the Arab world, Tamir has experimented with fantasy, folklore, and stream-of-consciousness narrative. He has produced five collections of stories, of which one, *Tigers on the Tenth Day* (1985), has been translated. Nizar Qabbani (b. 1923) worked as a diplomat before moving from Syria to Lebanon. Initially, he was enormously popular as the poet of love. As the years have passed, however, he has increasingly turned in his verse from love to oppositional politics. Qabbani shares some of Adonis's suspicions of Western culture and is particularly hostile to Existentialism: 'The sense of hopelessness which is imposed on our literary heritage is not Arabic: it was made in France, and we have imported its contagious crimes.' He prefers to write poems with uplift, in praise of Nasser, in praise of the Egyptian crossing of the Suez Canal in

1973, in praise of the Palestinian organization Fatah, in praise of militant revolutionary action.

The ruling regimes in both Iraq and Syria have tended to favour novels and stories which use historical themes to dramatize contemporary issues. (In recent years, the Iraqi government has been particularly keen on sponsoring inspirational novels and poems about war.) In the stereotypical novel of social uplift, a beautiful girl will symbolize the new life which can be glimpsed on the horizon and the hero will return to his work after his adventures more determined than ever before boldly to confront the challenges which face him and his generation—what has been referred to as 'boy meets tractor' literature. In poetry, the traditional medieval verse genres of *madih* (panegyric) and *hijja* (satire) retain their vitality in the Arab world today, being favoured by the supporters and opponents of the region's regimes respectively.

The greater part of North African literature written by Arabs has been written in French: Paris is Arab North Africa's publishing capital. On the other hand, it is the policy of the governments in the region to promote Arabic. Algeria, in particular, has made Arabization the centre-piece of its cultural policy (something which is resented by the Berber-speaking minority). A number of Algerian writers have moved over from French to Arabic, of whom the best known is Kateb Yacine (b. 1929). Traditionally educated at a Koranic school, he later went to live in France. In 1971 Yacine returned to Algeria and started to write in Arabic for the stage. His plays, which are aimed at large audiences, combine political education with drama. The Algerian novelists Abd al-Hamid ibn Haduqah (b. 1929) and al-Tahir Wattar (b. 1936) both write in Arabic. Wattar's early novels deal with the struggle against the French colonialists. *Al-Laz* ('The Ace', 1974) treats incidents in the struggle for independence in the 1950s and 1960s in a melodramatic and poetic way. More recently, Wattar has employed the imagery of folklore in *al-Hawwat wa' l-qasr* ('The Fisherman and the Palace', 1978) to criticize certain aspects of Algerian society. Ibn Haduqah's novel *Rih al-janub* ('South Wind') deals with an extremely common theme in modern Arabic writing—the struggle of a young woman to break free from her family and from society's patriarchal values, and to make a career for herself.

Arabic fiction in both North Africa and the Arab world generally is heavily weighted to specifically Arab issues and novels set outside the Arab world are quite rare. Genre fiction of any quality is rare also—a Syrian novelist, Imran Talib, has written seven science-fiction novels and other writers have occasionally used the paraphernalia of SF to disguise their political criticism, but Arabic SF can hardly be said to exist. Travel writing and history written to be read as literature are similarly poorly represented in the Arab world. By contrast, the quantity and quality of political and social critiques are striking.

For the most part books produced in the Arab world are cheap—and look it. Even a writer of Mahfouz's status will find his books luridly packaged with busty women and grizzled heroes posturing on the cover. A novel produced in Egypt might have a print-run of about 4,000 in large-format paperback. A lot of that will be exported to other Arab countries. If the print-runs are small, so are the rates of remuneration, and it is more or less unknown for a novelist to support himself by creative writing alone.

Writers in the Arab world also face a range of problems and dangers more or less unknown to their contemporaries elsewhere. The Syrian poet Nizar Qabbani lost his son to kidnappers and his wife to Israeli bombing. The novelist Ghassan al-Kanafani was murdered by the Israelis. The Lebanese poet Khalil al-Hawi committed suicide two days after the Israeli invasion in 1982. The poet Mahmoud Darwish spent time in Israeli prisons. So did Samih al-Qasim. Tawfiq Awwad was killed by Syrian shelling in Lebanon in 1989. Nawal al-Sadawi has been imprisoned in Egypt and has more recently needed round-the-clock police protection from fundamentalists. Naguib Mahfouz has been threatened with death by fundamentalists. Kateb Yacine has been sentenced to internal exile by the Algerian government. Censorship is routine. Islamic rigorists throughout the Arab world share a suspicion of the very idea of fiction, with its Western antecedents.

Many writers work in exile and it is noteworthy that in recent decades Paris and London have become leading centres of Arab intellectual life and publishing. Adonis and Darwish both live in Paris and the literary periodical *Karmel* is published there. The Egyptian Andrée Chedid lives in France and publishes her novels in French. Similarly, Amin Maalouf, a Lebanese exile in France, has made a reputation as the author of best-selling historical novels and fantasies. The literary magazine *al-Mawaqif* is currently published in London, where such important publishing houses as Riad al-Rayyes and al-Saqi are also based. The United States for its part has tended to attract academics—including Edward Said, Halim Barakat, Fuad Ajami, and Salma Khadra Jayyusi. Salma Khadra Jayyusi, a Palestinian poet and literary critic, is of particular importance for having established PROTA (Project of Translation from Arabic), which has prompted an impressive series of English translations.

FURTHER READING

Allen, Roger, *The Arabic Novel: An Historical and Critical Introduction* (New York, 1982).

Badawi, M. M., *A Short History of Modern Arabic Literature* (Oxford, 1993).

——(ed.), *The Cambridge History of Arabic Literature: Modern Arabic Literature* (Cambridge, 1992).

Cachia, Pierre, *An Overview of Modern Arabic Literature* (Edinburgh, 1990).

3

AUSTRALIA

PETER CRAVEN

THERE is no real substance in the belief that Australian writing only got going when national publishing began to sever itself from the essentially derivative, post-colonial, British variety in the 1970s. Australia's three most formidable writers of fiction (four if one includes the short-story writer and memoirist Hal Porter) were active long before that date: Patrick White (1912–90) wrote three of his most ambitious novels in the 1950s, and Martin Boyd's (1893–1972) *Langton Quartet* was largely composed during this same period. Christina Stead (1902–83) wrote her masterpiece in the 1940s though it was not discovered by her compatriots until 1966.

In 1960 White, the only Australian ever to win the Nobel Prize for literature and the greatest writer in any genre which the country has produced, was at the height of his powers and the author of four novels which, by the middle of the decade, were accepted in Australia as modern classics. White's first Australian novel was written on the voyage back to Australia after his years of war service and of London expatriation. *The Aunt's Story* (1948) is a story of derangement and mystical intimation which also has elements of social comedy: its protagonist Theodora Goodman is presented not only as a seer but as an eccentric in a colonial upper-class milieu. It is a novel notable for its use of virtuoso polyphonic techniques, for the fierceness of its sense that 'nothing can be whole or sole that has not first been rent', and for its dramatic structure.

White's next book, *The Tree of Man* (1955), is very consciously an epic of common life, albeit infused with a bush-country lyricism. It looked to Australian eyes to be White's masterpiece even if its eloquence provoked the abuse of one of the most notable poets (and critics) of the period, A. D. Hope (b. 1907), who dismissed it as 'illiterate verbal sludge', a slur that White, who talked of 'howling dingoes of critics', never forgot. The story of Stan and Amy Parker was that of an Everyman/Everywoman couple, more sacred to a supposedly egalitarian Australia than elsewhere, and told in a throbbing prose poetry and with a sense of the dignity of common life unparalleled in any previous Australian work.

It was followed by *Voss* (1957), the story of an explorer who perishes in the attempt to penetrate the desert but who is exalted by his telepathic (and telepathically reciprocated) love for Laura Trevelyan. *Voss* has brilliant clashes of colour and dissonances of tone as White establishes the Adelaide world of Laura with an Austen-like finesse while giving deliberate touches of historical dryness to the prose describing Voss's expedition. This works both to distance and to give credibility to what might otherwise be the outlandishness of his theme. *Voss* is closer to being technically flawless than any novel of White's first maturity.

The presence of a German hero in *Voss* points ahead to the most ambitious of all White's novels, *Riders in the Chariot* (1961), with its symbolically named Jewish figure of sanctity and sacrifice, Himmelfarb, and its group of striving souls—including the apparently mundane Mrs Godbold and the Aborigine Alf Dubbo—who seek to penetrate the Cloud of Unknowing but find themselves the prey of a suburban mob in Sarsaparilla. The hectic, Dostoevskian quality of this novel and its densely laden symbolic pattern make it a book which has always troubled the Australian sleep, not least because its religious intensity is played out against a background of suburban satire, which is uncontrolled, never amiable, and imperfectly observed.

If *Riders in the Chariot* is a headlong attempt to write the grandest kind of novel, it should be remembered that Australian poetry had been subject to a similar impulse. The poetry of Judith Wright (b. 1915), Kenneth Slessor (1901–71), and A. D. Hope during this period was enthralled by rhetorical grandeur (and, it may be, transfigured by it). The spirit of Yeats was present still, not only in the nearly overt homage of Wright's *Woman to Man* sequence (1949) but even in the mock-Augustan glories of much of Hope. Something similar may even be true of the hard-lined splendour of James McAuley (1917–76), who as a young man had mocked the Apocalyptic school by creating a hoax poet, Ern Malley (1944), and endowing him with something of the eloquence of McAuley's own first book, *Under Aldebaran* (1946). Even his anthology pieces from this period are touched with such sacramental fires and ceremonial ferocities that the spirit of mock Gothic never seems far away.

This was a conservative generation of writers in more than its mythopoeia and its strong sense of traditional literary forms. The most notable literary magazine of the 1940s and 1950s had been the left-leaning *Meanjin*; McAuley, however, became the editor of the radical right *Quadrant* in the mid-1950s and a Catholic convert of the firebrand variety. In the 1960s Australian writers of the first rank were likely to be closer to Catholicism than to Communism.

Much of this changed some time in the late 1960s, and it was then that—belatedly—Christina Stead received her due as a writer. *The Man Who Loved Children* (1940) was written in America and raises the vexed question of expatriation as a paradigm of the complex fate which dominates Australian intellectual and artistic life. It is one of the great autobiographical novels yet it transposes Stead's Sydney harbourside childhood to Annapolis and Maryland; and her quintessentially Australian father David Stead—one of whose letters is incorporated into the book unchanged—becomes the balefully magnetic Sam Pollitt, a man who tends to speak 'no language'. It is a magnificent work all the same, a rendition of the darkness as well as the joy of childhood, and so balanced between the two that it is hard to categorize it as either optimistic or pessimistic. It is also, in its way—though Stead would have hated the appellation—a deeply feminist novel, and as such both savage and sunlit. Stead's major work of the 1960s was *Cotter's England* (1966). She came back to Australia after her husband died, and spent her last years in the country which had formed her. She was a woman of the Left all her life. (The Victorian Premier intervened personally to prevent her posthumous *Ocean of Story* from winning a literary prize he had himself initiated.)

If Stead is the 'American' face of Australia, Martin Boyd is fascinated by the problem of how to represent the country's British and aristocratic traces. His *Langton Quartet* spans several generations, beginning in Melbourne in the middle of the nineteenth century and involving a landed family, British to the boot-heels but boasting a central figure with intimations of a spirituality deeper and broader than anything a pallid Protestantism could muster. *The Cardboard Crown* (1952) began the sequence, which was completed by *When Blackbirds Sing* a decade later. The dominant figure in the first volume is Alice Langton, whose diaries dramatize central conflicts involving adultery as well as the small horrors and joys of family life. The later books in the sequence are dominated by the figure of her grandson Dominic, the protagonist of *A Difficult Young Man* (1955). Boyd's achievement is to create a credible representation of cultivated Australians' lives seen in a fiercely aristocratic moral perspective. If he can seem like a small-scale realist, he also has the virtues of his limitations: a mastery of social comedy and of dialogue. He is, in his best work, a more consistent stylist than either Stead or White, with their shared weakness for a surging rhetoric. Boyd is probably the least fashionable but most accessible Australian writer of his period and the one whose reputation is most likely to rise.

Few of the achievements of Australian writing would have been possible if the writers had had a better sense of where things were going, historically. Take one of the more celebrated pieces of Australian fiction. In 1964 George

Johnston (1912–70) began a trilogy the best-known part of which is the first, *My Brother Jack*. To set its prose alongside that of Patrick White is to be reminded of the constrictions of Australian social realism at the time when Johnston was apprenticing himself as a writer. There are powerful things in *My Brother Jack*, the story of an artistic younger brother measuring himself against a tough sibling, in a context of familial brutality, and much that is valuable in its successors, *Clean Straw for Nothing* (1969) and *A Cartload of Clay* (1971), which dramatize the love of the hero for his second wife, and his subsequent disenchantment, as well as the time they spend in London, Greece, and Australia. The writing, however, is often pedestrian and the perspective merely dogged.

Charmian Clift (1923–69), Johnston's wife and the model for the character of Cressida in the trilogy, was a lesser novelist but a far more elegant writer. Apart from her two books about life in Greece, *Mermaid Singing* (1956) and *Peel Me a Lotus* (1959), her best work is the journalism that was collected in *Images in Aspic* (1965) and *The World of Charmian Clift* (1970).

It is arguable that the watershed in Australian cultural history came with the Second World War, which isolated artists from the escape route of expatriation and made them more aware of their national past. Nowhere is the impulse to 'make it old' more apparent than in the work of Manning Clark (1915–91), the first volume of whose *History of Australia* was published in 1962; it continued to appear, in six volumes, until 1987. Clark sought to see Australian history through the lens of what he took to be the great faiths of Europe, Catholicism, Protestantism, and the spirit of the Enlightenment. The upshot was an idealist history inclined to present the Australian past as a collective tragicomedy of a thousand flawed individuals. Clark's style has a parodistic modernity all its own which a harsh judge might label as decadent. His prose is full of echoes of the Prayer Book and of A. E. Housman, yet it also contains disconcerting swerves and lapses into a kind of vocal impersonation of the historical characters that crowd the narrative.

Clark's *History* is the grand Australian narrative to end them all and it had an incalculable effect on the late 1960s generation who encountered it at school and university. If Clark began as a liberal revisionist, sceptical of left-wing pieties, he ended—a generation later—as a kind of millenarian socialist. His influence is very apparent in one of the pre-eminent novels of the time, Thomas Keneally's (b. 1935) *Bring Larks and Heroes* (1967), which with its convict theme and its Gothic style applies the language of Patrick White to the material Manning Clark had imagined more persuasively than any of his predecessors. It is the story of an Irish corporal who becomes implicated in a plot to turn a penal colony into an enlightened republic rather than the kind of hell on earth where men may be flogged to death. Keneally's second novel, it seemed to hail the arrival of a novelist who might become a successor to White; its rhetoric is as confident as White's and its dramatic impact comparable, despite its being much shorter, to that of a novel like *Voss*.

Australian theatre at this time was still relatively impoverished, despite the success of Ray Lawler's (b. 1921) *The Summer of the Seventeenth Doll* (1955) and such worthy plays as Richard Beynon's (b. 1927) *The Shifting Heart* (1960) and Alan Seymour's (b. 1927) *The One Day of the Year* (1962). When a truly Australian drama did emerge only a few years later, it was notable either for its naturalism or for its dark comedy. The key figure was Barry Humphries (b. 1934). Australia tends to feel equidistant from both America and Britain, and to be the inheritor, if not the victim, of a linguistic imperium. This has meant that the country has always produced fine satirists. Humphries is probably the best writer for the stage Australia has had, as well as one of its greatest stage performers. He was born into a settled middle-class family in Melbourne with pretensions to refinement and has brought to the stage all the social gestures which can make Australian life seem absurd, not only to its British cousins but also to Australians themselves. Humphries was still at school when A. A. Phillips wrote his famous essay against what he called the 'Cultural Cringe', in which he said that inside every Australian there is a menacing Englishman wearing a permanent expression of distaste. Humphries represents precisely this kind of Anglo-Australian schizophrenia but does so at such a level of accomplishment that self-disgust and snobbery are transfigured into comic delight. This is true, in various ways, of his best-known characters, Dame Edna Everage and Sir Les Patterson, though Humphries's satire modulates into tragicomedy in his depiction of the greatest of all his characters, Sandy Stone, a dwindled Leopold Bloom in a dressing gown who has taught a generation of Australians about their capacity for self-deprecation and of the pathos of clinging to drab refinements of language.

There has been much other good comic writing in Australia. Perhaps the best is the political journalism of Mungo MacCallum (b. 1913), though one should not forget the columnist Charmian Clift. One of the most notable comic novels of the time is *A Salute to the Great McCarthy* (1970) by Barry Oakley (b. 1931), which pays homage to Australian Rules Football. Another distinguished comic writer, with his own distinctive Jewish humour, is Morris Lurie (b. 1938), whose *Rappaport* (1966) and *Rappaport's Revenge* (1973) are among his best books.

Humphries's own paradoxical relation to Australia—of someone living both there and in Britain—is like a cartoon version of the expatriate's situation: incapable of enduring the provincialism of a society for whom the expatriate remains a brighter star than he or she can ever be abroad. This is true of Germaine Greer (b. 1939) and Robert Hughes (b. 1938). Greer published *The Female Eunuch*, with its account of her Australian childhood, in 1970; in its way it is the most politically powerful book ever written by an Australian. Robert Hughes's *The Art of Australia* (1966) was a sparkling performance (though one played out for a national audience); but perhaps because he lives in New York rather than London Hughes has remained more at ease with Australia, both in his manner and, more particularly, in his imagination.

Humphries's Australia is the country of twenty-five years ago: it is an image that has worn badly. A worthy novel of the 1960s like *The Slow Natives* (1965) by Thea Astley (b. 1925) can seem now like a period piece, with its portrait of an alienated youth growing up in an alienated family. The book seems victimized by the suburban life it takes as its focus, as if a formidable literary talent were forcing itself to do the work of soap opera and imagining it to be realism simply because the ritual stereotypes (bored wives, children who want to be punished, gay opportunists) had never before been tested in the light of day.

A more formidable though still only half-acknowledged figure is Peter Mathers (b. 1931), whose two anarchic comic novels *Trap* (1966) and *The Wort Papers* (1972) seem to have less in common with any other Australian writing than they do with the best of the country's shaggy dog stories, Joseph Furphy's *Such is Life* (1903). There is also a sense in which Mathers initiates a move away from realism, so giving him a claim to be considered as the first Australian Post-Modernist.

Something akin to Post-Modernism asserted itself in poetry at the end of the 1960s, in a movement now known as the Poetry of '68, which seems linked primarily to free form, Americanness, and getting rid of the iambic thump and neat rhymes of earlier poets.

Of these, the most significant to arise between the generation of McAuley, Hope, and Wright, and the supposed moderns, was Francis Webb (1925–73), a writer of extraordinary complexity and metaphysical depth who was haunted not only by the image of the Mother of God and the suffering of Christ which his Catholicism had bequeathed to him, but by the fear that he was the defiler of those images. Webb was clinically mad for most of his poetry-writing life and belonged to the period when institutionalization reigned. For all its tortuousness, however, his poetry is not debilitated by the schizophrenia which afflicted the mind that brought it into being. *Socrates and Other Poems* appeared in 1961, bringing together poems which had been written during Webb's periods in hospital in Britain. It includes such accomplished short pieces as 'Bells of St. Peter Mancroft' and 'Five Days Old', as well as a notable poem about the Australian explorer Edward John Eyre. Webb's last book *The Ghost of the Cock* (1964) includes a scarifying and compassionate sequence based on his own predicament, 'Ward Two'. Webb is one of the major figures of Australian poetry. The combination of difficulty and strangeness in his work, as well as its fierce authenticity of vision, give it a different kind of authority from the Keatsian silkiness of Kenneth Slessor or the dominant poets of the 1950s, whose preference for strict forms seems, in part, wilful and 'Romantic'.

Webb was aided and helped back to Australia by David Campbell (1915–79), a bridger of the generations whose unemphatic lyrics were admired by traditionalists and new poets alike. Vincent Buckley (1925–88) was another figure of complex allegiances, in thrall to a Yeatsian eloquence but feeling the tug also of a poetic notation which could encompass a sense of self prey to various intimations of incoherency and loss. His most noted sequence and his most celebrated poem is 'Golden Builders' (1976). In the poems written in the decade before his death a new wiriness enters, competing with the Virgilian note and complicating it.

Buckley was at the centre of a group of poets at Melbourne University who remain active and prominent. Chris Wallace-Crabbe (b. 1934) is a poet of considerable play of mind and versatility; Peter Steele (b. 1939) is most notable for his wit in verse (and for the paradoxes of his intensely literary essays); Evan Jones (b. 1931) in his post-Auden way may well be the best poet of the group. Buckley's chief ally from this period and a poet of great formal rigour and concise, sometimes savage, wit is the Tasmanian Gwen Harwood (b. 1920).

John Tranter (b. 1943) is the most central (in literary political terms) and most influential of the Poets of '68. His career shows a concerted attempt to achieve distinction through sheer will-power and by milking every resource in the poet's power. His poetry is self-reflexive and touches on morally weighty matters, rehearsed and never quite disowned. Tranter himself seems somewhat uncertain about how much sense it is supposed to make and its Post-Modern sleekness is enhanced by the fact that the gulf between referentiality and the hermeneutic ghosts that shadow it is never as great as it might be. His first book, *Parallax*, was published in 1970. He had fled Australia a few years earlier but he is one of the first Australian writers to seem inconceivable in any other setting.

Although Tranter has done everything he can (and more) to exploit his
poetic talent, in his best work he has remained the poet he started out as.
The urban world of the mind that his poetry reflects came into literary
consciousness at about that time.

Tranter's own work has been equalled, if not surpassed, by some of his
contemporaries, however. Martin Johnston (1947–90), who died tragically
young and had his work edited posthumously by Tranter, was the author
of *Cicada Gambit*, an extraordinary Post-Modern novel. He also produced,
in the last year of his life, some of the finest lyrics ever written in Australia.
Robert Adamson (b. 1943) is an autodidact, as well as a latter-day Romantic; his verse is as full of the smells and atrocities of his beloved Hawkesbury
River as it is of Mallarmean notions of poetry's centrality: *The Clean Dark*
(1989) is a powerful, representative volume of his work. Another poet,
Robert Harris (1951–93), wrote distinguished work and, at the end of his
life, a masterpiece, *JANE, Interlinear & Other Poems* (1992).

In Bruce Beaver (b. 1928) Australia produced a poet who kicked against
the pentameter and modernized himself without being self-conscious about
it—even though one of his earlier books, *Letters to Live Poets* (1969), showed
a man, long afflicted by mental illness, clutching for sanity in the face of
what he took to be self-extinction. Beaver's work eschews eloquence, yet
is quintessentially modern and conversational. This is as true of his harrowing verse autobiography, *As it Was* (1979), as of his recent more speculative
and exultant poetry.

From the late 1960s there was a drift away from the mythopoeic, away
from the symbols of the bush country. This is discernible in the later work
of Patrick White. *The Solid Mandala* (1966) is the story of two brothers, one
cosmically inclined and 'mad', the other schizoid yet 'sane'. The book displays not only White's interest in the ideas of Jung but his willingness to
experiment with black comedy and kitchen-sink realism. It is the least characteristic and the most unstable of his major works, representing a descent,
not in quality but to a greyer, tighter mode of realism. After *The Solid
Mandala* White never again sounded the biblical note of *The Tree of Man*.
His next novel, *The Vivisector* (1970), dedicated to the artist Sydney Nolan,
is the story of a working boy who is adopted by a rich family and goes on
to become a great painter. The novel focuses on Hurtle Duffield's relationship to his mundane sister Rhoda, his love affair with the beautiful Boo
Hollingrake, and the nature of Duffield's art. It is a dark and brilliant characterization, free from the seedy realism of *The Solid Mandala* but more
concentrated in its effects and thinner in texture than a novel like *Voss*.

The Eye of the Storm (1974) is a novel centred on an old, rich woman who is dying, and may be read as a homage to the novelist's own mother, a baleful and indelible influence on him. Her memories are brought to life around her as she lies on her deathbed, watched by her son, an expatriate and eminent actor, and by her daughter, now a Catholic and a European aristocrat by marriage. The tension between these three characters, at once comic and grave, is brilliantly sustained.

Whatever it was in the air that now made it easier to write about contemporary life is potently, if skeletally, there in the stories of Frank Moorhouse (b. 1938), which seemed strikingly new to contemporary audiences, as bespeaking a shift in the way life could be represented. The stories in *Futility and Other Animals* (1969) and *The American's Baby* (1972) may seem dated now, but they have a rapidity and economy, a sense of space around any gesture or utterance, which makes them unlike any previous Australian short fiction. The characters (not least the fatuous American, Becker) are stick figures, but vivid stick figures. Moorhouse allows the world of Sydney bars and dives to speak and manages to treat sex as a glittering obsession.

His subsequent work has been patchy. *The Electrical Experience* (1974) is the disjointed story of a dreary soft-drink salesman in a country town that yields the satisfactions neither of the novel nor of the short story. *The Everlasting Secret Family* (1980), on the other hand, is a hard-hitting story of homosexual slavery (of a young boy to a politician) which is tautly written and verging on pornography, but with an element of drama which often eludes Moorhouse. Of his most recent work, *Forty/Seventeen* (1988), with its powerful delineation of middle-aged sexual infatuation and rueful retrospection, and a notably successful use of discontinuous narrative, is probably his best book to date. He is at present writing a multi-volume sequence of novels with a League of Nations setting. The first of these, *Grand Days* (1993), is flawed by its archness and its lugubrious use of circumstantial detail, though it has been highly praised.

Another short-story writer who made a great impact at much the same time as Moorhouse was Peter Carey (b. 1943), with collections called *The Fat Man in History* (1980) and *War Crimes* (1979). His reputation depends less on these, however, or on the slender and striking *Bliss* (1981), than on the crowded, fabulistic novels of the later 1980s, to which I shall return.

If there is one book which seems to sum up the changes that took place in the 1970s it is Helen Garner's (b. 1942) *Monkey Grip* (1977), the story of a young woman hippie who is in love with a junkie. It is a rough-hewn work, based in part on the sort of material one might find in a diary, but it takes a fresh look at the world of sex and entanglement, and, indeed, of

love. It was misunderstood by its first readers, who either admired or rejected it as the crudest form of realism. In fact, Garner is a master of dialogue and has a marked ability to establish a scene and hold it for precisely
the right amount of time, as her subsequent, admittedly costive, career has
shown.

Monkey Grip was followed by two novellas, published together, *Honour*
and *Other People's Children* (1980), less vigorous perhaps, but showing greater
artistry. *The Children's Bach* (1984) is a novella of fewer than a hundred
pages, very compressed and a work of high realism. It is the story of a
happy, rather dowdy couple who are subjected to sexual pressure from two
worldlings intruding on them from a sleazier part of society, and who, in
their distress, achieve an epiphany. This was followed by a slender volume
of short stories, *Postcards from Surfers* (1985), greyer and less rounded, though
some of the stories it contains are among the best to have been written in
Australia. *Cosmo Cosmolino* (1992) represents a departure for Garner, into a
world, adapted to the Australian inner city, of some form of 'magic realism'. It may read like a return of the repressed, of the religiosity and nightmares that might still lurk in the head of an ageing hippie, though it is more
properly understood as an expansion of Garner's possibilities as a writer,
beyond those of her earlier realism.

Garner began publishing as it happens in the aftermath of Gough
Whitlam's Labour government. Whitlam was a colourful and a cultivated
figure and the fact that he and his party could be elected to power in
Australia indicated the extent to which the nation had changed. It was
Whitlam who established the Australia Council, a generous and far-sighted
body whose responsibility was to support the arts. The vast majority of
Australian writers lean to the Left, politically, and many of them—including a number of the highest reputation—depend on the Literature Board
for their livelihood. They have to, because in a small country good writing
cannot be expected to sell in quantities sufficient to ensure the writer an
income.

It is difficult to overestimate the cultural role of government (or its capacity to mismanage its subsidies). It is possible to find poets, for instance,
who have done well out of the public purse. Les Murray (b. 1938), for one,
is said to have received around half a million dollars in grants over the
years, though in his case few would begrudge it because he is the most
technically inventive and talented poet the country has produced. The near
universality of this opinion is undermined only by recurrent doubts about
what exactly he is saying. Northrop Frye once said of Murray that 'in terms
of rhythm he can do anything'. Early in his career he was perceived as

something of a 'bush conservative', a view he did nothing to discourage with his pronouncements in favour of the parochial, and his dismissive remarks about internationalism and about such particular heroes of modernism as Ezra Pound. John Forbes (b. 1950), who is probably the most expert critic of the opposite camp, took up the implications of the title of Murray's early collection, *The Vernacular Republic* (1976), in saying that 'The trouble with Vernacular Republics is that they presuppose that the Kingdom of correct usage is elsewhere.'

Murray has had enormous international success in carrying his bushman persona abroad, together with the poetry of which it is the emanation. The highest acknowledgements of his pre-eminence have come from his fellow poets, and more particularly from those who are antipathetic to part of his project. These include Peter Porter (b. 1929), an expatriate who belongs perhaps more to the history of British poetry, but who is claimed as Australian by both poets and readers, and who remains the only Australian-born poet of his generation who might be thought superior to Murray. Not, it should be said, as a technician, though Porter is a formidable one, but because of the depth of feeling the poetry reflects and the range of material, both comical and stoical, which it contains. A poem like 'Non Piangere Liù', for instance, from the collection *The Cost of Seriousness* (1978), reveals a gravity and plangency that are beyond Murray.

John Forbes himself is the most consistent and the most frugal of the poets promoted (and occluded) by John Tranter. It was evident by the early 1980s that here was a poet of a jewel-like precision who was also a deflationary humorist, with an underlying seriousness that was often overlooked. The worst that can be said of Forbes is that he developed his aesthetic philosophy early and that most of the poems in his slender *New and Selected Poems* of 1992 follow the same pattern. In twenty years or so of writing, and despite a reputation established when he was in his twenties, he has apparently written only a hundred short lyrics worth preserving.

Forbes's 'domesticated surrealism', as Peter Porter has labelled it, would have been inconceivable without the influence of what we now call Post-Modernism. Murray Bail's (b. 1941) novel *Homesickness* (1980) may be seen as leading the way in this respect. It is the caricatural story of a group of tourists, grotesque in both their singularity and their sameness, who travel the world, visiting not the sites that history and human experience have honoured but bizarre simulations of them, junk museums in which tourism itself has become the idol. Bail is an uncompromising artist who uses a painstaking, at times awkward, prose to produce absurdist visions, alternative universes complete in themselves. His second novel, *Holden's Performance*

(1987), makes comparable play with the world of newspapers and has a central figure equally as vacuous as the collectivity of *Homesickness*.

In the last fifteen or twenty years, Australia has produced its fair share of fabulists and anti-realists. If Patrick White's penultimate novel, *A Fringe of Leaves* (1976), looked like a return to historical drama, with its retelling of the Eliza Fraser story, then his last major work, *The Twyborn Affair* (1979), involves a case of double sexual identity and takes liberties with the time-scale. Much in the story of Eddie/Eadith, who is both jackaroo and London brothel madam, is fantastic, but much, too, is realistic, and convincing. The novel shows what other directions White might have gone in if a romantic and slightly old-fashioned realism had not been his strong suit. It was the fictional swan-song in which White mythicized his homosexuality, and it was followed by his grand and savage autobiography *Flaws in the Glass* (1981). Years later, there came two codas, a story about a senile Graeco-Australian female aristocrat, *Memoirs of Many in One* (1986), and *Three Uneasy Pieces* (1987), a set of minimalist essays.

It would be wrong to take too seriously the question of who has inherited Patrick White's crown since his death in 1990. David Malouf (b. 1934) is one contender. He is at his most successful as a writer of novellas rather than in his novels. *The Great World* (1990) concerns two men held in the infamous Japanese Second World War prison camp of Changi; while his most recent book, *Remembering Babylon* (1993), is a more overtly lyrical but hardly any more successful study of a white man living with the Aborigines. Malouf's finest piece of fiction is perhaps his first, *Johnno* (1975), in which an artistic and ironic narrator remembers the wild young man, now dead, who at once troubled and enthralled his youth. The prose is flawless and the characterization beautifully sly and fresh. His most highly thought-of work, however, is *An Imaginary Life* (1978), which treats the relationship between the exiled poet Ovid and a Wolf Boy and is a work of great plangency and semi-articulated feeling. *Child's Play* (1981) makes saturnine play with the figure of a cultivated terrorist, and *Harland's Half-Acre* (1984) is a transitional work, which recapitulates much of the lyricism of the early Malouf but is tugged irresistibly towards larger themes. Malouf is also an accomplished poet—urbane, lyrical, and ironic—though his poetic work has not received the same attention as his fiction.

Elizabeth Jolley (b. 1923) is a fascinating figure in contemporary Australian literature. She is British born and bred but claimed as an Australian writer. Her recent work, the trilogy formed by *My Father's Moon* (1989), *Cabin Fever* (1990), and *The Georges' Wife* (1993), makes a striking contrast, in its classicism and restraint, with the savage, sometimes tragic style that earlier made her famous. Jolley has been writing since the 1950s but the dun-coloured realism in favour at the time meant she then wrote only for herself. When she finally emerged, with novels like *Miss Peabody's Inheritance* (1983), it was as a dark female comedian, with a wild streak of pity and pathos that made her unlike any other Australian writer. Jolley is the only novelist currently working on a scale anything like White's, both in the interrelatedness of her fictional worlds and in their range. Her mixture of cartoon and tragedy, and the games she plays with narrative, are congenial to the contemporary appetite for self-reflexiveness, but the power of her work lies elsewhere: in its sense of the grief behind the comedy, of the grotesqueries of life, of the necessity for sacrifice, of the deep bonds between women and the difficulty in dragging them into the light. *The Well* (1986), for instance, is a masterpiece, both grey and complex, while the trilogy, in which Jolly abandons both Australia and black comedy, is a ravishing work of fictionalized autobiography.

Amy Witting (b. 1918) is another older writer who has gained a readership only with age. She was published early on in the *New Yorker* but did not achieve fame in Australia until the publication of *I for Isobel* (1989). This is a powerful group of stories, cruel and compassionate by turns. Witting's earlier novel *The Visit* (1977), and a book of short stories, *Marriages* (1990), further reveal her talent. *A Change in the Lighting* (1994), the story of a woman who leaves an unfaithful husband, combines social comedy with an extraordinary portrait of near breakdown. Witting's work is best seen in relation to that of her contemporaries, Jessica Anderson (b. 1916), whose best known book is *Tirra Lirra by the River* (1978), and Thea Astley, much of whose later work is very fine.

Of younger women who have made their mark on the novel, Amanda Lohrey (b. 1947) is outstanding. *The Morality of Gentlemen* (1984) deals with union disputes during the Cold War period, and *The Reading Group* (1988) is a study of sexual and political entanglement which led to its author being threatened with litigation. Lohrey is not afraid of large-scale effects and her novels have a colour and a boldness often lacking in Australian fiction.

Peter Carey has shown he is unafraid of the fabulous, first in *Illywhacker* (1985), then in *Oscar and Lucinda* (1988). If the first book is picaresque, the second, with its strong 'magical' elements, is overtly Post-Modern. It is one of the few literary novels regarded by the general public in Australia as a contemporary classic. Carey's next book, *The Tax Inspector* (1991), treats the subject of child molestation in a style that is surprisingly 'thin' for a writer of his experience. *The Unusual Life of Tristan Smith* (1994) is an attempt to make a novel out of the two poles of his imagination, one of which is

Australian, the other more at home in New York. It is hard for Carey to appear in Australia as the master fiction writer he aspires to be because the prose in which his extravaganzas are couched is too imprecise.

A writer rather more in the tradition of White (and admired by him) is Kate Grenville (b. 1950). Her most notable book so far is *Lilian's Story* (1985), the story of a young girl who is constantly beaten by her father and then, in young womanhood, is raped by him. It succeeds, despite its sombre subject, in being a lyrical evocation of childhood and a luminous representation of the madness which overtakes (although it does not extinguish) the heroine, Lil Singer. Grenville's other books include *Dreamhouse* (1986), an erotic thriller set in Tuscany, and *Joan Makes History* (1988), which includes a narrative expanding on the subject-matter of *Lilian's Story* as part of the continuing saga of the Singer family. That saga is further extended and complicated in *Dark Places* (1994), in which Albion Singer, Lilian's unlovable father, tells his story. This is a novel as unsettlingly bleak as *Lilian's Story* is buoyant in the face of tragedy, and clearly the work of a significant writer. With her full-throated rhetoric and her willingness to risk unevenness and disarray, Grenville comes as close as any Australian writer alive to the mainstream tradition of White and Stead.

Two significant playwrights emerged during the 1970s: David Williamson (b. 1942) and Jack Hibberd (b. 1940). Hibberd's *A Stretch of the Imagination* (1973) is a monologue in which an old derelict philosophizes in the bush before he dies. If this has affinities with Beckett it has affinities also with Australian traditions of stoicism and of stand-up comedy. In recent years, Hibberd has given up the stage for medicine, whereas Williamson has gone on to become the nation's one highly successful commercial playwright. His best plays are the early ones: *The Removalists* (1972), the story of two brutal policemen; *Don's Party* (1973), a slice of sleazy life taking place on election night in 1969; and *Travelling North* (1980), which is about a man facing old age. Williamson has a splendid ear for dialogue and an adept stage sense, though his later work has seemed meretricious.

Poetry in the 1980s was strongest in the area of longer works. Alan Wearne (b. 1948), John A. Scott (b. 1948), and Laurie Duggan (b. 1949) have each created long poetic works of some significance. In 1986 Wearne published *The Nightmarkets*, a political novel, many years in gestation, written in a free adaptation of sonnet form. It tells the story of a worldly, though liberal, politician striving to create a new party, and is transparently based on aspects of three real politicians from the conservative side, one of whom did indeed found a new party. The world is a shadowy one, involving sex and prostitution, but alive with the spirit of 1970s activism and Leftism. This verse novel is of an authentically epic length and written in a fractured syntax and a vernacular style full of neologisms.

John Scott's poetry is often self-reflexive, quoting and modifying his previously published work. His books include *The Quarrel with Ourselves* and *Confession* (1984), *St. Clair: Three Narratives* (1986, revised ed. 1990), and *What I Have Written* (1993). The latter is billed as fiction and set out as prose, but its strategies are essentially continuous with Scott's poetry and it could just as easily be described as a sequence of prose poems.

Laurie Duggan is a poet of satirical and lyrical bent, who has translated Martial with great *élan*. His major work is undoubtedly *The Ash Range* (1987), a long, partly documentary poem about East Gippsland, the area from which Duggan's forebears came. The language is lapidary and without any hint of affectation.

Other poets who have produced work of high accomplishment include Gig Ryan (b. 1956), who writes sharp, atonal love poems; Kevin Hart (b. 1954), with his melancholic meditations on mortality and faith; and Peter Rose (b. 1955), who writes elegant lyrics in a style clearly influenced by Peter Porter. The poets influenced by, and allied to, Les Murray are in some respects less venturesome. Among the more distinguished are Robert Gray (b. 1945), Geoffrey Lehmann (b. 1940), Alan Gould (b. 1949), Geoff Page (b. 1940), and Jamie Grant (b. 1949).

Black writing has not as yet fully reflected the enormous increase in self-awareness among the Aboriginal people, and the sense of white Australian guilt which has led to government legislation in favour of blacks. The best-known black writers include Sally Morgan (b. 1951), whose *My Place* (1987) is the moving, semi-fictionalized account of a young woman seeking to come to terms with her black roots and the desecrations to which her people have been subjected. Mudrooroo (Colin Johnson) (b. 1939) is the author of *Wild Cat Falling* (1965), the first novel to be published by an Aboriginal writer, and of *Master of the Ghost Dreaming* (1991) and *Wildcat Screaming* (1962). He has also published collections of verse. The best-known black poet remains Oodgeroo (Kath Walker) (1920–93). No Aboriginal writing in English, indeed, has the authority or interest of the song cycles translated in anthologies such as R. M. Berndt's *Love Songs of Arnhem Land* (1976), or in Rodney Hall's *Collins Book of Australian Poetry* (1981) and Les Murray's *New Oxford Book of Australian Verse* (1986). The greatly increased interest in Aboriginal culture is perhaps most strongly displayed in the theatre, in plays like Jack Davis's *No Sugar* (1985), and in rock music and other performing arts.

The outstanding young playwright is Stephen Sewell (b. 1953), a dramatist of immense ambition who writes towering, only just stageable plays
about the horrors of late capitalism and of family life. *Dreams in an Empty City*
(1986) links together his twin preoccupations with Marxism and Christianity,
while *Sisters* (1991) is a scarifying, almost circular dispute between two sisters.

Tim Winton (b. 1960) is easily the most eminent of the younger novelists. He has learned from the American Catholic writer Flannery O'Connor,
and seeks to show the action of grace in the everyday. He is, at the same
time, full of a kind of homespun blarney. His major works are *That Eye, the
Sky* (1986) and *Cloudstreet* (1991). His most recent novel, *The Riders* (1994),
is the story of a man searching Europe, with his young daughter, for his
vanished wife. The riders who appear and reappear throughout the narrative are like some forlorn motif from Celtic mythology.

Some of the most imaginative Australian writing has long been in non-
fiction. Hal Porter (1911–84) was one of the country's greatest short-story
writers, and a not inconsiderable poet who also wrote plays. But it is his
three volumes of autobiography, *The Watcher on the Cast-Iron Balcony* (1963),
The Paper Chase (1966), and *The Extra* (1975), which may constitute his literary monument. The prose is almost excruciatingly purple and Porter
tends to show other people in all their humiliating nakedness, while appearing to glamorize himself. The overall effect, however, is complex and tends
to undercut the authorial persona. The three books are powerful and wholly
strange.

The best of the expatriates are a long way from the gorgeous cockatoo
manner of Hal Porter. Clive James's (b. 1939) memoirs, especially the first
volume, *Unreliable Memoirs* (1980), are comic writing of some splendour.
Germaine Greer's *Daddy, We Hardly Knew You* (1989) is the chronicle of the
author's quest for her father, in which she appears, graphically, as a beset
harridan, a tremendous piece of self-portraiture. Much the best of such
works of non-fiction in recent years, however, is Robert Hughes's *The Fatal
Shore* (1987), an impassioned and magnificent account of Australia's convict
origins, written in an epic, novelistic style that brings a grim history to
highly coloured life.

The resurgence of Australian publishing since 1975 has also encouraged
literary biography. Mary Lord's *Hal Porter: A Man of Many Parts* (1993) and
Michael Heyward's *The Ern Malley Affair* (1993) are excellent accounts of
their subjects, and Hazel Rowley's *Christina Stead* (1993) and Brenda Niall's
Martin Boyd, A Life (1988), together with David Marr's *Patrick White* (1991),
have contributed inestimably to our knowledge of our major writers.

The breakdown of the distinction between fiction and non-fiction has been crucial to the development of Australian writing in recent years. In the homespun, minimalist work of Gerald Murnane (b. 1939), for instance. Murnane writes a form of abstract, self-reflexive fiction concerned with landscape and with the mental space an individual may find himself in as he contemplates it. His work, from *The Plains* (1982), the story of a photographer lost in some territory of the mind, to *Velvet Waters* (1990), a group of short stories, is an obsessive treatment of linked themes. Murnane's prose is rhythmically monotonous at first but he achieves extraordinary variations out of such apparent sameness and his overall manner has great richness. His finest work is arguably *Inland* (1988). His earlier works, *Tamarisk Row* (1974) and *A Lifetime on Clouds* (1976), reflect, at a more realistic level, the author's obsessions with horse-racing and the iconography of the Catholic Church.

John Bryson's (b. 1935) *Evil Angels* (1985) is centred on one of the most famous cases in Australian legal history: the conviction and imprisonment of Lindy Chamberlain for the murder of her infant daughter Azaria in the Northern Territory, the country's fabled desert centre. The book actually played a part in getting the case reopened and thus in securing Chamberlain's eventual release and exoneration. It was barely noticed at the time of its first publication what an impressive example *Evil Angels* is of perspectival writing, as well as of forensic argument.

Louisa (1987) by Brian Matthews (b. 1936) is an attempt, by a distinguished literary critic, to write a speculative autobiography, one that leaves space for things the author does not know about himself. It is an exhilarating cross between Post-Modernism and a shaggy dog story.

Post-Modernism, indeed literary theory in general, has been taken more seriously perhaps in Australia than elsewhere because the universities loom larger in cultural life than they might (or should). Drusilla Modjeska (b. 1946), a former academic and a theorist, has written two remarkable books. One, the near-novel *Poppy* (1990), recounts the life, mental breakdown, and resurgence of the narrator's mother, while at the same time providing an intellectual commentary on the material to create a poised and sustained examination of the inner life using the methods of social comedy, almost in the manner of a modernist 'anatomy'. Its successor, *The Orchard* (1994), is a more controlled work, sometimes essayistic in the grand American manner and sometimes intimately, or self-consciously, fictionalized.

Australia retains the illusion of having a single literary culture, with the consequence that middle-brow writing occupies a great deal of whatever space is available. The consequence of that, however, is that truly ambitious or imaginative work is all the more distinctive.

4

BRAZIL

JOHN GLEDSON

BRAZILIAN literature since 1960 has been dominated by political and social changes of great depth and, at times, violence. The military coup of 1964, and the subsequent 'coup within a coup' in 1968, which brought the pro-American Right to power, extended the practice of torture of political dissidents, and instituted severe censorship, delivering a traumatic shock to intellectuals as well as many others; and the 'economic miracle' of the late 1960s and early 1970s led to a sudden and massive urbanization, and the growth, in the south of the country above all, of a huge working class.

There is no simple correlation between these events and literary movements, which often reacted to them at a distance—or covertly, given the presence of censorship, which had a crucial role between 1968 and 1975, and cannot be ignored either before or after those years. The larger patterns of history have their equivalents in literature, however, and, to an extent, allow us to identify the central authors. Certainly, Brazil provides no simple parallel to the Spanish American 'boom' (which became a publishing phenomenon in Europe when censorship in Brazil was at its worst): a relatively large number of its authors have been translated, but none (apart from Jorge Amado, who is a case apart) has achieved the international cachet of García Márquez, Manuel Puig, Carlos Fuentes, or Vargas Llosa. Essentially, Brazilian writers still address themselves to a home market.

A previous generation, which the critic Roberto Schwarz called the 'fazendeiros do ar' (the farmers of the air), and who had, often nostalgically, recalled their rural past from a relatively comfortable urban exile, were slowly being superseded. Some, however, wrote important work in the 1960s and 1970s. The greatest Brazilian poet of the century, Carlos Drummond de Andrade (1902–87), published a series of volumes, collectively entitled *Boitempo* ('Oxtime', 1968–79), which marks his most complete and detailed return to Itabira, the small mining and agricultural town where he was brought up: together, the 200-odd poems make up a vivid picture of a rural world belonging to the early years of the century.

In 1966 João Cabral de Melo Neto (b. 1920), the leading poet of the next generation, published *A educação pela pedra* ('Education by Stone'). These poems, all of them tightly knit in structure with an 'exposition' and a 'conclusion', and with brilliant twists of logic and imagery, rank among his finest, but since then his work has become less inventive and more nostalgic (as witnessed in the title of one of his later collections, *Museu de tudo* ('Museum of Everything', 1975). The other dominant figure of the 1950s, João Guimarães Rosa (1908–67), published some delightful short stories in his experimental, poetic style, in particular *The Third Bank of the River and Other Stories* (1962), but nothing to match the Joycean ambition of *The Devil to Pay in the Backlands* (1956).

The most remarkable hangover from this previous generation, however, was Jorge Amado (b. 1912), whose novel *Gabriela, Clove and Cinnamon* (1958) was a huge commercial success, and led to a large number of variations by Amado on the same formula: essentially 'small-town' settings in the provinces, traditional values which include, and are spiced up by, comedy and a relaxed 'Brazilian' openness towards sex. Nostalgia forms a vital element in this essentially escapist literature: the formulaic manner in which Amado exploits it, and the fact that his apparent political correctness with regard to issues of sex and race hides more antiquated attitudes, results in something very close to soap opera in both tone and quality. Later novels like *Dona Flor and her Two Husbands* (1966), *Tent of Miracles* (1969), and *Tieta* (1977) were immensely successful, and have had a crucial role in forming the image of Brazil in the outside world: translation of Amado is almost automatic. For many years his novels were invariably best-sellers; they still sell well, but have been overtaken recently by the almost equally meretricious Rubem Fonseca, a writer who deals in modern, urban violence.

Autran Dourado (b. 1926) is an interesting transitional figure. His novels and stories are set in the same rural world (and the same state, Minas Gerais) as the poems of Drummond de Andrade, and they, too, look back to a traditional world. *The Voices of the Dead* (1967) ends with the arrival of the first motor car in Duas Pontes (Two Bridges) where Dourado sets much of his fiction. But it explores this world with a Faulknerian feeling for its secrets, for the tensions, frustrations, and ultimately the violence produced by subservience and mistrust, in a hierarchical society which has still not rid itself of the inheritance of slavery (abolished in 1888).

Dalton Trevisan (b. 1925), who also began to publish in the 1950s, and continues to the present day, witnesses to another side of this gradual refocusing of Brazilian society. His (very) short stories, some of the best of which have been collected in *The Vampire of Curitiba and Other Stories* (Curitiba

is the capital city of the southern state of Paraná, and was then very provincial and 'colourless'), evoke a world of small-time urban drop-outs, of
family quarrels and sexual 'perversities'.

The most obvious moment of change in the literary atmosphere came,
however, with a short story which dramatized, with unforgettable brutality, the vast gap between rich and poor. 'Feliz Ano Novo' ('Happy New
Year') by Rubem Fonseca (b. 1925) recounts the invasion of an upper-class
party by a gang of thieves, which ends in rape, murder, and defilement.
Published first in 1973, it was then banned, which only heightened its
popularity and influence: it gave Fonseca the success which he has since
exploited in best-selling thrillers such as *High Art* (1983), often starring Man-
drake, his chess-playing detective.

In the mid-1970s, as censorship was slowly lifted, it became possible to
write the truth about repression, revolt, and in particular about the widespread use of torture by the authorities. Since books were freed sooner than
newspapers, journalism migrated into literature. *A Celebration* (1976), a lively
experimental novel by Ivan Angelo (b. 1936), is much the most readable,
amusing, and acute view of Brazil at the height of the crisis, in 1970. Focusing on a group of intellectuals in Belo Horizonte, the capital of Minas
Gerais and Brazil's third-largest city, Angelo constructs a plot which nevertheless involves the urban working class, landless peasants fleeing from
drought, the police, and others. He combines a racy, slangy style (excel-
lently conveyed in the translation) with varied narrative techniques, which
reflect his healthy doubts about the whole enterprise of summing up a
society in the throes of such sudden change. His *The Tower of Glass* (1979)
is a more thoughtful and in a sense more abstract series of short stories,
equally as good as the earlier novel, and sharing with it a sure-footed appreciation of the ways in which authority is imposed in class contexts, in a
society where much is understood by gestures and by reading between the
lines.

Another novel (or series of three linked short stories), by the film critic
Paulo Emilio Salles Gomes (1916–77), *Three Women*, is a brilliant satire,
recounted by a member of the São Paulo *haute bourgeoisie*, on the frivolity
and snobbery of his class, revealing as accurate an ear for language as that
of Angelo. It is significant that in the 1970s both Angelo and Salles Gomes
should have produced books which are compromises between short-story
collections and novels: there was a vogue at that time for short fiction,
much of it ephemeral, because of a genuine sense that events were happening so fast as to make too ambitious a summary premature. This went with
the political disillusionment that followed the defeat of the left-wing guerrilla

movements of the late 1960s, chronicled most vividly by Antonio Callado (b. 1917), himself an important journalist and one of the most courageous opponents of military repression, in *Quarup* (1967) and *Don Juan's Bar* (1971). These two novels contain the best portrayals of the political atmosphere of the period: the first concentrates on the repression of the sugar-workers in the north-east in 1964, the second on a motley gang of middle-class urban guerrillas in the late 1960s.

In poetry, the ideological extremes were more absolute, and the results less inspiring. The 1960s were dominated by the concretist poets, the brothers Haroldo (b. 1929) and Augusto (b. 1931) de Campos, whose experimental, international style aimed at bringing Brazil up to date: a good deal of their energy was dedicated to translating authors like Mallarmé, Joyce, Pound, Mayakovsky, etc. Much of their critical work, and their translations, had healthy effects in widening the horizons of Brazilian poetry, but the lack of syntax and of colloquial language in their concretist constructions (and the extraordinarily doctrinaire and intolerant tone of some of their pronouncements) in the end produced a mystified sense of frustration.

One result was the rise of the so-called 'mimeograph' poets, who distributed their works in the street, in reaction against the 'cultural élitism' of the concretists; but much of this poetry, though it had important consequences in the late 1970s and 1980s, was ephemeral and over-personal. At one stage the (not entirely ridiculous) notion arose that real poetry had emigrated into popular song, which, in such figures as Chico Buarque de Holanda and Caetano Veloso, was going through a golden age, in part because of its combination of political protest and the ability to reach huge numbers of people. The real genius of Chico and Caetano should not be underestimated. In particular, Caetano's lyrics, their adventurous clashes between old and ultra-modern, their often simultaneously self-indulgent and sardonic romanticism, a style half-mockingly called *Tropicalismo*, had enormous repercussions.

In the 1960s, when political theatre was still allowed to operate (within certain limits), this youth-oriented frustration found expression in a revival of the modernist Oswald de Andrade's (1890–1954) play *O rei da vela* ('The Candle King'), which involved a particularly aggressive form of audience participation. Roberto Schwarz sees the avant-garde theatre in this period as limited to a left-wing middle-class audience, which was prevented by the political situation from exploring such uncomfortable questions as that of class conflict, and was inclined instead to moralize simplistically over abstractions like 'freedom'. More recently, Brazilian theatre has been the victim of the immense popularity of television and soap operas: the most successful plays have tended to be political and, in a wider sense, generational

in theme. Playwrights such as Gianfrancesco Guarnieri (b. 1934) and
Oduvaldo Vianna Filho (1936–74), whose *Rasga coração* ('Rip Heart', 1974),
his most successful play, dramatizes the clash between a Communist father
and his environmentalist son, dominated the small theatrical world in the
1970s. Augusto Boal (b. 1931), who worked in the political theatre of the
1960s, but was exiled between 1971 and 1986, is undoubtedly the most
influential product of this movement in the rest of Latin America and beyond, with such works as *Theatre of the Oppressed* (1974).

The major writer of the 1960s and 1970s was apparently marginal to
these developments, though less so than she liked to pretend: in fact, it
would be easy to argue that she was pivotal to the whole period under
discussion. Clarice Lispector (1920–77) was the daughter of Ukrainian Jewish immigrants. Married for many years to a diplomat, and influenced by
English-language women writers, above all by Katherine Mansfield, she
returned to Rio, and separated from her husband, in 1960. In that year she
published her first collection of short stories, *Family Ties*, which remains
one of the classics of the period. Set almost entirely in middle-class Rio,
these stories recount, with extraordinary vividness and sympathy, and a
liberal use of a kind of controlled interior monologue, crises in the lives of
women of varying ages (from 15 to 89) and situations (childless or not, with
more or less happy marriages, etc.). 'The Imitation of the Rose', the most
tragic story of all, dramatizes the gradual re-descent into madness of Laura,
a woman who is so hemmed in by her stifling background and conventional Catholic upbringing that she cannot see beyond them. She has never
been allowed an inner creative life, but finds one in the only way she knows
how, by losing contact with reality. In the 1960s Lispector published some
ambitious novels, including *The Passion According to G.H.* (1964), in which she
attempts to give her insights a greater intellectual and even quasi-religious
significance (though the 'Passion' is anything but conventionally Christian);
but her shorter works remain for many readers the most inspiring. During
the last two decades of her life, partly no doubt as a result of living in close
contact with her readership as a journalist (her extraordinary newspaper
articles, which might include a short story one day, a childhood memory
the next, a lyrical and sarcastic evocation of the capital, Brasilia, the next,
were collected as *Discovering the World*), she developed a quirky, humorous,
sarcastic, and highly poetic style which is in itself a remarkable achievement: she said that she enjoyed the Portuguese language because she had
to fight with it every day.

In the 1970s Lispector profited sooner than most from the freedom
offered by the lifting of censorship, and published a collection of stories,

The Stations of the Body (1974, translated with *Where You Were Last Night* as *Soulstorm*), which many saw as pornographic and where the high emotion of *Family Ties* is replaced by a kind of blunt, offhand cynicism. Just before her death from cancer in 1977, *The Hour of the Star* was published: a short novel that can be seen as a critique of the social realism which became fashionable in the 1970s after censorship was lifted. One half of it tells the deliberately banal story of an infuriatingly passive girl, Macabea, who has migrated from the impoverished north-east of Brazil to Rio, who loses her awful boyfriend to her best friend and, after having had a brilliant future foretold for her by an extraordinary kitsch clairvoyante, Madame Carlota, is run over by a Mercedes. The other half of the story, however, has the male, middle-class narrator questioning his own motives and identification with his character, in ways which bring into question the whole concept of a realism that is able to cross class boundaries.

A powerful and a surprisingly popular writer, Lispector has had a vast influence on those following her, both women and men. After her death, her reputation suddenly grew outside Brazil when the French feminist writer Hélène Cixous took her as a model; partly because of this (one-sided) view, she must now rank, along with Jorge Amado, as the most influential Brazilian writer of the century. *The Hour of the Star* in particular can be seen as a pivotal work. By posing a challenge to social realism and, indeed, to realism as such, and by questioning the roles of reader and author within the fiction itself—it even reproduces Lispector's handwritten signature on the first page—the book challenges the conventional relationships between readers, narrators, texts, and authors, and confirms the discomfort underlying the euphoria of the years immediately after the lifting of censorship, a discomfort and disillusionment which later political events only served to emphasize.

Two other powerful writers belong to more or less the same generation as Lispector. Darcy Ribeiro (b. 1922), an anthropologist and more recently a politician, wrote a most vivid novel about the indigenous peoples of Brazil in *Maíra* (1976), which dramatizes their plight through the dilemma faced by Ava/Isaias, the son of a tribal chief who has been taken to Rome and made into a Catholic priest in order to convert his people. The novel deals with many other issues, too (including those of Protestant missionaries and the destruction of the Amazon forests), and contains some extraordinary accounts of tribal mythology. Lygia Fagundes Telles (b. 1923), is the widow of Paulo Emilio Salles Gomes, and, like him, at home in the world of the São Paulo middle class. More conventionally realist than Lispector, her stories and novels are nevertheless powerful accounts of the stuffiness and repressiveness of this milieu. Two novels (*The Marble Dance*, 1954, and *The Girl in the Photograph*, 1973) as well as her stories (*Tigrela and Other Stories*, 1986) have been translated. In recent years, in novels like *As horas nuas* ('The Naked Hours', 1989), which focuses on a drunken old actress, Telles's subject-matter has become more frightening and her style more experimental.

This kind of disintegrating world can also be found in the short stories of Caio Fernando Abreu (b. 1948), which are often set in São Paulo or in the author's native Rio Grande do Sul, and portray the metropolis in a language as colloquial and as controlled as that of Ivan Angelo: the sexual revolution, drug and alcohol addiction, the desperate search for protection and comfort in religion, sex, or love, all these may seem obvious themes in a country where the afflictions of the First World and those of the Third have a nasty habit of combining. What is impressive about Abreu, however, is the vitality and conviction with which he brings his characters to life, and his ability to celebrate (as in a story of homosexual initiation, 'Little Monster') as well as to reveal horror, as in a story about AIDS, 'Beauty' (both stories are in *Dragons . . .* (1988), his only collection to have been so far translated into English).

Fagundes Telles and Abreu are two authors among many who are trying to come to grips with the confusing—and discouraging—situation of Brazil in the 1980s and early 1990s. In fact, for all their experimentalism of method, they are two of the most successful writers in remaining both honest and realist, in responding to the challenge posed by *The Hour of the Star*. Political uncertainty and disillusionment followed the euphoria of the movement for direct elections in 1984, with the death of President-elect Tancredo Neves prior to his inauguration in 1985, and with the failure, since then, of either weak or corrupt civilian administrations to control inflation, to alleviate poverty, or to give even a minimum of credibility to the political system. The result was a widespread mood of pessimism and cynicism, and a lack of any sense of direction, which are reflected with surprising directness in Brazilian culture. The great underlying, permanent fact is the terrible social inequality in the country—Brazil is the most unequal country on earth—which gives an extra urgency to all the questions posed earlier by Lispector.

It is difficult even so to identify literary trends with any certainty. To begin with, there have been some significant failures. In terms of quality, if not sales, there has not, for example, been a really successful historical novel. Márcio Souza's (b. 1946) *The Emperor of the Amazon* (1976), an account of Brazil's grabbing of the territory of Acre from Bolivia in the early part of the century, suffers, as do his later novels set in the same area, from an unnecessary, forced use of 'magic realism' and satire. Even more discouraging, given his impressive début with *Sergeant Getulio* (1971), is João Ubaldo Ribeiro's (b. 1941) *An Invincible Memory* (1984; the original title would have been literally translated as 'Long Live the Brazilian People'), which, in spite of its ambitious sweep, covering both the nineteenth and twentieth centuries, is little more than a series of historical and even racial stereotypes (the pushy, treacherous mulatto, for instance).

A much more serious engagement with history is Silviano Santiago's (b. 1936) *Em liberdade* ('At Liberty', 1981), a fictional recreation of the life of the great 1930s novelist Graciliano Ramos after his release from gaol during the Vargas dictatorship. By focusing on the real issue of censorship and the freedom of the writer, and by showing a greater sense of historical perspective—he also goes back to the late eighteenth century, and the 'suicide' of a poet involved in an independence movement in 1789, when Brazil was still a part of the Portuguese Empire—Santiago has produced in this novel something much more valid and disturbing.

Arguably, the main characteristic of recent fiction is the perspectivism used to such good effect in *Em liberdade* (and in Santiago's later *Stella Manhattan* (1985), which is set during the years of the military regime, among exiles in New York). By 'perspectivism' I mean that use of differing perspectives on a central problem which serves to relativize the writer's own claim to authority and certain knowledge. In one way or another, writers have often tried to put frames round their work, either by using unreliable narrators (as in Fagundes Telles's more recent work), or by the author himself adopting a knowing, debunking attitude. Another favourite device for avoiding realism has been to choose a social setting that is somehow strange and atypical of the country as a whole. Some writers have set their work amidst Brazil's many immigrant communities. Milton Hatoum's (b. 1952) impressive *The Tree of the Seventh Heaven* (1989) is set amongst the Lebanese community in Manaus, the capital of the Amazon region. It is concerned with the fate of a single family, but the plot points in several directions and it fails to reach a definitive conclusion in any of them; it makes up for this by containing heady evocations of oriental and tropical tastes in fruit or cooking, and by the strangeness of many of the characters. Other writers who have concentrated successfully on immigrant groups are Raduan Nassar (b. 1935) in *Lavoura arcaica* ('Archaic Farming', 1975, revised 1982) and Moacyr Scliar (b. 1937) in *The Centaur in the Garden* (1980), who write about Lebanese and Jewish communities respectively.

Another reaction to the crisis in realism is exemplified at its purest by the fiction of João Gilberto Noll (b. 1947), only two of whose stories seem so far to have been translated into English. *Harmada* (1993) is a typical example of Noll's work, a 'novel' of some 120 pages, with no chapter-divisions, recounting a few tenuously connected episodes in the life of an unnamed man. He moves from a sexual orgy, in which desire leads continually to frustration, to a lunatic asylum to involvement with a group of actors, at a tempo which can speed up or slow down at the most unexpected moments. Noll aspires, in the words of one commentator, to an 'invertebrate language, one which involves no main beam to support it, which doesn't want to go anywhere, which liquefies itself on the dim canvas of the blind man'. This is to take up Lispector's challenge with a vengeance, and one cannot help wondering how much further this kind of refusal of meaning can be taken, fascinating and paradoxically readable as Noll's work is.

That its bleak scenario corresponds to something in the Brazilian literary air is confirmed by Lya Luft's (b. 1938) *The Red House* (1988), which contains an even stranger collection of grotesques, among whom the miserably unhappy narrator moves, cut off from her husband, her son, and her prospective lover. This novel, too, ultimately refuses to use plot to create tension, but with less success than Noll.

In 1991 a literary sensation was caused by the publication of *Turbulence* by Chico Buarque de Holanda (b. 1944), a hugely popular composer and singer. It, too, reflects this same atmosphere: an indeterminate urban setting, an equally indeterminate narrator, and a plot which moves between the ultra-rich and the ultra-poor, between the violent city and the corrupted (drug-producing) countryside, to end in a pointless, accidental death. Here, the symbolism is more obvious: this is intended as a metaphor for the current state of Brazil. In this way, the desire *not* to represent actuality seems to have travelled in a full circle, something that Lispector would perhaps in the end have recognized as inevitable.

These same doubts and conflicts can be found in recent poetry also, superseding, fortunately, the old polarization between the concrete and the mimeographed poets. Many of those who have recently come into prominence have entered late on their poetic maturity, but this is in itself a healthy sign, suggesting that they have rejected the facile self-dramatization which is always one of the poet's temptations. Perhaps the most characteristic of them is Francisco Alvim (b. 1938), whose short poems, which often contain an oblique hint of violence, belie their own complexity: often they are in the form of a dialogue or are at least implicitly spoken, and they hint at contexts at which the reader has to guess. Many of these implied contexts—social, political, cultural—are Brazilian, so that Alvim's poetry can be fiendishly difficult, if not impossible, to translate.

This tension between public worlds—of officialdom, commercialism, sexual or family conventions, etc.—and private language is something which the best poetry needs to generate, and Alvim is not the only contemporary Brazilian poet to achieve it. Armando Freitas Filho (b. 1940) takes materials from a popular culture superficially alien to poetry, and recycles them in allusive ways, intertwining them with a kind of intimacy which, like the poetry itself, seems truncated and frustrated. Sebastião Uchoa Leite (b. 1935), who is closer in sympathy to the concretists, nevertheless employs their sophisticated literary self-consciousness in a deliberately self-destructive way and, again like Lispector, criticizes his own perverse fascination with realism.

Assertively feminine, let alone feminist, voices are a relatively rare and recent phenomenon in Brazilian poetry. Now, however, that women have found something definite and specific to say, they are making a mark. Two very different poets stand out. Adélia Prado (b. 1935) is consciously domestic and religious in her imagery, and thus apparently conservative, conforming to the stereotype of the provincial housewife; but within this role she has displayed a flamboyance and assertiveness that have made her poetry widely accessible. Ana Cristina César (1952–82) is much more the urban sophisticate, the conscious feminist—one of her poems has the ironic title *A teus pés* ('At your feet'). She writes about her own inner conflicts as a woman, in a conversational style much closer to that favoured by recent Anglo-American poets.

FURTHER READING

Brasil, Emanuel, and Smith, William Jay, *Brazilian Poetry: 1950–1980* (Middletown, Conn., 1983).

Gledson, John, 'Brazilian Fiction: Machado de Assis to the Present', in John King (ed.), *Modern Latin American Fiction: A Survey* (London, 1987).

Lowe, Elisabeth, *The City in Brazilian Literature* (Madison, NJ, 1982).

Patai, Daphne, *Myth and Reality in Brazilian Literature* (Madison, NJ, 1982).

Perrone, Charles, *Masters of Contemporary Brazilian Song: MPB 1965–1985* (Austin, Tex., 1989).

Schwarz, Roberto, *Misplaced Ideas: Essays on Brazilian Culture* (London, 1992).

Stern, Irwin (ed.), *Dictionary of Brazilian Literature* (Westport, Conn., 1988).

5

CANADA

SANDRA DJWA

I N the past thirty years Canadian writing in English (with which I shall be exclusively concerned here: Quebec literature has a tradition of its own) has come of age. Up until the 1950s the major genre was poetry; the 1960s saw the rise of the novel; drama emerged in the 1970s; after 1980 there was a flurry of autobiographical writing. Nor should one forget literary criticism, strong in Canada thanks to the influence of two leading figures: Marshall McLuhan (1911–80), who was hailed as a guru of the new 'information age' after publication of *The Gutenberg Galaxy* (1962) and *The Medium is the Message* (1967); and Northrop Frye (1912–91), whose work has been extraordinarily influential, largely because of the synoptic intelligence of books such as his *Anatomy of Criticism* (1957), *The Great Code* (1982), and the 'Conclusion' to the first *Literary History of Canada* (1965), in which Frye established a paradigm for Canadian criticism when he asserted that the country's poetry (and, by extension, writing) was characterized by a 'deep note of terror' and a 'garrison mentality'—the response of the pioneer to the wilderness.

Today, the novel is the most significant genre. Margaret Atwood, Robertson Davies, Alice Munro, Rohinton Mistry, Mordecai Richler, and Carol Shields have all received Governor-General's Awards and all have been short-listed for the Booker Prize, Michael Ondaatje winning it in 1992. A recent survey suggests that Atwood is now the second most widely read living novelist at British universities, a far cry from the 1960s, when many Canadians expatriated themselves to Britain in order to develop their art. Elizabeth Smart, Mavis Gallant, Leonard Cohen, Margaret Laurence, Richler, Robert Kroetsch, and Timothy Findley all then lived and published abroad, but by 1975 most had returned to Canada.

The foundations for change were laid in the 1960s, when a strong feeling of Canadian nationalism developed, building up to the 100th anniversary of Confederation in 1967. Canadian literature began to be studied at the universities, classic texts were republished, and unprecedented financial support was given to artists, writers, and publishers through the newly established Canada Council (1957). New journals and small presses mushroomed.

The year 1967 was a key one in the development of drama, when James Reaney's (b. 1926) *Colours in the Dark* (1969), John Coulter's (1888–1980) *The Trial of Louis Riel* (1968), and George Ryga's (1932–87) *The Ecstasy of Rita Joe* (1971) were all commissioned for the Centennial celebrations. John Herbert's (b. 1926) *Fortune and Men's Eyes* (1967) did well in New York and was produced in London in 1968. The main images of this new drama are those of the dispossessed: Rita Joe, an Indian woman, is caught in the legal web of a Vancouver courtroom; *Fortune* takes place in a prison; the Irish Donnellys, in Reaney's play *Sticks and Stones* (1976), which was the first part of a trilogy, are beset by the society around them. David French's (b. 1939) *Leaving Home* (1972), the major dramatic work of the period, depicts a Newfoundland outport family adrift in urban Toronto.

Because the rise of Canadian drama coincided with a new nationalism, the history play was an important part of the developing repertoire. Sharon Pollock's (b. 1936) *Walsh* (1972–3), and Coulter's *Louis Riel* both present an anti-establishment view of history, accentuating the violence done historically to the native or First Nations people. Other plays, like Rick Salutin's (b. 1942) *1837: The Farmer's Revolt* (1973) and John Gray's (b. 1946) *Billy Bishop Goes to War* (1978), emphasize Canadian heroes.

The 1970s saw the establishment of production workshops for new plays, notably Toronto's Theatre Passe Muraille, Tarragon, and New Play Centre, and Vancouver's Tamahnous. The production of Tomson Highway's *The Rez Sisters* (1986) marked the first major production of a First Nations playwright. A sequel, the wonderfully titled *Dry Lips Oughta Move to Kapuskasing* (1989), explores the possibility of spiritual renewal through the aboriginal myth of the 'trickster' figure.

In the mid-1960s the philosopher George Grant (1918–92) argued in *Lament for a Nation* (1965) that Canada had been destroyed as a viable nation state by the ideology of American liberalism, backed by the resources of technology and capitalism. Grant's concerns were to be echoed by nationalist poets and novelists for the next two decades, especially by Atwood and by Dennis Lee (b. 1939) in his long poem *Civil Elegies* (1968). The most popular poetic form was the long poem, in which a documentary realism was combined with national myth-making, as in E. J. Pratt's (1882–1964) *Towards the Last Spike* (1952). This strain was augmented in the mid-1960s by the more personal narrative poems of Earle Birney, Irving Layton, and Al Purdy, which place a greater emphasis on colloquial language and a poetry in which the structure and form of the writing enact the process of life itself.

Birney's (1904–95) best books include *Ice Cod Bell or Stone* (1962), *Near False Creek Mouth* (1964), and *Collected Poems* (1975). 'November Walk Near False Creek Mouth', his finest single poem, begins with a walk along Vancouver's English Bay, which slips into a meditation on life, evolution, and death, counterpointed by the tide: 'The beat is the small slap slapping | of the tide sloping slipping.' Despite Birney's keen eye for parodic juxtapositions (a 'star', a 'wrinkled triad of tourists', and a 'kewpie doll' provide a contemporary gloss on the Magi), this is a profoundly despairing poem in which the narrator recognizes the 'unreached unreachable nothing | whose winds wash down to the human shores | and slip shoving'.

Dorothy Livesay (b. 1909), P. K. Page, Margaret Avison (b. 1918), Jay Macpherson (b. 1931), and Phyllis Webb were other poets who consolidated their reputations at this time. Macpherson's witty poetry in *The Boatman* (1957), the sexual frankness of Livesay's *The Unquiet Bed* (1967), and the psychological profundity of Page's *Cry Ararat* (1967) were admired and imitated by younger writers. Margaret Avison, however, is the most impressive poet of the period. Characteristic of her work is 'Snow', in *Winter Sun* (1960), with its extended metaphors involving sight and seeing, including its arresting opening statement: 'Nobody stuffs the world in at your eyes. | The optic heart must venture: a jail-break | And re-creation.' *The Dumbfounding* (1966) celebrates her religious conversion and *Sunblue* (1978) celebrates the Christian year. These are poems in which light is the animating principle, as being the sun/Son of God. What most readers will recognize as the sheer joy of being alive—'The diamond-ice-air is ribbon-laced | with brightness'—is for Avison the sheer joy of Being in its sacramental context. She is most convincing as a poet when responding to the sweep and energy of the physical world.

Alfred Purdy (b. 1918) published *The Crafte So Longe to Learne* (1959) as Alfred Purdy, but became Al in order to write *The Cariboo Horses* (1965), *North of Summer* (1967), and *The Collected Poems of Al Purdy* (1986). This change of name signifies a shift in his style, from the imitation of English poetry to a more colloquial North American voice: 'At 100 Mile House the cowboys ride in rolling | stagey cigarettes.' Purdy's sense of pioneer history and landscape in such poems as 'The Country North of Belleville' helped to foster a new poetry of place in younger poets like Atwood and John Newlove (b. 1938). Newlove and Patrick Lane (b. 1939) are both western poets in the Purdy tradition. In *Black Night Window* (1968) Newlove celebrates 'The Pride', or the making contact with the land through Indian myth—'the knowledge of | our origins, and where | we are in truth, | whose land this is | and is to be.' Lane, whose collections include *Albino Pheasants* (1977) and *Old Mother* (1982), wrote 'The Weight' as a response to 'The Pride': in his work Nature is more brutal, and the heritage one of redneck ancestors: *'Jesus* | you wanted to know | something of your history | eh?'

Before 1960, the tradition in the Canadian novel had tended to conflate identity with place, as in Stephen Leacock's satirical portrait of Ontario, *Sunshine Sketches of a Little Town* (1912), or the gritty prairie realism of Sinclair Ross's (b. 1908) *As for Me and my House* (1941). Similarly, the new nationalism shaped a generation of novelists committed to exploring their 'ancestral roots'. Sheila Watson, Laurence, Kroetsch, and Rudy Wiebe mapped the west; Robertson Davies, Munro, and Timothy Findley wrote about Ontario; Richler and Cohen wrote of Montreal. Some writers followed Leacock and began to establish their own invented territories— Laurence's Manawaka, Davies's Deptford, Munro's Jubilee.

Robertson Davies (1913–95) first became known as a playwright and satirist. His novels, set in a small Ontario town, reflect the influence of Leacock but Davies's satire has a sharper edge, often exploring the multiple aspects of 'truth' through the use of several narrators to describe the same incident. The novels follow the chronology of a life: the first group—the Salterton trilogy, *Tempest-Tost* (1951), *Leaven of Malice* (1954), and *Mixture of Frailties* (1958)—describe a young man or woman, often associated with the arts, attempting to find his or her way in an inhospitable society; the second group, the Deptford trilogy—*Fifth Business* (1970), *The Manticore* (1972), and *World of Wonders* (1975)—focus on the mature individual, fortyish, coming to terms with his or her self; while in the third group, the Cornish trilogy— *The Rebel Angels* (1981), *What's Bred in the Bone* (1985), and *The Lyre of Orpheus* (1988)—the main characters are older, and the mood is retrospective.

Davies's best single book, *Fifth Business*, is a psychological romance. Dunstan Ramsay, a schoolmaster, tells the story of an ordinary life which is revealed to contain unexpected heights and depths, as behind the ordinary one catches a glimpse of the extraordinary. Davies sees mankind as muddling along in the 'middle order' of existence, while also introducing both angels and demons into his fiction. His devils (Liselotte Vitzlipützli of the Deptford trilogy, and the lapsed Father John Parlabane of the Cornish trilogy) are often the best of his creations. His novels are marked by wit, strong plots, and appealingly bizarre characters.

Mordecai Richler (b. 1931) left Canada for Europe in 1951. During a ten-year stay in England he wrote a series of linked novels, notably *The Apprenticeship of Duddy Kravitz* (1959). Duddy is a young man without

scruples—'Where Duddy Kravitz sprung from the boys grew up dirty and
sad, spikey also, like grass beside the railroad tracks'—who escapes from the
Montreal ghetto. *Cocksure* (1968) is reminiscent of Philip Roth's *Portnoy's
Complaint*, but Richler's satire is blacker and verges on the absurdist. *St
Urbain's Horseman* (1971) is his most balanced novel, the satire being coun-
terpoised by what the novelist sees as a desirable normality. Here, as in the
later novel *Joshua Then and Now* (1980), Richler dramatizes a decent man's
attempt to answer some of the riddles of human existence. *Solomon Gursky
Was Here* (1989) is large, ambitious, and sprawling, a farcical romp based on
the improbable thesis that a Jewish antecedent of the wealthy Bronfman
family in present-day Montreal was a survivor from the early nineteenth-
century Franklin expedition to find the North-West Passage. Richler returned to live in Canada in the 1970s and in *Oh Canada! Oh Quebec! Requiem
for a Divided Country* (1992) he attacks Québécois nationalism and the move
towards separatism.

Sheila Watson (b. 1909) and Leonard Cohen (b. 1934) were among the
early experimental novelists. Watson's *The Double Hook* (1959) has become
a cult book among younger writers and is remarkable for the way in which
it combines the description of landscape, myth, and the use of local dialect.
It begins like a narrative poem and owes much to T. S. Eliot's *Waste Land*
and the myth of the Fisher King, except that Watson's is a Fisher Queen:

> In the folds of the hills
> under Coyote's eye
>
> lived
> the old lady, mother of William
> of James and Greta . . .

The plot develops from the actions of this old lady, a Fisher Queen in the
arid waste land of Chilcotin. Her son James is a reluctant quester. Watson's
cast of half-white, half-Indian characters is supervised by Coyote, the Amerindian god, and by the redemptive God of Catholicism.

Cohen began as a poet—his *Selected Poems* were published in 1968—then
became a novelist in *The Favorite Game* (1963) and *Beautiful Losers* (1966). He
is now best known as a popular composer-singer. The thesis of *Beautiful
Losers* is that the experience of failure is indispensable for the creation of art,
a 'beautiful' failure being exemplified in the lives of such losers as the narrator, his Indian wife Edith (a figure representing both the Egyptian goddess Isis and the Iroquois saint Catherine Tekakwitha), and his guide and
lover 'F.' Cohen helped to change both the subject-matter and the technique of the Canadian novel by his use of myth, by linking sexuality with

art, and by his poetic language. He also introduced a surrealist or Post-Modern note, by mixing real and fictional characters, and using a narrator who reflects on his own narration.

Canadian nationalism coincided in the 1960s with the upsurge of feminism, and novels by women tended to explore women's issues within a nationalist framework. In 1971 Margaret Laurence suggested that what Canadian writers had done was 'to come to terms with our ancestral past, to deal in this way with themes of survival and growth, and to record our mythology'. A year later Atwood published *Survival: A Thematic Guide to Canadian Literature* (1972), a forceful but idiosyncratic repudiation of 'the victim role'. Noting that every national literature has a central symbol, Atwood argues that for Canada the appropriate symbol is the collective victim struggling for survival against a hostile nature and a colonial environment.

Laurence (1926–87) was the major novelist of the 1960s and 1970s. Like Robertson Davies, she writes psychological studies of character in a small town, but in her case the locale has shifted to the prairies and to Manawaka, a fictionalized version of her Manitoba birthplace. Four of the five Manawaka books—*The Stone Angel* (1964), *A Jest of God* (1966), *The Fire-Dwellers* (1969), all structured around biblical myths, and a collection of linked short stories, *A Bird in the House* (1970)—were all as it happens written in Britain, where Laurence went to live in the 1960s.

No character in Canadian fiction fights harder for survival than Hagar Shipley, the raging old woman of *The Stone Angel*, generally recognized as the first completely successful character in Canadian fiction. Like the stone angel in the cemetery that stands above the prairie town, Hagar is proud, unbending, and unable to love. Laurence's strengths as a novelist are revealed in the middle and last chapters of this novel, in which past and present commingle, and Hagar achieves self-knowledge: 'I must always, always, have wanted that—simply to rejoice. How is it I never could?' Similarly, Rachel, in *A Jest of God*, and Stacey, in *The Fire-Dwellers*, struggle towards an understanding of their situation as women.

The Diviners (1974) is Laurence's most important book, a large, risky, experimental novel which moves away from realism into such techniques as MEMORYBANK MOVIE, a flashback inserted as a set-piece into the narrative. The novel brings together themes, characters, and elements of plot from her earlier work but approaches them from a new perspective: that of Christy Logan, a garbage collector, whose view of the seamy underside of the small town is passed down, together with his Scottish tribal folklore, to a young orphan, Morag Gunn. This is novel as meta-history, in which

Laurence has set out to make a large statement about life in Canada. It has an epic sweep, touching on such historical episodes as the settling of Scottish pioneers on the prairie, and on the displacement of the Indians and the *métis* or people of mixed race. Part of the impulse that generates *The Diviners*, she has said, is 'the need to give shape to our own legends'. This shaping is both oral, as when Logan tells his stories about Scotland, and literary. Morag Gunn, the orphan, becomes a successful writer, but recognizes ultimately that she, like old Royland the water diviner, has lost 'the gift', and she returns home 'to write the remaining . . . words, and to set down her title'. That title is, of course, Laurence's own title, *The Diviners*. Laurence's Canadianism, her sense of place, and her honesty in describing the situation of women helped to shape a whole generation of writers. She was the first woman novelist to be read widely by Canadians.

Robert Kroetsch's (b. 1927) western trilogy—*The Words of my Roaring* (1966), *The Studhorse Man* (1969), and *Gone Indian* (1973)—moves similarly from realism towards myth and fable. Kroetsch's strength is his gift for telling tall stories, his exuberant comedy, and his Post-Modernist game-playing with technique, as in *The Ledger* (1975), a verse collection which makes play with various uses of the word 'ledger'. His best book, *The Studhorse Man*, is a tall tale with Homeric parallels. An Alberta rancher, Hazard LePage, sets out on an 'odyssey', looking for suitable mares for his great blue stallion Poseidon. Much of the book's raunchy humour centres on parallels between the horse's imposing member and the member of the Studhorse Man himself, which is known as 'Old Blue'. The book is also loosely based on variants of the Isis myth, but in Kroetsch's version the goddess Demeter is a male, whose role is that of LePage's biographer and rival in love. The prevailing tone in others of Kroetsch's novels—*Gone Indian*, *What the Crow Said* (1978), *The Puppeteer* (1992)—is that of parody.

The 1970s were a strongly political decade, in which relations between Quebec and the other provinces became fractured over constitutional issues. It was also a decade which saw the consolidation of 'English-Canadian' and feminist traditions in Canadian writing.

Margaret Atwood (b. 1939) now became the best-known contemporary writer. As a poet first of all: *Double Persephone* (1961) was followed by other collections, *The Circle Game* (1966), *The Journals of Susanna Moodie* (1970), and *Procedures for Underground* (1970). Atwood's poems are almost equally divided in their subject-matter between considerations of female–male relationships and the new nationalism. Susanna Moodie was a woman pioneer who is transformed by Atwood into an ancestral spirit inhabiting the land,

and the *Journals* was the single most influential book of poetry to be published in the 1970s, generating, in imitation, more than a dozen collections of poems on pioneer life.

Atwood is also a strong feminist. The epigraph to *Power Politics* (1971) is a bitter recognition of the politics of sex and of the destructiveness, from a woman's point of view, of the sexual connection:

> you fit into me
> like a hook into an eye
>
> a fish hook
> an open eye

In later collections, *You Are Happy* (1974) and *Two-Headed Poems* (1978), Atwood returns to the war (and occasional peace treaties) between the sexes. In *True Stories* (1981) and *Interlunar* (1984) she is increasingly concerned, as suggested by the brutality of poems like 'A Women's Issue', with atrocity reports from Amnesty International. Her *Selected Poems: 1966–1984* appeared in 1990.

Since 1974, however, Atwood's focus has shifted to prose. At its best her fiction combines intelligent, witty, social satire with high seriousness. She writes moral fables that are structured poetically by a series of dominant metaphors and which, unlike realistic fiction, work on the deeper level of myth and allegory. *The Edible Woman* (1969), *Surfacing* (1972), *Life before Man* (1979), and *The Handmaid's Tale* (1985) are novels which criticize the society they depict through a central metaphor. In *The Edible Woman*, for example, it is the metaphor of woman as a commodity, as a piece of cake waiting to be eaten. Much of the comedy depends on ideas about fertility goddesses such as Atwood had earlier used in her verse. Thus Leonard Slank is terrified of 'Birth. Fecundity. Gestation . . . It's obscene', but is none the less 'led flower-garlanded to his doom' as consort to Ainsley, would-be Great Mother, and her 'goddam fertility-worship'. The protagonist, Marian, meanwhile, trying to find her way in life as a woman, discovers that her 'mind was at first as empty as though someone had scooped out the inside of my skull like a cantaloupe'.

Surfacing, one of Atwood's best novels, is built around a complex of metaphors—a drowning brother, a dead frog, an aborted foetus, a lost father—all of them associated in a young woman's mind following a climactic descent into water, which is also a descent into her subconscious. The connections she makes between them lead her into madness as she searches for her identity as woman, daughter, and mate. Atwood's wit is apparent in *Life before Man*, in which two women are characterized as prehistoric dinosaurs, one vegetarian, the other flesh-eating, scrapping over a mate. In *Bodily Harm* (1981), Rennie, a disaffected Toronto travel writer, blunders into a Caribbean revolution. *The Handmaid's Tale* is a frightening dystopian parable set in the twenty-first century in Gilead, in a society whose patriarchal structure is enforced by 'Aunts' and 'Guardians' and where young women like the narrator, Offred (= Fred's handmaid), become child-bearing mistresses to the powerful males. *Cat's Eye* (1988), a moving retrospective novel, explores the relations between women, especially adolescents. Atwood's most recent book, *The Robber Bride* (1993), is somewhat formulaic, the protagonist, Zenia, being too obviously based on the figure of Hecate. Her collections of stories include *Dancing Girls* (1977), *Murder in the Dark* (1983), *Bluebeard's Egg* (1983), and *Wilderness Tips* (1992), the last of these dealing with themes of ageing, betrayal, and death.

Alice Munro (b. 1931) ranks second to Atwood as the most important fiction writer of the 1970s and 1980s. Born in a small town in Ontario, she has been influenced by the women writers of the American South. Her dominant form is that of the linked short story, and her subjects are always filtered through women's perceptions: their recognitions, betrayals, continuities, as they impinge on friends, lovers, and others. What is new is Munro's acknowledgement of the strange world lying just beyond an ordinary reality.

Her first book, *Dance of the Happy Shades* (1968), was followed by *Lives of Girls and Women* (1971), a series of stories which chronicles the development of Del Jordan as both woman and artist. Munro treats the growth of intelligence and sexuality matter-of-factly, yet within the exaggerated framework of adolescence. A scene in which Del loses her virginity, almost by accident, is wonderfully well done, as is a chapter in which she literally fights with her lover for her independence. The motif of the artist is introduced in the first chapter, with recollections of the child attempting to catalogue a house, 'a whole rich, dark, rotting mess of carpets, linoleum, parts of furniture, insides of machinery, nails, wire, tools, utensils'. This cataloguing impulse is maintained throughout the book to the final chapter, where Del puts forward an aesthetic very close to that of Munro: 'I would try to make lists . . . And no list could hold what I wanted, for what I wanted was every last thing . . . held still and held together—radiant, everlasting.'

Munro's next collection of linked stories, *Something I've Been Meaning to Tell You* (1974), explores questions of the relative power of men and women. *Who Do You Think You Are?* (1978) is an episodic novel chronicling the interconnected lives of the young Rose and her stepmother Flo. In a pivotal

chapter, 'The Beggar Maid', Rose learns that neither she nor her husband
can fulfil the other's fantasy, and their life becomes a battleground. Ten
years after divorcing, they encounter each other in an airport terminal: 'He
made a face at her. It was a truly hateful, savagely warning, face . . . Was
this the face they all wanted to make? To show somebody . . . everybody?
They wouldn't do it, though . . . Special circumstances were required . . . the
sudden, hallucinatory appearance of your true enemy.'

It is in this precise documentation of psychological violence that Munro
excels. The question that pervades her fiction is whether art can discover
and illuminate the springs that animate human behaviour. She ends *Lives of
Girls and Women* with a metaphor, of 'deep caves paved with kitchen linoleum', the caves being the unknown depths of the psyche, as overlaid by
the mundane. Successive titles like *Something I've Been Meaning to Tell You*
and *Who Do You Think You Are?* offer an index to the kind of fiction that
Munro writes—colloquial, but artless only in appearance. In the last decade
she has published *The Moons of Jupiter* (1982), *The Progress of Love* (1986), and
Friend of my Youth (1990), darker stories reflecting the rootlessness of contemporary life.

Rudy Wiebe (b. 1934) was born into a small Mennonite community
in Saskatchewan, and writes about the Canadian west. *The Blue Mountains
of China* (1970) is a moving experimental novel narrated by a series of
Mennonite voices, all of them different. *The Temptations of Big Bear* (1973)
and *The Scorched-Wood People* (1977) are major works of the decade, experimental in form, in which Wiebe successfully recreates the Indian and *métis*
past. He is attempting, he says, to see a face (Big Bear is 'a little, ugly,
proud-spirited man'), to comprehend a voice, and to move into the 'finer
labyrinths opened by those other senses . . . smell, the tinct of sweet grass
and urine; taste . . . the hot, raw buffalo liver dipped in gall'. Of his recent
novels, *A Discovery of Strangers* (1994) is based on historical accounts of the
first Franklin expedition (1819–21) in search of the North-West Passage.

Timothy Findley's (b. 1930) literary territory is that risky no man's land
where real and fictional characters meet. Preoccupied with themes of innocence, violence, and insanity, he sees a dualism in human consciousness:
just beyond reason is the fearful and irrational, which is ready to inundate
the psyche. *The Wars* (1977) is his best book, spare, well made, convincing,
the story of a young Canadian who disobeys his British commanding officer
on the Western Front during the First World War. Robert Ross is either a
hero or a traitor, depending on one's perspective. That war, in which over
60,000 young Canadians lost their lives, left an indelible mark on the national
psyche and contributed later to demands for Canadian independence. *The*

Wars reflects this: 'You begin at the archives with the photographs . . . maps and letters; cablegrams and clippings . . . *The war to end all wars.*' Behind the narrator stands the author, whose relationship to the archives is personal: Robert Ross is a composite character who draws some characteristics from Findley's own soldier-uncle, but carries the name also of Oscar Wilde's Canadian lover. In his memoir *Inside Memory* (1990) Findley explains why he refused, when urged, to omit a scene in which Ross is raped by his fellow officers: 'Robert Ross and his generation of young men were raped, in effect, by the people who made that war.' *The Wars* gains its power from the psychological truth of the individual characters and its realism—in describing the camaraderie, mud, cold, and madness of the trenches.

Not Wanted on the Voyage (1984) is a fable, a subversive version of the ark story in the book of Genesis, with a gin-loving farm wife, Mrs Noyes, and her abusive husband Noah. Findley's highly regarded *Famous Last Words* (1981) takes as its central character Hugh Selwyn Mauberley, a writer, from Ezra Pound's poem of the same name. The story is told through a number of time-frames, the last of them in May 1945, as two soldiers debate over Mauberley's dead body in Austria. One soldier is convinced that he was a traitor; the other reserves judgement, wanting to read the evidence of four rooms whose plaster walls have been covered with transcriptions from Mauberley's journals of 'a low, dishonest decade', and another room in which the ceiling is covered with symbols from the painted prehistoric cave at Altamira in Spain. Findley's subject in this engrossing book, in fact, is the 1930s and the flirtation with Fascism by the British upper classes.

In the 1980s the traditional literary genres begin to overlap. Eli Mandel's (1922–92) *Life Sentence* (1981), for example, is a mixture of autobiography, criticism, travel journal, and poetry; Michael Ondaatje published *Running in the Family* (1982), which contains autobiography, a travel journal, and (one suspects) fiction; Mavis Gallant's *Home Truths* (1981) are short stories with biographical overtones; P. K. Page's *Evening Dance of the Grey Flies* (1981) contains a futuristic fiction 'Unless the Eye Catch Fire . . .' (recently made into a play), while her *Brazilian Journey* (1987) is a combination of autobiography, travel diary, and art commentary.

The rationale for this overlapping process can be gleaned from remarks made by the poet George Bowering (b. 1935) in the 'Prologue' to a novel, *Burning Water* (1980), a fictionalized account of Captain George Vancouver's search for the North-West Passage: 'In the late sixties I was a poet, so I wrote a poetry book about [George] Vancouver and me. Then a radio play about us . . . But I was not satisfied. The story of the greatest navigational voyage of all time was . . . [a] narrative. So I began to plan a novel, about us.' The impulse is still to tell a story and to map a place, but the autobiographical element, the 'us', is now explicit.

The foundations of autobiographical writing were laid in the 1970s by John Glassco's (1909–81) delightful fictionalized *Memoirs of Mountparnasse* (1970), and by Charles Ritchie's (b. 1906) published volumes of diaries, beginning with *The Siren Years* (1974). Of the writers mentioned earlier, Laurence, Findley, and Purdy have all published literary memoirs, as has George Woodcock (b. 1912), whose three-volume autobiography, concluding with *Walking through the Valley* (1994), contains observations on his own writing and on that of other Canadian writers, as well as on his role as a promoter and editor of Canadian literature. Joan Givner's (b. 1936) artfully constructed *Self-Portrait of a Literary Biographer* (1994) combines personal journal, autobiography, and critical insights on the problems she encountered when writing biographies of Mazo de la Roche and Katherine Anne Porter.

Biography, too, may be seen as having helped to establish a Canadian canon: books such as Maria Tippett's (b. 1944) *Emily Carr* (1979), Douglas Spettigue's (b. 1930) *F.P.G.: The European Years* (1973), Claude Bissell's (b. 1916) *The Young Vincent Massey* (1981), and William Christian's (b. 1945) *George Grant* (1994). Or, among biographies of literary subjects: Elspeth Cameron's (b. 1943) *Hugh MacLennan* (1981), Sandra Djwa's (b. 1939) *The Politics of the Imagination: A Life of F. R. Scott* (1986), and Rosemary Sullivan's (b. 1947) *By Heart: Elizabeth Smart, A Life* (1992).

The form most favoured by poets in the 1980s was once again the long poem. Phyllis Webb's (b. 1927) *Wilson's Bowl* (1980) contains her 'Letters to Margaret Atwood', in which she abandons her old sense of failure and confronts Atwood's more powerful muse, the female earth-gods. Don Coles's *The Prinzhorn Collection* (1982) recapitulates the psychological history of Dr Prinzhorn, who was the 'curator' of a madhouse within the larger madhouse of Nazi Germany. Daphne Marlatt's (b. 1942) *What Matters* (1980) and *Anahistoric* (1988) present such aspects of a woman's experience as sex and childbirth within a semi-biographical, semi-theoretical framework. George Bowering's *Kerrisdale Elegies* (1984) is a loose reworking of Rilke's *Duino Elegies*, offering contemporary equivalents for the original metaphors and situations, and mixing autobiography with history. This, indeed, is Bowering's best work, in which he mediates between his own domestic life and the larger questions of life and art raised by Rilke. His novel *Burning Water* (1981) moves similarly between autobiography and history as, writing and researching in Trieste, he ponders such questions as what he will have for dinner. History meanwhile undergoes revision as his historical subject, Captain Vancouver, is given a lover; his opposite number, the Spanish ship's captain Don Juan Francisco de la Bodega y Quadra, who, like Bowering himself, enjoys good food and wine. Bowering's *Selected Poems: Particular Accidents* appeared in 1980.

Important collections were published by such established poets as F. R. Scott (1899–1985), Page, and Webb. Page's (b. 1916) *Evening Dance of the Grey Flies* and *The Glass Air: Selected Poems* (1985) contain gentle, assured poems in which the poet comes to terms with ageing and death, and in which the concept of transfiguration is central: 'As grass and leaves grow black | the grey flies gleam— | their cursive flight in gold calligraphy.' 'After Reading *Albino Pheasants*' raises questions about the 'irrepressible' imagination:

> I fear flesh which blocks imagination,
> the light of reason which constricts the world.
> *Pale beak . . . pale eye . . . pale flesh . . .* My sky's awash.

Page's vision, her insistence on the role of the imagination, and her control of poetic form are all shown to fine advantage in these two books.

Don Coles (b. 1928) is an important but underrated poet. His tone is wry, oblique, often melancholy or nostalgic, and his work contains fresh and surprising observations. He is capable of humour, also, in poems such as 'Natalya Nikolayevna Goncharov', in which the great Russian writer Pushkin contemplates his bride-to-be, Natalya:

> *Odalisque,*
> *Risque.* All directions to this
> Lavish property, his. Such
> White abundance. Her thighs. She
> 'Doesn't like poetry'. When they.
> When she opens them. Ah. The Church.
> Bless it. Soon. Can she talk?

The speaker's confusion of syntax and sex, of verse and body, prefigures his inevitable disillusionment. Cole's selected poems, *Landslides*, appeared in 1986; his *Forests of the Medieval World* in 1993.

New reputations were established in the novel in the 1980s, and others were extended. Mavis Gallant (b. 1922) is a major writer who has lived in Paris since 1950 and who has published two novels and a number of collections of short stories: *My Heart Is Broken* (1964), *The Pegnitz Junction* (1963), *The End of the World and Other Stories* (1974). *From the Fifteenth District* (1973) contains 'The Moslem Wife', a marvellous tale of two English expatriates, the hardworking Netta and her flighty husband Jack. The chorus to their enduring mismatch is provided by Dr Blackley, a man with a speech defect which causes him to put an extra syllable into his words ('It is all a matter of stu-hyle . . . Oh, well in the end it all comes down to su-hex.'). With the publication of *Home Truths* (1981), which contains stories of Canadians both at home and abroad, Gallant asserted her patrimony: 'A Canadian is someone who has a logical reason to think he is one. My logical reason is that I have never been anything else.' *Home Truths* is informed by a savage irony: Montreal here is a grey, cold city, inhabited by bloodless English people who make cruel choices for reasons which seem woefully inadequate to the young orphan, Linnet Muir, whose biography overlaps with that of her creator. Janice Kulyk Keefer's (b. 1952) outstanding collection of short stories, *Travelling Ladies* (1990), shows the influence of Gallant.

One of the most impressive of the new novelists is Carol Shields (b. 1935). Her novel *The Stone Diaries* (1993) takes the form of an autobiography, complete with genealogical tables, photographs from a family album, and a story which goes from a birth, by way of a grotesque, far from average life, to a death. Shields's narrator is charming in her matter-of-factness: 'My mother's name was Mercy Stone Goodwill. She was only thirty years old when she took sick, a boiling hot day, standing there in her back kitchen, making a Malvern pudding.'

Jack Hodgins's (b. 1938) *Spit Delaney's Island* (1976) is a collection of short stories in which Spit, a fortyish survivor, starts by saying of himself, 'This here's one bugger you don't catch with his eyes shut,' then promptly loses wife, children, and his peace of mind. The stories in this volume and in two subsequent novels, *The Invention of the World* (1977) and *The Resurrection of Joseph Bourne* (1980), as well as a second collection of short stories, *The Barclay Family Theatre* (1981), introduce the Barclay family, Maggie Kyle and her six larger-than-life sisters. Hodgins's Vancouver Island characters, especially Maggie and the messianic evangelist Donal Keneally, are figures drawn from the tall tales of the frontier days. His books incorporate Irish comedy, parody, mystery, biblical allusion, and scatological humour. His recent work includes a realist novel, *The Honorary Patron* (1987), and a historical romance, *Innocent Cities* (1990).

Michael Ondaatje (b. 1943) now ranks second to Margaret Atwood among Canadian novelists. He was born in Sri Lanka, but came to Canada in 1962. Ondaatje is also a poet, whose poems, like his later novels, are notable for their violent, often surreal imagery. He is at his best as a poet when writing about a figure from history or myth. His poetry is collected in *There's a Trick with a Knife that I'm Learning to do: Poems 1973–1978* (1979). *The Collected Works of Billy the Kid* (1970) is a mixture of prose, poetry, and drama, as well as a collage of lists and photographs, with a blank page to represent a photograph of Billy himself. The characters are drawn from history, but the portrayal is ambiguous as Ondaatje's tone shifts from admiration to disgust to parody: 'Poor young William's dead | with a fish stare, with a giggle | with blood planets in his head.' His recent collections of poetry include *Secular Love* (1984) and *Elimination Dance* (1991).

His first novel, *Coming through Slaughter* (1976), is the story of Buddy Bolden, a celebrated early New Orleans jazz musician, who eventually went mad. Ondaatje tells his story through a montage of historical record and actual and imagined dialogues. His next prose work was *Running in the Family*, an account of a return visit to Sri Lanka. This is a mixture of reminiscence, exotic family history, and the poet's account of his search for his roots. It is a richly perceptive book which cuts sharply from scene to scene, leaving the reader to interpret the images. This same perceptiveness is given a Toronto context in *In the Skin of the Lion* (1987), a story told through the consciousness of a child.

Ondaatje's most recent novel, *The English Patient* (1992), is partly based on the reports of members of a British Geographical Society expedition, who are searching for the hidden oasis of Zerzura in Gilf Kebir in southern Egypt. The novel is a poetic meditation on exploration, on history, and on war, as well as containing two separate love stories and several converging plot lines. All this is held together in the consciousness of Hana, the child of Ondaatje's previous novel, who is now a nurse, looking after a dying man in Italy. Hana reflects on her affair with an Indian army officer, Kapir Singh, and this turns into another journey into exoticism as her lover's back becomes a map of the holy places of Sikh India. The climax of the book, however, is her dying patient's reliving of the death of his lover Katharine at Zerzura, a scene evoking primitive myth and ritual. He carries the dying woman into the Cave of Swimmers and tries desperately to revive her, calling on the jackal-god of the underworld: 'Then the terrible snarl, violent and intimate, came out of her upon me. A shudder through her whole body like a path of electricity. She was flung from the propped position against the painted wall. The creature had entered her and it leapt and fell against me.'

This fine novel is often seen as differing in both subject and treatment from other contemporary Canadian fiction; actually, it is close to the mainstream. *The English Patient* is a meditation on history and war somewhat in the manner of Findley's *Famous Last Words*; and the scene in the painted Cave of Swimmers evokes both Findley's and Kroetsch's references (in *Gone Indian*) to the painted cave at Altamira, as well as Atwood's powerful depiction, in *Surfacing*, of the primitive ingestion of the gods by the novel's female narrator. And the dying patient's elegiac summation, that 'we die containing a richness of lovers and tribes, tastes we have swallowed, bodies we have plunged into', is very reminiscent of Leonard Cohen, on whom Ondaatje wrote a critical study back in 1970.

In the last decade Canada's immigrant writers have begun to explore their cultural roots through novels and autobiography. Sometimes their subject is the life they have left behind: for example, the India of Rohinton Mistry's (b. 1952) splendid collection of short stories *Tales From Firozsha Baag* (1987) and his equally fine novel *Such a Long Journey* (1991); or the Russia of the London-based Michael Ignatieff's (b. 1944) *The Russian Album* (1987), an eloquent search for his family's Russian past which shades into reflections on self and identity, as does Ignatieff's subsequent novel *Asya* (1991). Ignatieff, who describes himself as a Canadian expatriate, is a writer of considerable power: his *Scar Tissue* (1993) is a moving novel about death and dying.

Sometimes again, the subject is the immigrant experience, West Indian in Neil Bissoondath's (b. 1955) *A Casual Brutality* (1988), Italian in Nino Ricci's (b. 1959) *Lives of the Saints* (1990). Alternatively, the experience of immigrants may be seen in retrospect, over two or three generations, as in Joy Kogawa's (b. 1935) poetic novel *Obasan* (1981), which looks back from the perspective of a second-generation Japanese at the internment and dispersal of Japanese families in Canada during the Second World War, or Sky Lee's (b. 1952) *Disappearing Moon Café* (1990), which describes the lives led by Vancouver's Chinese over three generations. The description of Indian experience by whites has now been superseded by such First Nations writings as Thomas King's (1943) wry and gentle stories in *Medicine River* (1989), and by his novel *Green Grass, Running Water* (1993), as well as by an anthology edited by him, *All my Relations: An Anthology of Contemporary Native Fiction* (1990).

FURTHER READING

Atwood, Margaret (ed.), *The New Oxford Book of Canadian Verse in English* (Toronto, 1982).

Frye, Northrop, *The Bush Garden: Essays on the Canadian Imagination* (Toronto, 1971).

Hutcheon, Linda, *The Canadian Postmodern: A Study of Contemporary English-Canadian Fiction* (Don Mills, 1988).

Keith, W. J., *An Independent Stance: Essays on English-Canadian Criticism and Fiction* (Erin, 1991).

Lecker, Robert (ed.), *Canadian Canons: Essays in Literary Value* (Toronto, 1991).

New, W. H. (ed.), *The Literary History of Canada*, iv (Toronto, 1990).

Stouck, David, *Major Canadian Authors: A Critical Introduction to Canadian Literature in English* (Lincoln, Nebr., 1988).

Wasserman, Jerry (ed.), *Modern Canadian Plays*, i and ii (Vancouver, 1993–4).

6

CHINA, TAIWAN, AND HONG KONG

ALISON BAILEY

PRIOR to 1949, Chinese literature emanated from one major source: the Chinese mainland. After 1949, once the Communists had taken control of the mainland, the Nationalists fled to Taiwan. Radical ideological and cultural divergences between the rival Chinese states then played a significant role in the development of two literatures, even if there are, also, remarkable similarities, founded on responses to a shared heritage. Hong Kong represents yet a third source of Chinese literature, both creatively and as a conduit through which writing unobtainable elsewhere can be published or bought. Finally, after the Tiananmen Massacre in 1989, a new avenue for Chinese literature opened up through exile.

Traditional culture has proved at once a source of pride and a burden for modern Chinese writers, who have been trying to come to terms with it since the middle of the nineteenth century. Fiction, in particular, has always been at the centre of bids for modernization. Back in 1902 Liang Qichao* (1873–1929), an influential reformer, exclaimed, 'If you want to revitalize a country's populace, you must first revitalize that country's fiction.' Since then, the connection between fiction and national salvation, supported by traditional views of literature's function as moral arbiter, and by the literati's traditionally close ties to government, has become increasingly explicit.

Vernacular fiction, formerly despised as a 'popular' genre, became the dominant genre of the twentieth century. Believed by reformers to embody and convey the dynamism of modern societies in the West and Japan, it was perceived as the medium through which mass education and the inculcation of modern ideas were to be achieved. Writers took it on themselves to be China's saviours, and this preoccupation has dominated literary discourse throughout the century.

* The PRC Pinyin romanization system has been used throughout, except for Taiwanese names. With Chinese the surname precedes the given name. It is customary for Chinese writers to use pen-names: writers' real names appear here in brackets.

The New Culture, or May Fourth, movement (c.1917–27) challenged orthodoxy in radical ways and has shaped social and cultural discourse ever since. With 'Science' and 'Democracy' as their keywords, reformers promoted Westernization and attempted a total rejection of China's cultural past. The classical language, for so many centuries the élite mode of expression, was replaced by a vernacular which eschewed the elegant, concise indirection of its literary ancestor and was strongly influenced by Western syntax. The short story, an imported genre, became the dominant literary form, best able to convey the intensely lyrical subjectivity typical of May Fourth fiction. The first-person narrator appeared for the first time in vernacular fiction and autobiographical modes prevailed. Writers like Lu Xun (1881–1936) were fired with the desire to expose China's problems and employed a form of 'critical realism' with which to do it.

By the 1930s and 1940s Chinese writers had become increasingly left-leaning and the lyrical short story was largely superseded by satirical works and by long novels with rural settings that espoused collective rather than individualist values. Satire soon declined in influence, however, because it was considered unpatriotic and too negative. Left-wing writers began to emulate Soviet-style Socialist Realism, whose aim was not simply to reflect reality but to shape it, through the promotion of a particular Marxist ideology. This, with certain variations, was to become the predominant fictional form on the mainland until after Mao Zedong's death in 1976.

THE MAINLAND

In 1942 Mao Zedong laid down prescriptive rules circumscribing mainland Chinese literature for the next forty years. Literature's primary function was to be political: aesthetic and entertainment values were largely suppressed. The writer's audience was to be workers, peasants, and soldiers, to whom his or her work must be easily comprehensible, promoting the Party spirit and reflecting the 'real life' of the people. This last meant depicting a bright, idealistic future, little if any psychological probing, and increased numbers of exemplary protagonists of the right class background. Bourgeois individualism, critical realism, and satire were to be avoided, as were Westernized styles: 'national forms' based on oral literature and folk-songs were to be adopted. The palatable, if simplistic, agitprop works of the peasant writer Zhao Shuli (1906–70) became the epitome of the Mao ideal.

After 1949 writers on the mainland came under increasing and eventually overwhelming Party control. A massive bureaucracy was set up which led campaigns, initiated and dominated literary debates, and co-opted large numbers of writers through a system of providing salaries, housing, privileges, and status. Many younger writers were committed to the ideals of the Party, and were willingly enlisted.

A mounting number of campaigns aimed at ensuring conformity of thought, and alternating positive and negative views of the role of intellectuals, meant, however, that this 'golden age' was short-lived. The number of new titles published after 1949 went down drastically. Even so, the massive purges of the Anti-Rightists' campaign of 1957–8 took many by surprise. Approximately half a million people, including a large number of writers, were labelled as Rightists and sent to prison, to labour camps, or into internal exile, some for over twenty years. Many ex-Rightists, rehabilitated in the late 1970s, played an important role in the development of contemporary Chinese fiction.

In the mid-1960s ideological splits disguised as literary debates heralded the Cultural Revolution (1966–76), a mass campaign initiated by Mao in order to seize power from less hard-line opponents. It tore the country apart. Enormous numbers of people underwent 'criticism and struggle' sessions, many involving brutal treatment. Families and colleagues denounced and betrayed each other. Enforced separations, imprisonment, and suicides were all too common. Urban intellectuals and cadres were sent to the countryside 'to learn from the peasants', leading lives there of hardship and uncertainty. Leading cultural and political figures were beaten, imprisoned, and killed. These traumatic events still reverberate today and had profound implications for the literature of the succeeding decades.

Eventually factional violence was perceived to be out of hand and the army intervened. The Party restored order by sending rebellious urban youth (*zhiqing*) into long-term exile in the countryside. The mixed experiences of this generation became the subject-matter of a large number of works after the Cultural Revolution was over and they had returned home. Many of the most important recent writers are former Red Guards or 'rusticated youth'.

Literature suffered badly during the Cultural Revolution. Only one major novelist emerged, Hao Ran (Liang Jinguang, b. 1932), a writer whose long novels carefully reflect prevailing policy but whose occasionally stirring prose, with its strong debts to traditional fiction, could not prevent his work joining him in obscurity when his Party backers fell in 1976. Literature was absolute in its moral certainty: no ambiguity or irony was allowed. Certain classics and translations of modern Leftist writers abroad were available to a privileged few, including many young people amongst whom they circulated illictly. Some underground works were hand-copied and passed around in the later years of the Cultural Revolution, but the works of Mao formed the dominant canon.

A new period of comparative freedom of expression began after Mao's death, as the Maoists and the more reform-minded faction headed by Deng Xiaoping fought for power. In 1977 a pro-intellectual story by a young writer, Liu Xinwu (b. 1942), entitled *Banzhuren* ('The Class Teacher') was published in the most important of the Party's literary journals. This indifferently written story was an event of major political significance, representing as it did the first sign of a thaw. In 1978 another story was published, this time in a Shanghai paper, which heralded a flood of similar tales of suffering during the Cultural Revolution. *Shanghen* ('The Scar') by Lu Xinhua (b. 1954) is a melodramatic account of a young woman's alienation from her counter-revolutionary mother. A maudlin tale with a politically correct happy ending, or 'bright tail', its sentimental tone proved no barrier to its success. It established itself as the forerunner of an officially backed genre of literature of the 'Wounded' or 'Scarred' (*Shanghen wenxue*). 'Wounded' literature is characterized by its rhetorical excess and its themes of the exposure of suffering and resolution, as well as by its remarkable uniformity. Mostly written by members of the generation of millions of young people who had been 'rusticated' and were now returning in force to the cities, it provided a sanctioned form of catharsis, for writers and readers alike.

'Wounded' literature focused on the traumatic experiences of the Cultural Revolution in terms of unrelieved darkness. Prior to 1982, much of it dealt with persecution, corrupt cadres, honest peasants, hard work and no pleasure, rape, suicide, and hopelessness. There was at first little questioning or apportioning of blame, except for Mao's wife and cohorts, although over time Mao's initially sacrosanct role has been increasingly undermined. The prescribed positive endings give ground for hope thanks to Party support and the protagonists' desire to serve the New China. Kong Jiesheng's (b. 1952) stories from this period are representative.

After this came a re-evaluation, with several writers feeling the need to show that life in the countryside had not necessarily been one of unrelieved hardship and that not everyone had been a victim: many had volunteered to go and felt their experience had been valuable. Shi Tiesheng's (b. 1951) nostalgic idyll *Wo yaoyuande Qingpingwan* ('My Faraway Qingpingwan', 1983) is a good example of this tendency, whose most engaging example, however, is Ah Cheng's *Qiwang* ('The Chess King', 1984), which I will consider below.

The years 1978–9 marked the Democracy Movement, largely initiated by disillusioned ex-Red Guards. One of the most important publications to surface during this was *Jintian* (*Today*), a journal which published fiction and poetry by writers destined to become internationally renowned (it is now published in exile under the editorship of the poet Bei Dao (Zhao Zhenkai, b. 1949)). *Today* and its contributors had a profound impact on Chinese writing. Bei Dao, Chen Maiping, and others wrote fiction which was highly innovative and experimental, but it was their poetry which was to break moulds and undermine the all-pervasive Maoist discourse. The 'Misty' or 'Obscure' poetry (*menglong shi*) of such as Bei Dao, Gu Cheng, and Shu Ting was highly disturbing to orthodox critics because it broke with the 'realist' mode they wrongly considered to be traditional in China and turned instead to private symbolism and to Western modernist models.

Also significant was the renewed emphasis on the self in this poetry and fiction. Maoism had given priority to the community over the self and individualism became associated with bourgeois reaction. In the wake of the massive disillusionment and loss of ideals after the Cultural Revolution, however, a new 'I' emerged, or the 'self as hero'. The late 1970s also saw the return of the Rightists to the fold: tens of thousands were finally released from labour camps or allowed to return from exile in the hinterlands. A number of previously silenced writers began writing again, focusing on the ideals of the 'golden age', on their experiences and feelings when denied by the Party, and their tentative joy at being re-accepted. In general, the fiction of these ex-Rightists displays a remarkable level of loyalty to the Party in its reformed state and great optimism for China's future.

Ex-Rightist authors include Wang Meng (b. 1934) and Zhang Xianliang (b. 1936), both of whom have achieved international recognition. Wang Meng remained a Party loyalist and idealist until recently. Despite his conformist views his fiction is experimental, or even modernist, although Wang Meng himself seems reluctant to accept this label because of its negative connotations. He prefers to locate his experiments within a Chinese tradition, although his work is strongly influenced by Russian and Soviet models. The 'self as hero' makes a frequent appearance in his early post-rehabilitation fiction, much of which seems to be based on his own experience. His 1979 novel, *Buli* (*Bolshevik Salute*) can be read as a sequel to a controversial story of 1956, *Zuzhibu xinlaide nianqingren* ('The Young Newcomer in the Organization Department'), which brought about his exile. Breaking with the chronological narrative characteristic of post-1949 fiction, *Bolshevik Salute* moves back and forth between past and present in a carefully structured way, chronicling the highly subjective reflections of an idealist Rightist—a radical and controversial departure at the time.

Wang Meng has continued to experiment with chronology and with interior monologue in such short stories and novels as *Hudie* ('The Butterfly'), *Chun zhi sheng* ('Voices of Spring', 1979), and *Huodong bianrenxing* (*Movable Parts*, 1987). He has come under attack for the perceived obscurity of his work which, orthodox critics argue, makes it incomprehensible to the masses. His style is noted for its rhetorical flourishes, its flamboyant play with different linguistic registers, and the swiftly changing thought processes of his protagonists. Western readers may find his writing florid and self-indulgent, but many Chinese critics praise the innovative way in which he plays with the language, creating an aesthetic effect far removed from the concision of most classical Chinese genres and from the simplicities of the Maoist era.

Zhang Xianliang's prison-camp novels, especially *Nanren yiban shi nüren* (*Half of Man is Woman*, 1985), caused a tremendous stir in mainland China. Forming a series, and semi-autobiographical in nature, they focus on the ruminations of an intellectual Rightist narrator named Zhang during and after his twenty years of hard labour. One has to assume that it is the controversial nature of the subject-matter, combining details of the Chinese gulag with episodes of lust and impotence to allegorize the plight of the Chinese intellectual, that has brought him so much attention. His prose is often laborious and overly intellectual, while his symbolism is rather heavy-handed. The narrator is profoundly ambivalent in his attitude towards women, who seem to represent a China alternately yearned for and rejected or rejecting.

A much underrated but far better account of an intellectual's plight in virtual captivity during the Cultural Revolution is Yang Jiang's (b. 1911) *Ganxiao liuji* (*Six Chapters from my Life 'Down under'*, 1981). Yang Jiang's model is the delicate and moving early nineteenth-century memoir by Shen Fu, *Fusheng liuji* (*Six Records of a Floating Life*). Like its predecessor, Yang Jiang's work is subtle in its play of memories and of repetition. Deliberately understated in its detailing of fruitless hard labour and painful partings, Yang Jiang's spare and classically concise prose is a highly effective medium for exposing the absurd and terrible ironies of that time.

Understated too are the short stories of Chen Ruoxi (Ch'en Jo-hsi, b. 1938), a writer from Taiwan who returned to help the Motherland. Unfortunately for Chen, her stay coincided with the Cultural Revolution. Unable to write before leaving again, she then produced some of the first and best accounts of that period. Her work's main significance lies in its cool documentary style, which makes it of historical or sociological rather than literary interest; none the less, her writing is effectively quiet and undramatic, dwelling on the small incidents that underline the absurdities of that upside-down world. Her narrators allow a sense of initial dismay to develop into mounting disbelief and horror at the things people do to each other in the name of revolution. The title story of her best-known collection *Yin xianzhang* ('Mayor Yin', 1978) is a fine example of her work.

The early 1980s saw a comparative easing of literary restrictions, although successive campaigns against writers and against modernist experimentation ensured a certain degree of conformity. Many writers, such as Gao Xiaosheng (b. 1928), were engaged in 'reform literature', extolling the merits of modernization and the gradual dismantling of central control in industry and agriculture. Others were more critical or promoted the needs of special interest groups, particularly scientists and intellectuals. Zhang Jie (b. 1937) has been seen as an advocate for women, particularly divorcées, with her novella *Fangzhou* ('The Ark', 1981). Her work is technically accomplished and often satirical in nature. Along with the majority of 'reform' writers, she continued to write within accepted confines, although her work sat less easily with the authorities than that of some. The overall effect of 'reform' literature was subtly, and often unconciously, to assist in the process of delegitimizing Party authority.

A far more profound threat to literary orthodoxy came from the influx of light reading, martial-arts fiction, love stories, crime stories, and pornography. Moral, didactic, and ideological guidelines were severely shaken. The number of translations of foreign works increased dramatically, including much Western popular literature. Political reforms and an increased openness encouraged more debate.

The year 1985 was a key one, when a number of different trends emerged almost simultaneously, the effects of which are still being felt. These included the influential 'Roots' school of fiction, avant-garde experimentalism, and experiments in other forms such as oral literature.

The works of Ah Cheng (Zhong Acheng, b. 1949) represent a breakthrough. He was sent to the countryside during the Cultural Revolution. There, he seems to have been an inveterate story-teller, swapping stories for food, a major preoccupation in his work. In 1984 he was persuaded to publish his most famous story, 'The Chess King', which was followed closely in 1985 by two more stories in the same series, *Haizi wang* ('King of the Children') and *Shu wang* ('King of the Trees'). Like many of his contemporaries, Ah Cheng writes about the life of urban youth in exile in the countryside. Where he differs from them is in his adept handling of philosophical themes, particularly Daoism and Confucianism, and his adaptation of traditional language to modern circumstances. His work is free of the didacticism so typical of post-1949 literature. This, along with his lack of bitterness and refreshing humour (thin on the ground in contemporary Chinese literature), has made him very popular with a large readership outside the mainland.

'Roots' literature has its basis in the desire of 'rusticated youth' to come to terms with its experiences and in an attempt to understand or redefine Chinese culture. Writers began looking for—and creating—a mythic or idealized 'China' through an exploration of past traditions, peasant life, local cultures, and marginal areas where, ironically, the majority Han Chinese culture is least dominant. Ironically, too, most 'Roots' writers are urban-based, so that there is a distance, mental, geographical, and often temporal, between them and the worlds they describe.

From 1985 on, 'Roots' literature became a major force. Its best-known writers include Jia Pingwa (b. 1952), with his accounts of peasant life and rural reform in remote Shangzhou; Zhaxi Dawa (b. 1959), with his exotic Tibetan tales; and Zheng Wanlong's (b. 1944) rather brutish frontier stories. Rural or border area settings seem to have the effect of freeing writers from their inhibitions. Masculinity, violence, and male sexual prowess come to the fore, in far more explicit detail than ever before, while women (most 'Roots' writers seem to be men) remain symbols of ambivalence, to be treated with brutality or desired as sexual objects or mothers of sons. For example, the 'Roots'-influenced Liu Heng's (b. 1954) novella *Fuxi Fuxi* (1988) blends ancient Chinese myth with a claustrophobic account of sexual obsession, quasi-incest, and fathers' desire for male heirs. Death inevitably follows sexual transgression, but the male protagonist's bizarre death by drowning gives him an ironic immortality as his highly visible genitals pass into legend.

'Roots' literature contains a plethora of marginal figures imbued with symbolic complexity: mutes, primitives, idiots, the insane, the impotent, and the maimed. The work of Han Shaogong (b. 1953), a former Red Guard and 'rusticated youth', is typical. His landscapes and people, although nominally rooted in remote mountainous regions of Hunan and drawn from his vision of ancient Chu culture, seem to be allegorical in nature, posing questions about China and the Chinese character that go beyond regionalism. His most famous early stories, *Guiqulai* ('The Return', 1985) and *Langaizi* ('The Blue Bottle Cap', 1985), deal indirectly with the aftermath of the Cultural Revolution. 'The Return' describes the bewildering visit a young man makes to a remote village, where he is welcomed by villagers certain he is someone else. Denying this at first, the narrator eventually seems to concede that he might once have been this other person, but the question of his identity is left uncertain. The story hinges on memory, alienation, and the loss of self, as the protagonist collaborates in the dislocation of his own identity and accepts almost unconcernedly his role in a murder.

Han's most controversial works, *Ba Ba Ba* ('Dad Dad Dad', 1986) and *Nü Nü Nü* ('Woman Woman Woman', 1986), deal explicitly, if allegorically, with the 'fossilization of the Chinese race'. 'Dad Dad Dad' is set in an isolated mountain village apparently untouched by modern life and rife with superstition and cruelty: a microcosmic 'China'. At the centre of the story is an idiot, Bing Zai, whose sole vocabulary consists of the words 'Dad, Dad', which he aims at any man in sight, and 'Fuck your mother'. Bing Zai becomes in turn the butt of the villagers' cruelty, a sage, and a failed sacrifice. Around him the villagers fight battles with the neighbouring village and embark on an exodus after a mass self-inflicted poisoning of the weaker members. Bing Zai survives, presumably as an indication that the whole stupid cycle of destruction and ignorance will continue. In 'Woman Woman Woman' an old woman suffers a stroke and becomes tyrannical before evolving backwards into a monstrous, caged fish and dying in mysterious circumstances. The narrator, a devoted nephew, retreats into yearning for a life uncomplicated by anything except doing the washing-up.

The peasant-born 'Roots' writer Mo Yan (Guan Moye, b. 1956) sets his stories and novels in rural Shandong. In the West he is best known for his family saga *Honggaoliang jiazu* (*Red Sorghum*, 1987), which is a powerful and nostalgic record of recent Chinese history as it affects one family. It offers a glorious vision of heroes and brave women who dwell in a fabulous traditional world unlikely ever to have existed except in imagination. Life is often brutal but described in sensuous, epic detail. More rooted in contemporary China is his *Tiantang suantai zhi ge* (*Paradise County Garlic Song*, 1988), based on an actual rural riot against excessive local taxes in 1987. Mo Yan's often shockingly violent short stories deal with themes of impotence, obsession, and a limited redemption: rural life is not depicted nostalgically but imbued with a dark, sour aftertaste.

Other tendencies appearing after 1985 include the urban 'hippy' or 'Stray youth' fiction of Liu Suola, Hong Feng (b. 1957), and others, which many Chinese critics have condemned as nihilistic. Wang Shuo (b. 1958) continued the trend towards an uncommitted, cynical fiction that was enormously popular for a time with young readers. Characterized as 'hooligan' literature, his writing is iconoclastic and, a rare phenomenon, humorous.

Describing a counter-culture of young people living on society's margins, Wang Shuo delights in language play, revelling in the intricacies of Beijing slang and parodying officialese. As an entrepreneur free of literary hierarchies, he has been able to preserve an independence unavailable to other Chinese writers until very recently. Wang Shuo's work is seen by some as irredeemably vulgar and anti-intellectual, but he has made a contribution towards freeing contemporary Chinese fiction of didacticism and its intellectual focus. A recent attempt to emulate his popularity in a different style has been the controversial (and temporarily banned) best-seller *Feidu* (*Ruined City*, 1993) by Jia Pingwa. This knowing, prurient novel deliberately bowdlerizes sex scenes in imitation of censored versions of its model, the sixteenth-century classic *Golden Lotus*. Tracing the sexual adventures of the artist/writer as entrepreneur, it epitomizes the materialist spirit characterizing the new Chinese market economy.

A writer much discussed and translated in the West is Wang Anyi (b. 1954), who deals with formerly taboo subjects such as sexual obsession and adultery. She has ventured into 'Roots' territory with a charming novella *Xiao Baozhuang* ('Baotown', 1984), but her recent work is often set in urban Shanghai and details the materialistic desires and selfish passions of Shanghailanders. An accomplished writer, artfully artless, her work can seem too detached and concerned more with technique than emotional depth. None the less, she is important for her role in expanding the territory of contemporary mainland fiction.

Further expansion came from 'avant-garde' writers such as Can Xue, Ma Yuan, Ge Fei, Su Tong, and Yu Hua, whose works undermine the hegemony of realism. Yet these writers often display the same preoccupations with the Chinese past and character as their more conventional colleagues over the generations. Where they differ is in their refusal to suggest solutions to China's problems, or hope. The 'self as hero' is virtually absent as the younger writers turn to formal experimentation to shape their fictions. Reflexivity becomes a keynote, seen for example in Ma Yuan's influential *Xugou* ('Fabrication', 1985). Kafka, the Japanese novelist Kawabata, and Borges are important models for these writers, but many find inspiration, too, in the classical Chinese tradition of strange, supernatural tales laconically told. Because their work is puzzling and élitist, 'avant-garde' writers reach a very limited audience.

Can Xue (Deng Xiaohua, b. 1953) burst onto the literary scene in 1985 with a very brief, much anthologized story *Shanshangde xiaowu* ('The Hut on the Hill'). This story encapsulates many of the preoccupations treated in more detail in her two novels *Canglaode fuyun* (*Ageing Clouds*, 1986) and

Huangnijie (*Mud Street*, 1987). 'The Little Hut' is not directly about the Cultural Revolution or about living under an authoritarian regime but is infused with their horrific after-effects. It is pervaded by an atmosphere of paranoia and constriction. The home and, more specifically, the body are attacked from both within and without: the senses are impaired or act as vehicles of pain, veins throb like 'worms under the skin'. There are barriers everywhere, but all of them permeable. Can Xue's work as a whole deals with madness, dreams, and isolation and she is the highly accomplished forerunner of a new wave of young writers who take her themes of mental violence a step further, alienating many readers with their explicitly gory descriptions of physical violence and their seemingly total detachment.

Su Tong (b. 1963) and Ge Fei (b. 1964) are preoccupied with history, creating fictive histories of a semi-imaginary China. Su Tong writes family histories, such as *Qi qie chengqun* ('Wives and Concubines', 1990), which focus on sexual transgression, violence, and psychological distress. Influenced by the work of the 1940s writer Zhang Ailing, his work shares her predilection for detail and a claustrophobic atmosphere. Ge Fei's rural stories deal with memories and fragmented histories in a China where strange, supernatural events are treated as part of the ordinary fabric of life. In *Qing Huang* (1988) the narrator embarks on an oddly directionless quest in which one story leads to another, adding to the mysteriousness of this strangely detached pastoral tale. *Mizhou* ('The Lost Boat', 1987) has the same sense of detachment and the same lyrically timeless rural setting. Indistinct memories of the protagonist's childhood and adolescence add to the mystery surrounding his ultimate fate, unknown until the last lines of the story though predictable since the prologue.

Quite different is the brutal and horrific violence of Yu Hua's (b. 1962) work, although his manner, too, is detached. Yu Hua subverts the entrenched value systems of Chinese culture, but without comment. He mixes fantasy and a strange, flat realism without distinction, leaving one with few recognizable signposts. He parodies genres such as the classical Chinese romance (*Gudian aiqing*, 'A Classical Romance', 1988) or the detective story (*Hebian de cuowu*, 'Mistake by the River', 1988), subverting both their form and their conventional meanings. In *Xianshi yizhong* ('One Kind of Reality', 1988) he undermines the myth of the Chinese family in a story of arbitrary violence and revenge utterly devoid of normal human emotions, as one of two brothers is dissected in a satirical and explicit fashion by jolly doctors chattering happily over their work. In *Yijiubaliu nian* ('1986', 1987) a mad ex-prisoner and fugitive from the Cultural Revolution returns to a family that does not recognize him. Already obsessed with ancient tortures, his madness grows as he starts to inflict mutilations on himself. Yu Hua provides a radical critique of Chinese culture by rendering explicit the violence he sees as inherent within it.

TAIWAN

Issues of modernity, Western influence, and the burden of a traditional patriarchal culture have all been treated by Taiwanese writers, who are as profoundly imbued with a sense of social mission as their mainland cousins. Similar themes emerge: the relationship between fathers and sons, questions of national character, food, sex, and the urban/rural divide. Problems of rapid modernization and consumerism have been aired, there has been experimentation in fictional form and language, and modernists have clashed with committed realists. Censorship and political oppression, too, were common in Taiwan until very recently.

Where Taiwan differs has been in its history. A Japanese colony from 1895 to 1945, the island was cut off politically, linguistically, and culturally from the mainland. Many islanders were educated in Japanese rather than Chinese. The influx of mainlanders after the war led to bloody (and officially unacknowledged) repression of the native Taiwanese population, who feel no personal ties to the mainland. Many were persecuted in the past for their belief that Taiwan should be independent, but supporters of autonomy have grown in numbers and power in the last decade, when there have been influential, if not entirely successful, moves towards creating a Taiwanese-language based literature without ties to the Chinese literary tradition.

The 1950s were mainly characterized by anti-Communist works and by a conscious break with, or even suppression of, the recent past. Western literature, particularly modernist works, filled the gap. In the 1960s Taiwanese poets and novelists began to experiment with a form of modernism that stressed the values of liberal humanism and the autonomy of the literary work. Many of the modernists were caught up in the May Fourth challenge to the past and were often critical of traditional ethical values. After the early 1970s modernism was superseded by the extremely vocal 'Nativist' school, who, for all their vehement anti-modernism, have themselves assimilated many modernist techniques.

Pai Hsien-yung (b. 1937) is Taiwan's most renowned writer. Pai led a privileged existence among the exiled mainlanders of his parents' generation, and they became the focus of his short-story collection *Taibeiren*

(*Wandering in the Garden, Waking from a Dream: Tales of Taipei Characters*, 1971). These stories centre on the homesickness felt by the exiles as they try to adjust to a diminished present. Memories, the ghosts of a lost past invading the present, and the traditional Chinese theme of transience help to give them their power of evocation. Over time they have developed an aura of faded exoticism, which only enhances their charm.

Pai's work is full of allusions to the techniques of traditional Chinese literature, as can be seen most clearly in his *Niezi* (*Crystal Boys*, 1983), a novel about the underground gay scene in Taipei. This makes conscious use of China's most famous pre-modern novel, *Story of the Stone*. Narrated by a young gay hustler from a broken family, *Crystal Boys* describes the lives of the night-time inhabitants of New Park, which, like the garden in the eighteenth-century classic, is both a haven from, and vulnerable to, destructive incursions from outside. The characters of the novel are searching for surrogate fathers, sons, or brothers, trying to create new families or communities that will subvert rather than reinforce a patriarchal society. Against a background of festivity, as well as dire poverty, they tell stories of desire and longing, though sex is less important to them than food, familial affection, and brotherhood. A profoundly sentimental novel, in the best sense, *Crystal Boys* offers an alternative vision of a world which, for all its poverty and pain, allows its inhabitants freedom and redemption.

Wang Wen-hsing (b. 1939) has been responsible for introducing the works of many modern Western writers into Taiwan. He is best known for two novels, *Jiabian* (*Family Crisis*, 1973) and *Beihaide ren* (*Backed against the Sea*, 1981). *Family Crisis* was a best-seller which challenges patriarchal assumptions through a Freudian account of a young man's search for the father he had earlier caused to run away from home. The novel has two narrative lines, in fact, one dealing with the son's memories of growing up and his changing feelings for his parents, from love to distaste, the other recounting his fruitless quest.

The foregrounding of language and novelistic technique found in *Family Crisis* reaches a climax in *Backed against the Sea*, in which a dubious former soldier delivers a monologue on, among other things, food, sex, poverty, and fate. This novel has been described as the 'most radical, sustained achievement of modernism in Chinese literature'. A mocking, scatological critique of the effects of modernity on Taiwan, it is divided into three sections: the narrator's wildly-ranging ruminations about virtually everything, from poetry to fortune-telling; his accounts of a madhouse office building where bureaucrats scurry around and beat each other up without reason; and his encounters with four prostitutes, which are alternately comic and sad, terrifying, somnolent, and joyous. Wang also plays with language, inserting meaningless phrases, altering parts of Chinese characters, and interpolating foreign words. *Backed against the Sea* is a profound and funny book, but one which deeply alienates most Taiwanese readers. A sequel is in progress.

Taiwan's increased diplomatic isolation was an important factor in the emergence of Nativist literature in the 1970s. Nativist writers are left-leaning, and see modernization and Westernization as a threat to the integrity of rural Taiwanese culture. Their works are mainly set in villages and small towns, nostalgically lauding the beauties of the countryside and its simple way of life. A few influential Nativists have advocated reunification with mainland China, but the majority have been closely associated with the independence movement. In recent years, several have abandoned writing for political activism while others have rejected writing in Chinese in favour of Taiwanese.

Hwang Chun-ming (b. 1939) is the most enduringly successful Nativist. His stories from the 1960s deal with the adverse effects of modernization. His protagonists are usually poor, uneducated, baffled individuals struggling to survive and to make sense of a world they find increasingly incomprehensible and hostile. The gentle humour and regretful tone of his rural stories turns into something harsher in those set in small towns or cities. His best story in this vein is *Erzi de da wan'ou* ('His Son's Big Doll', 1968), in which a sandwich-board man battles to keep his hated job, all too aware that he cuts an absurd and pathetic figure. Hwang is a vivid writer, with a cinematic ability to establish an atmosphere in a few swift strokes and with lively dialogue. His later work has become increasingly satirical. *Saiyounala, zaijian* ('Sayonara, Goodbye', 1977), for example, records an ironic encounter between a self-doubting Taiwanese businessman and his Japanese clients, who want to obtain 'scalps' of pubic hair from every prostitute they sleep with. The story forms a powerful criticism of Taiwanese fears and perceived Japanese ambitions.

Ch'en Ying-chen (Ch'en Yung-shan, b. 1936) is one of the few Nativist writers to want reunification with the mainland. A long-time opponent of the government, he spent over seven years in prison for his beliefs. A Christian and a socialist, he often deals in his work with the dilemmas faced by individuals caught between their ideals and the need for action. Ch'en favours a sentimental 'critical realism' in which to express his didactic opinions. *Shanlu* ('Mountain Road', 1984), for example, focuses on a dying woman who has sacrificed her comfort to give succour to a comrade's poverty-stricken family, only to see her ideals undermined by the insidious pleasures of materialism. Ch'en's earlier works, also romantic in tone but less tendentious, are more successful. They include *Wo de didi Kangxiong* ('My Younger Brother Kangxiong', 1960), another account of ideals betrayed; the tragicomic *Jiangjun zu* ('A Race of Generals', 1964), and *Diyi jian chaishi* ('My First Case', 1967), which uses a mysterious suicide to explore the gaps in understanding between exiled mainlanders and native Taiwanese.

During the 1980s, both modernists and Nativists became less influential. Younger writers seemed to have absorbed lessons from both movements. Satire and black humour now emerged as significant trends, as well as an increased awareness of women's issues.

David Wang has suggested that recent Chinese literature has been overburdened by the 'self-righteous outcries and bitter sentiment' to be found in the work of writers like Ch'en Ying-chen. He sees some hope of salvation through the 'radical laughter' of Wang Wen-hsing, Wang Chen-ho (1940–90), Huang Fan (Huang Hsiao-chung, b. 1950), and others. Wang Chen-ho was a Nativist who preferred parody and burlesque humour to the seriousness of his colleagues. Scatological, carnivalesque images and language dominate his work and he employs a richly varied language culled from a wide range of sources. His most famous early story is the mocking yet sad tale of a *ménage à trois* involving three unsavoury people, *Jiazhuang yiniuche* ('An Oxcart for Dowry', 1967). Notable among his later work is the political satire *Meigui, meigui, wo ai ni* (*Rose, Rose, I Love You*, 1984), which makes fun of small-town pretensions against the backdrop of a newly opened brothelbar serving American GIs.

Huang Fan also employs black humour, although more subtly than Wang Chen-ho. The story that first brought him fame was the ironic *Lai Suo* (1979), which cynically contrasts the loss of idealism of a Taiwanese Independence movement leader with the *naïveté* of a rank-and-file member, recently released from prison and trying to adjust to the new, materialist Taiwan and to redeem his guilt at the suffering he has caused his family. Frequent time-shifts and shifts of scene compound the protagonist's confusion as he stumbles from one awkward situation to another. Huang Fan's work is refreshingly free from the sentimentality that spoils so much modern Chinese fiction.

Li Yung-p'ing's (b. 1947) *Jiling chunqiu* (*Chronicles of Jiling*, 1986) was heralded as a major literary event. It is beautifully written, in a vivid, concise Chinese shorn of loose, Westernized syntax. The book consists of twelve interrelated stories that combine to form a 'novel', providing multiple perspectives on the ramifications of a shocking rape committed in a small town. *Chronicles* does not intervene or explicitly condemn the actions and words of the protagonists. And like the language in which it is written, the setting is stripped of specific local markers: the town could be anywhere in a timeless China, yet is described meticulously enough to place the work within a Nativist tradition.

Li Ang (Shi Shuduan, b. 1952) attacks prevailing traditions and mores from a feminist point of view. One of Taiwan's most popular writers, she focuses on the status and sexual consciousness of women, and has often shocked orthodox critics by her explicitness in descriptions of sexual violence and desire. Her novel *Shafu* (*The Butcher's Wife*, 1983) is a relentless catalogue of violence, blood, and suffering, and at the same time an indictment of traditional Chinese society. The story centres on the pathetic Lin Shi, married to a pig butcher who rapes and abuses her until she is finally driven to slaughter him—like a pig. The story is told in flashback, as Lin Shi wanders dazedly through her life, finding pleasure only in frantic bursts of eating. Both she and her husband are symbolic characters, she in her abject helplessness and he in his almost irredeemable repulsiveness. Chinese superstitions and the destructive power of gossip also come under attack, in the vicious figure of Aunty Ah Wang.

The Butcher's Wife remains perhaps Li Ang's most powerful work because in it her symbolism, imagery, and meaning work together to enhance the overall effect. In her later work, such as the novels *Anye* (*Dark Night*, 1985) and *Miyuan* (*Maze*, 1991) and the short story *Yifeng weiji de qingshu* ('A Love Letter Never Sent', 1986), her ambitious treatment of contemporary society seems overburdened with significance. *Dark Night* deals with the sexual entanglements of a group of people against a background of financial wheeling and dealing. *Maze* explores a woman's sexual desires and her attempts to recover a personal and national past by restoring her ancestors' elaborate garden. Li Ang remains one of Taiwan's best writers, provocative and ambitious, and an important leader of the trend to move away from explorations of 'old' China or Taiwan's ties to the mainland to focus on contemporary life on the island.

HONG KONG

As a British colony since 1842, and remote from the Chinese centre politically, culturally, and linguistically, Hong Kong's Chineseness is often perceived to be ambiguous. Different waves of immigration (and exodus) have added to the complexity of the picture. Hong Kong has often been described as a cultural desert where commercial interests predominate, but recently commercial confidence has allowed a re-evaluation of Hong Kong's relationship with the Chinese mainland. The press is free and active, and often (though not always) hostile to Beijing. Hong Kong has published work by many writers unable to publish in the People's Republic.

Up until recently, Hong Kong literature has been dismissed as negligible. mainly popular trash, but a sudden literary boom has led to more optimistic predictions for the (pre-1997) future. Very few writers have emerged, however, to suggest that this optimism is justified. Established literary figures still make their presence felt: Ni Kuang, a prolific science-fiction and martial-arts writer, Jin Yong (Louis Cha), and Liu Yichang (Liu Tongyi, b. 1918). Liu Yichang is the author of an influential novel, *Jiutu* (*The Drunkard*, 1963), which was one of the first works of Chinese fiction anywhere successfully to employ modernist techniques, and which is a telling critique of the low status of literature in a commercialized and deracinated Hong Kong. Liu suggests that only popular literature can survive in such a society.

Women writers have emerged in the new boom, especially Xi Xi (Zhang Yan, b. 1938), whose short stories in particular are impressive. Often employing a first-person narrator, she explores the inner workings of the female mind in subtle and moving ways. Her themes are those of isolation, alienation, and identity, and her detached style works successfully to underline them. Her best story is *Xiang wo zheyangde yige nüren* ('A Girl Like Me', 1982), which describes the dilemma of a mortuary cosmetician whose boyfriend wants to know what she does for a living.

Jin Yong (Louis Cha, Zha Liangyong, b. 1924) remains Hong Kong's best-known writer, read voraciously throughout Chinese communities worldwide. His prolific output is of a very high standard and his martial-arts fiction is able to appeal to high- and lowbrow tastes alike. He once wrote that the enormous popularity of martial-arts fiction lies in the fact that it 'is a Chinese genre. And Chinese, of course, like to read Chinese genres.' His novels have a strong sense of history and an equally strong patriotic vision of 'China'. His interpretations of traditional Chinese genres seem to cut across the geographical and ideological barriers separating Chinese communities with a success no other contemporary writer has yet achieved.

FURTHER READING

Anderson, Marston, *The Limits of Realism: Chinese Fiction in the Revolutionary Period* (Berkeley, 1990).
Best Chinese Stories (1949–1989) (Beijing, 1989).

Chang, Sung-sheng Yvonne, *Modernism and the Nativist Resistance: Contemporary Chinese Fiction from Taiwan* (Durham, NC, 1993).

Duke, Michael S. (ed.), *Contemporary Chinese Literature: An Anthology of Post-Mao Fiction and Poetry* (Armonk, NY, 1985).

——*Modern Chinese Women Writers: Critical Appraisals* (Armonk, NY, 1989).

Larson, Wendy, and Wedell-Wedellsborg, eds., *Inside Out: Modernism and Postmodernism in Chinese Literary Culture* (Aarhus, 1993).

Martin, Helmut, and Kinkley, Jeffrey (eds.), *Modern Chinese Writers: Self Portrayals* (Armonk, NY, 1992).

Widmer, Ellen, and Wang, David Der-wei (eds.), *From May Fourth to June Fourth: Fiction and Film in Twentieth-Century China* (Cambridge, Mass., 1993).

Zhao, Henry Y. H., and Cayley, John (eds.), *Under Sky Underground: Chinese Writing Today*. 1 (London, 1994).

7

CZECH REPUBLIC AND SLOVAKIA

IGOR HÁJEK

WHEN, in late December 1958, two weeks after its publication, Josef Škvorecký's (b. 1924) first novel, *The Cowards*, was withdrawn from the bookshops and its author banned, it looked like the end of an all too brief period of grace in Czechoslovakia. Over the previous two years a remarkable thaw had occurred after the Stalinist freeze, enlivening both the Czech and the Slovak cultural scenes. In literature, quite a few new names had been introduced, some of whom were to stay in the forefront of interest for the next forty years: notably Miroslav Holub (b. 1923), Ivan Klíma (b. 1931), and Milan Kundera (b. 1929).

The political backlash, when it struck, was quick and thorough. The cultural community of the country was purged from top to bottom: editors were dismissed, books were sent straight from the printers to the pulping mill, films were locked away in safes. Compared with what was to befall them a decade later, however, the punishment meted out to the budding reformers was fairly mild. Most of those who lost their jobs were moved to positions where they would have less opportunity to take daring decisions. The managing director of the publishing house that had brought out *The Cowards* became the head of a film production group, while the editor-in-chief was transferred to the State Publishing House for Children's Books. The heretics were dispersed and suppressed, but not quite destroyed.

The pressures for reform soon began to build up again, however, and, beset as it was by economic and political difficulties, the country's leadership was unable to resist them for long. The door against which unorthodox or sobered-up Communist intellectuals were pushing, in close association with non-Communist colleagues who had not surrendered their independence for a dubious promise of paradise on earth, was opening ever wider: by the mid-1960s, the right of a 'democratic' and 'humanist' culture to exist side by side with the socialist one was officially recognized.

In a State that remained essentially totalitarian, art had to take on a role as substitute: it made up for the absence of free public institutions where social and political issues could be publicly aired. Film, poetry, drama, and even painting provided an outlet for the pent-up frustrations and grievances of a large part of the population. Literature was especially well suited for this purpose, writers being by definition the most articulate of people; in any case, the Czech public was well versed in looking for meaning between the lines in what it read. Reading was growing more pleasurable, too; once the suffocating doctrinaire controls were relaxed, new talent burst out and the quality of writing improved beyond recognition.

The first steps in a new direction were taken in the early 1960s by young writers with a keen perception of the present. They infused their prose with a lyrical sincerity and freshness which contrasted with the impersonal Socialist Realist works of the previous decade, which had been composed to a stultifying formula. Some treated similar subjects to the novels of the 1950s, but—within the limits of what was now being tolerated—far more pessimistically. Contemporary life was presented in less attractive and more realistic colours, while problems that previously a fictional Party Secretary would have dealt with by a flick of his finger were now left painfully unresolved.

One of the most popular books of this kind was a short novel by Jan Procházka (1929–71), *Zelené obzory* ('Green Horizons', 1960), in which a young agronomist comes into conflict with the set ways of a backward agricultural co-operative. Procházka did not question the foundations of the ruling ideology, but Ivan Klíma came close to doing so in *Hodina ticha* ('The Hour of Silence', 1963), an early attempt at a political novel, in which he portrayed the damage done to human relations in the 1950s collectivization drive.

The signal that things were really taking a turn for the better was the readmission into public view of three writers. In 1963 a conference on Franz Kafka rehabilitated this Prague-born German-Jewish writer, who had hitherto been seen as the embodiment of decadence, the very opposite of the revolutionary optimism that socialist writers were supposed to instil in their readers. As Kafka's work became available again in a country where any mention of the existence of censorship would itself be censored, it was not difficult for readers to recognize that some of the realities of Communism were reminiscent of Kafka's nightmarish fantasies. In the same year Vladimír Holan (1905–80), a recondite metaphysical poet, officially ostracized for the past fifteen years, was awarded the title of National Artist.

The third writer had been banned for a shorter period than the other two: five years after *The Cowards* scandal, which had threatened to seal the fate of any liberalizing attempts for a long time to come, Škvorecký was permitted to publish again. Two long short stories, *The Emöke Legend* (1963) and *The Bass Saxophone* (1967), were both marked by nostalgia, a prominent facet of his fiction, but they also contained features of special significance in relation to the times. In the first story, the character of an intruding, obnoxious man symbolized the brutal vulgarity given free rein under Communism, while the other story affirmed the supremacy of life and art, in this case the art of jazz music, over any ideology.

The capacity to reflect aspects of the socio-political environment in personal terms, which also obviated any hassles with the censorship, was well demonstrated by Kundera in his short stories, later collected as *Laughable Loves* (1963–8). In the cleverly composed story 'Nobody Will Laugh', for instance, he traces the farcical tricks employed by a college lecturer to shake off an unpublishable author convinced of his own genius. The stubborn, relentless pursuit of the carefree young academic by the would-be author, culminating in the former's ruination, personified in the minds of many Czech readers the ponderous obstinacy of their rulers. From this point of view, Kundera could later claim that his novel *The Joke* (1967) was a love story, although few would argue that its plot, closely knit as it is into the political history of Communist Czechoslovakia, could take place against any other background. Similarly based on recent experience was *The Axe* (1966) by Ludvík Vaculík (b. 1926), a novel which describes the all too familiar corruption of a dream of happiness and justice for all: while struggling to realize it, the narrator's idealistic father is transformed from a respected man into one shunned even by his relatives.

Soul-searching work of this kind was mostly written by authors who had themselves in their younger days succumbed to the idea of a grand social plan and who had subsequently witnessed its perversion. They did not entirely discard the failing doctrine, but indicated their doubts as to whether the ideal could be redeemed.

The 1960s, however, also saw the emergence of authors who either attempted to examine certain features of the dominant ideology from outside its confines or ignored it altogether. In his plays Václav Havel (b. 1936) adopted some of the techniques of the Theatre of the Absurd, but many of the grotesque absurdities he paraded on stage were in fact inspired by the experience of everyday life all around him. Both *The Garden Party* (1963) and *The Memorandum* (1965) exposed the emptiness of the cliché-ridden language of bureaucracy and its dehumanizing effects. Once Havel's satires were produced in the West, however, the home-grown, Czech variety of alienation was recognized as an offshoot stemming from widely spread roots.

In fiction, a penetrating analysis of the socialist, neo-bourgeois lifestyle came from a chemical engineer, Vladimír Páral (b. 1932). In a series of brilliantly constructed novels starting with *Veletrh splněných přání* ('The Fair of Dreams Fulfilled', 1964), of which only two, *Catapult* (1967) and *The Four Sonyas* (1969), have appeared in English, and written in a style reminiscent of a scientist's research report, he highlighted the moral defects engendered by the modern rat race, which up until then had been supposed to plague only Western consumer societies. Páral got away with his implied criticism because, like a magician performing a disappearing act, he evaded any mention of the almighty Party that in real life was in total control of every aspect of individual and social existence and therefore ultimately responsible for the syndrome that he described. This was a device to be gratefully adopted and mastered by other writers in the 1970s and 1980s.

While Páral skilfully steered clear of politics and ideology, Bohumil Hrabal (b. 1914) was one of those who simply ignored them. Whenever he got into difficulties with censors and editors, it was because of the eccentric nature of his writing. His first collection of short stories was pulped in 1959, but as a sign of the creeping relaxation they appeared at long last in 1963— Hrabal's literary début at the age of 49. Another collection of stories, *Pábitelé* ('The Palaverers'), followed in 1964 and after that a new book appeared nearly every year until 1969. Hrabal was a new phenomenon in Czech literature. A robust story-teller and an intellectual hedonist, he picked up anecdotes in Prague taverns among beer drinkers and people living at the edge of society and transformed them into surreal, bizarre tales illuminated by an ecstatic amazement at the miraculous diversity of human character and life. For a long time, Hrabal's popularity in the West rested on the Oscar-winning film version of his more conventional wartime story *A Close Watch on the Trains* (1965), but since then most of his best work has been translated into English.

One of the novel features of Hrabal's prose was the use of slang and colloquialisms that would have been unthinkable a decade earlier under the puritanical rules of Socialist Realism. By paying increased attention to style and by engaging in linguistic experiment, writers were reacting against the drab language of Stalinism. The titles of the first two books by Věra Linhartová (b. 1938), *Prostor k rozlišení* ('Room for Differentiation', 1964) and *Meziprůzkum nejblíže uplynulého* ('Intermediate Research of the Immediate Past', 1964), themselves indicate the level of abstraction her texts were aiming for.

Artistic experimentation of various kinds found a fertile ground in Slovakia, where literature in the 1960s did not blend with politics to the same extent as in the Czech part of the country; the Slovaks were interested more in asserting their national identity than in liberal reforms. Of the younger generation of Slovak writers, Ján Johanides (b. 1934), Jozef Kot (b. 1936), and Jaroslava Blažková (b. 1933) wrote innovative fiction that was very much in tune with that of their Czech counterparts.

Even seemingly hermetic writing could not be entirely separated from the circumstances in which it came into existence. Nor could it feel entirely safe to write in this fashion in conditions where art was treated in principle as an instrument of propaganda and where repressive practices could be reverted to at a moment's notice. A refusal to comply with current demands was itself an act of artistic courage. Marxism attributed an enormous importance to the education of the masses, and in this context literature acquired exaggerated weight and attracted excessive attention. In many ways, this was a continuation of the role which it had played for centuries in many countries of Central and Eastern Europe: that of a medium through which national aspirations were voiced.

A feud thus developed between the rulers, apprehensive of the effect that unorthodox books could have upon the population, and those writers who saw themselves as the tribunes of the people. They became the main challengers of the regime, which resisted the notion that concessions might make it more acceptable. Instead, the authorities once again tried to turn the clock back. The conflict which came to a head in 1967 split the political establishment: when the hard-liners lost, the forces of reform were released. During the first seven months of 1968, later to be known as the Prague Spring, writers were relieved of their traditional obligation to imbue their work with that which could not be openly stated. When censorship was abolished, the media took full advantage of their new freedom of speech; there was no longer a need for public issues to be discussed in a disguised, metaphorical way. Not too many books were written as writers took the opportunity to express their opinions directly. By now the Writers' Union was publishing more than a dozen periodicals, which set the standard not only for literary criticism, but also for quality journalism. Some of the best writers applied their skills in this field. Ludvík Vaculík, already a national hero for the speech he had made at the 1967 Writers' Union Congress, enhanced his standing further by excellent reportage and by his classic manifesto of civic rights *Two Thousand Words* (1968).

The Prague Spring was the culmination of an effort to transform Communism into something more suitable for human beings to live under, and united nearly the entire intellectual and artistic community. The struggle against the regime had been conducted largely by means of ideas expressed through words and images, and when the political experiment was crushed by invading Soviet tanks, the wrath of the victors was turned against the creators of those words and images.

The purges which affected cultural life in the Czech regions, and to a lesser degree in Slovakia, in the early 1970s, and the represssion they suffered over the next twenty years, exceeded anything experienced before. Particularly harsh measures were directed against literature: many of the best-known names disappeared almost overnight as writers were banned or went into exile. In both instances they became unmentionable: whole print-runs of books were destroyed if a proscribed name as much as appeared in a footnote. The nation was in a state of shock which writers, equally traumatized, were unable to reflect: the single exception was Vaculík, who in the *The Guinea Pigs* (1977), a novel where a deceptively cheerful narrative hovers above a sea of despair and foreboding, captured the mental horror caused by the sudden descent of irrationality and the ensuing reversal of white into black and of truth into falsehood.

In these new circumstances, Czech literature soon divided into three streams. In the first stream were books published with official blessing, the majority of them of inferior quality and limited interest, produced by second-raters rushing to replace their silenced fellow authors. Nearly all of this writing has deservedly remained unknown abroad. The banned writers, thrown back on pre-Gutenberg methods, had to organize their own publication with the help of typewriters and carbon paper. Over the years this activity developed into a sophisticated alternative culture with its own critical journals, exhibitions, and dramatic performances staged in private flats. For the next two decades, it was virtually the only visible manifestation of the existence of dissenting opinion, which, even so, could not be expressed in overtly political terms. Instead of voicing their opposition to the regime, artists and writers exposed the questionable values on which it was based. Nowhere is this better presented than in Havel's three one-act plays *Audience* (1975), *Private View* (1975), and *Protest* (1976), which illustrate the way character is corroded in morally corrupt conditions. Other suppressed authors used various means to render a similar testimony, whatever the subject, while the quality of their writing itself served as an indictment of the rule of the mediocre.

Their work would have been less widely known had it not been for the initiative of publishers in exile like Index in Cologne, or 68 Publishers in Toronto, which was run by Škvorecký and his wife. They printed the books of banned and exiled writers, many of which were subsequently smuggled back into the home country. The 1970s and 1980s were a peak period of

Czech literature: never had so many books been translated into foreign languages. Kundera, Škvorecký, and Klíma, who all acquired the reputation of major novelists, were joined in Western readers' awareness by Arnošt Lustig (b. 1926), Jiří Gruša (b. 1938), Pavel Kohout (b. 1928), and others. Miroslav Holub was acclaimed as one of the world's finest living poets. In 1984 the Nobel Prize was awarded to Jaroslav Seifert (1901–86). Regrettably, his poetic style, which maintains a precarious balance between an overpowering emotional intensity and lyrical sweetness, makes his work virtually impossible to translate without approaching dangerously close to sentimentality. The Nobel Prize was commonly regarded, however, as honouring the entire besieged Czech literary community, of which Seifert was the revered senior.

Muzzled at home, Czech writers thus achieved considerable popularity abroad, where their work also appeared in dozens of anthologies, its attractiveness no doubt in part enhanced by its exotic flavour. The authentic atmosphere of lurking fear in a neo-Stalinist state could be savoured at a secure distance: there is a difference between being actually harassed by the secret police and reading about what living in a state of constant anxiety does to the human psyche. On the other hand, Ivan Klíma enjoyed success in the West by writing about everyday experiences that were not so sinister and often treating them with irony and humour, as in his short-story collections *My Merry Mornings* (1985), *My First Loves* (1986), and *My Golden Trades* (1992). Even in novels that are concerned in one way or another with the ethical twists and turns of the individual conscience—*Love and Garbage* (1990), *Judge on Trial* (1991), *Waiting for Darkness, Waiting for Light* (1994)—he allows the circumstances of the times to intrude only when the plot depends on their doing so.

Nor did the first two books that Milan Kundera, now banned in his own country, published abroad comment directly on the increasingly oppressive and repellent nature of the regime in Prague. *Life is Elsewhere* (1974) takes its title from a slogan written up on walls during the student uprising in Paris in May 1968. The novel rejects lyricism, which it sees as a mark of immaturity and as a potential source of evil once people become blinkered by a revolutionary romanticism. With the sarcastic detachment of someone who, not too many years before, had himself won acclaim for his lyric poetry, Kundera follows his hero Jaromil's rise from over-enthusiastic adolescent avant-gardist to Party propagandist bard, and his consequent moral descent to secret police informer. Kundera also casts doubts on prevailing myths of motherhood through the character of the young poet's possessive mother. His second novel written in exile, *The Farewell Party* (1976), is set in a Bohemian spa town, where the paths of a group of people have accidentally crossed and where they now try to sort out their complicated relationships. Fate intervenes, however, with its usual tragicomic playfulness, frustrating their intentions and imposing its own resolution.

Recent Czech history was more prominent in two later books, *The Book of Laughter and Forgetting* (1980) and *The Unbearable Lightness of Being* (1984). The first is a collage of loosely connected variations on related themes, in which historical fact is mixed with philosophical reflections and real people appear side by side with fictional characters, the author occasionally stepping in himself. This 'polyphonic' approach was to become Kundera's hallmark, allowing him to present a many-sided picture of contemporary reality with space, too, for some strongly expressed personal opinions. *The Unbearable Lightness of Being* was similarly inspired by the plight of Czechoslovakia under Soviet occupation and further enhanced Kundera's reputation throughout the world. Once again, the narrative—based on the relatively simple story of a couple who return home from exile in the West—is shaped out of seemingly incongruous elements that Kundera blends into an impressive study of human values.

These two novels were first published in Canada. When copies were smuggled into Czechoslovakia, they provoked a sharp samizdat debate among both banned and exiled writers and critics (in the official press, Kundera's name could not even be mentioned). Objections were raised against the use he had made of political themes, many feeling that Kundera's presentation of life in the Czechoslovakia of the 1970s and 1980s lacked authenticity, that he had no real understanding of the mental suffering and physical harassment inflicted by the regime on those who refused to conform. Others argued that his novels could not be judged by conventional criteria, according to how closely they reflected contemporary life; rather, they should be read as intricate metaphors constructed so as to pose questions and advance arguments.

Meanwhile, a more traditionally realist picture of the ironies and absurdities of life at home was supplied by Vaculík in his *feuilletons*, occasional pieces that were disseminated in typewritten copies. Some of these were later collected as *A Cup of Coffee with my Interrogator* (1987). The title piece of this volume gives a first-hand insight into the danger of growing friendliness between the oppressor and the oppressed, a theme which also inspired Havel's play *Temptation* (1988).

Work by Czech authors continued in these years to arouse a fair degree of interest and to meet with a favourable response. Škvorecký, now living in Canada, continued the saga of his *alter ego* Danny Smiřický, in *The Miracle*

Game (1972) and *The Engineer of Human Souls* (1977). These two novels cover a turbulent quarter-century of history and offer a Western reader an inside view of momentous events from the unusual and illuminating angle of an East European consciousness.

Equally stimulating was the audacity with which both 'dissident' and exiled writers used literature as a means of asserting basic values of truth, decency, and freedom. The political system that they confronted embodied symptoms of the same decay that could be found universally in contemporary life. As nurtured by totalitarianism, however, these symptoms were magnified to a grotesque and terrifying extent. Women writers in particular reacted sensitively to the pervading callousness. Many of the subtle short stories of Eda Kriseová (b. 1940), for instance, are marked by her abhorrence of a mindless and pernicious consumerism and by an almost physical empathy with a nature devastated by pollution and by human recklessness.

The state into which the country had sunk could not be entirely overlooked even by those writers officially allowed to publish. To state the obvious fact, that the way the country was being governed was itself responsible for its condition, was out of the question. Instead, Páral's method of causing the omnipotent and ubiquitous Party to seem to disappear was refined and applied by a number of ambitious younger writers. In their novels all manner of ills—corruption, mismanagement, and widespread depravity—were exposed with a boldness the 'dissidents' could not have aspired to, but the blame for them was attributed exclusively to individuals. The trick of isolating criticism of society from any suggestion that politics was to blame was developed to perfection, so that readers were left with a strange sense that something was missing: the society depicted in these novels was familiar in its details and easily recognizable, yet seemed also to float in the vague atmosphere of a fairy-tale.

These books were not of high literary quality in the main: their value is that of sociological documents. Even genuinely talented writers such as Zdeněk Zapletal (b. 1951) had to abandon precise observation for an obligatory amnesia as soon as they ventured onto a broader social context. The reader of his remarkably well-written *Půlnoční běžci* ('Midnight Runners', 1986) may wonder, for instance, why all the characters have a gap in their personal history, until he realizes that these blank spots all occur around the tabooed year of 1968.

Such difficulties could be avoided by refusing to become involved at all with the present or the recent past. This had long been the strategy of Hrabal; none the less, once he was allowed to publish again in the mid-1970s, he had to mutilate his work in order to make it acceptable. Originality was regarded as subversive. Only in the late 1980s was a 'grey zone' established which provided a refuge for writers who existed on the fringes of official-dom and took no part in the activities of the dissidents. If there was a message in their work, it was mainly one of deep disgust, but well hidden by a seemingly innocuous subject-matter and more often than not by an abstruse style of writing. Thus these writers, too, were presenting their experience of Czech society in personal terms, as Kundera had in the 1960s. And as with Havel two decades earlier, so now the plays of Daniela Fischerová (b. 1946) and Karel Steigerwal (b. 1945), or the prose of Alexandra Berková (b. 1949), explored the limits of what the authorities would tolerate.

In Slovakia in the 1970s and 1980s the situation developed differently. The repression there took milder forms; only a few Slovak authors went into exile and there was hardly any dissident movement. Many writers tacitly accepted the prevailing conditions and forbore expressing any ideas or undertaking any activities that might have had unwelcome repercus-sions. They showed less moral commitment than their banned Czech col-leagues so that, paradoxically, Slovak fiction of this period most resembled that being written in the West in its concentration on the private world of the individual. Writers such as Jozef Puškáš (b. 1951) or Dušan Mitana (b. 1946) demonstrated a fine command of their craft, but apart from their technical skill were not really to be compared with the more profound though not easily fathomable new work published by Johanides from the late 1970s.

Once Communism collapsed in Czechoslovakia in November 1989, it was expected that readers who had spent the past twenty years hunting for clandestine or smuggled copies of banned books would flock in their thou-sands to bookshops, unrestricted at last in their urge to satisfy their craving. The expectations proved unrealistic. The increasing number of private publishers who started bringing out hitherto forbidden books in huge print-runs soon found that the taste of a fickle public had changed and that they had to compete with the new wave of trash that was flooding the market. The experience of the former dissidents in standing up to oppression proved alien to the acquiescent attitude of the silent majority: their popularity quickly evaporated, as was shown by the results of the first free elections held in Czechoslovakia in 1991. With the exception of Havel, who was elected President of the Republic, and a handful of others, writers were pushed into the background by professional politicians and entrepreneurs. It did not help that many writers were known as leaning towards the Left, while the country as a whole veered sharply to the Right.

Once the initial turmoil had subsided, a new phase of Czech literature began to unfold. The rapid weakening of the links with Slovak culture, after the division of the country into two in 1993, had only marginal effects. The major change was internal: in seeming reaction against the preceding decades, the centuries-old tradition of social or political commitment was vehemently rejected. Instead, a new generation of writers set out on the path of experimentation. Unimpeded by censorship or political supervision, they could now indulge themselves by publishing virtually anything. Kafka enjoyed yet another influential come-back in the ironic short stories of Jiří Kratochvil (b. 1940) and Czech Surrealism was resurrected in the work of Pavel Řezníček (b. 1942). Moralizing was replaced by playfulness and intricacy of style, as in the whimsical prose and poetry of Michal Ajvaz (b. 1949) or the erudite and convoluted novels of the literary theorist Daniela Hodrová (b. 1946). Overwhelmed by the deluge of trash on the one hand and bewildered by some fairly hermetic writing on the other, Czech readers welcomed a light-hearted look back at the tragic period from which the country had just emerged: *Báječná léta pod psa* ('The Blissful Years of Lousy Living', 1992) by Michael Viewegh (b. 1962) became the first post-1989 best-seller.

In many instances, the reception of Czech authors at home differed from that they enjoyed abroad. Hrabal, who has been widely translated into English, was treated on his eightieth birthday in 1994 as a classic who could hardly be held in higher esteem. Škvorecký, too, quickly regained his former popularity, though the critics, if not the public, were slightly less kind to Klíma. The new young poets, searching for a metaphysical Absolute and for novel verbal ways in which to express it, had little appreciation for the rationality of Holub, who had been universally praised in the English-speaking world. Particularly complex was the reputation of Kundera, who at first insisted that his works should be published over a period of time in the order in which they had been written. When he relented and his most recent novel, *Immortality* (1990), was published in its original Czech (in 1993), nearly the entire literary community, despite its previous reservations, acknowledged Kundera as a novelist of world stature. The ferment that followed the end of Communism has yet to produce his equal.

FURTHER READING

Goetz-Stankiewicz, Marketa (ed.), *Good-bye, Samizdat* (Evanston, Ill., 1992).
Harkins, William E., and Trensky, Paul I. (eds.), *Czech Literature since 1956: A Symposium* (New York, 1980).

112   **Igor Hájek**

Liehm, Antonin, and Kussi, Peter (eds.), *The Writing on the Wall* (New York, 1983).
Modern Slavic Literatures, ii (New York, 1976).
Novák, Arne, *Czech Literature* (Ann Arbor, 1976).
Pynsent, Robert B. (ed.), *Modern Slovak Prose* (London, 1990).
Trensky, Paul I., *Czech Drama since World War II* (White Plains, NY, 1978).

8

ENGLAND

JAMES WOOD

ENGLISH writing in the 1960s and 1970s resembles a Victorian house whose windows have all been smashed: a solid structure timidly vandalized. Torn between nostalgia and rebellion, tradition and experiment, English writing of this period often lapsed into symmetrical failures: its Victorian solidity seems uninspiring and its experimentation only wanly successful. The Dickensian robustness of Angus Wilson's (1913–82) novels, for instance, is not robust enough; but neither is his attempt to modernize or Post-Modernize the Dickensian tradition; Iris Murdoch's (b. 1919) twentieth-century version of Tolstoyan realism has not been realized, nor could it have been, perhaps; but her philosophical dance around that realism has not been springy enough, and has attracted no partners; A. S. Byatt's (b. 1936) desire to write what she calls 'self-conscious realism' seems too self-conscious and not real enough.

These are in part the inevitable disjunctions of the Post-Modern writer, attempting to write at once solidly and playfully. But there has been a larger failure at the heart of the language, a failure to be open to contemporary energies, to be free from tradition while also stealing from it. Philip Larkin (1922–85) is probably the only major figure of English writing in the last thirty years, with V. S. Naipaul (b. 1932) and Harold Pinter (b. 1930) as perhaps the major figures in fiction and drama, respectively.

Larkin dominated the age through voice, phrasing, and language. His lines are now a kind of running bass of English literary culture. Indeed, they have petrified into epigram: 'On me your voice falls as they say love should | Like an enormous yes.' His elegiac cadences can be heard in most of his poetic heirs (like Michael Hofmann (b. 1957) and Glyn Maxwell (b. 1962)):

> We slowed again,
> And as the tightened brakes took hold, there swelled
> A sense of falling, like an arrow-shower
> Sent out of sight, somewhere becoming rain.
>
> ('The Whitsun Weddings')

Larkin had wanted to be a novelist before he became a poet, and indeed wrote two novels. His poems are not just lyrics, but small fictional enclosures. Like few other poems of the contemporary era, Larkin's gleam in the memory with fictional narrators and characters—Mr Bleaney, for example, who preferred 'sauce to gravy', or 'The fathers with broad belts under their suits | And seamy foreheads'.

His greatest character, however, was himself, the bored, fearful elegist who was both more and less than his poems suggest. Larkin was the man who watched England from behind a train window, who removed his bicycle clips in church in awkward reverence, who advised against having children, who resignedly worked in an office with his 'loaf-haired secretary', and who missed the boat of 'sexual intercourse' ('Sexual intercourse began | In nineteen sixty three | (Which was rather late for me)'). That the real Larkin who lived and worked as a librarian in Hull was not entirely the same as the poetic presence was suggested by the appearance of letters published after his death, in 1992: the real Larkin was much blacker and more scabrous. A measure of his self-transformation is the poem 'Posterity', in *High Windows* (1974), which imagines a conversation between two academics, one of whom is writing about Larkin's work. The poem's crabbed irony works (just), because the 'Larkin' under discussion—'One of those old-type *natural* fouled-up guys'—is registered as a fiction, a creation. The point of the poem is that there is nothing 'natural' about this fouled-up guy—he is a wily construct.

Larkin made use of an elegiac tradition of Englishness, and became its acutest definer. More precisely, he ironized that tradition of disappearance. To Edward Thomas's Georgian vision of a dreamily absent rural station, 'Adlestrop' ('Yes. I remember Adlestrop'), Larkin counterposes a more rugged 'No, I have never found | The place where I could say | *This is my proper ground.*' Larkin would be, as the title of his first major collection suggested, 'less deceived' than an earlier generation of England's elegists— not undeceived, just more ironically fond of those deceptions. Larkin's elegist in his poem 'The Whitsun Weddings' (the title poem of his 1964 volume) sees England with a combination of virginal awakenedness and elegiac sleepiness. (In his poem 'In The Stopping Train', first published in 1977, but in no way a rival to Larkin's power, Donald Davie (b. 1922) also figures the train as an agent of elegy and missed opportunities: 'Time, the exquisite torment! | His future is a slow | and stopping train through places | whose names used to have virtue.') In his poem, Larkin sees 'canals with floatings of industrial froth; | A hothouse flashed uniquely.' But all this is disappearing; newly married couples get onto the train, and though Larkin gestures

towards 'all the power | That being changed can give', it is impossible not
to feel that more is ending than is beginning: 'the wedding-days | Were
coming to an end.' As the train approaches London, 'now fields were build-
ing plots, and poplars cast | Long shadows over major roads', and Larkin's
narrator imagines 'London's postal districts packed like squares of wheat',
a lovely image that turns the poem into an English pastoral elegy.

In using the train as his vantage-point, it is not unlikely that Larkin
recalled Edward Thomas's elegiac trips around England before the 1914–18
war, described in *The Heart of England* (1906). Like Larkin, Thomas sees a
land transformed by new buildings and streets, and concludes that they are
impossible to write about, 'so new that we have inherited no certain attitude towards them, of liking or dislike'. Larkin's most Thomas-like elegy is
the poem 'MCMXIV', which is generally read as a straightforward elegy for
a national innocence destroyed by the Great War. Less obviously, it suggests the difficulty of elegy, because we cannot adequately evoke the lost
England whose passing we mourn. The poet finds he can re-enter the past
only through a kind of vivid cliché: 'The crowns of hats, the sun | On
moustached archaic faces . . . The tin advertisements | For cocoa and twist':

> Never such innocence
> Never before or since,
> As changed itself to past
> Without a word—the men
> Leaving the gardens tidy,
> The thousands of marriages
> Lasting a little while longer:
> Never such innocence again.

Ted Hughes's (b. 1930) version of 'MCMXIV', in the poem 'Six Young
Men', uses the old photograph as a relic of incommunicability: 'Six months
after this picture they were all dead.' But Hughes's vigorous mourning is
very different from Larkin's elegy, in ways that are characteristic of both
poets. Where Larkin proposes a great divide, a world absolutely changed
and a past absolutely lost, Hughes feels a continuation that is both grotesque—a kind of offence—and majestic: 'And still that valley has not
changed its sound | Though their faces are four decades under the ground.'
In Hughes's poem, the dead soldiers take their place in nature's endless
cycle of violence; and this nature is Hughes's England, its ancient 'inner
map'.

In place of Larkin's train window, which distances the poet, Hughes's
commonest vantage-point is the eye, the retina, or 'the mind's-eye'. Through

it, he sees an English nature which is partly nonconformist English (D. H. Lawrence) and partly Americanized space (Emerson, Whitman). Hughes's early poetry, in *The Hawk in the Rain* (1957), *Lupercal* (1960), and *Wodwo* (1967), was original partly because of the uses it made of an American violence of diction. But Lawrence and Gerard Manley Hopkins have been the biggest influences on Hughes—the Lawrence who contrasted the 'close, hedged-and-fenced English landscape' with 'The great circling landscape' that 'lived its own life' of Mexico and New Mexico. Hughes's Lawrentian landscape is both bare and populated, for it is through nature (animals, plants, rocks) that man speaks; and through its violence that man speaks his own violence. In 'Pike' the poet looks into a pond of pike and reflects that it is much more ancient than England's monasteries: 'Stilled legendary depth: | It was as deep as England.' In his poem 'Thistles' the plants are seen as rebellious Vikings with 'gutturals of dialects', who refuse to be silenced but return 'Stiff with weapons, fighting back over the same ground'. It is a vision of history-as-nature, a cycle of repeated struggle and defeat. In 'Relic' the poet evokes a beach, not as Larkin's untalkative strip, but as a place where natural things 'Continue the beginning'. This is a violent Eternal Return of false starts (perhaps given body elsewhere in Hughes's work in his fondness for images of stillborn ewes and aborted piglets).

Hughes has never really developed as a poet, neither in vision nor in language. His diction has become increasingly hysterical ('Honeysuckle hanging her fangs'), while his vision has often been bullying and reductive: 'Everything is inheriting everything' is the portentous last line of 'Root, Stem, Leaf'. But this absolutism undermines what is best in Hughes's poetry: his vivid originality with metaphor and ability to make us see something distinctly—e.g. a cranefly, with its 'bamboo fuselage . . . And the simple colourless church windows of her wings'. Cloaked in his dark essentialism, his animals and plants—his ferns and thistles, his pike and pigs, his hawks and crows—begin to resemble each other, as if everything *were* inheriting everything else.

Larkin's irretrievable past is so partly because it is necessarily seen through the words of others, including other works of literature; it is our own words that are not forthcoming. A Post-Modern age has made explicit use of Larkin's suggestiveness in this respect. Some of this use has been mediocre, opportunistic, or programmatic, but some of it also has been worthwhile. A. S. Byatt, in her novel *Possession* (1990; I shall come back to it), Peter Ackroyd (b. 1949), whose novels have rarely been anything more than wan pastiche, and the poet Geoffrey Hill (b. 1932) have all, in their different ways, seen an England recalcitrantly mediated by writers before them. For

Hill, the most gifted contemporary English poet after Larkin, this is a country both immediate and mystically remote: 'Landscape is like revelation; it is both | singular crystal and the remotest things.' Hill's finest work, *Mercian Hymns* (1971), joins together contemporary England and the gnarled historical landscape of King Offa, blending the two into a language at once churchy, ornate, and full of comedy: 'His maroon GT chanted then overtook. He lavished on | the high valleys its *haleine*.'

Basil Bunting's (1900–85) long, dense modernist poem *Briggflatts* (1966) also constructs an ancient kingdom out of literature and lore. It strives to speak what Bunting calls 'a Northumbrian tongue' on behalf of a Northumbria made up of such legendary figures as Eric Bloodaxe the Viking. But the poem's formal intimacy is as much homage to Bunting's mentor, Ezra Pound, as it is to the illuminations of the Lindisfarne Gospels (one of Bunting's avowed inspirations). There are echoes of Wordsworth's *Prelude*. *Briggflatts* is sometimes impressive but often tedious. Its strangeness has to do with its belatedness—it is the only long modernist poem to have been written in England in these years.

When the narrator of William Golding's (1911–93) pastoral novel *The Pyramid* (1967) returns to the village of his childhood, Stillbourne, he discovers that the old 'hazed-over' road sign has been replaced by a new blue-on-white one, visible 'at a distance of half-a-mile'. But the past has not been updated so much as obliterated by this renovation. For 'I saw that Stillbourne was like anywhere else after all.' The village has been released out of the private possession of memory into the collective absence of elegy.

In his novel-cum-autobiography *The Enigma of Arrival* (1987), the British-Trinidadian novelist V. S. Naipaul describes a season spent in the heart of rural England, on the estate of an old manor house in Wiltshire. It is a book of great, winding patience, written in a kind of creeping, caterpillar prose, a book of great beauties, and tediousness too. Naipaul encounters what seems to him at first an unchanging, literary landscape: 'like something out of an old novel, perhaps by Hardy or out of a Victorian country diary'. One of the men he encounters seems a 'Wordsworthian figure'. But Naipaul slowly discovers that in this place—part manor, part military firing range (it is next to Salisbury Plain)—'Change is constant.' His own presence in that landscape is an aspect of that change. Reflection on this draws Naipaul on to tell again the story of his own coming to London from Trinidad in 1950 (a narrative he has shaped and reshaped in both fictional and autobiographical form in book after book). Naipaul, who fed hungrily on Dickens as a child, confesses that the London he expected to find was that of Dickens, a fantasy city. *The Enigma of Arrival* tells the story of the destruction of various kinds of illusion. Naipaul soon discovers that he does not know London at all; it is not the city of Dickens any more than Wiltshire is the landscape of Hardy. Nevertheless, his rebellion against those illusions is a kind of homage to their power; indeed, his literary career, entirely spent in England, is the greatest homage to those illusions—for he has striven to turn it, in books like *Finding the Centre* (1984), into something almost heroically fictional or objectified, like the career of a picaresque hero.

So the English landscape is both unliterary and always soaked in literature. In 'From Kensal Rise to Heaven' (in *Acrimony*, 1986) one of the most talented poets of his generation, Michael Hofmann, sees London with a cold, illusionless eye, characteristic of much English writing in the 1980s. 'Dogs vet the garbage before the refuse collectors.' But the old literary mediation persists, amongst the stabbings, the Chinese take-aways, the 'building, repair and demolition':

> In an elementary deception, the name of the street
> is taken from a country town, and when I get up
> I find my education is back to haunt me: Dickens House,
> Blake Court, Austen House, thirteen-storey giants.

In Muriel Spark's (b. 1918, in Scotland: see also the Scottish chapter in this volume) novel *The Ballad of Peckham Rye* (1960), England's past is raised only to be mocked, like most things in the book. The novel tells the story of Dougal Douglas, a Scotsman who has come to work in Peckham. Dougal is a devil-figure, a diabolical con-man, whose presence in Peckham causes death and destruction. One of his tricks is to know more about people than they know themselves, and he sets about researching the history of Peckham. The results suggest a history both lofty and bathetic—and probably untrue, since Dougal Douglas is anything but reliable: 'Mendelssohn wrote his Spring Song in Ruskin Park. Ruskin lived on Denmark Hill. Mrs Fitzherbert lived in Camberwell Green. Boadicea committed suicide on Peckham Rye, probably where the bowling green is now . . .' A tunnel is discovered under Peckham Rye police station, and Dougal is sure that it leads to an old nunnery. By the end of the novel, it is discovered to be just a dead end, a 300-yard corridor; history, we gather, leads nowhere.

The Ballad of Peckham Rye is an interesting and original novel, though, like most of Spark's work, spindly, heartless, and brief. It is not 'realist', because the fable or ballad-like nature of the project tends to compact narration and character in non-realist ways. Moreover, Dougal Douglas has agreed to write the autobiography of a retired singer and actress, Maria Cheeseman, and it becomes clear that he is insisting, against her wishes, on inserting a fictional chapter or two into the book. These fictional chapters, we learn, will recount Dougal's own exploits in Peckham. He is thus that classic modernist or Post-Modernist hero: he is writing the novel we are reading. When a gang of thugs break into his lodgings, they discover a mysterious list entitled 'Phrases suitable for cheese'. This is in fact a list of clichés, which Dougal intends to make use of in Maria Cheeseman's autobiography. Since most of the protagonists use clichés, this is a kind of joke at the novel's expense. Dougal's success in Peckham has much to do with his originality in a place habituated to cliché.

Spark's novel is characteristic of much English writing since 1960—an experiment contained within an old-fashioned commitment to character and realism. Angus Wilson's novel *No Laughing Matter* (1967) has vividly real characters who also like to play family theatricals, parodying Shaw and Beckett; Margaret Drabble's (b. 1939) later novels are solidly narrated but also contain a kind of Virginia Woolf-like stream-of-consciousness, and authorial interventions; William Golding's novels are what he himself called 'fables'; and Angela Carter's (1940–92) are often versions of fairy-tales. In addition to which there were more obvious cases of rewriting: Anthony Burgess's (1917–93) best book, *Nothing Like the Sun* (1964), is an intensely Joycean novel about Shakespeare; Jean Rhys's (1894–1979) *Wide Sargasso Sea* (1966) brilliantly fantasizes a West Indian life for Mrs Rochester, the character in *Jane Eyre*. This was certainly not a dull time for the English novel.

Nevertheless, it often seems poised uncomfortably between experiment and nostalgia. Some of these contradictions can be found in Iris Murdoch's influential polemic 'Against Dryness', first published in 1961. Murdoch's essay, in ways that are interestingly similar to her fiction, moves uneasily between philosophy and aesthetics. Arguing against what she sees as the tendency of modern philosophy, Murdoch demands a vision of man seen not as solitary or free but 'against a background of values, of realities, which transcend him'. Sunk in this overwhelming reality, we will always be tempted to deform it by fantasy, to wish it away, or to turn it into a manageable game. But, argues Murdoch, freedom is never absolute but always calibrated—there are degrees of freedom. And real freedom is not solitariness but a renewed sense both of other people and their mysteries ('the opacity of persons'), and of the 'transcendence of reality'. This, says Murdoch, was the vision of the great nineteenth-century novelists.

At this point, and not entirely convincingly, Murdoch leaves hold of philosophy and jumps into her aesthetic net. Most twentieth-century fiction, she says, has been a species of fantasy; it has been either

crystalline or journalistic; that is, it is either a small quasi-allegorical object portraying the human condition and not containing 'characters' in the nineteenth-century
sense, or else it is a large shapeless quasi-documentary object, the degenerate descendant of the nineteenth-century novel, telling, with pale conventional characters, some straightforward story enlivened with empirical facts.

What we need, argues Murdoch, is not better art, but truth: 'We need to
return from the self-centred concept of sincerity to the other-centred concept of truth.' This truthfulness must necessarily produce better art. Most
modern English novels, she writes, are not *written*. If art is to be truthful
once more, prose must 'recover its former glory, eloquence and discourse
must return. I would connect eloquence with the attempt to speak the
truth.'

Murdoch's essay is an important document, partly because it illuminates
so much of what is both admirable and misshapen in her own art; and
partly because it illuminates so much of the productive and valuable anarchy of recent English writing. What is striking about Murdoch's fiction is
how her best novels embody the contradictions of her essay, but, through
their imaginative energy and self-wrestling, render those contradictions comparatively unimportant.

Murdoch's fiction is riven between a metaphysical objection to form
(because form tidies things into the 'crystalline'), and an artist's awareness
that art cannot do without it. And this tension is further complicated by her
fondness for both controlling myths and symbolism—which tend to assert
their own shaping tidiness. Under these strains, many of her novels are
flattened into allegorical maps of whimsy and feints. In *The Bell* (1958),
which is set in an Anglican lay community, the novel's considerable social
density—in the relations of the members of the community with one
another—is submerged by the symbolic weight of the bell, which is made
to represent the solid mystery of the real; with the effect that the *actual*
solid mystery of the real drains away. In other novels, like *The Sandcastle*
(1957) and *A Severed Head* (1961), a mythic structure seems to hold greater
aesthetic importance than the heavily manipulated characters.

In her best work—which would include *A Fairly Honourable Defeat* (1970),
The Sea, the Sea (1978), and *The Philosopher's Pupil* (1983)—Murdoch makes
productive use of her own mistrust of art's powers to dramatize a confrontation between the artist and the saint; and between egotism and selfless-
ness. Charles Arrowby, in *The Sea, the Sea*, is a theatrical impresario who
has retired to a seaside village. In Murdoch's bestiary of enchanters and
Prospero-figures, he is a relatively benign manipulator (unlike the more
sinister philosopher, John Robert Rozanov, in *The Philosopher's Pupil*).

Charles's delusions of power are pitted against the selfless Buddhism of his cousin James. But James has genuine, rather than merely figurative, magical powers of manipulation, and is certainly an ambiguous saint. It is difficult not to agree with A. S. Byatt, in her book on Murdoch (*Degrees of Freedom*, 1965, revised 1994), that in her later novels she has been suggesting versions of 'a revitalized, demythologized religion'. This religion is an extension of Murdoch's reverence for otherness and for the reality of other people. As she has put it, 'the total obliteration of your present being would mean that the world would exist and not you.' What is yearned for is the death of the ego. *The Sea, the Sea* proposes James's death-haunted Buddhism as one religious possibility; in *The Philosopher's Pupil* Father Bernard believes in a Tolstoyan Christianity of the here-and-now, one premissed (like Tolstoy's) on a belief in the dead but not risen Christ; he may be seen as an heir of Carel, another priest without a god in *The Time of the Angels*.

A. S. Byatt is herself a pivotal figure here; in her work, as if through a glass hull, one can see the choppy currents of English writing in the last thirty years. There is about it an ambitious ungainliness. By temperament, but also by programme, she has been eager to experiment—one finds realism, parody, allegory, a fiction of ideas and a fiction of sensuousness, moralism, fairy-tale, campus farce, Victorian pastiche, post-structuralist theory (her best-known novel, *Possession* (1990), combines Victorian pastiche and the work of the French feminist theorist Luce Irigaray).

Byatt's project, thus far, has been more important than her achievement, When she started writing fiction in the mid-1960s, she found much contemporary English writing both intellectually reticent and verbally enfeebled. Her great influences were George Eliot and Iris Murdoch (with Wordsworth and Coleridge in the background). She had no time for the brutish negations of her immediate precursors (Kingsley Amis, C. P. Snow, and even the Angus Wilson of the 1950s had decided that Woolf and Joyce must be driven out of town, the better, one imagines, to empty the saloon-bar for their own philistinism), and had attended Frank Kermode's influential seminars on narrative and structuralist theory at University College London in the late 1960s.

Byatt's wish has been to restore to English fiction a lost density and a lost intelligence. As she has written, she believed in T. S. Eliot's 'dissociation of sensibility' when she left school; and though she now knows too much to see it as anything more than a vivid metaphor, her own writing has been an attempt to heal that dissociation—something she locates at the heart of language itself. She has written, borrowing Eliot's image, that in her fiction she wants to make abstract thought as real as smelling a rose. She longs for immediacy, but knows that language is always rhetoric, and that literature in this century has made this abundantly clear to us. More than this, while part of her imagination yearns for a visual immediacy, the other part constantly peels away into analogy, allegory, metaphor, and relations with other texts. She is incorrigibly literary, but seeks to escape this condition.

The result, in her fiction, is an attempt to write what she calls 'self-conscious realism', a contradiction that is both her subject and, alas, her substance. Certainly, one does not have to dig deep for themes in Byatt; her work is, in this respect, a shallow grave. Her second novel, *The Game* (1967), is a clever assault on the notion of realism as a transparency, as a detached recording of life. Critics have seen it as Byatt's dramatizing of her own relationship to her sister Margaret Drabble, then as now a best-selling writer of middle-brow domestic fiction. Julia, a best-selling novelist, is happy to characterize her fiction as 'honest comfort for the masses, that's all it is, and fodder for the sociologist'. She claims 'no more than the virtues of an accurate recorder'. But when Julia writes a novel about her sister Cassandra's life as a don in Oxford, Cassandra realizes that 'you can both destroy and create reality with fiction'. In an interview, Byatt was bluntly explicatory: 'Cassandra sees writing as artifice and Julia sees writing as natural, and Cassandra is a better writer than Julia.' Elsewhere, Cassandra wants to heal the dissociation of sensibility: 'sit still and let everything run into everything else. We need a sense of being undifferentiated . . . I keep chasing metaphors. Out of a desire for an impossible unity.' Metaphor both binds together different things and reminds us that these different things are only likenesses, hence not really bound together.

Byatt's third novel, *The Virgin in the Garden* (1978), was the first of a projected tetralogy about the 'second Elizabethan Age'. In north Yorkshire a group of people are celebrating the coronation of Elizabeth II by performing a verse drama about Elizabeth I. Byatt is seeking, in her own words, to represent a 'paradise' before Eliot's dissociation of sensibility, 'in which thought and language were naturally and indissolubly linked'. The second novel in the series, the much more successful *Still Life* (1985), is informed by a line from the American poet William Carlos Williams, who wrote that there are 'no ideas but in things'. She wanted this novel, in contrast to its predecessor, to be 'very bare, very down-to-earth . . . to give the "thing itself" without the infinitely extensible cross-referencing of *The Virgin*'. Her plan was to write a novel stripped of metaphor, in which words denoted things plainly and exactly. However, 'I found that this was in fact impossible for someone with the cast of mind I have.'

Intelligence is Byatt's greatest problem as a writer. She has never learned

how to subjugate it. She has a greater commitment to character than perhaps any of her major contemporaries—to the patient unfolding of motive
and psychological change. *Still Life*, for instance, represents an important
attempt to describe, through a kind of intellectual autobiography, the education, both academic and sentimental, of a young, intelligent post-war
woman, Frederica Potter. We follow Frederica—from Blesford Grammar
School, through Cambridge, and out into the London of the late 1950s—in
the knowledge that we are witnessing a generation and a decade: the decade of Byatt's own education and coming-of-age. But Byatt's characters do
not live: they are mummified in strips of ratiocination. They are less the
dynamic sources than the arrested victims of thought. Hers is a failure of
tone and language, and an almost wilful flight from immediacy—for all her
apparent yearning to capture it. Almost every character in *Still Life* is made
to take up a correct position on the question of language-as-rhetoric. The
vicar, Daniel (Frederica's brother-in-law), for example, has given up using
metaphor in his sermons: 'he had come . . . to mistrust figurative language.
He never now made a sermon from metaphor, nor drew analogies: he
preached examples, cases, lessons.' And even when Byatt is not sorting out
her characters' intellectual positions, her description—as animation—is ordinary; indeed, her prose manages to be at once rich and strangely inanimate:

Daniel did not change. He wore the same black clothes—baggy corduroys, heavy
sweater, working man's jacket—that he had worn through the sixties and seventies. Like many hirsute men he had thinned a little on top where once his black fur
had been extravagant, but he had a plentiful and prickling black beard, and his body
was still compact and very heavy.

If one compares Byatt's detailed description of Daniel with V. S. Pritchett's
(b. 1900) swift, selective description of his father in his autobiography *A Cab
at the Door* (1968), one can see the difference between will (the determination to notate), as it appears in Murdoch and Byatt, and instinct (the instinctive capturing of personality): 'I loved seeing the sad voluptuous pout of his
lips as he carved a joint and the modest look on his face when, at my house,
he passed his plate up and said, as his own mother had before, "Just a little
more." It should have been his epitaph.' Pritchett's autobiography (a sequel, *Midnight Oil*, was published in 1971) contains some of the best English
writing of the last thirty years. In it he tells the very English story of a
working-class boy's escape from his family into literature; it is dominated
by the portrait of his Dickensian father, whom he likens to Mr Micawber—
he was a Christian Scientist with impractical business projects and a bedroom full of tinned food in preparation for Armageddon.

In the passage I have quoted, Pritchett's advantage over Byatt is partly, of course, that he is portraying a Dickensian 'character' or caricature: his father's theatricality is what makes him vivid. But even so, one notices that where Byatt hoards, Pritchett selects; moreover, that the passage catches his father not frozen in habiliments but in a moment of movement—not just physical but emotional, for in one comic detail Pritchett illuminates a soul caught in a strategy of ordinary greed and mild self-deception (the 'voluptuous pout' giving the lie to the 'modest look'). The final sentence fixes not the father but the scene as symbolic; and slyly makes the father into a creature of legend in the most domestic of contexts.

It is in her Booker Prize-winning novel *Possession* (1990) that Byatt has come nearer than in any previous work to converting her weaknesses into plausible necessities: abandoning the struggle for realistic density and the evocation of character, she produced what she called a 'romance'. In this vibrant tale of 1980s academics in search of two (fictitious) Victorian poets, Randolph Henry Ash and Christabel LaMotte, we cannot expect her contemporary characters to be anything but shadows compared with the magisterial and overwhelming reality of the Victorians—and, in particular, the reality of the thousands of lines of pastiche Victorian verse Byatt has written for the novel. Her foregrounding of her own academicism as the book's subject gives it a certain verve as campus farce and Post-Modern frolic. But the suspicion arises that the book is not quite 'light' enough to be a truly frolicsome romance, that it is still yearning for the conventions of realistic density. *Possession*'s romance is too heavy, and its 'realism' emerges too often as botched caricature.

Margaret Drabble, like her sister—though at a lower intellectual pressure —has been writing a kind of 'self-conscious realism' since the mid-1970s: solid frames containing attempts at a density of character and society, but also full of authorial interventions, stream-of-consciousness, and outrageous coincidences and connections clearly intended as a deliberate affront to a late twentieth-century 'plausibility'. Her novels of the 1960s—like *The Garrick Year* (1964) and *The Millstone* (1965)—were over-praised at the time because of their novelty of content. (They dealt frankly and at a popular level with the frustrations of married domesticity as experienced by young middle-class women.) Drabble's ninth novel, *The Realms of Gold* (1975), was much more ambitious, and inaugurated a new phase in her writing. Since then, in particular in her vast trilogy *The Radiant Way* (1987), *A Natural Curiosity* (1989), and *The Gates of Ivory* (1991), she has striven to write large books soaked in social and political data (often using contrasting families from the North and South of England).

The Realms of Gold is probably the best of these novels. It attempts to render England through a system of controlling metaphors. Its centre of consciousness is an archaeologist called Frances Wingate, famed for her discovery of a buried Saharan city. Over the course of the novel we read of her relationship with her lover, a married lecturer, and encounter her relatives in the North. The maundering structure, though vulnerable to criticism, at least builds up a wide portrait. Furthermore, Drabble uses her metaphors subtly, without too much bullying—the buried Saharan city is also the buried northern city of Frances's childhood, a place lost in time, backward, neglected; by implication, the novel form itself is the archaeological means by which this ruined land is to be excavated.

Unfortunately, Drabble has no style capable of integrating her musings and observations. The writing is a kind of trade fair of different styles: loose, unpressurized stream-of-consciousness, repetition, and pointless puns serving no larger purpose: 'He had known they were ancient, he said to himself, as he scrambled back down the hill to his hard scrambled eggs.' Like her sister, Drabble has a weakness also for condescending interventions. In *The Radiant Way* and its successors, her chosen northern town is simply called 'Northam', whereas Drabble's southerners get to live in a very specific London. As one critic has remarked, Drabble's frequent authorial interventions have the effect of 'dismantling her structures well before they have become solid enough for us to take an interest in them'.

The political influence behind Drabble's novels has been Dickens. Indeed, Pritchett's description of his father reminds us of Dickens's perseverance as an influence on much English writing since 1945. Angus Wilson (who wrote a critical book about him) is the most obviously indebted; but V. S. Naipaul's early comic novels are intensely Dickensian, and some of Muriel Spark's comedy has a Dickensian vividness. Pinter's use of vernacular comes from Dickens via T. S. Eliot's *Sweeney Agonistes*. In a younger generation, Paul Bailey (b. 1937) and Martin Amis (b. 1949) have made use of Dickens—the first for the theatrical, shabby-genteel background of much of his fiction, especially the semi-autobiographical *Gabriel's Lament* (1986), the latter as a source for grotesquerie and caricature. The cockney theatricality of Angela Carter's (1940–92) early and late novels has clear roots in Dickens also.

Dickens's theatricality and power of caricature have been the lasting influence. Pritchett, who with Virginia Woolf has been the century's great English critic of fiction, has written illuminatingly about Dickensian comedy as reflective of the truest English character. He sees this comic theatricality as an egotism, a solitariness, and a kind of madness ('eccentricity is, in fact, practical madness'). Pritchett's own characters in his fiction are just such solitaries, going through life supported on a cushion of inner fictions. Dickens's great creations are 'solitary pronouncers':

All Dickens's characters, comic or not, issue personal pronouncements that magnify their inner life . . . They are strange, even mad, because they speak as if they were the only persons in the world . . . Our comedy, Dickens seems to say, is not in our relations with others but in our relation with ourselves, our poetry, our genius.

In a fine image, Pritchett writes that Dickens saw that his characters 'were people whose inner life was hanging out, so to speak, on their tongues, outside their persons'.

Muriel Spark is where we best find an unconscious Dickensian theatricality. Like Dickens's characters, Spark's actually change very little in the course of her books, and are entranced by their own sense of themselves as legendary figures: Miss Brodie (in *The Prime of Miss Jean Brodie*), like Mr Micawber, is in love with her small collection of maxims and motifs.

A good example of a natural rewriting of Dickens can be found in one of Spark's later novels, *A Far Cry from Kensington* (1980), which is set in the shabby-genteel world of London publishing in the 1950s. Milly, the owner of the boarding-house in which the novel's narrator Mrs Hawkins lives, is a frankly Dickensian caricature. From this flow her ample gaiety and also her limitations as a character. When the next-door neighbours argue, Milly leads Mrs Hawkins to a window from where they watch the argument; she turns life into a stage: 'Milly, always with her sense of the appropriate, dashed down to her bedroom and reappeared with a near-full box of chocolates. We sat side by side, eating chocolates and watching the show.' Milly enjoys life as spectacle; and, like a Dickens character, she mythologizes her acquaintances into a parliament of selves (as David Copperfield does when practising at home with his family his job as a parliamentary sketch-writer; 'and night after night, we had a sort of Private Parliament in Buckingham Street'). Near the end of the novel, Milly and Mrs Hawkins go to Paris. In the Louvre, Milly remarks on the likenesses between the portraits and her friends: 'Now, Milly remarked that the Mona Lisa was "the image of Mrs Twinny", by which observation I was first amazed and then impressed for, indeed, Mrs Twinny, the wife of our odd-job neighbour, bore a decided resemblance to the Mona Lisa.' The narrator's tone is hardly different from David Copperfield's: Milly domesticates the Louvre, but also turns her friends into portraits, a Private Parliament.

Spark's theatricality is natural; Angela Carter's, by contrast, is determined.

Carter started writing in the 1960s at about the same time as A. S. Byatt (her first novel, *Shadow Dance*, appeared in 1966, and her second, *The Magic Toyshop*, in 1967). Like Byatt, she is a writer whose rebelliousness may be more important than her final achievement. Again, like Byatt, she found herself with little that was usable in her immediate literary tradition (she once wrote, in an essay on Katherine Mansfield, that the period of Mansfield's creativity, 1902–23, 'now looks as though it was England's last artistically vital one'). She had a lively interest, however, in popular art-forms—fairy-tales, music hall, pantomime, puppetry—and found herself attracted to the demotic and theatrical in Dickens and Shakespeare. She also fed on the liberties of various forms of Surrealism, but also the magic realism of García Márquez and Günter Grass, and the Post-Modern paranoia of Thomas Pynchon. Such influences are apparent in her very earliest work, as she rolls up the old heavy carpet of realist narration and unrolls instead her own brighter mat: of a menacing fairy-tale. Often, Carter's prose is brilliantly suggestive, at once playful and black: 'May progressed slowly. The white lilacs in the churchyard where Honey said Ghislaine had been raped and hurt browned at the edges and reeked of halitosis and finally dropped down dead.' The England of Carter's early novels is both real and stagy, a Gothic suburb of the mind full of crumbling antique shops, sinister houses on hills, and peopled by weird puppeteers and manipulators, like the crazed Honeybuzzard in *Shadow Dance*, or the misogynist toy-shop owner in *The Magic Toyshop*.

These early novels take the form of surrealist fairy-tales or fables, but with a strong theoretical undertow. In what is possibly her best novel, *The Magic Toyshop*, Carter tells the story of a 15-year-old orphan who leaves her magical childhood home in the country for a sinister Gothic house on a hill in south London. In this house are a mute aunt, who communicates by chalking words on a slate, and a viciously patriarchal uncle, who bullies his new acquisition, the young orphan, into taking part in his amateur dramatics. The story has a feminist pressure—the uncle, we are told, likes 'silent women'—and Melanie's escape from the house at the end of the book may be seen as an escape from the house of the 'fathers'. *Love* (1971), which is the portrait of a wayward middle-class depressive, explores the theoretical work of the psychoanalyst Joan Riviere, in particular her notion of femininity as masquerade.

Carter was open about the polemical and theoretical purpose of her work. She told an interviewer in 1984 that her character Tristessa, the transvestite movie star in *The Passion of New Eve* (1977), was created 'in order to say some quite specific things about the cultural production of femininity', adding that 'I've tried to keep an entertaining surface to the novels, so that you don't have to read them as a system of signification if you don't want to.'

Carter's fictions, however, drench us in signification, and their theoretical coerciveness—embodied in the books as a tendency towards over-explicit statement, allegory, and symbol—seems to be, not just the inevitable price paid by a Post-Modern self-consciousness, but an artistic failure. Much of Carter's work is about life as display or spectacle—about signification, in fact. But she overdoes her theme by making her books not just theatrical but pieces of theatre overrun by actors: Honeybuzzard in *Shadow Dance* has a collection of false noses and vampiric teeth; the wicked uncle in *The Magic Toyshop* has his own puppet theatre; the heroine of *Nights at the Circus* (1984), Fevvers, is a cockney circus performer; and the two sisters at the heart of *Wise Children*, Nora and Dora Chance, are former music-hall dancers. Carter's books are not theatrical, like Spark's, but theatricalized, seemingly determined to remind us of their liveliness.

The Dickensian demotic appears much more naturally—though without any loss of Post-Modern knowingness—in Harold Pinter's two best plays, *The Caretaker* (1960) and *The Homecoming* (1965). Unlike Carter, Pinter's liveliness, although clearly willed, seems to be organically generated by his language. Pinter, it may be argued, is the only successful verbal innovator of his generation, and one of the few (along with perhaps Martin Amis) to possess his own voice ('Larkinian' and 'Pinteresque' are the only two such epithets of this period). Pinter's language, an odd *mélange* of T. S. Eliot stage-cockney (one recalls Eliot's 'I knew a man once did a girl in' in *Sweeney Agonistes*) and absurdist comedy, is both experimental and antique, sometimes plausible and often highly stylized.

Likewise, the world of his plays moves in and out of the real. *The Homecoming* is in part a violently ironic assault on England's relation to the past. Teddy arrives home in London suddenly, with a wife of several years standing whom the rest of his family have never met. He teaches philosophy in an unnamed American university. His family—a vicious old patriarch, an uncle, and two brothers—is misogynistic, insular, and vaguely menacing. Teddy's homecoming, we discover, is not simply to his family but to his close-minded country, obsessed with its once-victorious past: the play is full of glancing references to the last war, to 'bombsites' and 'rubble'; one of Teddy's brothers, Lenny, while talking about Venice, adds inconsequentially: 'If I'd fought in the war I'd've gone through Venice . . . good old Venice.'

This past-hauntedness inheres most strongly in the play's language, which is what gives it its strange vividness. Lenny's 'good old Venice' sounds odd not just because it is clear that Lenny has never been to Venice, but because the locution belongs to another age and another city—'good old London' or 'good old Blighty' would be more likely. Similarly, when Max, who is a bully and may have been a child-abuser, threatens Teddy with 'a cuddle and a kiss like the old days', the language is quaintly pantomime-like, but the threatened cuddle is not—there is nothing quaint in these 'old days'. The old days indeed are a close-minded family, for Teddy discovers that because he has left England there can be no homecoming; he has become invisible. His family, though repeatedly told otherwise, decide that he and his wife have just married. Teddy tells them near the end of the play, with apparent satisfaction: 'You're way behind, all of you.'

Pinter's language, however, is very much of the present; it is a literary slang fattened on contemporary swill. It is an ironic container of the old, certainly, but receptive to a new language of bureaucratic cliché, bourgeois pretence (Teddy is asked 'Did you have a big function?'), and academic specialism (when Teddy and Lenny argue about philosophy, Teddy complains that 'that question doesn't fall within my province'). It is a literary vernacular with a cockney or Jewish-cockney tilt, at once demotic and comically portentous ('He's had more dolly than you've had cream cakes'; 'You wouldn't understand my points of reference'). Pinter's absurdist routines—an argument over a cheese sandwich, or the tramp's repeated invocation of the place-name 'Sidcup' in *The Caretaker*—can seem repetitive and too flimsy to take the philosophical weight apparently asked of them. But he is one of the few writers of this period who has truly enlivened the literary language.

Perhaps Dickensian theatricality is doomed to be merely imitative in our age. Certainly, Angus Wilson's varied and distinguished fiction suggests that this is so. Wilson described his own virtues and limitations as a writer with unconscious acuteness in his allegory of English muddle *The Old Men at the Zoo* (1961). The wife of that novel's narrator, who is a brilliantly heartless mimic, rebukes him: 'Yes, darling, but everybody you describe is ridiculous and a bit sad . . . You do see very funny things in people and you have got feeling, but you paint the whole that way.' Wilson, as critics have always noted, was a mimic of great brilliance; his best writing is certainly in his speech (especially his monologues), for outside dialogue he was no stylist. He has a capacity for Dickensian caricature, though he lacked Dickens's sense of the fantastic, and he lacked Dickens's monstrously vivid descriptive powers. He seems a very English writer, with an acute social receptivity (he is a fine describer of embarrassment) but no metaphysical hunger.

His early stories from the late 1940s and early 1950s were brilliant satires on a new post-war bourgeoisie; during the next twenty years he widened his art into social panorama and experiment, but kept close to the talents that made his first books so good: his mimicry and his morally sensitive satire. Indeed, if one looks at the novels he wrote during the 1960s and 1970s—*The Old Men at the Zoo*, *Late Call* (1964), *No Laughing Matter* (1967)—one concludes that Wilson became trapped by his mimicry. Too often, he stops, as it were, at the mimetic threshold: he does not push through into the internal corridors of his characters to see how they function. At his worst, his portraits do not have the gross vitality of Dickensian caricature, nor the artistry; they lack both depth and pathos.

This is certainly true of the grotesques who run the zoo in *The Old Men at the Zoo*. Wilson's determination to render them as vivid grotesques simply produces a kind of willed vulgarity of phrasing: 'He paused, then leaning his short stubby arms on the huge desk, he loomed towards me, a blubbery shapeless old mass.' These characters do not really live for us even as grotesques. Wilson is forced to insist on their strangeness by likening them to zoo animals. 'Leacock swung round from the window, his toucan eyes rounder than ever with anger . . .' Of Lord Godmanchester, the newspaper magnate who runs the zoo, we are shown 'His huge shapeless rhino's bottom as he ambled out of the room'.

The Old Men at the Zoo is a dystopia—it is 1971 and Europe is on the brink of war. The book is a kind of satire on England's political class, using the London Zoo as a microcosm of the state, much as the New Town of Carshall figures as a microcosm of a new England in *Late Call*. The novel adapts, as it were, Orwell's remark that England is a family with the wrong members in control. In Wilson's version, England is a zoo with the wrong animals in charge. The explicitness is everywhere—the linking of humans and animals, or in plain statement: 'I saw the muddle as an old men's muddle, the obstinacy, shiftiness, laziness and weariness of a lot of old men faced with an emergency of violence and suffering.' This zoo is hierarchical, like England: aristocrats/tycoons (Lord Godmanchester), technicians and administrators (Simon Carter, the secretary of the Zoo and the novel's narrator), innovators, reactionaries, and faithful retainers like the humble Filson, whose son is killed at the start of the book by a sick giraffe; when Carter says that there must be an inquiry, Filson is too loyal to the institution to countenance such exposure.

Simon Carter is torn between his talents as a naturalist (he is a specialist on badgers) and his priggish efficiency as an administrator. He subjugates the first to the second, as he becomes increasingly involved with the zoo's removal from London to the Welsh borders. In his critical book *The Wild Garden* (1963) Wilson expounded this dualism as the central theme of the novel with a zeal that suggests just what is over-explicit about the novel's allegory. The struggle between the need for 'contemplation and social activity', he writes, is today's central paradox for the humanist. Wilson points out the neat irony that the only moment that Carter gets undisturbed to observe his badgers comes at the end of the book, when he must shoot them to save himself from death by starvation. 'The contradictory (and, as it seems to me, inescapable) circle is complete.' The book has a similar neatness, and once Wilson's political ideas wash away, only the thinnest artistic sediment is left.

Late Call (1964) is a much stronger work. Certainly, Sylvia Calvert, the novel's centre of consciousness, is Wilson's deepest portrait. Sylvia, with her tiresome 'character' of a husband, Capt Arthur Calvert (wounded in the Great War), relinquishes the south-coast hotel she has run for years, and moves to the New Town of Carshall, to live with her widowed son Harold. The novel's simplicity is one of its most attractive features. Sylvia encounters a new England of angry young men, new concrete towns, and new mores (one of Harold's sons leaves home and announces his homosexuality by letter), and through her discomfort, boredom, and aimlessness, Wilson carries gracefully much of the same thematic load that he dragged too heavily through *The Old Men at the Zoo*.

No Laughing Matter is Wilson's most ambitious book: an attempt at a portrait of our century seen through one family. It is both traditional and experimental. On the one hand, it is a huge family saga that moves steadily through the decades from the 1910s onwards, crowded with rounded characters from the Matthews family, whose paths we follow happily enough— Marcus, who becomes a gay art-dealer, and who is politicized by his relationship during the 1930s with a Jewish man; Quentin, who becomes a left-wing journalist during the Spanish Civil War, and then a political chat-show host in the televisual 1960s; Margaret, who becomes a fashionable novelist. On the other hand, the novel is decidedly anti-realist: all of the children are mimics, and they have a family tradition called 'The Game' in which they imitate their parents in invented dramatic scenes. The novel frequently turns from third-person narration to dialogue laid out as playscript. The Matthews family's penchant for games, amateur dramatics, and camp role-reversal turns a realist saga into a Post-Modern circus.

If the novel fails, ultimately, it is not because it attempts too much formally, but because it attempts too little humanly. Wilson's characters, for all their delights, tend to dissolve into their histrionics; and the reader feels that this text is still old-fashioned enough to want character-depth. Though we spend hundreds of pages in the company of the Matthews children, we never know them as we know the characters in great novels of the family. We do not know them because Wilson's narrative, for all its apparent intimacies, does not ask us to; it does not struggle with its characters—it simply confirms them. This is partly a weakness of the saga-form, which bundles the Matthewses through experiences that seem not invididual but merely representative: Quentin goes off to the Spanish Civil War, Marcus takes a Jewish lover, and Margaret becomes a society novelist—because the 1930s somehow expect it of them. But even without this formal smother-ing, Wilson's characters lack individuation because they are conceived statically; they do not change very much. Each new happening, each new decade, brings a repetition of the essence of each character, not a challenge to that essence. Wilson has a nice warmth towards his creations, and some of this is infectious; but there is a more important lack of astringency.

The most talented inheritor of Dickensian comedy of the last thirty years has been V. S. Naipaul. Indeed, of his generation this writer has been the only really successful innovator in fictional form. Most of his books explore, in various ways, the situation of the 'colonial', or apparently 'marginal', man (in several books this exploration has been explicitly autobiographical). Naipaul's comedy and pathos as a novelist arise from his deep understand-ing of the complex and awkward yearning of the margin for the centre, and the nightmares and enigmas of arrival at the centre.

He has often been criticized as a reactionary, because of his abrasive portraits of Caribbean life (see the chapter on West Indian writing in this volume) and his long allegiance to the literature of the centre (Dickens, Conrad, Flaubert, Gogol). In fact, he has a delicate sense of the comic calculus of imperial condescension and colonial ambition. In his first novel, *The Mystic Masseur* (1957), his comedy is mild and warm, and lightly satirical of both Trinidadian aspiration and English pomposity. Ganesh, the *shlemiel* of this novel, has become a familiar Naipaul figure—clumsily yearning for greatness, convinced that his life is a train of destiny, while Naipaul shows it to be a carnival of accidents. A failed masseur, he becomes, thanks to a series of preposterous events, Trinidad's most famous mystic, and finally a member of the island's legislative council. The fiercest satire here is poured on Indersingh, a Trinidadian just returned from corrupting Oxford, who wears blazers and says 'old man'.

Naipaul's fourth book, *A House for Mr Biswas* (1961), is still his greatest. It has influenced writers with a fondness for the magical or surrealist such as Salman Rushdie, not just because of its sweeping comic range, but because it is a vessel of the fantastic (Biswas is born with six fingers). Its comedy is continually pushing away from the referential. Biswas's yearning—to be something great, something more than a henpecked shop sign-writer—is what gives the book its deep comic pathos. Where Ganesh plays with fate, Biswas is in rebellion against it. Again, Naipaul squeezes comic sap out of the disjunction between the margin and the centre. When Biswas starts work as a journalist, he corresponds with the Ideal School of Journalism, Edgware Road, London, which advises him to write about 'the Romance of Place-Names (your vicar is likely to prove a mine of colourful information)'.

Naipaul's characteristic humour is bathos, a grinding together of high and low registers which has been influential in much contemporary Anglo-Indian comic writing: 'When he got home, he mixed and drank some Maclean's Brand Stomach Powder, undressed, got into bed and read some Epictetus.' The tone of absurdly injured pride, the teetering mock-heroic pomposity is funny.

Naipaul's later work has swerved away from comedy, however; it has become more sombre, more political, and more transparently autobiographical. It has also become experimental. In *In a Free State* (1971) he brings together three novellas about exile—one set in Africa, one in London, one in Washington, DC. On either side of this trilogy, he appends a frankly autobiographical prologue and epilogue—a few pages apparently torn from his travel notebook. In the Washington story, Santosh, a servant who accompanies his master from Bombay to Washington, discovers with great sadness that, in America, freedom means, in both senses of the phrase, that 'nobody cares what you do'. In later autobiographical books Naipaul has tended to make his own life-story an archetype of colonial experience.

English fiction in the 1960s, as we have been seeing, explores all kinds of innovation in form, complicated notions of realism, and flirts with real experiment. Why—apart from occasional successes such as *Biswas* and *The Homecoming*—does much of this fail to ignite? A certain parochialism is one reason, an inability to rise out of material contexts and up into some upper atmosphere of the soul. An English love of allegory, and symbol, is another, tending to push the writer towards over-explicitness. This is seen clearly enough in William Golding's work. Golding's fables contain an unremarkable philosophy (that 'humans produce evil as naturally as bees produce honey', as he put it); or rather, they contain a philosophy which needs the kind of self-dramatizing that the fabular cannot offer. What is fabular about them is often what is most weak—the conch shell standing for parliamentary democracy in *Lord of the Flies* (1954), the colour-coded black and white of good and evil in *Darkness Visible* (1979). In his best book, *The Spire* (1964), which is about a hubristic priest who is determined to build the great spire of a cathedral left unnamed but clearly Salisbury, Golding turns his weaknesses into burnable energy. The entire book is symbolic, but the symbol is so transparent that it becomes dynamic: or as the American writer Eudora Welty put it on another occasion, 'one way of looking at Moby Dick is that his task as a symbol was so big and strenuous that he *had* to be a whale'.

If 1960s fiction was innovative in form, in the 1970s and 1980s new fictional *languages* appeared. Partly this had to do with the breaking up of the apparent coherence of English literary culture: Scottish writing, making full use of vernacular language and dialect, began to appear; Salman Rushdie, born in India and one of the most influential novelists of the last fifteen years, constructed a new language of Magic Realist fantasy and Anglo-Indian compounds; in poetry, Irish poets like Seamus Heaney, Paul Muldoon, and Tom Paulin were using Irish vernacular to enliven their adjectives and adverbs. Even English poets like James Fenton (b. 1944) were bypassing Larkin for the livelier, less insular influence of W. H. Auden.

The largest shift, however, was a turning outwards both to European models and to America. The most interesting poet of the 1980s, Michael Hofmann, is the son of a German novelist, and his great influence is Robert Lowell; when the Poetry Society, in 1994, asked twenty leading British poets to name their main twentieth-century influences, the favourites were both American: Elizabeth Bishop and Robert Lowell.

The importance of this double shift cannot be overemphasized, for it has probably changed 'English' literature for ever. Of course, English writers did not somehow strip themselves of native traditions, nor would they have wanted to. Martin Amis's early novels (*The Rachel Papers*, 1973, *Dead Babies*, 1975, *Success*, 1978) brought a new savagery to English fiction, but Amis's prose has its roots in Fielding and Dickens, as well as in Saul Bellow. Equally, though the world of Ian McEwan's (b. 1948) first two books, *First Love, Last Rites* (1975) and *In Between the Sheets* (1978), has obvious connections to Jean Genet and William Burroughs, his prose has an English control and composure (part of his sinister novelty as a writer lies in his unwillingness to allow his prose to follow the anarchy of his dark subject-matter); more than that, his sensitivity to embarrassment recalls Angus Wilson (one of his teachers at the University of East Anglia) as does his acute sense of the class-colouration of English life.

In *The Innocent* (1990) McEwan in part defines Leonard Markham's humble and faintly comical background through his invocation of the place-name 'Dollis Hill', Leonard's London home before his arrival in Berlin.

Behind this one hears not just Pinter's repeated 'Sidcup' in *The Caretaker* (McEwan uses the name 'Leonard' much as Pinter squeezes the same name for comedy in *The Homecoming*), but Henry James's self-questioning in an entry in his *Notebooks* for October 1896: 'Don't I get an effect from *Folkestone?*'

McEwan may well be the best novelist (not stylist) of his generation, and certainly one of the few who—particularly in his early work—can be said to have created a 'world'. This is a world of incest, rape, pornography, sado-masochism, sexual power-games, bondage, and corpses; more precisely, it is overwhelmingly a world of male desire uncontrolled; of the Freudian worm in the English apple. In a story called 'Homemade', a male narrator recalls the night he lost his virginity—to his 10-year-old sister; in 'pornography', the opening story of the collection *In Between the Sheets*, O'Byrne, a pornographer's apprentice, is two-timing a couple of nurses. While in bed with one of them, he realizes that he enjoys being sexually humiliated and abused. Eventually, the two nurses take their revenge, in a weird rewriting of Lawrence's story 'Tickets Please', by amputating his member. The story closes with O'Byrne both relishing and dreading the agony ahead. In 'Dead as They Come' McEwan leads us through an expert construction of a male chauvinist's love for his new, and mute, wife, 'a perfect mate', whom he eventually kills. The story's irony is generated by the knowledge the reader is given that this woman is in fact a shop-window mannequin: we are shocked by how naturally murderous the discourse of ordinary husbandly misogyny sounds. In *The Innocent*, Leonard Markham, posted to 1950s Berlin, begins to fantasize, while having sex with his lover Maria, that he is an English soldier conquering a defeated German.

Some of these stories are gripping; others seem one-joke ideas, or slight ('Dead as They Come' is an example); others still seem exploitative. Kiernan Ryan, in the first full-length study of McEwan's writing, argues against this last charge, claiming that 'one of the strengths of McEwan's stories is their willingness to address the implications of their unsavoury obsessions . . . his best tales confess the ambiguity of their attitude and oblige us to reflect on the mixed motives governing our own response as readers.' This is surely right, and it is this ambiguity that lends the stories their queasy power. But Ryan's argument does not mean that the stories and early novels do not, after all, exploit: they exploit their material so as to get us to do what Ryan says they do; and they exploit us in order to turn their vilenesses into 'ambivalences'. How we value this activity, and the kind of interest we are willing to invest in these kinds of ambivalence, will determine what we think of this early work.

McEwan's later novels are more ambitious. In *The Child in Time* (1987), he creates a haunting dystopia, a vision of England twenty years hence which is nevertheless recognizably Thatcher's England of the 1980s. *The Innocent* deals with secrets and the building of post-war Europe, a world partly returned to in *Black Dogs* (1992). One by now familiar problem with these three later books is that they are too explicit in respect of their themes and weigh themselves down with symbolism. *The Child in Time*, for instance, intelligently explores notions of time—how unstable it is, how we live all time at the same time, how the past is always in us—and edges towards mysticism. But everything in the novel converges on this time-theme like a collapsing tent: when Stephen, the novel's hero, tells the story of how his shop assistant mother met his father, we cannot but notice that they met when he brought back a faulty clock he had bought in her store; Stephen's friend Thelma is a physicist who lectures him on the instability of time; and so on.

Black Dogs, which uses the memory of two black dogs seen fleetingly during a honeymoon in France as a symbol of modern Europe's dark past, is McEwan's most ambitious attempt to link the private and the public. Bernard Tremaine, a literalist and a Labour MP, and his wife June, a religiose mystic, constitute the binary structure of the novel; or as their friend Jeremy, the book's narrator, tells us early on, a little too bluntly: 'Rationalist and mystic, commissar and yogi, joiner and abstainer, scientist and intuitionist, Bernard and June are the extremities, the twin poles along whose slippery axis my own unbelief slithers and comes to rest.' This opposition strikes the reader as facile, and one might say that the rest of the novel attempts to excuse or to complicate it (though crucially, in the end, never to disown it, for what power *Black Dogs* has would evanesce if this opposition were thoroughly dismantled). June has been haunted ever since the day in 1946 when she saw the two huge black dogs. Her determination to see them as symbols (they 'prompted the thought of a message in a dumbshow, an allegory for her decipherment alone . . . They emanated meaning') for Nazi evil is disavowed by the staunchly literal Bernard. But the novel appears to insist on our believing in June's interpretation even as Bernard contradicts it. Its settings reinforce that interpretation: the modern Europe we are given is a Nazi-threatened Europe, for Bernard accompanies Jeremy to Berlin just as the Wall is coming down, and there they confront a gang of neo-Nazi youths.

Over-calculation is the bent arrow in McEwan's very full quiver of talents. In *The Innocent*, for instance, Leonard Markham has arrived in mid-1950s Berlin to help British Intelligence work on the building of a secret surveillance tunnel which will travel underneath the border with the East. When Leonard first begins to fantasize about dominating Maria during sex (which McEwan helpfully calls 'excavations'), the novel is not slow to tighten the symbolic net: 'He was in a tunnel whose only end was his own fascinating annihilation.' From this moment onwards, McEwan repeatedly connects the surveillance tunnel—and hence the machismo of spying—with warped masculinism.

The secrets being guarded in Berlin are never, so we discover, the final secrets—there is always a further level of repression—and in Berlin this is institutionalized. As one of Leonard's colleagues remarks: 'everybody thinks his clearance is the highest level there is, everyone thinks he has the final story. You only hear of a higher level at the moment you're being told about it.' This is a moment of textual self-description too good to be true for a book that is essentially a spy thriller; but it is also a deeply revealing moment in McEwan's work. The over-explicitness is not surprising. But there is something self-confounding about it: for a novel which needs to tell us so insistently that no one ever has the final story has gathered to itself a finality of its own; *it* at least has the final story, which is that there are no final stories.

No writer of his generation has been more influential (in both good and bad ways) on younger writers than Martin Amis. It is his prose style that has been influential—not the earlier Dickensian verve of *The Rachel Papers*, but the later Americanized prose of *Money* (1984), *London Fields* (1989), and his book of journalism about America and American writers, *The Moronic Inferno* (1987). (It says everything about the nature of Amis's influence that his book of journalism has had a wider impact than any of his novels.) Amis's Americanizing of his style, under the influence of Saul Bellow, coincides with a general shift in British (and Western) culture towards the products of American Post-Modern popular culture. America is the locus of Post-Modernity and its discontents—vulgar films, trashed cities, the congestions of cliché and other degradations of language, the clotting of the soul with cultural debris, the submersion of the individual. Amis's work has been almost captively responsive to these developments.

Any reader familiar with Bellow's work will hear its radiant emergencies in Amis's. Bellow may have given Amis his theme (as well as his fondness for italics) when he has a character say in *The Adventures of Augie March* (1953): 'The big investigation today is into how *bad* a guy can be, not how good he can be.' From Bellow, Amis gets much of his streaming syntax and parenthetical interruptions; his glamorous plurals, adjectival massing, often in triplicate; his compounds (compare Bellow's 'perpetual event-glamour' with Amis's description of a tennis star as 'shining with money-dignity and hardened achievement'); and the redundant, but apparently urgent, use of the word 'human' (compare Amis's 'I kept wondering how it went, humanly' with Bellow's 'feeling the lack of almost everything you needed, humanly').

Nevertheless, part of the reason for Amis's influence is that his comic style combines this Americanized knowingness with some of the traditional ironies of English comedy. In Amis's writing, many of the things which have been appearing as weaknesses in recent English writers—authorial intervention, allegory, symbol, over-explicitness, facetiousness—are turned into virtues, through the robust self-consciousness of his performance. This is his importance as a writer: at his best, he turns English prose inside out— he is like someone wearing his clothes the wrong way round and triumphing over our embarrassment through his swaggering confidence. He is a reminder that, though flawed as a novelist in all kinds of ways, a writer with real literary energy can do almost anything he likes.

Unlike some of his English predecessors, Amis has learned that authorial intervention depends on building a playful relationship between a self-conscious author and a self-conscious reader. In *London Fields*, for example, via his surrogate-author Mark Asprey, he intervenes to tell us something about his monstrous thug Keith Talent: 'Keith's account of the football match. I've heard such summaries from him . . . At first I thought he just memorized sections of the tabloid sports pages. Absolutely wrong. Remember—he is modern, modern, despite the heels and the flares. When Keith goes to a football match, that misery of stringer's clichés is *what he actually sees.*' By vigorously voiding Keith of any human value, Amis turns such explicitness into not only a joke but a necessity. Since Keith is not just a symbol but a victim of cliché-saturation, it becomes the writer's task to fight his battles for him. The prose, not the world, becomes the container of value.

At the local level, inversion is what drives Amis's comic recitatives: 'Death seems to have solved my posture problem—and improved my muscle tone. What jogging and swimming and careful eating never quite managed, death is pulling off with no trouble at all. I recline with burger and fries, while death completes its own stay-fit programme. And with none of that sweating and grunting which some of us consider so unattractive.' And paradox is the secret of his comic compound words ('tithe-mogul', 'money-dignity'). In *Time's Arrow* (1992) Amis makes inversion into the actual form of the book, and tells the life of a Nazi war criminal backwards, as if it were a film being reversed.

Amis's weakness as a writer is that, for all the transparency of his know-ingness, he remains heartlessly knowing about his characters, always an adjective ahead of his subjects. He has said that he would sacrifice any-thing in a book for a fine phrase; the result is that his caricatures, like the monstrous pornographer John Self in *Money*, and Keith Talent, have a Dickensian brutishness, but never move us as Dickens's gargoyles do. Never-theless, his achievement is formidable. His urban England of cliché, money, pornography, and apocalyptic weather is one of the few genuinely *realized* worlds in modern English writing, and one of the few to have the authentic lineaments of the contemporary. More importantly perhaps, his descriptive powers, and in particular his powers of metaphor, are greater than those of any of his contemporaries. At his best, those powers create images that perfectly match the comic bleakness of his late twentieth-century vision—as when he describes London pigeons and their 'criminal balaclavas', or a typical London park: 'the untouchable youths in their spikes, the meteor-ology of the sky, the casteless old wedged into benches . . .'

An Amis-like vitality can be seen in Jeanette Winterson's (b. 1959) first novel *Oranges Are Not the Only Fruit* (1985), whose proximity to the English comic tradition has to do with its perfect manipulation of voice. Its heroine and narrator, the young Jeanette (it is explicitly autobiographical), tells us about the strangest of worlds—lower-middle-class Evangelical Christian-ity—in a tone of innocent bewilderment. Pushed through the narrator's stylistic funnel, Christianity is registered as a kind of ridiculous child's play. Winterson's style is a surrender to the comic incomprehensibility of this world; but in the folds of the young Jeanette's glibness lies her rebellious-ness, for her lesbianism will eventually force her exclusion from that world (the novel is also a traditional English story of working-class escape).

Winterson has done nothing better than this first book; indeed, she has become a bibliographer's definition of nostalgia since each new book has been poorer than the last. *The Passion* (1987) and *Sexing the Cherry* (1989) have used Angela Carter's example to explore fairy-tale, cross-dressing, and time-travel. But where her first novel was vibrant with its self-sufficient liveliness, these later books hide within them, like an accident victim who is nothing but metal plates and rods, steely axioms and inflexible aphorisms: 'Bridges join but they also separate'; 'Pleasure and danger. Pleasure on the edge of danger is sweet.' This habit culminates in *Art & Lies* (1994), which is little more than a sermon on behalf of the kind of fiction Winterson now seems to want to write.

The aimlessness of Winterson's *œuvre* may reflect a larger anarchy. Eng-lish writing, like Whitman's poet, now contains multitudes. Post-Modern story-telling (Angela Carter, Winterson, Graham Swift's *Waterland*, 1983) coexists with the more traditional narration of novelists such as Anita Brookner (b. 1928) or Kazuo Ishiguro (b. 1954). In poetry of the last decade, Auden has been chosen over Larkin as the strong precursor. At a time that has been necessarily political, when nationhood has begun to seem an activity rather than an attribute, Larkin's melancholia and traditional forms have seemed less usable than Auden's Anglicized modernism. Glyn Maxwell, the best poet of his generation, writes about what Auden called 'England, this country of ours where nobody is well'. His first book, *Tale of the Mayor's Son* (1990), has a very Audenesque cast of police officers, civil servants, and city slickers. The poet has a Larkinian ordinariness—'I walk, mild citizen | of what's suggested'—but is in fact no mild citizen at all, but keen to skewer his country with Auden's pincers: 'Educated in the Humanities, | they headed for the City, their beliefs | implicit in the eyes and arteries of each . . . Who knows when | they made their killings during that hot spell' ('The High Achievers').

In a time when Englishness itself was becoming unstable, it is noticeable that novels of Englishness—rather than English novels—began to appear. These were books that insisted on a factitious English tradition (like Peter Ackroyd's *English Music*, 1992) or a forced and explicit English symbolism or imagery (such as A. N. Wilson's *The Daughters of Albion* (1991), which closes with its protagonists singing 'Jerusalem' on a hilltop near Stonehenge). What most of these books proved was that English writing in the last thirty years has largely failed to tell convincing national stories. Some of this failure may stem from the weight of tradition.

The two novels of Alan Hollinghurst (b. 1954), however, *The Swimming Pool Library* (1988) and *The Folding Star* (1994), remind us that nationalism in art is like a medieval town: it radiates outwards from a neglected centre. It cannot be bullied into existence. In their frank treatment of homosexuality, their word-games, and their self-consciousness, they inherit the muted experimentalism of the 1960s; but they also have a Henry Jamesian solidity of architecture and language, and a Larkinian air of elegy. They suggest that the best fiction of the next twenty years will thrive on an avant-gardism of *content* (the expansion of what can be allowably said) rather than of form.

In *The Folding Star*, a 33-year-old teacher, Edward Manners, goes to a Flemish city and falls in love with one of his pupils. In the novel's middle section Edward returns to his childhood town just south of London for the funeral of his first boyfriend, who has died in a car-crash. Edward recalls his lost childhood, a memory 'of summer dusks, funny old anecdotes, old embarrassments that still made me burn, boys' cocks and kisses under elms that had died with my boyhood's end'. The softened syntax and phrasing is almost shamelessly English, and reminds us of A. E. Housman and Edward Thomas—though one should not miss the sly insertion of 'boys' cocks' into this pastoral bed. Later in the same section, Edward remembers a family summer ritual—watching the Wimbledon tennis tournament on television with the windows open and the curtains closed, occasionally hearing 'the sonic wallow of a plane distancing in slow gusts above'. One admires the unobtrusive way Hollinghurst expands this domestic rite, links it to a national ritual, and then turns the experience into an English literary genre (elegy): the moment, recalls Edward, seemed 'an English limbo of light and shade, near and far, subtly muddled and displaced'. We have been returned, in a stroke, to Larkin's elegiac limbo, to the describable and indescribable England of Edward Thomas, gently stretched to include new data, new experiences, new lives and sexualities. From Dickens's Private Parliament to Hollinghurst's Private Wimbledon: this is the private history—sexual and familial—of a nation.

FURTHER READING

Bergonzi, Bernard, *The Myth of Modernism and Twentieth Century Literature* (Brighton, 1986).

Bradbury, Malcolm, *The Modern British Novel* (London, 1994).

——(ed.), *The Novel Today: Contemporary Writers on Modern Fiction* (London, 1977).

Everett, Barbara, *Poets in their Time* (London, 1986).

Haffenden, John, *Novelists in Interview* (London, 1985).

Richetti, John (ed.), *The Columbia History of the British Novel* (New York, 1994).

Tredell, Nicholas, *Conversations with Critics* (Manchester, 1994).

9

FRANCE

JOHN TAYLOR

As the twentieth century draws to a close, French literature seems in a confusing state. The lamenters most often attribute this to the absence of 'great writers' who, having captured the international limelight, would compensate for the deaths of, say, Albert Camus (1913–60), André Breton (1896–1966), François Mauriac (1885–1970), André Malraux (1910–76), Jean-Paul Sartre (1905–80), and Simone de Beauvoir (1908–86). Other commentators add that no literary avant-gardes have stirred up world-wide excitement as intense as that created by the surrealists before the Second World War, by the existentialists after that war, or by the practitioners of the New Novel during the 1950s and early 1960s. Contemporary French literature, especially as it is perceived abroad, provokes bewilderment and even pity, as if the thematic boldness and stylistic experimentation expected of French novelists and poets, ever since the days of Flaubert and Baudelaire, were now provided exclusively by a handful of structuralist or post-structuralist philosophers, critics, and psychoanalysts. The prestige accorded, especially in British and American universities, to the theories of Roland Barthes (1915–80), Jean Baudrillard (b. 1929), Hélène Cixous (b. 1937), Gilles Deleuze (b. 1925), Jacques Derrida (b. 1930), Michel Foucault (1926–84), Jacques Lacan (1901–81), Jean-François Lyotard (b. 1924), and others has created the impression indeed that it is thinkers, not novelists or poets, who have kept French literature alive.

It suffices, moreover, insist the detractors, to look at other eminent literary figures from Sartre's generation. Nearly all of them are considered to have produced their finest books before the 1960s. René Char (1907–88), for example, may well best be remembered, not for his concise, oracular poems, but for his more transparent Resistance notes and aphorisms, *Leaves of Hypnos*, published in 1946; the last great accomplishment of Francis Ponge (1899–1988), in his quest to describe 'objects-in-themselves', was his collection *Soap*, which dates back to 1967; the most stunning 'inner' and 'imaginary' voyages of Henri Michaux (1899–1984) were products of youth or middle age; the best work of Raymond Queneau (1903–76) likewise ends with *Exercises in Style* (1947) or *Zazie on the Metro* (1959); and *Prisoner of Love* (1986), the poignant last novel of Jean Genet (1910–86), published after twenty-five years of silence, and tracing—through his commitment to the Palestinian cause—his spiritual search for his unknown mother, merely constitutes the exception proving the rule.

This perception of moribundity describes less a factual situation than incurious ways of thinking about French writing. For no other literature have critics been so inclined to draw up linear histories whereby one outstanding name or group succeeds another on a time line. This limiting view, with its implicit belief in periodic manifestations of genuine novelty and with its reliance on bursts of highly publicized polemics, has of course been encouraged by the successive calls-to-arms of influential authors. Dominant personalities (Sartre, for the existentialists; Alain Robbe-Grillet (b. 1922), for the writers associated with the New Novel; Philippe Sollers (b. 1936), for those involved with the review *Tel quel* (1960–82)) have established lists of authors 'to be read' and 'not to be read' (as Breton once phrased it on the back cover of a surrealist magazine), promulgated the aesthetic guidelines governing the group, disputed style and content with adversaries both living and deceased, all while excluding former companions who expressed wayward opinions. Observers within and especially outside France have been tempted to follow this lead, considering French literature to be a dialectic of conceptual conflicts in which individual writers could be fitted into definable movements of ideas. Critics have accordingly emphasized the expression of 'concepts' or 'theories', whether aesthetic, moral, metaphysical, or political, as the primum mobile of French literature—and as its sole aim.

Following on the controversies raised by the New Novel, the ever widening influence of French structuralist and post-structuralist theories has reinforced this emphasis. In some circles, debating these often provocative approaches to reading has displaced the curiosity once reserved for the discovery of new or neglected authors. That such theories—which deny definition to the authorial 'I', for example, or seek to lay bare the underlying, potentially incoherent assumptions of literary texts—were initiated and developed mainly by French thinkers has suggested that no serious writing could be going on simultaneously in France. Disseminated abroad in sometimes simplistic versions, these theoretical writings have convinced critics (though rather few French writers) that French literature has been taken over by theory. The intellectual enthusiasm fostered by contemporary French philosophy has diverted attention from, has even belittled, poetry and prose that do not lend themselves so readily to theoretical appropriation.

In his prescient diatribe *La Littérature à l'estomac* ('The Literature of Bluff',

1950), Julien Gracq forewarned of the emergence of a 'literature of magisters'. In the eyes of non-French critics especially, such writing sprouted like a fascinating thicket during the three decades following the Second World War. For too many readers, this thicket still conceals an entire forest.

This is not to say that the experiments carried out by the writers associated with the New Novel and even *Tel quel* bore no fruit or exhibit no lasting interest. However, a larger perspective reveals that the literary problems obsessing several of these authors—narrative point of view, temporality, the relation between 'subjects' and 'objects', factual indeterminacy, the justification of 'characters'—are symptoms of much deeper philosophical mysteries to which several other French writers or poets were then and still are acutely sensitive.

Encompassing the problems defined by the New Novelists yet also including other territories not explored by them is the vast question of subjectivity and what, in its various forms, is called 'presence'. The continuing vitality and challenge of French literature lies in the seriousness and extraordinary variety of responses that have been given to these central philosophical problems. During the past twenty years, what above all unites contemporary French writers of disparate, even opposing aesthetic positions—including some of the New Novelists—is their invigorating practice of autobiography. When Robbe-Grillet himself turned from his chillingly impersonal fictions to the writing of *Ghosts in the Mirror* (1984), the first of a three-volume series of memoirs paradoxically entitled *Romanesques* (a title translatable roughly as 'Fictions'), he declared: 'I have never spoken of anything but myself.' Conjuring up enigmatic figures from his past, fragmentary childhood memories, sado-erotic visions, and bits of literary gossip, Robbe-Grillet now proposes, as he puts it in the third volume, *Les Derniers Jours de Corinthe* ('Corinth's Last Days', 1994), what he calls an 'an autobiography . . . conscious of its inherent incapacity to constitute itself as one, conscious of the fictions that necessarily traverse it, of the shortcomings and aporias that undermine it, of the reflexive passages that break up the anecdotal movement, and perhaps, in a word, conscious of its unconsciousness.'

Marguerite Duras (1914–96), also linked to the New Novel, offers a more telling example. An autobiographical tendency is visible as early as *The Sea Wall* (1950), a first recounting of her Indo-Chinese childhood. In her earlier novels and plays she makes fiction from the intense amorous feelings with which her work has become synonymous. Depicting adultery, incest, and other forms of transgressive love, her recent writing is complemented by events from her past or present life, which, some real, others obsessively reprocessed by her imagination, add a potent mythographical charge.

Whether dealing with an adolescent affair with a rich, 27-year-old Chinese man, as in *The Lover* (1984) and its more powerful reworked version *The North China Lover* (1991), or giving an erotically charged account of a relationship with a younger man, as in *Blue Eyes, Black Hair* (1986) or *Yann Andréa Steiner* (1992), the passions on which Duras concentrates are extreme, desperate, illicit—and sublime. As she remarks in *The Malady of Death* (1982), she seeks to mirror those 'sudden rifts in the logic of the universe' from which the 'sentiment of loving' results.

Wielding one of the most original (and parodiable) styles in contemporary writing, Duras experimented constantly with dialogue and narrative structure during the 1960s and 1970s. *Hiroshima mon amour* (1960), *The Ravishing of Lol V. Stein* (1964), *Destroy, She Said* (1969), *India Song* (1976), and *The Truck* (1977), initially written as scenarios or at least with eventual stagings or filmings in mind, show astonishing gifts for enigmatic dialogue and probe the rapport between words and visual images. These departures from the more classical forms of *The Sailor from Gibraltar* (1952) and *Little Horses of Tarquinia* (1953) draw attention to the uniqueness and the strangeness of the act of writing. Her most lasting achievement lies in her powerful evocations of fatal desire and inconsolable love. In her best pages, she adds to the long-standing excellence of French love poetry and prose.

Like Duras, Claude Simon (b. 1913), the winner of a not sufficiently fêted Nobel Prize in 1985, has displayed an increasingly visible autobiographical propensity. His work displays a rigorous thematic unity, from his novels of the 1960s, *The Flanders Road* (1960), *The Palace* (1962), and *Histoire* (1967), to his grandiose later novels devoted to the perceptions of an individual caught up in a war that takes him far from home. In *The Georgics* (1981), descriptions of his service as a cavalryman absurdly protecting French borders from German tanks in the Second World War (a subject also dealt with in *The Flanders Road* and *L'Acacia* ('The Acacia', 1989)) contrast with fictional episodes based on the archives of a distant, seemingly historical ancestor. This ancestor, a minor noble, sides with the Jacobins during the French Revolution and fights as a general in the Napoleonic Wars. Simon's discovery of his documents and correspondence in an abandoned mansion also enters into the 'mesh' of events making up the by-no-means linear plot(s). Faithful in this regard to a typical device of the New Novel (to which Simon has otherwise been abusively associated: he is best defined as a dauntless innovator in the long line of French realists interested in war, history, nature, and manual labour), the novel reveals the process by which it is being fabricated. *The Georgics* also borrows from, and comments on, George Orwell's Spanish Civil War book *Homage to Catalonia*. Simon adds recollections of his own participation in that war to what he had already written in *The Palace*, then examines Orwell's belated discovery that the Republican cause had been betrayed.

This Tolstoyan probing of an individual's relationship to the political contingencies of his day and to the sweeping forces of history is condensed in *The Invitation* (1987), a satire recounting Simon's disgruntlement during an official visit to the Soviet Union of Mikhail Gorbachev. Although Simon responds with uncharacteristic rapidity to recent personal experiences, he continues to challenge his readers with a densely textured style capturing that state of 'semiconsciousness', as 'after a sleepless night', in which 'the senses perceive everything (as) separate, isolated one from the other, in a woolly unreality, vaguely unbelievable'. The perception-crowded convolutions of Simon's sentences suggest that an object, an event, a person, or an instant of time can be only fragmentarily perceived, never in any global, coherent way.

Simon's stylistic teachings have been carried on by François Bon (b. 1953), the author of several novels weaving a complex web of interpretations around a single sordid event. The event so disappears into the interpretations that the essence of the plot becomes the web itself. In *Décor ciment* ('Cement Scenery', 1988), for example, a man is beaten to death on a housing estate. As in his previous novels—*Le Crime de Buzon* ('Buzon's Crime', 1986), *Limite* ('Limit', 1985), or *Sortie d'usine* ('Factory Exit', 1982)—Bon gives a quasi-theatrical structure to the story, dividing the text into three parts, each of which consists of a succession of monologues. Often setting his novels in squalid surroundings and amidst down-and-outs or other social marginals, Bon 'palps' the 'cement skin' of the city (as a character remarks) and feels the 'fragility' underneath.

In her striking short stories Annie Saumont (b. 1927) similarly applies an incisive, innovative style to grave social or psychological problems. Displaying split personalities or simply having their heads 'not screwed on quite right', Saumont's disquieting characters, as in *I'm No Truck* (1989), are brought to life by means of shifting perspectives in the narration, bursts of direct speech, oddly punctuated, conjunction-less syntax, and revealing uses of personal pronouns. Like Nathalie Sarraute (b. 1902), who was also associated with the New Novel, Saumont exposes the *sous-conversation*, the 'innuendos', 'implied meanings', and 'ulterior motives' that lie behind or 'beneath' ordinary conversation. Sarraute, the pioneering author of *Tropisms* (1939) and *The Age of Suspicion* (1956), had long been notoriously sceptical about the possibility of creating fully rounded characters; yet she unexpectedly comes up with an apparently justifiable one—herself—while recounting her own past in *Childhood* (1983).

In subject-matter, if not in style, Bon's novels seem permeated by the investigative spirit of the *polar*, the French detective novel or murder story. No one has so subtly assimilated the technical qualities of this genre as Patrick Modiano (b. 1945). Returning time and again in his unified *œuvre* to a period of history he did not experience directly, the Second World War, Modiano plays with a paradoxical, autobiographical dichotomy: he shifts between what he has witnessed during his lifetime and what he imagines himself witnessing in a 'previous life' similar to (but not quite like) his present one. In *Honeymoon* (1990), for instance, which like his other novels involves an 'investigation', Modiano unwinds an 'invisible thread' connecting one event to the next. The mysteriously lacunary plot gradually leads the narrator to certain discoveries about his past during the German Occupation, to which the author returns obsessively in all his work. Positing a world governed by such 'threads', by unforeseeable coincidences and overlooked details, by 'missing persons' and uncertain identities, Modiano teaches that the unassimilated horrors of the Holocaust underlie our present. He centres present-day feelings of uprootedness, estrangement, and existential anguish—even in those individuals who, like himself, were born after the war—in the still unmeasured effects on our consciousness of those evil days. In accordance with his themes of evanescence and amnesia, Modiano's characters are intentionally ghostlike, haunted by the past. Whatever specific events build the suspense, the motives behind only some of the acts, words, and gestures are revealed; other motives remain indecipherable.

Like nearly all contemporary French novelists, Modiano, a writer hypersensitive to detail and ambience, rarely approaches the 'real' with the forthrightness of a Balzac or even a Flaubert. Jean Rouaud (b. 1953), the author of a vivid family chronicle, *Fields of Glory* (1990), is a rare throwback to those wry, acerbic, sometimes compassionate observers of provincial France. In *Adieu* (1988) Danièle Sallenave (b. 1940), the author of *Phantom Life* (1986) and other novels in a more experimental vein, similarly sets in a quiet corner of the countryside a touching series of conversations between a 37-year-old photographer and his 83-year-old great-uncle. The narrator affectionately pokes fun at the old man, who persistently confuses 'Roman' and 'Romanesque' when speaking of architecture and who washes himself with an *eau de toilette*. Yet Sallenave chooses not to provoke our disgust at the seedier aspects of old age. Central among the complex and varied themes of this short book is that the great-uncle, despite the drabness and ordinariness of his existence, has his dignity.

Unlike Rouaud and the Sallenave of *Adieu*, however, most French writers are less interested in reality than in how it is mediated through the mind. In *Aerea in the Forests of Manhattan* (1985), for example, Emmanuel Hocquard

(b. 1940) transforms the legendary wanderings of Ulysses into an unusual dreamlike sequence of short, fragmentary texts involving intriguing shifts in settings and enigmatic characters who appear only to disappear. Not surprisingly, the introspective narrator's feelings are revealed less in what he does than in his thoughts or in his perceptions of the outside world. Although this delicate, almost fragile novella is purportedly 'fictional', Hocquard's story-line is strikingly personal in tone and no fabricated details of any kind seem to fill the natural lacunae of reverie and memory.

Of the many other writers for whom the real remains at once alluring and problematic, Julien Gracq (b. 1910) has undergone a revealing metamorphosis. His literary heritage stems from Surrealism (a fertile seed-bed of challenging contemporary writers) and, beyond that, from English and German Romanticism. This influence is especially visible in his first novel, *The Castle of Argol* (1939), noted for its anachronistic Gothic qualities. Beginning, however, with his first volume of critical essays, *Préférences* (1961), and especially with *Lettrines* (1967; *lettrines* are, among other things, the characters used to indicate a textual reference) and *Lettrines II* (1974), two collections of relatively short personal memories, literary perceptions, and travel notes, Gracq turned from fiction to criticism, and from criticism to autobiography. The most memorable example of this evolution is *Les Eaux étroites* ('The Narrow Waters', 1976), an essay-like narrative blending commentary on books read, childhood memories, and perceptions of the passing landscape, the text gently cadenced as the narrator's skiff slowly descends the Evre, a tributary of the Loire. Gracq's reconciliation with his own past and with the present real world becomes still more visible in *Autour des sept collines* ('About the Seven Hills', 1988), his ill-humoured recollections of a trip taken to Italy, and in *Carnets du grand chemin* ('Notebooks of the Open Road', 1992), a more heterogeneous book.

Gracq is admired above all for his style. His melodious, adjectival departures from the school-learned canons of concision are summed up in *Grève désolée, obscur malaise* ('Desolate Shore, Obscure Malaise', 1947), an essay by Maurice Blanchot (b. 1907), one of the most celebrated critics of the postwar period. Blanchot, who has published little fiction since his influential novels of the 1940s and 1950s, concludes that in Gracq's case 'writing badly means writing well'. This simple observation is one of many that could be cited in illustration of the extraordinary esteem given to stylistic originality (or purity) in France.

Yet a linguistic dilemma has also become increasingly acute. In *Journey to the End of the Night* (1932) Louis-Ferdinand Céline (1894–1961) gave powerful credentials to the use of the spoken language. In his wake, many writers have explored the possibilities of everyday vocabularies and speech patterns. Céline's intrepidity has been carried to extremes by Pierre Guyotat (b. 1940), the author of *Eden, Eden, Eden* (1970) and *Prostitution* (1975), as well as by Jean-Louis Cordebard (b. 1945), who in *Le Sommeil de Magdebourg* ('The Slumber of Magdeburg', 1989) uses an intentionally archaic, extravagantly alliterated language. In *Petite Chronique des gens de la nuit dans un port de l'Atlantique Nord* ('A Short Chronicle of Night People in a North Atlantic Port', 1988) Philippe S. Hadengue (b. 1932) employs a painfully halting, oddly skewed syntax to reflect the narrator's suffering. His tense, idiosyncratic style continues to mirror guilt, grief, humiliation, existential uprootedness, and the 'original sin' of birth in *La Loi du cachalot* ('The Sperm Whale's Law', 1993), a metaphysical novel going well beyond its gloomy harbour setting and its murder-story plot. Language is twisted into startling evocations of the natural backdrop to the tragedy. The almost tangible 'night' becomes a protagonist, as does Time itself, an aqueous substance in Hadengue's imagery. Both these disturbing 'short chronicles' are in fact long allegories of inflicted and self-inflicted wounds that bring an individual face-to-face with himself.

Many younger writers (of more classical stylistic sensibilities) look to Gracq, or to Ponge, as inspiring and exacting models of descriptive writing. The former's prose serves as a touchstone for Patrick Drevet (b. 1948), the sensitive and sensuous author of a moving childhood memoir, *My Micheline* (1990). Devoted to yearly trips taken, as a boy, with his mother, Drevet's memoir is not chiefly concerned with ordinary realism (despite the topographic precision of the author's reminiscences). Drevet's 'geography' is a thoroughly intimist one in which every landscape carefully observed or fleetingly perceived enters into his quest for 'the foundations of Being'. Drevet has written several novelistic meditations on adolescence, homoeroticism, landscape, and our inner sense of passing time: *Le Gour des abeilles* ('The Bee Pond', 1985), *A Room in the Woods* (1989), and *L'Amour nomade* ('Nomadic Love', 1991).

Hubert Haddad (b. 1947) has also benefited from his long dialogue with Gracq's prose. He is the author of several hallucinatory novels, of which *Oholiba des songes* ('Oholiba of the Dreams', 1989) stands out. Focusing on the metaphysical lesions left in the soul of a New York photographer forty-five years after the murder of his family by the Gestapo, this compelling novel passes from horrific recollections of the past to exact perceptions of the real world—and back again. The orphaned hero eventually embarks on a search for his origins, a quest which culminates dramatically on the shores of the Dead Sea.

Like much of Drevet's work, the solemn novels of Pierre Bergounioux (b. 1949) are rooted in a provincial childhood. Autobiographical works such as *L'Orphelin* ('The Orphan', 1992) or *La Toussaint* ('All Saints' Day', 1994) are marked by psychological portraits of his ancestors and by odd metaphors taken from the languages of accountancy and the natural sciences. The novelty of Bergounioux's methodical, dark-toned writing lies not only in his unusual reworking of the concept of original sin (transformed into negative psychological traits that one 'inherits' from one's forebears), but especially in his gropings for a path leading out from its perennial curse. In his relentless dwelling on the past, his work movingly investigates the fundamental question of whether it is possible to live fully and freely in the present. In *Marin mon cœur* ('Marin my Treasure', 1992) Eugène Savitzkaya (b. 1955) takes the opposite path, by emphasizing the unfathomable uniqueness of one's immediate ascendants or descendants in the 'chain of being'. Using allegorical imagery taken from nature, Savitzkaya speculates on the way his baby son perceives the world.

In a disquieting triptych consisting of *Hôtel Splendid* (1986), *Forever Valley* (1987), and *Rose Mellie Rose* (1987) Marie Redonnet (b. 1948) concentrates on orphanhood and on the lives of woman narrators coming to grips with their destiny in stark, backwater settings.

The 'realism' of such authors is filtered by reminiscence, daydreaming, desire, philosophical cogitation, or, in Savitzkaya's and Redonnet's cases, by fable and metaphor. Similarly, in Gracq's *La Forme d'une ville* ('The Form of a Town', 1985), inspired by years spent as a boarder in a Nantes *lycée*, the sensuous configuration that the city takes on decades later in the author's mind is more important than any presumably objective facts that a realist would have wished to confirm. In Gracq's concern with the 'contour of intimate rêveries', the locus of whatever fiction is created is no fantasy world; the fiction results, not from artifice, but from the distorting mirror of memory.

Gracq seeks the 'presence' of Nantes in these distortions. With Yves Bonnefoy (b. 1923), a poet likewise influenced by Surrealism, the term 'presence' takes on a powerful, indeed mystical resonance. He has elucidated the term in numerous essays, notably *The Act and the Place of Poetry* (1959) and *L'Arrière-pays* ('The Hinterland', 1972), and his poetry and prose can be considered less often as retrospective evocations of an experienced plenitude than as searches for the possibilities of having such experiences, of arriving at or inhabiting a 'true or genuine place' where 'presence' might be encountered.

Like several major French poets, Bonnefoy struggles to unify opposites.

His work embodies contrasting themes, such as darkness and light, negation and affirmation, the fascination with death as opposed to the forces of life. Equally crucial is the poet's attempt to create a justifiable poetics out of the disparate theoretical stances inspiring his work. In his view, Rimbaud and Mallarmé still inform, however invisibly, the writing of French poetry. Bonnefoy focuses especially on Rimbaud's proclamation that he has 'come back to earth' and intends to 'embrace a rugged reality'. Yet this urgent reconciliation with the everyday material world eventually induced Rimbaud to abandon poetry. Bonnefoy, who reiterates his faith in the reality of the earth and enveloping cosmos—in their most elemental manifestations indeed (he typically permutes words such as 'tree', 'fire', 'water', 'light', 'star', or 'stone', thereby 'cleansing' them of their well-worn connotations)—must ask himself the same radical question: if the experience of 'presence' is ineffable, is writing not unjustifiable? Bonnefoy sees Mallarmé as following, in contrast to Rimbaud, an ethereal path eventually terminating in an affirmation of language as our sole reality. With this intuition, Mallarmé foretells the elaboration of the deconstructionist point of view, wherein writing is an arbitrary, authorless construct of signs. Bonnefoy does not entirely reject what Mallarmé calls a 'pure notion', but vigorously searches for a justifiable authorial 'I'. This search continues to obsess, not only Bonnefoy, but also French novelists and poets of various aesthetic inclinations.

Not surprisingly, Bonnefoy assigns to poetry the task of offering 'hope'. In his earlier poems, he often depicts himself at a 'crossroads': he cannot be sure he has chosen the right path, the one leading to a locus of 'presence'. Yet his more recent 'ensembles' of verse, such as *In the Shadow's Light* (1987) and *Début et fin de la neige* ('The Beginning and the End of the Snow', 1991), not to forget the limpid prose texts gathered in *Rue Traversière* (1977 and 1992) and *La Vie errante* ('The Wandering Life', 1993), seem to indicate that it is possible to commune with a presence at once transcending and incarnate in our earthly experience. Such books confirm Bonnefoy's major role as an explorer and a reclaimer of a vast field of literary investigation which many late twentieth-century French writers, in disgust or discouragement, have handed over to post-structuralist philosophers or theologians: the critical and creative inquiry into the essence of language and the spiritual significance of the cosmos.

A similarly serious project, in a very different form, unifies the unclassifiable poetry of Edmond Jabès (1912-91). His many individual volumes are organized into a series of 'books' (*The Book of Questions*, 1963-73, *The Book of Resemblances*, 1976-80, *The Book of Limits*, 1982-7, and *The Book of Hospitality*, 1991), which in turn compose an ultimately unfinishable Book of Books. Jabès's vision, quasi-biblical despite his apparent atheism, differs radically from Mallarmé's conception of 'The Book' as the 'Orphic explanation of the Earth'. '[My books] become unreadable', Jabès told an interviewer, 'if one tries to find some certainty in them.' The poet explores the possibilities of Judaism 'after the death of God', all the while continuing to call him to task, to name him, or to equate him with the Void.

Jabès situates his quest for the Book in a world marked not only by God's presumed 'absence'—the key term, in stark contrast to Bonnefoy's 'presence'—but also by the 'obliteration' of the Jews by the Nazis. Yet the two poets converge in their aspiration to discover, then offer, a glimmer of 'hope'. Jabès's mission implies the responsibility of engaging with the philosopher Theodor Adorno's statement that 'after Auschwitz one can no longer write poetry'. Although it may be impossible to come to terms with the horror, the poet, by his 'perpetual questioning', which itself constitutes a response to Adorno's challenge, seeks to make 'the unsayable infinite somehow a legible, audible finite'. 'Once life stops questioning death, and death questioning life,' adds Jabès, 'there is no more hope.'

The Book of Questions is the keystone of his œuvre. An open work par excellence and, like his subsequent Books, a stylistically heterogeneous collection of poems, maxims, dialogues, songs, questions, fables, and thoughts, the text mixes Jabès's voice with those of innumerable imaginary rabbis who wrangle over philosophical and theological questions. These inquisitive sages poignantly represent the historic dispersion of the Jewish people, a theme reinforced by allusions to the death-camps, to the poet's own exile from his native Egypt, to every human being's basic 'foreignness', indeed to language's fundamental 'foreignness'. 'The book is my world, my country, my roof and my riddle,' declares the writer, who methodically reveals the 'invisible wounds' and ontological rootlessness with which all Jews—and inevitably all human beings—are born. The desert, too, is a recurrent symbol, resembling the 'silence and whiteness' of a page over which the poet and the reader remain alone with their thoughts. In this paradoxical, labyrinthine poetry that constantly subverts one's most intimate certitudes, there are few concrete images, except in striking, haunting fragments recounting the story of Yukel and Sarah, a writer and his lover, whose lives, devastated by Nazism, conclude respectively in suicide and madness.

A writer of pages equally as paradoxical as those of Jabès is Michel Fardoulis-Lagrange (1910–94), a leading dissident from orthodox Surrealism and the least-known major writer in contemporary French literature. In his work, the underlying ontology of everyday occurrences is explored in a unique style blending oracular concision, odd narrative stances, and vertiginous abstractions. Besides his collection of short poems, *Prairial* (1991), which commemorates those mysterious moments when 'one returns to the threshold of causes', the best introduction to his challenging work is *In Benoni's Time* (1958), a novella whose occasional touches of humour and intermittent recourse to realist story-telling guide one through the more abstruse regions of Fardoulis-Lagrange's mind. An excellent introduction, too, is *Les Caryatides et l'albinos* ('The Caryatids and the Albino', 1959), a novella in which the author contemplates two caryatids on the Cours Mirabeau in Aix-en-Provence and simultaneously meditates on the presence of an albino girl sitting next to him.

Like Gracq, Bonnefoy, Char, and other writers who came of age under the tutelage of Surrealism, Fardoulis-Lagrange was obliged to reinterpret, for himself, what Breton called 'the small quantity of reality', and to determine to what extent he would retain Surrealism's metaphorical and irrational propensities. In *L'Observance du même* ('The Observance of Sameness', 1977) and *Théodicée* ('Theodicy', 1984), the slightest, most banal occurrences (two boys leaving a house and 'not knowing how to traverse time despite the great velocity of the clouds in the sky') provide the impetus with which to explore the question of how 'subjectivity' screens us off from Being (which he calls 'The Simple', emphasizing its 'sameness', 'invariability', and 'timelessness'). As in ancient tragedy and Greek paganism, Fardoulis-Lagrange establishes in his fictions a backdrop composed of ongoing mythic dramas and timeless rituals.

Characteristically, in *L'Inachèvement* ('The Incompletion', 1992) a procession of children carrying the sacred remains of an eagle meets up with a group of adults who have spent hours deciphering hermetic inscriptions on the dimly lit back-room walls of a bookshop. As in *Le Texte inconnu* ('The Unknown Text', 1948), Fardoulis-Lagrange develops the notion of an 'unknown text' that must be interpreted, an image paralleling Jabès's invisible, ungraspable 'Book of Books'. Often set in childhood and obliquely, if perhaps deceptively, autobiographical, Fardoulis-Lagrange's books (such as the particularly rich *Memorabilia*, 1968) also explore 'plenitude', 'immanence', and the 'elimination of consciousness' in their attempts to arrive at 'the origin' of 'what can be uttered'. In a far-reaching book-length interview with Eric Bourde, *Un art divin, l'oubli* ('A Divine Art: Oblivion', 1988), he refers to the German Romantics in a way that describes the dense texture of his own writings: 'Philosophy seems to be the superstructure of a poetry to which philosophy none the less grants sovereignty'—a maxim that captures the spirit of much of the profoundest French writing of today. Like Gracq, and in a different way Char, whose later poems—in *The World as*

Archipelago (1962), *Bareness Lost* (1971), or *Aromatic Huntsmen* (1975)—probe the ontological foundations of man and nature, Fardoulis-Lagrange represents a marginal yet persistent Germanic undercurrent in French literature.

Likewise informed by this undercurrent, and notably by Heidegger (especially the latter's concept of 'revealed truth'), is André du Bouchet (b. 1924). Like Bonnefoy in quest of those elusive instants of 'presence' and like Fardoulis-Lagrange absorbed in the problem of consciousness as a paradoxical hindrance to communion with the 'ground of Being', du Bouchet builds his syntactically twisted, lapidary, aphoristic poems around only a few recurrent natural elements. In *Air* (1951, 1986) he writes that he desires to 'push down with all my weight on the weakest word so that it will burst and deliver its sky', a proposition that induces him to break up his poetry all over the page. His thematic range, as illustrated in *Dans la chaleur vacante* ('In the Vacant Heat', 1961), *Qui n'est pas tourné vers nous* ('Who Is Not Turned Toward Us', 1972), *Rapides* (1980), or *Ici en deux* ('Here in Two', 1986), might seem very narrow were it not for the depth of his ambition: the exploration of 'the muteness—as if matt—of matter'. This phrase underlines the difficulties, indeed the consciously imposed contradictions, inherent in du Bouchet's search for a fusion of 'here' and 'there', of 'presence' and 'absence', of 'immanence' and 'transcendence', of disparate sense impressions. 'I write as far as possible from myself,' he maintains, adding that he aspires to remain 'farther from [himself] than from the horizon'.

Philippe Jaccottet (b. 1925) also searches in his poetry for a 'space' we cannot 'enter' yet which is suddenly 'revealed' to us—an 'elsewhere' situated in the 'here and now'. One of the finest observers of landscape and the natural world, Jaccottet seeks not the permanence of a place or an object, such as the suddenly withering peonies in *Après beaucoup d'années* ('After Many Years', 1994), but rather traces of fleeting beauty and possible spiritual significance. In his view, a genuine locus of presence is unattainable, yet the ever-doubting poet also knows that he can at least 'depart'—from nothing, from nothingness. To this end, he must efface himself. 'Do not be deceived,' he notes in *Cahier de verdure* ('Notebook of Greenery', 1990), 'It is not I who have traced these lines, | but rather, on a given day, an egret or the rain, | on another, an aspen, | provided that a beloved shadow cast light on them.' 'Attachment to self increases the opacity of life,' he adds in *Seedtime* (1971, 1984), yet this appeal to subjectlessness must be distinguished from that of a du Bouchet or a Fardoulis-Lagrange. Jaccottet's 'I' remains affirmed, with the discreet, modest touch of a haiku poet.

Jacques Réda (b. 1929) seeks 'presence' in an utterly different locale: in the 'ruins' of modernity. He is the contemporary master of the classical alexandrine in his poetry and the author of subtle, tender, ironic works of prose devoted to his wanderings in the Parisian suburbs and the least-visited regions of 'la France profonde'. 'Promener', 'promenade'—these are favourite words of the author of *Recommandations aux promeneurs* ('Recommendations for Strollers', 1988), *Le Sens de la marche* ('Facing Forwards' or else 'The Meaning of Walking', 1990), and *Aller aux mirabelles* ('Picking Cherry Plums', 1991). In this last book especially, a masterpiece of gentle, tongue-in-cheek autobiographical prose, Réda reveals himself to be an invigorating celebrator of the small, significant things of life, a vivid perceiver of 'the astonishing existence of others', and a melancholic reminiscer. Returning to his provincial home town for a long weekend after 'six years of . . . unfulfilled promises', he links up anecdotes, character sketches and ruminations on ageing, death, family life, and—just once or twice—writing.

Réda seeks 'presence' in ordinariness and especially in humdrum places 'rejected' by modern civilization. 'Impoverished towns' or unsightly 'old hillocks', he specifies in an essay devoted to his mentor, Charles-Albert Cingria (1883–1954), 'because of . . . their unflinching resistance on the borders of annihilation and their muted pagan vehemence, teach us to desire, and to be aware of the potentialities of, a total recuperation'. This search for a 'total recuperation' concludes both in marvelling at chanced-upon minor miracles and in Wordsworthian meditations devoted as often to man's role in the cosmos as to his place in a hostile cityscape. Beginning with *Amen* (1968), and especially with *The Party is Over* (1970), Réda's wit competes with the sombre ruminations and sudden illuminations of a soul sensitive to the ephemerality of life, to the certainty of death, and to touching, unexpected manifestations of human dignity. He is a leading representative of what is usually called 'la littérature intimiste'.

Equally intimist are several travel writers, of whom Nicolas Bouvier (b. 1929) stands out. His masterwork *The Way of the World* (1963) is devoted to a youthful trip through Yugoslavia, Greece, Turkey, Iran, Afghanistan, and India. Setting off in 1953 in an old Fiat, Bouvier and his artist-sidekick travel with deliberate slowness, often settling down for a few months in one town. 'Loafing around in a new world', remarks Bouvier, 'is the most absorbing occupation.'

The novelist Jean-Marie G. Le Clézio (b. 1940) has likewise introduced themes of otherness into his recent novels and essays, often set in Mexico, Central America, or Africa. He portrays human beings—and himself—as irremediably errant, as 'ontological desperadoes' (as he puts it in his first novel, *The Interrogation*, 1963), condemned by their obsession with death and their fundamental dissatisfaction to search for a means of quenching their thirst. This thirst is spiritual. In *The Ecstasy of Matter* (1967) Le Clézio evokes a 'long religious journey that will probably never end.'

The Westerner's relationship to foreign mentalities and landscapes is explored in a quite different way by Claude Ollier (b. 1922), another writer linked to the New Novel. Ollier first became known for his eight-volume fictional cycle *Le Jeu d'enfant* (Child's Play', 1958–75). The cycle interweaves recurrent characters and events into a complex investigation set in alien settings: the North African mountains, New York City, Norway, even a planet named Epsilon. In subsequent works such as *Marrakch medine* ('Marraksh Medina', 1979) and *Mon double à Malacca* ('My Double in Malacca', 1982), Ollier continues to blur the distinction between fiction, autobiography, and documentary.

Two outstanding older intimist writers are Jean Follain (1903–71) and André Hardellet (1911–74), both of whom were writing important books at the time of their deaths. Follain's prose and poetry offer affectionate, enigmatic vignettes of Parisian and provincial life. Like Réda, he is sensitive to the brutal disappearance of the 'old France'; confronted with the smallest proof of time passing, he produces an emotion treading a fine line between melancholy and anxiety. In the posthumously republished *L'Épicerie d'enfance* ('The Childhood Grocer's', 1986), his most charming work of prose, Follain sets his Norman childhood against the violent changes wrought by modernity. More typical is his discreet spying on human beings in their most private moments. This master explorer of *pudeur*, of 'loves shining only for an instant', creates in his poems a delicate sensuality. At first glance deceptively transparent, Follain's short poems leave one with a sense that everyday life is full of riddles—the goal of nearly all intimist writing.

Hardellet's work, as evinced in *Le Seuil du jardin* ('At the Threshold of the Garden', 1958), *Lady Long Solo* (1971), *Donnez-moi le temps* ('Give Me Time', 1973), and *La Promenade imaginaire* ('The Imaginary Stroll', 1974), is a visionary attempt to discern 'traces' of past time beneath the surface of reality. Peering through a 'rift' or 'crack' discovered in the surface of the perceived world (stepping through half-open *portes-cochères* is a favourite activity), Hardellet 'witnesses' events that belong to periods before he was born, usually the Second Empire. He thereby gains access, by means of what he calls 'voluntary remembering', to a fragment of the collective unconscious, to a 'hibernating memory that denies the passing of time'. Interested in multiple identities (he uses coded near-homonyms of his own name for characters or narrators), he also draws out the melancholy of these extraordinary experiences. His touching, earnest prose, full of wonder, yearning, and appeals to the reader's complicity, is representative, not only of a search for another form of 'presence', but also of the most intimist branch of what the French call 'la littérature fantastique', a sometimes rather dark-toned fantasy literature. Even in Hardellet, the present can be depicted as potentially threatening and human beings as mere puppets of fate or of some otherworldly, conspiratorial force.

Although not an explicitly autobiographical writer like Hardellet, Georges-Olivier Châteaureynaud (b. 1947) has created a similar kind of French 'magic realism' in a disquieting novella, *Les Messagers* ('The Messengers', 1990), as well as in his novels and several collections of short stories. In this novella an adolescent vagabond meets up with a 'messenger' who is unaware of the contents of the message he is bearing. After bizarre nocturnal adventures, the boy unwittingly inherits the messenger's mission: carrying the message from one destination to the next, with only the slightest hopes of one day being able to deliver it. 'As if dislodged from himself,' he finds himself thrown into 'a hidden order that looks to him like a chaos'. Châteaureynaud evokes the frightening metaphysical implications of this 'hidden order'.

Compared to Réda, Follain, and Hardellet, Charles Juliet (b. 1934) typifies a more austere, soul-searching genre of intimism. He is admired for the four volumes of his *Journal* (1978–94) and for his several volumes of limpid, terse poetry, notably *L'autre chemin* ('The Other Path', 1980, 1991), *Fouilles* ('Excavations', 1980), and *Ce pays du silence* ('This Land of Silence', 1992). The tortured sincerity and transparency of his verse distinguishes him from many contemporary poets. Ever accessible and direct, his skeletal, discreetly metred poems explore solitude, fear, individuation, egotism, love, and expectation. 'Waiting hollows out | this fault line | that cuts me off | from what I would need | to experience,' he writes in *Approches* ('Approaches', 1981), and his verse traces in an almost diary-like fashion the itinerary of a man struggling to get beyond existential despair and to attain inner peace. Intensely introspective, Juliet's writings affect one as if they were personal letters. Indeed, the most moving introduction to his sensibility is *Dans la lumière des saisons* ('In the Light of the Seasons', 1991), a collection of four affectionate letters sent to a 'distant friend' in the United States. Throughout his work, he seeks to learn how to 'adhere' to 'what he is'. His self-dissecting efforts are inspired by hopes of eventually finding an affirming, positive path, an aspiration that describes more contemporary French writers than is commonly acknowledged.

The exalted, ecstatic poetry of Jean-Philippe Salabreuil (1940–70) likewise seeks a path, defined by him as a life-encompassing, ultimately life-sacrificing search for those 'words truer than the world and what it contains'. In three startling books, *La Liberté des feuilles* ('The Freedom of Leaves',

1964), *Juste retour d'abîme* ('Now that the Abyss has Returned', 1965), and *L'Inespéré* ('The Unhoped-For', 1969), Salabreuil transforms the hopelessly banal everyday world into a luminous realm. A cosmic, mystical drama is recounted as if it had been experienced in the recesses of the poet-seer's heart. Based on an intense private symbolism, his poems increasingly refer to an alluring 'angel' whom the poet desperately seeks to 'rejoin'. Could this obsessional imagery be drawn from specific memories? One imagines dramatic events heralding the end of purity and innocence: the irreparable loss of childhood, a son's separation from his mother, the bitter ending of an adolescent love. All three 'narratives' (as opposed to 'collections') allude painfully to tragic separations and impossible reconciliations. By *The Unhoped-For*, life itself has become the unattainable 'beloved', a 'red gown blazing' between 'the angel' and 'Being'.

One kind of French writer seems to reject the idea that literature can or should lead from itself to any other destination. Of the recent books by Robert Pinget (b. 1919), none is more typical of a certain contemporary sensibility than *Monsieur Songe* (1982), not to mention its sequels, *Le Harnais* ('The Harness', 1984) and *Charrue* ('Plough', 1985). Described by the author as a mere 'diversion', a series of short chapters evokes the thoughts and deeds of a fussy old man, his servant, and his niece. Monsieur Songe is no rounded character, but neither is his identity as unstable as that of Pinget's earlier fictional creations. A not-quite-spiritually-vacuous Everyman, Monsieur Songe has none the less been given a hearty dose of absurdity and mediocrity.

Similarly nondescript 'non-heroes' appear in the fictions of Jean-Philippe Toussaint (b. 1957), the author of *The Bathroom* (1985) and *Monsieur* (1986). Both books chronicle less the wilful adventures of their unaggressive, surprisingly charismatic main characters than the way adventures happen to them. The world confronts them in all its illogicality, and the daily incidents in which the protagonists (always passively) get involved are only vaguely connected. As in two subsequent novels, *L'Appareil-Photo* ('The Camera', 1988) and *La Réticence* (1991), Toussaint's prose is sprinkled with offhand, tongue-in-cheek allusions to scientific theories obliquely pertinent to his literary vision. 'Quantum theory', notes the narrator of *Monsieur*, 'destroys the notion that physical description can be accurate and that its language can represent the properties of a system independently of observational conditions.'

Like Toussaint, Jean Echenoz (b. 1947) has written several novels that parody both traditional literary genres and even the New Novel itself. *Le Méridien de Greenwich* (1979), *Cherokee* (1983), *L'Équipée malaise* ('The

Malayan Undertaking', 1987), *Lac* ('Lake', 1989), and *Nous trois* ('The Three of Us', 1992) are take-offs, sometimes simultaneously, on the detective novel, the adventure novel, the spy thriller, the sentimental love story, and the science-fiction novel. Discreetly absurd details (such as the spy microphones implanted in the thoraxes of bluebottles in *Lake*) are described with great naturalness, while exceedingly slight characters disport themselves in only slightly more substantial settings. What is relatively 'durable', Echenoz seems to say, is 'place', never human endeavours.

Gothic Romance (1984), by Emmanuel Carrère (b. 1957), taps this same vein. Based on *Frankenstein*, as well as on the biographies of Mary Shelley, Percy Bysshe Shelley, Byron, and John Polidori, it poses as a historical novel. The kitsch of whodunits and sci-fi thrillers is ironically introduced into the plot. As in *The Moustache* (1986), Carrère turns our common-sense experience of passing time inside out, while making a farce out of the philosophical questions that Mary Shelley asks so earnestly. The so-called 'return to story-telling' in contemporary French fiction, a phenomenon widely discussed during the early 1980s, sometimes comprises insubstantial characters such as these, and playful subversions of literary genre. A sequence of events is only taken so far: eventually the fragment of 'plot' is cast into a temporal or spatial setting that calls its verisimilitude into doubt.

By contrast, a desperate urgency runs through the work of Louis Calaferte (1928–94). The author of *Septentrion* (1963), arguably the most highly accomplished erotic novel of the post-war period (along with Bernard Noël's (b. 1930) *The Castle of Communion* (1969)), Calaferte is also a self-styled 'Christian anarchist' who has transcribed his spiritual progress and literary views in five thick volumes of *Carnets* ('Notebooks', 1980–93). His vast *œuvre* includes 'Intimist Plays', 'Baroque Plays', several book-long poems and collections of poetry, as well as eighteen works of prose. These vary in style from *Requiem des innocents* ('Requiem for the Innocent', 1952), a first novel recounting the author's adolescence in a squalid quarter of Lyon, to collections of disquieting short prose: *Portrait de l'enfant* ('Portrait of the Child', 1969), *Hinterland* (1971), *Limitrophe* ('Border Zone', 1972), *Ébauche d'un autoportrait* ('Rough Sketch for a Self-Portrait', 1983), *Promenade dans un parc* ('Stroll in a Garden', 1987), *L'Incarnation* (1987), *Memento Mori* (1988). In this latter genre Calaferte has forged a tense, dreamlike, sometimes fabulous, sometimes microscopically realistic prose that dissects, as he puts it, 'what, in me, is the world' more often than 'this accident, of the world, which is me'. Calaferte's resolutely introspective writings teem with images of the body and the mind in their cruellest, lewdest, basest, or most mediocre postures. With Christian morality as an invisible, ideal backdrop, Calaferte 'prospects the cavern', examining the 'foundations of human nature', the 'domains where sex, violence, and blood rule as absolute masters'.

Although he comes from a quite different literary background, Jude Stéfan (b. 1930) also explores the overlapping domains of eros and death. At once extremely contemporary and turned towards the past, his poems remain in constant dialogue with ancient or modern mentors, from Catullus to Pavese. From the longer poems of *Suites slaves* ('Slavic Suites', 1983) to the shorter forms of *Libères* (1970; the title is a neologism), *Laures* ('Lauras', 1984), and *Élégiades* ('Elegiads', 1993), not to forget the stunning 'contra-haikus' of *Stances* (1991), Stéfan renews traditional forms by means of a musical, syntactically intricate, refined 'baroque' style. Few can rival his erotic poems in their powerful evocations of violent, ephemeral pleasures, set against the inexorable deterioration of the body.

His stories, gathered in *Les États du corps* ('The Bodily States', 1986), *La Fête de la patronne* ('The Madam's Party', 1991), and earlier collections, revolve around a half-invented adolescence in Italy and a career as a *lycée* teacher in Normandy. Fictive sisters and recurrent adolescent companions link most of the stories (which *seem* autobiographical), as Stéfan explores the most serious aspects of human relationships. Incest, sexual initiation, and suicide are frequent themes. In his percipient essays, he locates the essence of the short story in extraordinary situations in which something happens—'an accident, a rape, a disappearance'—which 'can make us understand that . . . we are born in order to die'. Noting, in an autobiographical sketch, that his pessimism is 'even worse' than that of the aphorist E. M. Cioran (1911–95), Stéfan none the less achieves a compelling ambiguity: he artfully plays with romantic emotions, evoking in his most memorable stories the possibility of an 'absolution from selfhood' or of a 'last chance to be saved by love'. Whereas du Bouchet and Fardoulis-Lagrange see the dissolution of subjectivity as a means of experiencing ontological 'presence', Stéfan suggests that one can hope, at best, for a transitory blending with 'someone who is not you'. The questions of subjectivity and presence, around which so much contemporary French literature revolves, are thus placed on a spiritually horizonless emotional level. His stories and poems, indeed, rehabilitate the emotions as a valid path for prolonged literary and philosophical exploration.

Pascal Quignard (b. 1948), influenced by his readings in Greek and Latin literature, is similarly engaged with the questions of eros and of death. He has produced an impressive variety of books, from his multi-volume series of *Petits Traités* ('Short Treatises', 1981–90), a collection of brief observations about language and writing, to a confessional novel about egocentrism and ennui, *The Salon in Württemburg* (1986). He has also written several 'brief lives' of musicians, artists, and philosophers. A good example of these is *Albucius* (1990), the portrait of a Roman writer of erotic and 'juridical' novels. Weaving obscure strands of erudition into a lacunary, half-historical, half-fictional tapestry quite unlike the classical 'historical novel', Quignard convinces us that this sensuous, scathing, bitter writer is our own aesthetic and moral contemporary. By gathering together 'the fragments, the quotations, the ruins' of Albucius' life and work (and revealing at the same time how they are gathered, thereby destroying any illusion of verisimilitude), Quignard resuscitates a 'troubled, tormented' author. 'Quare scripsisse,' wonders Albucius, 'what's the point of having written?' Like other books by Quignard, this compelling novel-essay-biography—with its aftertaste of a transposed autobiography—revolves around this unanswered question.

Guy Debord (1931–94), the mastermind of the International Situationist movement, likewise probes this enigma in *Panegyric* (1989), the most remarkable pure autobiography of recent times. Of obvious interest to anyone studying the radical political movements of the past three decades, *Panegyric* graphically sums up 'troubled times, extreme divisions in society, and immense destruction', not to mention the major role the writer himself played in these 'troubles', notably in the May 1968 student and worker uprisings. Unlike nearly all other reminiscences written by former revolutionaries, *Panegyric* is the work neither of an ageing social crusader nostalgic for the good old days at the barricades, nor of a turncoat repenting his errors. This concise but rich and provocative memoir is the product, rather, of a political philosopher whose pen has never been more scathing.

The revived genre of the Suetonian 'life', as practised by Quignard and also by Pierre Michon (b. 1945), who has devoted sensitive studies to Rimbaud, Joseph Roulin (Van Gogh's postman-friend), and several others, appears in a different guise in the New Fiction movement, a group of writers officially founded in 1992 with the publication of Jean-Luc Moreau's provocative manifesto and anthology *La Nouvelle Fiction*. Several novels written by the seven founding members (Haddad, Châteaureynaud, Frédérick Tristan (b. 1931), François Coupry (b. 1947), Jean Levi (b. 1948), Patrick Carré (b. 1952), Marc Petit (b. 1947)) can be described as 'fictive autobiographies'. Sharing a literary heritage of German Romanticism, the English Gothic novel, the oriental tale, spiritualism, speculative philosophy, and Surrealism, the writers explore in their different ways the perennial Romantic themes: fate, the soul, the dreamworld, the presence of 'invisible realms', the myths underlying reality. Tristan, the best known of the group, has constructed a self-referential fictional world in which separate novels are linked through common characters.

In the work of all the New Fictionists, the interaction between characters constitutes mere steps in the ultimately solitary hero's individuation or in his progress toward some sort of spiritual and philosophical enlightenment. Even more than with the formalism of the New Novel or *Tel quel*, the New Fictionists' most profound quarrel is with realism. Common to them all is a scepticism about the solidity of the real world; hence their desire to 'deviate the real' into a 'parallel universe' disquietingly similar to (or sometimes ludicrously different from) our own.

The 'initiatory novels' of Michel Tournier (b. 1924) are not far removed from the spirit of the New Fiction. In *Friday* (1967), *The Erl King* (1970), *Gemini* (1975), and *The Four Wise Men* (1980), Tournier makes use of German philosophy and of myths or legends from a variety of backgrounds. In his intellectual autobiography, *The Wind Spirit* (1977), he explains how myths opened a passage for him between the abstract harmonies of metaphysical systems and a novelistic form that would be dynamic, yet 'traditional' and 'reassuring'.

Georges Perec (1936–82) is another writer who 'deviates the real' or the personal into parallel fictional worlds, notably in his 'autobiography' *W, or The Memory of Childhood* (1975). By alternating autobiographical chapters with the episodes of an eccentric plot involving 'a community concerned exclusively with sport, on a tiny island off Tierra del Fuego', Perec attempts to pin down a few fragments of a past of which he claims to have 'no personal memories'. It eventually becomes clear that he is constructing an allegory of Nazism (his mother was murdered in Auschwitz). Hidden personal allusions are in fact sprinkled throughout the work of this author, who has achieved astonishing verbal exploits: a 500-word palindrome; an exceedingly complex novel, *Life a User's Manual* (1987), whose plot is engendered by means of calculations based on a '10 × 10 magic square'; not to mention the pangrams, anagrams, isograms, acrostics, and crosswords that he produced after becoming a member of the Ouvroir de Littérature Potentielle (OuLiPo) in 1967. His OuLiPian experiments can be seen as attempts to retrieve the possibility of writing by gaining control over subjectivity and arbitrariness, by eschewing mimesis and expressionism, as well as by wrestling with the most basic elements of a written language: the letters of the alphabet. One of Perec's most abstruse feats was to compose a long series of autobiographically allusive poems as variations on only eleven letters; another was his *e*-less novel, *A Void* (1969).

Besides the continuing interest aroused by *Things* (1965), a fictional study of a young couple immersed in the consumerism of the 1960s, or by *A Man Asleep* (1967), Perec's future reputation must ultimately rest on *Life a User's Manual*. Research based on the author's manuscripts and papers has shown how elaborate the 'constraints' used to construct the novel are: each chapter consists of a description of a room, in a building consisting of a hundred rooms, and the order in which rooms are described, and in which particular things in each room are evoked, is likewise based on intricate mathematical formulas. The main plot, in a book containing many sub-plots and plots-within-plots, concerns the life of a millionaire, Bartlebooth. At the age of 25 he decides to take painting lessons for ten years. Thereafter, he spends the next twenty years travelling and painting water-colours in seaside towns at the rate of one a fortnight. He sends the water-colours back to a jigsaw-puzzlemaker, who turns the paintings into puzzles. Once he has returned home, Bartlebooth spends his last twenty years reassembling the puzzles, each of which is then sent to another specialist, who removes the original painting from the wood support. A chemical solution dissolves the paint and the clean sheet of paper is returned to the millionaire.

Some of Perec's diabolically ingenious fabrications may leave one weary, even cold, yet *Life a User's Manual* movingly crowns his lesser efforts. The objectivity and neutralized emotions of his descriptions gradually build into an overwhelming feeling of emptiness, of the void, once the artifice behind the fiction is suddenly exposed. Meticulously structured, the novel is dismantled in a sleight-of-hand ending and shown to consist of mere scaffolding: the preconceived rules by which it had been fabricated in the first place.

Another member of the OuLiPo, Jacques Roubaud (b. 1932), has also produced a variety of works, running from collections of verse to his whimsical prose trilogy *Our Beautiful Heroine* (1985), *Hortense is Abducted* (1987), and *Hortense in Exile* (1990). More impressive are his autobiographical books, *Le Grand Incendie de Londres* ('The Great Fire of London', 1989) and its sequel *La Boucle* ('The Loop', 1993). The first takes off from his failure to follow through on an ambitious idea born of a dream: a novel that would have been called 'The Great Fire of London'. His young wife's premature death put an end to the project, and in passages that first may seem randomly arranged yet which are in fact intricately organized (by means of 'interpolations', 'bifurcations', and other 'ramifications'), Roubaud portrays himself writing, mourning, meditating on his abandoned project, working on the subtle metrics of medieval poetry, and passing through the exigencies of everyday life. In his minute descriptions of the outside world, both before and after his wife's death, or in his sensitive evocations of his shifting moods, Roubaud stoically searches for the true locus of emotion. Similarly, *The Loop* wanders through the multidimensional labyrinth of the author's family memories and relationships.

Deep mourning for his wife also underlies Roubaud's even more moving work *Some Thing Black* (1986), a collection of eighty-two elegiac poems commemorating a life once shared, the material appurtenances of cohabitation, his beloved's body (and corpse). In remarkable images of love and respect, the poet stubbornly refuses to avoid the physical, intellectual, and emotional reality of her death: 'I practise no comparison | I advance no hypothesis | I go under by my fingernails.' No catharsis or religious faith provides consolation and relief, although a fragile serenity inhabits some of the sublime final poems. In his despair, all the poet can do is continue to 'name' his beloved, an act that makes her 'anterior presence . . . shine'. The tensions inhabiting French literature since the 1960s coalesce in this remarkable sequence: the unexpected invasion of the personal and even the tragic into the universe of pure literary forms.

FURTHER READING

Brosman, C. S. (ed.), *French Novelists since 1960* (Detroit, 1989).
Caws, M. A., *The Inner Theatre of Recent French Poetry* (Princeton, 1972).
Roudiez, L., *French Fiction Revisited* (Naperville, Ill., 1991).
Stamelman, R., *Lost beyond Telling: Representations of Death and Absence in Modern French Poetry* (Ithaca, NY, 1990).

10

GERMAN-SPEAKING COUNTRIES

RHYS WILLIAMS

THE writing covered in this chapter comes from four European states: East and West Germany, Austria, and Switzerland. Rather than try and cover it in national terms, I shall point up stylistic trends and themes that have been widely shared since 1960 among writers in the German language. The end of the Second World War in 1945 did not mark a 'Nullpunkt', or 'Year Zero', for German writers. The writing of the immediate post-war period displayed affinities with that of the 1930s: of the 'inner Emigration' (non-Nazi writers who remained in Germany), or else of exile. Writers of the generation of Hans Werner Richter (1908–93) and the slightly younger Alfred Andersch (1914–80), co-founders of the 'Gruppe 47', found themselves looking to American (Hemingway and Faulkner), French (Camus and Sartre), and Italian (Vittorini, Pavese, Moravia) literary models. They saw themselves as opponents of the Adenauer government, criticizing above all its policy of rearmament and of integration into the West, which cemented the division of Germany into two; nevertheless, in the cultural sphere, they endorsed the very programme of 'Westintegration' that they purported to oppose politically. The writing of the 1950s—the novels of Hans-Erich Nossack (1901–77) and Gerd Gaiser (1908–76), the early works of Heinrich Böll (1917–85) and Siegfried Lenz (b. 1926)—introduced ahistorical existentialist ideas to a public understandably suspicious of both history and politics. Only Wolfgang Koeppen (b. 1906), with his trilogy *Tauben im Gras* ('Pigeons on the Grass', 1951), *Das Treibhaus* ('The Glasshouse', 1953), and *Der Tod in Rom* ('Death in Rome', 1954), and Arno Schmidt (1914–79), whose linguistic originality, egocentricity, vehement anticlericalism, and Joycean inventiveness attracted a small, yet influential, band of fanatical admirers, have survived the changes in literary taste which the politicization of the 1960s brought about.

Since 1960 politics have played a significant role in German writing. Germans, both East and West, have looked unquestioningly to their writers to act as the conscience of the nation, to define their nationhood, to offer intellectual leadership. As a consequence, writers have been taken much more seriously by the State: the right-wing politican Franz-Josef Strauβ's notorious dismissal of West German writer-intellectuals as 'rats and blow-flies' is merely the obverse of the high regard in which writers were and are held. By the same token, the East German state protected and fostered its writers, expecting them to contribute through their work to the success of the socialist experiment; it was only the expulsion of Wolf Biermann from the German Democratic Republic in 1976 which ended the uneasy consensus there between government and writers.

The West German literature of the 1960s was inaugurated in 1959 with the publication of Günter Grass's (b. 1927) *The Tin Drum*. This novel marked a new departure on a number of counts: first, it confronted the immediate German past, not by dehistoricizing it, but by locating historical events in a specific place and time. Grass's Danzig is German and intensely personal, as he evokes the sights, sounds, and smells of the city. Simultaneously, however, an omniscient narrator reports on a third-person character, Oskar Matzerath, an evasive, self-exonerating figure who is compelled in turn to recount his past in the form of a confession. The shift in narrative voice, the ambivalence of the book's moral stance, the decision to recall a German Danzig while fully acknowledging the existence of a Polish city of Gdańsk, all help to make *The Tin Drum* an extraordinary contribution to a new sense of East German–West German identity. Anglo-Saxon reviewers and critics who stressed Grass's 'surrealist' imagination failed to acknowledge how surreal actual German history had been. The novel's politics adumbrate Willy Brandt's 'Ostpolitik', or 'opening to the East', well before the question of West Germany's relations with its eastern neighbours had come to supplant 'Westintegration' as a central concern. Grass was to rework the Danzig theme in his next two successes, *Cat and Mouse* (1961) and *Dog Years* (1963).

The startling originality of *The Tin Drum* signalled a new direction for German writing to take. Böll's *Billiards at Half-Past Nine*, which also confronts the legacy of the recent German past, and Uwe Johnson's (1934–84) *Speculations about Jakob*, whose subject is the political realities of the GDR, appeared in the same year as *The Tin Drum*; and the following year saw the publication of Martin Walser's (b. 1927) first major novel, *Half Time*, and of Peter Weiss's (1916–82) *Leavetaking*.

As himself a native of Danzig, Grass embodied the problem of the German past and, more tellingly, the German present. Despite the platitudes mouthed by the governing Christian Democrats about reunification, every political and economic alliance forged by the Adenauer government had

seemed to take unification further away; the writers, under Grass's tutelage, began to see the socialist SPD as the party of both cultural unity and
internal reform. Paradoxically, the erection of the Berlin Wall in 1961 marked
the beginning of the end for the cultural division of Germany.

Despite valiant attempts in the East to maintain cultural unity—in the
late 1940s Alfred Kantorowicz's periodical *Ost und West*, and in the early
1950s Peter Huchel's show-piece periodical *Sinn und Form*—by the second
half of the decade each state was looking to its own allies. While even
radicals in the West extolled French or Italian models (both politically and
culturally), their counterparts in the East looked to the Soviet Union for
inspiration. In the 1960s things changed. Younger writers were no longer as
suspicious of ideology as those who had experienced National Socialism at
first hand, and they became critical of the consumerism of West Germany,
seeing it as a more or less wilful suppression of, or over-compensation for,
past guilt. Siegfried Lenz now began to explore the issues of the past more
directly: *Stadtgespräch* ('Gossip in the Town', 1963) examines the moral
issues of political commitment, while *The German Lesson* (1968) attempts to
explain the psychological deformations of the present as the product of the
German past; even Lenz's later novels, *Das Vorbild* ('The Model', 1973), *The
Heritage* (1978), and *Training Ground* (1985), still operate within the thematic
complex of the 1960s in their exploration of the legacy of National Socialism, and their questioning of what it means to be German.

Lenz's writing remains characteristic of the successful phase of the Gruppe
47. Convened and chaired by Hans Werner Richter, this had established
itself by the early 1960s as a dominant force in German literature. Despite
Richter's insistence that political programmes and ideologies had no
place in the literary debates which the Group staged with increasing self-
consciousness, its political thrust was leftist and anti-authoritarian, or certainly anti-government. The building of the Wall posed some problems, the
writers not wanting to protest too vehemently, fearful of being manipulated into participation in Cold War politics—the broad support for the
SPD which emerged in the mid-1960s encouraged more radical intellectuals
indeed to dismiss the Group as essentially conservative. So representative
of West German literature had it become by the mid-1960s, however, that
it travelled abroad—to hold its meetings in Sweden in 1964 and in the USA
(Princeton) in 1966. By now it did not merely represent German writing in
the West, but had become a media circus. Writers could be made or broken
by their public performance. At the Princeton meeting the internal divisions
which had always been present became explicit: the young Austrian writer
Peter Handke launched a savage assault on the 'descriptive impotence' of

the Group. The following year a group of left-wing students demonstrated against its political irrelevance, even as it tore itself apart in debates on the socio-political relevance of literature.

Ostensibly, the reason no more meetings were held was a direct result of the Warsaw Pact invasion of Czechoslovakia in 1968, the next meeting having been planned for Prague. Political events in West Germany had also played a major part: the Grand Coalition of 1966 saw the SPD gain power, albeit in coalition with the CDU. Opposition to the government inside Parliament became virtually impossible, and the sense of political impotence spawned the student unrest of the late 1960s. Massive protests, especially in Berlin, against the shooting of the student Benno Ohnesorg during the visit of the Shah of Persia in 1967, against the introduction of the Emergency Legislation, and against the assassination attempt on the student leader Rudi Dutschke, created an atmosphere of crisis into which writers were drawn. It was in the late 1960s that the seeds of the German urban terrorism of the 1970s were sown.

The writing of the late 1960s did not always succeed in recapturing the verve and originality of such major authors as Grass, Böll, Martin Walser, Peter Weiss, and Uwe Johnson. After his *Danzig Trilogy*, Grass embroiled himself more directly in political actualities with *Local Anaesthetic* (1969) and *From the Diary of a Snail* (1972). The former employs a course of dental treatment as a metaphor for political activism and protest. The dust-jacket illustration suggests that a small pain (a finger held in a candle flame) may act as an anaesthetic, or as a distraction from more serious surgery: the question is raised whether one is justified in burning a dog alive in Berlin as a protest against the Vietnam War. Political protest as direct action may all too easily be confused with mere youthful aggression, as the narrator recalls from his own past, and from the wider German failure to oppose National Socialism. The private and public spheres, the contemporary and the historical, are neatly interwoven in such a way as to relativize the act of protest, yet the moralizing tone suggests a refusal to take direct political action seriously.

In *From the Diary of a Snail*, Grass again mixes the personal with the public, intercutting an account of his travels around Germany to support the SPD on the hustings with domestic debates within the Grass family; the narrative is further interspersed with an account of the experiences both of Danzig Jews in general, and of a single Jewish character who is saved from the Holocaust by being hidden in a cellar. Once again, the novel's didacticism, and Grass's desire to intervene constructively in the political debate, seem to inhibit the sheer exuberance and inventiveness characteristic of *The*

Tin Drum. Not until *The Flounder* (1977) was his delight in story-telling to reappear.

Heinrich Böll's progress through these years displays a not dissimilar shift towards topicality, although it is the essentially humane, rather than the directly political, which Böll extols. *Billiards at Half-Past Nine* (1959) and *The Clown* (1963) largely offer spiritual values as an antidote to the materialism of the West German 'economic miracle', but *End of a Mission* (1966) and *Group Portrait with Lady* (1971) take issue more directly, more specifically, and with a sharper satirical edge, with the authoritarian State. At the same time, Böll was developing a more complex and ambitious narrative technique: *End of a Mission* culminates in (and embodies) a 'happening', while *Group Portrait* has a narrator who often fails to find out all he wants to know about his heroine, Leni Pfeiffer.

In *The Lost Honour of Katharina Blum* (1974) Böll engages in the ferocious debate surrounding the Baader–Meinhof terrorist group, and his 'gentle anarchy'—the subversive political stance which underlies all his novels—is here transformed into a bitter assault on the practices of the gutter press. The overheated atmosphere which German terrorism managed to create in the mid-1970s had had the effect of radicalizing Böll into a passionate defender of civil liberties. If *Katharina Blum* explores the police state from below, *Safety Net* (1979) seeks to present it from the inside, focusing on the pressures imposed on a publishing magnate and his family by the security measures necessary to protect them against terrorism. By the end of the 1970s, however, literary tastes had undergone fundamental changes, and Böll's techniques and strategies, virtually unchanged from the late 1950s, failed to convince German critics.

Martin Walser, whose *Half Time* (1960) was one of the noted successes of the new West German literature, retained in his later fiction the hero, the modern Everyman and commercial traveller Anselm Kristlein, through whose experiences he had earlier dissected the commercialism and relentless competitiveness of the Federal Republic and uncovered its psychological deformations. In the sequel, *The Unicorn* (1966), Kristlein becomes an unsuccessful writer, with the task of writing a book about love. His quest to recall his own past loves becomes a catalogue of failure, yet one which illuminates the social realities of West Germany and exposes his own sense of alienation from them. Walser's literary development was towards greater formal experimentation, a development echoed in his political ideas, as his enthusiasm for the SPD gave way to a strong sympathy with the reconstituted West German Communist Party (DKP). By the end of the 1960s, his support for the Anti-Vietnam campaign and for the establishment of a

Writers' Union had alienated him from many right-wing and liberal critics and found expression in *Die Gallistl'sche Krankheit* ('Gallistl's Disease', 1972), and in *Jenseits der Liebe* ('Beyond Love', 1976).

Walser was not to redeem himself with a broader reading public until 1978, when *Runaway Horse* reminded his readers of his skill in exposing the discreet charmlessness of the bourgeoisie. The hero of this novella was to reappear in *Brandung* ('Surf', 1985), a German campus novel, set in the kind of North American milieu familiar to readers of David Lodge. Walser turned briefly to a German–German theme in *Dorle und Wolf* (1987), a book which earned him a wide acceptance in more conservative circles. With its assumption that Germans in a divided country are 'halbierte Menschen', ('people split in two') it transformed Walser, somewhat unexpectedly, into an advocate of German unity, or, at the very least, into an author who wished to have his say about the issue of German identity. In *Jagd* ('The Hunt', 1988), he returns to the bourgeois world of Lake Constance; his hero Gottlieb Zürn is besieged by offers from women, which he finds it all too easy to resist, finding instead a kind of salvation in the bosom of his family. Rebellion against society has become a resigned acceptance.

Peter Weiss first made an impact in 1960 with his surrealistic *Der Schatten des Körpers des Kutschers* ('The Shadow of the Coachman's Body'); he then received a positive reaction to two more conventional, autobiographical works: *Leavetaking* (1961) and *Vanishing Point* (1962). The enormously successful drama *Marat/Sade* (1964), with its conflict between radical individualism and the desire for political change, seemed to epitomize the debates that had accompanied the politicization of literature in the 1960s. His documentary drama *Die Ermittlung* ('The Investigation', 1965), based on the trial of camp-guards from Auschwitz, inaugurated open discussion of German responsibility for past crimes, and, together with Rolf Hochhuth's play *The Representative* (1963), launched a spate of documentary dramas dealing with political and moral issues. His *Viet Nam-Diskurs* ('Discourse on Viet Nam', 1968), *Trotzki im Exil* ('Trotsky in Exile', 1970), and *Hölderlin* (1971) succeeded in alienating him simultaneously both from the right-wingers who then supported American foreign policy, and from orthodox Marxist-Leninists. The tension between a personal aesthetic and political commitment which underlies Weiss's work dominated political discussions among the younger generation in West Germany in the 1960s and early 1970s, when he was held in veneration. His monumental three-volume *Die Ästhetik des Widerstands* ('The Aesthetics of Resistance', 1975–81) offers at once a history of left-wing thought in Germany from 1937 onwards, both political and aesthetic, and an intensely personal self-examination.

Another writer whose reputation was enhanced by his later writings is Uwe Johnson. *Speculations about Jakob* (1959), written in the GDR but published in the Federal Republic, focuses on a young East German railway worker who is killed by a train, having been to the West to visit his lover, Gesine Cresspahl, whom the secret police had hoped to recruit as a spy. The novel concerns the efforts of the characters to reconstruct the last month of Jakob's life. The extensive use of flashback, unidentified interior monologue, and the book's complex structure bewildered many early critics, even though the logic of events can be reassembled fairly precisely by a careful reader. The characters themselves, immersed in the atmosphere of mistrust created by the Cold War, are forced to speculate and in so doing come to embody the reality of a divided Germany only partly penetrable to those caught up in its complexities.

In *The Third Book about Achim* (1961) and *Two Views* (1964) Johnson continues to supply variations on the theme of the two Germanies, which was clearly an intensely personal preoccupation. The oblique narrative, which draws the reader into a pursuit of the truth, along with an uncompromising search for new narrative possibilities, established his growing reputation. The publication of his novel *Anniversaries* in four volumes (1970, 1971, 1973, and, after much delay, 1983) marked Johnson out, however, as perhaps the most talented of all post-war German writers. Living now in New York, Gesine Cresspahl draws her daughter Marie into a process of education which interweaves the pressures of the present (New York and an American perspective on the world filtered through the *New York Times*) and memories of the past (Gesine's parents' life in Richmond in the 1930s, and subsequently in Mecklenburg, both before and after the war). The novel contains 367 chapters, one for each day of a year in the life of an American city from 20 August 1967 to 20 August 1968; but it contains also a set of anguished reflections on personal guilt, on the Nazi experience, on the GDR, on American capitalism, culminating in the swiftly crushed possibility of 'socialism with a human face' in the Prague Spring of 1968.

The first post-war generation of writers in East Germany is well exemplified by the novelist Christa Wolf (b. 1929). Her first major success, *The Divided Heaven* (1963), was produced under the auspices of the Bitterfelder Weg, an official effort to encourage authors to describe the world of GDR industry—positively—from within. (Another noted example of this genre was Brigitte Reimann's *Ankunft im Alltag* ('Arrival in the Everyday', 1961)). Coincidentally, the West German 'Gruppe 61', founded by Max von der Grün (b. 1926), had just set out a programme also encouraging writers' closer involvement with the world of industry; Max von der Grün's own novels, *Irrlicht und Feuer* ('Will o' the Wisp and Fire', 1963) and *Stellenweise Glatteis* ('Black Ice in Patches', 1973), were written with this in mind and achieved wide popularity. Where Bitterfeld was concerned, Western critics were, not surprisingly, swift to denigrate what they regarded as state propaganda, though a closer reading of *The Divided Heaven*, in particular, suggests that the book's mixture of public and private concerns, and its narrative complexity, militate against any crudely propagandistic purpose.

Certainly, Christa Wolf's next novel, *The Quest for Christa T.* (1968), in which a somewhat conformist narrator, all too aware of the difficulties of writing, sets out to recreate the life of an unconventional friend who has died an untimely death, was well received in the West. It seemed to offer at least an indirect challenge to official views on the relationship between individual fulfilment and social responsibility. Emboldened perhaps by this 'subjective authenticity', Wolf then embarked on a journey of self-discovery in her autobiographical *A Model Childhood* (1976), a visit to her birthplace, now part of Poland, triggering reflections on the Nazi past and its legacy in the GDR.

The publication of this book coincided with the expulsion from the GDR of the protest-singer Wolf Biermann (b. 1936), an expulsion that marked a watershed in the relationship between the East German State and its writers. The gradual thaw which had permitted the publication of *The Quest for Christa T.*, Ulrich Plenzdorf's *The New Sufferings of Young W.* (1973), or even Volker Braun's *Unvollendete Geschichte* ('Unfinished Story'; albeit only in the journal *Sinn und Form* in 1975) was followed by a period of disillusionment and cynicism. After 1976 many GDR writers applied for, and were granted, permission to leave the country. In the aftermath of the Biermann Affair, major figures like Jurek Becker (b. 1937), Sarah Kirsch (b. 1935), and Günter Kunert (b. 1929)—all of whom had signed a letter of protest to the authorities in the official Party organ, *Neues Deutschland*—along with a host of lesser-known writers, moved to the West. By thus emasculating the voice of protest, the authorities ushered in a period of relative repression and helped to create a literature of dissidence. Those writers who remained in the GDR, such as Christa Wolf, Stephan Hermlin (b. 1915), Stefan Heym (b. 1913), Günter de Bruyn (b. 1926), Volker Braun (b. 1939), Heiner Müller (b. 1929), and Franz Fühmann (b. 1922), began to question with a growing openness and insistence the political assumptions or Party loyalties which had sustained them through the previous decades.

The shift towards subjectivity in the GDR, as evidenced by Wolf, was matched by parallel developments in the West. Whether it is more appropriately defined as 'Neue Subjektivität' ('New Subjectivity'), or 'Neue

Innerlichkeit' ('New Inwardness'), and whether it is seen as a rejection of politics, or as an extension of politics into the personal sphere, the new literature marked a break with the 1960s, becoming autobiographical in its concerns, and frequently adopting the form of a diary, a letter, or a confession. There had been hints of this new trend in the late 1960s: in Rolf Dieter Brinkmann's novel *Keiner weiß mehr* ('Nobody Knows Any More', 1968), Wolfgang Bauer's *Magic Afternoon* (1968), and Peter Handke's early plays and prose works.

Handke's *The Goalkeeper's Fear of the Penalty* (1970), *Wunschloses Unglück* ('Unhappiness without Desire', 1972), *Der kurze Brief zum langen Abschied* ('The Brief Note Bidding a Long Goodbye', 1972), and *The Left-Handed Woman* (1976) signalled the end of the literature of Gruppe 47. Even writers of an older generation seemed now to be inspired to emulate the new mode: Grass's *From the Diary of a Snail* (1972), Uwe Johnson's *Eine Reise nach Klagenfurt* ('A Journey to Klagenfurt', 1974), the Swiss writer Max Frisch's autobiographical *Montauk* (1975), even Wolfgang Koeppen's *Jugend* ('Youth', 1976) displayed, to a greater or lesser extent, a concern with personal feelings. Biographies of parents abounded: Handke's *Wunschloses Unglück* attempts to give literary expression to his painful memories of the suicide of his mother; Karin Struck's *Klassenliebe* ('Class Love', 1973), a cult success among younger readers, and *Die Mutter* ('The Mother', 1975) attempt a new, direct expression of emotion. Christoph Meckel (b. 1935), whose *Suchbild: Über meinen Vater* ('The Quest for my Father', 1980) combined a private settling of accounts with his father, a noted literary figure of the 1930s, with broader anti-authoritarian accusations levelled against an older generation, epitomized the 'Väterliteratur' or 'Father Literature' of the late 1970s and early 1980s. This generation is seeking less to recapture an empirical world than to satisfy a thirst for experience, and to fulfil a quest for identity. Disillusioned with contemporary politics, these younger writers are looking for a new kind of political experience in and through the private and personal. This was the generation of the student movement, but also of urban terrorism.

Their point of departure is the self. If their parents' generation had refused to talk about their past, had been characterized by what Alexander and Margarete Mitscherlich defined in their classic study of 1967 as a typically German 'Unfähigkeit zu trauern' ('inability to mourn'), then this new generation would seek out confrontations and conversations with their parents.

This combination of elements—inter-generational conflict, the search for personal authenticity, political protest, alternative lifestyles—shaped the new literature. Peter Schneider, first with *Lenz* (1973), then with . . . *schon bist du ein Verfassungsfeind* ('. . . and You're an Enemy of the Constitution', 1975), his immensely successful *The Wall Jumper* (1982), and finally *Vati* ('Daddy', 1987), succeeds unerringly in putting his finger on all these highly topical themes. Uwe Timm (b. 1940) in *Heißer Sommer* ('Hot Summer', 1974) combines a subjective vision with an ironic account of the student movement. Peter Schneider's brother Michael Schneider (b. 1943), F. C. Delius (b. 1943), Hugo Dittberner (b. 1944), Hermann Peter Piwitt (b. 1935), Jürgen Theobaldy (b. 1944), Helga M. Novak (b. 1935), Elisabeth Plessen (b. 1944), and Verena Stefan (b. 1947) offer in their sometimes radically different ways their own personal experiences as a model of the kind of awareness which each reader is being encouraged to develop for him- or herself. Jürgen Theobaldy's anthology of poetry *Und ich bewege mich doch . . . Gedichte vor und nach 1968* ('And I still move: Poems before and after 1968', 1977) not only underlines the subjective focus of the cultural revolution, but also embodies the rediscovery of lyric poetry as a popular genre.

A mere catalogue of 'subjective' writing poses as many questions as it resolves: there is a world of difference between Christa Wolf's 'subjective authenticity' in a context in which the prevailing ideology was aggressively 'objective', and the kind of self-indulgent posturings which marked extreme examples of the West German 'New Subjectivity'. Politically, in the West at least, 'subjectivity' was justified, in right-wing circles, as a return to 'pure' literary values after the aberrations of political commitment; it was seen as both a retreat from politics and a new form of politics.

'Subjectivity' may be variously defined in terms of subject-matter—as a sometimes prurient interest in extreme forms of self-indulgence and self-abuse, from the drugs and terrorist scene depicted by Bernward Vesper (b. 1938) in *Die Reise* ('The Trip', 1977), via the case-studies in schizophrenia which underlie some of Handke's interests, to the desperate battle with alcoholism contained in Ernst Herhaus's *Kapitulation: Aufgang einer Krankheit* ('Capitulation: Development of an Illness', 1977). It is also a formal category, a mode of literary perception, found even in the remarkable documentary literature of the late 1960s and early 1970s, in Erika Runge's *Bottroper Protokolle* ('Bottrop Protocols', 1968) or Günter Wallraff's startling revelations about the industrial exploitation on which the Federal Republic's economic miracle had been based: *Wir brauchen Dich: Als Arbeiter in deutschen Großbetrieben* ('We Need You: Working in German Industry', 1966), *13 unerwünschte Reportagen* ('Thirteen Undesirable Reports', 1969), the *Neue Reportagen* ('New Reports', 1972), the extraordinary revelations about the practices of the popular newspaper the *Bild-Zeitung* in *Der Aufmacher: Der Mann der bei 'Bild' Hans Esser war* ('The Lead Story: The Man Who Worked for "Bild" as Hans

Esser', 1977), or even his exposé of the conditions in which Germany's foreign workers existed, *Ganz unten* ('Right at the Bottom', 1988). All these reportages depend for their effect on the authenticity of the experiences described, an authenticity guaranteed, it seemed, by Wallraff's talent at insinuating himself into the situations which he describes.

The New Subjectivity in a narrower, more precise, sense is best exemplified, however, by the work of three authors: Nicolas Born, Peter Handke and Botho Strauß. Born, after an early foray into prose with *Der zweite Tag* ('The Second Day', 1965) and two volumes of poetry, *Wo mir der Kopf steht* ('What I Have a Mind For', 1970) and *Das Auge des Entdeckers* ('The Discoverer's Eye', 1972), achieved prominence with his second novel, *Die erdabgewandte Seite der Geschichte* ('The Dark Side of the Story', 1976). This is a kind of love story, in which the narrator's attempts to leave his girlfriend, and the complexities of their relationship, become a metaphor for his failure to relate to the Berlin world which surrounds him. His sense of disorientation and estrangement drives him to make desperate efforts to cling on to the banal domestic routines which offer him, however tentatively, a hold on experience. All explanations other than his own emotions have proved insufficient, and even these prove fallible. Born's next novel, *The Deception* (1979), presents, through the central character of a reporter, Georg Laschen, a not dissimilar world of chaos and disintegration, for which the setting of the book, a war-torn Beirut, operates as an elaborate metaphor.

As for Peter Handke, literature was, from the very beginning, a means of gaining personal insights, as his 1967 essay 'Ich bin ein Bewohner des Elfenbeinturms' ('I live in an Ivory Tower') argues: literature is not concerned with re-creating, or providing information on, an external social or political reality, but with 'poetic thought', which creates the world anew, disrupting ossified ways of knowing and perceiving. Although Handke had pursued these aims since the mid-1960s, his work in the 1970s is more radical than that of his contemporaries. *Die Stunde der wahren Empfindung* ('The Hour of True Perception', 1975) presents, as its title suggests, a kind of epistemological crisis. Gregor Keuschnig, a press attaché at the Austrian Embassy in Paris, is jolted out of his habitual modes of perception by a dream he has of murdering an old woman. The dream forces him to try and find a new coherence in his life, a new self-definition which calls into question all the assumptions on which his life has been built. Later, confronted by three disparate objects (a leaf, a fragment of mirror, and a hairslide), Keuschnig rediscovers the world of things; the functional nature of these objects falls away and they acquire a mystical significance as 'things in themselves'.

That Handke's work should have been labelled 'neo-Romantic' is scarcely surprising. In *The Left-Handed Woman* (1976) Marianne, having given up a brutal relationship with a man, Bruno, opts for a life outside any normal social context. We are given little insight into her feelings, but observe her from the outside, our distance as readers mirroring her own distance from normal social obligations. Handke's is not a feminist vision; solidarity with the like-minded is denied Marianne; she is permitted only the alternative of a life in isolation, albeit with her child. In *The Weight of the World* (1977) Handke describes only his own isolation, viewed this time from within. In a series of diary notes he rejects the conventional social and psychological determinants of experience, offering instead a 'pure' subjectivity of seemingly arbitrary observations and perceptions. The result is contradictory, for we can follow Handke's method precisely because his experiences remain communicable, being conveyed in a socially and psychologically shaped language. Subsequently, Handke has drawn back from the brink of incommunicability: his next books, *Slow Homecoming* (1979), *Die Lehre des Sainte-Victoire* ('The Lesson of Sainte-Victoire', 1980), and *Die Kindergeschichte* ('The Children's Story', 1981), suggest, in their different ways, a return to more conventional narrative, though the sense of isolation, the quest for identity, and for a quasi-mystical transcendence, recur. The element of repetition is a feature also of *Der Chinese des Schmerzes* ('The Chinaman of Pain', 1983), where a murder jolts the central character out of his habitual responses to the world.

Botho Strauβ first achieved prominence as a dramatist. In his early novels he displays a similar retreat into subjectivity, but a profound awareness also of its deficiencies. *Marlenes Schwester* ('Marlene's Sister', 1975), for example, is a psychological study of an obsessive relationship between two sisters, though the identity of the 'sister' of the title is created entirely by Marlene. Strauss's fiction is marked by a self-conscious blurring of the distinction between reality, dream, and fictionality. In *Theorie der Drohung* ('The Theory of Threat', 1975) the first-person narrator, who is also a writer, gradually becomes obsessed by a woman, to the point where he acquires her identity. His efforts to write, with the intention of protecting himself in this way from her lies, lead him, however, to the realization that every sentence he writes has been written before by someone else, and that he thus embodies the 'death of the author' seen as an original source. *Die Widmung* ('The Dedication', 1977) depicts the efforts of Richard Schrouback, abandoned by his girlfriend, both to define his own isolation and to win back her love. The book which he writes is also an act of self-destruction, a dissection which fails to reach the one reader for whom it is intended.

Rumor ('Upset', 1980) offers another variation on the theme of obsessive interdependence (between an alcoholic father and his gravely ill daughter) and of the self-destruction of a personality. Like all Strauß's central figures, the father is a story-teller; his fiction that he is a factory owner, and can offer work to a group of illegal immigrants, leads to his arrest, an outcome he himself appears to have initiated. In this novel the autonomous subject is revealed as an illusion, being shaped by biological and social determinants, as well as by language. In the minimalist *Paare Passanten* ('Couples Passers-by', 1981) an observer detects in passers-by the desperate efforts they are making to bestow meaning on their behaviour—their attempts to claim authorship of their own biographies as it were. Strauß's bleak, analytical view of human relationships and of human isolation leads him in the end into a form of mystical neo-Romanticism, best exemplified in his longest, most ambitious, and most complex novel, *Der junge Mann* ('The Young Man', 1984).

For women writers, the 'New Subjectivity', or the conviction that the personal *is* the political, was bound to focus attention on the ways in which destructive political and social pressures impinged on them privately. The emergence of a Women's Movement, and the development of a feminist aesthetic among literary theorists, also helped women's writing to come to the fore. Karin Struck's early novels marked a new departure, in which social and feminist perspectives were merged, and the preoccupation with the 'generation of the father' inspired such books as Brigitte Schwaiger's *Lange Abwesenheit* ('Long Absence', 1980) and Ruth Rehmann's *Der Mann auf der Kanzel* ('The Man in the Pulpit', 1979). More radical in their feminism and more aware of the problems of defining sexuality in other than male categories are Verena Stefan's *Häutungen* ('Shedding', 1975) and Christa Reinig's *Entmannung* ('Emasculation', 1976), whose title evokes not only the physical act of castration but the central character's gradual adoption of the female gender.

In Austria, Barbara Frischmuth and Elfriede Jelinek have continued a powerful feminist tradition established by Ingeborg Bachmann's novel *Malina* (1971): Frischmuth's trilogy of novels *Die Mystifikation des Sophie Silber* ('The Mystification of Sophie Silber', 1976), *Amy oder die Metamorphose* ('Amy or the Metamorphosis', 1978) and *Kai oder die Liebe zu den Modellen* ('Kai or the Love of Models', 1979) intercut empirical realities with supernatural elements which offer the characters a vantage-point free from immediate social determinants. In *Die Liebhaberinnen* ('Women as Lovers', 1975) and *Die Klavierspielerin* ('The Piano Teacher', 1983) Elfriede Jelinek gives a bleak portrait of the mechanisms of oppression which determine the lives of women. In the second of these novels the central character is made a slave to music by her mother, inducing in her brutal sado-masochistic sexual responses that are formulated in the most uncompromising terms.

The two major political developments of the 1980s in both East and West Germany were feminism and ecology, themes which became inseparable for Christa Wolf. *Kein Ort: Nirgends* ('No Place on Earth', 1979) marks her response to the GDR after the expulsion of Biermann as a hopeless society in which the kind of individual self-fulfilment which existed, at least by implication, in *The Quest for Christa T.* has given way to a mood of anti-utopianism. Although projected back into the early years of the nineteenth century, the novel depicts the failure of two exemplary writers, one male (Heinrich von Kleist), the other female (Karoline von Günderrode), to cope with the pressures imposed by their society. Wolf also contributed a short story to the collection *Geschlechtertausch* ('Gender Exchange', 1980), in which three noted women writers (Wolf, Sarah Kirsch, and Irmtraud Morgner) explore gender differences in three variations on the theme of sex-change. Wolf's next work, *Kassandra* (1983), and some lectures that went with it (published in English as *Cassandra: A Novel and Four Essays*), conflate the ecological and feminist arguments, though it is also possible to interpret Wolf's Troy in the novel as a metaphor for the GDR. Cassandra's prophecies of doom are not believed; the matriarchal society which appears to offer a possible escape from the problems of the present falls victim to a new patriarchal age and the destruction of Troy is complete.

The growth of the Peace Movement in the West and of an unofficial Peace Movement in the East forms the background to much German writing of the 1980s. The discovery of the worst effects of acid rain, and, a little later in the decade, the nuclear accident at Chernobyl, helped to reinforce the mood of what Hermann Glaser has called 'Katastrophismus'. Wolf's *Störfall: Nachrichten eines Tages* ('Accident: A Day's News', 1987) represents an attack on technological hubris, on the Faustian, i.e. masculine, desire to pursue knowledge and dominate an essentially female nature. The text is part pure narrative, part essay, part female intuition and part male analysis, and it represents her farewell to the GDR and to old ideas of the technological superiority of the Eastern bloc as symbolized by the Soviet Union's launching of the first manned space flight. That understandable, if naïve, belief in technology and industrial productivity has now become a despairing attack on the technocrats of both East and West. In a work which echoes Grass's *Headbirths* Wolf interweaves the political and the private, in the full knowledge that the distinction between the two has become an ecological irrelevance: Chernobyl and its effects permeate the private sphere; there is no detached moral position from which anything may be judged.

In the 1980s the German novel began to confront the global implications of industrialization with growing insistence. Again, there were antecedents: Thomas Bernhard's *Frost* (1963) not only established his wider reputation as a writer, but revealed an extreme of pessimism for which madness is the only rational response to a meaningless existence. Tankred Dorst's *Eiszeit* ('Ice Age', 1973) similarly is frequently interpreted as offering self-destruction as the only legitimate response to the burdens of both the present and the past. In his *Der Untergang der Titanic* ('The Sinking of the Titanic', 1978) Hans Magnus Enzensberger anticipates the literary preoccupations of the following decade, skilfully interweaving the present moment of the book's composition with his experiences in Cuba in the late 1960s and the 1912 sinking of the Titanic, in order to explore the dialectic between the old Enlightenment optimism and the new dangers facing the world. Max Frisch's *Der Mensch erscheint im Holozän* ('Man in the Holocene', 1979) symbolizes, through the mental decline and memory loss of the central character, the end of history and of civilization: Geiser's increasingly desperate efforts to cling on to memories and snippets of his once encyclopaedic knowledge are matched by the gradual disintegration of the landscape of the Ticino where he lives, as torrential rain prompts landslips and presages climatic change on a global scale. Günter Kunert's volume of poetry *Abtötungsverfahren* ('Deadening Process', 1980) also was widely seen as signalling a new Ice Age, a new 'catastrophism'.

Günter Grass's novels, too, later took up both feminist and ecological arguments. *The Flounder* (1977) celebrates the essentially female role in human history, exploring male–female relations from the Stone Age to the present. The belief in social and political progress (however slow) which had previously characterized Grass's work now gives way to a sense of gloom and despondency, a development which marks *Headbirths, or The Germans are Dying out* (1980), in which a married couple, both teachers, cannot in the current political climate bring themselves to conceive a child, concerned as they are with the issue of over-population in the Third World. The book takes up other topical issues, too, such as nuclear reprocessing and pollution, as well as containing Grass's reflections on the German past. *The Rat* (1986) offers a similar conflation of past, present, and future. Its point of departure is a post-nuclear world, in which the mistakes of the past (our present) may be explored. Grass here is also exploring his own past as a writer, his allusions to *The Tin Drum* and *The Flounder* being set against apocalyptic visions of the end of Enlightenment. He refuses to retreat into the purely subjective, however; it is simply that his hopes for a change in values, hopes which had long inspired his political commitment to the SPD, have proved illusory.

Writing in the GDR in these years shared many of the same features as West German literature. In *Headbirths* Grass recalls meetings between West and East Berlin writers from the early 1970s onwards: Grass himself, Nicolas Born, Peter Schneider, Christoph Meckel read and discussed their work with Jurek Becker, Sarah Kirsch, Günter Kunert, and writers of a younger generation in the East, Hans Joachim Schädlich (b. 1935) and Thomas Brasch (b. 1945). There were parallel developments where feminism was concerned: the documentary tendency was taken up by Maxie Wander, whose *Guten Morgen, du Schöne* ('Good Morning, Baby', 1977) more than equals the achievements of Erika Runge in its exploration of the gap between the official status of women in the GDR and social and individual realities. Irmtraud Morgner's *Leben und Abenteuer der Trobadora Beatriz nach Zeugnissen ihrer Spielfrau Laura* ('The Life and Adventures of the Troubador Beatrice, Recorded by her Accompanist Laura', 1974) introduces fairy-tale figures into the midst of the banal realities of GDR life in a masterly way, while *Amanda* (1983) explores, albeit in the subjunctive mood, the possibility of a more humane sense of global responsibility developing in the face of a nuclear holocaust.

While the previous decade had seen a mutual recognition in both East and West Germany of the qualities of the other's literature, GDR writing in the 1980s is marked by an increasing sense of disillusionment and political pessimism. With hindsight, it is possible to read it as presaging the collapse of the increasingly fragile consensus there. One outstanding example may suffice to show this: Christoph Hein's *Der fremde Freund* ('The Distant Lover', 1983), published in the West as *Drachenblut* ('Dragon's Blood'). The central character and narrator, Claudia, a divorced doctor, is a victim of male sexual aggression; her relations with her parents, her neighbours, her colleagues, are cool and detached; she has learned by bitter experience to protect her vulnerability behind a façade of indifference; her obsession with photography is revealed as a surrogate act of creativity, a process she can terminate at will. Claudia's encounter with Henry exposes her to genuine emotion, however, and it is his death that has provoked the retrospective account of her life which we are reading. At the core of the book she returns with Henry to the world of her childhood and recounts the betrayal of her only true friend, Katharina, in the early 1950s. By implication, Claudia's failure to confront this betrayal is the explanation for her later alienation and cynicism. Her compromise with the authority of the

State has damaged her capacity for normal relationships of trust. The background to the love affair with Henry is a soulless block of flats, a monument to socialist housing policy; the sense of being observed, or spied upon, becomes a recurrent motif, political espionage and sexual voyeurism merging in an oppressive system of control. Far from being able to heal the sickness of her society, Claudia herself suffers from its characteristic ills.

Hein was to follow this very successful novel with *The Tango Player* (1989), in which the central character Dallow, having been imprisoned for playing a satirical song, the words of which he barely noticed, finds it impossible to reintegrate himself into GDR society on his release. Unable any longer to play the piano, he embarks on a desperate attempt to make sense of his 'crime' and is finally reappointed to his post only when a colleague falls into disfavour for an ill-judged political remark. The mechanisms of political control are once more laid bare by the psychological distortions which they demand. Hein's two books both diagnose the ills of the GDR and serve as its epitaph.

Notions of Post-Modernism, particularly as elaborated on by French theorists, dominated discussion of German writing in the 1980s. The discovery of the body as a corrective to the disappearance of the individual subject is reflected in the work of Jelinek, but also of Anne Duden and Bodo Kirchhoff. With the apparent collapse of left-wing utopianism, the function of literature has shifted: confronted with what the political philosopher Jürgen Habermas has called the 'Neue Unübersichtlichkeit' (only inadequately rendered as 'New Impenetrability'), and with the 'end of history', literature prises itself out of its social context and becomes autonomous. Post-Modernism operates with images, metaphors, and symbols, but is not concerned with what they stand for; they serve only the purpose of what Heinz Ludwig Arnold dismissively calls 'individuelles Überlebenstraining' ('individual survival training'). Again, there are antecedents for this development: Wolfgang Hildesheimer's *Marbot* (1981), for example, the biography of an invented historical figure; or Patrick Süskind's extraordinary *Perfume* (1985), a skilful pastiche of a whole variety of literary styles; or Christoph Ransmayr's *The Last World* (1988), whose central character is in futile search of the Roman poet Ovid and the manuscript of his *Metamorphoses*; or Bodo Kirchhoff's *Infanta* (1990), in which a male model wanders into a Philippine village during a revolution and is captivated by the sheer exoticism of it all, before being killed in a meaningless accident.

Flight from an over-structured Western society has become a recurrent literary motif, spawning a number of works set in exotic milieus, such as Uwe Timm's *The Snake Tree* (1986), in which Wagner, the Western missionary of technology, is vouchsafed insight into the destructive forces of the so-called civilization which he brings and opts instead for a passive acceptance of the natural forces which surround him. At its most extreme the counter-landscape is a barren waste, as in Guntram Vesper's poem 'Nordwestpassage' ('North-West Passage', 1980). Sten Nadolny's *The Discovery of Slowness* (1983), which is based on the life of the British explorer John Franklin, presents Franklin's deliberate prudence as a necessary antidote to the hectic world of industrial London. Ransmayr's *Die Schrecken des Eises und der Finsternis* ('The Horror of the Ice and the Darkness', 1984) is similarly based on an Austro-Hungarian polar expedition of 1872–4. An encounter with the nat-ural world in Italy is central to Brigitte Kronauer's *Berittene Bogenschütze* ('Ridden Archer', 1986), whose hero Matthias Roth succeeds in transform-ing his sense of isolation into a personally productive, intensely experienced, observation of nature. Nature may presage death, but with the awareness of death comes a heightened awareness of life.

With the fall of the Berlin Wall on 9 November 1989, followed by Ger-man unification eleven months later, the German–German issue once more dominated literary debate. West German critics began a post-mortem on GDR literature, apportioning blame and discovering some new heroes, and suggesting that its faults (as well as its strengths) could be put down to the effects of censorship. The publication in June 1990 of Christa Wolf's *Was bleibt* ('What Remains') unleashed an acrimonious discussion of her stand-ing in particular, and that of GDR literature in general. The text was, it appears, first written in 1979, at a time when, in the wake of the Biermann Affair and her signing of the protest letter, Wolf had been under surveil-lance by the State Security Service ('Stasi'). She revised it for publication in 1989. The account she gives of the surveillance, and of the atmosphere of ill-concealed oppression, appears authentic enough, though the decision to publish it after the fall of the Wall aroused deep resentment, not only among Western critics, but also among writers who had left the GDR in the late 1970s and early 1980s. It seemed to indicate that Wolf wished now to be numbered retrospectively among the dissidents. Grass leapt to her defence, but Biermann set the issues in a wider context, arguing a general failure among East German intellectuals to resist the blandishments of power, or the attractions of *littérature engagée*, as it had been propounded both in the GDR and in the West from the mid-1960s onwards.

The literature of the new, unified Germany is as yet difficult to assess. Of the noted publications of the last few years one might pick out Erich Loest's *Die Stasi war mein Eckermann, oder: Mein Leben mit der Wanze* ('The Secret Police played Boswell to my Johnson: or, My Life with the Bug', 1991), a bitter, belated, account of Loest's own treatment in the GDR. Günter de Bruyn, after minor successes with *Buridans Esel* ('Buridan's Ass', 1968), *Preisverleihung* ('The Award', 1972), and *Märkische Forschungen* ('Research in the Mark Brandenburg', 1979), achieved a much greater success with his confessional autobiography *Zwischenbilanz* ('Provisional Stocktaking', 1992); while Wolfgang Hilbig's '*Ich*' ('I', 1993) is a book in which a writer-spy is directed to inform on a character code-named 'reader'. Grass, who remained an obdurate opponent of unification, produced in *Unkenrufe* (1992, literally translated as 'The Call of the Toad', but perhaps better conveyed as 'Voices of Doom and Gloom') his own pessimistic response to it.

Now that GDR literature has ceased to exist in its own right, critics have begun to question whether it will survive, whether the qualities it exhibited were so conditioned by the unique circumstances under which it was produced that it will come to seem either irrelevant or incomprehensible. The last word could be left, perhaps, to Volker Braun, a writer who elected to remain in the GDR and formulated his response in the poem 'Das Eigentum' ('Property', written in July 1990). The opening line expresses a mixture of disorientation and puzzlement: 'Da bin ich noch: mein Land geht in den Westen' ('Here I still am: my country is moving to the West'). The middle section of the poem acknowledges the problem which writers from the former GDR will encounter: 'Und unverständlich wird mein ganzer Text' ('My whole text is becoming incomprehensible'), and the last line expresses a powerful, though not, it must be said, universally shared, sense of loss: 'Wann sag ich wieder *mein* und meine alle' ('When will I ever again say *mine*, and mean everybody's').

FURTHER READING

Bullivant, K., *Realism Today: Aspects of the Contemporary West German Novel* (Leamington, 1987).
—— (ed.), *After the 'Death' of Literature: West German Writing of the 1970s* (Oxford, 1989).
—— *The Future of German Literature* (Oxford, 1994).
Burns, R. A., and van der Will, W., *Protest and Democracy in West Germany: Extra-parliamentary Opposition and the Democratic Agenda* (London, 1988).
Demetz, P., *After the Fires: Writing in the Germanies, Austria and Switzerland* (New York, 1986).
Parkes, K. S., *Writers and Politics in West Germany* (London, 1986).
Reid, J. H., *Writing without Taboos: The New East German Literature* (Oxford, 1990).
Thomas, R. H., and Bullivant, K., *Literature in Upheaval* (Manchester, 1974).
—— and van der Will, W., *The German Novel and the Affluent Society* (Manchester, 1968).
Wallace, I. (ed.), *The Writer and Society in the GDR* (Tayport, 1984).

11

GREECE

PETER MACKRIDGE

F OR the first fifteen years after the Second World War Greek literature was dominated, in prose, by more or less fictionalized narratives of recent events—the war against the Italians in Albania in 1940–1, the Axis Occupation of 1941–4, and the Resistance—and, in poetry, by fairly direct, non-lyrical statements expressing the existential struggle born of a sense of defeat. Although the novelists emerged largely from right-wing or centrist backgrounds, and many of the poets—particularly the younger ones—belonged to the Left, the writing of both groups was equally marked by the traumatic experience of the Civil War, whose most violent period lasted from 1946 to 1949, when the defeat of the Communist-led Left led to the imprisonment or exile of tens of thousands of Greeks.

Around 1960, changes began to show themselves in literature, probably under the influence of such international developments as the gradual political and sexual liberalization that accompanied the thaw in the Cold War. By this time most of Greece's political prisoners had been released; the Greek Left were faced by the realization not only that they had been definitively defeated in their own country but that their beloved Soviet Union had not been the land of liberty they had believed in for so long; and the events of the 1940s were receding sufficiently into the background to enable writers to treat the present and recent past of Greece in a more innovative literary form while still largely adhering to realism. In this brief period, from about 1960 to the imposition of a military dictatorship in 1967, Greek literature enjoyed a remarkable flowering, with poetry, as before, outweighing prose in both quality and quantity.

It was at this time that the three dominant poets of the 'Generation of 1930', George Seferis (1900–71), Odysseas Elytis (b. 1911), and Yannis Ritsos (1909–90), produced some of their most mature work. Seferis, who had brought Greek poetry into the limelight by winning the Nobel Prize for literature in 1963, published his final book of poems in 1966 under the title *Three Secret Poems* (his *Collected Poems* came out in English in 1982). This dense, visionary poetry crystallizes Seferis's sense of the age-old tragedy played out under the dazzling Greek light and ends with the mystical expression of a purificatory burning of all matter which will make way for a rebirth into a new life.

Elytis's huge, complex poem *The Axion Esti* (1960), equally inspired by the sufferings of the Greeks during the wars of the 1940s, presents a lyrical autobiography of the poet-as-Greece, from a childhood that is integrated with the landscape, to a descent into a hell of suffering, and finally to a rebirth in which the elements of Greek landscape and tradition are glorified for having been sanctified by suffering. Here Elytis continues the Greek tradition in which the poet presents himself as the voice and conscience of his people, particularly in times of oppression.

Ritsos, who must have been one of the most prolific poets the world has ever known and whose lifelong allegiance to Communism made him no less attached to Greek tradition than Seferis and Elytis, produced the bulk of his no fewer than seventy-five books of poetry in the years 1960–90 (his *Selected Poems* appeared in translation in 1974). During the 1960s he produced much of his most effective work, chiefly in two contrasting modes: short, witty epigrams with vivid surrealist imagery, beginning with the two volumes of *Martyries* ('Testimonies', 1963–6), and long, meandering monologues spoken by mythological figures, most of them members of the Atreides family, whose stories are made to bear an uncanny resemblance to those of the Ritsos family; the frequent references to the Trojan War clearly symbolize the Greek Civil War of the 1940s. These monologues, collected as *The Fourth Dimension* (1972), which reflect the disillusionment felt by Ritsos and other Greek leftists after the events in Eastern Europe in 1956, are none the less a plea for greater tolerance.

The poetry of Seferis, Elytis, and Ritsos, among others, reached practically the entire Greek population in the 1960s in brilliant musical settings by the composer Mikis Theodorakis. In 1960 a fourth member of the 'Generation of 1930', the surrealist Andreas Embirikos (1901–75), published a collection of amusing short poetic narratives entitled *Amour Amour* (*Grapta*).

The voices of Elytis (who won the Nobel Prize in 1979), Ritsos, and Embirikos have continued to be prominent to the present day: 1991 saw the publication of Ritsos's posthumous collection *Arga, poly arga mesa sti nychta* ('Late, Very Late into the Night') and a collection by Elytis, *Ta elegia tis Oxopetras* ('The Oxopetra Elegies'), both of which are concerned with the imminent advent of death and have enjoyed significant commercial success, while Embirikos's eight-volume erotic novel *O Megas Anatolikos* ('The Great Eastern') appeared posthumously in 1990–2 amid exaggerated public interest in the repetitive details of the characters' sexual exploits.

Much of Greek literature since the Second World War has been deeply marked by a sense of belonging to a defeated camp, a sense that the struggles and sufferings for the sake of a brighter social future have been in vain. Yet, rather than being a cause for lamentation, this has often led poets, on a communal level, to a sense that, as survivors, they have a duty to write on behalf of their lost comrades by conveying a political and social lesson; and, on a personal level, to condense their experience self-mockingly into short, terse poems. This is the case with several poets of what is conventionally known as the 'generation of defeat', notably Manolis Anagnostakis (b. 1925; *The Target*, 1980) and Titos Patrikios (b. 1928), whose poetry—intelligent, unlyrical, and lacking in surrealistic imagery—frequently meditates on the role of poetry in society.

Others of this generation reacted differently. Takis Sinopoulos (1917–81; *The Landscape of Death*, 1979, and *Selected Poems*, 1981) produced longer poems in narrative mode haunted by the dead, the horror, and the madness of the Civil War, in which he served as a medic in the government army. D. P. Papaditsas (1922–87), Miltos Sachtouris (b. 1919), and Ektor Kaknavatos (b. 1920), who emerged from a background in Surrealism, have generally turned their backs on contemporary history in their mature poetry; indeed, they seem to be promoting poetry as a means of resisting an over-burdensome history. Papaditsas went on to produce *En Patmo* ('In Patmos', 1964), an account of a visionary experience that was to form the subject-matter of the rest of a poetic *œuvre* whose expression is abstract and philosophical. The short poems of Sachtouris (*Selected Poems*, 1982, and *Strange Sunday*, 1984) contain obsessively repeated nightmare images of malfunctioning human beings and animals, while Kaknavatos has explored his temporal and spatial relation with the universe through remarkable imagery taken from geology, palaeontology, mathematics, chemistry, and astronomy. Sachtouris and Kaknavatos are among the very few of the poets mentioned so far who have truly experimented with language.

Greek prose, too, flourished in the 1960s as never before. The two best-known novels are perhaps *The Third Wedding* (1963), by Kostas Taktsis (1927–88), and the trilogy *Drifting Cities* (1960–5), by Stratis Tsirkas (1911–80). Taktsis's novel is one of the most enjoyable in the language; it is the hilarious, yet at times tragic, story of two women's interconnected lives, told by the heroines themselves against the background of Greek history in the first half of the twentieth century. The Greek family has never quite recovered from Taktsis's exposé of it as an organ of repression and a network of possessiveness, hatred, and jealousy; *The Third Wedding* also points up the lack of humour that has usually characterized Greek literature.

Tsirkas's three novels, set in Jerusalem, Cairo, and Alexandria during the

Second World War, set out to tell the story of the betrayal of the Greek Left by the Communist Party itself, but also succeed in presenting, through a complex technique involving alternating narrators, a vivid and arresting picture of the Middle East as a hotbed of international sexual and political intrigue during this period. At the same time, the short stories of Dimitris Hatzis (1913–81), *To telos tis mikris mas polis* ('The End of our Small Town', 1963), chronicle, from a Marxist viewpoint, the breakdown of the old Ottoman social structures in a northern Greek town under pressure, first from an international capitalist economy, then from the German Occupation.

One of the most remarkable newcomers to prose in these years was Vasilis Vasilikos (b. 1934), whose trilogy of novellas *The Plant, The Well, The Angel* (1961) humorously explores the existential anxieties of a confused younger generation living under the shadow of the Bomb and frustrated by the restrictions imposed by family and society. Vasilikos's novel *Z* (1966), subtitled 'imaginary documentary of a crime', is a non-realistic reconstruction of the real murder of a left-wing politician in Thessaloniki in 1963, in which the villains are presented as dinosaurs. Two other important young prose writers based, like Vasilikos, in Thessaloniki, and who made their appearance in the 1960s, were Yorgos Ioannou (1927–85) and Yorgos Heimonas (b. 1939). Ioannou's collections of prose pieces, which hover between fiction, reminiscence, and essay, chart, through the persona of an isolated and easily disgusted individual, the personal and communal experiences of pre-war dictatorship, followed by a decade of war, which have led Greece to its present state. By contrast, Heimonas has been one of the most innovative prose writers of the period since 1960 in a series of books, for example *The Builders* (1979), in which horrific experiences are narrated in a fragmented language that owes much to the author's experience as a psychiatrist. Nevertheless, Greek literature of the period lacked an avant-garde, and it is indicative that the most experimental magazine of the 1960s, which promoted the survival (or revival) of Surrealism, was called *Pali* ('Again').

The military dictatorship of the Colonels (1967–74) marked a break in Greek literature, at least in part because of the imposition of a preventive censorship for its first two and a half years, which closed down all but the most conservative literary magazines and drove most serious writers to refuse to publish their work at all. Very little prose was published, while poetry took on a role it had been playing in Eastern Europe, namely that of finding a sober and concise expression for a poetic truth opposed to the cack-handed and delirious oppressiveness of the regime's own language. At this time Greek literature (particularly poetry) became aware once more of its role as the voice of the oppressed nation; an awareness particularly apparent in the collection of anti-junta poetry and prose published under the title *Eighteen Texts* (1970), which demonstrated that the dictatorship had brought about a reconciliation between the opposed camps of the Civil War by housing Communist and anti-Communist writers between the same covers.

No doubt under the pressure of the dictatorship and of his self-imposed exile in France, Elytis produced in 1971 three new books of lyrical poems, after a silence of several years; and Ritsos, after being silenced for five years by imprisonment, house arrest, and censorship, used the experience of confinement to publish several collections of poems from 1972 onwards. Most remarkably, the years of dictatorship saw the emergence of a large group of young poets who were first known as 'the poets of *amfisvitisi*' (a Greek word denoting a challenge to accepted values) and later as the 'Generation of 1970'.

But before dealing with their work, a word about the intervening generation of poets. Unlike many of the poets that preceded them, Nikos Karouzos (1926–90), whose first book appeared in 1961, and Kiki Dimoula (b. 1931), whose best work has appeared since the 1970s, do not seek redemption in political engagement but express the pain of existence and an awareness that redemption—if it is to be found at all—is not to be attained in the physical world. Karouzos's tragic vision during the last fifteen years of his life was of the inadequacy of language, which he came to see as a parasite on reality, standing between us and absolute Being and preventing us from making direct contact with it. Dimoula's language is more experimental, involving dislocations of syntax and paradoxical juxtapositions of images as she pleads to be vouchsafed a sudden, unexpected experience that would redeem her from the repetitiveness of habit.

Two poets linking this middle generation with the 'Generation of 1970' are Katerina Anghelaki-Rooke (b. 1939; *The Body is the Victory and the Defeat of Dreams*, 1975, and *Beings and Things on their Own*, 1986) and Tasos Denegris (b. 1935). Anghelaki-Rooke's poetry is dominated by a consciousness of the body and its mortality: the body constitutes the confines of our world; mental states are dependent on its state, while the internal organs are constantly working towards death; and love is a search, through the body, for redemption from its confines. Denegris, in his darkly humorous glimpses of the urban scene, makes extensive use of the imagery of modern culture—football, American music, cinema, and drugs—that became centrally important to some of the younger poets from the 1970s onwards. The large number of talented young poets who emerged during the dictatorship, born between 1943 and 1952, had little or no direct memory of the Civil War that had indelibly marked the older generations. Furthermore, for the first time in the history of Greek literature, women now began to be as prominent as men (if not more so).

The 'Generation of 1970' was marked by a number of new influences, some of them international, others peculiar to Greece: the events of May 1968 in Paris and youth protest in general; the new Western adulation of youth and the creation of the generation gap; pop music; the permissive society and women's liberation; the Cold War and the threat of nuclear annihilation; the military dictatorship in Greece (itself a product of anti-Communist hysteria) with its censorship and its brutal suppression of dissent; and the rapid urbanization of the country (the neighbourhood, with its courtyards and corner-shops, giving way to apartment blocks and supermarkets) coupled with its technologization (television first became an integral part of Greek life under the Colonels, who used it as a crude instrument of propaganda), its growing material prosperity, and its consumerism. Elytis, a much older poet, drew on influences such as these in *Maria Nephele* (1978), a long, complex poem which became a best-seller and which pitches two voices antiphonically one against the other, that of a young girl and that of an older man.

Although some of their early poems are directly interpretable as a protest against the military regime, these poets have avoided both the political commitment and the metaphysical search for redemption characteristic of their elders. Instead, they accept the impossibility of faith and of any objective truth. In their search for self-knowledge their poetry is often satirical, ironic, humorous, playful, even flippant, and lacks any tragic or nostalgic tone; their language is generally colloquial, avoiding both traditional lyricism and—with some exceptions—avant-garde experiment, although the legacy of Surrealism is apparent in their constant substitution of an incongruous image for what the reader has been led to expect. If Theodorakis's music was suited to the poetry of the Generation of 1930, the musical counterpart of this new poetry was the songs of Dionysis Savvopoulos, which express the incongruous impact of American culture and modern technology on the stagnant provincialism of the Colonels' Greece.

The most prolific of the young male poets of the 1970s is Yannis Kondos (b. 1943; *Mercurial Time*, 1978; *Danger in the Streets*, 1979; *The Bones*, 1985), whose early poems express opposition to political oppression, but who goes on, through an often humorous use of surrealistic images and events, to express fears and anxieties emanating from an unspecified source, but also a suspicion that such natural phenomena as parts of his body or emotions

are as artificial as the man-made objects around him. Like his hero Kostas
Karyotakis, who committed suicide in 1928 and whose self-deprecating image
of the 'inglorious poet' has provided a model for the 'Generation of 1970',
Kondos also writes about the problems of poetic expression and about the
mendacious words of others.

Poetry is also the subject of some of the poems of Nasos Vagenas
(b. 1945; *Biography*, 1978), whose tone is deliberately prosaic and often
humorous, and who has recently been experimenting in traditional metre
and rhyme—largely abandoned in Greek poetry since the 1930s. The playful and self-conscious poems of Yannis Varveris (b. 1955), with their constant references to a future of old age and death, are also based on a strong
iambic rhythm. Lefteris Poulios (b. 1944) shows most clearly the influence
of American poets, particularly the Beats, with his persona of an indignant
voice crying in the modern urban wilderness. Vasilis Steriadis (b. 1947)
depicts the substitution of modern technology for human body-parts and
emotions, while Michalis Ganas (b. 1944; *Concerning the Ascension*, 1984) is
exceptional in alternating in his imagery between a contemporary urban
dystopia and a nostalgic return to his rural birthplace with his elegies on
loved ones who have passed away. The other poets of his generation evince
little or no rapport with the rural landscape.

Of the women poets, Natasa Hatzidaki (b. 1946) experiments most extensively with a language related to modern consumer technology and pop
culture, while Pavlina Pamboudi (b. 1948), particularly in her collection with
the provocative title *Aftos ego* ('He I', 1977), presents [her]self as separate
from [her]self by using the masculine adjective when referring to the 'I' of
the poems; this sense of alienation is frequently found in contemporary Greek poetry. Pamboudi's books are typical of Greek women's poetry
of the late 1970s and 1980s in that they consist of sequences of connected
narrative-like texts (often laid out in prose form) rather than collections of
separate poems.

Three other outstanding women poets who have produced sequences of
prose-poems are Maria Laina, Rea Galanaki (both b. 1947), and Jenny
Mastoraki (b. 1949). Laina's and Galanaki's poetry is concerned to mark out
a woman's space in the world. Mastoraki, after a brilliant début with the
humorous and self-ironic poems of *Diodia* ('Road Tolls', 1973), went on to
a kind of poetic autobiography covering the period from birth to marriage
in *To soi* ('The Family', 1978), which playfully, self-mockingly, and sometimes surrealistically depicts the horrors faced by a girl growing up in a
repressive Greek family. Since then Mastoraki has become more experimental, presenting in *Istories ya ta vathia* ('Tales of the Deep', 1983) horrific

images of violence, torture, and slaughter—disturbingly equated with love—
in a rich and densely poetic language replete with medievalisms, neologisms, and multiple references to earlier Greek texts; and in *M' ena stefani fos*
('With a Garland of Light', 1989) sensuous, surrealistic images of sleep and
death suffused with quotations from the nineteenth-century Greek poetic
tradition.

Two particularly prolific novelists who cover the whole period from 1960
to the 1990s are Alexandros Kotzias (1926–92) and Menis Koumandareas
(b. 1931). Kotzias's career began in 1953, with the publication of the first of
seven novels, which were followed from 1987 onwards by the first four of
a projected series of seven novellas that was cut short by his accidental
death. In his effort to depict what he called the Thirty Years War between
Left and Right, Kotzias consistently portrayed the kind of vicious character
who was responsible for the violence that has permeated Greece's recent
history, and his brand of realism, which often involved the use of the characters' own voices as narrators, demanded a correspondingly violent language. His *Antipiisis archis* ('Usurpation of Authority', 1979) centres around
a violent, foul-mouthed agent of the Security Police under the Colonels'
junta. In *Jaguar* (1987), however, he moved with the times (it has become
fashionable for male writers to write in female voices) by focusing on the
contrasting experiences of two female characters who had been on opposite
sides during the Civil War. Koumandareas, despite the realism of his depictions of contemporary Athenian *petit bourgeois* life, has written sensitively of
subtle relationships, like that between a married woman and a younger
man in *Koula* (1978).

The novel *To kivotio* ('The Crate', 1974), by the poet Aris Alexandrou
(1922–78), is a landmark in the development of Greek fiction in its relation
to the dominant theme of recent history. Ostensibly the written apologia of
a soldier in the Communist army who has been arrested by his own side
in the closing stages of the Civil War, this novel uses historical events and
situations as a pretext for a philosophical challenge to the traditional notions
that narrative discourse is capable of embodying an objective truth. The
empty crate of the title, which the narrator and his comrades have transported on a dangerous but futile mission, has been interpreted as symbolizing
not only the failure of the Communist idea in Greece, but also the emptiness of the linguistic signifier. *To diplo vivlio* ('The Double Book', 1976), by
Dimitris Hatzis, is another novel by a Communist which deals with the
problematics of narrative, this time in connection with a social problem
strangely absent from Greek fiction: that of economic emigration.

In the 1980s, for the first time in Greek literary history, new novels came to outnumber volumes of poetry, and many of the leading novelists were women. Novels began to sell large numbers of copies, and several writers who had previously made their name in poetry or the theatre became successful novelists.

A survivor from an earlier generation is Alki Zei (b. 1928), a writer of children's books whose first novel for adults, *Achilles' Fiancée* (1987), was an immediate success. It tells the story—partly through her own memories and partly in the words of a third-person narrator—of a woman who is thrown in with a Resistance leader during the German Occupation, thinks she has fallen in love with him, and goes to join him in exile in the Soviet Union after the Civil War; disillusioned with his narrow-minded adherence to Communist dogma, she takes their daughter back to Greece, from where she is forced to flee when the Colonels take over; finally she realizes how history and politics have controlled her existence and denied her any freedom of choice. A similar self-realization under the pressure of historical circumstances is the theme of *Fool's Gold* (1979), by Maro Douka (b. 1947), in which a young woman comes to an awareness of her autonomy in the process of telling the story of her experiences since the beginning of the dictatorship; her involvement in the Resistance and with various lovers has hitherto hindered her development as a free individual.

History and tradition are treated in a new way by several novelists of the 1980s. In *Astradeni* (1982), by Evgenia Fakinou (b. 1945), a girl from the provinces charts her traumatic transition to the menacing metropolis of Athens. Fakinou's second novel, *The Seventh Garment* (1983), opposes tradition to modernity by narrating the story through the interior monologues of three women, each representing a different generation with its contrasting experiences and its different interpretations of the same events. *History of a Vendetta* (1982), by Yorgis Yatromanolakis (b. 1940), although set in Crete in the inter-war period, against the background of Greek political history, is—like 'The Crate'—more concerned with the problematics of narrative than with telling a story. *O vios tou Ismail Ferik Pasa* ('The Life of Ismail Ferik Pasha', 1989), by the poet Rea Galanaki, is a re-creation, without a trace of chauvinism but full of symbolism, of the true story of a Christian Cretan who was abducted to Egypt in the 1820s, became a Muslim, and eventually found himself back in Crete as Commander-in-Chief of the Egyptian forces fighting the Christian insurgents. All these novels challenge the traditional view of history as a linear process.

In poetry, younger writers who emerged in the 1980s have adopted a more private and intimate tone, making many references to earlier literature and writing in a generally more formal style. In prose, they have tended to depict solitary characters in search of love against a realistic background of bars and discos.

Literature is still very much in demand in Greece. Novels now achieve bigger sales than ever before, and there is a market for poetry in elegantly designed little volumes. Excellent literary magazines continue to contribute to the promotion of poetry and short stories, as well as to critical debate on contemporary and earlier literature. Translations of works by young Greek writers are constantly appearing in other European countries, but very few have broken through the language barrier into English.

FURTHER READING

Beaton, Roderick, *An Introduction to Modern Greek Literature* (Oxford, 1994).

12

HUNGARY

RICHARD ACZEL

The Russians have gone. They've left all sorts of things behind. Above all: us. They've gone, and we've been left behind. What a relief, we sigh. Then we look around, and what do we see? Yes, at last we're at home in our own homeland—but it's hardly a relief.

THUS Péter Esterházy (b. 1950), one of Hungary's most interesting and talented contemporary novelists, writing at the end of 1989, the year that saw the collapse of Communism and the beginnings of the transition to parliamentary democracy throughout East Central Europe. Esterházy's caution is significant. As a writer who has proved consistently critical of his nation's political and historical preconceptions, he is quick to insist on continuities easily overlooked in the euphoria of political transformation. He belongs to a generation of writers profoundly distrustful of the rhetoric of political commitment and social progress that not only permeated official Hungarian culture in the period of state socialism, but which also has much deeper roots in the national literary tradition.

In Hungary—as in Central Europe in general—writers have played a key role in most of the major political upheavals of national history, from the revolution against the Habsburgs in 1848, through the anti-Soviet uprising of 1956, to the democratic transition of 1989. As Pál Gyulai, the great arbiter of literary taste in the second half of the nineteenth century, wrote exactly one hundred years earlier: 'For us literature and art are more significant than for the more fortunate nations of Europe—they are not only matters of civilization and enjoyment, but central tenets of our nationhood and sovereignty.' Much of what is best in recent Hungarian writing has developed out of the attempts of writers like Esterházy to redefine the 'us' in a way that challenges national conceptions of the tradition of literary *engagement*.

Those I have in mind are predominantly writers of various forms of prose, rather than poetry or drama. It is in prose that the most consistently challenging, innovative, and accomplished work has been produced over the past twenty years—which have seen narrative fiction displace lyric poetry from its traditional role as the leading genre. I shall begin, even so, with a brief consideration of the work of four poets, to illustrate not only how extra-literary concerns influence the way in which literary reputations are established and sustained in Hungary, but also what has been achieved by major writers who manage to transcend the limitations of the *engagé* tradition.

The first of these is Sándor Csoóri (b. 1930), who has enjoyed a position of great literary influence over the past twenty-five years. In 1987 a critic claimed: 'With the death of Gyula Illyés, the mantle of poetry's spokesman for the Hungarian nation has descended on Sándor Csoóri.' This claim may be a little far-fetched, but it reflects a perception that has considerable currency in Hungary. Like Illyés, who was a leader of the populist movement in the 1930s and a major moral voice in post-war literature, Csoóri comes from a peasant background and sees the idiom and values of folk literature as the essential ingredients of a distinctive national culture. In this way, he identifies himself with a strong tradition of literary populism, which had already developed into a coherent and distinctive 'popular-national' school by the nineteenth century. Csoóri's populism nurtures an essentially romantic conception of national character, informed by the traditional life and values of the peasantry. Much of his poetry is concerned with the disintegration of this 'organic community' in an increasingly urban, industrial, and cosmopolitan world.

Csoóri's reputation has more to do, however, with his vivid and powerful essays, and with his public role as an outspoken champion and guardian of national values. In 1983, for example, he wrote a courageous and polemical introduction to a documentary study of the plight of the Hungarian minority in Slovakia. The volume was published in New York, and banned in Hungary, and was thus never widely available to Hungarian readers. The gesture, rather than the contents, of Csoóri's introduction was, however, much discussed in the press, and the fact that he was subsequently prohibited from publishing in Hungary for a year did much to enhance his popularity.

Another poet whose reputation seems inextricable from his political role is György Petri, considered by many to be the finest living Hungarian poet. Much of his poetry is shaped by a certain pathos of political protest, and because of its critical character he was banned from publishing for much of the 1970s and 1980s. As with Csoóri, Petri's encounters with the authorities during the Communist period are undoubtedly one explanation of his popularity. At its best, however, his verse can be both intellectually stimulating and profoundly moving. His first collection, *Magyarázatok M. Számára*

('Explanations for M.', 1971), in which a deceptively straightforward, almost prosaic love poetry serves as a basis for serious, if often deeply ironical, philosophical speculation, probably remains his best work to date. The more overtly political verse he wrote in the 1980s is generally limited both in focus and by its didacticism. Since 1989 Petri has been struggling to find a new voice. His most recent volume, *Sár* ('Mud', 1993), reflects the new uncertainties of the post-Communist period at a more attractively abstract level. The opening poem sets the tone, beginning with the words: 'We're on the move again. That is, we continue to stand still.'

The two finest representatives of post-war Hungarian poetry are without doubt János Pilinszky (1921–81) and Sándor Weöres (1913–89). Pilinszky was a devout Roman Catholic and the profoundly—if unconventionally—religious character of his poetry met with the disapproval of the Stalinist regime. By the 1970s, however, he was widely recognized as one of the most important poets of the century.

Pilinszky's poetry recreates a world of unremitting spiritual suffering and existential anguish, only partly mitigated by religious faith. Much of his inspiration derives from his experience as a prisoner of war in Austria and Germany in the last years of the Second World War. Through his stark, undecorative, yet highly inventive imagery, he sustains an intensity of self-awareness. This is particularly evident in the later volumes, *Kráter* ('Crater', 1976) and *Apokrif* ('Apocrypha', 1981), the title poem of the latter volume being one of the most powerful lyric poems in the language.

Weöres, who published more than twenty-five volumes of poetry during his lifetime, is widely recognized as the master craftsman of post-war poetry. His verse is characterized by its extraordinary thematic and stylistic range—from the profoundly philosophical to the comic—and by its unparalleled technical virtuosity. He continually recreates his elaborate personal mythologies as his work shifts between the idioms of primitive ritual and folk-song, and the invention of sophisticated literary personae. The enormous power with which Weöres identifies with these is best illustrated by *Psyché* (1972), a collection of verse and prose that is offered as the autobiographical work of an imaginary woman poet of the early nineteenth century. Although Weöres drew frequently on the forms and themes of folk poetry, and Pilinszky on the imaginative world of earlier 'visionary' poets, neither can be classified as belonging to a particular school, and the enduring value of their work transcends any considerations of ideological allegiance or commitment.

Turning to contemporary prose, one is bound to begin with the work of György Konrád (b. 1933), who remains the most internationally celebrated

Hungarian writer of the post-war period. Again, his literary achievement has been somewhat overvalued for reasons having nothing to do with literature. Konrád in fact enjoys a higher reputation abroad than he does at home. All of his four novels—three of which were banned or only published after a considerable delay in Hungary—have appeared in English, French, and German translation, along with such sociological and political works as *The Intellectuals on the Road to Class Power* (written with Iván Szelényi, 1979) and *Antipolitics* (1984). This international attention far exceeds that afforded to other, more accomplished Hungarian writers, and is partly to be explained by Konrád's perceived significance as an intellectual dissident under the Communist regime.

He established an international reputation with his first novel, *The Case Worker* (1969), which appeared in English translation in 1974. This remains his finest achievement as a novelist. It is a powerful and humane indictment of urban suffering at the lower end of the social scale and is based largely on Konrád's own observations as a sociologist in the 1960s. His first-person protagonist, a social worker in Budapest, is brought to realize that his interventions into the lives of others—however well intentioned—can never relieve them from their misery. The 'case worker', who describes himself as an 'agent of indifference and mediocrity', is finally unable even to imagine the 'better world' his activity as a reformer seems to demand: 'the world is what it is, nothing can change it.'

This resignation is characteristic of the Central European conception of history, which informs much of Konrád's work. It is best summed up in an 1989 essay entitled 'The Viewpoint of the Victim': 'In Central Europe, history is merely a mundane term for Fate . . . Fate does not approach with old-fashioned, tragic majesty, but comes upon us like a drunken driver.' Most of Konrád's fictional characters can be seen in one sense as the victims of history, from the case worker and his clients, to the town planner of his second novel, *The City Builder* (1977), whose bizarre Cartesian maxim, 'I plan therefore I am', is as much the product of an excessively rationalistic social system as is the town on which his plans are imposed.

In Konrád's third novel, *The Loser* (1980), this sense of the historical subject as victim is expressed in more overtly national terms. After living through three of the most traumatic eras in the nation's history—the Second World War, the Soviet occupation, and the 1956 uprising—Konrád's protagonist ends up in a mental institution, where he is told by his doctor: 'We are not a nation that makes history. Our revolutions have failed, in wars we always end up on the losing side . . . We served the Turks, then the Germans, and now the Russians.' Konrád's characters, however, are generally not only the products of the system they serve but also to some degree complicit with them.

In his most recent novel, *The Garden Party* (1989), his sense of the arbitrariness of history is reflected in his treatment of narrative. The writer sits in his garden, where various characters—some real, some imagined—come and go, either telling their own stories or evoking stories within the writer-narrator. In place of a single plot, histories alternate and merge with fragments of meditation and intellectual autobiography. The novel thus becomes the site of a kind of dialogue between narrative fiction and the essay, the genre in which Konrád has produced his most interesting work since *The Case Worker*.

He is a witty, ironical, highly polemical essayist, 'an alternative thinker by profession' who takes issue with all forms of ideological fundamentalism. One of the few collective allegiances he is prepared to sanction without qualification is that of a 'European republic of letters'. 'I want', he claims, in an essay entitled 'Barbarizáció' ('Barbarization', 1989), 'to be a suspicious cosmopolitan who, to the grim disapproval of local collective sensibilities, blows subversive and foreign ideas like bubbles into the deep blue sea.' In the same breath, however, he can define himself as a 'patriotic and cosmopolitan Hungarian Jew' who thinks with two heads, 'one Eastern, the other Western'. For Konrád, this ambiguity is a crucial constituent of what he sees as the Central European condition: 'We live . . . on the border between two civilizations, where we are bound to compare everything with a matter-of-fact relativism.' It is this relativism that makes identity, like history, forever negotiable and uncertain, and perhaps, ultimately, a concept devoid of meaning. As the protagonist of *The Loser* says, early in the novel: 'What I call "I" has dried up, like water from a can.'

A similar preoccupation with the arbitrariness of history and the instability of the historical subject can be seen in the work of Miklós Mészöly (b. 1921). Mészöly established his reputation as a major innovator with the publication of his first novel, *Az atléta halála* ('The Death of an Athlete', 1966), in which the widow of an athlete tries to write his biography. Her thoughts on, and investigations into, her husband's life are presented without any attempt to classify them, and both life (as narrative) and character (as a fictive construct) remain essentially open-ended concepts.

Mészöly's best works are his short stories and novellas. They are typically set in a small Central European town, surviving precariously on the borders of history, with the narrator functioning as a kind of archivist faced with the impossible task of piecing together the disconnected fragments of an ambiguous past. In this vein, Mészöly's most powerful work is *Forgiveness*

(1983), a novella which begins and ends with a band of smoke left suspended above a country town by a passing train. The narrative spans four months in the life of a local clerk-cum-archivist, into which several key events in the town's history are interwoven: the subterranean reproduction of its layout in a complex of graves after a disastrous plague in the seventeenth century; the trial of a former mayor in the early 1920s; the discovery of a naked corpse in an apparently untrodden cornfield. These historical fragments mysteriously punctuate the equally fragmented experience of the clerk and his family without any suggestion that there is a meaningful or causal relationship between past and present. The novella ends with the clerk literally dreaming of a 'highflown sentence' with which to beg his wife's forgiveness for an act of infidelity. Even in his dream the sentence refuses to pass his lips; but now the possibility at least of forgiveness has been entertained and this fragment can join the others on an equal footing.

Mészöly's attitude to history leads him to question the integrity and continuity of the narrative act itself. This scepticism is developed still more radically in the work of Péter Esterházy, which extends the interrogation to question the stability of the narrating self. At first sight, the opening words of Esterházy's second novel, *Függo* ('Dependent', 1981), would seem to contest any rejection of subjectivity: 'I narrate, I and this "I" is not some fabricated character, but the novelist, who knows his business, a bitter, disappointed man.' When one realizes, however, that this apparently confessional opening is in fact a quotation from the Diaries of the Austrian writer Robert Musil, the irony of such a statement becomes clear.

Esterházy's wish to test the boundaries between narrative and discursive prose was already manifest in his first novel, *Termelésiregény* ('A Novel of Production', 1979). The novel is in two sections: a hilarious pastiche of Stalinist 'workplace fiction' is followed by a lengthy account of the narrator's everyday life as an author, provided in the form of endnotes by his fictitious literary secretary, Goethe's amanuensis Johann Peter Eckermann. The novel juxtaposes a variety of historical styles and textual borrowings, and demonstrates not only Esterházy's inexhaustible linguistic virtuosity but also his desire to explore historical continuities. The way in which parliamentary reports from the nineteenth century merge with political rhetoric from the Stalinist 1950s suggests a circular conception of history, typical of the scepticism of Esterházy's generation.

After *Termelésiregény* he embarked on a major creative undertaking that took seven years to complete: a series of stylistically diverse experimental novels and shorter 'fictions' which were finally published in a single volume entitled *Bevezetés a szépirodalomba* ('An Introduction to Literature', 1986).

This offers a remarkably rich and inventive exploration of a great range of prose styles, and its title constitutes a direct challenge to what Esterházy sees as the extra-literary expectations of an over-politicized readership. This is not to say that 'Introduction to Literature' is any less political than the 'Novel of Production'; rather, that here the boundaries between the political and the aesthetic are not taken for granted but foregrounded and made problematic. Many of the texts in the volume are dated 16 June, for example, the date on which, in 1958, the politician Imre Nagy was executed for his role as leader of the revolutionary government of 1956. But 16 June is also a key date in modernist fiction: it is James Joyce's 'Bloomsday', the day on which the action of *Ulysses* takes place, and Esterházy has used it to highlight the fictional status of his own writing.

Among the most powerful items in 'Introduction to Literature' are *Kis Magyar pornográfia* ('A Pocket Hungarian Pornography', 1984) and *Helping Verbs of the Heart* (1985). The first of these is a splendid satirical essay on the ideological prostitution of literary language that seeks to liberate the writer from the perverse roles thrust upon him by two centuries of didacticism: the writer as prophet, as educator, as social reformer, as national psychotherapist. In the first section, the writer is called on to perform a circumcision. 'You must help me,' his patient pleads, 'after all, you are the engineer of the soul' (a reference to Stalin's famous definition of the writer's role in society).

Helping Verbs of the Heart is perhaps the most immediately accessible of Esterházy's novels. It describes the illness, death, and funeral of the writer's mother. The first part of the book is narrated by the bereaved son, the second by the mother, who returns to mourn her lost child in dreams and memories that paint a vivid picture of her youth in pre-war Hungary. These two narratives are counterpointed by a third text, printed in capital letters at the foot of the page and consisting largely of literary quotations. Even here, however, where Esterházy's writing appears to be at its most intimate and confessional, the emphasis is on differentiating between the writing subject and the biographical self. The novel's preface is a seemingly confessional account of the author's reasons for writing; it is, however, taken verbatim from the German writer Peter Handke's *A Sorrow beyond Dreams*.

A later novel by Esterházy, *The Book of Hrabal* (1990), further complicates these ambiguities of authorial and narratorial identity. In this case they are implicit in the book's title. Hrabal is the Czech novelist Bohumil Hrabal, who occasionally speaks in the novel in the first person. The central part is narrated, however, by Anna, the wife of a Hungarian novelist. Watched over by a pair of angels who receive their instructions by walkie-talkie,

Anna, who is pregnant with her fourth child, is contemplating an abortion. Finally, she decides to have her baby and the scene shifts to Heaven, where God is taking saxophone lessons from Charlie Parker. The novel closes, ambiguously, with the 'stupendously botched and vulgar', yet somehow 'simple and complete', sound of God's saxophone blasting incomprehensibly through the Universe.

Esterházy's most recent 'novel', *The Glance of Countess Hahn-Hahn—down the Danube* (1991), is a combination of narrative, essay, and spoof travelogue. It is in fact a conflation of two journeys down the River Danube, one by a young Hungarian aristocrat, who has been 'kidnapped' by a mysterious double-agent uncle, the other by a professional traveller, undertaking a voyage of discovery for a 'contractor', with whom he communicates by telegram. Much of the traveller's description of the region he traverses becomes a half-frivolous essay on the contradictions inherent in the notion of 'Central Europe'. Indeed, *The Glance of Countess Hahn-Hahn* reflects Esterházy's growing interest in the essay-form as a way of accommodating the various discourses, genres, and voices which competed for precedence in his earlier work.

Another major novelist whose work has been heading in the same direction is Péter Nádas (b. 1942). In his case the essay has come to represent the only way out of a 'creative crisis' which led him to abandon fiction altogether. Since the publication of his monumental *A Book of Memoirs* (1986)—justly considered to be the finest post-war Hungarian novel—Nádas has focused almost exclusively on non-narrative prose forms. There is irony in this: in the two novels he had published, he seemed to breathe new life into the genre.

Both books register a sense of crisis, however, concerning the limitations of the novel form. The first, *Egy családregény vége* ('The End of a Family Novel', 1977), is a lyrical study of the significance of family history and tradition in the life of a young Hungarian Jew growing up in the 1950s. It ends in a profound crisis of personal and historical identity, reflected in a breakdown of narrative cohesion. Unable to identify with his father, who had made moral and political compromises in the Stalinist era, the narrator is brought to realize that the traditions which governed his grandfather's generation belong irretrievably to a world that no longer exists. Historical continuities are ultimately regarded as dubious fictions, and the genre of the family, or genealogical, novel as no longer viable for the Central European writer at the end of the twentieth century.

Nádas's second novel, *Emlékiratok könyve* ('A Book of Memoirs', 1986), on which he worked for eleven years, also tackles themes of memory, personal identity, and historical continuity. It consists of three apparently separate narratives, or memoirs: the story of a Hungarian student in East Berlin in the 1970s; an adolescent boy growing up in Budapest in the 1950s; and a German novelist living and writing at the turn of the century. Only at the end of the book do we learn that the first and second narrators are one and the same person, and that the third is his fictional creation. The closing chapters are written by a childhood friend of the composite narrator, after the latter's seemingly meaningless death. The friend is able to reconstruct the sequence of the complex narrative, but even he cannot restore the logic of development that the memoirist had sought to extract from his memories. He is ultimately forced to admit: 'even after a most thorough-going examination of the notes I could not decide what course he would have made the plot take.'

Emlékiratok könyve seems to have stretched the boundaries of narrative invention to limits beyond which Nádas feels now unable to go. The book is a masterpiece, and, as such, hard to follow. In a subsequent essay, he has posed the question 'whether there mightn't be a connection between my own creative crisis and the historical crisis of the novel as literary form'. The question is relevant to all the novelists considered here. For all of them, the experience of their national or regional history has led to a loss of faith in both the continuities of narrative and the stability of the narrating subject. Their dilemma has come increasingly to resemble that of Musil's essayist in *The Man without Qualities*: 'He has a vague intuitive feeling that this order of things is not as solid as it pretends to be; nothing, no ego, no form, no principle, is safe, everything is in a process of invisible but never-ceasing transformation, there is more of the future in the unsolid than in the solid, and the present is nothing but a hypothesis that one has not yet finished with.'

Musil's reflections take on a new significance in the context of the political transition in Hungary. The events of 1989 have two large implications for writers there. First, the collapse of the old regime has not led to the publication of many major works that could not have appeared during the years of state socialism. This is largely because, during its last two decades, the literary censorship was considerably more liberal than elsewhere in the Communist bloc. With the important exceptions of the work of Konrád and Petri, most of the best writing produced in the 1970s and 1980s was published by the state publishing houses. Indeed, the chances of publishing innovative or experimental work were probably greater before 1989, when publishing was heavily subsidized by a state apparatus which—paradoxically perhaps—entertained no anxieties about intellectual élitism. Today,

Hungarian writers face a very different economic reality, where the most active censor is the free market. Thus Konrád joined several other distinguished writers in contributing to the first Hungarian edition of *Playboy* in 1990, while seeing his novel *The Loser* remaindered less than a year after its first publication.

A second implication concerns the continuing importance of politics in the making and breaking of literary reputations. The President of the new Hungarian Republic is a dramatist, Arpád Göncz, and the poet and essayist Sándor Csoóri was a key adviser to the first post-Communist government. Another influential literary figure, the populist dramatist and short-story writer István Csurka, was a founding member of the first governing party, the Hungarian Democratic Forum. At the other end of the political spectrum, Konrád's party, the Free Democrats, subsequently formed a coalition government with the restructured Socialist Party, after that party's overwhelming victory in the April 1994 elections.

Such are the ironies of Hungarian politics and the kinds of 'commitment' they continue to command. Against this background it is not surprising perhaps that a writer like Esterházy should, back in 1984, have remarked in a now famous phrase: 'It might be more reassuring if the writer thought less in terms of the people and the nation, and more in terms of subject and predicate.' Seven years later, a leading critic commented: 'If you find the plays of Arpád Göncz lacking in dramatic tension or stylistic originality, your reservations may be taken as a criticism of his political party. Any criticism of the inflated rhetoric of Csurka, on the other hand, may be taken as an attack on the [pre-1994] coalition Government.' Esterházy, one can safely assume, is yet to be reassured.

FURTHER READING

Czigány, L., *Oxford History of Hungarian Literature: From the Earliest Times to the Present* (Oxford, 1984).

Pynsent, R. B. and Kanikova, S. I., *Everyman Companion to East European Literature* (London, 1993); also published as *Encyclopedia of East European Literature* (New York, 1993).

13

INDIA

RICHARD CRONIN

V. S. NAIPAUL pointed out in 1964 that Indian literature in English had ceased to exist: 'The only writer who, while working from within the society, is yet able to impose on it a vision which is an acceptable type of comment, is R. Prawer Jhabvala. And she is European.' He ought to have been right. That Indians had chosen to write in English must then have seemed simply a historical accident, a product of the Raj that would not long survive its passing. The government of India had committed itself to Hindi as the national language, and those who wrote in one of India's twelve other major languages felt themselves engaged in a struggle against, not the pretensions of English, but the encroachments of Hindi. English remained as the first language of only one tiny and sadly disadvantaged Indian community, the Anglo-Indians.

The Indian government that assumed power after Independence in 1947 was remarkable, amongst much else, for its literary talent. Its President, Radhakrishnan (1888–1975), was a philosopher of rare eloquence, and its Prime Minister, Nehru (1889–1964), had published in 1936 an autobiography startlingly different in its humanity and in its painful pursuit of self-knowledge from the more usual political memoir. There was the Marxist intellectual Krishna Menon (1898–1982), and there was C. J. Rajagopalachari (1878–1972), whose English prose translations offer a fine introduction to the two great Indian epics, the *Mahabharata* and the *Ramayana*. Outside the government there was Gandhi (1869–1948), whose autobiography, *The Story of my Experiments with Truth* (1927), is the best corrective to the reverentially anodyne accounts of Gandhi that have resulted only in trivializing his achievement. It seemed an irony of history that such a government was fated to inaugurate an Indian nation in which the vitality of English as a literary language would slowly atrophy.

India's three significant novelists in English continued to write. In books such as *Untouchable* (1935) and *Coolie* (1936), Mulkraj Anand (b. 1905) had shown how the Indian novel in English might become a powerful expression of social concern. Raja Rao (b. 1909), India's first modernist, had, as early as 1938, shown in *Kanthapura* how English could be moulded into rhythms expressive of a distinctively Indian experience, and R. K. Narayan (b. 1907) had already invented Malgudi, the small south Indian town that he has explored in more than a dozen novels until it has become a fictional world which, in its completeness and its delicacy of texture, outdoes Trollope's Barsetshire or Hardy's Wessex.

But these are writers who grew up in British India, heirs to a culture in which Indian and British elements were interfused. Nirad Chaudhuri (b. 1897) is one of that culture's most distinguished products, and his *Autobiography of an Unknown Indian* (1951) is the definitive account of how it formed not just his mind, but the mind of his generation. The bitterness evident in Narayan's later novels, in *The Vendor of Sweets* (1967) and *A Painter of Signs* (1977), and the apocalyptic pessimism that marks (and mars) the second instalment of Chaudhuri's autobiography, *Thy Hand Great Anarch!* (1987), are, literally, miles apart. Narayan's serenely equable temperament has been invaded by spleen in Bangalore, whereas Chaudhuri's characteristic mordancy has been intensified into gloomy hysteria in Oxford, but both, one suspects, are the responses of writers living in a world that seems increasingly less familiar to them, a world they are in danger of no longer recognizing.

Of the three novelists, only Raja Rao has continued to develop. In *The Serpent and the Rope* (1960) and the more recent *The Chess Master and his Moves* (1987), Rao explores the relationship between the West and the East in a manner that might have proved a decisive influence on his successors had he not, by his dense philosophical digressions and his uncompromisingly symbolic method, so successfully shielded himself against the temptation of reaching out to a wider audience.

It must have seemed a safe prediction in 1964 that the future of Indian literature lay with the Indian languages, where there have been significant achievements. But in fact, Naipaul spoke too soon. The most fertile period of Indian writing in English began in 1981, and has since shown no sign of coming to an end. There seem to be four reasons for this. First, the establishment of Hindi as the national language was fiercely resisted by speakers of other Indian languages, particularly in the south. In consequence, English has maintained a role as a common language. Second, even as the British Empire was dissolving, the United States was establishing itself as the dominant power across the greater part of the globe, a fact that in itself did much to sustain the status of English. Third, since 1947 there has been a substantial migration from India to the English-speaking countries of the West. Hanif Kureishi's (b. 1954) *The Buddha of Suburbia* (1990) is only the

first of what will inevitably be a growing number of important novels by
writers born in the West that explore the experience of living within an
Asian community, whether in Britain, Canada, the United States, or Australia.

The fourth reason is Salman Rushdie (b. 1947). In *The Great Indian Novel*
(1989), an irreverent chronicle of modern Indian political history, Shashi
Tharoor (b. 1956) pauses when he reaches 15 August 1947, to note the
'children being born at inconvenient times of the night who would go on
to label a generation and rejuvenate a literature'. It is a graceful tribute and
a proper one. Modern Indian literature was born in 1981, when Rushdie
published *Midnight's Children*.

The *fatwa* issued against Rushdie in 1989, announcing that his novel *The
Satanic Verses* represented a blasphemy so grave that it would be a righteous
act for any Muslim to murder him, has made him, for reasons that no one,
least of all Rushdie himself, will rejoice in, the most important writer of the
second half of the twentieth century. But even before 1989, it was to Rushdie
that Indian writers in English were indebted for their new-found confidence. At the beginning of I. Allan Sealy's (b. 1951) *The Trotter-Nama* (1988),
the narrator notices a fellow passenger on his plane, a distinguished looking
man fastidiously sipping a glass of dry white wine. 'There's a proper writer,'
he thinks, 'must be an islander.' At the end of the novel, he meets him
again at the reception desk of an international Indian hotel, staring at the
ceiling in a silent pantomime of exasperation as he muses on some particularly gross manifestation of Indian inefficiency. It is from Rushdie that Sealy
has acquired the nerve to meet Naipaul's baleful stare with so unabashed
an effrontery.

It is a confidence that seems not to have transmitted itself to poets.
India's two most distinguished modern poets, Nissim Ezekiel (b. 1924) and
A. K. Ramanujan (b. 1929), were both children of the Raj, 'Macaulay's
children', as Ramanujan puts it, rather than 'midnight's'. Ezekiel has stayed
in India: 'I have made my commitments now. | This is one. To stay where
I am.' He has built his achievement on his recognition of himself as an
outsider, as a Jew in a nation of Hindus, Muslims, and Sikhs, but also, just
as important, as the exponent of a poetic language which, in its technical
accomplishment and its dry exactitude, distances him from his surroundings. In his fine autobiographical poem 'Background, Casually' he remem-
bers schooldays lived in terror of the 'undernourished Hindu lads | Their
prepositions always wrong'. Ezekiel has experimented with poems in Indian
English:

> I am standing for peace and non-violence.
> Why world is fighting, fighting

Why all people of world
Are not following Mahatma Gandhi,
I am simply not understanding.

This, however, is a language not only confined to comedy, but condemned
to be patronizing. Nevertheless, of Indian poets in English, Ezekiel alone
has produced a handful of poems that have that rarest of all qualities, in-
evitability. His 'Poet, Lover, Birdwatcher', for example:

To force the pace and never to be still
Is not the way of those who study birds
Or women. The best poets wait for words.
The hunt is not an exercise of will
But patient love relaxing on a hill
To note the movement of a timid wing;
Until the one that knows that she is loved
No longer waits but risks surrendering

A. K. Ramanujan has lived for many years in Chicago. He is an accomplished translator of Tamil poetry, and there is a sense in which all his verse
has the quality of brilliant translation. He makes his poems out of memories of the south India of his childhood and of his family, but the poems
are always charged with his sense of his separation from his subject-matter.
The separation is not only geographical but linguistic, and in his best poems
Ramanujan makes a virtue of this. The title poem of his first volume, 'The
Striders' (1966), describes some 'bubble-eyed' American water insects:

See them perch
on dry capillary legs
weightless
on the ripple skin
of a stream.

His poetic language, too, perches on the skin of the experience that it
records, and the effect can be oddly compelling.

The first significant Indian poet in English was a woman, Toru Dutt
(1856–77), and women poets since the 1960s, Kamala Das (b. 1934), Mamta
Kalia (b. 1940), and Eunice de Souza (b. 1940), have turned to English again,
attracted, I suspect, because they find in English a neutral space that will
accommodate more easily than their Indian languages an attempt to redefine their experience as women. Kamala Das, whose autobiography *My
Story* frankly and powerfully records the experience out of which the poems
were born, writes with an urgency and a passion that are sometimes restrained, as when she grieves for the undemanding love that her grandmother once offered to her:

That woman died,
The house withdrew into silence, snakes moved
Among books I was then too young
To read, and my blood turned cold like the moon.

More often she broods with self-lacerating contempt on the sexuality that
compels her again and again to act out the bitter comedy of love:

Notice the perfection
Of his limbs, his eyes reddening under
The shower, the shy walk across the bathroom floor,
Dropping towels, and the jerky way he
Urinates. All the fond details that make
Him male and your only man.

But, whether men or women, Indian poets in English are forced to make
capital out of a predicament, to forge a poetic language in a country where
the English language is not continuously revitalized by its vigorous use in
the life of every day, where, as Rajagopal Parthasarathy (b. 1934) puts it in
his 'Under Another Sky': 'The sun | has done its worst. Skimmed | a lan-
guage, worn it to a shadow.' Some, such as Arun Kolatkar (b. 1932), have
responded by becoming bilingual poets. Kolatkar's English has a vitality
that derives, one suspects, from his practice as a poet in Marathi. But
Parthasarathy has made a more radical decision. In his essay 'Whoring after
English Gods' (1976) he announced that his 'prolonged and tempestuous
affair with the English language' was over, and that henceforward he would
write in Tamil.

It ought to be as debilitating for the novelist as for the poet to write in
a shadow language, but in fact Indian novelists in English seem to have
been invigorated by precisely the predicament from which the poets suffer.
In *Midnight's Children*, Saleem Sinai, Rushdie's hero, spends his childhood
years in a middle-class Bombay enclave built on a hill, and hence safely
removed from the teeming life of the city below. When Saleem leaves his
exclusive little colony, he travels enclosed in the family car that takes him
to his exclusive English-medium school or to the cinema, where he watches
American films. One day, Saleem loses control of his bicycle, and hurtles
downhill, crashing into a procession of strange and intimidating men. It is
a language march: Marathis protesting that Bombay should be ceded to
Maharashtra, and that Marathi replace Gujarati as the official language. The
protestors are incomprehensible to Saleem. Marathi is his worst subject at
school, and his Gujarati is just as bad. In this episode Saleem is the true
representative of all Indian novelists in English. He mounts his bicycle—so

very English a machine—and crashes into India, with its teeming masses, who stare into his face and speak to him in languages that he cannot understand. The men are kind enough to him, addressing him good-naturedly as a 'little princeling', a 'young nawab', a 'lord', but their good nature is secured by their confidence that his life is utterly irrelevant to theirs. The language that Rushdie uses to represent India in itself reveals him as unrepresentative.

As the march indicates, in India language is a passionately contested political issue. Rushdie points out in *Midnight's Children* that, in 1956, Nehru divided India into six states: 'But the boundaries of these states were not formed by rivers or mountains, or any natural features of the landscape. Language divided us.' English was not the language commonly spoken in any of these states, but it does not follow that it offers a disinterested linguistic perspective within which such divisions might be healed. Saleem Sinai might be spared the hatred that the Marathi demonstrators feel for Gujaratis, but that is only because his English education has removed him too far from them to make him a proper object of hatred.

Because knowledge of English is not an instrument of geographical division, it functions all the more powerfully in India to establish social divisions. 'I spoke English with my parents,' Homi Seervai, the narrator of Boman Desai's (b. 1950) *The Memory of Elephants* (1988) tells us, 'and Hindi with the servants.' Jaya, in Shashi Deshpande's (b. 1943) *That Long Silence* (1988), knows that she was selected for the doubtful honour of marrying her husband because he wanted a wife 'who can speak good English', and was prepared to forgo a dowry to achieve his end. Balraj Khanna's (b. 1944) *Nation of Fools* (1984) tells the story of Omi, who moves with his family to Chandigarh, and learns to speak in a passable imitation of the Cambridge-returned Professor Raj Kumar, who speaks English so well 'you can hardly understand what he says'. Omi's reward is to win social acceptance by the 'Simla pinks', the golden youth of Chandigarh, who have been educated in one of the exclusive hill-station boarding-schools, and are distinguished from the rest of the population by their fair complexions and their command of English.

Most Indian novelists in English are recurrently afflicted by a sense of the absurdity of their enterprise. In Upamanyu Chatterjee's (b. 1959) *English, August* (1988), Agastya Sen, who has succeeded in joining the Indian Administrative Service, is sent for his training year to Madna, a dreary provincial town. He spends the year lying on his bed, staring at the ceiling of his guest-house bedroom, listening to his cassette recorder, smoking dope, and masturbating. His life in Madna is a bitter parody of the dislocation between the urbanized Western consciousness that Chatterjee shares with his hero and the town to which Sen has been posted, and it leads Chatterjee to question whether English literature has any valid place in India at all: 'Why is some Jat teenager in Meerut reading Jane Austen?' In his second novel, *The Last Burden* (1993), he tells how a father is careful to inculcate in his sons the habit of 'discounting, even pooh-poohing, the worlds of their own languages'. When his sons' Jesuit school threatens to change the medium of tuition to Hindi, he writes furiously to the Principal: 'I do not pay your school fees just so that tomorrow my sons for a living have to teach Hindi in a tinpot primary school.'

Such novelists are haunted by the fear that, as one of Chatterjee's characters puts it, there may be no 'universal stories', that each language may be 'an entire culture', and that their own language maroons them within a culture that is not Indian at all. Chatterjee's solution is to rewrite English. The central character of his first novel is accused of speaking an English 'unique in its fucked-up mongrelness', but it is in the second novel, *The Last Burden*, an exhilaratingly bilious account of an Indian family bound more tightly to each other by rancour and resentment than a less eccentric family might be by love, that Chatterjee finds a wholly individualized prose— dictionary words, 'sudorific', 'fenestral', interspersed with scabrous modern slang, all enclosed within a syntax baroque in its studied formality. The father, Shyamanand, indulges in a factitious nostalgia for the family life of his own misremembered childhood, 'an earlier, illusorily genial world (in which Shyamanand and his siblings had nested together in parsimony, balefulness and rancour), wherein, mawkish that he is, he reckons that the bonds of family had been sturdier, and parents more revered'. Shyamanand and his family speak to one another, presumably, in Bengali, but Chatterjee seizes the opportunity allowed him by his English to invent for the family a language as eccentric, as zestfully mordant, as the personalities of its members.

More usually, it is the remoteness of the novel's language from its subject-matter that is exploited. Here, Ruth Prawer Jhabvala (b. 1927) showed the way. She has described in her essay 'Myself in India' how she lived when she was there, retreating from the climate and from the people into the air-conditioned, shuttered solitude of her Delhi flat. Her language carries that chilly aloofness into her novels and stories, so that her characters, Indian and Western alike, remain always at a clinical remove, a distance preserved by the fastidious, slightly styptic prose that records their doings. In *How I Became a Holy Mother and Other Stories* (1981) she divides her characters into two groups, the seekers and the sufferers. But this is not a distinction she maintains. The people who interest her are the exiled, who spend their lives looking for a home, and the spiritually wounded whose lives are spent looking for a cure. Both quests seem futile, so that even her best characters, Sarla Devi of the novel *Get Ready for Battle* (1962), for example, who has preserved her social conscience, and the energy to resist injustice, in the end retain dignity only to the extent that they have retained the capacity to suffer.

For Jhabvala, living in India and writing about it are both activities that require an unremitting exercise of bad faith. 'The most salient fact about India is that it is very poor,' she writes, with the consequence that it is not possible to dine well in one's comfortable Delhi flat without wilfully blinding oneself to the existence of thousands who enjoy neither food nor shelter. India, as Jhabvala describes it, is a country where moral blindness is the essential condition of survival. Her most typical characters are prosperous urban Indians whose lives are spent studiously cultivating their ignorance of the country in which they live, characters like the government minister in the short story 'Rose Petals', whose car is stopped by a disturbance in which slum-dwellers are feebly protesting against their forcible eviction. The minister distracts himself from the scene outside the car windows by gabbling nervously about the unaccountable variations in performance between different models of the same car. Jhabvala holds such people in fierce contempt, but she is always guiltily aware that it is a contempt she might just as properly direct at herself.

She is interested, too, by the procession of Westerners who, since the 1960s, have trekked to India, impelled by their dissatisfaction with Western materialism. She charts with a somewhat malign satisfaction the discovery by characters such as Child, the sannyasi from the English Midlands in *Heat and Dust* (1975), that in a country where people starve, materialism has a sharper edge than anything Wolverhampton can offer. But even in such characters Jhabvala recognizes aspects of herself, for she too, she confesses, finds something 'spiritual' in India, something incongruous with the wretchedness and degradation of Indian poverty—a spirituality she glimpses most often when she listens to Indian music. 'I am irritable and have weak nerves,' Jhabvala writes of herself, and it is that nervous irritability that invigorates her Indian fictions. In her essay 'Myself in India' she describes a hysterical cycle in which she—in common, she claims, with most Western residents in India and with many Indians—is trapped. Her experience of India becomes, from time to time, intolerably intense, and generates only a desire to escape, but if she takes a plane to Europe, she finds that for her the West has lost its reality, and she lives as if in a dream until she returns to India.

The Ivory–Merchant films with which she has occupied herself as a scriptwriter since she finally left India for New York might suggest to some that she remains trapped. Away from India, she has assisted in nostalgic re-creations of a Western past which, despite the meticulous accuracy of the period trappings, gain their limp charm by remaining utterly unreal. Her best work was done in India, and it was never stronger than when she found a character infected by her own hysteria, a character such as the narrator of the short story 'An Experience of India', the Western wife of a foreign correspondent, who periodically leaves the luxury of her Delhi flat and goes in search of the real India. Her expeditions culminate in dismally brutal sexual encounters from which she retreats to her husband and his air-conditioning. It is a cycle that ends only when her husband walks out, and she is left confronting with terror and excitement the emptiness of her future.

Other novelists have developed Jhabvala's themes. Nayantara Sahgal (b. 1927), for example, in a novel such as *Rich Like Us* (1985), examines and exposes the survival strategies of prosperous urban Indians, and in *Plans for Departure* (1986) she explores the experience of a young European woman in Edwardian India in a manner that recalls *Heat and Dust*. As one would expect of Nehru's niece and an outspoken critic of Indira Gandhi, Nehru's daughter, Sahgal's novels have a firm grasp of Indian politics that Jhabvala cannot match, but they are not stamped, as Jhabvala's fiction is, by the impress of her own awkward and unaccommodating personality.

Anita Desai (b. 1932), too, lacks Jhabvala's irritability, but her novels remain quite distinctive. Where Jhabvala's cool English prose establishes her at an acerbic remove from the India of which she writes, Desai writes from a distance at once contemplative and imbued with a kind of pathos. Her most memorable characters, Bim in *Clear Light of Day* (1980) and Nanda Kaul in *Fire on the Mountain* (1977), live apart from the excitements and the turmoil of modern India. Bim lives unmarried in the family house, a se-cluded bungalow in Old Delhi's Civil Lines, and there leads a life given over to history, which she teaches, and memory—sad memories many of them, of family miseries and of her rupture with her beloved elder brother, but irradiated now and then by a happy memory, jewel-like in its clarity and brilliance. Nanda Kaul lives at a still greater distance. In her widowhood, she has retired to an unfashionable hill station, and looks down on the plains from the heights of the Himalayan foothills. She remembers her married life, spent in studiously failing to notice her husband's adultery, and enjoys the chill luxury of a widowhood in which she can at last live for herself alone, until Rakha, a young girl, comes to stay and drags her back into the world of human responsibility.

Bim's brother once had the ambition of becoming a great Urdu poet, a second Iqbal. The dream comes to nothing, but in a later novel, *In Custody* (1984), Desai tells the story of Deven, whose great passion, although he is obliged to make a living as a lecturer in Hindi, is for Urdu poetry, and of how he finds himself compelled to take responsibility for the welfare of the last great Urdu poet of India. Something of Desai's feeling for Urdu may stem from her recognition that in independent, post-partition India Urdu shares with her own English both a rich cultural heritage and the status of a language under threat. Nur's poems are 'perfect, unblemished shapes', his life is a drunken chaos. Between the two stretches the gap that, one suspects, Desai recognizes as separating her own fastidious, lyrical talent from the chaotic and violent bombardment with which India assaults the senses of anyone who walks along a city street: a gap that her novels explore, and move, tentatively, towards resolving.

Jhabvala, Sahgal, and Desai are novelists who happen to be women, rather than women novelists, and the same might be said of Kamala Markandaya (b. 1924). It is Shashi Deshpande (b. 1943) who, in her most recent novels, has set herself the task of breaking what she describes in the title of the first of these as *That Long Silence* (1988). Both this novel and its successor *The Binding Vine* (1993) focus on the life of a woman writer. Jaya, in the earlier novel, finds her voice only when her husband leaves her. Before this she has been constrained by commercial pressures, by the magazine editor who dismisses her attempts as 'middle-class stuff, women's problems . . . too distanced from real life', by her husband's anguish when she publishes a story about 'a man who could not reach out to his wife except through her body', but most of all by her own, internalized inhibitions, by her inability to free herself from the demand that she restrict herself to 'feminine' emotions: 'A woman can never be angry; she can only be neurotic, hysterical, frustrated.' Her husband is proud enough of the success of her 'Seeta' stories, comic episodes in the life of a scatty middle-class housewife, who, as her name reminds us, remains for all her modernity continuous with the traditional ideal of Indian womanhood. (In the *Ramayana*, Seeta is the devoted wife of Rama, and still functions as the classical model of wifely virtue.) On her marriage, her husband gave her the name of Suhasini. Her task is to abandon that name in favour of the name she was born with, Jaya, which means victory.

In *The Binding Vine* Urmila begins the novel grieving for the death of her infant daughter. Two projects reawaken her interest in life, however. She discovers the diary and unpublished poems of Mira, her husband's mother who died in childbirth, and resolves to publish them. Both the diary and the poems record a married life in which Mira was repeatedly raped by her husband. Urmila's second project is to win justice for Kalpana, who lies throughout the novel, silent and unconscious, the victim of a violent rape by, it emerges, her brother-in-law. Even Kalpana's own mother believes that her daughter has been dishonoured rather than the rapist. Mira and Kalpana are divided by history and by social class, and Urmila is separated from both by her own relatively happy marriage; but the novel works to dismantle these distinctions. Urmila, unlike Jaya, is not permitted to emerge from her story victorious, but with a bleak sense that 'the binding vine' of the novel's title—a phrase from one of Mira's poems that represents all those emotions that tie women to their roles as wives and mothers—will continue to render women subject to, and sometimes the victims of, male power.

Mira writes her poems in Kannada and her diary in English, which seems to her entirely natural. Deshpande herself is more suspicious of such dichotomies. She is aware that her own feminism is Western in its origins, and offers her a perspective that is liable, if she is not vigilant, to make her treatment of the experience of Indian women as exploitative as that of other Western industries processing Indian raw materials. She marks her recognition of this danger by including in *The Binding Vine* a feminist film maker, Priti, who is anxious to make a film of Mira's life until a modern case of suttee—the custom by which widows are burnt on their husbands' funeral pyres—occurs and offers her a more piquant subject-matter.

English, as its defenders in India are apt to say, is India's window on the world, with the inevitable result that all Indian novels in English explore the relations between East and West. It is unsurprising, then, that so many Indian writers should take as their theme a journey to the West: *A Passage to England*, to borrow the title of Nirad Chaudhuri's account of his own journey (1959). The most monumental account of such a pilgrimage is that of Ved Mehta (b. 1937), whose life work, an autobiography, six volumes of which have so far been published (1971–93), traces a journey from his parents' house in Lahore, where he was blinded by an attack of meningitis when he was 3, to the Dadar School for the Blind in Bombay, and thence to a school for the blind in Little Rock, Arkansas, until, in the most recent volume, he arrives as a student at Oxford.

Younger writers, Sara Suleri (b. 1953), whose *Meatless Days* (1989) is a meditation on her emigration from Pakistan to America, Amitav Ghosh (b. 1956) in *Shadow Lines* (1988), and the dazzlingly precocious Amit Chaudhuri (b. 1962) in *A Strange and Sublime Address* (1989) and *Afternoon Raag* (1993), prefer to fracture time and move sinuously between continents, so that the text becomes a picture of a consciousness forever in transit between different orders of experience. Their concern is, as Chaudhuri puts it, with 'jotting down the irrelevances and digressions that make up our lives', 'trying to pin down a sensation into its exact formula of words', an enterprise that gathers energy as the books move between continents. Chaudhuri puzzles over the discrepancy between the Bengali alphabet that he can read only stumblingly, with its letters 'intimate, quirky, graceful, comic, just as he imagined the people of Bengal to be', and the alphabet that he uses himself, or the difference between Western music that remains, like his own novels, 'printed upon the page' and an Indian raag in which 'each singer has his own impermanent longhand with its own arching, idiosyncratic beauties', so that the recital is a matter of 'constant erasures and rewritings' until at the end it is 'erased completely'. At this point, the phrase 'Indian writer' becomes either a misnomer or a paradox, and one is forced to recognize what Rushdie calls 'the folly of trying to contain writers inside passports'.

With *Midnight's Children*, Rushdie established what has remained since 1981 the most distinctive pattern for the Indian novel: the family chronicle that is also a history of the nation, a distorted autobiography that embodies in equally distorted form the political life of India. Saleem Sinai, born as the clock strikes the midnight hour that inaugurates India's independence, comes to understand that he embodies in his own person the life of the new nation. Saleem's egomaniacal pretension registers Rushdie's recognition of the madness of his own enterprise, to contain within a single novel the life of a nation of 600 million people. This is an ambition that Rushdie, born in India, but who emigrated with his parents to Pakistan, and was educated in Britain, where he has lived most of his adult life, seems peculiarly disqualified from entertaining. The spectre that haunts almost all Indian novelists in English—the fear that the language that they are using renders their novels somehow inauthentic—becomes the ghost that animates the intricate machine of Rushdie's novel. Saleem offers his own voice as representative of all India's citizens, a mad act of faith that sustains the huge and multitudinous fiction until, at the last, he begins to crack under the pressure of trying to contain so much, and such diverse, experience. The novel ends as Saleem explodes into 600 million silent fragments, the number of the unimaginably vast population on behalf of whom he had attempted to speak. His is a necessary madness, for India is, as Rushdie puts it, an 'imaginary country', a country that could never have existed 'except by the effort of a phenomenal collective will—except in a dream we all agreed to dream'.

Saleem's dream is at once proof of his madness, and the exercise demanded of every one of India's millions of citizens if the dream that is the
Indian nation is to be maintained, and the largest democracy in the world
is not to disintegrate. The action of *Midnight's Children* moves from India to
Pakistan to Bangla Desh, acknowledging an India that failed to be adequately
imagined even at its inception, and establishing an idea of the nation that
is properly defended not by politicians, whose devotion to a monolithic
idea of truth is inevitably divisive, but by novelists, whose imagination
rejoices in a human diversity that politicians seek only to control. In his
novel *Train to Pakistan* (1956) Khushwant Singh (b. 1915) produced a sad
and humane memorial to those who died in the partition riots. He ends his
monumental and passionate *History of the Sikhs* (2 vols., 1963, 1966) by
calling for the establishment of an autonomous Sikh homeland. It is as if
Indian unity has become a notion so difficult that it can no longer be sustained, except in writings that address themselves not to historical facts but
to the truths of the imagination.

Since 1981 a remarkable group of young novelists has emerged, all of
them indebted to *Midnight's Children*. I. Allan Sealy in *The Trotter-Nama*
(1988) and *Hero* (1991), Boman Desai in *The Memory of Elephants* (1988), and
Shashi Tharoor in *The Great Indian Novel* (1991) acknowledge themselves
as Rushdie's children, sharing with him an ambition to imagine a nation
that is authorized rather than invalidated by the quirky individuality of the
writer. Tharoor's book is a parody of the greatest of the Indian epics, the
Mahabharata, which tells the story of the war between the five Pandavas
and the Kaurava clan and arrives at the conclusion that the only victory
possible for human beings is that of a man over himself. Tharoor traces the
history of India from the beginnings of the Independence movement to the
assassination of the Prime Minister, Indira Gandhi, in 1984. He favours
joyously awful puns ('the rigged veda', 'the bungle book'); signals his suspicion that Nehru might not have seen India very clearly by representing
him as the blind Dhritarashtra, father of the Pandavas, who has an affair
with the splendidly named British aristocrat Georgina Drewpad; reasserts
Gandhi's claim to central importance by renaming him Gangaji after India's
sacred river; and ends his novel with the apotheosis of Morarji Desai, who,
despite his political failings and his habit of drinking his own urine, is, for
Tharoor, the true modern counterpart of Yudhishtir, the most spiritual of
the five Pandavas.

Boman Desai's interest is less with India as a nation than with his own
Parsi community, but the 'memoscan', a device allowing the past to be
experienced as the present, invented by his hero Homi Seervai has the same

function as the telepathy with which Rushdie credits Saleem. Homi had invented the machine so that he might experience still the sexual ecstasy he had found with the girlfriend who had discarded him, but the device allows him to reconstruct the whole of his Parsi heritage, so that by the end of the novel he can say: 'I had done it: I had brought them all together in one place at one time, made a whole of all the scattered pieces.'

I. Allan Sealy's *The Trotter-Nama* is as inexhaustibly inventive as Rushdie. Sealy is an Anglo-Indian, and traces the history of his community in a chronicle of seven generations of the Trotter family, told by the seventh Trotter, who is a forger of Indian miniatures, and the inventor of a hitherto unknown school of eighteenth-century miniaturists. Sealy's own ambition is similar, to reinvent the Anglo-Indian community. He takes the Anglo-Indian experience of being outsiders in two communities, of being, as Queenie, wife of the sixth Trotter, discovers, outlandishly white in India, and outlandishly brown in Britain—'the process had started in the aeroplane when she went to powder her nose about half-way between Delhi and London'—and reimagines it as conferring on Anglo-Indians a unique centrality, so that the second Trotter, Mik, can masquerade both as Kipling's hero, the most vigorously imagined British embodiment of India, and, when he dyes himself blue by bathing in vats of indigo and takes to sporting with milkmaids, as Krishna, best loved of the gods of Hindu India.

Such novels are impelled by an excited sense of the immensity of their subject-matter. In his first novel, *Such a Long Journey* (1991), Rohinton Mistry (b. 1952) tells the story of Gustad Noble, learning painfully to reconcile himself to the disappointments of his life as he enters old age. In a British novel such a theme would encourage a muted, attenuated treatment, but Mistry's novel is Dickensian in its fullness, marked throughout by Mistry's desire to allow the richly various life of Bombay to infiltrate his story. It is clear that he shares the grandiose ambition of the pavement artist, 'a B.A. in World Religions', who, at Noble's request, transforms the wall outside Noble's apartment block—previously only a surface for passers-by to relieve themselves against—into a gigantic mural on which all the world's religions are represented. India contains so much that it seems only a small step to extend an ambition to become the novelist of India to one of representing the world. Like so much else in the Indian novel, it is a development predicted in *Midnight's Children*, in the peepshow-wallah, Lifafa Das, who stuffs his magic box with more and more pictures in a desperate attempt to make good the boast with which he tempts his customers, 'See the whole world come see everything!', or in the miniature painter who is afflicted by 'gigantism', his pictures getting bigger and bigger as he tries to cram more and more into them, or by Saleem Sinai himself, who chooses as his time capsule, containing the personal bits and pieces that will remind future archaeologists of his existence, a battered tin globe.

Sealy's seventh Trotter, shadowy and disreputable though he may be, has become, as if through a process of natural evolution, a citizen of the world, acquainted with all five continents. His second novel, *Hero*, whose central character is translated from a first career as a film star to a second as prime minister, moving from one fantasy world to another with only a short intervening period when he acquaints himself with the 'middle dimension' of reality, is inspired by the Indian film stars, N. T. Rama Rao and others, who have found a second home in politics, but just as importantly by the revelation that an American film actor might find his way to the White House.

Sealy, like Rushdie, has lived much of his life outside India. He is an Indian writer, but also, in Rushdie's sense of the term, an immigrant writer, whose experience has thrust modernism on him by confronting him with a world that cannot be comprehended by any unitary notion of reality. But the culture of India itself is bewilderingly pluralistic, which may explain why its writers have found it easier than writers of different origins to make use of immigrant experience. In Bharati Mukherjee's (b. 1940) first novel, *Wife*, an Indian woman uprooted in New York goes mad. In her later fiction she chooses rather to celebrate the freedom available to the deracinated to become the person one chooses to be rather than to remain the person one is born.

It would be pointless to argue over whether Mukherjee, fiercely proud of her American citizenship, is more appropriately regarded as an Indian or an American writer (see the United States chapter later in this volume), and in this she is characteristic. Vikram Seth (b. 1952), for example, is the author of *The Golden Gate* (1986), a verse novel that describes the adventures in love of a group of Californian yuppies, and of *A Suitable Boy* (1993), recognized by Khushwant Singh as an unmatched portrait of India in the 1950s. Together with Rushdie, Seth is the most remarkable talent to emerge from India in the past fifteen years, and he could scarcely be more different. Everything Rushdie writes, even the disappointing successor to *Midnight's Children*, *Shame* (1983), is stamped his by the idiosyncrasies of his prose. Seth uses an equal linguistic virtuosity to make himself invisible, which may be why he can be so admirable a translator of Chinese poems while his own poems remain so undistinguished. Rushdie insists that his experience of cultural displacement has forced modernism on him. In Seth the same experience has produced a variety of Post-Modernism, a devotion to the traditional distinguished from pastiche by a knowing self-awareness; the copy of *Buddenbrooks* tossed aside by a character in *A Suitable Boy* as impossibly long and unreadable, or Seth's personal appearances as an anagram in *The Golden Gate*, where Kim Tarvesh, a disenchanted postgraduate student, is occasionally glimpsed lurking disconsolately on the periphery at parties. Seth knows better than his critics the charges to which he is vulnerable; that, like Janet Hayakawa, the sculptor of *The Golden Gate*, his is 'a facile versatility', prompting the question, 'Where has she been these thirty years?' The books themselves are the best answer to the accusation. In *The Golden Gate* his debt to Charles Johnson's translation of *Eugene Onegin* allows him to look at California, spiritual home of the Beats, through the prism of stanzaic verse, and to distance himself from his material without ever condescending to it. The only comparable achievement is, coincidentally, that of another of Pushkin's translators, Nabokov, in *Pale Fire*. In *A Suitable Boy*, Seth's traditionalism allows him to rediscover character. Mrs Rupa Mehra becomes too substantial, too vivid a presence to be confined within a novel: she is at once infuriating and endearing, a benevolent Indian version of Mrs Bennet in *Pride and Prejudice*, a comparison that Seth is typically careful to suggest by equipping her daughter with a Jane Austen novel to read on a train. *The Golden Gate* and *A Suitable Boy* share a theme. Both reject the Western ideal of passionate romantic love in favour of the more secure happiness to be found in a relationship built on calm affection: an exemplary theme, indicating the character, one suspects, of Seth's own relationship with his craft.

Vikram Seth is a writer of a new type. It is as if Indian, and Chinese, and American cultures are all available to him by virtue of his own transparency. Rushdie is a global novelist in a quite different sense, possessed of an imagination so vigorous that it leaps over national and cultural barriers. In the second of his great novels, *The Satanic Verses* (1988), Zeeny Vakil campaigns against the demand for 'authenticity' in Indian art, insisting on the 'eclectic, hybridized nature of the Indian artistic tradition'. Rushdie is himself Vakil's most distinguished disciple, and *The Satanic Verses* his most complete attempt to embody this ideal. The 'Satanic verses' themselves are the heterodox Koranic verses repudiated by Muhammad, and those in which the poet Baal satirizes the Prophet: Browning's 'Pied Piper of Hamelin', the doggerel set to Hindi film tunes with which Gibreel instructs the modern prophetess Ayesha, and the insidious childish verses—'Violets are blue, roses are red | I've got her right here in my bed'—with which Saladin drives Gibreel mad with jealousy. They are also, as Rushdie allows William Blake to remind us, any verses of whatever kind, for all poets, all fiction makers, are of the devil's party. Rushdie's Mahound, like all prophets, responds to the multiplicity of the world by defiantly insisting, 'one, one, one', and all poets, like Rushdie's Baal, must reject him. But in *The Satanic Verses* Mahound and his modern counterpart, the prophetess Ayesha, are honoured even as they are rejected, for Rushdie accepts the reality of religious faith, and celebrates a world made up of competing realities. It is a dangerous world, because if these alternative realities confront each other rather than 'jostling on Tube stations, raising their hats in some hotel corridor', then it is 'uranium and plutonium, each makes the other decompose, boom'. It is a sad irony that it should be this novel that brought about just such a confrontation, for its central point is that it is as necessary to find some way of living tolerantly in such a world as it is to find a way of living with nuclear fission.

At the end of *The Satanic Verses*, Salahuddin Chamchawala returns to Bombay, which serves to remind us that it was Rushdie's experience of a country always in danger of disintegration that first gave him his vision of the world, and that it is the survival of India on which his optimism ultimately depends. Rushdie had the good fortune to be born in an 'imaginary country', a country that could continue to exist only for so long as it could be imagined.

FURTHER READING

Mukherjee, Meenakshi, *The Twice Born Fiction: Themes and Techniques of the Indian Novel in English* (New Delhi, 1971).
——*Realism and Reality: The Novel and Society in India* (New Delhi, 1985).
Rushdie, Salman, *Imaginary Homelands: Essays and Criticism 1981–1991* (London, 1991).
Walsh, William, *Indian Literature in English* (London, 1990).

14

IRELAND

PATRICIA CRAIG

IN an essay of 1983, entitled 'Ireland at Swim', Denis Donoghue quoted a passage from Yeats's *Memoirs*: 'Practical movements are created out of emotions expressed long enough ago to have become general, but literature discovers; it can never repeat. It is the attempt to repeat an emotion because it has been found effective which has made all politically provincial literature . . . so superficial.' Donoghue extends the insight to present-day Ireland, and to Northern Ireland in particular, about which, he says, 'discussion . . . is interminable and frustrating. No one is thinking. Everyone is merely repeating an emotion he has found effective: effective in the sense of making him and his position familiar.'

Both Yeats and Donoghue were well aware that Irish literature was, and to an extent still is, bedevilled by a similar impulse; that it is those authors who have broken away from nationalist (say) or other social assumptions whose work has always achieved the greatest impact. At the time he was writing, in 1910, Yeats knew that the enemy of progressiveness was a certain vapid type of patriotic verse: e.g. 'The troops live not that could withstand the headlong charge of Tipperary.' By 1910, in fact, neither artless patriotism, nor, for that matter, artless pastoralism, was a tenable sentiment in Irish writing (though these modes did not altogether die out), as the ironic way of looking at things, and its attendant complexities, supervened. After Yeats came Patrick Kavanagh: Kavanagh, in 1941, was writing a 757-line poem about the charmlessness of Irish country life:

The wind leans from Brady's, and the coltsfoot leaves are holed with rust,
Rain fills the cart-tracks and the sole-plate grooves;
A yellow sun reflects in Donaghmoyne
The poignant light in puddles shaped by hooves

which came to be seen as something of a landmark, being both a riposte to all the insipid bucolics who went before (the hankerers after a cottage in a bog), and an indicator of things to come. In the wake of Kavanagh's 'The

Great Hunger', we reach, eventually, the urbanities superimposed on country themes by such dextrous contemporary writers as Seamus Heaney and
Paul Muldoon.

Landmarks were few enough, in the middle part of the century. Censorship in the South, and two brands of puritanism in the North, had brought
about a situation in which it was easier for writers to opt for the ideological
truism—religious or political or cultural: to write with their instincts rather
than their intelligence, or, in other words, to repeat an emotion (as Yeats
had it) because it had been found effective. The nonconformists, in this
respect, are the really interesting authors: Flann O'Brien bringing his exor-
bitant wit to bear on every aspect of Irishness, for example.

The Dolmen Press in Dublin, founded by Liam Miller in 1951, quickly
got down to the business of fostering a proper—that is, an exacting—
approach to poetry, issuing in due course first collections by Richard Murphy,
Thomas Kinsella, and John Montague. In 1955, after a silence of seventeen
years, Austin Clarke published *Ancient Lights* (under his own imprint of the
Bridge Press), and showed himself to be as strong a social critic as ever,
though with a knottier and more derisive manner replacing the lyricism of
such early poems as 'The Straying Student'. Social criticism: this is one of
the two major concerns of Irish writers in the twentieth century, whether
the tone is glum, angry, ironic, or ebullient.

The other notable enterprise in contemporary Irish writing is the retrieval, or acknowledgement, of some facet of the past, generally for the
purpose of savouring the sense of national distinctiveness. But first it is
necessary to take a look at the more widespread—indeed, inescapable—
practice of social criticism, as this suggested itself to Irish writers confronted
on all sides by balefulness or stagnation. The year 1955 also saw the publication of Brian Moore's *The Lonely Passion of Judith Hearne*, the first in a series
of three fine novels displaying extreme exasperation with the author's native
Belfast. Each of the three is centred on a particular kind of failure, social in
Judith Hearne, sexual in *The Feast of Lupercal* (1958), and intellectual in *The
Emperor of Ice-Cream* (1966); and they add up to an energetic indictment of
some of Northern Ireland's mid-century ills.

Moore is an important novelist, in the first place, because he brought an
adult sensibility to bear on the issues he gets to grips with; before him, you
find little or no reputable fiction in the North, beyond the earliest (childlike)
novels of Michael McLaverty, *Call my Brother Back* (1939) and *Lost Fields*
(1942). Moore is important also as an identifier of blight; in particular, of
sexual blight. In this last he is not alone: it is a forceful motif running
through the work of Kavanagh, Austin Clarke, and others—'Celibacy is our

best rule still'—and reaches a culmination in John McGahern's novel of 1965, *The Dark* (his second novel).

The Dark is an account of an awful Irish adolescence, of a motherless boy growing up in the back of beyond with a brutal father and some cowed sisters, and a possible vocation for the priesthood which is scuppered by an addiction to masturbation: 'Bless me, father, for I have sinned . . . I committed one hundred and forty impure actions with myself.' *The Dark* is a very accomplished novel which gains something of its power from its dispiriting tactic: we are spared no detail of semen in socks, the lathering of bare buttocks, ringworm sores on cattle. The only refuge of McGahern's dithery young hero is an outdoor lavatory, past a bed of rhubarb stalks, where he can sit in the dark and ponder such matters as the possibility of his life's being merely 'a haphazard flicker between nothingness and nothingness'. When Brian Moore posits 'a nation of masturbators under priestly instruction' (in *Fergus*, 1970), his intention is humorous as well as scathing, while McGahern at this stage is deeply committed to a downbeat view. It is somehow all of a piece with the mood of the book that he should suffer for having written it, as well as suffering in it (I am assuming that there is an autobiographical element to *The Dark*). The novel was banned in Ireland and the author dismissed from the teaching post in a Catholic school which he had held for ten years.

Clearly, puritan Ireland, to cite John Montague's irresistible parody of Yeats, was not dead and gone at this stage, though the forces were marshalling that would see it on its way. Possibly Montague's mockery hurried on the process. Montague himself seems to have come a long way since 1951, and his demand then for a literature reflecting 'Catholicism as a living force in Irish life'. (His implication was that the Anglo-Irish Protestant impulse in literature had run its course, as indeed, by 1951, it had.)

Before the 1960s—Kavanagh notwithstanding—outcries against puritanism were intermittent and muted: Louis MacNeice and his friend and BBC colleague W. R. Rodgers, ex-Presbyterian minister of Loughgall, Co. Armagh (to take those examples), shared an anti-puritanical drive. MacNeice died in 1963 and Rodgers six years later, by which time puritanism in Ireland was a dwindling force (though it has never died out altogether), as the effects of social change and exposure to liberal influences began to make themselves felt. In the North, which is a special case, continuous upheaval became the overwhelming destructive factor, requiring both repudiation and elucidation in literature: 'Sixty-nine the nightmare started,' as one Ulster poet, James Simmons, wrote. (I will take a closer look at this departure in a minute.)

Among the prescient voices raised around 1960 was at least one female voice, that of Edna O'Brien from Co. Clare, whose robust, romantic outlook encompassed a refusal to shirk sex (an attitude that got her banned in Ireland). *The Country Girls* (1960) and *The Lonely Girl* (1962) are works of considerable charm and sharpness; she never hesitates to sound a plaintive note, it is true, but at this stage the plaintive element is overlaid with comedy. No one has written better about hapless country girls coming a cropper at their small-town convent school, or getting a taste for sophisticated life in 1940s Dublin.

The time was certainly ripe for a contemporary female voice, Ireland throughout the century having been bedevilled by misogyny to a remarkable degree. De Valera's Ireland, in particular, was a place in which it could thrive. Two of the most striking examples of anti-feminism, however, come from the North. Maurice Leitch (b. 1933) has set himself the task of scrutinizing blight and decay, from the run-down linen mills of *The Liberty Lad* (1965), his first and most engaging novel, to the Protestant terrorism, graft, and brutality of *Silver's City* (1981), which opens with a bungled assassination and ends with a stabbing. *Poor Lazarus* (1969) brings misogyny to the fore. Women, in this novel, are likened to 'discarded pieces of rubbish', accused of ruining any social gathering by 'changing the atmosphere in that subtle yet bullying way that [they] always have', and generally held to be an obstacle to a decent life. If they are used for a sexual purpose it is with revulsion, resentment, and to gratify an urge towards mastery. Leitch deserves credit, I suppose, for identifying this abuse among all the others in front of him—sectarianism, say, or economic decline—but endless contempt for women, highlighted for whatever reason, does have a dispiriting effect.

In the novels and stories of Anthony C. West (1904–89) the same characteristic produces a more alarming effect, as well as engendering disbelief. West's *The Ferret Fancier* (1963) and *As Towns with Fire* (1968) were mystifyingly greeted with a chorus of praise as soon as they appeared, the first being appropriated to a classic Irish tradition of rural writing (or the parochial sex-and-slaughter mode), the second—about a reluctant Co. Monaghan RAF man during the Second World War, whose mind becomes so deranged that he plans to set up home with his wife and children in a barrel in the woods—drawing forth from critics a barrage of praise such as 'brilliance', 'poetry', 'genius', and the like. The truth is that both these books are deadly and solipsistic. They are also crammed to bursting with women's breasts and bottoms. 'Knickerbockers full of behind and green pullover stuffed with breast', 'a fine-skinned white breast', 'a round plump bottom': such images occur on every page. You cannot avoid the impression that busts and bottoms are constantly being thrust in West's hero's face. At any rate, these parts are all he sees.

These aberrant outpourings do not offer much in the way of subtlety or illumination, but they do have a thing or two to tell us about the low estimation of women in Ireland, and about the temptations of over-writing. Fortunately, around the same time, more heartening developments were taking place. Thomas Kinsella's call, in 1966, for a literature—in the wake of Joyce—that would simultaneously revive an Irish tradition and admit the modern world, did not go unheeded (either in poetry or in prose).

William Trevor (b. 1928), for example, was about to turn to Ireland for his subject-matter, after the sedate, distinctly English, comic realism of his earlier books. His collection of stories *The Ballroom of Romance* (1972), and in particular the title story, points up a kind of Irish inertia, incisively expressed. 'The small towns of Ireland are what I know best,' Trevor has stated: towns like Youghal and Mitchelstown and Skibbereen, with their modest houses, their pubs selling Murphy's Stout, their Coliseum cinemas and Atlantic Hotels, and hardware stores bearing names like Keogh's.

Flamboyance and whimsy, qualities traditionally associated with Irish writing, are quite alien to Trevor. What you notice first of all about his style is the glint of irony or exactitude shining through even his grimmest imaginings. Assurance and decorum never falter, but they come, impressively, with an edge of comedy or calamity. As the Irish element in Trevor's work has come increasingly to the fore, so his range has been extended in a number of ways. Reverberations from the Northern troubles, for example, have a place, while history, especially social history, forms a complicated framework to his Irish novels, *Fools of Fortune* (1985) and *The Silence in the Garden* (1988). It is not that he has fallen under the spell of what Sean O'Faolain called 'that old curse and bore of modernising Ireland, our revered, unforgettable, indestructible, irretrievable Past', just that he is making it his business to tackle the whole murky question of bygone social arrangements in the country, and their political implications.

The Silence in the Garden, for example, presents an Anglo-Irish house on an island off the coast of Cork: a house owned by a single family, the Rollestons, since an act of usurpation established them on the island in the seventeenth century. They built the house to replace an earlier castle, then leased the lands to tenant farmers up until the 1840s, when the Famine and its accompanying wretchedness caused the resident family to waive its rents, to the detriment of later generations. Conquest, administration, disaffection, distress: these are bare facts indeed, but Trevor's details of past iniquities or inequalities amount to a good deal more than historical annotation. Such facts, indeed, serve to indicate both the theme of the novel—that of making amends, in one way or another—and its plan, which involves the formation of an ironic pattern. The proper fate of such 'big houses' as the Rollestons' is to 'return to the clay': this resonant concluding phrase of the novel echoes the view of an earlier Trevor character, the nineteenth-century butler Fogarty in the masterly story 'The News from Ireland' (1986), who resents the prolongation of a way of life irreconcilable with conditions in the country.

A more common fate of the Irish 'big house' is to linger on, suffering colourful dilapidation. From Maria Edgworth's 'the wind through the broken windows . . . and the rain coming through the roof' to Caroline Blackwood's Dunmartin Hall (in her novel *Great Granny Webster*, 1977), with puddles in the corridors and warped doors, the Anglo-Irish house has characteristically fallen a victim to disrepair (Thomas Kinsella has a fine description of ruined Woodstock in his poem 'Tao and Unfitness at Inistiogue'). The image of disintegrating grandeur, indeed, has proved so useful that even novelists of the present are reluctant to let it go. Aidan Higgins, writing about barrenness and decay in 1930s Ireland, fixes on a big house, Springfield, and the three sisters who inhabit it, to focus his theme in *Langrishe, Go Down* (1966). Jennifer Johnston, John Banville, and Molly Keane have adapted this most persistent of Irish motifs to their own purposes. These purposes need not involve either an elegiac note, or an attitude of denunciation. Political comment is no longer *de rigueur*, as Keane shows in *Good Behaviour* (1981), a biting comedy of manners set mostly during the Black and Tan/Civil War period, which excludes the entire dimension of Republican unrest. There is never a trench-coated gunman about the avenues, or a blazing mansion to summon up from its owners reserves of aristocratic phlegm.

If, however, you take the big house as a symbol of conquest or oppression, you may find your proletarian hackles rising, as Michael Hartnett (b. 1941) does when he attends a musical evening at Castletown House, in Co. Kildare:

> I stepped into the gentler evening air
> and saw black figures dancing on the lawn,
> Eviction, Droit de Seigneur, Broken Bones:
> and heard the crack of ligaments being torn
> and smelled the clinging blood upon the stones.

These vivid lines invite comparison with the class-revolt of the English poet Tony Harrison, whose 'Stately Home' includes 'paintings of beasts they'd shot at or they'd rode, | cantered grabbed acres on, won local stakes, | once all one man's debatable demesne'. The Irish experience, though, adds national to class outrage, whenever the past and its legacies come up for consideration: something that tends to happen quite often, even at present and despite the modernizing impulse which overtook the country around 1970 (with concomitant freedoms which came too suddenly, in many instances, and went to the nation's head). Looking to the past to enrich or illuminate some aspect of the present: this testifies to the continuing hold over Irish imaginations of a pungent history, a sense of unique wrongs.

The pattern created by the fusion of literature and history is continually being adapted, however, to accommodate contemporary feelings about bygone events. John Montague's *The Rough Field* (1972), for example, possesses a contemplative calm which offsets its immersion in resonant discontinuities, 'shards of a lost tradition', as Montague has it, many of them—the Gaelic place-names of Co. Tyrone, for instance, the Rough Field, the Glen of the Hazels, the Heights of the White Stone—recoverable if not restorable, and all contributing to the glamour of disaffection.

Place-names, indeed, are important, as Brian Friel's enlightening play *Translations* demonstrates. Set in the 1830s, this treats the business of standardization, of renaming, by which an anodyne English is superimposed on the recalcitrant syllables of the original Gaelic, by British army cartographers engaged in an Ordnance Survey of Ireland. Friel is concerned with the loss, or erosion, of national identity, as Montague is, but approaches it from a different perspective, reaching back to a crucial moment in the past when discontinuity became inevitable, when something snapped. *Translations* carries an ironic ring, with implications for the present, asking one to imagine a British army battalion in Co. Derry, say, 'translated' back to pre-Famine Donegal. The power of an enterprise like Friel's, or Montague's, depends on its working at an inexplicit, as well as a straightforward, level.

The Rough Field, in which Montague lays claim to a lot of highly charged local lore, is made up of a series of interconnected poems, and includes the spellbinding 'Like Dolmens Round my Childhood'. This piece of transfigured reminiscence, which was probably written a decade or so earlier, around 1960, has been tentatively singled out by Derek Mahon as 'the first contemporary Ulster poem', and has a place among the landmarks dotted about the field of Irish poetry of the last thirty years, along with poems like Thomas Kinsella's 'Nightwalker', Seamus Heaney's 'Tollund Man', Derek Mahon's 'A Disused Shed in Co. Wexford', Michael Hartnett's 'A Farewell to English', Michael Longley's 'Wounds', Paul Muldoon's 'Immram' or 'Gathering Mushrooms', Paul Durcan's 'Making Love outside Áras an Uachtaráin', Ciaran Carson's 'The Irish for No'. It is not that these particular poems are necessarily more profound, or more resourceful, than others by the same authors, just that, for some reason, they set off reverberations of a more than usual intensity. They are all influential poems, as well as getting to the heart of contemporary concerns, in one way or another.

Most of the poets named in that list are Northern Irish, which brings us on to one of the most debated matters in the field of Irish letters of recent years. Has there, or has there not, been a 'Northern Renaissance', starting in the 1960s and still continuing; and if so, what is its connection with, first, the Troubles, and second, the arrival of Philip Hobsbaum in Belfast in 1962? Thomas Kinsella, in his *New Oxford Book of Irish Verse* (1986), dismisses the whole idea as a journalistic figment, claiming those Northerners whose work he admires, such as Mahon and Heaney, for the country as a whole, and not just for a fraction of it. This is an attitude, I imagine, from which few Northern writers would wish to dissociate themselves. The fact remains, however, that, after the stagnant years of the 1940s and 1950s, the province suddenly found itself nurturing an outbreak of literary talent, which coincided with political upheaval.

Coincided is the word. It was not the violence in the streets that sparked off an instantaneous poetic response, or engendered the expertise needed to make any kind of sense of it. (When the response *was* instantaneous the effects were usually deplorable, as in an anthology such as Padraic Fiacc's *The Wearing of the Black* (1974), which is all undigested outrage.) It was rather that the cataclysm and its concomitant pressures made themselves felt in literature in oblique and subtle ways. Indeed, the effectiveness or otherwise of the response depended on the quality of the sensibility brought to bear on the events.

The second idea about poetry in the North—that certain key figures had served an apprenticeship under Philip Hobsbaum (born in Bradford), and that this put them and their successors poetically on the right tack—equally will not stand up to scrutiny. Hobsbaum arrived at Queen's University, Belfast, in 1962, and promptly set up a Creative Writing group (soon known simply as 'the Group'). According to Michael Longley, writing about the Group in an *Honest Ulsterman* of 1976, Hobsbaum's stars from the beginning were Seamus Heaney and the playwright Stewart Parker; neither Simmons nor Mahon was a regular attender at meetings; and Longley himself, though he went along fairly frequently, was somewhat at odds with the aesthetic purveyed there. Hobsbaum's contribution to the burgeoning poetic activity of the time was to generate 'an atmosphere of controversy and excitement'; and this was somehow piled on top of controversy and excitement emanating from other sources: for example, from the Civil Rights agitation which was just getting under way. A democratic, anti-sectarian spirit was in the ascendant, heralded in works like Sam Thompson's play *Over the Bridge* (1960), about bigotry among shipyard workers, and carrying a distinct humanistic burden.

The reasons why the optimism of the decade petered out in disaffection and disarray are properly discussible in the context of social, rather than literary, history, but it is a curious fact that by the end of the decade North ern Ireland had ceased to be a backwater, in ways both admirable and reprehensible. In *For All That I Found There* (1973), Caroline Blackwood posits the notion of a monumental boredom—the boredom of the suburbs, dead Ulster Sundays, bowler-hatted businessmen, the grey mists lingering over the loughs—finally generating its own antidote: an intriguing idea. At the same time, and more encouragingly, the province was casting off the image of philistinism that had dogged it for more than a century. It had ceased to be a place where nothing happened, in actuality or in the arts.

By 1970, first collections of poetry by Heaney, Longley, and Simmons had appeared; and a second quartet of Northern poets—Frank Ormsby, Carson, Tom Paulin, and Muldoon—was coming up fast behind. What Hobsbaum's Group had bequeathed to everyone even peripherally associ-ated with it (and their successors) was a feeling for craftsmanship (as opposed to unadulterated self-expression), and this ensured an astonishing degree of accomplishment from the start. Such influences as were detectable in the early work of these poets were on the whole salutary—Larkin rather than Dylan Thomas, MacNeice rather than W. R. Rodgers—and soon diminished, in any case, as the poets' individual voices gained in strength. Heaney, for example, becomes more complex and allusive with every volume: to chart his progress from *Death of a Naturalist* (1966) to *Seeing Things* (1991) is to think in terms of the actual journey he made from countrified Castledawson in Co. Derry to Oxford and Harvard, where he has been a professor—but with nothing discarded, nothing left behind. With Heaney, it is always a case of accretion, not elimination.

Longley and Mahon—both born in Belfast, both products of Trinity College, Dublin—showed their mastery of urbane poetic strategies from the word go. Mahon's bleak subject-matter, his visions of dereliction and detri-tus, is transfigured by lyricism and wit; he came out quickly, and from a cosmopolitan standpoint, as a strong critic of the warped element in North-ern Irish life, while not being entirely unsusceptible to the lure of the purely local: 'Portrush, Portstewart, Portballintrae | *Un beau pays mal habité.*' Mahon's single best-known poem is his 'Disused Shed in Co. Wexford' (from the 1975 collection *The Snow Party*)—a shed, incidentally, originally located in the grounds of the burnt-out hotel in the novel *Troubles* (1971) by J. G.

Farrell, to whom the poem is dedicated (Irish writing discloses many such instances of connection and cross-fertilization). Something about the 'Disused Shed'—its focus on 'mushrooms | crowd[ing] to a keyhole', perhaps, or 'lost people' (those lost in history or through atrocity, pleading to be delivered from inarticulacy), struck a chord with poetry readers.

Longley's 'Wounds' (from *An Exploded View*, 1973), though less well known, produced a similar effect, with its potent juxtaposition whereby the violence of the First World War is brought hard up against the dingier violence of present-day Belfast. As far as Longley's more recent work is concerned, it is hard to think of anything more lyrical or versatile than 'The Linen Industry', for example, with its evocative opening lines ('Pulling up flax after the blue flowers have fallen | And laying our handfuls in the peaty water'); or more electrifying than 'The Butchers', in which the terrorist 'butchers' of the Shankill Road are filtered through Homer.

James Simmons (b. 1933) has always taken things more easily (though he is as astute a social critic as any of his peers). His aim is to write in as relaxed a mode as possible. Virtue, as far as Simmons is concerned, resides first in an ability to see things for what they are; and then, by and large, to tolerate them. He is an opponent of euphemism, aloofness, and affectation. His effects are often, but not always felicitous: a pamphlet, for example, provokingly titled 'Sex and Rectitude' (1993), is more wilful than judicious in its treatment of a harrowing subject (the end of a marriage conjoined with the lynching of two soldiers in West Belfast). However, Simmons brought a new directness and demotic vigour to Irish poetry ('Our youth was gay but rough, | Much drink and copulation'), at a time when these qualities assumed all the force of a rallying call.

It is a far cry, indeed, from the neurotic demotic of a poet like 'Padraic Fiacc', say, all jagged edges and hysterical abbreviation, back streets and boneyards and unfortunates lying all over the place in blood, piss, pus, and slime. This is not social criticism, but social melodrama. Fiacc, born Joe O'Connor in 1924, has his admirers, those who find merit in lines such as these: 'Will the wound ever close | On the boy of ten | Far out in | The drowning man | Has a deep | Rooted bad dream.'

Fiacc confronts the 'Troubles' head-on, and this has won him acclaim from those who believe it is salutary to call a bullet-mangled body a bullet-mangled body, and leave it at that. It is one option open to chroniclers of the Ulster affray, but not the most subtle or illuminating. You need an idiosyncratic approach like Paul Muldoon's ('There's more to living in this country | Than stars and horses, pigs and trees, | Not that you'd guess it from your poems'), or Paulin's abrasive eloquence, to do full justice to the topic.

Or even the unflinching steadiness of a poet like John Hewitt. Hewitt, born in Belfast in 1907, is an upholder of decency and order, planter integrity and regional patriotism:

> I take my stand by the Ulster names,
> each clean hard name like a weathered stone;
> Tyrella, Rostrevor are flickering flames:
> the names I mean are the Moy, Malone,
> Strabane, Slieve Gullion and Portglenone.

This was written in the early 1950s; it needs to be read with the 'Postscript' of 1984 to get the sharpest flavour from its innocent enumeration of cherished localities. From a 'Troubles' vantage-point, the listed place-names take on a different connotation and effect, 'summoning pity, anger and despair, | by grief of kin, by hate of murderous men | till the whole tarnished map is stained and torn, | not to be read as pastoral again'.

In one of his poems, Tom Paulin comes up with the phrase 'this local stir' to clarify an aesthetic practice that owes a good deal to a sense of continuity and local singularity. Hewitt and Heaney 'trace us back | to the Rhyming Weavers'; that is, they see themselves to some degree as existing within a tradition peculiar to the North of Ireland but without embracing any of the restrictions this implies. 'The Rhyming Weavers' (Hewitt's title for a selection of verses by some eighteenth- and nineteenth-century artisan poets of Antrim and Down, which he edited) represent an aspect of social and political history on which the aesthetics of Hewitt and Heaney, and of Paulin himself, can converge. Radicals, Republicans, United Irishmen, or Irish Luddites—these self-taught versifiers and social critics were egalitarians to a man, and as such attractive to Irish left-wing authors of the late twentieth century on the look-out for literary precursors untainted by sectarianism.

Paulin's appropriation of these and other 'Lagan Jacobins' forms the dominant motif for his collection *Liberty Tree* (1983):

> Memory is a moist seed
> And a praise here, for they live,
> Those linen saints, lithe radicals
> In the bottled light
> Of this limewashed shrine.
> Hardly a schoolroom remembers
> Their obstinate rebellion

Liberty Tree bears out Paul Muldoon's assertion that 'history's a twisted root, | with art its small, translucent fruit | and never the other way round'—

that 'art' evaporates if it is pressed into political service and that this is
something to be pondered in a time of crisis, whether the crisis is precipit-
ated by Franco, Hitler, or misrule in Northern Ireland.

But what of misrule in the South, the gauche State with its Catholic
ideology, its censorship and anti-feminism, and its bourgeois ethic geared
to discomfit the fosterers of Irish spirituality? Southern Ireland does not lack
its social critics, either. As Thomas McCarthy (b. 1954) writes in the poem
'Returning to De Valera's Cottage' (in *The Sorrow Garden*, 1981), 'We kicked
the heap of weeds | with our heels and cursed the narrowness of the path.'
And Paul Durcan (b. 1944), in the title poem of his collection *Going Home
to Russia* (1987), lists a few of the things he is glad to see the back of:
'Goodbye to the conscientious politicians of Ireland . . . Goodbye to the
penniless, homeless, trouserless politicians | Goodbye to the pastoral liber-
als and the chic gombeens.' Durcan is an inspired commentator on social
matters, whose hallmark is an amused amazement at the oddity and banality of Irish life. Neither his garrulous, foot-off-the-ground approach, however, nor his instinct for ingenuity, nor his irrepressible comic vision,
undermines the essential seriousness of his purpose, which is to deride—
where necessary—and irradiate the realities of the day. Durcan's latest
collection, *A Snail in my Prime* (1993), puts the emphasis on personal rather
than social matters, as well as showing a new, attractive gravity and an
enticing strangeness.

Durcan's more characteristic ease of manner and jokiness have sometimes proved a dangerous example for poets less resourceful than himself.
Rita Ann Higgins and Julie O'Callaghan, for example—both exponents of
the facile feminist vernacular mode—go in for a very watered-down Durcan-
esque wryness: 'Ya gotta garnish your recipes. | Cut out pictures from
magazines | Like *McCall's* or *Family Circle* | and always make your dishes
| look like in the photographs.'

The recognition of anti-feminism as a social abuse cried out for, and has
received, more vigorous treatment in literature. *A Life of her Own*, Maeve
Kelly's title for a collection of stories published in 1980, lays claim to a basic
right that took a long time to emerge. These particular stories are 'traditional', that is countrified, to the extent of being peopled by rural women
who wear men's boots and carry buckets of pigswill.

At the same time, however, the urban shift in Irish writing was becoming more and more apparent. A cosmopolitan assurance shines through all
the work of Julia O'Faolain, for example, whether she is writing about
medieval nuns or modern Ireland—*No Country for Young Men* (1980) is an
ambitious novel about political violence and the recovery of the past, moving

between 1921 and 1979. Eavan Boland (b. 1944), another Dubliner, is a poet exceptionally alert to the 'simplified images of women in Irish poetry', and the need for writers of the present to repudiate them—indeed, if they are women, to make the leap from emblem to executant, and speak for themselves. The revisionist impulse that revolutionized Irish historiography in the 1960s was extended to cover (among other things) the past treatment of women in literature, and of literary women: both fine, even if the practice has led to the over-rating of authors such as Kate O'Brien. Irish feminists, indeed, have found plenty to cheer, as well as agitate, them.

As so much has changed in Irish social life over the last thirty-odd years, resulting in considerable loss as well as gain, the tendency to look back—for whatever purpose—has found proliferating outlets, from the unadorned memoir to the more complicated act of retrieval, or lament. For straightforward social detail, no one has done better than Florence Mary McDowell in her accounts of growing up in an Antrim mill village in the 1890s—*Other Days around Me* (1966) and *Roses and Rainbows* (1972)—which contain much information about what country people ate around the turn of the century, how their houses were furnished, and how they got about.

Moving along the line of increasing density, we eventually come, via the Dalkey playwright Hugh Leonard's *Home by Night* (1979) and Max Wright's *Told in Gath* (1990), to Denis Donoghue's *Warrenpoint* (1991), a memoir whose charm resides in its clarity of expression and idiosyncratic approach—Donoghue keeps inviting other authors into his vicinity for purposes of comparison, or to amplify or endorse some perception of his own. His by now famous observation that, as a child in a Northern Catholic family, 'A Protestant was as alien to me as a Muslim', points up the full horror of sectarian segregation, and the consequent creation of a Protestant or a Catholic *mentality*. To get the other side of the picture, it is only necessary to look at the equally odd upbringing experienced in an equally fanatical community by a young Plymouth Brother at the same period. Going to the cinema for the first time as a grammar schoolboy, Max Wright found it 'as different and as awful as a Roman Catholic church'.

In an early poem by Seamus Heaney, the exiled Joyce is glimpsed indulging his faculty for recall: 'Blinding in Paris, for his party-piece | Joyce named the shops along O'Connell Street.' Such ineradicable attachment to one's starting-place is the subject of Ciaran Carson's very pointed and quizzical poem 'The Exiles' Club', in which a group of Irish-Australians reconstruct the Falls Road. Carson's striking series of Belfast poems—starting with a riot squad and ending with a metaphorical snowfall—joins with Anne Devlin's story 'Naming the Names' (1986) in expressing complicated feelings about the vanished Falls. The story repeats the street names like a shibboleth: 'Once more they came back for the names, and I began: Abyssinia, Alma, Balaclava, Balkan, Belgrade, Bosnia, naming the names: empty and broken and beaten places. I know no others.'

Carson's superb poem 'Hamlet', in which past is fused with present, Ireland with England, loss with reclamation, is lucidly committed to the integrity of its evocations:

> The sleeve of Raglan Street has been unravelled; the helmet of Balaclava
> Is torn away from the mouth. The dim glow of Garnet has gone out
> And with it all but the memory of where I lived. I, too, heard the ghost:
> A roulette trickle, or the hesitant annunciation of a downpour, ricocheting
> Off the window; a goods train shunting distantly into a siding
> Then groaning to a halt; the rainy cries of children after dusk.

But the poem also invokes other realities: a booby-trapped corpse, with accompanying bomb-disposal expert.

Realities of the day are the thing. In his introduction to the *Picador Book of Contemporary Irish Writing* (1993), Dermot Bolger (b. 1959) is all for admitting the contemporary world into Irish literature, while believing strongly that 'tradition' needs to be reinvented, not revived. The time has come, Bolger holds, to exclude priests, donkeys, pure peasant lasses, and repression, and to take account of such facts of life as the conversion of Dublin, by the mid-1980s, into the heroin capital of Europe.

Bolger is also in favour of allotting a place in literature to Dublin's post-war housing estates. It is not only Roddy Doyle (b. 1958) who has latched onto the dramatic (and demotic) possibilities of these anarchic agglomerations, all low behaviour and unquenchable spirit. But whereas Doyle's achievement is to coat chicanery, boorishness, squalor, and so on with the thickest possible overlay of charm, charm is the last quality Bolger has in his sights. One of his objectives, exemplified in his novel *The Journey Home* (1990), is to point up the shocking state of Ireland, and to this end, he enlists every possible enormity: the book is full of characters injecting themselves with drugs, committing suicide in lavatory cubicles, suffering exploitation and violence, becoming twisted and hopeless. And the scene of these miseries is a devastated city, where the hero of the novel watches dawn breaking 'over the tombstones in the cemetery across the carriageway'. At his best, Bolger is a forceful social critic, but his portrayal might have been fashioned with greater sharpness, less bludgeoning.

Patrick McCabe's (b. 1955) novel *Carn* (1989) charts the effects of social change on an archetypal Southern Irish town, not far from the border. The 1960s have brought prosperity of a kind, and bungalows, dance halls, and

housing estates fill the empty spaces. With the 1970s, however, and a recession, the spirit is knocked out of Carn. The spectre of emigration rises up
again. Situated where it is, the town's vicissitudes are complicated by neo-
Republicanism. Support for the IRA is viewed first in one light, then in
another. Northern activists cross the border with ease, and local sympathiz-
ers are roped in to lend a hand with intimidation.

It is hard to keep terrorism out of contemporary Irish writing, though
some authors have managed it. One of these is John Banville, who is more
interested in mythological or scientific resonances, as in *Mefisto* (1986), or in
confronting chaos and imposing some kind of order on it. One consequence
of the concern with terrorism perhaps has been the development of the
thriller. Over the last quarter of a century a spate of thrillers has poured
out, most of them of very inferior quality. Indeed, the endless ineptitude of
these works—usually set in a characterless city called Belfast, and featuring
IRA godfathers, brutality, and tormented undercover agents—has provoked
impatience with the terrorist theme. Fiction writers have proved less adept
than poets when it comes to suggesting the complexities of the whole issue,
though Brian Moore, as one might expect, raised the Belfast thriller to a
new level of tension and expertise in his *Lies of Silence* (1992). Yet even this
novel does not, in Seamus Heaney's words, 'set the darkness echoing'.

In an interview a few years ago, Benedict Kiely (b. 1919) put his finger
on one of the insidious effects of continuous terrorism: 'Every city and
every town has its own pattern and rhythm, and that would seem to be
destroyed in Belfast.' His own novella *Proxopera* (1977) had already adum-
brated the idea of distortion and pollution in Irish life. 'Proxopera' is a word
coined by Kiely to denote the terrorist operation carried out by proxy—
'Proxopera for gallant Irish patriots fighting imaginary empires by murdering the neighbours'—and in the book he has exchanged his usual ebullience
for a grimmer, more biting style. It is set in Co. Tyrone and concerns a
retired schoolmaster, a Mr Binchey, who finds himself sitting at the wheel
of a car 'bearing death and ruin to the town he loves'. The car is loaded
with a bomb in a creamery can, and Mr Binchey is driving it because his
son, daughter-in-law, and grandchildren are in the hands of gunmen. Clearly,
some virtue has gone out of a world in which such coercion is commonplace. On his enforced mission of destruction, Mr Binchey thinks back to a
time when a creamery can was a harmless, even a lovely object; and this
is somehow the most morose and bitterest thought of all.

Over the last twenty-odd years, there has been a renewed interest in
Irish-language poetry, and some of Ireland's most significant reclamations
and renunciations have had to do with the language issue. We have, for

example, Thomas Kinsella's translations of poems assembled in a dual-language anthology called *An Duanaire: Poems of the Dispossessed 1600–1900* (1981). During the three centuries covered in this book, the destruction of Gaelic Ireland was deplored even as it was taking place, in the mordant verses of poets like O Bruadair and O Rathaille, and also in the more mellifluous *aislingí*, or 'vision poems', which proliferated during the eighteenth century.

All this is part of the heritage of every Irish writer, even if it is only available to some of them through the medium of translation, and even if—as many commentators have pointed out—to trace the fortunes of the language is to unfold a story of discontinuity and disuse. It has never died out completely, but its survival has been precarious. Breandán O hEithir, for example, wrote in the 1940s of being fed up with the whole 'cottage-in-the-corner-of-the-glen' fixation in Gaelic fiction, and was consequently exhilarated when Máirtín O Cadhain's great comic novel of 1949, *Cré na Cille* ('Churchyard Clay'), was published. In this, half the characters are already dead and buried—like the Irish language itself throughout the greater part of the country—but nonetheless capable of malice, entertainment, and a vigorous turn of speech.

The poet Máirtín O Direain (1910–88) likewise found himself somewhat at sea, by his own account, before his first collection came out in 1942. 'We were greatly handicapped by having no proper models,' he wrote; no one writing in Irish had hit on a means of 'tackling contemporary problems in contemporary style'. Acknowledging the deficiency, however, opened up all kinds of possibilities. Ever since, poets and other writers in Irish have been at pains to show themselves no less amenable to the avant-garde than anyone else. One need only turn to recent dual-language anthologies such as *An Tonn Gheal* ('The Bright Wave') or *An Crann Faoi Bláth* ('The Flowering Tree') to see that no poetic device of the present, from ellipsis to paradox, has passed them by.

In 1975 the Limerick poet Michael Hartnett (b. 1941) made a decision to turn his back on English. His work in Irish, however, has become increasingly close-textured and intense; one misses the sharp wit and astringency of the poem in which he announced the crucial decision, 'A Farewell to English', with its moments of strong evocation: itinerant seventeenth-century poets, for example, in 'sugán belts and long black coats | with big ashplants and half-sacks | of rags and bacon on their backs'. Hartnett is also the usual translator into English of Nuala Ní Dhomhnaill (b. 1952), who has claimed the freedom to be as domestic, erotic, and enigmatic as her Northern contemporary Medbh McGuckian (who writes in English).

It was Paul Muldoon, however, who translated Ní Dhomhnaill's poem 'Ceist na Teangan' ('The Language Issue'), which begins 'I place my hope on the water | in this little boat | of the language', and goes on to envisage the delicate construction of iris leaves and bitumen ending up in the lap of 'some Pharaoh's daughter'. This is a small poetic conceit whose optimism does not seem ill-founded. What Ní Dhomhnaill and others are showing is that the Irish language affords plenty of scope for exuberance, word-play, contemporary preoccupations, and a special kind of Irish urbanity.

FURTHER READING

Andrews, Elmer (ed.), *Contemporary Irish Poetry* (London, 1992).
Cahalan, James M., *The Irish Novel* (Boston, 1988).
Dawe, G., and Foster, J. W. (eds.), *The Poet's Place* (Belfast, 1991).
Donoghue, Denis, *We Irish* (Brighton, 1986).
Foster, John Wilson, *Forces and Themes in Ulster Fiction* (Dublin, 1974).
Johnson, Dillon, *Irish Poetry after Joyce* (Bloomington, Ind., 1985).

15

ISRAEL

BRYAN CHEYETTE

IN a typical contribution to the Hebrew Writers' Association conference in 1968, Hayim Hazaz (1893–1972), a doyen of Hebrew literature, voiced his dissatisfaction with contemporary Israeli writing: 'It goes without saying that Israeli literature should be a responsible literature . . . Above all, books shouldn't be mere books, writers shouldn't be anonymous, shouldn't be lukewarm, comfortable people . . . they should be heroes of a national struggle, of a class-war, of culture; people of conviction and responsibility.' Hazaz's own contrived, overly rhetorical fiction, especially his novels of ideas, often bears out this programmatic statement, and contrasts unfavourably with the enigmatic modernism of his contemporary S. Y. Agnon (1888–1970). Agnon won the Nobel Prize for literature in 1966 for an *œuvre* which, in its use of parables and its pervasive if unexplained *Angst*, is closely akin to Kafka. Much of Agnon's fiction was published posthumously and, because of this, has continued to influence a good deal of contemporary Israeli literature.

Although somewhat anachronistic by 1968, Hazaz's call to arms none the less captured something of the heroic spirit of the founding 'Generation of 1948', whose *engagé* fiction was an uncomplicated aspect of Jewish nation-building. By the time the State of Israel was founded, in 1948, many Hebrew writers—whose parents had often, like Hazaz, been born in Eastern Europe—had plainly transported Soviet Socialist Realism into the Middle East. Their literature was, above all, a way of advancing the embryonic Jewish State by documenting the pioneering achievements of themselves and their parents in rural Palestine. Their readership was small, with only 700,000 Hebrew-speakers in 1948, but their impact on subsequent generations of Hebrew writers and readers was immense.

Unlike what had been written previously in Galicia and Russia, much of this literature denigrated the Diaspora, which in turn helped to reinforce a sense of 'normalization' in the new-born State of Israel. Instead of Diaspora values, these writers tended to promote the 'Canaanite' idea of a new

Hebrew nation based on the life-affirming qualities of the local landscape. Working on the land, it was argued, would reshape a Jewish future with little reference to an 'abnormal' Jewish past. As handmaidens to the nascent State, these determinedly parochial 'sabra' (or native) writers promised a future of absolute fulfilment, where ideals and realities would merge. By 1968, as the defensive tone of the quotation from Hazaz indicates, there was a strong reaction against such an overbearingly prescriptive and unapologetically domestic literature. Indeed, the move away from the self-satisfied certainties of the 'revolutionary' founding generation can be said to characterize Israeli literature since the 1960s.

By 1970 the influential critic Gershon Shaked was promoting what he called a radical 'new wave' in Hebrew literature. This 'new wave', publishing mainly in the 1960s, challenged the strongly held convictions of the previous generation of writers, with its cathartic ideal of secular redemption. I shall concentrate initially on these 'new wave' writers, who include Yehuda Amichai (b. 1924), Aharon Appelfeld (b. 1932), Amalia Kahana-Carmon (b. 1930), Amos Oz (b. 1939), and A. B. Yehoshua (b. 1936). These authors, with the lamentable exception of Kahana-Carmon, have deservedly achieved a wide readership in translation and are rightly considered to be among the most important writers in Israel today.

Oz and Yehoshua are often coupled together as the *enfants terribles* of their generation. Both began publishing self-consciously symbolic short stories in the late 1950s and 1960s in which they aspired to establish the limits of the national rebirth and the flaws inherent in any such collective achievement that fails to alter the rudimentary conditions of human existence. Both were born in Jerusalem, although Oz moved to a kibbutz when he was 15 and Yehoshua to the city of Haifa in his late twenties. Whereas Oz has described the role of the Israeli novelist as being akin to that of a witch-doctor—exorcizing the demons of his tribe—Yehoshua speaks of himself as a communal psychotherapist exposing the repressed fears of the nation. Instead of peopling their fiction with characters living at the supposed centre of national life, they have looked to the margins, for displaced outsiders whose inner lives have remained untouched by synthetic notions of progress. Above all, both writers exemplify a modernist reaction to the upstanding social realism of an earlier generation—a reaction which took place in Israel half a century after the equivalent response in Europe and America.

The stories in *Where the Jackals Howl* (1965), Oz's début collection, are set in a mythical kibbutz which lies in a plain surrounded by mountains. Beyond the artificial lights and barbed wire, marauding jackals symbolize those bestial powers which threaten the façade of order and decency preserved in these islands of assumed civilization. This sense of fear and menace, which is the prevailing mood of Oz's early fiction, transcends the obvious geopolitical realities of Israel's precarious foothold in the Middle East. His central characters are, in fact, most likely to be strangely attracted to the dark and terrifying forces which encircle the kibbutz. The title of Oz's first full-length work of fiction, *Elsewhere, Perhaps* (1966), evokes a vital presence beyond the bounds of kibbutz life which is both a deeply felt craving and a continual refrain in the novel. This theme is taken up again in *A Perfect Peace* (1982), which contrasts Yonatan Lifshitz's longing to leave his kibbutz with the idealistic Azariah Gitlin, who wishes to contribute to this seemingly enlightened project.

Such symbolic differences have become the staple of Oz's fiction. The antagonism between fathers and sons is especially fierce in his novels as such Oedipal rivalry is perceived to be a conflict in which the father-figures give birth not merely to their offspring but also to the State. His second novel, *My Michael* (1968), an instant best-seller in Israel, transfers a claustrophobic sense of entrapment away from kibbutz life to the city of Jerusalem, which is Oz's other major setting. This outstanding novel is his most achieved depiction of an unhappy marriage, representing a larger national divide, memorably articulated in the passionate first-person narration of Hannah Gonen. Hannah thinks of Jerusalem as a 'landscape pregnant with suppressed violence' and, like Oz's kibbutzniks, she becomes increasingly attracted to the unexplored 'dark' regions. Her intense fantasies revolve particularly around a set of Arab twins whom she knew in her youth. The novel concludes with one of her recurrent visions of these twins—coupled with the wail of a jackal—as they are about to launch a guerrilla raid in Israel. Hannah sees their movements as 'a hushed run, a caress full of yearning' and becomes completely enraptured by these all too apparent forces of destruction.

By the end of *My Michael*, Hannah's main 'reality' is her fantasy-world, which serves as an indictment of the rationality and calm of her husband Michael. He is a geologist concerned with studying the 'volcanic forces' active beneath the world's surface, a profession deftly symbolizing those unconscious elements which are excluded from the all-encompassing convictions of Oz's fatherly nation-builders. This reconciliation of opposites, or incorporation of the 'other' into the Israeli national consciousness, has become the main preoccupation of Oz's later fiction. His epistolary novel *Black Box* (1987) contains a polyphony of discordant voices and lacks, significantly, any central narrator, just as there are radically antagonistic voices to be heard also in his collection of essays *In the Land of Israel* (1983). His most recent fiction, however, is characterized by rather predictable, monomaniacal central figures such as Yoel Ravid in *To Know a Woman* (1989), or the eponymous anti-hero in *Fima: A Novel* (1991), who embody respectively either the limits of masculine rationality or the unreality of messianic thinking. In both cases, the lack of any fertile inner life gives rise either to arid certainties or to hopeless fanaticism.

Yehoshua's earliest stories, in contrast to those of Oz, were almost wholly allegorical. They broke entirely with the tenets of the Generation of 1948 and deliberately left out any identifiable Israeli reality. In this, they were closest to the fiction of Agnon or Aharon Appelfeld. At the same time, Yehoshua's first collection of fables, published in 1962, was probably over-influenced by his four-year stay as a young man in the Paris of Jean-Paul Sartre and Albert Camus. In these stories he is especially concerned with the existential plight of those whose sense of self is bound up with the need to live in the shadow of an impending disaster. Thus, in the best of them, 'The Yatir Evening Express' (1959), the inhabitants of a remote mountain village collaborate to derail an express train so that they can, for a short while, have some contact with the outside world. At the point of destruction, amid the screams of the dying and the wounded, the villagers achieve a kind of transcendence and the central figure of the story makes love to the woman who has instigated the catastrophe. Human contact is attained by a dionysiac release which goes beyond the artificial structures of society.

Yehoshua's next volume of stories, *Facing the Forests* (1968), is a remarkably accomplished mixture of the naturalism and symbolism characteristic of his later writing. One story concerns a nameless husband who ends up slumped on the roadway, contemplating his disaffected wife's return in her car to crush him. Another pathological male figure considers murdering his ex-lover's child so that he will once again share her life. Such is the price that Yehoshua's irredeemably alienated protagonists must pay to go beyond the gulf of estrangement. In the exemplary title story of this collection, the neurotic inability to make contact with others—outside a murderous context—is given a compelling political dimension. 'Facing the Forests' concerns an *Angst*-ridden graduate student who communicates with an Arab mute by helping him to burn down a forest planted by the Jewish National Fund on the site, he learns, of an abandoned Palestinian village. The destruction of the forest is both a radical critique of the founding generation, who repressed the Arab 'other' in their midst, and a broader plea that the unhealthy 'silences' at the heart of Israeli society be addressed. Yehoshua's deceptively simple prose is designed to articulate an unconscious world which invariably floats to the surface in his expressionistic fiction. His stories and novellas have been republished in translation in one volume, *The Continuing Silence of a Poet: The Collected Stories of A. B. Yehoshua* (1988), an event rightly compared in importance with the publication in translation of Agnon's *Twenty-One Stories* (1970).

Unlike Oz, Yehoshua has established his reputation as one of Israel's pre-eminent writers with his short fiction. His first two novels, *The Lover* (1977) and *A Late Divorce* (1982), both develop the bleak interior landscapes of his earlier work. As with Oz's *Black Box*, they are constructed around a series of distinct narrative voices intended to embody a fragmentary and decentred Israeli society. By the time of *Five Seasons* (1987) and *Mr Mani* (1990), however, Yehoshua, like Oz, had moved away from his previous commitment to symbolism and fantasy and instead embraced a blend of social and psychological realism situated in a more extensive historical context. In *Mr Mani* the multiplicity of perspectives in his earlier work has been augmented by five historically specific but interrelated monologues; while in *Five Seasons* Molkho's coming to terms with his wife's death is similarly composed around five disparate periods and locations. Yehoshua's world is, for the most part, more intensely focused than that of Oz and he has recently added a considerable breadth of setting to the depth of his characterization.

Aharon Appelfeld is foremost among those who, like Yehoshua at his best, have added fruitfully to the strand of Hebrew modernism inspired by Kafka and Agnon. Born in Romania, he was sent to a concentration camp at the age of 8, from which he escaped and spent the next three years hiding in the Ukrainian backwoods before being rescued by the Red Army. His mother was killed by the Nazis and he was subsequently reunited with his father in Israel in 1960.

These biographical details hardly need to be borne in mind, however, when reading Appelfeld's contemplative, haunting novels which, above all, refuse to make easy connections or straightforward narratives out of his childhood experiences. His biography is, as he has repeatedly stated, an 'unbelievable story' and the uncommon restraint of his fiction, at its most consummate, engulfs the past not in historical explanation but in the profound silence of someone who is obliged to say that which can barely be said. No Hebrew writer before or since has captured so plangently the lives truncated by the Holocaust. His stories of the 1960s, still largely untranslated, were some of the first rigorously to challenge the facile catharsis of a health-giving Zionism, which refused to accept that there were historical traumas that could not be 'normalized' by the Jewish State.

Appelfeld's Hebrew prose is the self-conscious product of someone who learned his adopted tongue only as a teenager. He deliberately writes as an outsider, paring his language to the bone to avoid the clutter of local allusions. For this reason, he is uniformly regarded as the most European of Israeli writers, one whose deliberately skewed vision corresponds to the fate of those who have become the flotsam and jetsam of history. His best-known longer fiction, published in the 1970s, established the victims of anti-Semitism—rather than the heroic Israeli 'sabra'—as an enduring concern of Hebrew literature. *Badenheim 1939* (1974), which brought him an international readership, enacts the painful alienation of a minutely observed European Jewry in the 1930s, desperately trying to find a rational *modus vivendi* in a brutally irrational world. His masterpiece, *The Age of Wonders* (1978), begins with a child's-eye view of an assimilated Jewish family in a small Austrian town in the 1930s. Thirty years after the war, in book 2 of the novel, the boy, or his ghost, revisits his home town. The precarious link between the first-person narrator of book 1 and the figure of Bruno in book 2 crystallizes the fraught relationship that Appelfeld has with his horrendous past. The impossibility of adequately capturing his 'unbelievable' history and the concomitant need to relive it in his fiction is at the heart of his poetic later novels. The best of these—*The Retreat* (1982), *Tzili* (1983), and *The Healer* (1985)—have all been widely translated.

It is a sign of the continued marginality of Amalia Kahana-Carmon in the largely male canon of Hebrew writing that surprisingly little of her work has been translated. Born in Tel Aviv, she is universally regarded, after the poet Leah Goldberg (1911–71), as Israel's most distinguished woman writer. Her intimate, nuanced fiction deliberately avoids the symbolic pretensions of her male counterparts, who aspire to represent either the pioneering glories, or the dark underside, of Jewish national revival. Kahana-Carmon's idiosyncratic style and her intense focus on the private have, from her earliest short fiction in the 1960s, been associated with the writing of Virginia Woolf, an association that she has explored ironically in both her fiction and her criticism. Much of her innovative prose technique, and her vivid depiction of the uncanny configurations that make up the ever-changing moods of her heroines, are taken from such early feminist modernists as Woolf, Katherine Mansfield, and Dorothy Richardson. Narrative incompletion, momentary connections with the 'other', and a fluid, often forlorn, woman's consciousness specifically relate her fiction to these earlier writers.

As with Virginia Woolf, Kahana-Carmon has been commonly accused by male critics of being merely a delicate or unconventional observer of intriguing minutiae rather than a grand commentator on life and death. Her response to this criticism has been to show both the necessity and the

impossibility of engaging as a woman with a society centred around romantic, masculine values. In an early story, 'N'ima Sassoon Writes Poems' (1966),
a schoolgirl craves a moment of intimacy with her teacher. Kahana-Carmon
portrays romantic love as an unrealizable instant of absolute revelation,
only to withdraw ironically from such a conventional view as the story
comes to a pointedly uncertain climax. N'ima Sassoon is destined to become a poet, whose subject is precisely her inability to speak in the received
language of Israeli society—which neatly prefigures Kahana-Carmon's own
gently subversive later fiction.

For the most part, the best Hebrew writers who began publishing in the
1960s and 1970s developed a poetic prose style which was in stark contrast
to the social realism of the 1948 Generation. Although he belongs chrono-
logically to that earlier generation, Yehuda Amichai's response to their
documentary-like fiction and verse was one of a free-wheeling Surrealism.
He published his first two, prize-winning, volumes of poetry before the
1960s, but was already writing prose that helped subsequently to define the
hybrid forms and experimentation of contemporary Israeli fiction.

Amichai's first and only collection of short stories, *The World Is a Room
and Other Stories* (1961), and his important novel *Not of This Time, Not of This
Place* (1963), both had a substantial impact on a younger generation of
Israeli prose writers. The stories have been likened to random excerpts
from a diary as they conspicuously lack any reference to a coherent reality
outside the determining but nebulous consciousness of the narrator. When
describing the War of Independence in 'The Battle for the Hill', for instance,
Amichai deliberately blurs the boundaries between civilian and army life in
such a way that the language of love becomes irrevocably bound up with
that of war. In another characteristic story, 'The Times my Father Died', a
child's awareness of the world is used to demonstrate the irredeemable gulf
between his father's stable, Orthodox past and an insecure, unbelieving
present.

This story echoes Amichai's momentous novel *Not of This Time, Not of
This Place*, which takes as its theme the dislocation of a young Israeli from
his German-Jewish past. In 1936, at the age of 12, Amichai himself left
Germany with his devoutly Jewish family for Palestine and settled in Jerusalem, and his complex, experimental novel has a divided central figure
who is simultaneously both in Israel and in pre-war Germany. This dual
consciousness enabled other Hebrew writers, for the first time, to address in
a mature and textually sophisticated manner the subject of the Holocaust
and Israel's complex relationship to Jewish victimhood.

Since 1971 Amichai has concentrated almost entirely on his poetry and he
is now universally regarded as Israel's most eminent poet. An understanding

of his prose is the necessary backdrop, however, to the obsessive pre-occupations of his poetry. In both poetry and prose, Amichai's abiding concerns and extravagant use of metaphor revolve around the intermingling of the sacred and the profane, around a son's Oedipal flight from an Orthodox Jewish father, and the creation of an elegiac and increasingly besieged persona. The desperate need to retain or recover a sense of personal integrity in a world beset by wars and bloodshed remains, above all, at the heart of Amichai's loosely structured and more embittered later verse. He pays explicit homage to T. S. Eliot, Dylan Thomas, and W. H. Auden and his war poetry has been rightly compared to Wilfred Owen's. As with many 'new wave' writers, he moves anxiously from expressing a nation's unconscious—'When I was young, the whole country was young. And my father | was everyone's father'—to capturing a momentary sense of self that lies beyond words.

Israeli poetry, as Amichai demonstrates, has followed the path of the Israeli novel in reworking the prevalent norms of the founding generation of the Jewish State. Natan Zach (b. 1930), above all, has formulated in his essays and his verse an influential new poetics, in opposition to the more ideologically motivated figures of Natan Alterman (1910–70) and Avraham Shlonski (1900–73), who dominated Israeli poetry up until the 1960s. Zach, who was closely followed by Amichai and David Avidan (b. 1934), led the way in incorporating a Hebrew vernacular and slang into his poetry, thus opening it up to the modern world. His firm grounding in English and German literature meant that his deceptive lucidity had a universal appeal, in contrast to the more ingrained concerns of an earlier generation. Among other poets, two Holocaust survivors, Abba Kovner (1918–88) and Dan Pagis (1930–86), are both well known in translation, mainly through their exceptionally moving and meticulous autobiographical verse. After Amichai, T. Carmi (b. 1925) is probably the most internationally recognized Israeli poet. His terse, indirect poetry, which is always grave and impersonal, contrasts with the more expansive and disputatious writing of Amichai.

In recent years, the fragmentation and displacement of the founding myths of Israeli society have continued apace in the work of an impressive number of writers. Two authors, in particular, exemplify this sustained demythologization. In their very different ways, Yaakov Shabtai (1934–81) and Yoram Kaniuk (b. 1930) have both published novels which no longer simply undermine the idea of a Jewish national centre; they write as if such a centre never really existed. Both authors were born in Tel Aviv but they concentrate on the margins of experience to the extent that in their fiction even this most Israeli of cities becomes unreal.

Before his untimely death, Shabtai published *Past Continuous* (1977), which is widely regarded as the most important of all Israeli novels. This astonishing, Proustian work, which consists of a single extended paragraph in the Hebrew (but not in the translation), so decentres its characters and the city of Tel Aviv that they appear to be constantly on the verge of disintegration. Rather than attempting to locate a single national unconscious, like Oz and Yehoshua, *Past Continuous* revolves around three disparate but ostensibly familiar individuals who are relentlessly differentiated in an endlessly variable social setting. As Shabtai's three central figures self-destruct, the novel's hypnotic narrative refuses to settle on any one of them, thus leaving little behind, apart from the book's prodigious formal achievement, to withstand the 'madness' of contemporary Israeli society.

Since the early 1960s, Kaniuk has published a steady stream of iconoclastic and grotesque novels. Taken as a whole, his *œuvre* offers a series of jagged, indigestible images of a society where uncertainty has become the dominant condition. Unlike Shabtai, who took the formal inventiveness of 'new wave' writing to its limits, Kaniuk has refused to be confined by high culture and has, like many of his contemporaries, combined the old conventions of *belles-lettres* with popular cultural forms, such as the detective novel or journalistic satire. A typical early novel, *Himmo, King of Jerusalem* (1962), blends commonplace romanticism with an almost Beckettian intensity to recount the love of a woman for the 'wonderful mouth' of a wounded soldier who has lost his arms and legs in battle. *His Daughter* (1987) recounts Miriam Krieger's suicide and her obsessive love for a young soldier who was accidentally killed before she was born. In this novel Kaniuk stresses the debilitating effects on its inhabitants of a country which belongs to what he calls the 'domain of death'. Like Shabtai in *Past Continuous*, he replaces the life-affirming, redemptive impulse of the Zionist dream with the 'smell and aura of death', an unknowable realm which unwittingly guides the actions of both writers' dislocated protagonists.

Since the late 1970s, the social realism of the 1948 Generation and the largely symbolist response of the 'new wave' writers have both been surpassed by a proliferation of literary innovators. This can be seen, for instance, in the enchanting 'magic realism' of Yehoshua Knaz (b. 1937), or the delicate historical dystopias of Yitzhak Ben-Ner (b. 1937), or the timeless Borgesian parables of Yitzhak Oren (b. 1918). The drama, too, has flourished in the person of Yehoshua Sobol (b. 1939), whose heretical plays *The Soul of a Jew* (1982) and *Ghetto* (1984) have been performed throughout the world. Both plays capture something of the passionate re-examination of the Jewish past, in relation to an iniquitous present, characteristic of contemporary Hebrew writing in general. Even though a good many novelists and poets, such as Amichai and A. B. Yehoshua, have written plays, the drama has not attained the heights of poetry or the novel.

Since the 1980s the most interesting Israeli literature no longer has pretensions to represent a single, unified nation. Virtually all contemporary writers have taken into account the inability of a polarized society to be encompassed within any one narrative. Groups and cultures hitherto thought of as 'other' in respect of the largely European, masculine norms of the Jewish State have begun increasingly to tell their own distinctive stories, and in a nuanced, vernacular Hebrew drastically at odds with past definitions of what it means, linguistically, to be an Israeli citizen. These examples of the 'other' include the Sephardi (non-European Jewish) fiction of Sami Michael (b. 1926) and the Palestinian plays, poetry, and fiction of Emile Habibi (b. 1919) and Anton Shammas (b. 1950)—all writers who have successfully challenged both the European hegemony of the Hebrew language and, by implication, the State of Israel.

A significant number of non-Hebrew-speaking Jewish writers, led by Philip Roth (b. 1933) and Clive Sinclair (b. 1948), have also engaged impressively with the State of Israel in their fiction and essays, while some Israeli writers, such as Simon Louvish (b. 1947), have published in a variety of languages outside Israel. With Shammas and Habibi writing in both Hebrew and Arabic, the notion that the Hebrew language should be confined exclusively to the Jewish people, or to the contentious borders of Israel, is under serious attack. Amos Oz summed up this feeling in his collection of essays *The Slopes of Lebanon* (1989), when he described himself as an 'exile in my own land'. There is, in other words, a growing crisis of confidence with regard to what exactly constitutes the proper subject-matter of Israeli writing. Women writers—Ruth Almog (b. 1936), Shulamit Hareven (b. 1931), and Shulamit Lapid (b. 1934)—have accentuated this predicament by assiduously challenging the previously dominant male canon and concerns of Hebrew literature, which is undergoing a profound crisis of identity.

This uncertainty has given rise to a genuinely open and varied literature equal, at its best, to anything produced in Israel in the past three decades. David Grossman (b. 1954) is undoubtedly the most gifted writer of the new generation. His exceptional books of reportage *The Yellow Wind* (1987) and *Sleeping on a Wire* (1992) have established him as an unflinching commentator on Jewish–Palestinian relations. His knowledge of both Hebrew and Arabic contrasts startlingly with the unpleasant parochialism of Yehoshua's *Between Right and Right* (1980) and Oz's more limited, though stimulating, *In the Land of Israel*.

Grossman's essays are at pains to break down what he calls the 'simple stories' that inform the Israel–Palestine conflict and, for this reason, his three novels all have a self-conscious story-teller as a central figure. In them, he replaces the 'simple stories' with magnificently diverse narratives that expose the dangerously reassuring myths by which one people justifies its rule over another. In his most recent novel, *The Book of Intimate Grammar* (1991), Grossman's scope is unusually circumscribed, however, as if he had concluded that his essays were the place for grand historical generalizations.

In contrast, his first novel, *The Smile of the Lamb* (1983), was the first major work of fiction to be primarily concerned with Israel's troubled presence in the West Bank and Gaza Strip. The four protagonists in this speak, initially, in their own compelling voices in apparently disconnected chapters: a bewildering shift between differing and competing stories that counters those in the Middle East who would wish their own convictions to dominate. The crude divide between warring peoples is replaced by a shared sense of loss, which finally unites Grossman's disparate characters. This structure was further developed in his outstanding second novel, *See Under: Love* (1986), which takes as its subject-matter the refusal of Israeli society to acknowledge the damage done to its national psyche by the Holocaust. This novel, too, is divided into four diverse chapters, ranging from a superbly achieved Israeli child's-eye view of the Holocaust, to a phantasmagoric evocation of the Polish-Jewish writer Bruno Schulz (see the Polish chapter in this *Guide*), and concluding with an unexpected encyclopaedic summary of the previous sections.

In this way Grossman intertwines history and fantasy to help us to see through the stale 'certainties' of the past. By the end of *See Under: Love*, his own narrative persona simply wishes 'for a man to live in this world from birth to death and know nothing of war'. As the 32-year-old Grossman had already seen four wars when this book was published, the naïvety of this sentiment is meant to shock. But while his fiction might well be shockingly avant-garde, his growing prominence at home and abroad indicates, above all, that he can reach a large audience. An average Israeli novel will sell around 20,000 copies and an average poetry collection 15,000 copies, an extremely high readership in a country that has only about 3.5 million proficient readers of Hebrew. Judging by the popularity even of experimental works, Israel needs more than ever the solace of literature.

FURTHER READING

Alter, Robert, *After the Tradition* (New York, 1969).

Fuchs, Esther, *Israeli Mythogynies: Women in Contemporary Hebrew Fiction* (New York, 1987).

Shaked, Gershon, *The Shadows Within: Essays on Modern Jewish Writers* (Philadelphia, 1987).

Sinclair, Clive, *Diaspora Blues: A View of Israel* (London, 1987).

Sonntag, Jacob (ed.), *New Writing from Israel* (London, 1976).

Yudkin, Leon, *Beyond Sequence: Current Israeli Fiction and its Context* (London, 1992).

16

ITALY

PETER HAINSWORTH

BETWEEN the late 1950s and the mid-1970s, Italy became a modern European country. The abruptness of the transition made itself felt particularly in the early 1960s, startling, perhaps traumatizing, most of the country's inhabitants, writers included. Most of those who were to be the significant names of the period were already well into their careers when the 'boom' or 'economic miracle' burst upon them. Some were already well known before the war. They now found themselves living through radical changes: the loss of the old peasant cultures, with their dialects and traditions, unconstrained urban expansion (especially in the north), rapid industrialization, the growth of consumerism and modern media. In short, the country went through a now familiar process of assimilation to modern economic and social patterns and structures.

For most of the 1960s and 1970s Italian writers were largely occupied with coming to terms with this revolution and the political turmoil surrounding it, confronting, dodging, interpreting, and reinterpreting what was happening, assessing and reassessing their own roles, and that of literature in general. In all this one thing was clear: the tradition of Italian letters—élitist, self-referential, linguistically and stylistically remote—in which they had grown up was undergoing a shake-up. There had been various attempts over the preceding century and a half to create a 'national-popular literature' (as the Marxist philosopher Gramsci called it). Whether or not that was still a real possibility in the 1960s, there were now more people actually speaking the national language (as opposed to dialect), there were more readers, and literature itself was turning into a marketable commodity, though for a while it seemed it might also be an instrument of revolution. The writer was pushed out from the study or literary café into the public eye and transformed into activist, pundit, commentator, star. Only in the 1980s would the generation who had dominated Italian literature since the war fade away, their younger contemporaries from the 1960s see the literary and political controversies subside, and a new generation appear who would find the situation more or less normal, if not natural.

One of the most serious efforts to break out of the ivory tower had been made in the immediate post-war years, when *impegno*, or political commitment, had been the rule and neo-realism the style that went with it. The aim was to create a literature, principally fiction, with popular appeal, which showed the reality of life in Italy for the unprivileged majority, and its underlying political and social imperatives. By the mid-1950s, *impegno* and neo-realism were both in trouble, however. Those writers who had not already done so left the Communist Party in 1956, in the wake of the invasion of Hungary, though a critical, leftish stance would remain the norm. Neo-realist fiction itself risked being nostalgic, schematic, and surreptitiously literary, in spite of its earthy pretensions, much as the film-makers with whom the novelists often collaborated tended to be poetic and romantic. The uneasy contradictions at work meant that most novels were in fact unapproachable for the mass of readers. At the same time many writers felt imprisoned by their realist chains and looked to other forms of expression, even when they wanted to write explicitly about modern Italy.

Neo-realism was not, however, the dead end it has often been said to be. The fiction of Vasco Pratolini (1913–91), for instance, centres on popular life in Florence. In 1955 he published what was easily taken as a Stalinist Socialist Realist novel: *Metello* is the story of a turn-of-the-century worker who comes to political consciousness and takes part in the then optimistic struggle for socialism. As an allegory of the 1950s, the novel is embarrassing. But it was only the first volume in a cycle of three novels on the twentieth century as experienced by the people of Florence, and as a historical novel it has considerable richness. The cycle itself is an unusually large-scale venture for a literature which has always favoured short novels and short stories. The second volume, the enormous *Lo scialo* ('Waste', 1960), is the only modern Italian novel which examines with any concreteness and depth the rise of Fascism in the 1920s and its first decade in power. In it Pratolini achieves a complex representation of dramatic events covering two decades; he makes his own political position clear, but his analysis is neither doctrinaire nor simple.

Other novelists, too, continued successfully in the neo-realist manner well beyond its official death in the mid-1950s. Carlo Cassola (1917–87), for instance, always kept political and historical rhetoric at a distance in his deliberately grey novels of the Tuscan countryside, most famously in *Bebo's Girl* (1960). Though he himself eventually moved in the direction of campaigning fiction, his more interesting early work seems now almost to point to the minimalism of the 1980s.

For Alberto Moravia (1907–90), on the other hand, *impegno* and neo-realism were just one stage in a career that was already becoming increasingly mainstream. He had been a strong presence in Italian literature since his precocious, and outstanding, first novel, *A Time of Indifference* (1929). In the post-war years he published various novels and stories concerned with the malaise and bad faith of bourgeois or Fascist society, against which he set the unrestrained vitality of popular life and sexuality. *Two Women* (1957) is his main attempt at a committed neo-realism. Like many of Moravia's books it is too long, but it also suffers from a schematic design (a mother and her unnaturally pure daughter made conscious of the reality around them through war and rape), and an over-explicit message of the need to accept freedom, responsibility, and death. Some of his later novels, such as *The Empty Canvas* (1960), mark an interesting return to the theme of bourgeois alienation, though with *The Two of Us* (1971) he tried an up-to-date mix of sexual comedy and student protest.

Moravia has also been admired for his short stories since at least the time of his first *Roman Tales* (1954), and for stories about women (*Boh*, 1976), which have been claimed, by some Italian women at least, to show a remarkable understanding of female sexuality. Where he shone in his later years was as a film critic for the weekly *L'Espresso* and as a travel writer who produced informed, questioning accounts of visits to India, China, and Africa.

There were ways out of neo-realism other than that taken by Moravia. Italo Calvino (1923–85), the 'squirrel of the pen', as Pavese had called him, was already darting between imaginative freedom and the demands of *impegno* in his first published novel, *The Path to the Nest of Spiders* (1947). For some years after that, his writing continued to have an explicitly political side to it, though he kept shifting towards reflection on the complexity of modern life and on the difficulties of giving a sense to everyday experience. This can be found in the ironic short stories he wrote, in the manner of Maupassant, and in short novels which are on the face of it social critiques: *A Plunge into Real Estate* (1957), and *La giornata di uno scrutatore* ('A Day in the Life of a Scrutineer', 1963).

But Calvino also followed a different tack. He collected and reworked Italian folk-stories in his *Italian Folktales* (1956), and produced his own modern urban fairy-stories with *Marcovaldo* (1963), in which an innocent but by no means stupid workman confronts the inhumanity of the modern city. By now he had already written the three fantastic novels which he brought together as *I nostri antenati* ('Our Ancestors', 1960): *The Cloven Viscount* (1952), whose protagonist is split into his good and bad halves by a cannon-ball; *The Non-existent Knight* (1959), whose hero is nothing more than an inexorable will contained inside a suit of armour; and *The Baron in the Trees* (1957), in which a young eighteenth-century nobleman climbs into the trees in a fit of pique and stays there for the rest of his life. In some ways this trilogy is like *Alice in Wonderland*: comic, even absurd, full of action, read with pleasure probably by children, yet also intelligent and disquieting in its implications. Unlike *Alice*, however, and without taking away from its own *lightness* (a quality Calvino set much store by), it is immensely self-aware. As we shall see, Calvino still had a long way to go as a writer, but for many readers the trilogy is his masterpiece.

Beppe Fenoglio (1922–63) might have stayed with the run-of-the-mill grimness of his early novel of Piedmontese peasant life *La malora* ('Perdition', 1954). But when he turned to write about his experiences as a wartime partisan, he produced some of the most original fiction to spring from the Second World War. Picking up hints from Pavese and the early Calvino, he creates a world of tight-lipped young men risking everything playing lethal games in the hills at a moment when the choice between good and evil has been made and what remains is the ruthless, confused fight against a weakened but locally more powerful enemy. In Fenoglio's best stories, *Primavera di bellezza* ('Springtime of Beauty', 1959) and *Il partigiano Johnny* ('Partisan Johnny', 1968), existentialist bravado acquires an almost epic air.

Thoroughly disregarding neo-realist principles, Fenoglio heightens the strangeness of the experience and of his fiction by heightening and distorting his language. Most strikingly, he makes the most of his long-standing cultivation of English literature, often Anglicizing his Italian or even writing whole passages in an idiosyncratic English. Much of his work (including *Il partigiano Johnny*) was unfinished and unpublished when he died. Only in the later 1960s did his reputation begin to grow towards its current heights.

A greater, and older, novelist also had to wait for recognition. Carlo Emilio Gadda (1893–1973) had been enjoyed by the *cognoscenti* since the early 1930s. He became a name to conjure with (initially as a byword for difficulty) after the appearance of his two major novels, both much worked on, both unfinished. *That Awful Mess on the Via Merulana* (1957) is a kind of detective story set in 1930s Rome, but the investigation into the murder of a beautiful, well-off, and barren *signora* becomes an attempt also to track down *il male* (evil or sickness) through the constantly changing complexities of life. A crime is eventually solved which may have little (or a lot) to do with the main crime.

There is a similar openness and a similar pursuit of *il male* in *Acquainted with Grief* (1963); only here, though it is foreseen, the main crime has yet to happen. It is in a way the same crime as in the earlier book, but explicitly matricidal now and the element of authorial self-laceration is apparent. At the same time the novel is anything but self-indulgent, with its angry, wounded protagonist wasting his life in a fictional South American country that is really post-1918 Italy and with his ageing mother, who has been emotionally destroyed and alienated (as Gadda's mother was in reality) by the death of her second, and favourite, son in the First World War.

Far more than any other twentieth-century Italian author, Gadda combines humour, intellectual depth, emotional power (often, but not always, the emotion is rage), self-exposure, and objectivity in a constantly shifting kaleidoscope of styles and perspectives. The knots and tangles (to use two of his favourite images) he describes are in the external world itself and Gadda, who was an engineer by profession, never lost the belief that they had to be investigated as scientifically as possible. In the early 1960s and for some time after, however, it was primarily his baroque language-games that impressed younger writers. Gadda seemed to offer the prime example of how familiar linguistic chains could be successfully broken: a far better example than other still active writers of the older generation. Tommaso Landolfi (1908–79), for instance, was writing anti-novels displaying a distinctive metaphysical irony, and Dino Buzzati (1906–72) was still producing impressive Kafkaesque short stories, but neither had anything like the same impact as Gadda.

In the most acclaimed and commercially successful fiction of the boom years, the dominating mood was that of nostalgia, though by no means unalloyed. The first Italian best-seller after 1945 was *The Leopard* (1958), the novel which, together with three shorter stories, makes up the *œuvre* of the Sicilian nobleman Giuseppe Tomasi di Lampedusa (1896–1957). The novel is set in the last century, soon after Garibaldi's invasion of Sicily, and the setting is aristocratic. Its sumptuous, decadent tableaux were emphasized in Visconti's film version, though in the novel Lampedusa and his *alter ego* protagonist, the powerful, ageing Principe di Salina, see everything through ironic, weary eyes. What disturbed large numbers of the progressively minded was that the novel dealt apparently with the end of an epoch, yet saw the coming of the new, united Italy merely as a continuation of old practices under different banners, and with somewhat less style. It was (and remains) all too recognizable a picture.

Lampedusa's bitter-sweet pessimism chimes with that of Giorgio Bassani (b. 1916), who, as a publisher, first accepted *The Leopard* for publication. Bassani's own novels and stories, eventually somewhat misleadingly published together as *Il romanzo di Ferrara* ('The Novel of Ferrara', 1973), are mainly semi-autobiographical evocations of bourgeois Jewish life in Ferrara in the pre-war years. The earlier books, up to and including the most celebrated of them, *The Garden of the Finzi-Continis* (1962), have an idyllically leisurely air. Bassani's finely sensitive and intelligent prose savours each of the places and moods which he re-creates, and allows each of his almost invariably melancholy characters to take on definition and at the same time to retain the core of mystery which is their *raison d'être*. But the idylls have a sepulchral, painful quality. Although Bassani mentions it directly only infrequently, the deportation and death of the Ferrarese Jews in 1943 is a constant presence. Beyond that definitive disaster, and obscurely linked with it, there is an undertow of personal unease. *The Garden of the Finzi-Continis* preserves a convincing tension between Bassani's younger fictional self—weak, self-obsessed, a victim, and yet a survivor—and Micol, the object of his affections, who, though simultaneously precious and prescient in character, exudes vitality.

In his subsequent novels, *Behind the Door* (1964) and *The Heron* (1968), the traumas are laid all too painfully bare. Since then Bassani has mostly written poetry, though the continuity between his verse and his fiction is evident. The poems are laid out like epitaphs—the most impressive collection is actually entitled *Epitaffio* (1974)—and have a monumental air, even when they take off from everyday incidents. It is a distinctive poetry and one which has not been as fully appreciated as it deserves.

During the 1960s Bassani was more read in Italy, though less known abroad, than Primo Levi (1919–87), whose best-known work pivots explicitly on his first-hand experience of the death-camp of Auschwitz. The first, limited edition of *If This Is a Man* had originally appeared in 1947, but came more to public attention in the later 1950s. It is the story of Levi's deportation and imprisonment in Auschwitz in the last two years of the war and was followed by a sequel, *The Truce* (1963), recounting the liberation of the prisoners and their subsequent long and painful journey home. Both books are less documents than attempts to testify—to re-create and to interrogate an intolerable past from the perspective of a liberal humanism that somehow still survives, though incurably hurt. The power of the writing comes partly from its sobriety; Levi shocks by not setting out to do so and accuses simply by representing what was done in the camps, not by any direct denunciation of the perpetrators. By making constant comparisons or contrasts with our normal, common experience, he brings us to share in his own dreadful experience, even if ultimately that far exceeds our comprehension. The only real answer to it that Levi offers is to remember, with respect and with affection, the remarkable body of people who experienced it with him.

In the first flush of consumer civilization in Italy, these horrors seemed remote, and Levi himself looked for ways to go beyond or outside writing about the Holocaust. In *The Periodic Table* (1975), for instance, he brings his training as a chemist to bear on personal reminiscence and anecdote in an attempt to cross the divide between the scientific and the humanistic cultures. He also wrote a novel about Jewish partisans in Eastern Europe, *If Not Now, When?* (1982).

But the nightmares were always there. The most painful and testing of his later books is the last, *The Drowned and the Saved* (1986), published not long before his suicide, in which he returns to the question of the camps at a moment of dawning awareness that Fascism was once again becoming a force in Europe. At least as disturbing, and in some ways more personally revealing, are Levi's poems, collected as *At an Uncertain Hour: Collected Poems* (1984). Here he eschews, as one would expect, any form of modernism and in the best of them achieves a distinctive sombreness, his tortured humanism now acquiring a powerful new resonance as it merges with cadences and formulas derived from Jewish ritual.

Some authors in these years looked backwards in more arduously literary and more mythopoeic ways. Elsa Morante (1918–85) was as much an anti-bourgeois as her long-time husband Alberto Moravia, but, unlike him, put stress on the visionary capabilities of the writer and the fantasy lives of the psychologically deprived. She is at her most lyrical and tormented in *Arturo's Island* (1957). In *The World Saved by the Little Children* (1968) she actually moves into free verse and, as the title suggests, displays an irrational optimism about those people who turn their back on modernity. In *History: A Novel* (1974) the 'Happy Few' have become a mentally feeble mother, a small, doomed child born of rape, and animals—all victims of the unending violence of history (specifically the Second World War) but creatures in whom innocence or joy can briefly bloom. Here, for once, Morante aimed at narrative on the large scale, and with popular appeal. She risks being sentimental in some places and bluntly didactic in others (and agreed to the book being ruthlessly marketed). The result was a best-seller. Still, *History* has pace, lyricism, and a moral power which, if anything, has grown in the light of recent European events.

By comparison, the other myth-making novel of the decade, *Horcynus Orca* (1975) by Stefano D'Arrigo (1919–92), which seemed much more sophisticated at the time, has lost its sparkle. It, too, has a wartime setting, this time in Sicily. It opens with the appearance of the sea-monster of the title to a refugee sailor and maintains a riotous mixture of myth and history throughout, as well as of neologisms, dialect, and standard Italian. D'Arrigo owes much to Gadda, but ends up being linguistically precious where Gadda is not so.

All the authors I have named so far were responding to modernity, if to a large extent by rejecting it. But there was also a strong current in literary culture which aimed at meeting the new Italy head-on in appropriately modern literary forms. Elio Vittorini (1908–66), who was more guru than creative writer in his last years, proposed in a famous article that modern capitalism was best handled in indirect terms, as the French (he claimed) were handling it in the *nouveau roman*. Not everyone agreed, but certainly a great deal of 1960s fiction, and quite a lot of the poetry, too, tried to mix social and political critique with literary modernism in various more or less unstable combinations.

The plots of many novels were centred on intellectuals and their troubles. Luciano Bianciardi (1922–71) charts the downward path of one deluded provincial in boom-years Milan in the ironic but heavy prose of *La vita agra, or It's a Hard Life* (1962). Lucio Mastronardi (1930–79), with his startling mixtures of different varieties of Italian, wrings more laughs from small-town hatred and despair in his novels about the town of Vigevano in the Po valley. Goffredo Parise (1929–86), in *The Boss* (1965), reduces a Chaplinesque dreamer to the point where he surrenders to a robotic existence and marriage to a mute, mentally damaged beauty as the only way of surviving in the new capitalism. Paolo Volponi (1924–94) depicts a similar crushing of human intelligence and imagination amongst the workers in *The Memorandum* (1962). Darker and more subtle in its mixture of comic and serious motifs is the work of Giuseppe Berto (1914–78), especially *Incubus* (1964), a novel in which the figure of oppressive authority is seen as existing more within the mind than in an objective social reality.

All of these novelists produced other interesting fiction (though Volponi saw himself primarily as a poet), but to a large extent they now seem to belong to the early 1960s. Since then, contemporary dilemmas have continued to be written about but in quite different terms. Dacia Maraini (b. 1936) and Oriana Fallaci (b. 1929), for instance, have tackled issues such as abortion and prostitution in an approachable, forceful way, while other writers who were also journalists, most notably Giorgio Bocca (b. 1920), have acted as the conscience of the nation on such matters as terrorism or the backward state of southern Italy.

The older novelists who came closest to the social reality, however, were those who approached it more obliquely. Natalia Ginzburg (1916–91) writes more or less as a neo-realist in her impressive Resistance novel *All our Yesterdays* (1952), written in the distinctive flat, conversational tone which for years caused her to be looked down on as an un-literary writer, as a 'women's' writer in the bad sense. In fact her manner derived from her early reading of Ivy Compton-Burnett and is as subtly stylized as that of Pavese (who was part of the same circle of writers and intellectuals in 1940s Turin). In short novels such as *Valentino* (1957) and *Sagittario* (1957) she carefully skirts direct confrontation with major contemporary issues. But in these everyday tragedies of middle-class Italians, men as well as women, which are played out in and around the home, she explores the psychological precariousness and impoverishment that seemed very quickly to be becoming the Italian norm. Her strongest book is *Dear Michael* (1973), a detached but compassionate letter-novel about a loose group of despairing, drifting characters, with at their centre the vaguely revolutionary Michele of the title.

In her later years, Ginzburg focused particularly on the issue of the family, especially in her last book, *Serena Cruz, o la vera giustizia* ('Serena Cruz, or True Justice', 1990), a pamphlet on the abuses of state power suffered by a little girl and the family which had (illegally) adopted her. Here, the continuity with her earlier work was evident. In her 1963 autobiography *Family Sayings* she had made the sayings of the title, and the habits and relationships that went with them, into a fragile safety-net against the disasters which, for a Jewish family like hers, were only just off-stage. This book also displays a quirky humour, which was probably one of the main reasons for its immediate success. The humour resurfaced in a more acerbic form in some otherwise slight stage plays, beginning with *Ti ho sposato per allegria* ('I Married You for Fun', 1966), which were quite successful at the time but have now slipped from view.

Ginzburg's close contemporary Leonardo Sciascia (1921–89) allowed his political and historical conscience much greater visibility. In his most famous novel, *The Day of the Owl* (1961), he became the first notable writer from Sicily to make the role of the Mafia in Sicilian life his main theme. Three subsequent detective novels were more disquieting because in them he played literary games with the genre as well as intimating at an all-penetrating corruption. First came a taut, self-defeating Mafia investigation, *To Each his Own* (1966). Then the uncertainties extended as the setting moved to a disguised mainland Italy with *Equal Danger* (1971). And a third stage seemed to be reached in the surreal *One Way or Another* (1974), in which the conflict between a rational investigation and criminal deviousness is reduced to a game of mirrors.

History, however, came close to confirming imagination in 1978 when the Red Brigades kidnapped and eventually murdered Aldo Moro, the Secretary of the Christian Democrat Party, a crime of which Sciascia produced a compelling analysis in *The Moro Affair* (1978). He returned to the vagaries of justice in later novels, notably in *Una storia semplice* ('A Simple Story', 1989), after a period during which he had seemed to be on the verge of making a full-time career in politics. In essays and articles of the late 1970s and early 1980s he wrote about the past of Sicily—of which he had already given impressive imaginative recreations in the stories of *Sicilian Uncles* (1958) and in novels such as *The Council of Egypt* (1963).

Sciascia's underlying thesis is an extension of that implied in *The Leopard*: that in Sicily there has been stasis or a defeat for reason at every moment in history when the rest of Europe has moved forwards. Sciascia's work as a whole offers bleak images of Sicily, both past and present, and ones that hover on the edge of cliché. But his example and encouragement (supplemented by the energies of his friend, the independent, Palermo-based publisher Elvira Sellerio) gave Sicilian writing a real boost. By the mid-1980s it had a higher profile in the country as a whole than it had ever had before.

In the 1960s the stance of writers such as Ginzburg, Sciascia, and many others was readily decried as politically and literarily unadventurous, while a funny, subtle commentator on shifts in Italian language and mores like Luigi Meneghello (b. 1922) was barely heard at all, no doubt because he was writing from exile in England. In the first half of the decade the writers and critics who voiced the loudest claims to up-to-dateness were those who made up the Gruppo 63 or the 'neo-avanguardia'. These writers wanted to de-provincialize Italian culture and they assimilated at speed the then nascent canon of international theory (Saussure, Adorno, Freud, Lévi-Strauss, *et al.*). Most of them also wanted a literary and intellectual revolution, and a political revolution, too, in a good many cases.

Perhaps surprisingly, much of what emerged from the debates and congresses of the Group retains its interest still. It was in this ambit that Umberto Eco (b. 1930) gave a first, and very powerful, shape to his thought in *The Open Work* (1967). And the now embarrassingly titled anthology *I novissimi* ('The Newest Ones', 1961) is still worth reading for the essays it contains on poetry, even if a good proportion of the poems themselves are only conceptually interesting—as perhaps they always were.

Inevitably the moment passed and the neo-avant-garde, which was anyway divided, fell apart. Some former members at least flirted with armed revolution. Nanni Balestrini (b. 1935) was wanted for questioning for several years on suspicion of being involved in left-wing terrorism; but he kept on writing and publishing. His poetry, once computer-generated, has become plainer and more forceful as the years have gone by. His fiction has kept a modernist air. He is at his most powerful and angry in *Vogliamo tutto* ('We Want it All', 1971), which depicts the strikes at the Fiat car factory in 1968 from the perspective of the young southern workers who were at their sharp end. There is still force, too, in *Gli invisibili* ('The Invisible Ones', 1987), which applies a similar collectivist technique to the intellectuals who earlier lived out the revolutionary imperative and saw it crumble away.

Most members of Gruppo 63, though, moved into academic life. Edoardo Sanguineti (b. 1930), for instance, who, like Balestrini, had been one of the contributors to *I novissimi*, became an outstanding literary critic as a professor at the University of Genoa. As a creative writer, apart from producing two novels or anti-novels, both of which are disturbing recastings of contemporary cultural debris, *Capriccio italiano* ('Italian Caprice', 1963) and *Il giuoco dell'oca* ('The Goose Game', 1967), he has concentrated mainly on poetry. His jokey, intelligent avant-gardism has lost in bite as the years have passed, but has gained in playfulness and humanity.

Other avant-garde writers, too, notably Alberto Arbasino (b. 1930) and Giorgio Manganelli (1922–90), explored the pleasures of modernism in fiction in knowing, often satirical ways. Arbasino's *Fratelli d'Italia* ('Brothers of Italy'), originally published in 1963 but revised often and thoroughly enough to be still winning prizes as a new novel in 1993, scourges the follies of the 1960s—for those able to keep abreast of its ironies. But many writers of that decade felt, or pretended to feel, deep suspicion of the novel as an irredeemably compromised bourgeois form and kept looking for alternatives or replacements.

Pier Paolo Pasolini (1922–75) veered between poetry, fiction, and, eventually, film. He had begun by writing delicate poetry in the dialect of Friuli, but made his name with his scandalous evocations of young tearaways in the Roman *borgate*, *The Ragazzi* (1955) and *A Violent Life* (1959), though the carefully calibrated dialogue made both novels difficult reading for most Italians. In the same years he was trying to write a poetry that was up to date in content but traditional in form. In his most famous collection, *Le ceneri di Gramsci* ('Gramsci's Ashes', 1957), the *terza rima* of Dante was the unexpected medium in which he voiced the incompatibility he felt between his commitment to the Communist Party and an anarchic vitality.

In the early 1960s Pasolini channelled the narrative—and ostensibly more popular—side of his imagination into film. He continued to write plays, some of which became the basis for his films (e.g. *Teorema*, 1968), and, semi-secretively, fiction too, his vast, unfinished allegory of consumerism, *Petrolio* ('Petroleum'), appearing only long after his death, in 1992. What he produced publicly was poetry. His verse was now casually discursive, taken up with major issues of the day yet simultaneously self-probing. At its best it shows great imaginative power. Just how interesting a poet Pasolini was is only now becoming clear as stock is taken of the vast corpus of his previously uncollected poems.

Pasolini was not just a novelist, poet, playwright, and film-maker. He intervened in every area of controversy he could, ranging from debates on the state of modern Italian to the significance of student protests (he was on the side of the exploited, working-class police against the pampered middle-class protesters). The last collection of his newspaper journalism to have been published during his lifetime, *Scritti corsari* ('Piratical writings', 1975), is a wonderfully energetic, readable, and incisive series of reflections on the state of Italy. Pasolini's murder robbed the country of a charismatic figure.

Other prominent rebels of the 1960s and 1970s survived to find themselves part of the cultural establishment. At the populist end of the scale is the playwright Dario Fo (b. 1926). Italian theatre has almost always flourished when its productions have originated in the theatre and not with writers as such. From the late 1940s almost until his death, the figure who brought most to the stage was the Neapolitan Edoardo De Filippo (1900–84), an actor-manager and playwright who became a national institution. As himself both clown, showman, and playwright, Dario Fo had much in common with De Filippo, but he was of the revolutionary Left and more than willing to step out of the theatre into television or (for a while) to put on performances in factories for the workers. He saw himself as using laughter to scourge the established order for its hypocrisy and violence, and succeeded in needling it enough at times for performances of his plays to be banned. In *Mistero buffo* ('Comic Mystery Play', 1973) he renewed political theatre by making the medieval jester-figure into the voice of contemporary popular protest, whilst *Morte accidentale di un anarchico* ('Accidental Death of an Anarchist', 1970) played an influential part in the controversy surrounding the death in police custody in 1969 of the anarchist Pino Pinelli. The problem for Fo was that (particularly outside Italy) such plays soon lost their topicality and became assimilated to pure farce. It is easy in retrospect to dismiss Fo the political activist, but the revolutionary impulse was what gave his best work its comic and dramatic force.

At the other, élitist end of the scale from Fo stands Franco Fortini (1917–94), latterly an academic, but best known as an independent intellectual, whose demanding essays interpret and interrogate the humanist current in modern Marxism. He is also a significant poet, who dismisses avant-gardist revolutions in poetry as specious, both politically and poetically. Fortini himself takes his cue from Brecht (whom he translated) and Mao Zedong (whom he once admired), and works with, rather than against, the Italian poetic tradition. The effect is of a sober self-consciousness, more impressive than engaging. In later years he became more obviously personal, and less authoritative, as he had to deal with growing old and with living in an Italy in which a capitalist culture seems to have triumphed.

All those who have written and published poetry in modern Italy have felt the presence of Eugenio Montale (1896–1981). In the early 1960s it was still possible, given a certain amount of pig-headedness, to speak of Montale in the same breath as Salvatore Quasimodo (1901–68), who was awarded the Nobel Prize for his morally serious but otherwise uninteresting poetry; or as Giuseppe Ungaretti (1888–1970), whose best work was long behind him. At that time Montale had published only three books in thirty-five years. But the 'provisional conclusions', as he termed the last two poems in *La bufera e altro* ('The Storm and Other Things', 1956), turned out to be drawing a line under the first half of his career and opening the second. From then up until his death (and since his death, too, thanks to a curious arrangement he made with Annalisa Cima, the young critic who was one of his last muses), Montale published poetry in abundance.

Its general thrust, signalled initially in a moving series of poems for his dead wife—given the name of 'Xenia' in *Satura* ('Medley', 1968)—was towards the prosaic, that is, towards emphasizing the absence of the insights (the 'occasions') that had motivated the earlier poetry, as well as the clogging presence of the paraphernalia and babble of contemporary society. The tone can be reactionary, tetchy, the language itself apparently throwaway, almost degraded, but what Montale calls a 'half-speech' ('mezzo parlare') is also at least half-optimistic. The larger insights may have gone and his memories of them may have to be reinterpreted (some of these later poems are in fact a creative reassessment of earlier ones), but insights keep coming, if only into the ways in which meaningfulness has been lost, or perhaps never existed. The old Montale, with his seat in the Italian Senate and his Nobel Prize, was also a Post-Modernist tragedian and gamester. Indeed, throughout the second phase of his career he was remarkably in tune with the work of many younger poets.

He had always been in tune with the older ones. Mario Luzi (b. 1914) and Vittorio Sereni (1913–83) followed something like Montale's own trajectory. In the post-war years they slowly emerged from the hermetic manner which had been the poetic norm since the 1930s. Luzi adopted a prosaic, hesitantly self-questioning vein that yielded its best results in *Nel magma* ('In the Magma', 1963) but has risked becoming repetitive in later collections. Sereni reached unexpected lyric heights the more casual his manner became, especially in his last collection, *Stella variabile* ('Variable Star', 1979).

Giuseppe Giudici (b. 1924), too, has something of the tone of the early Montale in his 1960s collections, which focus on the modern urban and industrial experience (rather like the novelists of the time). In his later verse he has achieved more strident effects by mixing patently literary motifs and a harshly prosaic language. Of more recent poets in this mode the most notable is Valerio Magrelli (b. 1957), who already in his assured first book, *Ora serrata retina* ('Blacked Outer Retina', 1979), is like an old Montale made young again, scoured of the crustiness but still centring his work on the unyielding strangeness of life and language.

Of other poets the most adventurous has been Andrea Zanzotto (b. 1921). His early poetry had the air of a late-in-the-day, backwoods hermeticism, though its mixture of surface melody and underlying disquiet was already distinctive. But with each succeeding volume the issue of modernity claimed more and more of Zanzotto's attention, until with *La beltà* ('Beauty', 1968) it invaded the fabric of poetry itself on a massive scale. Fragments of the old peasant life and culture, of traditional and modernist poetry and poetics, idyllic or not, were brought into violent collision with nuclear and consumerist nightmares, in a desperate search for an authentic poetry and feeling, which Zanzotto seemed to think was realizable, if anywhere, only in a half-nonsensical linguistic mishmash.

This novel form of modernism, much more complex than that of the Novissimi which it superficially resembled, continued in subsequent collections, though with unexpected modification. *Il Galateo in bosco* ('A Manners-Book in the Wood', 1979), which centres on the relationship between biological codes and human conventions, includes a sequence of virtuoso Petrarchan sonnets entitled 'Ipersonetto' ('Hypersonnet'). And a good part of Zanzotto's 1980s poetry, including moving elegies for Pasolini and Charlie Chaplin in *Idioma* ('Idiom', 1986), is written in a Trevisan dialect. Protected by this linguistic barrier, it has a directness and a vulnerability not to be found in his work in Italian.

Zanzotto signalled a sea-change. 'Difficult' poetry has continued to be written, but in an unassuming, linguistically unaggressive mode, at least by recent practitioners such as Gianni D'Elia and Antonella Aneddu, though Dario Bellezza (b. 1944) has managed to keep a violent persona as a *poète maudit* alive in both his verse and prose. Many poets have taken to using regular forms, even versions of a traditional poetic language, as in the startlingly artificial love poetry of Patrizia Valduga (b. 1953).

Dialect poetry, too, has escaped from the low status to which it had been traditionally relegated and its literary sophistication acknowledged. Some older poets have been given their due—such as Biagio Marin (1891–1985), who, in old age, and in the dialect of Grado, wrote lyrical verse concerned with the subjects of eternity and emptiness; or Ernesto Calzavara (b. 1907), who playfully mixes Veneto dialect, Italian, Latin, and on occasion oddments from other languages; or, most powerfully, and for most readers most difficult to penetrate, Albino Pierro (b. 1916), working in an obscure dialect of his native Lucania.

Other poets, now in their sixties, but still very active, include Franco Loi (b. 1930), who writes forceful, harsh lyrics in Milanese, and Franco Scataglini (1930–94), who use an antiquated form of the dialect of Ancona. Currently, indeed, there is a host of poets using dialect, happy, perhaps because of the steep decline in actual dialect use, to make the most of the mixture of security, nostalgia, and stylistic freedom which it offers them.

The most remarkable poetry to have appeared in recent years is quite different from this, however. Attilio Bertolucci (b. 1911), whose first book appeared in 1929, has come into his own in old age. Superficially straightforward in manner, and for years treated by critics as a provincial lightweight, Bertolucci had always tended to a reflective, discursive poetry, occasioned by his experience of everyday life in Parma and Rome. But a new strength showed behind the subtly graded tonal and temporal effects in *Viaggio d'inverno* ('Winter Journey') of 1971. Then in the 1980s he completed the first two parts of a large autobiographical novel in verse, *La camera da letto* ('The Bedroom', 1984, 1988). In a way this is a celebration of the ordinary, though an ordinary involving neurosis, passion, and war. Bertolucci puts the accent on the undramatic, allowing the rhythms of his irregular lines and his long, snaking syntax to suggest the pace of life going by, marked by larger events but determined mostly by a shifting network of smaller happenings.

From the mid-1970s onwards, the flight from the political and from polemic of any sort evident in poetry is evident in most other forms of writing, too. Literature became fun, at least in intention. This was a novelty. Though avant-gardist fiction had been playful, this tended to be swamped by the difficulty of the texts. The one author who had successfully combined lightness and seriousness was Calvino. In the 1960s he moved to Paris and became part of the OuLiPo group, of which Georges Perec was to become the best-known member. A change of direction, not entirely unprepared for in his previous work, is evident in *Cosmicomics* (1965), in which cosmic events such as the creation of matter are experienced by a character with the unpronounceable name of Qfwfq, who happens to have been present at them, along with his family.

Much of the work that followed, culminating in the multiple openings of *If on a Winter's Night a Traveller* (1979), played combinatorial games with different ideas and forms of fiction. Although the tricks Calvino played in some of his books—particularly the Tarot-based *The Castle of Crossed Destinies* (1973)—were too clever for some admirers of the earlier fables, an enormous number of readers found in the later Calvino a distinctively pleasurable exploitation of theoretical ideas. *If on a Winter's Night*, in particular, plays games with figures such as the Author (one Italo Calvino), the Critic, the Forger, the female Reader (Ludmilla), and the Reader ('you'), and brings everything to a satisfying fairy-tale conclusion when 'you' finally finds happiness by marrying Ludmilla.

There is perhaps more substance, however, in the stories and reflections of *Mr Palomar* (1983), which casts an absorbed, steady gaze—Mount Palomar is the site of a famous telescope in California—on often apparently banal or wayward happenings and quietly develops the strangeness inherent in them.

Calvino was the same sort of outsider as his eighteenth-century baron in the trees. Umberto Eco is an insider, though one who belatedly made an unexpected sideways move from theory into fiction. He had been in the public eye in Italy since the early 1960s as an innovative thinker about language, literature, and communication, though one who could also write effective, often very funny journalism—he had an early success with the satirical pieces of *Diario minimo* ('Minimal Diary', 1963), which include a scathing review of Dante's *Divine Comedy* as it might have appeared in a fourteenth-century Sunday newspaper. In 1975 he was appointed to the world's first professorship of semiotics at Bologna and published his fullest attempt at a comprehensive theory of signs in *A Theory of Semiotics*.

This was, however, a turning-point. Eco's subsequent writings, often published simultaneously in English and Italian, are partial studies and spring from the realization that a total theoretical systemization is not possible. His intellectual doubts are evident in his immensely successful medieval detective story *The Name of the Rose* (1980). In part this is an ironic comment on the failure of rational investigation, since Eco's detective hits on the solution to the mystery by accident, as well as a condemnation of all attempts, moral or intellectual, to control knowledge. But most readers were probably more taken with the novel's escapist and imaginative verve. Eco claimed that it began as bed-time stories for his children. He later tried to produce another popular-cum-intellectual success with *Foucault's Pendulum* (1988), a novel in which the phantom of a total intellectual system metamorphoses into a world-wide Masonic conspiracy. In this novel, however, his narrative skills were unable to carry the sheer abundance of out-of-the-way information, real or invented, though individual moments reveal his characteristically unpredictable humour.

The 1970s were widely felt to be a period of stagnation for the novel:

older writers were fading away and no new ones worth reading seemed to be emerging. Then, in the early 1980s, a whole series of new names suddenly appeared, and some slightly older ones found a new lease of life. They form a heterogeneous group in many ways, but with some characteristics in common: a fear of political heavy-handedness, a certain caution about being too modernist or obscure, and a sense of the importance of having a distinctive style. In spite of the publicity that was initially lavished on them, none of these writers has had anything like the success of Calvino or Eco, though a good deal of their work bears comparison with the best of what has been published in other countries.

Some have chosen the path of excess. Aldo Busi (b. 1948), for instance, has cultivated an outrageous public persona both inside and outside his writings, and succeeded in giving a virtuoso representation of northern Italian mores, gay and not-so-gay, in his first two novels, *Seminar on Youth* (1984) and *The Standard Life of a Temporary Pantyhose Salesman* (1985). In later books he has tended to become repetitious or opaque, however.

Altri libertini ('Other Libertines', 1980), the first and best novel of Pier Vittorio Tondelli (1955–91), made a precarious linguistic and existential carnival out of the lives and language of young drifters and drug addicts living on the edge of some nameless town, though his later books are less vital. Gesualdo Bufalino (b. 1919) is a more conventionally literary writer. His first novel, *The Plague-Sower* (1981), finished when he was 60, is a fictionalized memoir of a stay in a Palermo hospital for terminal TB cases just after the war, in which the writing is baroque but the humour and the pessimism Beckettian. It was followed by a string of other books, some of them exquisite evocations of the old Sicily, the best of them probably *Blind Argus, or The Fables of the Memory* (1984), which recalls a year spent as a schoolmaster on the Sicilian coast in 1955.

Another Sicilian writer, Vincenzo Consolo (b. 1931), similarly gives pride of place to his elaborate language and to playing games with the mechanisms of fiction, though his most compelling novel to date, *Il sorriso dell'ignoto marinaio* ('The Smile of the Unknown Sailor', 1976), does so in the name of a sceptical investigation into the brutal repression of an 1860 uprising by Sicilian peasants.

There are also minimalist writers. Gianni Celati (b. 1937) began in the 1970s with frenzied stories about innocent, demented outsiders. His more recent collections, since *Voices from the Plains* (1985), are impassive registrations of colourless, empty existences led in the featureless conurbations and ribbon-developments of the Po valley. Antonio Tabucchi (b. 1943) is similarly bare but more overtly sophisticated in his cultivation of surreal mystery and metaphysical malaise. Equally knowing, though aiming at a cooler, less neurotic tone, is Daniele Del Giudice (b. 1949), whose three quest novels—the best is *Lines of Light* (1985)—inquire indirectly into the relationship between the scientific and the literary imagination.

Three powerful women writers came into prominence in the 1980s. They all work within a broadly feminist perspective and explore avenues into the past, or its loss, in a way that male writers of the 1980s do not. Fabrizia Ramondino (b. 1936) writes about girlhood in wartime Naples in *Althenopis* (1981), and about the meaning of the events of 1968 for the various generations of a Neapolitan family in *Un giorno e mezzo* ('A Day and a Half', 1988). Rosetta Loy (b. 1931) also writes about childhood, though her strongest novel, *The Dust Roads of Monferrato* (1987), is ostensibly a nineteenth-century family saga. There is a degree of nostalgia in both Loy and Ramondino. Francesca Sanvitale (b. 1928) confronts pain more directly, especially in *Madre e figlia* ('Mother and Daughter', 1980), in which illness, guilt, and generational and sexual conflicts have a phantasmagoric intensity. In comparison, other novelists, such as Andrea De Carlo (b. 1952) and Francesca Duranti (b. 1935), who made names for themselves by playing knowing literary games, have not worn well.

It remains to be seen whether the redrawing of the political map which occurred in 1994, and which shifted the balance of power to the Right, will have lasting literary repercussions, or whether, as the 1980s suggest, writers in Italy have withdrawn permanently into themselves.

FURTHER READING

Caesar, Michael, and Hainsworth, Peter (eds.), *Writers and Society in Contemporary Italy* (Leamington Spa, 1984).
Baranski, Z., and Pertile, L. (eds.), *The New Italian Novel* (Edinburgh, 1994).

17

JAPAN

MARK MORRIS

O E Kenzaburo* was awarded the Nobel Prize for literature in 1994. Since the late 1950s, as part of a generation of talented writer-intellectuals, he has produced millions of words in the form of fiction, criticism, political essays, journalism, and several genres yet to be classified. Yet a number of ironies shadow his recent international recognition. Younger Japanese readers in particular find his writing alien and difficult: Oe is famously unread. And right before winning his Nobel Prize, Oe made public a long hinted decision to abandon the craft of fiction.

There is in such a statement little echo of the narcissism of Mishima Yukio (1925–70)—Oe's literary and political rival throughout the 1960s— who contrived to end his life with a spectacular suicide and his career with the four-part *The Sea of Fertility* (1965–71). Oe's sense of resignation reflects, rather, the fact that in Japan, as in many advanced capitalist countries, the culture of the written word is in retreat. In the context of contemporary Japan, such potential silence can only be interpreted as a rebuke directed at the institution of literature, which in recent years has, it seems, been invaded massively by both the values and the languages of the market-place, and gradually stripped of its once considerable imaginative and critical assets.

Nan to naku kurisutaru ('Somehow, Crystal') was a huge best-seller in 1981. Ostensibly a story about a fashion model and her love life, what made it a best-seller was its annotations, 442 notes detailing such things as brand names, trendy shops, cafés, and other items from the affluent landscape inhabited by its yuppie author, Tanaka Yasuo (b. 1956). Here, realized publishers and advertising men, was an entire pilgrimage route for the sort of self-conscious hyper-consumption which Japanese apologists were beginning to call Post-Modern living.

When Murakami Haruki (b. 1949) published his best-selling *Noruwe no mori* ('Norwegian Wood', 1987), more flair seemed to go into the packaging— contrasting red and green covers to catch the Christmas shoppers—than

---

* With Japanese names, the surname comes before the given name.

into the actual writing. The book sold in the millions. In a number of works, usually more memorable for their titles than their contents, Murakami has attempted both to market the 1960s and 1970s as consumable nostalgia and, at the same time, to efface them as history. The typically streetwise narrator of *A Wild Sheep Chase* (1982) remembers the good music and the good girlfriend of 1970. On the television appears a dramatic image of Mishima delivering his last soliloquy. 'The volume control was broken so we could hardly make out what was being said, but it didn't matter to us one way or another.' All the narrator feels is that 'the curtain was creaking down on the shambles of the sixties'.

Not so long ago, quite a few of Oe's generation might still have hoped that writing, and especially the high ground of experimentation represented by the best prose fiction, might help carry through an incomplete task of modernity, explaining social reality and contesting literary models of the present and the future. Japan is badly in need of such models. Surface affluence masks a society deeply concerned about its ravaged environment, and the corruption and arrogance of its ruling bureaucrats and politicians. Some people even claim that Japan no longer has a culture, merely advertisements and commodities circulating within an administered society of consumption under the alias of the Post-Modern.

Murakami's act of disavowal must not go uncontested, however, for the 1960s represent one of the greatest eras of Japanese writing. Both the 1960s and 1970s are remarkable in particular for an extraordinary variety of writing by women. Post-war reforms in education, and an expanding market for serious literature, helped to foster more than one generation of women who have exploded the old label of 'women's literature' as a somehow separate genre. In what follows, and despite their importance for understanding Japan's consumerist ideology, I shall pay little attention to authors of best-sellers such as Murakami or Yoshimoto Banana (b. 1964), whose novel *Kitchen* (1988) has been successfully marketed around the world.

The high ideals held in Japan about the potential role of fiction within the project of modernity were formed only over a long stretch of time: they represent the optimism of post- rather than pre-war Japan. Nevertheless, many aspects of current writing date back well beyond the war.

For a century past, Japanese writers have written *shosetsu* rather than novels or short stories. The term, borrowed from Chinese, had originally a pejorative sense of 'trivial tale, short anecdote'. By the late nineteenth century, however, as Japan learned more about Western culture, it came to refer to longer narratives and to mean something akin to 'novel'. Yet the *shosetsu* has never developed any clear set of generic boundaries. A *shosetsu* may be qualified as short or long, but whether it contains three pages or three hundred, it is still read, interpreted, and discussed as part of the same culture of prose expression.

The openness of the *shosetsu* form meshes closely with, and is in turn inflected by, the manner of its publication: serialization. From the 1890s Japan's daily newspapers began serializing works of prose fiction. Before long, a daily competing for its share of a growing urban readership might feature one or more *shosetsu* on the front page and include additional stories and essays inside. Although fiction diminished in importance as newspapers began to make most of their money from advertising rather than sales, *shosetsu* have been mainstays of the highly profitable weekly magazines since early this century. In the mean time, and still limping along today, a rather more sedate range of monthlies, focusing on literature or on a combination of social, political, and cultural issues, has long supported more experimental or avant-garde writing.

Book publication only really began to reach a mass audience in the mid-1920s. Paperbacks, which dominate today, joined the market during the 1930s, then took off through the 1960s. Overall, the practice of serialization has been so prevalent that the word *kakioroshi*—'fresh off the pen'—was coined to describe, and advertise, any book that had not first been through the network of daily, weekly, or monthly publication.

In contrast, if not really in competition, to the commercialized genres was *junbungaku*, or 'pure literature', which connects with a Western-inspired *shosetsu* tradition of the late nineteenth century. It is a generous category, and contained, until recently, most of the writers known outside Japan, where it has now been eclipsed by the manufacture of best-sellers. The major publishers, the vast bulk of whose income derives from sales of *manga* comics, keep a small number of serious literary journals alive and continue to publish *junbungaku* authors largely as a matter of prestige.

Before the war, *junbungaku* was sustained by a fairly small number of writers, critic-reviewers, and small and medium-sized publishers. A crucial historical function of this collective establishment, the *bundan* or 'literary circle', was the whole-hearted promotion of literature, especially prose fiction, as a worthy and even essential element of modern culture, in the face of old Confucian prejudices against fiction, the pressure of the market for mass production, and, increasingly, the willingness of the State to intervene and to censor. After the war, the opposition between 'pure' and 'popular' writing began to weaken. Popular writers were more free to aim higher, and *junbungaku* authors more willing to rub shoulders with them in the many literary periodicals that flourished after the mid-1950s.

One variant of the *shosetsu* deserving special mention is the *shi-shosetsu* or 'I-fiction'. This is more a modality of writing, reading, or evaluating texts than a definite genre. The 'I'—or 'he' or 'she'—of a *shi-shosetsu* is more likely to live out the pains of alienation, of not fitting into a liveable social role, than to express any a priori 'soul' or subjectivity. In a society given to consensus, it can be a risky, exposed practice. But just as *junbungaku* once shed a certain glow of legitimacy on the wider institution of literature, so 'I-fiction', with its conventions of authenticity and sincerity, has provided *junbungaku* with a special artistic and moral gravity.

A third modality of fiction that once existed close to *junbungaku*, but which had its sights on winning a mass audience, was the 'proletarian' literature movement. This brought together a wide range of left-wing, mainly young and middle-class writers during the 1920s and early 1930s. The movement was destroyed when Japan geared up for total war, leaving the literary field dichotomized into highbrow and pure versus popular. The return of the politically repressed was one of the key events that shaped the literature of the post-war years. Indeed, the violent intersection of the political with the literary is what marks the beginning of the 1960s.

In December 1960 Fukazawa Shichiro (1914–87) published a story called *Furyu mutan* ('Account of an Elegant Dream'). The narrator finds himself one day swept along amongst a merry crowd of Tokyo commuters to the grounds of the Imperial Palace. The revolution has broken out, to the rhythm of mambo bands and conga dancing. 'You could also hear the hiss made by the man selling balloons, inflating them with a bamboo tube. Right beside him the Crown Prince and Princess Michiko were stretched out on their backs, and they were just about to execute them at that very moment.' The narrator is somewhat startled to notice that the execution-er's axe is his: what a bother, it will get awfully messy. Down comes the axe, away rolls the Prince's head. Before his dream ends, the narrator will find himself engaged in a wrestling match with the long-dead Empress Dowager, widow of Emperor Meiji. A very funny, wicked story, it cost one human life and could have cost more.

People were in the streets during the early summer of 1960 on a scale never witnessed before. Millions of people throughout the country, and crowds numbering hundreds of thousands in Tokyo, were protesting against the imminent renewal of the Security Treaty which tied Japan to American Cold War policies and the threat of nuclear war. In mid-June, a student-led incursion into the grounds of the Parliament brought brutal repression: the police killed one student and severely injured hundreds more.

Left-wing activism generated an antithesis in the form of right-wing extremism, centred on ominously familiar themes of emperor-worship and ultra-nationalism. The day after the blood-letting at the Parliament, a Socialist politician was stabbed; the same October, the General Secretary of the Socialist Party was murdered in the middle of a speech. Against this background, there appeared not only Fukazawa's wild tale but, in January 1961, two other equally provoking *shosetsu*, Mishima's 'Patriotism' and a very young Oe's 'Seventeen'.

Mishima took a great deal of care over 'Patriotism'. A previous, longer work by him had been more or less damned by the *bundan* critics; at a time of personal crisis he was looking for a new direction. He turned to a highly romanticized vision of the far Right, taking his cue from a failed *coup d'état* of 1936. A young army officer misses his opportunity to join his fellow young 'idealists' in their desperate attempt to destroy corrupt politicians and restore the Emperor to direct rule. Unwilling to participate in the quelling of the rebellion, he prepares himself for *seppuku*, or ritual suicide. 'For a second or so his head reeled and he had no idea what had happened. The five or six inches of naked point had vanished completely into his flesh. . . . So this was *seppuku!*, he thought. It was as if the sky had fallen on his head . . . The pain spread slowly outward from the inner depths until the whole stomach reverberated.' He retches. 'Seemingly ignorant of their master's suffering, the entrails gave an impression of health and almost disagreeable vitality as they slipped smoothly out and spilled over into the crotch.' All the while, his young wife sits and witnesses the scene, then plunges a dagger into her throat.

Oe's 'Seventeen' is presented as the first-person monologue of a hopelessly awkward boy who, having just turned that age, veers from the confines of his miserable family outwards into the political turmoil of summer 1960. After a brief fling with the Left, he finds himself gradually won over by the virulent anti-Communist harangue of a veteran Fascist. As the story winds down, the boy and a small group of other misfits lay into the students surrounding the Parliament. The boy sacrifices his individuality in the name of the Emperor, made to feel invulnerable by the snappy uniform provided by the party. 'Mine alone this blessed age seventeen as, in the midst of the pain, the screams and shouts of terror, the gloom of a night fierce with dark abuse, I beheld His Majesty radiant in a vision of blazing gold.'

A continuation of the story appeared the following month, as *Sejii shonen shisu* ('Death of a Political Youth'). Oe's narrator is now arrested for the assassination of a prominent Socialist; before committing suicide in gaol, he has another ecstatic vision of the imperial godhead. While Oe may have taken hints from Sartre's story 'L'Enfance d'un chef' in creating this savagely ironic 'I-fiction', he clearly based it on the real-life 17-year-old assassin of the Socialist Party's General Secretary.

After Oe himself had received death threats, his publisher issued a public apology for having printed the story. Then another teenage terrorist broke into the home of Fukazawa's publisher, killed a maid, and seriously wounded the publisher's wife. The boy was 17, a member of a faction of the extreme Right. Fukazawa went into hiding under police protection, and his publisher, too, apologized. The repercussions of this wave of violence are still being felt. Neither 'Account of an Elegant Dream' nor 'Death of a Political Youth' has been reprinted, except in underground form.

Mishima wrote other works akin to 'Patriotism' and produced one imaginative parable, The Sailor Who Fell from Grace with the Sea (1964). But his books were now selling at best in the tens of thousands, not by the hundred thousand, as in the 1950s. By 1965 he had begun serialization of what was meant to be his greatest work, the four-volume The Sea of Fertility. The first volume, Spring Snow, recreates in lush detail the atmosphere of pre-war aristocratic life. The décor may be more convincing than characters such as the doomed young hero, Matsugae Kiyoaki, or Honda Shigekuni, his serious-minded friend. The latter was given the considerable task of reappearing in subsequent volumes, tracking his mystically reincarnated childhood friend through time and space. In the second volume, Runaway Horses, Kiyoaki has returned in the body of a young apprentice terrorist. Mishima is successful in reimagining the political tensions of the 1930s. His idealistic assassin Isao is a cardboard cut-out, yet the boy's irrevocable trajectory towards violence and suicide is terrifying to follow. Mishima fails to engage seriously with the final two parts of the tetralogy, however. He was increasingly caught up with, among other things, metaphysical pamphleteering, organizing his private army, and rehearsing for his own seppuku.

While still writing a university dissertation on Sartre's philosophy, Kurahashi Yumiko (b. 1935) published 'Partei' (1960). This is a short sketch, redolent with the Sartrean language of viscosity and despair, concerning the claustrophobia of political dogma—the target here is the far Left. A female student tries to prove herself worthy of party membership in the eyes of an ineffectual boyfriend. After an ignominious affair with an actual worker, she becomes pregnant, and ends up in gaol, where, alternating between fits of laughter and of vomiting, she repudiates both her boyfriend and his party. Back in her dormitory, a letter is waiting; it is from the party and accompanies her brand-new membership card. The irony is not very subtle, but it does seem more effective than in Kurahashi's longer work in the same vein, the Kafka-on-amphetamines parody *The Adventures of Sumyakist Q* (1969).

Writing and politics intersected also in the career of Kaiko Takeshi (1930–89) during the Vietnam War. His reportages from Vietnam were serialized in an influential mass weekly, then published as *Betonamu senki* ('Vietnam War Chronicle', 1965). He was an active member of the protest movement Beheiren, along with most intellectuals and writers (with the exception of Mishima). In *Into a Black Sun* (1968), Kaiko produced something close to Graham Greene's prophetic novel *The Quiet American*.

Away from the clamour of political confrontation, several of the most 'classical' twentieth-century authors were still at work. In 1968 Kawabata Yasunari (1899–1972) became Japan's first winner of the Nobel Prize, an honour that Mishima had coveted. Tanizaki Jun'ichiro (1886–1965) made certain he himself did not win it: he answered establishment efforts to convert him into the grand old man of literature by writing one of his most gleefully scandalous *shosetsu*, *Diary of a Mad Old Man* (1961–2). The early 1960s were especially productive for Kawabata. He turned out a gentle stream of touristic melodrama in *The Old Capital* (1961–2), then opened up the darker side of his talents in *The House of the Sleeping Beauties* (1961) or 'One Arm' (1964). It was the former, the aestheticizing Kawabata, not the latter, to whom the Nobel committee awarded its Prize. *House of the Sleeping Beauties* tells of a man's visits to a house that is divided into red velvet-lined chambers where young virgins lie in drug-induced sleep. In this castle of fetishism, old men come to lie beside the young women, to look and to dream, unembarrassed by their own ugliness and impotence. In 'One Arm' Kawabata seems to return to his roots in European modernism. Here the male narrator borrows a woman's arm for the night. He wanders furtively home through a dense and malevolent fog, there to marvel at the contours of his prize. He takes it to bed and eventually fits it to his own shoulder. Images and symbols abound, as do reveries about women in his past that are more openly sexual than the reflections on purity conjured up by the ageing narrator of *House of the Sleeping Beauties*. No clear pattern of meaning coalesces, however, around the surrealistic text.

Mishima praised *House of the Sleeping Beauties* as the most 'inhuman' *shosetsu* he had ever read; and 'One Arm' remains very mysterious. Both works seem saturated with menace, and with potential violence, wrapped tightly around woman as fetish; the former story ends with the death of one of the virgins. Years before, Kawabata had written a work about a psychopathic voyeur, so such erotic effects are clearly more than coincidental.

Tanizaki's *Diary of a Mad Old Man* is a grotesque comedy of ageing and obsession, themes that always seem death-haunted in Kawabata. Old Tokusuke falls for his son's wife Satsuko, a former chorus girl who knows how to play the old man's game. He is particularly obsessed by her gorgeous feet and will buy her anything in order to get at them. His final wish is to have a gravestone in the shape of Satsuko's foot. 'When she treads on my grave and feels as if she's trampling on that doting old man's bones, my spirit will still be alive . . . feeling the fine-grained velvety smoothness of the soles of her feet.'

During the late 1950s and 1960s, Mishima, Kawabata, and Tanizaki all found good translators and interested New York publishers. As a consequence they have been considered, in America and Europe, as somehow representative of Japanese culture. In Japan itself, probably only Tanizaki is felt to be capable of bearing such a weight of responsibility. The richness of his earlier works is still being brought to light in English and other translations.

A more literal sort of veteran writer was Ooka Shohei (1909–88). During the Pacific War he found himself in the Philippines. He wrote several notable works based on his experiences there as soldier and prisoner of war, the best known being *Fire on the Plains* (1952). He belongs to the contemporary age chiefly because of the massive *Reite senki* ('Chronicle of the Battle for Leyte', 1967–9). Basing himself on extensive Japanese and American sources, including diaries and memoirs, Ooka here forged his own documentary style to detail the way in which military incompetence and bureaucratic secrecy had sacrificed tens of thousands of lives in a hopeless cause. Serialized as it was during some of the worst years of the Vietnam War, Ooka's account did not need to spell out its historical relevance.

When in 1987 a large group of writers and intellectuals were asked to name the best ten books to have appeared since the war, first choice overall was *Black Rain* (1965–6) by Ibuse Masuji (1898–1993). The taboo on writing about the nuclear devastation of Hiroshima and Nagasaki had disappeared with the end of the American Occupation; and many readers have found Ibuse's account perhaps the most moving of all. *Black Rain* embeds the journal of a Hiroshima survivor within a larger story of the bomb's after-effects and the plague of radiation sickness. The narrator ultimately abandons an attempt to find his young niece a husband; known to have been in the city's ruins, she is shunned as a marriage prospect. As the book ends, she has begun to display symptoms of radiation sickness.

Before the war, Uno Chiyo (b. 1897) used the 'I-fiction' form to write *Confessions of Love* (1935). Much to the eventual chagrin of her lover of the time, it was a breathless retelling, in his persona, of the foolishness which had led him into a failed suicide attempt. Thirty years later, in *Sasu* ('Sting', 1963–6), a story that manages to be both unsentimental and gently sympathetic towards the failings of her husband and herself, Uno wrote a straightforward first-person narrative about a collapsing marriage, her own. She followed this classic *shi-shosetsu* with another almost as good, *The Story of a Single Woman* (1972). In 'Sting' she sums up one aspect of her character by means of a folk-tale concerning a turtle and a scorpion. Scorpion asks turtle for a ride out to sea, and promises not to be so stupid as to risk his own life by stinging. Poor turtle agrees—with the predictable result. To turtle's desperate 'Why?', scorpion replies sadly: 'Stinging is in my nature, I can't help stinging. Don't take it personally.'

One of the most complex works in the varied *œuvre* of Enchi Fumiko (1905–86) is *Namamiko monogatari* ('Tale of the False Oracle', 1965). Enchi was one of a disappearing kind of Japanese writer, the kind who could absorb modern Japanese and European fiction yet still feel connected to the matrix of story-telling created by the women story-tellers and writers of the age of *The Tale of Genji*. 'Tale of the False Oracle' opens with the author-narrator's claim to have rediscovered a manuscript from the eleventh century portraying the court where Murasaki Shikibu, the author of *The Tale of Genji*, served. Mixing her own narration and that of her invented manuscript with insertions from authentic classical texts, Enchi teases one into a spiral of texts and stories whose effect is to suggest that, whatever claims may be made as to a given story's truth or untruth, narration exists primarily for the sake of summoning up more stories. Much of the force of Enchi's work, as of Tanizaki's, lies on the surface of her language. Among her many shorter fictions, *Chisai chibusa* ('Small Breasts', 1962), a tale of incest and suppressed passion, reads more like a tribute than a challenge to Tanizaki.

In the 1960s Japan began to grow rich, and materialism to replace idealism. The three 'sacred possessions' everyone now wanted were a television, a washing machine, and a fridge. Increasingly, during the 1970s, they might even aspire to a house of their own in which to put them.

Kuroi Senji (b. 1932) is one of a group of writers who were by this time being characterized as an 'introverted generation.' The narrator of his story *Jikan* ('Time', 1969) is a white-collar employee, or *sarariman* ('salaryman'). He becomes haunted by a vision of a man in a raincoat, just at a point in his own life when he is struggling to find an equilibrium between the vivid experiences of his student days and the drab business world he inhabits at present. The vision eventually takes on substance: he sees the actual coat on an old friend, a man who has remained loyal to his troubled political past. That the story should come down on the side of a resigned acceptance of the status quo gives it representative value.

A man looks at a door. 'One of the numberless grains of wood lifts slightly, wave-like, whereupon all the little connected grains one after another hesitate then pulse, their peaks overlap, the whole forming a swell and gradually cresting until, curling up out of the planks like some eerie feeler, it just manages to hold in check its own woody substance.' Furui Yoshikichi (b. 1937) is one of the most impressive stylists to be writing in the contemporary language. In a passage such as this, from his story *Mokuyobi ni* ('On Thursday', 1968), he generates a text in which words, things, and meanings alike are set in motion and form new, sometimes menacing relations. Many of his characters inhabit a similarly unstable terrain, somewhere between the natural world of the countryside and one strewn with anonymous apartment buildings and sprawling underground stations. In 'Wedlock' (1970) a man and a woman live in a tiny apartment on the edge of the city, locked inside by the raucous voices of the labourers who lodge next door, by the prying eyes of an old woman who roves their marginal world like some displaced shaman, and by their own stifling relationship.

Furui's extraordinary *Enjin o kumu onnatachi* ('The Women Form a Circle', 1969) lies somewhere between essay and fiction. The narrator registers, with mounting unease, various scenes of women acting in unison. First, he comes upon a group of adolescent girls dancing in a ring; then some female students encircle the king as the chorus rehearsing a Greek play; another group of women perform a synchronized ballet of housework, outlined against the windows of their apartment block. Finally, the narrator looks back at his wartime childhood and, as incendiary bombs rain down, the women form a circle about a terrified small boy. Confronted by the evidence of women acting and communicating together in ways foreign to men, the narrator seems to hover between anxiety and a nervous admiration: a fair reflection of the way in which the more liberal men of Furui's generation were experiencing the expanding role in society of Japanese women.

The rapid changes associated with Japan's new prosperity had an enormous impact on families, and the nuclear, rather than the extended, family began to become the norm. One major work which dramatizes the erosion of traditional modes of authority is *Hoyo kazoku* ('Embracing Family', 1965), by Kojima Nobuo (b. 1915). The hapless protagonist of this novel, Shunsuke, has ignored his wife Tokiko in his pursuit of a career as an academic specialist in American literature. He finds out that she has had an affair with a GI. 'He should have been angry, but was instead crushed by a blinding truth: that was a woman standing there.' After husband and wife have quarrelled, Tokiko is ready for a show-down with the American; and Shunsuke has to go along as interpreter. The one thing the couple have in common is their devotion to the ideal of owning a modern, American-style house. The new house does not save them, however. The forceful Tokiko dies of cancer, and Shunsuke, weak though he is, gains a measure of dignity. Kojima's frequent humour at his expense is spiced with nostalgia for the old patriarchal order.

The work of Abe Kobo (1924–93) is filled with black humour and with nightmare. In *Woman in the Dunes* (1962) a man on an expedition to gather insects ends up 'gathered' himself: he is lowered down into a deep pit in the sand, where his fate is to help a woman who lives there to shovel back the inexorable tide of sand. This is a taut, open-ended parable about alienation and the search for meanings within a cycle of meaningless repetition, written in a language that Mishima likened to 'the hollow, desiccated, blank glare of high noon'.

Abe could write heavy-handed existential melodrama, as in *The Face of Another* (1964), or self-indulgent pastiche of Kafka, as in *Secret Rendezvous* (1977). More convincing is his variation on the theme of detection, *The Ruined Map* (1966). Abe's detective traverses an urban landscape studded with stereotypes of the genre: a shrewd ex-wife, a boss averse to taking risks, a younger woman who is impersonally seductive inside a smart apartment, with a lost husband and a shifty brother. Abe complicates the plot with the touch of a veteran fabulist and, perhaps, a few hints from the French *nouveau roman*.

From the early 1970s much of his energy went into the Abe Kobo Studio drama troupe, though he still managed, in *The Box Man* (1973), to push the *shosetsu* in the direction of the Post-Modern. A Beckett-like narrator here roams the city inside a home-made carapace: 'I am now looking around the inside of the box . . . a cube slightly more spacious than my own capacity . . . cardboard walls tamed by sweat and sighs . . . graffiti inscribed with a ballpoint pen all over in small letters . . . reverse tattooing . . . a not very prepossessing personal filigrain.' Abe opens this anti-novel—whose narrative is interrupted by strangely captioned photographs and weird chapter titles—with the report of a police raid against homeless vagrants sheltering in a central Tokyo park. Since 'cardboard cities' have sprung up in Tokyo in the 1990s in the wake of recession, *The Box Man* still retains its parodic bite.

As writers turned more to the personal, private aspects of contemporary experience, it was inevitable that 'I-fiction' would regain some of the status it had lost in the politicized atmosphere of the post-war period. One of the more dramatic examples of this revival is *Shi no toge* ('The Sting of Death', 1977) by Shimao Toshio (1917–86). Its publishing history is complicated, as it expanded over more than twenty years from a story into a long book— a logical consequence of the episodic and diffuse rhythm of serial publication, at which Kawabata was a master. The full work details the destructive dependency which binds a wife, driven to insanity by her husband's infidelity, to a man who seeks absolution through submission to his wife's pain and wilfulness. The husband bears the author's own personal name Toshio; his wife is called Miho, as was Shimao's wife in real life. Autobiographical fiction of this intensity invites full participation from its readers, who are asked to experience with him the author-narrator's dread of the next outbreak of Miho's madness.

Oe Kenzaburo's *A Personal Matter* (1964) is one of the most representative works of 1960s fiction. Like the same author's *Hiroshima Notes* (1965), it was intimately tied to a personal crisis. A young English instructor, Bird, dreams of escaping to darkest Africa, but his dreams come to an end with the birth of a son disfigured by a brain hernia. 'That long, tapered head! It sledge-hammered the stakes of shock into Bird.' This is Oe's own brain-damaged son Hikari (the name means literally 'light, radiance'), who reappears many times in his later books. *Hiroshima Notes* was Oe's earlier attempt to connect private suffering to public issues. It examines the fractious Japanese peace movement, registers the dignity of the A-bomb survivors, and wills meaning out of their continued suffering. Like so many friends of the family, those who have gone on reading Oe have followed, among his many themes, Hikari's difficult road to adulthood and his struggle for self-expression.

The 'I' who narrates Tsushima Yuko's (b. 1947) 'The Silent Traders' (1982) evolves a theory whereby stray cats have the advantage over ex-husbands: 'The children leave food on the balcony. And in return the cat provides them with a father. How's that for a bargain? . . . In their dreams, the children are hugged to their cat-father's breast.' In Tsushima's work, indeed, the family is pared down to its core, of women with children. She invokes elements of her own life—the death of a beloved brother who suffered from Down's Syndrome, her experience as a single mother, the death of her son—with imaginative freedom, but still within the intimate confines of the 'I-fiction' form.

Child of Fortune (1978) follows a single mother whose life seems to drift between the demands of her teenage daughter, a dull job, an ex-husband, and two male friends; memories of her dead brother provide little anchorage. Then she becomes certain that she is pregnant again. When she finally drags herself to the hospital, however, the pregnancy turns out to be a phantom one. Tsushima's plots are a bit like everyday life; they do not offer much by way of transcendence. If a work such as *Woman Running in the Mountains* (1980) is more accommodating and ultimately more positive about human relationships, that may be partly due to the fact that it was first serialized in a major daily.

The year before she wrote *Yoru no hikari ni owarete* ('Pursued by the Light of the Night', 1986), Tsushima's son had collapsed and died while taking a bath. In the sparest prose she recreates this incident, her panic and disbelief, and the ache of not being able to end her own life. She only permits herself the luxury of imagery when recollecting especially harrowing memories. Yet these stark revelations form part of a larger meditation on death which is, in its turn, linked to Tsushima's retelling of a heartbreaking romance from the classical era. Thus one travels with her, back and forth in time, participating in a healing process that depends on the telling of tales.

In 1945 the ending of state censorship meant writers might introduce sexuality more directly into their texts—provided the American censors did not intervene. Perhaps out of their sheer amazement at still being alive—3.5 million Japanese had died in the war—or as an antidote to the abstractions of political discourse, post-war writers took to depicting unabashedly carnal contact between their characters, rather than anything more nuanced. It was only later, from the late 1950s to the mid-1970s, that a series of obscenity trials indicated that the post-war State was willing, in an arbitrary fashion, to apply its puritanical pre-war laws against writers judged to have gone too far.

In *The Pornographers* (1966) Nosaka Akiyuki (b. 1930) created a form of porno-picaresque fiction. Two Osaka grifters make or sell porn of all kinds: tapes, films ('The Bulging Pillar', 'Peeping through the Pines', etc.), photographs, books. The central irony for the main character, Subuyan, is that when he at last finds true love, it is with some of the merchandise: an electric love-doll. Nosaka has written with brutal black humour about the hardships of life during the American Occupation. One of his most effective works is 'American *Hijiki*' (1967), whose adult narrator is haunted by grotesque memories of a boyhood spent scavenging, and occasionally pimping, in bombed-out Osaka. Once he has brought home what looked like dried seaweed, *hijiki*. It turned out to be GI-ration black tea. In a belated attempt to exorcize his past, he takes a rich American visitor to a sex-show, but his efforts at 'pecker nationalism' come to naught when the star male performer wilts in the presence of a foreigner.

In a variety of works, Kono Taeko (b. 1926) has explored sexuality and the articulation of self and others through the body. She depicts ordinary women made extraordinary by circumstances such as illness, childlessness, and/or the absence of a husband, and whose profound anxiety and self-loathing tend to be expressed in sado-masochistic rituals. She first gained attention with 'Toddler-Hunting' (1961), in which a woman hunts out the small sons of friends and buys them clothes to dress up in—little girls inspire physical revulsion in her. She is herself engaged in a relationship with a man of such violence that neighbours start to complain, and she becomes haunted by a frightening fantasy: that she is watching a father torturing his son. This core fantasy mixes the subjective and objective, as well as the female and male points of view, with a complexity that almost demands a psychoanalytical reading.

Kono employs another sort of phantasy in works like 'The Last Time' (1966) or *Fui no koe* ('Voice from the Blue', 1968). The protagonist of 'The Last Time' is on her way to a funeral when she hears a voice announce that she has only twenty-six hours to live. With maddening rationality, she busies herself about the house, getting her clothes ready for the garbage collectors, making lists, and leaving notes for the future reference of her husband and what she assumes will be his next wife. 'Voice from the Blue' is a psychological thriller which blurs the dividing-line between the psychological and the fantastic. A young woman sees a vision of her dead father hovering in mid-air. He seems to be granting her permission to carry out some unspecified task. In fact, Kono sends her off to suffocate her mother, kill her lover's son, and knife another man with mechanical precision. Faced with such violence performed by a female character, critics have hurried to supply symbolic readings of the novel. They have done little, however, to blunt the shock of Kono's vision of female rage set free.

Kono's longer works, such as *Kaiten tobira* ('Revolving Door', 1970) or *Miiratori ryokitan* ('Strange Tales of Mummy-Hunting', 1990), move at a slower pace, yet still draw energy from realistic, or unrealistic, scenes of sexual excess. 'Revolving Door' is a variant on the theme of partner-swapping, one which a number of writers tested out in the 1970s, such as Kurahashi Yumiko in *Yume no ukihashi* ('Floating Bridge of Dreams', 1971). Near the beginning of Kono's story, as a husband makes love to another woman in a room upstairs, his wife, reclining in a chair downstairs, suddenly senses him pushing hard down on her, intent on having rough oral sex. 'At the very moment she was about to cry out with pleasure, he was at her throat, and, unsatisfied, she was sealed in her agony. . . . If it's like this for me, how can *she* bear it?' Currents of sexual excitement and fear eddy throughout a dense, riddling text. 'Strange Tales of Mummy-Hunting' is, for most of its length and despite the incongruous title, a quiet reconstruction of middle-class life in wartime. Then, as the bombing worsens, so do the games of domination played out by a young wife and her doctor husband. Here Kono seems to have let herself become imprisoned by her early work, with sado-masochism as her thematic signature.

Tomioka Taeko (b. 1935) has written several key works, notably *Suku* ('Straw Dogs', 1980) and *Tochi utsu nami* ('Where the Waves Come in', 1983), seemingly calculated to undermine the stereotyping of women still common among male authors. Both stories centre on a middle-aged woman who, with gentle persistence, collects attractive young men. 'From the moment Eikichi came into the room,' says the wry narrator of 'Straw Dogs', 'all I thought about was what I'd need to do to have sex with him . . . I was interested—does simply having a fleshy bit of some person I hardly know actually go inside me really add up to a physical *relationship*?' In a different vein, Tomioka has written a powerful sequence of stories combining personal history, a canny ear for dialect, and motifs taken from folklore. Two of the best of these are 'Facing the Hills They Stand' (1970) and *Yuki no hotoke no monogatari* ('Tale of the Buddha in the Snow', 1987).

One of the most significant writers to emerge during the 1970s and 1980s was Nakagami Kenji (1946–92). He is best known for having staked out the margins of the 'outcast' communities of those whose 'low' occupations have placed them beyond the pale of Japanese society. In *Ichiban hajime no dekigoto* ('The Very First Event', 1969) and *Misaki* ('The Cape', 1975), as well as in longer works such as *Kareki nada* ('The Bay of Withered Trees', 1977), Nakagami brought 'I-fiction' into contact with his own family's world of working-class outsiders. Planted deep within most of the stories is the suicide of his violent, alcoholic older brother. In other *shosetsu*, Nakagami has adapted material from medieval legends as shaped by outcast performers.

The violence of patriarchy and the vitality of women is everywhere apparent in 'The Bay of Withered Trees'. The main character, Akiyuki, is faced with a riddle concerning the hazards of masculinity: can you consent to being a man, and a potential father, while loathing your own natural father and recognizing the justice and life-force only of women?

Nakagami has written also about the marginal figures engaged in male prostitution. *Sanka* ('Psalm', 1990) centres on a young man who works under the name Yves, servicing 'white pigs' and 'black pigs', women and men, in luxurious urban settings. Having transformed himself from country boy into well-paid sexual robot, he needs to guard against any irruption of human feeling while he is on the job. And on the job, for 364 pages, he

pretty much always is. 'Psalm' seems determined so to reify masculine
sexuality that it is all but annihilated.

When my grandmother started to tell one of the old stories, this is what she'd
say.—It was long ago, and even if it never happened, you've got to listen. And I,
with all my might, would pledge my assent with a grunt—Hrrmph!

For a long time now, Oe Kenzaburo has been moving from the centre to
the periphery of Japanese life, taking his readers to a mountain village on
the island of Shikoku. This is the village he himself grew up in, but also the
site of mythical events and a historical rebellion. It is a locus of hope. The
quotation above comes from *M/T to mori no fushigi no monogatari* ('M/T
and the Story of the Miracle of the Forest', 1986), in which this same scene
is repeated several times, like an incantation. It is an account of how narrative wisdom may be got from the mouth of a Matriarch who is telling
tales about a godlike Trickster; and it demands that stories be taken seriously. Oe mixes folklore and legend with elements of the 'I' persona that
readers will recognize from his earlier books. He has been reshaping this
narrative technique ever since *The Silent Cry* (1967), and has returned to it,
recasting it in a more realistic manner, in his most recent work, *'Sukuinushi'
ga nagurareru made* ('Till the "Saviour" Be Struck Down', 1993), which is
the first part of a planned trilogy called *The Green Tree Ablaze*. It contains
just about everything: ecology, reincarnation, the importance of rural co-
operatives, the power of narrative, the history of a famous writer and his
son, the miracles concealed within the routines of daily life, and herma-
phroditism, among other themes. Perhaps this is the beginning of the end
of Oe's prolific career. If so, he is going out throwing whole handfuls of
literary fireworks in the face of Post-Modern complacency.

FURTHER READING

Gessel, Van C., and Tomone Matsumoto (eds.), *The Showa Anthology: Modern Japanese
   Short Stories*, ii: *1961–1984* (Tokyo, 1985).
Hibbett, Howard (ed.), *Contemporary Japanese Literature* (New York, 1977).
Lewell, John, *Modern Japanese Novelists: A Biographical Dictionary* (New York, 1993).
Masao Miyoshi, *Accomplices of Silence* (Berkeley, 1974).
——, *Off Center* (Harvard, 1991).
Yukiko Tanaka and Hanson, Elizabeth (eds.), *This Kind of Woman: Ten Stories by Japanese
   Women Writers, 1960–1976* (Stanford, Calif., 1982).

18

NEW ZEALAND

IAIN SHARP

BEFORE 1980 the literary forms at which New Zealand writers excelled were miniaturist—the short lyric poem and the short story. Consequently, much of the best writing of those years can be found within the covers of a single volume, *The Oxford Anthology of New Zealand Writing since 1945* (1983). Since 1980 New Zealand writing has burgeoned, however, and the significant works of the 1980s and 1990s require a full shelf.

The desperate thinness not only of New Zealand literature but of New Zealand culture generally in the years immediately following the Second World War can be ascertained by glancing through the early issues of *Landfall*, the dominant literary magazine of the period. 'It is true that New Zealand is a long way from Europe,' sighed the fastidious editor, Charles Brasch (1909–73), in his introduction to the inaugural issue, which appeared in March 1947. 'But it is true also that the European tradition can take root here and grow, if we wish it to do so.' He expected the germination to be a lengthy procedure. Determined to set a high standard, in the first issue he presented the work of only two poets: Allen Curnow (b. 1911) and James K. Baxter (1926–72). There was no fiction at all, presumably because Frank Sargeson (1903–82), then the country's only worthwhile fiction writer, was suffering from writer's block.

Overwhelmingly Eurocentric in their thinking, Brasch's generation felt their isolation keenly and often bewailed the fact that they were a long journey by sea from anywhere interesting. Yet they also felt too connected to the local landscape to want to abandon it for good, like their one indisputably talented literary predecessor, Katherine Mansfield (1888–1923), who fled to England at the age of 20, never to return, except in her haunted imagination. Aghast as they frequently were at the philistinism which surrounded them, Brasch and his peers believed it was their responsibility to introduce a modicum of culture to their barbarous islands.

In the years since then, jet travel and new telecommunications have gradually brought New Zealand more into line with the rest of the world.

Changes in the national psyche always lag behind technological advances, however. Thus many New Zealand writers retain traces of the outpost mentality which they developed in their youth.

Frank Sargeson's influence is important in this regard. Uncompromising in his determination to devote himself full-time to writing, he lived in poverty almost all his adult life in a fibrolite bungalow in Takapuna, Auckland. Already regarded with suspicion by his neighbours, he had to be circumspect about his homosexuality in the days when this was still a criminal offence. Praised for their scrupulous realism when they first appeared in the 1930s and 1940s, his *Collected Stories* (1965) now read more like acts of revenge, relentlessly mocking the drab puritanism of 'respectable' New Zealand society and insisting on the superior warmth and integrity of outcasts, paupers, queers, eccentrics, and riffraff. In his later fiction, particularly the satirical novel *Memoirs of a Peon* (1965), which depicts the misfortunes of a would-be antipodean Casanova, Sargeson's prose is supple, varied, at times even baroque, but the stories which established his reputation are told in a simple vernacular style. Often the narrator is a barely articulate proletarian drifter who only half-understands the events he describes.

Of the many authors who have emulated Sargeson's tight-lipped early manner, the most impressive is the humane Dunedin-based moralist O. E. Middleton (b. 1925), whose best work can be found in *Selected Stories* (1975) and his two jointly published novellas, *Confessions of an Ocelot* and *Not for a Seagull* (1979). Others, however, have shared Sargeson's hostile opinion of New Zealand society, without wishing to imitate his narrative strategies. Among them are the gifted writers Maurice Duggan (1922–72) and Janet Frame (b. 1924), to whom, at the beginning of their careers, Sargeson offered his somewhat limited hospitality, allowing them, at different times, to live and work in the army hut behind his bungalow.

A restless experimenter, obsessed with problems of phrasing, Duggan was by nature even more of a pessimist than Sargeson. Perfectionists almost always lead unhappy lives, but Duggan's gloomy outlook was exacerbated by his alcoholism and his long battles against a succession of debilitating diseases (osteomyelitis, tuberculosis, and finally cancer). In Sargeson's fiction, there is no hope of a bright new dawn irradiating the cultural waste land, but at least the marginalized characters occasionally locate like-minded companions with whom they can share their laments. Duggan's lonely heroes are denied even this comfort. Yearning, dissatisfied, regretful, sometimes close to snapping point, they nevertheless lack the will to change. Duggan's *Collected Short Stories* (1981) make for melancholy reading, but they are models of meticulous craftsmanship.

Eccentric, poor, painfully shy, traumatized by the premature deaths of two beloved sisters in separate drowning accidents, Janet Frame was wrongly diagnosed as a young woman as schizophrenic. She spent almost all of her twenties in mental hospitals, where she was repeatedly subjected to ECT. Published while she was still a psychiatric patient, her first book, *The Lagoon and Other Stories* (1951; reprinted 1993), contains in embryo most of the themes of her subsequent fiction. She focuses on the lives of losers, loners, mad people, budding writers, and those on the verge of a nervous break-down. The joys of childhood give way to the pain and disappointment of adult experience. Imagination is hard to retain in a stiflingly conformist world.

Frame's propensity for delving into the dreams, anxieties, and delusions of mentally unstable characters has resulted in some strange and disturbing novels. Told from the perspective of Daphne Withers, *Owls Do Cry* (1957) traces the deterioration of the aptly named Withers family over a period of twenty years. Isolated during a storm and terrified by the possibility of attack by a prowler, Malfred, the heroine of *A State of Siege* (1966)—a retired art teacher, who lives alone in a beach house on an island near Auckland—gradually loses her grip on reality. In *Daughter Buffalo* (1972), Turnlung, an elderly New Zealand writer of doubtful sanity, travels to New York, where he engages in a brief sexual liaison with Talbot Edelman, a young Jewish doctor who specializes in the study of death. Possibly Edelman is a figure who exists only in Turnlung's disintegrating mind; or vice versa. With teasing similarities to her creator, the rambling narrator of *Living in the Maniototo* (1979) is a woman of many aliases who journeys back and forth between the United States and New Zealand, lampooning both with her satirical wit. Set in a North Island town which is under the influence of the mysterious Gravity Star, a cosmic force which overturns all ordinary no-tions of space and time, *The Carpathians* (1988) adds elements of science fiction to Frame's habitual metafictional games.

A one-woman revolution, over the last four decades Frame has greatly expanded the scope of New Zealand fiction with her bold innovations. Her most popular books, however, operate within the humanist-realist tradi-tion. For every one reader who has struggled through the opaque mysteries of *The Carpathians* and *Scented Gardens for the Blind* (1963), twenty are familiar with Frame's lucid, straightforward volumes of autobiography—*To the Is-Land* (1983), *An Angel at my Table* (1984), and *The Envoy from Mirror City* (1985). Although the supposed narrator is a character called Istina Mavet (the name blends the Serbo-Croat word for 'truth' with the Hebrew word for 'death'), *Faces in the Water* (1961; reprinted 1980) is essentially an auto-biographical account of Frame's harrowing asylum years.

The most considerable fiction writers who emerged a little after Frame, in the late 1950s and early 1960s, are Sylvia Ashton-Warner (1908–84), Ronald Hugh Morrieson (1922–72), Maurice Gee (b. 1931), Maurice Shadbolt (b. 1932), and Marilyn Duckworth (b. 1935).

Ashton-Warner spent many years teaching Maori children in remote rural schools. The rewards and disappointments of this experience, and the more general frustration of being a woman of artistic temperament in a boorish masculine society, underlie her first, and best, novel, *Spinster* (1958; new edition 1980). Haughty, egocentric, ever ready for a battle, she was often at loggerheads with the education authorities over her teaching methods. She describes her idiosyncratic techniques in *Teacher* (1963) and relives her struggles in *I Passed This Way* (1979).

Ronald Hugh Morrieson might fairly be described as an oddball. Apart from a single traumatic trip north to Auckland, he spent his entire life in the small Taranaki town of Hawera, where he taught the piano, played in dance bands, ogled women, got drunk, and was generally dismissed as a ne'er-do-well. His masterpiece *The Scarecrow* (1963; reprinted 1981) is a demented but effective mixture of Gothic horror, aberrant sexuality, and knockabout farce. Its opening sentence is the most celebrated in all New Zealand literature: 'The same week our fowls were stolen, Daphne Moran had her throat cut.' Morrieson's other notable success, *Came a Hot Friday* (1964; reprinted 1981), depicts the disaster-prone antics of a pair of lovable scoundrels as they try to swindle rustic gamblers.

A persistent decrier of the ill effects of puritanism and material greed, Maurice Gee is firmly grounded in the tradition of social criticism derived from Sargeson. His first novel, *The Big Season* (1962), a *Bildungsroman* whose hero is an *Angst*-filled small-town rugby footballer, is pedestrian, but since then his work has gone from strength to strength. *Plumb* (1978), *Meg* (1981), and *Sole Survivor* (1983) comprise a pleasingly complex trilogy, which covers nearly a hundred years in the history of the Plumb family and comments bitingly on the progress of European settlement in New Zealand. Gee's favourite technique is to build his novels around an elderly central character who reflects on past triumphs and defeats and eventually arrives at fresh revelations. *Crime Story* (1994) departs from this pattern, however, by presenting a multiplicity of viewpoints and a near-encyclopaedic range of criminal activity, from corporate fraud to manslaughter.

Although he was not one of Sargeson's protégés, Maurice Shadbolt has always shared Sargeson's preoccupation with capturing the nuances of national identity. His first book, a collection of short stories imperiously called *The New Zealanders* (1959; revised edition 1993), was much praised when it first appeared, but by the late 1970s Shadbolt's naturalistic techniques looked old-fashioned and the younger generation tended to think of him as little more than a worthy plodder. In recent years, however, he has transformed his previously colourless prose into a succinct, witty, muscular instrument and produced a splendid trio of tragicomic novels dealing with the nineteenth-century land wars between pakeha (i.e. European) settlers and the Maori tribes who defied British authority—*Season of the Jew* (1986), *Monday's Warriors* (1990), and *House of Strife* (1993).

The younger sister of the poet Fleur Adcock, Marilyn Duckworth first made her mark with *A Gap in the Spectrum* (1959; reprinted 1985), a novel distinguished, like all of Duckworth's work, by its economy, intelligence, and frank social observation. She wrote three more novels in the 1960s, then disappeared from sight, apart from a slim volume of poems, until the mid-1980s, while she raised four daughters and three stepchildren. She re-emerged with a pair of droll comedies about the difficulties of love, sex, and child-rearing: *Disorderly Conduct* (1984) and *Married Alive* (1985). Duckworth shares with Frame an interest in speculative science fiction: her next novel, *Rest for the Wicked* (1986), is set in a sleep research clinic which contains a machine for reading the inmates' dreams. She has subsequently continued to produce a book a year, all of them worthwhile. Narrated in part by a child molester, *Leather Wings* (1995) is the most disquieting of her later books.

Towards the end of the 1960s and throughout the 1970s, some of the younger New Zealand writers, to whom Sargeson and his struggles seemed antiquated, began to experiment with non-realistic modes of fiction they had learned from reading Borges, Beckett, Burroughs, Barthelme, Robbe-Grillet, Calvino, and other foreign writers. Their work is well represented in *The New Fiction* (1985), an anthology edited, with an enormously long, polemical introduction, by one of the key practitioners, Michael Morrissey (b. 1942).

The wiliest of the contemporary fiction writers, however, including Morrissey himself, have kept at least one foot in the humanist-realist camp while looking abroad for other possibilities. The South Island writer Owen Marshall (b. 1941) is exemplary in this regard. Duggan-like in his concern with technique, Marshall has read widely and is probably as conversant as any of his peers with Post-Modernism. Yet *The Divided World: Selected Stories* (1989) shows him attending diligently to the time-honoured business of creating credible characters and constructing plausible plots.

Damien Wilkins (b. 1963), one of the brightest hopes to emerge in the last few years, can also be located within the humanist-realist tradition. The central figure in his first novel, *The Miserables* (1993), is a young man who returns to Wellington from the United States for his grandfather's funeral and struggles to achieve an open-hearted response to his family without sacrificing his intelligence.

Good prose is not the strict preserve of fiction writers. Among New Zealand's historians there are some fine stylists. Outstanding are E. H. McCormick's wry *Omai: Pacific Envoy* (1977) and Ormond Wilson's myth-deflating *From Hongi Hika to Hone Heke: A Quarter Century of Upheaval* (1985)—as much for their mandarin syntax as their painstaking research. Dick Scott's *Seven Lives on Salt River* (1987) is a lively account of seven families in close contact with the Maori tribe Ngati Whatua in Northland during the early days of European settlement. Michael King's *Moriori: A People Rediscovered* (1989) is a heartfelt study of the small, culturally distinct group of Polynesians who have lived on the Chatham Islands (about 800 kilometres off the east coast of New Zealand) for centuries and suffered deprivation at the hands of both Maori and pakeha.

New Zealand poetry has been dominated by Allen Curnow for more than half a century. Few poets anywhere have been gifted with his combination of eye, ear, and brain. Typically, his poems proceed from the observation of a specific landscape. Seeing precedes saying: the self looks out on the external world and tries to make sense of the encounter. Often, however, Curnow's exact descriptions are accompanied by a simultaneous discourse on the theory of perception, mutability, the limitations of the mimetic process, the unbreachable gap between word and world. Even in his youth he was an expert prosodist, as his *Selected Poems, 1940–1989* (1990) confirms, but, if anything, his rhythmic control has improved with age. The marvellous long sentences of *Continuum: New and Later Poems, 1972–1988* (1988) can twist, pun, pivot, change direction, vault across stanza breaks, quote Shakespeare, and borrow snatches of French, Latin, and Italian without ever becoming jerky or seeming out of breath.

Curnow knows how good he is. Beneath the urbane, apparently casual, tone he assumes in interviews, one often catches the hint that New Zealand is big enough to contain only one poet of genius and that he is it. His pre-eminence has always been widely acknowledged, but also widely resented. Part of the problem is that he has written so effectively about the history of colonization and settlement that this subject-matter (the biggest available to a post-colonial writer) now seems peculiarly his own, leaving other ambitious poets with little to do, except bemoan his appropriation of it.

Almost from the publication of his first book, *Beyond the Palisade* (1944), which appeared when he was only 18, James K. Baxter was hailed as Curnow's most potent rival. Born into an uncommonly literate family by

New Zealand standards, Baxter was steeped in verse from infancy. Always prolific, he produced poems of every conceivable kind during his brief lifetime, but he tended by temperament towards the grandiloquent jeremiad. Like Sargeson, he never tired of castigating his countrymen, whom he dubbed 'Pig Islanders', for their meanness, prudery, and lack of imagination. He became a national celebrity during his last years, when he allowed his hair and beard to grow and set up a commune for the young and bewildered at Jerusalem, a tiny settlement on the banks of the Wanganui River, named by a nineteenth-century missionary with delusions of grandeur (the similarly diminutive Corinth and Athens are its near neighbours). Baxter's *Collected Poems* (1980) is a huge book: for most readers, the *Selected Poems* (1982) should suffice.

Kendrick Smithyman (1922–1996), who began his writing career about the same time as Baxter, is a wordy, unexcitable, unmusical poet, more concerned with teasing out conundrums than arriving at conclusions. After recovering from an early enthusiasm for Dylan Thomas, he settled into a mode that has served him well for four decades. He fashions clever, meandering, circuitous poems out of his prodigiously eclectic reading and his familiarity with the history and topography of the upper half of the North Island. His work is best sampled in his *Selected Poems* (1989).

A close inspection of the career of C. K. Stead (b. 1932), whose first poems appeared in literary magazines in the early 1950s, tells one much about the state of New Zealand literature in the last forty years. Opinionated and combative, Stead has been involved in almost all of the country's big literary controversies during this period. Although he has always identified himself as a New Zealander, pointing proudly to the fact that his earliest forebears arrived in the country in 1832, he insists, even more trenchantly than Curnow or Brasch, on the importance of the European tradition. London is still the centre of his literary map, although he also feels the lure of the United States and is troubled by the American cultural hegemony.

A tough-minded critic, Stead has never held back from reassessing his elders, sparring with his peers, and handing out badges for good conduct to his juniors. Against the temper of the time, which favours the advancement of hitherto disenfranchised voices, he believes there is such a thing as talent, which is distributed unequally and unpredictably, without regard to ethnic background or gender. He also believes the same standards of excellence should apply to all works of literature, irrespective of origin. This sounds eminently fair, until one asks how the standards of judgement are to be determined. Those in positions of power (generally in New Zealand, as elsewhere, affluent, well-educated, middle-class, middle-aged, white males, like Stead) tend, not always consciously, to establish criteria which favour their own productions.

Everything that Stead writes is distinguished by its clarity of expression. One of his early successes, *The New Poetic* (1964; revised edition 1987), is a study of Yeats, Eliot, and Pound. His own poetic practice began with Yeatsian pastiche, but later, under Pound's influence, he forsook conventional stanzaic patterns in favour of open form and, as he memorably put it, 'the accretion of radioactive fragments'. *Poems of a Decade* (1983) contains the best of his verse. *In the Glass Case* (1981) and *Answering the Language* (1989), his two volumes of essays, are indispensable reading for anyone with an interest in New Zealand's literary politics.

Throughout the 1960s Stead was a relentless opponent of New Zealand's participation in the Vietnam War. His dystopian first novel, *Smith's Dream* (1971; revised edition 1973), imagines a Vietcong-like resistance movement fighting against a Fascist dictatorship which has taken over New Zealand. *All Visitors Ashore* (1984), his second, and most enjoyable, novel, is essentially a veiled memoir of his literary apprenticeship in the 1950s. Surprisingly, given his frequent quarrels with Maori leaders, Stead's most recent novel, *The Singing Whakapapa* (1994), champions one of his nineteenth-century ancestors, who tried to put a stop to the Anglican Church's rapacious acquisition of Maori land.

Two of Stead's near contemporaries, Kevin Ireland (b. 1933) and Fleur Adcock (b. 1934), impressed early in their careers with their witty, unsentimental love poems. Adcock departed for England, where she had already spent much of her childhood, in 1963. Thereafter she has been only an occasional visitor to New Zealand. Ireland left New Zealand in 1959, travelled around Europe, and lived in London for more than twenty years as a Fleet Street journalist, but all of the books he produced during this period were published in New Zealand and he returned to Auckland in 1986. His later poems are unfailingly eloquent, but he is often content to settle for easygoing comedy. His *Selected Poems* (1987) contains most of his worthwhile work.

Vincent O'Sullivan (b. 1937) matches Stead in the range of his literary activities, as poet, playwright, critic, editor, short-story writer, novelist. As a poet, O'Sullivan is most convincing in the ruthless monologues of *Butcher and Co.* (1977). His riveting play *Shuriken* (1985) investigates the causes of the shameful machine-gunning of 122 Japanese prisoners of war at Featherston, near Wellington, in February 1943. His novel *Let the River Stand* (1993) is a dour masterpiece about the doomed love affair between two young eccentrics in the Waikato dairy-farming area in the 1930s.

Increasingly in the 1960s New Zealand poets discovered America and abandoned rhyme and regular scansion. Not that American influences had been wholly absent before—Curnow was fascinated by Wallace Stevens and Baxter by Hart Crane. The generation of writers born immediately after the Second World War, however, were saturated with American culture from birth. For them, the British Empire was a distant and rather comical concept. If, like Stead, they reacted with anger and indignation to the aggressive foreign policies of the Johnson and Nixon administrations, and in their hotter moments denounced the United States as an evil force, they nevertheless watched American movies, listened to American pop music, and pored eagerly over the works of Pound, William Carlos Williams, Olson, Creeley, Bly, Ferlinghetti, and Ginsberg.

The effects can be seen in *The Young New Zealand Poets* (ed. Arthur Baysting, 1973). Inevitably, over the two subsequent decades, some of these once young poets have lapsed into oblivion or else failed to live up to their early promise, like David Mitchell (b. 1940), who once seemed the most powerful of them. Alan Brunton (b. 1946), Murray Edmond (b. 1949), Russell Haley (b. 1934), Sam Hunt (b. 1946), Alan Loney (b. 1940), Bill Manhire (b. 1946), Bob Orr (b. 1949), and Ian Wedde (b. 1946) have all gone on, however, to produce considerable bodies of work.

Hunt, indeed, has become the best-known poet in New Zealand, but this is due less to the quality of his poems than to the vigour with which he has toured the country performing them. In recent years he has also contributed his versifying skills and flamboyant personality to television commercials. He has a good ear and is capable of writing incisively, but too many of the pieces in his *Collected Poems 1963–1980* (1980) and *Selected Poems* (1987) have a rather throwaway air. His is a less convincing voice than Ian Wedde's or Bill Manhire's.

Simultaneously immersed in hippie culture and smart enough to maintain a coolly ironic distance from it, Wedde was recognized early on in his career as his generation's most formidable spokesman. If some minds are naturally reductive, stripping the landscape down to the essentials, others tend steadily towards diversity and complication. Wedde is one of the complicators. Ever loath to be pigeon-holed, and ever keen to sabotage glib orthodoxies and expose the inadequacies of simplifying theories, his most valuable attribute may be his cussedness. Praised in the late 1960s and early 1970s for his exuberant excursions in open form, he responded by writing a sequence of sonnets, *Earthly: Sonnets for Carlos* (1975), and expressing an admiration for Auden in his interviews. *Driving into the Storm: Selected Poems* (1987) is a good introduction to Wedde's knotty and allusive verse.

In his protracted preface to *The Penguin Book of New Zealand Verse* (1985), which he co-edited with Harvey McQueen, Wedde argues that the liveliest New Zealand poems have always employed a 'demotic' rather than 'hieratic' tone, but, typically, he covers himself by assuming a very hieratic manner when defending the homespun balladry of whalers, sealers, gold-diggers, swagmen, and their successors. The Penguin anthology created much controversy when it first appeared, partly because of its ungrudging inclusion of poems in Maori (many of them by living writers) and partly because of its readiness to modify the canon by embracing a motley range of younger writers, removing a clutch of vapid, overly honoured dullards, and reinstating neglected writers from the past.

Wedde's brilliant, if rather chaotic, novel *Symmes Hole* (1986), which re-employs characters from Melville's *Omoo*, also presents an alternative vision of New Zealand history—one that puts the rambunctious nineteenth-century mariners back into the story, instead of focusing on the stalwart, land-owning pioneers. More recently, he has proffered some homespun balladry of his own in *The Drummer* (1993). No longer young enough to be deemed promising, but not yet old enough to be considered a grand old man, Wedde has drifted out of the literary spotlight he occupied with such authority and aplomb in the 1970s and 1980s. Nevertheless, he remains a powerful figure, and is no doubt capable of further surprises.

Born in the conservative far south, and educated at the University of Otago, where he studied the Icelandic sagas, Bill Manhire has always combined a lively awareness of pop culture and current literary trends with a level-headed appreciation of tradition. While most of his contemporaries were writing long, discursive, egocentric poems, Manhire established his reputation in the late 1960s with lean and cryptic lyrics. His poems deal with such domestic realities as courtship, marriage, and child-raising, but they are also open to surreal effects and flights of fancy. His sly sense of humour, which delights in deflating literary cant and pretension, is everywhere apparent in his work, most tellingly in his splendid prose miscellany *South Pacific* (1994). *Zoetropes* (1984) is a fine selection of his early poems, but admirers of his quirky ironies will also want a later collection, *Milky Way Bar* (1991) and *My Sunshine* (1996).

For the last fifteen years, Manhire has run a creative writing course at Victoria University in Wellington. Although he denies any intention of becoming a literary godfather, he seems none the less to communicate his ironic awareness to his students. Graduates of his course include Elizabeth Knox (b. 1959), Jenny Bornholdt (b. 1960), and Barbara Anderson (b. 1926). Knox's ambitious novel *Treasure* (1992) examines the progress of an evangelical Christian sect in both North Carolina and Wellington. Collected in three volumes, *This Big Face* (1988), *Moving House* (1989), and *Waiting Shelter* (1991), Bornholdt's charming poems manage to be simultaneously poised and humble, clever and kindly. Anderson's *Portrait of the Artist's Wife* (1992) satirizes the New Zealand literary scene and her *All the Nice Girls* (1993) is a shrewd novel about the problems of adultery.

In a small country like New Zealand, charismatic teachers like Manhire can exercise much sway. In the late 1960s and early 1970s, several of the contributors to *The Young New Zealand Poets* passed through the American poetry course established at Auckland University by Roger Horrocks and Wystan Curnow (Allen's son). At that time the course ended with Robert Creeley, but Horrocks and Curnow later extended it to include the writings of language-oriented Post-Modernists like Charles Bernstein, Ron Silliman, Lyn Hejinian, and Susan Howe. None of New Zealand's literary magazines was prepared in the early 1980s to discuss avant-garde work of this kind, so, in league with some of their former students, who were bedazzled by the theories of Barthes, Lacan, Derrida, and Co., Horrocks and Curnow started a journal of their own. The first issue of *And* landed on the sleepy literary establishment in August 1983, like a missile from Mars. If many of the literati were too hidebound, too simplistic, or too preoccupied with their personal difficulties to care about any of this literary theory, others, who had hitherto congratulated themselves on their familiarity with intellectual developments overseas, were suddenly made to feel ignorant and did not like the feeling.

Other members of the *And* group had probably studied the inspirational French and American texts with greater thoroughness, but Leigh Davis (b. 1955) soon emerged as its most effective literary terrorist. After graduating from Auckland University in English literature, instead of choosing one of the three customary professions (journalist, teacher, librarian), he entered the world of high finance, working first for the Treasury Department in Wellington and then for the country's leading merchant bank, Fay Richwhite. In 1983, resorting to a photocopying machine after Auckland University Press rejected his manuscript, he published *Willy's Gazette*, an extraordinary sonnet sequence saturated with allusions to Barthes's *Mythologies* which relentlessly satirizes literary devices that Davis considered obsolete, while still managing to celebrate his recent marriage, his shift from Auckland to Wellington, and the excitement he felt at transforming himself into a financier.

Davis's impeccable suits and gleeful determination to become a rich man infuriated most of the literati, who still expected artists and poets to register in public their unceasing opposition to Mammon, even if they were not actually starving and raggle-trousered, like James K. Baxter. Davis's penchant for applying the language of marketing to the literary scene also caused great offence. The most notorious of his peremptory formulations likened Allen Curnow to a 1957 Chrysler—a classic of its day, to be sure, but long since superseded. Fully ensconced today in the commercial zone, Davis has published nothing since 1987. Copies of *Willy's Gazette* are now almost impossible to procure, but two useful anthologies from the late 1980s, *The New Poets: Initiatives in New Zealand Poetry* (ed. Murray Edmond and Mary Paul, 1987) and *The Caxton Press Anthology of New Zealand Poetry 1972–1986* (ed. Mark Williams, 1987), include generous quantities of Davis's poetry.

Like the fiction writers, the smartest of New Zealand's poets keep one foot within the humanist-realist tradition. None so far has been willing to abandon the experiencing self as subject as thoroughly as the American Post-Modernists. For all its intellectual derring-do and reflexivity, *Willy's Gazette* does not part company entirely from the mode which has always dominated New Zealand poetry, that is, lyrics that recount personal epiphanies or sadnesses. Nor does the recent work of the poets who have been most affected by *And*'s promptings. Notable volumes in this connection include Alan Loney's *Missing Parts: Poems 1977–1990* (1992), Murray Edmond's *From the Word Go* (1992) and *The Switch* (1994), Graham Lindsay's *The Subject* (1994), and Michele Leggott's *Swimmers, Dancers* (1991) and *Dia* (1994).

Among the younger poets who have reached maturity in the 1990s, Gregory O'Brien (b. 1961) is outstanding. Blessed with an instinctive musicality, O'Brien's prolific work draws steadily on the three main passions in his life: Surrealism, family ties, and the Catholic Church. *Location of the Least Person* (1987), *Great Lake* (1991), and *Days beside Water* (1993) are his strongest collections to date.

Reviewing the first issue of *And*, unimpressed by its intimidatory tactics and wanting to strike back with a little intimidation of her own, the novelist Fiona Kidman (b. 1940) drew attention to what an exclusively male clique the contributors were. The editors were embarrassed enough by the charge of sexism to devote most of their third issue to women's writing. In spite of the pre-eminence of Katherine Mansfield and Janet Frame, New Zealand's male writers have generally tended to believe that literature (and poetry, in particular) is men's business. 'The fact that women writers are so poorly represented here is disheartening but, on the evidence of the submissions offered, justified. The majority of the verse submitted by women was reasonably competent but of a two-dimensional quality—too often clichéd or overly sentimental,' wrote Arthur Baysting in his introduction to *The Young*

New Zealand Poets. Confident enough of his own three-dimensionality to include himself as a contributor (no subsequent anthologist has thought it necessary to include him), he presented the work of only one woman, the delicate lyricist Jan Kemp (b. 1949).

By the middle of the 1970s, women demanded a bigger say. The most persuasive New Zealand writers to emerge during this time were Fiona Kidman, Lauris Edmond (b. 1924), Rachel McAlpine (b. 1940), and Elizabeth Smither (b. 1941), all of whom published their first volumes of poetry in 1975, International Women's Year.

Although Kidman's plucky, frank, and rather clumsy poems were warmly received, it was her semi-autobiographical first novel, *A Breed of Women* (1979), which won her a large following. Her finest work to date is *The Book of Secrets* (1987), a novel which examines the unenviable lives of three women trapped within a fanatical religious community in the far north of New Zealand in the nineteenth century.

Lauris Edmond has made up for a late start with a copious output over the last two decades, which includes radio plays, short stories, memoirs, essays, and a novel, as well as many volumes of poetry. In her *Collected Poems* (1994) she articulates with uncommon candour and sensitivity the warring claims of love for one's family and a longing for freedom. Her three-part autobiography—*Hot October* (1989), *Bonfires in the Rain* (1991), and *The Quick World* (1992)—provoked controversy because of its unflattering depiction of Edmond's dead husband. Her son Martin felt compelled to present a more sympathetic portrait in *The Autobiography of my Father* (1992).

McAlpine is a peculiarly uneven poet, alternately chatty and intense, banal and incandescent. She is generally at her best when incensed or grieving. Most of her best work is contained in her *Selected Poems* (1988).

Whimsical, temperate, always reticent about disclosing personal details, Smither's poems consist mostly of amused reflections on the world around her and the books she has read. Limited in emotional range but intellectually resourceful, she is like a more succinct Smithyman. *The Tudor Style: Poems New and Selected* (1993) is an excellent distillation of her work.

Anne French (b. 1956) first made her mark in literary magazines and anthologies while she was still in her teens, but she waited until the latter half of the 1980s before publishing full-length collections of her witty, well-shaped verse. In *The Male as Evader* (1988) she probes incisively into sexual politics.

Along with women, Maori writers, too, became much more visible in the 1970s. White New Zealanders of Brasch's generation, or even Stead's, had blithely assumed that traditional Maori culture was on its last legs and would soon be as extinct as the moa. Books, they believed, were beyond the ken of most of the indigenous people, whose moribund culture had always been oral. Maoris sometimes sang, but they did not write, except for a few honourable exceptions, like the poets Alistair Campbell (b. 1925) and Hone Tuwhare (b. 1922).

Highly acclaimed by the pakeha literary establishment, the poignant lyrics which Campbell wrote in the 1940s and 1950s owed much to the English Romantics. His later work, which includes novels and plays, as well as the verse gathered in *Pocket Collected Poems* (1996), is darker and more troubled by his personal demons (madness, marital problems, a pervasive sense of exile). Although he has lived in New Zealand since he was 8 years old, Campbell was born in Rarotonga. His mother was a Cook Island Maori of chiefly descent who married a Scottish trader. *Island to Island* (1984) is a deeply moving memoir which deals with Campbell's eventual return as an adult to the Cook Islands and his reassessment of the island relatives whom he wrongly imagined to have abandoned him.

Hone Tuwhare was praised in the 1960s for his tightly compressed nature poems. Later in his career, he became more expansive and colloquial, and gave free rein to his irreverent sense of humour. *Deep River Talk: Collected Poems* (1993) is a comprehensive collection of his best work.

The first book of stories to be written in English by a Maori was *Pounamu, Pounamu* (1972), whose author, Witi Ihimaera (b. 1944), went on to write the first two Maori novels, *Tangi* (1973) and *Whanau* (1974). All three of these titles refers to key concepts in Maori culture. *Pounamu* is a kind of jade used to make ornaments and tools; a *tangi* is a funeral ceremony; harder to translate accurately, *whanau* signifies the concept of the extended family in Maori villages. The central theme of all three books is the erosion of traditional Maori values as young people move increasingly to the cities. *Waiariki* (1975), an eloquent collection of stories by the Wellington-based Maori writer Patricia Grace (b. 1937), covers similar terrain.

Although an implied criticism of pakeha encroachments is omnipresent in their work, Ihimaera and Grace initially wrote more in sorrow than in anger, and their fiction seemed to pose no threat to their white readers. Indeed, liberals among the latter could afford to be generous, commiserating with the indigenes in their death throes. New Zealanders of European descent were taken by surprise, however, by the Maori renaissance in the late 1970s, when activists began to demand the teaching of Maori language and culture in schools and the return of tribal land seized without scruple by the colonial government in the last century.

The 1981 tour of the country by the Springbok rugby team from South Africa was a decisive turning-point in New Zealand's social history, dividing the citizenry like no event before or since. For decades New Zealanders had believed that the Springboks were the only worthwhile opposition for their sporting heroes, the All Blacks. By the beginning of the 1980s, however, South Africa was synonymous with racial oppression and, when die-hard rugby fans insisted that, politics be damned, the tour should go ahead, thousands of New Zealanders opposed to apartheid took to the streets in protest, leading to ugly clashes of unprecedented violence.

Pakeha liberals thought that the main concern was to express disgust at the lack of civil rights in South Africa, but Maori activists saw matters differently. They drew parallels with their own situation. If New Zealand has been lauded abroad as a haven of racial harmony, this is largely because elsewhere lynchings, riots, and massacres are the norm. Apartheid can take subtler forms. In theory, Maori people have enjoyed equal rights with Europeans since the signing of the Treaty of Waitangi in 1840. In practice, Maori people are now the urban poor; most pakehas have little contact with them and know next to nothing about how they live.

After 1981 books by Maori writers became much fiercer in tone. Donna Awatere's *Maori Sovereignty* (1984) is reminiscent of the mid-1960s tirades of such black Americans as H. Rap Brown and Eldridge Cleaver. Although they are more meticulously researched and composed than Awatere's wild call to arms, the essays of the eminent Maori academic Ranginui Walker (b. 1932), collected in *Nga Tau Tohetohe: Years of Anger* (1987) and *Struggle without End: Kau Whawhai Tonu Matou* (1990), are clearly the work of a very angry man. Witi Ihimaera's long, discursive, third novel, *The Matriarch* (1986), incorporates an accusatory reassessment of the history of European settlement. Although hers is essentially a humane and gentle voice, Patricia Grace, too, does not shrink from political confrontation in her recent fiction. In her finest novel to date, *Potiki* (1986), the *whanau* of a small coastal community battle against avaricious white property developers.

Since 1981, indeed, the novels which have made the biggest impact in New Zealand have all dealt with Maori–pakeha relations from one angle or another. Scandal contributed to the success of *Other Halves* (1982), a novel recounting a love affair between a white woman in her thirties and a teenaged Maori street boy. New Zealand readers were aware that the book's author, Sue McCauley (b. 1941), drew partly on her own romance.

Keri Hulme (b. 1947) is a writer of mixed Maori, Orkney, and English descent. Initially printed on poor paper by a women's collective with limited financial resources, after Hulme had refused to make the revisions proposed by established publishers, her first novel, *the bone people* (1983), was the subject of lively debate on its first appearance and even more so when it won the Booker Prize in 1985. Some find it gushing, incoherent, and indigestible; others a hypnotic affirmation of love's redemptive power. The truth, no doubt, is somewhere in between. Singularly resistant to plot summary, since dream sequences, bursts of hallucinatory verse, and snatches of tribal lore contribute greatly to the overall effect, *the bone people* explores the fraught relationships between three characters living on a remote stretch of the South Island: a female artist, a Maori factory worker, and his small, physically abused, foster son.

A proud literary outsider who frequently refers to his experiences in Borstal and prison, Alan Duff (b. 1950) is not a subtle writer, but he tackles contentious social issues which other New Zealand novelists have avoided. His most powerful book, *Once Were Warriors* (1990) and its sequel, *What Becomes of the Broken-Hearted* (1996), focus on Jake Heke, a brawling drunkard, and his battered kin. Utterly ignorant of his Maori heritage, Jake is a wife-beater living in a small town. One of his children becomes a gang member and is killed in a fight. Another is sent to Borstal for his part in a burglary. Another is raped and hangs herself. Accused by some critics of pandering to racial stereotypes, *Once Were Warriors* caused a huge uproar and sold in thousands. In 1994 the film adaptation quickly became the most popular movie ever to be screened in New Zealand, surpassing even *Jurassic Park*.

Although European interpretations of the Maori are now generally frowned upon, two recent books by pakeha historians have been universally respected for their fair-mindedness and painstaking research: *The New Zealand Wars and the Victorian Interpretation of Racial Conflict* (1986) by James Belich (b. 1950) and *The Treaty of Waitangi* (1987) by Claudia Orange (b. 1938). D. F. McKenzie's brief, densely argued monograph *The Oral Culture, Literacy and Print in Early New Zealand: The Treaty of Waitangi* (1985) also repays close study.

FURTHER READING

Alley, Elizabeth, and Williams, Mark (eds.), *In the Same Room: Conversations with New Zealand Writers* (Auckland, 1992).

Baysting, Arthur (ed.), *The Young New Zealand Poets* (Auckland, 1973).

Edmond, Murray, and Paul, Mary (eds.), *The New Poets: Initiatives in New Zealand Poetry* (Wellington, 1987).

Evans, Patrick, *The Penguin History of New Zealand Literature* (Auckland, 1990).

Jackson, MacDonald P., and O'Sullivan, Vincent (eds.), *The Oxford Anthology of New Zealand Writing since 1945* (Auckland, 1983).

Morrissey, Michael (ed.), *The New Fiction* (Auckland, 1985).

The Penguin Book of New Zealand Verse (Auckland, 1985).

Stead, C. K. (ed.), *The Faber Book of Contemporary South Pacific Stories* (London, 1994).

Sturm, Terry (ed.), *The Oxford History of New Zealand Literature in English* (Auckland, 1991).

Williams, Mark (ed.), *The Caxton Press Anthology of New Zealand Poetry 1972–1986* (Christchurch, 1987).

19

POLAND

GEORGE HYDE, WITH WIESŁAW POWAGA

THE fate of writing in Poland has traditionally been to articulate and shape the national consciousness through long periods of oppression and suppression, from the first partition in 1772 to the short-lived Polish Republic after 1918, the horrors of the German invasion in 1939 and the Second World War, and the Communist take-over that followed. Communism, hopelessly inefficient and in the end bereft of all effective authority, stopped the cultural clock and made it possible to resurrect the myths and archetypes of the Romantic and modernist eras, which were deeply intertwined with the sense of national identity, especially in its revolutionary guise. The Communists handled this heritage with care, and tried to turn it to their own political and quasi-political ends.

The Polish temperament also lends itself, however, to irony, game-playing, anarchic black humour, blasphemy, and what Poles refer to as a 'disinterested malice'. If in the 1960s the theatre kept returning to the Romantic classics, and recycling their characters, plots, motifs, and images, this was accompanied by an informed rediscovery of the roots of Polish Absurdism, Surrealism, performance art, Dada, and satire. Once the 'thaw' following Stalin's death (in 1953) had gathered momentum, there was a succession of productions of Witkiewicz's absurdist plays from the 1920s and 1930s, and many influential student and fringe theatre companies were inspired to emulate his vision and methods.

Although he was the foremost absurdist both before and after the Second World War, Stanisław Ignacy Witkiewicz (1885–1939) wrote a number of quasi-political fantasias which had to wait until the 1960s for their première. *Oni* ('They'), for example, was first produced in 1963, followed by lesser pieces like *Gyubal Wahazar* and *The Cuttlefish*. Witkiewicz's startlingly original novels also were reissued between 1957 and 1979.

Out of this revival there sprang Szajna's strident, semi-official Studio Theatre, and the masterly company of Tadeusz Kantor (1915–90). Kantor's 1973 production of Witkiewicz's *Nadobnisie i koczkodany* ('Lovelies and

Dowdies', also known as 'Dainty Shapes and Hairy Apes'), with its extraordinary use of the theatrical space—a significant part of the production took place not in the auditorium but in the cloakroom—was the occasion to test a new theory of the relationship between actors, text, and audience. Kantor is a representative Polish phenomenon (he dates the beginnings of his theatre from a couple of underground wartime productions). His loyal 'family' of actors worked with him day in, day out, in Kraków, on productions which he described as 'text-mincers' because they 'cut up' texts by, among others, Witkiewicz, Bruno Schulz, and Witold Gombrowicz, in order to reassemble them as collages and constructivist 'installations'.

These passionate deconstructions were imitated by lesser talents; but in their pristine forms they gave an altogether new currency to the authors in question. Schulz (1892–1942), for example, one of Kantor's key sources, was primarily a short-story writer. Sometimes called the 'Polish Kafka', he wrote, in Polish, from the margins of Galicia, about the part-Christianized Jewish communities there, about their way of life and bizarre dreams. A generation of young 'marginalized' Polish intellectuals, and innumerable hangers-on of the arts, found his Jewishness, his extreme introversion, and his sexual fetishism all equally fascinating and dangerous.

Witold Gombrowicz (1904–69) is a tougher nut for non-Poles to crack: an acerbic, ascetic formalist, he has a ruthlessly sharp eye for nonsense, pursuing it into all its favourite Polish hiding-places, and a few more besides. Kantor made particularly effective use (in *Dead Class*, 1975) of a schoolroom sequence in Gombrowicz's first novel, *Ferdydurke* (1937). This takes the form of a kind of extended exorcism of a half-remembered, half-dreamed school-time punctuated by ferocious rites of passage and humiliations, and encounters with moribund or aborted 'selves' that were never allowed to come to fruition. Accompanied by a new manifesto, and a panoply of *ad hoc* 'theories', *Dead Class* inaugurated Kantor's 'Theatre of Death'. The formalistic side of him speaks of the dead world of texts, fixed, rigid, and haunting, from which the living can never extricate themselves. Rejecting the Freudian unconscious, with its therapeutic imperatives, Kantor shows us how we are all inevitably 'haunted' and inhabit a layered 'spherical' space populated by ghosts that will never leave us alone for as long as we live. The showman in Kantor sets his ghouls twitching and parading obsessively, as if to say: stop us if you dare. In this way, the actors inhabit forever the textual world of the dead. The traumatized audience, on the other hand, eventually leaves the theatre but will keep re-running the dramatic experience, recognizing it as 'theirs'.

By the time of his death, Kantor had produced a body of theatrical work equal in quality to that of any contemporary director. His only possible rival in Poland was Jerzy Grotowski (b. 1933), whose eclectic fusion of Eastern and Western theatrical styles, and highly trained, athletic group of actors, provided him with a range of techniques that allowed him to undertake some remarkable experiments. By dissecting the classics of earlier periods, especially Polish Romanticism, and stripping his texts, right down to the bare armature of plot and gesture, Grotowski's work rapidly developed from workshop-style constructivism towards 'paratheatre'.

In general, forty years of Communist rule, far from annihilating theatre, stimulated it hugely, even to excess. Large sums of money were made available with very few strings attached, and an astonishing wealth of intelligent and imaginative work (as well as some opportunist rubbish) was produced which, if it engaged with the official ideology, did so with critical verve and insight.

This was more or less the case with poetry, too. Some leading figures emigrated, notably Czesław Miłosz, who, despite the censor's blackout exercised a great influence, especially in the 1970s, no less so with his prose, such as *The Captive Mind* (1953) or *The Land of Ulro* (1984), than with his poetry. Nevertheless a remarkable number of significant poets continued to write in People's Poland despite the censorship. Inevitably, the political situation was reflected in many of the poems most anthologized in the West, like Zbigniew Herbert's (b. 1924) 'Elegy for Fortinbras', where it coincided with themes that a non-Polish reader could identify with. But for every poem reworking, in some allegorical way, contemporary Poland's relation to her past aspirations and future hopes, there were dozens which, perhaps observing some self-denying ordinance, took domestic or parochial themes and locations as their main subject-matter. The range of styles and manners included Miron Białoszewski's (1922–83) minimalism on the one hand, and Wisława Szymborska's (b. 1923) sense of the specific tonalities of women's experience on the other (Białoszewski is notable also for having run a back-room studio theatre; for his atmospheric prose about the daily experience of provincial life; and for his Diary of the Warsaw Uprising).

In this 'mainstream' context, Tadeusz Różewicz (b. 1921) stands out as a poet who continued writing throughout the forty years of People's Poland (bearing the usual deep scars from the war) with scarcely a false or rhetorical note, picking his way along a moral tightrope of personal experience stretched between the huge edifices of Party and Church, and largely impervious to the rhetoric of both. Another poet contemporary with Herbert and Różewicz, but less well known outside Poland, Stanisław Grochowiak (1934–76), developed a kind of modern baroque style which goes well in Polish. Other poets deserving of mention are Tymoteusz Karpowicz (b. 1921), a latter-day product of the avant-garde, and Rafal Wojaczek (1945–71), one of the self-destructiuve cult figures who have always figured prominently in Polish writing.

The 'thaw' resuscitated some native talents and tendencies, and dramatically improved communication with the non-Communist world, including émigré writers. Adam Ważyk (1905–82) inaugurated a new era with his *Poemat dla dorosłych* ('Poem for Grown-Ups', 1955), an extended critique of the glaring cultural shortcomings of socialism, in whose wake there came a great flowering of talent. The extraordinary Alexander Wat (1900–67), for example, published two fine volumes of verse quite unlike his early Futurism, being both classical and meditative. A remarkably large number of these suppressed or marginalized talents went on developing intellectually and morally, reviving native strains of black irony, the grotesque, a fascination with language as a creative medium, and surrealist imagery; and they gained a significant following among the young. Exposure to the American Beat poets and their European counterparts meant that genuine folk idols were created, the most prominent among whom was Edward Stachura (1937–79), who was the kind of explosive figure that in Western Europe or the USA might have become a rock star.

One striking feature of the new Polish poetry has been the significant part played by women. Under Communism, women had (in theory) absolute equality with men; and in so far as child-rearing might prove an obstacle to this equality, the obstacle was removed by a benevolent State. Traces of a generous policy of maternity leave etc. still remain, and this is an area where the Church will intervene on the side of progressive opinion. Women's writing, therefore, while speaking out against hypocrisy and double standards, is just as likely to express resentment at the imposition of unwanted public and professional roles on women whose domestic and emotional lives were too demanding already, so that Wisława Szymborska's acerbic *Portrait of a Woman* reads like nothing more nor less than an average day in a woman's life. The women poets collected in the 1988 anthology *Ariadne's Thread* express such a wide range of emotions (even if they regularly return to the 'domestic') that one wonders if 'thread' is the right metaphor. But *political* feminism scarcely exists, even in the 1990s. Polish women seem actually to resist it.

The late 1960s and early 1970s saw the formation of a 'new wave' in poetry. Stanisław Barańczak (b. 1946), an eminent poet, translator, and scholar, played a major part in defining its objectives in terms of a concentration on the here and now, on things as they are, rather than on larger political and historical issues. At the same time, the milieux in which the new wave sprang up (the Kraków student press, the STU theatre, the group around the Poznań Theatre of the Eighth Day) meant that a lot of lively, critical young talent was directed towards, or against, the 'quality of life' in People's Poland (rather than the big political themes). Inevitably, it was not long before what started out as apolitical came under the scrutiny of the official 'organs'. As long as the older generation was showing its scars and keeping alive the traumas of recent history, and its intellectual successors were pursuing purely artistic objectives, or speaking in parables, the Party kept at a decent distance. As soon as young intellectuals began speaking out, however, about the potential of the new media, about the contemporary reality of a mass readership, about the thoughts and feelings of a real (and relatively well educated) younger generation, there were problems. These led to turbulence in the early 1970s, when Barańczak and others were forbidden to publish.

From this time also date the volumes reckoned now as defining the new wave aesthetic: Adam Zagayewski's (b. 1945) *Sklepy mięsne* ('Meat Shops', 1975); Barańczak's *Jednym tchem* ('In One Breath', 1970) and *Dziennik poranny* ('Morning News', 1972), Ryszard Krynicki's (b. 1943) *Organizm zbiorowy* ('Corporate Organism', 1975); and Julian Kornhauser's (b. 1946) *W fabrykach udajemy smutnych rewolucjonistów* ('In the factories we have the air of sad revolutionaries', 1973). A feature of all of this work is what Polish critics call its 'biographism': a preoccupation with recording the events of everyday life just as one experiences them. But what starts out as a kind of naturalism may end up as something else, as poets compose symbolic 'journeys round my skull' as a way of affirming the centrality of the individual. The exploration and assertion of the 'lyric self' becomes a lasting concern of these writers, especially the women. This in turn leads back to earlier kinds of protective irony. Parodies of official slogans and inscriptions also feature prominently, as well as a jargon that is presented (ironically) as the only language available. It is the contradiction between the personal and the public context that generates the irony, together with the sharp critical awareness always characteristic of Polish writers. Only as a dimension of personal reflection can writers get back to the 'big' themes.

After the period of martial law in 1981, and the moral victory of the Solidarity movement (preparing the way for the collapse of Communist rule), the prevalent political rhetoric, from whichever side of the fence it came, suddenly began to seem threadbare and old-fashioned. The new wave had had its day. A literary culture deeply entrenched in the heart of the national identity, and bitterly fought over with slogans, manifestos, and verbal and physical violence, fell into line with other European literatures, accepting that a mass civilization will inevitably produce a mass culture of a pluralistic kind in which the bearer of the word is no longer a prophet to be listened to in awed silence.

Donald Pirie's *Young Poets of a New Poland* (1993) shows just how far the poets have had to go to 'catch up' with an increasingly commercialized literary world. Pirie identifies—and perhaps gives too great a currency to— a 'New Privacy' movement centred on Gdańsk, in which a new preoccupation with inwardness manifests itself in obscure personal symbols and desperate, violent gestures. Krystyna Lars's (b. 1950) poem 'Giving Birth to a Knife', for example, links love and hate in a terrifying conjuncture; it could have been written anywhere, not just in Poland. And Grzegorz Musiał (b. 1952) finds no cure for his apocalyptic neuroticism in America's bland sensuousness. These poets write as if they can be reasonably sure that their paranoid obsessions (especially in the areas of sex and death) are shared by their readers.

If the women poets—like Anna Czekanowicz (b. 1952), Krystyna Lars, and Urszula Benka (b. 1955)—use even more sado-masochistic imagery, and seem even more conscious than the men of an eternal cycle of oppression and subjugation working itself out in life, feminist politics nevertheless remain conspicuous by their absence. The condition of women is simply offered as an extreme but representative case of the human condition. And this in turn may be symptomatic of a new response to the iconography of Catholicism (belief, in any proper sense of the word, may be waning fast, but as it does so, it releases a rich pattern of images). Some of these 'private' poets still tend to fall in behind 'Western' influences even as they recognize that a large part of Poland's problems in the 1990s spring from the fact that, however enthusiastically she embraces pluralism, her traumatic history still confronts her. One of the best contemporary poets, Bronisław Maj (b. 1953), managed during the 1980s to be both political and private, and to find a voice that was in keeping with the complex allegiances of the Polish literary tradition. The latest generation of Punk and post-Punk poets, the so-called 'Barbarians', managed a cleaner break.

The numerous sticking points in Poland's journey towards Western-style reforms show up even more clearly in the work of prose writers, and of the 'new' film-makers. After 1945, prose went down the same political and allegorical roads as verse and drama; more obviously so, indeed, because of the nature of its audience. The need to record wartime atrocities went hand in hand with the need to forge a literary style accessible to the new Communist mass society that remained to be created.

For novelists, as for poets, bearing witness to the recent past was the most urgent task. Writers like Jerzy Andrzejewski (1909–83), Zofia Nałkowska (1884–1954), and Tadeusz Borowski (1922–51) set themselves the task of recording the impact of Nazism in both theory and practice, and of the lasting psychological damage it had done. Andrzejewski rapidly became the most talked-about novelist of the time. His *Ashes and Diamonds* (1948) represented history as a fatality that had brought Poland to a point where only one choice was possible. The masterly film that Andrzej Wajda (b. 1928) made of this novel not only put Polish cinema on the map, it gave international audiences a charismatic and not altogether misleading glimpse of the national character.

In the period from 1949 to 1955, a highly prescriptive Socialist Realism marginalized all other kinds of prose writing, but with the 'thaw' new foreign influences helped to restore Polish fiction's speculative, metaphysical interests. One author in particular, Marek Hłasko (1934–69), took on the mantle of an 'outsider' figure for his contemporaries, with real artistic success—his *The Eighth Day of the Week* (1957; this is the extra day we need, but never get, in which to put everything straight) is a minor masterpiece and gave its name to Poznań's Theatre of the Eighth Day, the best of the 'unofficial' theatres of the 1970s.

One of the largest and most enduring talents of the time was Tadeusz Konwicki (b. 1926). He has a reputation among British readers, who have shown interest in his haunted landscapes full of unresolved conflicts and confrontations, dating back to the war, though coming also right up to the present. *The Polish Complex* (1977) starts in a queue outside a Warsaw jeweller's shop on Christmas Eve, where the crowd are waiting for Russian gold to arrive: a bitter contemporary gloss on the gifts brought by the Wise Men. Konwicki has seen the whole post-war period out: beginning as a Socialist Realist, he went through turbulent periods of changing allegiances, political persecution, and personal depression, always regaining his equilibrium in some new and different style of writing which exercised another part of his tortured personality. Throughout his career, he has also been engaged in film-making, most notably as an adventurous director. In all his work, a tough, sardonic manner carries him through many crises.

Many other writers besides Konwicki kept coming back to the war from strange personal angles, as if to subvert the official version of events which the Party kept refurbishing for its own purposes (it looks as if this trauma will outlast Communism, since important writers of the 1990s—Hanna Krall (b. 1937), for instance—are still doing the same). Konwicki has used this 'haunting' technique to represent other periods of Polish history, while other writers similarly have made telling points about the wounds that never heal because Polish history keeps repeating its saga of defeat and dismemberment. Konwicki's *A Dreambook for our Time* (1963) finds a parallel in novels by Roman Bratny (b. 1921), Andrzej Wydrzyński (b. 1921), Zofia Posmysz (b. 1923), whose *Pasażerka* ('Passenger', 1962) was turned into a fine, sadly unfinished film by Andrzej Munk, and others. The kinds of freedom discovered here in the treatment of historical time (*vis-à-vis* 'personal' time, and the 'official' march of history towards the classless society) re-opened some of the sacrosanct national themes treated very differently in the huge historical novels that bulk so large in Polish nineteenth-century writing; so that one can say that the Communist era revived the historical novel, as one might have expected, but only after passing it through a modernist prism: a characteristic Polish contradiction.

Another 'institutional' genre which was updated was the 'regionalist' novel of rural life. Konwicki has contributed to this trend as well (not least in *Bohin*, 1987). The enforced collectivization of agriculture was Polish Communism's biggest failure: the resistance of the peasants was so effective that the reforms, some of them necessary by anyone's standards, were not carried through.

Communist agricultural policy had literary consequences, however. The Gardzienice theatre group, whose name is taken from a small rural settlement not far from the eastern city of Lublin, made excellent capital out of the combined sense of apprehension and release that people (the 'audience') felt on being confronted by strange ritual events in some muddy field, with a crumbling barn for backdrop. The programme of the company includes not just performances/rituals, but also the revival of the communal artistic life of the village, in music, song, and story. The project was originally less utopian than it now sounds, given that the Communists were trying to preserve, centralize, and market a range of folk crafts, along with an idea of 'community'.

Perhaps the most intensely debated recent work of this tendency is Wiesław Myśliwski's (b. 1932) *The Palace* (1970). The ritual elements of this highly stylized narrative, while in no way embodying any real corpus of rural practice, contrive to suggest an 'organic' continuum between dream and natural rhythms.

The question of 'roots' is, of course, very much larger. Paweł Łysek's (b. 1914) stories of Silesia; Edward Redliński's (b. 1940) very popular novel *Konopielka* (1973), in which a woman coming to teach in a village wreaks havoc there by her unconventionality; or Erwin Kruk's (b. 1941) *The Mazury Chronicle* (1989), which deals openly with problems of ethnic identity in

Mazuria or the former East Prussia (and the mass exodus from there into Germany) are among the most significant works of this kind. And given how sensitive the Jewish question is in Poland, mention needs to be made of Julian Stryjkowski's (b. 1905) *Austeria* (1966), and Andrzej Szczypiorski's (b. 1924) *A Mass for the City of Arras* (1971) and *The Beautiful Mrs Seidenman* (1988), all of which deal with Polish–Jewish relations in a sympathetic but objective way. Writing about the Jewish experience that does not have directly to do with the Holocaust is gradually making its impact felt.

Some critics bracket the newer kinds of rural and regional writing with a distinctively Polish variety of 'faction', i.e. quasi-fictional documentary or reportage. As with other kinds of writing, this looks at first sight as if Poland were simply following in the wake of the USA or Britain, at a distance of some ten or twenty years; but this is only partly true. Polish 'faction' has a more comprehensive brief, in terms of a traditional truth-telling function: it offers an alternative reading of history, in a society where the press, and even most history books, have refused to tell the truth about certain key issues. Polish 'faction' is on the whole harder-hitting than its equivalent in the West. The author who has received most attention in this respect is Melchior Wańkowicz (1892–1974), especially for his book *Ziele na kraterze* ('Wild Flowers Grow on the Volcano', 1951). The biggest name in international terms, however, is that of Ryszard Kapuściński (b. 1932), who is sometimes treated simply as a journalist, but whose major reportages break new ground in their treatment of history. They have all been translated and enthusiastically received abroad, including his recent book about the fall of the Soviet Union, *Imperium* (1993).

Another genre still gathering momentum is the very distinctive Polish variety of science fiction. Stanisław Lem (b. 1921) has long been recognized as one of the world's leading SF authors. More recent writers include Jerzy Lipka (b. 1943) and Emma Popik, both of whom have used science fiction and fantasy to comment on contemporary life. With writers like Marek Huberath (b. 1954), Maciej Żerdziński (b. 1967), Andrzej Sapkowski (b. 1948), and Jacek Dukaj (b. 1974), we are in the realm of ground-breaking syntheses of fantasy, horror, and satire, which yet have their roots in real Polish experience—Huberath, for example, goes back to the concentration camps in order to return to portray contemporary Polish life with a fresh and lurid intensity.

There is now a general anxiety among Polish writers and critics that the political changes in their country will not prove propitious for the prolongation of what has been a remarkable creative flowering for a 'small nation' with a difficult language. State-funded publishing houses which once looked quite immovable have collapsed or been taken over. Journals with the most honourable credentials have gone bankrupt, or are hanging on with great difficulty, with the help of foreign advertising revenue. There are powerful indications of a radical swing in readership, away from serious literature to the kind of entertainment that accounts for the majority slice of the market in the capitalist world: indeed, a lot of the best-selling books are now translations, especially from English.

On the other hand, there are also new journals, new writers, and new kinds of writing: for example, the beginnings of a more 'interventionist' and at the same time popular kind of feminism—that of Maria Nurowska, for instance; or an unprecedented willingness to write about taboo subjects in a taboo language. Poles are not prudish, but until very recently they observed much stricter standards of literary decorum than we do. A book like Andrzej Stasiuk's (b. 1960) *Mury Hebronu* ('The Walls of Hebron', 1992), for example, was found shocking by many readers on account of its vulgarity. It is a kind of prison diary and pulls no punches.

In general, it is hard to believe that market forces in Poland will destroy a vibrant literary culture that has survived through hundreds of years of persecution.

FURTHER READING

Bassnett, S., and Kuhiwczak, P. (eds. and trans.), *Ariadne's Thread: Polish Women Poets* (London, 1988).

Czerniawski, Adam (ed. and trans.), *The Burning Forest: Modern Polish Poetry* (Newcastle upon Tyne, 1988).

Czerwinski, E. J., *Contemporary Polish Theater and Drama, 1956–84* (New York, 1988).

Eile, Sranislaw, and Phillips, Ursula (eds. and trans.), *New Perspectives in Twentieth Century Polish Literature* (London, 1992).

Halikowska, Teresa, and Hyde, George (eds. and trans.), *The Eagle and the Crow: Modern Polish Short Stories* (London, forthcoming).

Pirie, Donald (ed. and trans.), *Young Poets of a New Poland* (London, 1993).

Powaga, Wiesław (ed. and trans.), *The Dedalus Book of Polish Fantasy* (London, 1996).

20

PORTUGAL

MARIA GUTERRES

From 1925 to 1974 Portugal was a Fascist dictatorship, ruled first by Antonio de Oliveira Salazar and then, after Salazar had a stroke in 1968, by Marcelo Caetano, who essentially maintained the status quo. Salazar's was a repressive and brutal regime, which crushed all opposition in violent fashion. Writers could be penalized or imprisoned if their work was considered to be of a subversive nature.

The effects of this censorship were enormous. Some writers, in order to get their works published, practised a kind of self-censorship, but others were able to publish only after 1974. On 25 April of that year a bloodless Revolution took place, organized by a group of left-wing army officers (but supported by a large part of the army) who had taken part in colonial wars in Portuguese Africa, and wanted to put a stop to them. Portugal became a democracy, and a year later Angola, Mozambique, and other colonies became independent.

Salazar's legacy of poverty, illiteracy, and inequality has made it difficult for the country to modernize quickly, but since the Revolution, and its entry into the European Community in 1986, Portuguese society has undergone many changes. If the Revolution did not achieve the utopia so many left-wing writers had hoped for, at least it ended censorship and allowed books to be published that dealt with political events preceding the Revolution, and with the colonial wars.

From the 1940s onwards Portuguese writing had been dominated by the movement known as Neo-realism: a term used locally as a disguise for social realism and for alternative descriptions such as Marxist, socialist or Communist, which were forbidden by the censors. The Neo-realists themselves were in reaction against the Presença group of the 1930s, which had defended an aesthetic of art-for-art's-sake: they wanted a committed literature. They believed in the need to study the socio-historical process as the basis for their analysis of humanity and society, rather than trusting in intuition and introspection. In its first phase (from the late 1930s to the

1960s) Neo-realism was above all dedicated to the progress of one class—the proletariat.

But from the late 1950s onwards, although Neo-realist writers still believed in the ultimate ideal of a transformation of man and society, that belief became more complex and sophisticated. Writers began to be concerned with the middle classes and their problems, and the characters in their novels were more individualized. The majority of the writers who began or continued to publish in the 1960s, are, in one way or another, linked to Neo-realism, though it is also true that the first effects of Existentialism began to be felt in Portugal at this time, under the influence of Sartre and Heidegger, as well as, later, the effects of the French *nouveau roman*.

Carlos de Oliveira (1921–81) was a poet and prose writer who published his first book of poems, *Turismo*, in 1942. The themes which are constants in his work are already to be found here: solitude, love and death, childhood, and solidarity with the people. However, in *Cantata* (1960), *Micropaisagem* ('Micro-landscape', 1965), and *Entre duas memórias* ('Between Two Memories', 1971), he began to interest himself in other themes: memory and writing itself. In *Aprendiz de feiticeiro* ('Sorcerer's Apprentice', 1973) he describes how he had constructed *Micropaisagem*: 'For me, this work consists almost always in achieving a very spare text, deduced from itself, which sometimes forces me to transform it into a meditation on its own development and destiny . . . A text looking at itself in the mirror, seeing itself and "thinking itself".' In *Micropaisagem*, Carlos de Oliveira intertwines the themes of memory and of forgetting with that of writing, using only a limited number of images taken from the mineral world. Words are analysed, repeated, ordered, and elaborated differently from stanza to stanza, so as to reconstitute the genesis of the poem: 'The poem | attains | such concentration | that it transforms | lucidity | itself | to energy | and explodes | to come out | of itself.' Carlos de Oliveira is a poet who has had a profound influence on writers of younger generations.

Jorge de Sena (1919–78), essayist, short-story writer, literary critic, dramatist, and poet, is the author of a huge literary output; he was forced into exile in 1959, and spent many years as a teacher in Brazil and the United States. *The Poetry of Jorge de Sena* (1982), which includes poems from all his collections, illustrates the difficulties of his poetic language. This is characterized on the one hand by the socio-political concerns of Neo-realism, and on the other by his awareness of the individual and his presence in the world. Sena's is a conceptual and intellectual poetry, at times realist and satirical, in general anti-lyrical, though he was also a considerable love poet. Of his fiction, two works stand out: his novella *The Wondrous Physician*

(1977) and *By the Rivers of Babylon and Other Stories* (1989). The first is based on two medieval tales, which Sena combines and in which the Devil helps a young man by giving him miraculous powers in exchange for sex with the Devil himself: the story is a meditation on the conflict between good and evil, and the relationship between sin and responsibility. The title story of *By the Waters of Babylon* describes the last days of Camões, the greatest of all Portuguese epic and lyric poets, on whom Sena also wrote important critical essays.

One of the more significant writers who appeared on the scene in the 1960s is Luis de Sttau Monteiro (1926–93), who was both a novelist and a dramatist. In his fictional work he criticizes the bourgeois society of his time and its institutions, showing how the middle class and the State are interdependent. It is, however, as a dramatist that he is best known. When Sttau began to write plays, the Portuguese theatre, with few exceptions, was still under the influence of naturalism and the bourgeois drama. So he had to look elsewhere to find his own concept of theatrical technique. He found it in Brecht and John Osborne. Like José Cardoso Pires in his play *O render dos heróis* ('The Heroes' Surrender', 1960), Sttau chose in *Felizmente há luar* ('Happily There's Moonlight', 1961) a historical event through which to explore modern themes. Both writers use episodes from the nineteenth century—respectively, a rebellion in the north of the country in 1846, and the death in 1817 of Gomes Freire de Andrade, a general who rebelled against English rule in Portugal during the absence of King John VI in Brazil; both are events intimately connected with the rise of Liberalism in Portugal. As dramatized, they are only a pretext for a denunciation of the lack of freedom in contemporary Portugal, however. In *Felizmente há luar*, the people, whose role in the conspiracy was in fact minimal, form a permanent background to the action, being present on stage almost throughout. They are the moral yardstick against which all the actions of the play are judged; though, since they have no political power, their importance is only potential. In the Sttau play, Gomes Freire, who never appears on stage, is a kind of Christ-figure, and represents a criterion by which society as a whole is to be judged; he is both a political symbol in his own right and the beginning of a historical process. In this play, a successful conjunction of epic and drama, Sttau created a theatre which rejects facile emotions and appeals to the conscience of the audience. It is up to the audience to react to it in the way they see fit.

The other major contributor to the renewal of drama in Portugal was Bernardo Santareno (1924–80), who wrote eighteen plays, above all melodramas, between 1957 and 1979, and succeeded in creating a politically committed theatre, with popular roots. Not all his plays were successful, but *O Judeu* ('The Jew', 1960) stands out. Santareno, too, had discovered Brecht's epic theatre, and *O Judeu* is a didactic play, a faithful recounting of the life of Antonio José da Silva (1705–39), a famous eighteenth-century dramatist who was condemned as a heretic and burnt at the stake by the Inquisition. The narrator of the play, who also comments on its action, is the writer Cavaleiro de Oliveira (1702–83), who converted to Protestantism and spent most of his life in exile. Present on stage throughout, he advises the Jew to go into exile while there is still time. He contrasts the luxurious court life of King John V with the extreme poverty of his people, commenting sarcastically on the hypocrisy and fanaticism of both clergy and nobility, and the ignorance of the people, who believe that the Jews are the cause of all the nation's ills. By thus instructing the audience, the narrator encourages it to take action. At the end, King, court, and people applaud the burning just as they have earlier applauded the Jew's plays. The play ends with a cry from the narrator: 'Enlighten the people of Portugal!' *O Judeu* is a *tour de force*.

One of the writers most admired and read in this period was Fernando Namora (1919–89). Along with Carlos de Oliveira, he had initiated and consolidated Neo-realism, publishing his first novel in 1938. He wrote novels, poetry, essays, and memoirs, and is recognized as one of the most lucid observers of Portuguese society, both urban and rural. He published his last work a year before his death, and was for long a constant presence in the literary life of the country. Towards the end of the 1950s Namora moved away in his fiction from the ruralism of *O trigo e o joio* ('The Wheat and the Chaff', 1954) to a more urban, existentialist mode, critical of a decadent bourgeois society. In *O homem disfarçado* ('The Disguised Man', 1957) themes such as alienation, solitude, failure, *Angst*, and the loss of, and search for, identity appear, to be further explored in later novels such as *Domingo à tarde* ('Sunday Afternoon', 1961) and *Rio triste* ('Sad River', 1982).

Namora was a doctor and a cancer specialist, and in *Domingo à tarde* a doctor falls in love with a patient who has leukaemia, and lives with her for the last few months before her death. Though at the beginning the doctor sees his patients only as either curable or incurable, the novel recounts the process by which, through self-analysis and reflection on his past life, he achieves a vital transformation. *Rio triste* is an ambitious and successful novel, set in the 1960s, which contains a variety of perspectives: it has one narrator within the story, a second, omniscient one outside it, and also advances the story by means of letters and a diary. Here, two milieux are present: that of a middle-rank civil servant whose disappearance constitutes the enigma which the reader has to try to solve; and that of the literary, artistic, and journalistic world as it comes to terms with censorship, illegal strikes repressed by the police, emigration for both economic and political reasons, and the war in the colonies. This complex, multifaceted novel is Namora's masterpiece.

In the preface to his *Os desertores* ('The Deserters', 1967), Augusto Abelaira (b. 1926) wrote that 'there is only one novel inside me', and this novelist and dramatist has in fact devoted his work to the 'deserters' of contemporary society. All his novels are set in middle-class environments, in countries without political freedom. *A cidade e as flores* ('The City and the Flowers, 1959), which is set in Italy to avoid the censorship, is an attack on dictatorship. *As boas intenções* ('Good Intentions', 1963) attacks social inequality; and the institution of marriage is analysed in *Enseada amena* ('Pleasant Bay', 1966) and *Bolor* ('Mildew', 1968). In spite of their attempts to reach a more genuine existence, Abelaira's heroes remain trapped in their inauthenticity and are 'deserters' from a society itself in a state of collapse. *Sem tecto entre ruínas* ('Roofless among Ruins', 1978), published only after the 1974 Revolution though written before it, returns to the same themes. In this book Abelaira denounces the emptiness of a language which is a means, no longer of communication, but rather of avoiding silence. His characters, like the nation itself, are inert and static. The novel is circular, inasmuch as the final scene repeats the first, except that now the protagonist sees himself as he is seen by others. The characters are highly intelligent and cultured but alienated by their inability to act effectively in society. They are reduced to having amorous adventures in a hopeless, feelingless world where words have replaced meaningful actions.

Vergílio Ferreira (b. 1916) began publishing in 1949, as a Neo-realist, but soon came under the influence of Existentialism. Novels such as *Alegria breve* ('Brief Happiness', 1965) and *Nítido nulo* ('Clear Nothing', 1971) dramatize the main contentions of his work: an awareness, on the one hand, that there is no intimate, personal truth that might justify humanity's presence on earth, and, on the other, that all practical action in a social context is absurd. Artistic and aesthetic creation, and communion with other human beings, are more important than political action. The central character of *Nítido nulo* is in prison awaiting execution, and recalling his past. He has led a political revolution and has had a statue erected in his honour. But he has himself destroyed this statue on realizing that the present merely repeats the past: true freedom is revealed to be a state of mind. Ferreira's memoirs, *Conta corrente* ('Current Account'), published in five volumes between 1980 and 1987, are a vital source for understanding his work. He is a difficult writer, though well worth reading, for he is by far the best of the Portuguese existentialist novelists.

José Cardoso Pires (b. 1925), one of the most talented writers of his generation, achieved his first real impact with the short novel *O anjo ancorado* ('The Anchored Angel', 1958). This portrays a paralysed society, in which a frustrated and disenchanted generation loses itself in endless, circular discussions. *O hóspede de Job* ('Job's Guest', 1963) recounts, with a complete lack of sentimentality, the search of two men, one old, one young, for work in the impoverished south of Portugal, during the Salazar years. *O delfim* ('The Dauphin', 1968) is Pires's masterpiece, however, a novel that dismantles a number of national myths. In it the first-person narrator, who is both writer and hunter, recounts what has happened a year earlier, when he had known the main characters: the engineer (the dauphin of the title), his wife, and their manservant. It is the engineer himself—the word is more an honorific title than a job-description in Portugal—who is the creator of myths, and who comes under scrutiny and criticism. He incarnates the survival of a medieval mentality: rich, powerful, arrogant, superior, paternalistic towards his workers, he chases after other women while his own frustrated wife seeks solace with the manservant. In the end, she kills her lover and commits suicide, so leading to the destruction of the 'Lake House', the engineer's manor-house, which symbolizes his power and that of his class. Pires's *Ballad of Dogs' Beach* (1982) could only have been published after the Revolution, and is a novel about fear. It is based on a true story, set in the Salazar era, and is narrated by means of documents, police reports, newspaper cuttings, etc., so as to give the flavour of the time. In *Alexandra Alpha* (1988), Pires analyses the problem of Portuguese identity after the Revolution, by contrasting the past of the Fascist regime and colonial wars with the present Revolution, which has failed to realize the hopes that inspired it.

These are also the principal themes of António Lobo Antunes (b. 1942), a surgeon and psychiatrist who began to publish novels after the Revolution. *South of Nowhere*, originally published as *Os cus de Judas* ('Judas's Bums', 1979), is an autobiographical novel set in Angola during the colonial war there, but also a love story. The protagonist and narrator, a young army officer and typical left-wing bourgeois, analyses what the war is doing to him, and how it affects his personal and public life. He observes the corruption of the Portuguese who live there, the brutality, and his own fear and solitude. Once back in Portugal, he cannot understand why the colonial wars have not affected the people of the metropolis in the same way. The novel's success was no doubt partly due to its appeal to a younger, disillusioned generation of Portuguese readers. In *An Explanation of the Birds* (1981) and *As naus* ('The Ships', 1988), Lobo Antunes sarcastically analyses the decadence of Portuguese society since the collapse of the Empire, relentlessly demystifying all its failed heroes. He continues to be a very popular writer in Portugal, even though critics have not always been kind to him.

Almeida Faria (b. 1943) is a more original writer. His 'Lusitanian tetralogy'—*A Paixão* ('The Passion', 1965), *Cortes* ('Cuts', 1978), *Lusitânia* (1980), and *Cavaleiro andante* ('Knight at arms', 1983)—is structured around the rite of passage by which Portugal passed from authoritarianism to the saving grace of democracy. The four novels follow the fate of a middle-class family (the patriarchal, Salazarist father, the rebellious, militant son) through the events of the Revolution, which, however, turns out to be a false dawn. With Faria, as with other contemporary novelists, we begin to see the 1974 Revolution becoming one more myth in the country's history.

That Revolution came at a good time to advance the cause of women writers. In 1972 Maria Isabel Barreiro (b. 1939), Maria Teresa Horta, (b. 1937), and Maria Velho da Costa (b. 1938) published *The Three Marias: New Portuguese Letters*. This was banned by the regime, and its three authors were officially condemned, accused of an abuse of freedom and of having outraged public decency. After 1974 the verdict was quashed. The book's huge success was understandable, for it rebelled against the backward situation of women in Portugal, who were then mainly confined to the home and financially dependent on men: women were only given the vote in 1969. *New Portuguese Letters* is an epistolary novel, which reconstructs the life of the nun Mariana Alcoforado, the reputed author of the *Lettres portugaises* (1669—in fact, probably written by a Frenchman). *The Three Marias* uses this seventeenth-century nun as a symbol of women's oppression, in telling the stories of various modern victims of a patriarchal system. The novel's open eroticism was one reason why it was officially condemned.

Although the 'three Marias' have had a great influence on women's writing, other women writers before them had already made a considerable reputaton: Agustina Bessa Luís (b. 1922), for example, a writer of conservative values, who is the author of more than twenty novels. The best of these are *Fanny Owen* (1979) and *O mosteiro* ('The Monastery', 1980). Her novels, set amongst the decadent rural middle or upper classes, are almost devoid of dialogue, and given over to the detailed psychological analysis of her characters.

Lídia Jorge (b. 1946) is the most important woman writer to have appeared since Agustina Bessa Luís. Her novels focus on the problem of

Portuguese identity. *O dia dos prodígios* ('The Day of Miracles', 1979) is set in a village in the Algarve before and after the Revolution, and uses the language and culture of that region to show how little has changed in the life of the villagers, in spite of political upheaval. *O cais das merendas* ('Teatime on the Dockside', 1982) deals with the effects of tourism on the Algarve, and with the risks it poses to the local population, in terms of retaining their cultural identity. In *A costa dos murmúrios* ('The Whispering Coast', 1988) this same theme is combined with that of the colonial war in Mozambique. Words which had been reduced to 'murmurs', or spoken in hushed tones so that the wrong people should not hear them, words like 'war', 'domination', 'colonialism', and 'Fascism', often camouflaged beneath such alternatives as 'rebellion', 'multiracial societies', and 'overseas provinces', are now returned to the everyday language of the people. Lídia Jorge has made a highly original contribution to Portuguese fiction, above all by her juxtaposition, essentially demystifying in its purpose, of the traditional and modern aspects of contemporary Portugal.

The finest writer to have appeared in the past thirty years, however, is José Saramago (b. 1922). Saramago, who was self-taught, had several different jobs before dedicating himself to journalism and literature. He began by writing poetry and for the theatre, and was 55 years old before his first novel, *Manual of Painting and Calligraphy* (1977), appeared. Its central character is a 'mediocre' painter, who uses writing as a means of self-discovery: his encounters with the mistress of one of his sitters, who is a pillar of the regime, and then with the sister of a political prisoner, lead him towards the discovery of his real vocation as a writer, a discovery that coincides, on the last page of the book, with the 25 April 1974 uprising. *Levantado do chão* ('Lifted from the Earth', 1980) is a Neo-realist novel, based on real events, describing the lives of four generations of rural workers in the impoverished Alentejo. It takes us from the 1920s right up to the Revolution, and the subsequent occupation of the land by the peasants. Saramago gives great importance in this novel to the role of women, who are the guardians of memory and oral tradition, and whose achievement of self-awareness is a vital part of the collective struggle.

Baltasar and Blimunda (1982) is the translation of *Memorial do convento*— literally, 'The Memoir of the Convent', the convent in question being Mafra, just outside Lisbon, built by the spendthrift King John V in the 1730s to fulfil a religious vow. This tells the double story, first of the people who built this gigantic white elephant, and then of the construction of the 'passarola', a sort of flying machine, by the visionary Father Bartolomeu de

Gusmão. The building workers, not the clergy and nobility, are the heroes of the book, which also contains the story of the love affair between Baltasar, a soldier who has lost a hand and who ends up being burnt at the stake, and Blimunda, a clairvoyante. The novel is a spectacular evocation of the backwardness, superstition, and intolerance of Portugal in its economic heyday, as well as of the resistance of (some of) the people to the regime.

The Year of the Death of Ricardo Reis (1984) is Saramago's own favourite among his novels. It is set in Lisbon and evokes a different period of repression, that of the 1930s. It has two heroes: the poet Fernando Pessoa, who was by then dead, and Ricardo Reis, one of Pessoa's several 'heteronyms', or imaginary writers, each of whom was given his own style and outlook. Reis has recently returned from Brazil after the death of his creator. He has a sexual relationship with Lídia, a hotel maid, and a platonic relationship with Marcenda, a middle-class woman with a traditionalist father who suffers from a mysterious psychosomatic paralysis in one arm. As in *Manual of Painting and Calligraphy*, the oppressive atmosphere of the novel gradually reveals its political basis to lie in Salazar's dictatorship, but the counterpoint between this and the poets' discussions about life and literature, about the real and the ideal, and the nature of Portuguese history, make this novel an altogether richer and more integrated work than the earlier one.

Saramago has since written three more novels: *A jangada de pedra* ('The Stone Boat', 1986), *A história do cerco de Lisboa* ('The Story of the Siege of Lisbon', 1989), and *The Gospel According to Jesus Christ* (1991). The first two have not (so far) been translated, no doubt because of their more exclusively Portuguese or Iberian subject-matter. *A jangada de pedra* imagines the whole peninsula drifting free from Europe, and speculates as to its cultural unity. *A história do cerco de Lisboa* is a historical novel, set in the Middle Ages. *The Gospel According to Jesus Christ* is a retelling of the gospel story in radically materialist and unconventional terms, which, even in the (relatively) liberal atmosphere of today's Portugal, has brought the author into conflict with the (conservative) government, which refused to put the book up for a literary prize.

Saramago's novels have both strength and originality, both colour and that capacity to shock and envelop one in an exotic yet real atmosphere (even the drab Lisbon of the 1930s has its exoticism as described by him) that is the hallmark of the best Latin American novelists. Much of his power lies in his prose style, which has a powerful rhythm of its own, and which, by avoiding dialogue, manages to dilute the reality of his characters into their historical context.

FURTHER READING

De Sousa, A. G., and Warner, I. R. (eds.), *An Anthology of Modern Portuguese and Brazilian Prose* (London, 1978).

Macedo, H., and de Melo e Castro, E. M. (eds.), *Contemporary Portuguese Poetry: An Anthology in English* (Manchester, 1978).

Sadlier, D. J., *The Question of How: Women Writers and New Portuguese Literature* (Westport, Conn., 1989).

Studies in Modern Portuguese Literature (New Orleans, 1971).

21

RUSSIA

ROBERT PORTER

CONTEMPORARY Russian writing—writing *in* Russian, that is: I cannot be concerned here with writing done in the former Soviet Union in its various other languages—presents special problems of definition. Is one to deal with works being written and—promptly—published now? Or to include those finally being published in Russia, although they were written many years before when, for ideological reasons, they had no hope of publication? And what part does literature written and/or published hitherto only in emigration play in what is today a literary world governed primarily by the market-place?

The situation that seems to have emerged in the post-Communist era is one in which serious works exist in an uneasy and, as some Russian intellectuals see it, destructive symbiosis with popular fiction, outright trash, and pornography. Moreover, the sheer volume of serious literature published since Gorbachev relaxed controls after 1985 adds to the obstacles facing the would-be guide. Initially, it was questioned whether there was any such thing as a 'new' or 'young' generation of writers. In the late 1980s, mainstream literary journals (where, by tradition, the bulk of Russian literature first gets published) were too busy coping with the backlog that had built up during the era of stagnation under Brezhnev to address the work of newcomers; yet at the same time editors realized that they had certain obligations to the newcomers as well as to current *émigré* literature, not to mention previously unacceptable foreign writing which could now be made available in Russian translation. Problems of distribution and even paper production aside, Russians were now as free as they had been in the 1920s to read what they liked, and writers were free to resume in public the experimentalism practised by their predecessors decades before but which had been driven underground by the Socialist Realist decrees issued in 1932.

Given which, it is as well not to try and find any overall pattern or trend which might be visible to a future critic with the benefit of hindsight. Suffice it to say that a degree of 'normalcy' was now to be seen in the Russian world of letters, as the old bureaucratic structures crumbled (the Union of Soviet Writers, the censorship) and state prizes (notably the Lenin Prize) were discontinued, while new literary groupings emerged (for example *Aprel'*), a branch of the Pen Club was opened in 1989, and a Russian Booker Prize was established in 1992.

Hanging over Russian writing since 1985 has been the vexed question of 'dissident writers', a term I use with some reluctance, since all serious writers are dissidents to the extent that they challenge accepted norms and values. In the Soviet period, a great many writers were persecuted or proscribed to varying degrees and as such can be classed together as 'dissidents'; yet not very many of them took an overtly oppositional stance in the political sense. The comic writer Vladimir Voinovich (b. 1932) declared, with characteristic levity and irreverence, that after he was banned he did not fight for freedom, he enjoyed it. By 'dissident' I mean here any writer who attacked the Soviet establishment head-on, challenging its philosophy, its version of history, and its actions.

The most conspicuous example of this sort of dissident writer is Aleksandr Solzhenitsyn (b. 1918), but others whose most outspoken work was banned under Brezhnev include the novelist Georgy Vladimov (b. 1931) and the short-story writer Varlam Shalamov (1907–82), the memoirists Lev Kopelev (b. 1912) and Nadezhda Mandelshtam (1899–1980), and political theorists and civil rights activists such as Andrei Amalrik (1938–80), Vladimir Bukovsky (b. 1942), the twins Zhores and Roy Medvedev (b. 1925), and especially Andrei Sakharov (1921–89).

Will Solzhenitsyn ultimately be remembered for his fiction—*One Day in the Life of Ivan Denisovich* (1962), *The First Circle* (Frankfurt, 1968), *Cancer Ward* (Frankfurt, 1968)—or for his 'literary investigation' into the Soviet labour camp system and its history *The Gulag Archipelago* (Paris, 1973–5), which among other things lays the blame for the evils of Stalinism firmly at Lenin's door, or for his monumental cycle of historical novels *The Red Wheel*—the first version of the first volume of which is better known as *August 1914* (Paris, 1971)? Are his propagandistic works and his open letters, which sought to expose the evils of Communism and to renew Russia morally, the real kernel of his *œuvre*? Whatever the final judgement, Solzhenitsyn has exerted an undeniable moral influence throughout the world, in an age when morality is unfashionable or often seems hard to define. His is the voice of individual conscience and his writing tends to contain characters who are either wholly black or wholly white. The ending of *Cancer Ward* leaves us with the image of a monkey in the zoo, blinded by 'an evil man'—not by an 'enemy of the people' or an 'imperialist agent'. At last, two years after Stalin's death—which is when *Cancer Ward* is set—ordinary people are beginning, instinctively, once again to make clear-cut distinctions between right and wrong and are no longer duped by ideology.

Such adherence to rigid moral categories, coupled with a fundamentalist conception of literature as a vehicle for conveying authentic experience, would set Solzhenitsyn apart from many contemporary writers—and not least from his compatriot Andrei Sinyavsky (1925–97), who, together with Yuly Daniel (1925–88), was tried in 1966, served a prison term, and was then allowed to emigrate to Paris. Sinyavsky's writing illustrates another Russian literary tradition, that of the fantastic, the absurd, and the obscure. One of his stories, 'Phkhents', concerns a creature from outer space who crash-lands in the Soviet Union, and has to contort his limbs, practise self-censorship, and adapt his values in order to survive undetected. Sinyavsky also wrote a penetrating essay 'What is Socialist Realism?', which likened this officially sponsored theory to eighteenth-century classicism, and advocated in its stead the literature of the fantastic. The publication of these and other works in the West under the pseudonym Abram Tertz (they were eventually collected in one volume, *The Fantastic World of Abram Tertz*, New York, 1967) amounted in the eyes of the Soviet authorities to an act of sedition.

It was ironic that Sinyavsky's trial should have occurred in the same year that *The Master and Margarita* (1966–7; full text 1973) by Mikhail Bulgakov (1891–1940) burst onto the Soviet literary scene. Here was a novel that was as un-socialist and un-realist as anything by Sinyavsky, but it was permitted finally to appear, presumably because the author was long dead. *The Master and Margarita* tells a story of the Devil and his retinue creating havoc—philosophical and otherwise—in Stalin's Russia. The Devil, Woland by name, engineers deaths and disappearances, and provides a theatre audience with luxury clothes, only to render the hapless recipients naked once they leave the theatre. He mocks the notion of long-term economic and political planning. The macabre comedy is intertwined with extracts from a novel about Pontius Pilate by 'The Master', a writer who has relinquished his own name, shunned the world, and burnt the manuscript of his work. His beloved, Margarita, is recruited to officiate at Satan's Ball. In return, she and her lover are reunited, she is transformed into a witch, and as such takes revenge on the establishment critic who attacked the Master. His manuscript is restored to him, and we are told that 'manuscripts don't burn'. Arguably the greatest novel to have appeared in Russia this century, both baffling and entertaining, *The Master and Margarita* has caused a never-ending debate and inspired other works of the fantastic-grotesque variety, in particular *Al'tist Danilov* ('Danilov the Violist', 1980) by Vladimir Orlov (b. 1936).

Another major voice, at last able to be properly heard, was that of Vasily Grossman (1905–64). His enormous novel of the Second World War, *Life and Fate* (Lausanne, 1980, finally published in Russia in 1988), offered a controversial view of the Soviet war effort. The victory over Nazism demonstrated for Grossman not so much the superiority of socialism, nor even of Russians over Germans, so much as the victory of Russian nationalism—this meant, on Soviet territory, a victory over ethnic minorities, particularly the Jews, who became the victims of an anti-Semitic campaign in the post-war years. Perhaps even more controversial was the publication of Grossman's short novel *Forever Flowing* (Frankfurt, 1970), which offered not merely one more exposé of Stalin's labour camps, but more particularly an anatomy of an individual psychology labouring under coercion of various kinds—from which it emerges that there are various categories of collaboration with tyranny. Grossman's style is as realistic as Solzhenitsyn's, but he has a more developed sense of moral ambiguity. Perhaps the most powerful part of the book, however, is an extended essay which destroys any residual myths concerning the greatness of Lenin and places him in a broad tradition of Russia's history, with its tyrants and its serfs.

Another work which offered a version of Soviet history hitherto unknown officially was *Children of the Arbat* (1987) and its sequel *Fear* (literally 'Other Years', 1988) by Anatoly Rybakov (b. 1911). This novel depicts the gilded youth of the 1930s and the unjust repression of one of its members. Like Solzhenitsyn's *The First Circle*, it contains a close-up portrait of Stalin. Though arguably of more socio-political than artistic interest, it enjoyed widespread popularity in the late 1980s.

For Russian intellectuals perhaps the most startling act of rehabilitation was the publication in 1988 of *Doctor Zhivago* (Milan, 1957) by Boris Pasternak (1890–1960). Long known in the West and circulating clandestinely in Russia, this novel focuses not so much on the facts of history—though the action takes us in graphic detail from the 1905 Revolution through to the Second World War—as on the individual's life and conscience. Like Hamlet, or like Christ, Zhivago, whose name derives from the word for 'life', is fated to bear witness to his time and to rise above its corrupt politics. Personal sacrifice and renewal are at the centre of the work. In this way, without even deigning to dispute the historical record, Pasternak questions the very legitimacy of the Revolution.

Doctor Zhivago is controversial on several levels. In struggling to remain unsullied morally, the hero lays more store by his private life than by any public concerns. His private life, however, is ambiguous, torn as he is between a wife and a mistress, and between his profession as a doctor and his wish to write poetry. The book's structure, too, leaves something to be desired, with its many coincidences and a final chapter that comprises some of its hero's poetry. But it is by its lyrical qualities rather than any conventional narrative criteria that the novel should ultimately be judged.

Other 'dissidents' who were posthumously rehabilitated include Aleksandr Galich (1919–77). Able to publish only anodyne poems, plays, and film scripts for many years, he eventually joined the dissident camp when one of his plays was rejected. His substantive work comprises poems set to his own guitar accompaniment and performed at small, informal gatherings. He offers a rich array of Soviet types: the boorish nationalist and drunkard, for example, or the female Party functionary exuding Soviet snobbery. One of his most complex songs—and they often take on the dimensions of a narrative or playlet—is 'Song about Stalin' (in a full collection entitled *When I Return*, Frankfurt, 1981), where the despot as well as his victims hold centre stage. Galich was one of several such prominent poet-guitarists, the two other main exponents of the genre being Bulat Okudzhava (b. 1924), who also has a large body of prose fiction to his credit, and Vladimir Vysotsky (1938–80), both of whom were slightly more acceptable in Soviet terms. Regarding unequivocally dissident literature, one must mention also the Russian publication in 1987 of *Requiem* (Munich, 1963) by Anna Akhmatova (1889–1966), the cycle of haunting lyrics composed in the 1930s which, through their restrained passion, have become the most touching of all literary memorials to Stalin's victims.

Other reassessments of the Soviet past—*Novoe naznachenie* ('The New Appointment', Frankfurt, 1972) by Aleksandr Bek (1903–72), *Belye odezhdy* ('White Clothing', 1987) by Vladimir Dudintsev (b. 1918), and the novels of Yury Dombrovsky (1909–78)—begged the question of what exactly History is. Unsurprisingly then, when a Booker Prize for fiction was launched in 1992, the first winner, *Lines of Fate* (1992) by Mark Kharitonov (b. 1937), broached this very question. Kharitonov is one of the many honest foot soldiers of Russian literature whose development was stunted by the constraints of the pre-*glasnost* era. The 'plot' of his novel involves an academic, Anton Lizavin, who is obsessively researching a writer of the 1920s, one Semeon Kondratyevich Milashevich. He has discovered Milashevich's trunk, which contains all sorts of jottings, made on sweet wrappers. From these, and from the findings of other scholars and acquaintances, Lizavin is trying to construct a true picture of the writer and to interpret him accurately. However, he is persistently aware that he may be twisting the evidence.

New evidence supplements and threatens to supplant the historical record, and several interpretations of it are possible. Milashevich had spent time in the provincial town of Nechaisk (a location for some of Kharitonov's other stories), where Lizavin himself now lives, and we get episodes of local history, going back occasionally to earlier Tsarist times (Makary, tutor to Ivan the Terrible, figures even); but mainly the episodes come from immediately pre-Revolutionary Russia, the Revolution, and beyond. Even though the novel was written in 1981–5, the past seems to comment on the difficulties of the present (rampant inflation, economic ills generally, questions of ideology), and Lizavin's doubts about his research are reflected in his own personal life and his relationship to his family, which run parallel to those of Milashevich. Who was the woman in Milashevich's life? What happened to his son? What did he do before and during the Revolution?

Yury Trifonov (1925–81) had earlier posed similar questions in such novels as *The House on the Embankment* (1976) and *The Old Man* (1981), which were couched in sufficiently ambiguous terms to allow them to be published under the old regime.

The case of Trifonov opens up another question concerning the Brezhnev period. How are we to view the many worthy writers of those years who were able to pursue their careers, albeit with ups and downs? Some commentators found it wearisome that at first, in the new cultural climate ushered in by Gorbachev, such poets as Evgeny Evtushenko (b. 1933) and Andrei Vozneshensky (b. 1933) featured prominently. These were firebrands of the early 1960s who had enjoyed international reputations and yet were deemed to have trimmed their sails to the prevailing wind under Brezhnev. Talented, honest spirits, they none the less seemed to many to be compromised. Likewise, the school of 'village prose', which since the late 1950s had laboured to depict the unvarnished truth about deprivation in the countryside, while exalting the moral qualities of the peasantry in the face of a corrupting urbanization, now seemed distinctly *passé*. Moreover, this school's nationalist tendencies came to look unsavoury to the cosmopolitan and liberal-minded.

In the 1960s and 1970s Fyodor Abramov (1920–83), Viktor Astafiev (b. 1924), Vasily Belov (b. 1932), Boris Mozhaev (1923–96), and Valentin Rasputin (b. 1937) had beguiled their readers with their sympathetic portrayal of devout and stoical rustics who had borne the brunt of collectivization and war. Rasputin's *Farewell to Matyora* (1976), with its pronounced religious and environmental concerns, paints a heart-rending picture of a Siberian community destroyed to make way for a huge dam and power station. The sensitivity and human qualities on display in this novel can only be squared with the author's uncompromisingly reactionary pronouncements on nationalist issues and sexual mores by setting his moral preoccupations against the rising tide of criminality and incipient chaos that Russia has been exposed to in recent years.

In the Soviet era some non-Russian writers achieved prominence by choosing to write in Russian. Most notable among them are Chingiz Aitmatov (b. 1928), a Kirghiz whose novels blend local legend with contemporary issues in such a way as to suggest a degree of 'magic realism'. Novellas such as *Farewell, Gulsary!* (1966) and *The White Steamship* (1970) justly earned him a reputation as a sensitive, reformist writer, while his lengthier works—*A Day Lasts Longer than a Hundred Years* (1980) and *The Place of the Skull* (literally, 'The Execution Block', 1986)—though lacking the same cohesion, address such topical issues as *détente*, religious awareness, and drug and alcohol abuse. Fazil Iskander (b. 1929), an Abkhaz, came to fame with a short satirical work, *The Goatibex Constellation* (1966), but his *magnum opus* is *Sandro from Chegem*, a lengthy cycle of stories irreverent enough to ensure only its partial publication in 1973.

Iskander was seen as one of the more reliable proclaimers of decent values in the *glasnost* era, not least because of his involvement in the *Metropol* affair of 1978–9. *Metropol* was an 'almanach'—in Russia, this means an occasional literary anthology—produced by the more intrepid nonconformist writers of the time, who requested it be published without going through all the usual bureaucratic procedures, notably censorship. The authorities responded by foiling the planned 'launch' of the book and punishing the ringleaders: Viktor Erofeev (b. 1947) and Evgeny Popov (b. 1946) were expelled from the Writers' Union, others experienced varying degrees of difficulty in publishing, and three of the contributors—Vasily Aksyonov (b. 1932), Yuz Aleshkovsky (b. 1929), and Fridrikh Gorenshtein (b. 1932)—emigrated to the West.

Metropol established criteria that were to be of overriding importance in the post-Communist phase. The twenty-six contributors (twenty-five Soviet citizens plus the American novelist John Updike) declared in their preface that the only thing which had brought them together was the recognition that an author alone was answerable for his work, and that the right to enjoy such responsibility was sacred. This was the basis for a literary regime which was pluralist, in the best sense of the word, and politically suspect in the eyes of the Communist government solely because it was apolitical.

Any 'new' generation of writers arising after the years of stagnation would, wittingly or otherwise, have to take its cue from the contributors to *Metropol*.

One of these contributors took on himself the task of dispatching the entire Soviet legacy: the village prose writers, the conformist hacks, and the would-be reformists ('liberals'), who to the erstwhile outcasts looked uncomfortably like careerists. In his article 'A Wake for Soviet Literature' of 1990, Viktor Erofeev showed he had little time even for out-and-out 'dissidents', arguing, roughly, that they had been in the liberal camp under Khrushchev and that it had been largely a matter of luck whether or not individual works were published in Russia then, while dissident works published abroad died, in his view, through 'a surfeit of oxygen', presumably meaning that they attracted unwarranted attention in Russia and abroad because of their perceived ideological content. Erofeev contended that the moral and social imperative should be abandoned and that the way forward lay with 'alternative literature'. This could take its lead from 'the experience of Nabokov, Joyce, Zamyatin, Platonov, Dobychin, the *oberiuty* [a 1920s non-conformist grouping of Leningrad writers and artists], the creators of "the Russian absurd" '—i.e. all the outcasts of the early Soviet period whom many would classify as modernists.

Erofeev's article and the vociferous backlash it produced were only part of a widespread literary debate, but his supporters have a substantial creative achievement to their credit. 'Alternative literature' goes far beyond politics, it displays a cosmopolitan side, it is inventive, bawdy and outrageous, it has liberated the Russian language from the prudery of the former era, and has used parody as one of its chief weapons. It has its weaknesses too, of course, its pluralism allowing much scope for tastelessness and derivativeness. The best practitioners of 'alternative literature' seem prepared, however, to live with cheap imitators.

Viktor Erofeev has put his theories into practice in his creative writing: in a series of short stories and especially in his outrageous comic novel *Russian Beauty* (1990). This tells the story of a high-class prostitute, Irina Tarakanova, who has an affair with a literary bureaucrat. Her uncensored accounts of her sexual exploits are interwoven with her involvement in the 'dissident' movement, and in a bizarre scene she runs naked over the site of an ancient battlefield in order to 'save Russia'. Realism gives way to grotesque when she copulates with her deceased patron, conceives, and resolves to become reunited with him in death. Tarakanova is repeatedly referred to as Joan of Arc, and the novel contains irreverent parodies of, among others, Anna Akhmatova and Pushkin.

Other writers of 'alternative' prose include the *émigrés* Yuz Aleshkovsky, Fridrikh Gorenshtein, and Sasha Sokolov (b. 1943); and, of those living in Russia, Vladimir Sorokin (b. 1955), Vyacheslav P'etsukh (b. 1946), and Evgeny Popov. Sorokin specializes in short stories which start out in mock lyricism and then suddenly evoke disgust or revulsion by scenes of mutilation or coprophagy. He also writes novels that appeal to more traditional tastes, however, such as *The Queue* (Paris, 1985), which is constructed entirely out of the conversations of people waiting in line for scarce goods— they do not even know what they are queuing for and in their own fashion they are waiting for Godot. A recent novel by Sorokin, *Mesyats v Dakhau* ('A Month in Dachau', 1993), has been praised by some. Aleshkovsky's stories and short novels make hilarious fun of the discrepancies between official jargon and social aspiration on the one hand, and the banal self-seeking and self-justification of the common man on the other. He specializes in obscenity and underworld slang, while his plots have a penchant for the outlandish: *Nikolai Nikolaevich* (Ann Arbor, 1980) features a young criminal whose sperm is of such high quality that he is recruited to stock a research laboratory.

P'etsukh goes in for parody and historical fantasy. *Novaya moskovskaya filosofia* ('The New Moscow Philosophy', 1989) is a reworking of Dostoevsky's *Crime and Punishment*, while 'Rommat' (1990)—an acronym of romantic materialism, an alternative to the official philosophy of dialectical materialism—describes what might have happened in Russian history if the Decembrist rising of 1825 had succeeded. Popov is similarly inventive. His numerous short stories owe something to Zoshchenko, who enjoyed much popularity in the 1920s, yet it would be a disservice to call either of them satirists. Popov's comedy resides in his depiction of human incongruities— his unsophisticated Siberian characters experience wild swings of mood and go in for immoderate drinking and casual relationships.

One collection of stories is entitled *Veselie Rusi* ('Merry-Making in Old Russia', Ann Arbor, 1981), though the incidents are set largely in the Soviet Union of the 1960s and 1970s, the implication being that little has changed despite all the social engineering. Often Popov couches his scenes of domestic strife in terms of Russian fairy-tales, simultaneously undermining any chance of a happy ending and mocking the officially sponsored fairy-tales of Soviet ideology. His novel *The Soul of a Patriot* (1989), written and set at the time of Brezhnev's death in 1982, wittily captures the atmosphere of impending social upheaval, while treating us to snapshots from the author's own family history and his battles with the literary bureaucracy. Popov's second novel, with its punning title *Prekrasnost' zhizni: roman s gazetoi* ('The Splendour of Life: Novel [or Love Affair] with a Newspaper', 1990), consists in part of a collage of items taken from the old Soviet press arranged in such a way as to demonstrate the absurdity of public life.

One reason why there is so much parody in recent Russian literature is the fact that under Brezhnev public life had, in the eyes of many intellectuals, itself become a parody: a gerontocracy claiming to be the only true custodian of the future; a one-Party State preaching freedom, democracy, and peaceful coexistence while invading Czechoslovakia and Afghanistan; a government claiming scientific principles while presiding over an economy that was increasingly ramshackle; an ailing Marxist General Secretary who came to rely on a faith healer.

Alternative prose's pedigree in fact went further back than *Metropol*. Vasily Aksyonov established a reputation in the early 1960s as one of the 'young prose' writers (together with Anatoly Gladilin (b. 1935) and Voinovich), with works like *A Starry Ticket* (1961) and *Oranges from Morocco* (1963), in which somewhat insouciant youngsters use slang and are keener on foreign fashions and pop music than on the Five-Year Plan. In Aksyonov's case, this sort of writing eventually developed into works with a pronounced surrealist or Post-Modernist aspect, which could not be accommodated within Soviet literary norms. *In Search of a Genre* (1978) was published in the leading literary journal *Novyi mir*, but *The Steel Bird* (Ann Arbor, 1977) came out only in the USA, as did the major novel *The Burn* (Ann Arbor, 1980) and a political fantasy novel, *The Island of Crimea* (New York, 1981). Of all the writers who made up the 'third wave' of emigration from the late 1960s onwards, Aksyonov seems to have adapted most readily. Yet while his fiction has always displayed a fascination with the West, it should be remembered that he tried hard for many years to liberalize the Soviet system from within. His tolerance and aesthetic preoccupations are all the more arresting, given his family background—his mother Evgenia Ginzburg (1906–77) spent many years in labour camps and Siberian exile, eventually contributing her own two volumes, *Into the Whirlwind* (Frankfurt, 1967) and *Inside the Whirlwind* (Milan, 1979), to the all-important genre of memoir literature.

Occasionally, Russian literary history throws up a short work which proves to be pivotal; Pushkin's *The Queen of Spades*, say, or Dostoevsky's *Notes from Underground*. Something similar could be claimed for Venedikt Erofeev's short novel *Moscow Circles* (literally 'Moscow–Petushki', Paris, 1977). Unlike his formally educated and outwardly respectable namesake Viktor, Venedikt Erofeev (1938–90) was a drop-out, though utterly devoted to literature and music—and to alcohol. His account of a train journey from Moscow to the insignificant town of Petushki some 70 miles away quickly turns into a mock odyssey, as the hero-narrator evokes all manner of literary, historical, and political resonances in his drunken cerebral meanderings. His gregariousness comes close to the 'togetherness' (*sobornost'*) advocated by Slavophiles, while his interest in the individual as opposed to systems betrays a deep mistrust of any politics, especially revolutionary politics. Petushki, where the hero will find his 'salvation and joy', where 'the birds never cease singing and the jasmine does not fade', becomes an unobtainable human aspiration: the hero finds himself back in Moscow, where he is done to death by a gang of hoodlums. This is a novel sure to endure: its structure is circular so that it is, in a sense, unending; it quotes from texts of every age and culture—the Bible, Shakespeare, Pushkin, Blok—juxtaposing these timeless words with others more mortal from politicians and hack writers; and the whole is laced with a time-honoured, uninhibited Russian vernacular. Erofeev could not be published legally in his homeland until 1989, but his voice, already familiar to many throughout the intelligentsia, had a degree of authenticity which was to inspire many of the practitioners of 'alternative' prose. He revitalized all the linguistic registers that had been under threat for decades from highly prescriptive Soviet norms.

A backlash against prudery is one way of explaining some of the literature that came out after 1985. A more subtle view, however, is that of Andrei Bitov (b. 1937), who, with particular reference to Aleshkovsky, championed the use of obscenity in literature, after the linguistic mishmash of the Soviet years. In his own stories, though the obscene language is restricted, one finds precious little that could pass for mainstream Soviet literature. Only short extracts from his *magnum opus, Pushkin House* (Ann Arbor, 1978), were published legally under the old regime. Bitov was reading Nabokov's *The Gift* and *Invitation to a Beheading* while working on this novel, which is founded on parody, and painfully explores the ambivalent role of the intelligentsia in recent Russian history, centring on a love affair between Lyova and Faina, and the rivalry in love and career between Lyova and Mitishatyev. In Bitov the same stories can crop up in different books, and it may be that his *œuvre*—stories, novels, travelogues—should be considered as an organic whole, especially given his preoccupation with circular structures. Regard for harmony and for form is no bad thing in the cacophony of current Russian writing.

Of other prose writers, Vladimir Voinovich (b. 1932) is outstanding. His brilliant comedy of the Second World War *The Life and Extraordinary Adventures of Private Ivan Chonkin* (Paris, 1975), and its sequel *Pretender to the Throne* (Paris, 1979), are superior to his 'science-fiction' satire *Moscow 2042* (Ann Arbor, 1986). Ivan Chonkin is a village idiot who has the misfortune to find himself serving in the Red Army in 1941 (the year of the invasion from the West by the Germans). Detailed to stand guard over an aeroplane which has made an emergency landing in a remote village, Chonkin generates all manner of confusion through his disarming simplicity. At the same time, because he is innocent of the rigmaroles involved in army life, and in sharp contrast to the self-deluding bigwigs around him, Chonkin becomes a rounded and valuable human being: practical, loving, brave, and versatile.

Aleksandr Zinoviev (b. 1922), a philosopher turned creative writer, has produced an astonishing amount of satirical writing which combines narrative, dialogue, and disquisition, including *The Yawning Heights* (Lausanne, 1976), *Homo sovieticus* (Lausanne, 1982), and the delightfully entitled *Katastroika* (Lausanne, 1990). Vladimir Makanin (b. 1937) was one of the most respected of Soviet writers throughout the 1970s with his realistic and engaging stories of city life, but he gained a more international reputation with *Manhole* (1991), a fantasy which depicts one Russian society living above ground and another below it, and the 1993 Booker Prize-winning *Stol, pokrytyi suknom i s grafinom poseredine* ('A Baize-Covered Table with Decanter'), which, through the mind of a man awaiting trial, charts the all-pervasive paranoia induced by the Soviet experience.

In his novels *The Humble Cemetery* (1987) and *Stroibat* ('The Construction Battalion', 1989) Sergei Kaledin (b. 1949) describes in coarsely comic tones some of the seamier aspects of Russian life—grave-digging and peacetime military service. Oleg Ermakov (b. 1961) became an overnight success in 1989 with his gruesome stories about the war in Afghanistan, in which he had fought. His first novel, *Znak zverya'* ('The Sign of the Beast', 1992), similarly shows the Russian soldier at odds as much with his comrades as with the enemy.

Under the Soviet regime women had the worst of both worlds: they were liberated to do a man's job yet remained saddled with the extremely conservative Russian male view of them as housewives and mothers. Somewhat paradoxically, women writers did not come into their own in Russia until the twentieth century, but when they did, the best of them seemed to range far beyond the immediate issues raised by feminism. The work of poets like Akhmatova and Marina Tsvetaeva (1892–1941), or of memoirists such as Nadezhda Mandelshtam and Ginzburg, banned for many years, equalled anything written by men. By contrast, the baldly feminist works of, for example, the Bolshevik Aleksandra Kollontai (1872–1952), at the beginning of the Soviet era, or *A Week Like Any Other* (1969) by Natalya

Baranskaya (b. 1908), though heartfelt and justified, hardly rank as great literature.

When literary controls all but disappeared, the new wave of women writers was not overtly feminist. Indeed, one of the most prominent of them, Tatyana Tolstaya (b. 1951), somewhat antagonized Western feminist opinion with forthright statements to the effect that literature was androgynous. Yet her stories gained immediate success, for here was a talent that soared above social considerations, preferring instead, through her considerable powers of description, to inject light and imagination into situations that are for the most part utterly real. Occasionally Tolstaya indulges in the fantastic, as in the story 'A Clean Sheet', in which the hero undergoes an operation to remove his worldly cares, but suffers morally as a result. However, she specializes primarily in the evocation of childhood memories or in producing novel perceptions of mundane household objects, so that life, despite all its frustrations, always offers something new: the eponymous hero of 'Peters', henpecked, downtrodden, and driven at one point close to suicide, is left at the end pondering on the multifarious wonders of life. Tolstaya's first collection *On the Golden Porch* . . . (1987) was followed by *Sleepwalker in a Fog* (1988).

Arguably, the most powerful and disturbing writer in Russia today is Ludmila Petrushevskaya (b. 1938). Long known as a playwright (though her plays were performed only in workshop theatres in the Soviet period), she has since published stories and short novels which display Dostoevskian qualities, as in a major collection *Bessmertnaya lyubov'* ('Immortal Love') that appeared in 1988. In often cramped and overcrowded milieux, Petrushevskaya's characters frequently suffer from some physical, or more especially mental, infirmity; personal morality and questioning force their way to the fore as history and politics recede. Although there are allusions to other writers in her work, Petrushevskaya herself does not practise parody, unlike so many of her contemporaries. She may force her characters to act out a parody of some noble or adventurous story, as in 'The New Robinsons', or her characters may make self-aggrandizing comparisons, but their chief characteristics are delusion and mediocrity. The heroine-narrator of *Time: The Night* (1992) is an unhinged, interfering hack writer who persistently likens herself to Akhmatova. A similar middle-aged heroine-narrator in 'Our Crowd' (1988) likewise insists that she is clever, that she understands everything, and, more chillingly, that what she does not understand 'does not exist'.

Through her characters and situations, Petrushevskaya generates all manner of moral dilemmas, and the reader is hard put to it to apportion blame amidst all the wrongdoing. A recent collection, *V sadakh drugikh vozmozhnostei* ('In the Gardens of Other Possibilities', 1993), contains a story featuring a deranged mother who conceals her pregnancy and delivers the child herself, only to abandon it under some stones by the roadside; the child is rescued and returned to her, her family (two older children and a blind father) engage a lawyer to defend her, but the mother ignores her baby, and 'behaves like a stupid child, covering her face with her hands as if afraid—even of the little one who only needs forty grammes of milk and nothing else'. This, indeed, is another recurrent motif in Petrushevskaya, of adults being reduced to children—another collection of stories is entitled *Skazki dlya vsei sem'i* ('Fairy-Tales for All the Family', 1993).

Other women writers have paraded their sexuality more overtly, or the circumstances that their gender has predestined them to. The *émigrée* Julia Voznesnskaya's (b. 1940) *The Women's Decameron* (Tel Aviv, 1987), an essentially amusing, lightweight work, shows women airing their opposition to men and telling one another bawdy stories. Her second novel, *The Star Chernobyl* (New York, 1987), was less successful, as an attempt to fictionalize the real-life drama of the 1986 nuclear accident. (She was not alone in so doing: the journalist Vladimir Gubarev (b. 1938) gained prominence by writing a play, *Sarcophagus* (1986), on the same theme: an interesting indication of how promptly Russian writers are now influenced by market forces and topical issues.)

Nina Katerli (b. 1934), Viktoria Tokareva (b. 1937), and Valeria Narbikova (b. 1958) have, each in her own way, continued the very strong tradition of women's fiction. Katerli's stories are often set in her native Leningrad/ St Petersburg and are either starkly realistic or else supernatural. 'The Monster' (1983) has a dragon living alongside ordinary human beings in the same flat in a mutually supportive but not altogether pleasant relationship. 'Polina' (1984) explores the personal and sexual lives of two contrasting women. Tokareva often presents us with self-reliant, or even pushy, urban and professional heroines who can also display some of the characteristics associated with the stoical heroines of 'village prose'. By contrast, Narbikova has gained a certain notoriety with fanciful and fantastic stories involving a good deal of sexual explicitness. Her verbal dexterity notwithstanding, the emphasis in her writing on emotional turmoil may lead one to feel that she lacks substance, although her novella *Okolo ekolo* (the title is untranslatable) only failed to make the short list for the 1993 Booker Prize on a technicality. The other woman writer on the list was Lyudmila Ulitskaya (b. 1938), who, like Petrushevskaya and Tokareva, was initially known for her plays. Her novel *Sonechka* (1992) is a nostalgic portrayal of a family life that is both decent and happy despite the austerity of the post-war Moscow in which it is set.

The Russian stage, too, has enjoyed a new lease of life since 1985. Some of the novels alluded to above have been successfully dramatized, notably *Moscow–Petushki*, and there have been film and stage versions of key works by such writers as Abramov, Mozhaev, and Rasputin. Petrushevskaya's best-known plays include *Three Girls in Blue* (1983) and *Cinzano* (1989). Nina Sadur (b. 1950), much influenced by Petrushevskaya, had a collection of her plays published in 1989. The title piece, *Chudnaya baba* ('The Weird Peasant Woman'), presents a country 'healer' who resorts to myth when confronted with the 'real' world. Sadur makes overt gestures to Gogol, so illustrating that the Theatre of the Absurd has deep roots in Russian literature.

Aleksandr Galin (b. 1947) had several successful plays to his credit under the old order before gaining wider recognition with *Stars in the Morning Sky* (1987), which concerns a group of prostitutes expelled from the capital for the duration of the 1980 Olympic Games. Another play of 'social protest' typifying the first years of *glasnost* was *A Man with Connections* (1987) by Aleksandr Gelman (b. 1933), which deals in uncompromising terms with the personal and public damage wrought by a highly centralized command economy. In *Brestsky mir* ('The Peace of Brest-Litovsk', 1987) and *Dal'she . . . dal'she . . . dal'she!* ('Onward . . . Onward . . . Onward!', 1988), Mikhail Shatrov (b. 1932), Party member and author of several plays about Lenin and the Revolution, astounded audiences with a revisionist view of events that rehabilitated Trotsky, Bukharin, and other prominent victims of Stalin, and had Stalin himself acting the buffoon.

Russian poets today are in danger. Free to write what they like as poets are in any other liberal society, they face competition from rival literary genres and from the media. Their traditional role as the nation's conscience could well disappear. For the time being, however, poetry still holds a special place in Russia and its vitality is undeniable. As Gerald Smith has written: 'Poets may simply be drowned out by the newly unleashed electronic mass media, or upstaged by a liberated and commercialized entertainment industry. On the other hand, as the Poet fades away, the poems themselves may have a better chance.' Be that as it may, emigration is more traumatic for poets than for prose writers, for it deprives them not only of their primary audience, but also of their life-blood, the everyday sounds of their native language.

The achievement of Joseph Brodsky (1940–96) is thus all the more admirable. Tried for 'parasitism' in 1964, and hounded into exile in the West in 1972, he was awarded the Nobel Prize for literature in 1987, just as his work had started to be published legally in his homeland. Brodsky is indubitably the leading poet of the age. Influenced by Donne, Eliot, and Auden, and, nearer home, by the Acmeists—at first hand in the case of Akhmatova in her final years—he is still very much his own man. The connections between his verse and his worldly circumstances can appear as arcane as they do in the case of, say, Mandelshtam; however, a fierce moral awareness breaks through in his writing—as in his Nobel Prize address, where he declares that evil is always a bad stylist, or in his contention that 'It is better to be a total failure in democracy than a martyr or *la crème de la crème* in tyranny.'

Brodsky often seems obsessed with the notion of time, of how one age might relate to another, of what time can do to an individual, and of how language can forge links between different epochs. A lengthy lyric, 'Fifth Anniversary (4 June 1977)' (Frankfurt, 1983), marking his first five years in the West concludes:

> I have nothing to say to the Greek or the Varangian.
> Since I no longer know what earth I will lie in.
> Squeak away, squeak away, pen! Use up the paper.

Another lyric, 'Only ashes know what it means to be burned out' (dated 1986, published 1990), insists that 'we' will not be entirely obliterated, that a future archaeologist may be revolted by the 'carrion' he finds, but 'carrion is freedom from cells, freedom | from the whole: an apotheosis of particles.' Brodsky has generally been seen as more innovative formally than some of his colleagues, and he has tried his hand at writing verse in English. His battles are not political—they involve rather a defence of the word against the huge, amorphous notions that the contemporary world produces, particularly the concept of 'empire'. In Brodsky's view the Russian language has been the main victim of Communism: 'This country had all the makings of a cultural, spiritual paradise, a real vessel of civilization. Instead, it became a drab hell.' Such a view might be dismissed as chauvinistic, but it can also be seen as an extension of the Acmeists' 'longing for world culture', to which Brodsky whole-heartedly subscribes. Finally, one should note that his starting-point is always the individual voice rather than external phenomena: 'a poet's biography is in his vowels and sibilants, in his metres, rhymes, and metaphors.'

Other *émigré* poets include Aleksandr Galich (see above), Dmitry Bobyshev (b. 1936), Lev Loseff (b. 1937), Yury Kublanovsky (b. 1948), and Natalya Gorbanevskaya (b. 1936), who became firmly associated with the civil rights movement, especially by her public protest on Red Square at the time of the 1968 invasion of Czechoslovakia. One of her lyrics, 'Towards a Discussion about Statistics' (Frankfurt, 1986), might be taken as a response to works like Solzhenitsyn's *The Gulag Archipelago* and the growing torrent of revelations in the newly liberalized Soviet press:

> We won't argue. An extra million
> condemned, tortured, battered,
> is no more than a number. The million tears
> haven't flowed together, haven't caused a flood,
> and haven't thawed the permafrost . . .

Another of her poems, 'Oh my poor, decrepit, fallen into childhood, Europe . . .' (Paris, 1979), expresses the not uncommon view among Russian *émigrés* that the West seems unaware of its impending doom: 'this my verse over your grave | is only a proof of my powerless | and perpetual love . . .'

The 'third wave' of emigration was of such a magnitude and intellectual quality that it was hard for writers who remained at home, or for anyone else, to denigrate it. Indeed, it was argued by some that in the 1970s the literary centre of gravity in fact shifted from East to West. However, poets domiciled in Russia still had a major part to play: Gennady Aigi (b. 1934), Bella Akhmadulina (b. 1937), Boris Slutsky (1919–86), Oleg Chukhontsev (b. 1938), Yunna Morits (b. 1937), and those more particularly associated with the *glasnost* era such as Olga Sedakova (b. 1949), Elena Shvarts (b. 1948), and Dmitry Prigov (b. 1940).

Broadly speaking, Sedakova is a poet of the spirit. The mystical element in her work has led her to engage in a kind of dialogue with English-language poets, as for example in her 'Journey of the Magi', which picks up on images in Eliot's poem of that title; and in 'The Grasshopper and the Cricket' she uses a line from Keats as an epigraph: 'the poetry of Earth is never dead.' Sedakova's 'Fifth Stanzas' has been praised for its 'combination of philosophical complexity with exact physical presence'. *The Silk of Time* is a good bilingual anthology of her work (Keele, 1994).

The intensely personal stance, which kept Sedakova largely unpublished in Russia until the late 1980s, finds a different expression in Shvarts:

> I tasted once
> the milk of a woman friend,
> the milk of a sister—
> not to slake my thirst
> but for the liberty of my soul.
> She squeezed the milk from her left
> breast into a cup,

and in this simple vessel
it sang, foamed slightly.

This is the opening of 'Remembering a Strange Treat' (New York, 1985), and it illustrates Shvarts's preoccupation with the body, birth, and corporeal mutation—eyes become pearls, the Virgin in 'The Virgin Rides on Venice, and I on Her Back' (New York, 1985) becomes by turns a hag or a giantess. In another poem a woman asks God to take her rib and make a friend for her, 'not a man, not a woman, not something in between, | but an angel'. In 'Sale of a Historian's Library' (New York, 1985), the librarian travels back in history, assuming the personae of various men and women alike (Marie Antoinette, Marat).

Prigov is a leading representative of the 'conceptualists', a movement which came to the fore in the late 1980s and whose work frequently depends for its effects on word-play, parody, and irony. Prigov, an erudite, many-talented man who trained as a sculptor, has reputedly published only a small amount of his writing to date. He specializes in short, absurdist poems, several of which centre on the figure of the Soviet policeman. One has an eagle flying overhead and the poet asking if its name is Stalin. Or is it a swan and is its name Prigov? In twelve short lines Stalin's name occurs three times and Prigov's four; Stalin is lying in the ground and Prigov is looking askance at both eagle and swan.

The lesson of this brief summary has to be that in Russian writing the personal has now triumphed over the political. Many of the later works cited here adopt a first-person narration or parade the name of the author. Fragmentation and confusion there may be, but the Russian writer is now master in his or her own house, such as it is. Existential themes have displaced social ones. One might detect in this a transition from a literature concerned with 'Life' (*zhizn'*) to one concerned with 'Being' (*byt'yo*), and a re-merging with modernist traditions as they exist elsewhere in the world. Could this mean that the new Russian writers will leap-frog over the foreign writers who have shown them the way—as some have argued the best nineteenth-century Russian writers did? Or is it, to borrow the title of one of Brodsky's poems, 'the Autumn cry of the hawk'?

FURTHER READING

Brown, D., *The Last Years of Soviet Russian Literature* (Cambridge, 1993).
Chukhontsev, O. (ed.), *Leopard I, Dissonant Voices: The New Russian Fiction* (London, 1991).

Duffin Graham, S. (ed.), *New Directions in Soviet Literature* (New York, 1992).
Erofeyer, V. (ed.), *The Penguin Book of New Russian Writing: Russia's Fleurs du mal* (Harmondsworth, 1995).
Kelly, C., *A History of Russian Women's Writing 1820–1992* (Oxford, 1994).
——(ed.), *An Anthology of Russian Women's Writing 1777–1992* (Oxford, 1994).
Porter, R., *Russia's Alternative Prose* (Oxford, 1994).
Shneidman, N., *Russian Literature 1988–1994: The End of an Era* (Toronto, 1995).
Smith, G., *Contemporary Russian Poetry: A Bilingual Anthology* (Bloomington, Ind., 1993).

22

SCANDINAVIA

JANET GARTON

FOR many years after 1945, Scandinavian writers were preoccupied with the subject of the Second World War and its repercussions: with the Finnish winter war against Russia, the German occupation of Norway and Denmark, and the compromised neutrality of Sweden. The late 1940s and 1950s were dominated by war literature, and some major contributions even came in the 1960s, such as the Danish Communist Hans Scherfig's (1905–79) attack on his country's betrayal of its Communists in *Frydenholm* (1962), or the investigation of Sweden's treatment of Baltic refugees in *The Legionnaires* (1968), by Per Olov Enquist (b. 1934). Yet, broadly speaking, by the early 1960s writers were more concerned with formal experimentation. As the decade advanced, however, other political concerns came to the fore.

THE 1960s

SWEDEN

Modernist experimentation predominated earlier in Sweden than in either Denmark or Norway. As early as 1960 came a reaction against aestheticism in the form of a manifesto, *Front mot formens tyranni* ('A Stand against the Tyranny of Form'), written by, among others, Sonja Åkesson (1926–77), one of the foremost practitioners of 'nyenkel' poetry—verse that is characteristically low-key and colloquial, concerned with the minutiae of everyday life and with drawing attention to the insidious power of the mass media and advertising over people's thoughts.

Confrontation between the individual and the State became a growing preoccupation during the 1960s. At a time when the country was being held up to the world as a model welfare state ('the middle way'), its writers were beginning to question the benevolent paternalism which, for the best of reasons, could erode individual freedom. Not all such writing was overtly political; some writers, like Torsten Ekbom (b. 1938), used formal experiments such as collage to build up a critique of social manipulation (*En galakväll på Operan*, 'A Gala Evening at the Opera', 1969). Such works were élitist in their appeal, and are little read now; directly political writers had more popular success and lasting influence.

Swedish literature is more open to international currents than that of Denmark and Norway, more ready to extend its horizons beyond its own backyard. Growing knowledge of the problems of the Third World and the exploitative nature of Western capitalism combined later in the decade with the Vietnam War to persuade many Swedish writers that the indirect medium of fiction was no longer an adequate response. One of the principal movers here was Jan Myrdal (b. 1927), who began as a novelist in the 1950s, but concluded after 1960 that fiction was a form of lying which distracted people from taking action to change the world—'Readers might as well smoke hash.' His *Report from a Chinese Village* (1963) is a documentary account of a trip to China and an attempt to present Mao's new society in an unbiased manner; this was followed by critical assessments of Western society and of his own role as an intellectual (*Confessions of a Disloyal European*, 1964). Since the 1960s Myrdal has become an increasingly vituperative, self-appointed scourge of Swedish complacency.

Sara Lidman (b. 1923) was another writer to abandon fiction for reportage. From committed novels about apartheid in South Africa in the early 1960s she moved to a documentary account of a visit to Vietnam in *Samtal i Hanoi* ('Conversations in Hanoi', 1966). This is an unapologetically emotional defence of the valiant Vietnamese, faced by the American war machine. Following this, she too returned to an examination of Swedish society in *Gruva* ('The Mine', 1968), a study of the lives of miners in the far north; having been criticized for bias in the Vietnam book, she made strenuous attempts to present the facts objectively, but her support for the miners against the company officials is unmistakable. After the 1960s Lidman returned to fiction, with a popular historical series about her native Västerbotten of which one volume, *Naboth's Stone* (1981), has so far been translated. Lidman's poetic style and colourful characters make this an absorbing study of nineteenth-century rural society.

Poets, too, demonstrated increasing political awareness. Göran Sonnevi (b. 1939) was one of the instigators of the debate in 1965 with his poem 'Om kriget i Vietnam' ('About the War in Vietnam'), comparing the remote war with a peaceful Swedish idyll:

> Here hardly anybody dies
> for other reasons than personal ones. The Swedish

economy doesn't kill
many any more, at least
not in this country.

Björn Håkanson (b. 1937) writes intense anti-war poetry in *Kärlek i Vita Huset* ('Love in the White House', 1967), and Göran Palm (b. 1931) follows Myrdal and Lidman in his decision to abandon poetry for direct comment. His study of the exploitation of the Third World, *En orättvis betraktelse* ('Unjust Observations', 1966), is supported by statistical evidence, as is *Indoktrineringen i Sverige* ('Indoctrination in Sweden', 1968), an indictment of biased cultural attitudes.

A consciousness of being Swedish, and of Sweden's role in the modern world, informs the work of many writers even when they are not writing about contemporary events. 'Swedes possess the world's only portable consciences, they travel around as professional moralists,' declares a character in Enquist's *The Legionnaires*. The narrator's investigation in this novel of Sweden's treatment of Baltic refugees in 1945 springs directly out of a visit to Mississippi in 1966; his stance as a detached observer of racial conflict prompts an exposé of anti-Russian prejudice beneath the tolerant surface of Swedish society.

Another quasi-documentary account of a historical event, the doomed attempt to fly over the North Pole in a hot-air balloon in 1897—*The Flight of the Eagle* (1967) by Per Olof Sundman (1922–92)—is an implicit comment on Swedish nationalism and the rivalry with Norway's Nansen which made the explorers take unjustifiable risks. Sven Delblanc (1931–92) writes in *Nattresa* ('Night Journey', 1967) about the need to humanize Western society, and in *Åsnebrygga* ('Bridge of Asses', 1969) about his experience of America in the late 1960s. P. C. Jersild (b.1935) examines the power of bureaucracy and its dehumanization of individuals in *Grisjakten* ('The Pig Hunt', 1968) and *Vi ses i Song My* ('See You at My Lai', 1970).

NORWAY

Several major pre-war figures were still dominant in Norwegian writing during the 1960s. Johan Borgen (1902–79) continued to explore the struggle to define the self in the intriguing *The Red Mist* (1967), and the poet and novelist Tarjei Vesaas (1897–1970) wrote works like *The Ice Palace* (1963), a delicately observed study of adolescence in which the frozen winter landscape becomes an image of the breakdown of communication. Two established poets produced major collections: Rolf Jacobsen's (1907–94) *The Silence Afterwards* (1965) and Olav H. Hauge's (1908–94) *Dropar i austavind* ('Drops in the East Wind', 1966). Hauge's deceptively simple verses hint at a wealth of experience:

> Today I saw
> two moons,
> one new,
> and one old.
> I set great store by the new moon.
> But no doubt it's the old one.

A forerunner of the new political writing in Norway was Jens Bjørneboe (1920–76), a polemicist who carved out his own path in bitter opposition to the establishment. His novels and plays are harshly critical of authoritarianism, which he saw as endemic in Western society; the judicial and educational systems were among his targets. In 1966 he published the first novel of his central trilogy *Moment of Freedom*, a study of 'the problem of evil' which ranges widely in time and space, from medieval European witch-hunts to the conquest of the Aztecs and Incas. Like Myrdal and Lidman, Bjørneboe does not restrict his attentions to his own society, but allows his view of it to be fruitfully informed by awareness of a wider context. His last novel *The Sharks* (1974) is at once an exciting story of mutiny and shipwreck and a study of a twentieth-century society in miniature, riven by racial and class conflicts.

With the exception of Bjørneboe, the most interesting event in the mid-1960s was the arrival on the scene of a group of young modernists, centred around the literary journal *Profil*, which featured many of the writers who were to dominate Norwegian literature over the next two decades: Dag Solstad (b. 1941), Tor Obrestad (b. 1938), Espen Haavardsholm (b. 1945), Jan Erik Vold (b. 1939), and others. Solstad, perhaps the most gifted of them, produced short stories typical of their programme. His *Spiraler* ('Spirals', 1965) depicts a nightmarish existence where invasions from unknown forces continually threaten; this was followed by *Svingstol* ('Swivel Chair', 1967), which describes the very opposite—relentlessly predictable lives lived out in surroundings dominated by material objects of impenetrable solidity.

Poetry was a part of the modernist movement too. Jan Erik Vold experimented not only with words and metrical forms but with media; his performances of poetry with jazz began in the 1960s, and have continued since, making him a popular entertainer. His whimsical poems of everyday life, like those from *Mor Godhjertas glade versjon. Ja* ('Mother Goodheart's happy version. Yes', 1968), are recited in a singsong style which makes the familiar arresting:

My new blue duvet
deserves a poem yes
so warm so big so
light blue I got it
from mum for Christmas . . .

This is a long way from contemporary *Angst* about Vietnam. A few writers in Norway were intensely involved in political protest, however, like the poet and essayist Georg Johannesen (b. 1931): 'He who says: Look at that rose | is leading you away from | the bloodstains on the road.' Yet it was not until the end of the 1960s that political writing became fashionable in Norway, when some members of the 'Profil' group decided to join AKP (m–e), a Marxist-Leninist branch of the Communist Party, and to dedicate their writing to making Norway a Communist society—a conversion described in Solstad's *Arild Asnes 1970* (1971), which explores the dilemma of an intellectual, Arild Asnes, who is faced with the choice between independence of thought and Party loyalty. The early 1970s saw a plethora of political novels in Norway—not all of great literary merit. They were mainly concerned with deconstructing Norwegian society, and verged at times on the parochial in comparison with the broader view taken by Swedish writers.

DENMARK

Modernism in Denmark was a flourishing movement in both poetry and prose. A new generation of writers made their début, and have been central in Danish literary life ever since: a generation characterized in 1967 by Thomas Bredsdorff as *Sære fortællere*, or 'strange storytellers'. One of the strangest was Villy Sørensen (b. 1929), whose *Harmless Tales* (1955) are full of surreal episodes, in which people divide and metamorphose, and speech obstructs communication. A dumb boy can convey his feelings only through music, a blind girl cannot see unless her eyes are full of tears. Sørensen is also a classically trained philosopher and a social commentator, who later proposed an influential 'new model' for Danish society in *Revolt from the Centre* (1978).

The combination of modernism and philosophical speculation is characteristic of others of this generation in Denmark, whose writers have always tended more towards the theoretical and metaphysical than those of Norway and Sweden. Peter Seeberg (b. 1925) found creative inspiration in Wittgenstein before writing *Eftersøgningen og andre noveller* ('The Investigation and Other Stories', 1962), a series of sketches of individuals isolated in their own small universe, each one trapped by his own fixed ideas.

Combining his writing with work as a museum director, Seeberg has a dual vision of objects as both historical artefacts and an arbitrary framework for a fragmented existence.

Svend Åge Madsen (b. 1939) has from the start created his own universe and demands that the reader join in its creation: *Besøget* ('The Visit', 1963) provides alternative solutions to an existential crisis. Later novels like *Days with Diam* (1972) take this idea further: the plot subdivides like a maze in which the reader must make a choice at each junction. Those who embark on reading Madsen either give up at an early stage or tend to become fanatics.

For a more reader-friendly Danish modernist one might turn to the ubiquitous Klaus Rifbjerg (b. 1931), perhaps the central figure in the Danish literary world over the last thirty years. Since his début in the 1950s, Rifbjerg has produced a steady stream of books; in the 1960s alone, he published nineteen works of which he was sole author—novels, stories, poetry, plays— and he has written and produced many films and stage shows, and performed in various media. He rarely produces an uninteresting work. As a poet he heralded 1960s modernism with *Konfrontation* (1960), a collection in which idealism is confronted by cynicism and the world is no longer a sum, merely a collection of parts, as in the poem 'Terminology':

> Yes, yes, yes, now I'm coming
> down to you
> words.
> Trumpet: breathless.
> Forest: withered.
> Caryatid: antique.
> Love: lie.
> Halleluja: burp.
> Poetry: where's my truss?

His classic study of the emotional chaos of adolescence and repressed sexuality, *Den kroniske uskyld* ('Chronic Innocence', 1958), is a set text in Danish schools. *Operaelskeren* ('The Opera Lover', 1966) depicts the love of a mathematician for a musician and the way in which his carefully calculated life is challenged by creative forces that get out of control.

Loss of control, in some cases leading to madness, is symptomatic of social crisis in the work of Leif Panduro (1923–77), whose popular novels, full of black humour, are constructed like detective thrillers and are often set in mental asylums. In *Den gale Mand* (1965)—the punning title means either 'The Madman' or 'The Wrong Man'—the story pivots on uncertainty as to whether the narrator, who is accused of blowing up Copenhagen Cathedral, is wrongly accused or schizophrenic. In many of Panduro's works the inescapable conclusion is that modern society exhibits more symptoms of insanity than the inmates of the asylum.

Pre-eminent with Rifbjerg among Danish poets in the 1960s are Hans-Jørgen Nielsen (b. 1941) and Inger Christensen (b. 1935). Nielsen's poems in *Konstateringer* ('Taking Note', 1966) and *output* (1967) go a step beyond Rifbjerg's suspiciousness of 'large words' to a questioning of meaning in general: words are simply raw material, with no reference to any reality beyond, and one might just as well programme a computer to write poems for all the significance which emerges. The poet is no longer a privileged seer but a builder of blocks of language. Christensen is concerned with language in *Det* ('It', 1969), a text which builds from a single word to explore the process of writing, as well as the inexplicable nature of a world where fear is the dominant emotion—fear of being alone and fear of being with others—and 'there is nothing to do but say it like it is'.

Commitment of a kind is evident in writing like Christensen's, whose reaction to contemporary events is implicit in the fear of smashed faces, of horror, and of death; but direct political commentary is less in evidence in Danish writing than in Norwegian or Swedish. On the other hand, the modernism of the 1960s showed itself capable of renewal and development into the 1970s, even in the works of politically aware writers like Ivan Malinowski (b. 1926), whose poetry combined formal experiment with indignation at human barbarity.

FINLAND

The Second World War still dominated Finnish writing in the 1950s, producing novels like the internationally renowned *The Unknown Soldier* (1954) by Väinö Linna (b. 1920), a biting criticism of the propaganda of war. Nearly all the novels of Veijo Meri (b. 1928) are rooted in the experiences of the Second World War, such as *The Manila Rope* (1957) and other books published in the 1960s. The image of life as a journey permeates much of what he has written: a journey which follows a meandering course full of bizarre events, and leading ultimately nowhere.

The 1950s and early 1960s are also marked by poetic modernism, represented by writers like Paavo Haavikko (b. 1931), with his arresting images and free rhythms. (Some of his poetry has been translated in Anselm Hollo's *Selected Poems of Paavo Haavikko and Tomas Tranströmer*, 1974.) He has also produced novels and plays, such as *The Superintendent* (1968), a study of the tension between the individual and the State and the corrupting influence of power. Bo Carpelan (b. 1926), from the Swedish-speaking minority in Finland, wrote modernist poetry in the 1950s which gradually moved towards more concrete expression, until his poems became almost verbal photographs, as in *The Courtyard* (1969). Carpelan is also known as a novelist, particularly for *Axel* (1986), a historical novel based on the life of his great-uncle, who was a friend of the composer Sibelius, and describing musical life and political struggle in nineteenth-century Helsinki and St Petersburg.

Political struggle is never very far from the surface in Finnish writing, with the constant awareness of the country's position as a buffer state between Russia and the West. Early in the 1960s it surfaced strongly in the poetry of Penti Saarikoski (1937–83). Poems like 'What's Going On Really?' (1962) employ colloquial language, newspaper headlines, and overheard remarks in a humorous barrage of images. Like many Finnish writers, Saarikoski took a Marxist rather than Maoist line, but became increasingly disillusioned with Party totalitarianism. The theatre also became a forum for political comment in the 1960s, with cabarets, revues, and lively experiments such as Arvo Salo's (b. 1932) *Lapualaisooppera* ('The Lapp Opera', 1966), a hard-hitting satire about the use of force as a political weapon.

ICELAND

Halldor Laxness (b. 1902) was still pre-eminent in Icelandic literature during the 1960s, as both novelist and playwright. His intense nationalism and championship of the rights of the individual to follow his own conscience rather than obeying authority or dogma inform novels like *Paradise Reclaimed* (1960), the story of a farmer tempted by the promise of a paradise on earth in Mormon America, but who decides that his own paradise lies back home in Iceland. *Christianity at the Glacier* (1968) is a study of life in a remote Icelandic village, where official Christianity gets short shrift but practical care for one's neighbours binds the community together.

THE 1970s

The political ferment of the late 1960s had repercussions in many countries, not least in producing a greater understanding of the links between personal and political life. Nowhere is this more evident than in the area of gender, and the early 1970s saw a powerful resurgence of feminism. New

348   Janet Garton

women writers emerged in all the Nordic countries to put gender issues at
the forefront of debate, and at the same time to produce exciting new
literary forms and perspectives.

NORWAY

The first new Norwegian feminist to make a stir was Bjørg Vik (b. 1935),
who published short stories with titles like 'Cries for Help from a Soft Sofa'
(1966). Her early tales shocked some readers with their frank depictions of
women's sexuality, but are just as remarkable for their focus on the quiet
desperation of bourgeois family life. Vik was one of the prime movers
behind the journal *Sirene* ('Siren'), which began to appear in 1972, taking up
gender issues in education, business, and politics, as well as in art and
literature. Her short-story cycle *An Aquarium of Women* (1972) traces the
socialization of girls into well-trained 'little women', the mid-life crises of
women struggling with the double burden of paid and unpaid work, and
their attempts to create a new lifestyle in the face of prejudice. Vik is one
of the few women who has made a name also as a playwright, on both
stage and radio, with plays like *To akter for fem kvinner* ('Two Acts for Five
Women', 1974), in which five friends try to come to terms with their very
different lives as modern women.

The women writers of the early 1970s did not make their breakthrough
as a group but as individuals. Liv Køltzow (b. 1944) took up feminist politics with the novel *Hvem bestemmer over Bjørg og Unni?* ('Who Decides What
Happens to Bjørg and Unni?', 1972), a demonstration of how individuals
can resist the machinery of state power; her later works provide a more
sophisticated analysis of male–female relations. Cecilie Løveid's (b. 1951)
first major success came with *Sea Swell* (1979), a meditation about a woman's
life which is also a meditation about language and its constraints: 'So many
languages. Is it easier to have a language without words? Without colour?
One with a fine "touch me" structure? One with warm "come into me"
calls. Or a language which rises up like a racing cycle in a rainy street in
town.'

Awareness of the way language structures thought at a subconscious
level is a central theme of many feminist writers in Norway. Gerd Brantenberg (b. 1941) is an outspokenly political lesbian writer, who created an
inverted society in her satirical novel *The Daughters of Egalia* (1977). Having
first attempted to write the novel in 'normal' language, she realized that the
society she was trying to describe, in which women had been the dominant
sex throughout history, would have developed matriarchal rather than

patriarchal linguistic norms, and set about creating them. Society is composed not of men and women but of 'wim' and its derivative, 'menwim'. The result is initially comic, but this strange world gradually comes to seem more and more natural. With novels like this and the absurdist *What Comes Naturally* (1973), Brantenberg has contributed much to the mood of tolerance towards alternative sexuality which is such a feature of contemporary Scandinavian society.

Male writers meanwhile often took little account of gender in these years, focusing instead on class and on more general socio-geographical problems. The 'Profil' group now produced their most committed works, often in documentary or report form. Tor Obrestad's *Sauda! Streik!* ('Sauda! Strike!', 1972) was a widely discussed documentary novel based on a strike at the Sauda aluminium works in 1970. Dag Solstad's *25. septemberplassen* ('The 25th of September Square', 1975) was an ambitious attempt to describe the development of social-democratic Norway from 1945 to the 1972 Common Market referendum, through the experiences of a working-class family whose members move from unquestioning loyalty to the bosses to opposition to capitalist profiteering. Later in the decade, Solstad moved his focus back to the Second World War, with a trilogy of novels which indicted Norwegian class betrayal.

The novelist, poet, and playwright Edvard Hoem (b. 1950) produced one of the best political novels of the time, *The Ferry Journeys of Love* (1974). This demonstrates the effect of centralization policies on a group of islanders and the importance of solidarity; at the same time it is a fantastic account of an invented stretch of coastline, with characters who take over the action and a narrator who is unable to keep his distance, but is called to account by his creations. Kjartan Fløgstad (b. 1944), too, combines fantasy with political awareness in *Dollar Road* (1977), which traces the evolution of a rural farming community into a modern industrial society. It is an entertaining story, full of burlesque and picaresque episodes, and at the same time a linguistic *tour de force*, contrasting all the different registers of the Norwegian language. Fløgstad has since consolidated his reputation as an intellectual author, poles apart from naïve social realism.

Knut Faldbakken (b. 1941) was aware of problems of gender and of urban capitalism from early on in his career, though he took an individual approach to them. *The Sleeping Prince* (1971) describes the sexual fantasies of a frustrated middle-aged spinster; one follows the story with fascination as her eccentricity builds into paranoia. In *Twilight Country* (1974) Faldbakken portrays the disintegration of modern society, as life on a rubbish-tip becomes a struggle for survival among outcasts from a civilization choked by its own debris. He is one of the most widely translated of modern Norwegian authors, and has recently been accused of leading a 'male backlash' against feminism; the male narrator of the sexually explicit *The Honeymoon* (1982), for example, feels victimized by his ultra-feminist, sexually voracious wife.

DENMARK

Sexual tolerance went further in Denmark than anywhere else after censorship was abolished in 1967, and feminism found fertile ground. The somewhat older writer Tove Ditlevsen (1918–76) was an inspiration, with novels based on her own anguished life and her bad conscience at being both a woman and an artist; her suicide was mirrored in novels of women's lives in which this complicated balancing act had become too much to cope with: novels like *Fuglen* ('The Bird', 1974) by Jette Drewsen (b. 1943), and *Le* (1977) by Herdis Møllehave (b. 1936—Le is the name of the central character, but also, ironically, the Danish word for 'laugh').

The younger generation, however, had a more positive attitude. The name of Suzanne Brøgger (b. 1944) became synonymous with sexual freedom when she published books like *Crème fraîche* (1978), a quasi-autobiographical sexual odyssey which comes complete with a recommendation by Henry Miller. In earlier books like *Kærlighedens veje og vildveje* ('The Right and Wrong Paths of Love', 1975), however, Brøgger proposed not just an annexation by women of traditional male freedoms but a different way of living, a kind of love built not on pairing and the nuclear family but on openness to experience and uncertainty: 'To believe that women have it in mind to "take over" society with its patriarchal values, standards, symbols and language, shows a phallocratic lack of imagination. Women do not wish to get on top. Our goals have never been that low.' There is a tension in Brøgger's writing between intimacy and aloofness which can produce contradictions, but she has sparked off many lively debates in Denmark.

More traditional story-tellers are Dea Trier Mørch (b. 1941) and Kirsten Thorup (b. 1942). Mørch is an artist as well as a writer; her popular books are often illustrated by her own woodcuts. *Winter's Child* (1976) is a collective novel set in the maternity ward of the national hospital, and follows the experience of pregnancy and birth of women from different backgrounds; it is a sociological survey and a study of female solidarity, with drawings which emphasize the shared experience of giving life. Thorup's best-known works are the series of novels about Jonna, beginning with *Lille Jonna* ('Little Jonna', 1977). This is the story of a family from a provincial underclass which experiences the narrow-minded prejudice of a conservative rural society. The novels portray a fascinating gallery of characters but concentrate on the maturing of Jonna, whose struggles with her sense of inferiority are described with warm involvement.

Thorup was drawing on her own background to depict lower-class life in rural Denmark. Most writers, in Scandinavia as elsewhere, are middle-class; the women's movement, however, helped to make it possible for the traditionally silent classes to speak out. Grete Stenbæk Jensen (b. 1925) wrote *Konen og æggene* ('The Woman and the Eggs', 1973) about her experience of working in an egg factory, with low pay, poor conditions, and overwhelming tiredness.

Where men writers are concerned, the modernists remained at the centre. Klaus Rifbjerg's novels of contemporary life, centring on individual psychological crisis, continued with works like *Anna (I) Anna* (1969), the story of a pathologically repressed woman, and *Leif den lykkelige jun.* ('Lucky Leif Junior', 1971). In this novel Rifbjerg returns to the theme of *Chronic Innocence*, as Leif attempts to lose his innocence but proves unable to integrate sexual, class, and racial differences into his world-view.

The poet Henrik Nordbrandt (b. 1945) became a major figure, though hardly part of the national tradition; he has lived a large part of his adult life in Greece and Turkey, and has consciously rejected what he sees as the cold rationality of the North for the sensuousness and mystical experience of the South. His love poetry avoids romantic cliché and depends on concrete awareness of the presence of the other:

> Now I can no longer use you
> as a rose in my love poems:
> you are much too large, much too beautiful
> and much too much yourself.

SWEDEN

As in Denmark, women from the working class made their mark as writers. Maja Ekelöf (1918–89), in *Rapport från en skurhink* ('Report from a Slop Bucket', 1970), combines her experiences as a cleaner with her reflections on international politics; and Marit Paulsen (b. 1939), in *Du, människa?* ('Think You're a Human Being?', 1972), portrays the double discrimination against women as low-paid workers and as the wives of workers.

The new feminism made less of an impact in Sweden than it did in Norway and Denmark, no doubt because the country already had relatively advanced policies on gender. Earlier writers like Lidman and Åkesson remained prominent, as did Birgitta Trotzig (b. 1929), who could hardly be called a feminist, being a Catholic and holding more traditional views about a woman's role. Kerstin Ekman (b. 1933), originally a writer of detective stories, began in the 1970s to write a series of historical novels tracing life in Katrineholm from the 1870s to the present day. The focus is on the women, from the destitute but dogged Sara Sabina Lans, who supports her whole family in *Häxringarna* ('The Witches' Circles', 1974), to Anne-Marie in *En stad av ljus* ('A Town of Light', 1983), who in clearing out her house comes to terms with her family and her past. The series conveys an image of a woman's world that is opposed to the male ethos of competition, stressing instead the values of nurture and the creation and preservation of life.

Among male writers, political radicalism became in many cases more muted after the failure of the hopes of 1968. The disillusionment is clear in Enquist's *Sekonden* ('The Second', 1971), a documentary novel which traces the history of the Swedish working class through that of a sporting family whose most famous member, a hammer-thrower, was discovered to have set world records using an under-weight hammer. By the end of the 1960s, sport had become subject to commercial and political pressures, and was no longer an opportunity for self-development and teamwork. In later works Enquist explores historical topics; his play *The Night of the Tribades* (1975) looks at Strindberg's life and his love / hate relationships with women, while the novel *The March of the Musicians* (1978) takes up the theme of Swedish emigration to Brazil in the early years of the century.

Sven Delblanc also moved from political to historical novels with his semi-autobiographical 'Hedeby' tetralogy (1970–5): the history of a Swedish community from 1937 to 1946. It is far from a traditional epic, since the narrative voice moves around among the characters, and addresses the reader directly. Delblanc returned to the same family with another tetralogy in the 1980s, to try to exorcize his personal ghosts. P. C. Jersild focuses on contemporary society in his study of a child alone in Stockholm in *The Children's Island* (1976), and uses his experience as a doctor to write about illness and death in a modern hospital in *The House of Babel* (1987). The ethical dilemmas and dangers of modern technology are explored in *A Living Soul* (1980), in which events are narrated by a disembodied brain floating in a tank, destined for an experiment in cloning brains to be used as computers.

Per Gunnar Evander (b. 1933) began writing in the 1960s, but has always avoided direct political comment. Some of his novels can be read as having a political slant, however, like *Uppkomlingarna* ('The Upstarts', 1969), in which a man who is trying to write a political novel is invaded by several illegitimate sons; they torture him, telling him at the same time that they are proud to have a father 'whose condition mirrors that of the world'. Like many of Evander's early novels, this one plays an elaborate game with the reader; it is a fictional documentary, in which the narrator is called Per Gunnar Evander, has met the central character, and can provide 'facts' about his life. In the 1970s Evander wrote more realistic novels, such as *Måndagarna med Fanny* ('Mondays with Fanny', 1974), which became a successful film.

The poet Tomas Tranströmer (b. 1931) began to make a name for himself abroad in the 1970s. He has been widely translated into English, acquiring considerable popularity in the United States; his *Collected Poems* were published in English in 1987. His precise observations of nature and the personal tone of his free verse invite comparison with Walt Whitman.

FINLAND

Here there was no noticeable surge of feminist writing in the early 1970s; Finnish women had traditionally worked outside the home, and there was less perceived discrimination. One of the most important new feminist writers was the Swedish-speaking Märta Tikkanen (b. 1935), who took up the themes of institutionalized discrimination and sexual politics in the novel *Manrape* (1975), in which a woman who has been raped takes her revenge by raping the man in return, only to have her crime dismissed by the police because it is adjudged not to be possible for a woman to rape a man. Tikkanen had a major success with *The Love Story of the Century* (1978), an ironically titled poem cycle which is a brutally frank account of life with her alcoholic husband, the author Henrik Tikkanen, and at the same time an account of her own life as a writer and her discovery of a private female space to which she can retreat:

> Whilst your words beat against the mask
> I hung it up
> on the chair facing you
> and went on my way singing
> hidden by all your words
> which bounced back silently
> from the mild smile
> in the chair

Tikkanen has continued to demonstrate, in poetry and prose, the links between public and private life, as in *Rödluvan* ('Little Red Riding Hood', 1986), where the universal myth is subverted as the Wolf meets his match.

The Swedish-language poet Tua Forsström (b. 1947) published her first collection of poems in 1972; some of her lyrical celebrations of grief and loss have been translated in *Snow Leopard* (1990). Sirkka Turkka, Satu Marttila, and Arja Tiainen are among the Finnish-language women poets who began their careers in the 1970s. In a tetralogy which begins with *Vetää kaikista ovista* ('Friends and Enemies', 1974), Eeva Joenpelto (b. 1921) describes a society in transition between the old ways and the new, in which the men are often weaker and more inclined to stick to well-worn paths, whilst the women respond to the challenge of change.

ICELAND

In Iceland, Svava Jakobsdóttir (b. 1930) became a feminist figurehead. She began as a novelist and short-story writer in the 1960s and moved on to become an MP in the 1970s. Her stories provide startling juxtapositions of the realistic and the fantastic. The novel *Leigjandinn* ('The Lodger', 1969) is a symbolic account of the effects of the American military presence in Iceland, described in terms of the pressures it exerts on a housewife. The more recent *Gunnlaðar saga* ('The Story of Gunnlöd', 1987) draws on the medieval Eddic poem *Hávamál*, in which the male god Odin steals a sacred cup from the fertility goddess Gunnlöd, to provide a commentary on modern Icelandic society, dominated by business and military interests. Svava also had considerable success as a playwright in the 1970s.

AFTER 1980

The critic Oystein Rottem has characterized the 1980s in Scandinavia as 'the decade of fantasy', when writers abandoned political documentaries and reclaimed the fantastic as the proper sphere of creativity. It is a shift of emphasis which is apparent in several major works from this decade.

NORWAY

Committed writers like Dag Solstad and Edvard Hoem now changed the focus of their attention. Solstad embarked on novels with a more personal slant, where historical materialism is subordinated to the adventures of the central character-narrator, as in the fantastically titled *Gymnaslærer Pedersens beretning om den store politiske vekkelsen som har hjemsøkt vårt land* ('Teacher

Pedersen's Account of the Great Political Awakening Which Has Afflicted our Country', 1982). Ironic and inventive, this novel is as much about language as about politics. After an unsuccessful attempt at recording the history of Communism in the 1970s, Hoem moved in *Ave Eva* (1987) to a story of love and jealousy interwoven with Strindberg's *Miss Julie* in *Prøvetid* ('Rehearsals', 1984) and a study of rootlessness and despair.

Mari Osmundsen (b. 1951), whose first novel in 1978 was a politically correct account of trade unions and strikes, became a writer of fantastic tales with *Gode gjerninger* ('Good Deeds', 1984) and *Familien* ('The Family', 1985). The former, set in modern Oslo, tells of a young woman who is a witch with a personal demon, while the latter centres on a house of women, a place of creativity and sanctuary in a competitive male world, before moving finally into a wild zone where witches, pin-up girls from magazines, and lost children can live harmoniously together.

Bergljot Hobæk Haff (b. 1925) incorporated fantasy into her novels from the start, as in *Bålet* ('The Fire', 1962), the story of the fight for a woman between two male figures resembling Christ and Satan. During the political 1970s she was a marginal author, but she has come into her own in recent years in novels like *Den guddommelige tragedie* ('The Divine Tragedy', 1989), in which Christ again plays a central role, this time as a black child born to illiterate parents in South Africa, with a harassed God and an impatient archangel Gabriel as observers of his fate. Herbjørg Wassmo (b. 1942) is also something of an exception to the rule; her trilogy from the 1980s, beginning with *The House with the Blind Glass Verandah* (1981), is a realistic and harrowing account of the life of the 'German bastard' Tora and her sexual abuse at the hands of her stepfather; it was an enormous popular success.

Amongst authors who began publishing in the 1980s, various forms of fantasy have flourished. Short stories by Lisbet Hiide (b. 1956) and Sissel Lie (b. 1942), entitled respectively *Alices særegne opplevelse av natt* ('Alice's Peculiar Experience of Night', 1985) and *Tigersmil* ('Tiger Smile', 1986), are feminist fables where women are wild cats and stalk men in the jungle of the night; Lie's *Lion's Heart* (1988) allows a woman to travel back in time to experience life with the sixteenth-century French poet Louise Labé. Jan Kjærstad (b. 1953) often uses the detective story format as a basis for a novel which soon departs from credibility, as in *Det store eventyret* ('The Great Adventure', 1987), or *Homo Falsus* (1984), in which a woman murders men by the novel method of seducing them so intensely that they are absorbed into her body at the moment of orgasm.

Detective stories and spy novels are as popular in Scandinavian as they are in English literature. Louis Masterson, the creator of the detective Morgan Kane, is a pseudonym of the Norwegian writer Kjell Hallbing (b. 1934).

DENMARK

The most recent—and rather unlikely—success for a Danish author in English has been that of the thriller writer Peter Høeg (b. 1957). The investigator in his *Miss Smilla's Feeling for Snow* (1993), the small but deadly Smilla Jaspersen, is a Greenlander whose understanding of the different qualities of snow helps her to solve a crime; the untranslatable Greenlandic terms for snow are also an opportunity for Høeg to deliver a critique of Scandinavian colonialism and the linguistic deprivation of an ethnic minority.

Henrik Stangerup (b. 1937) was best known during the 1970s for his work on films, and his novels at that time drew their inspiration from the world of the media. After a financial and emotional collapse, he turned in the 1980s to historical individuals, whose lives take on the aura of myth. *The Road to Lagoa Santa* (1981) tells the story of the Danish biologist P. W. Lund, his researches in Brazil, and his mysterious illness, whose causes Stangerup suggests lie in the shadows of his puritanical past, which his exile to the colourful sensuality of Brazil cannot exorcize. *The Seducer* (1985) recreates the wild career of the nineteenth-century critic P. M. Møller, who was an enemy of Kierkegaard and the inspirer of his *Seducer's Diary*.

Dorrit Willumsen (b. 1940) explores myths about men and women, and about love. She is a modernist rather than a feminist, interested in exploring consciousness rather than changing society. Many of her works take a man as the central character, and are about the absence of love, which is the centre around which everything rotates. People without souls are replaced by robots or dolls, as in *Programmeret til kærlighed* ('Programmed for Love', 1981), where a (female) researcher is set the task of producing 'the perfect woman'—a sexy robot.

Of the new writers, the poet Pia Tafdrup (b. 1952) made her presence felt as an original voice from her first collection in 1981. Her poetry, of which the collection *Spring Tide* (1985) has been translated into English, expresses what she calls 'the syntax of desire', a spontaneous sensuality in which the lover is the world and the woman's body opens up in unashamed joy:

> I am the one
> who porous to your impulses
> opens up in desire
> everywhere and all at once
> to exist in the world.

Two authors from a previous generation had to wait until the 1980s to make their breakthrough in Sweden, when their inventive talents found a welcoming public: Torgny Lindgren (b. 1938) and Göran Tunström (b. 1937). Lindgren's stories have a quasi-biblical flavour, and are often narrated in an archaic, poetic style which underlines their function as fables or allegories of modern life. *Ormens väg på hälleberget* ('The Way of the Serpent upon the Rock', 1982) is a historical tale of sexual abuse and the dark forces it arouses, set in a nineteenth-century rural town. *Bathsheba* (1984) uses the biblical story of David and Bathsheba to comment on the misuse of power.

Göran Tunström has set several of his more recent novels in his home province of Sunne; but local colour is more of a backdrop to an existential drama in books like *Juloratoriet* ('The Christmas Oratorio', 1983) and *Tjuven* ('The Thief', 1986), in which individuals are the victims not of social change but of their own repressions and guilt.

Among those who have come to the fore in the 1980s, a popular author is Niklas Rådström (b. 1953), whose novels, like *Skuggan* ('The Shadow', 1982) and *Den helige Antonius frestelser* ('The Temptations of St Anthonius', 1986), are full of invented documents and references, fictional editors and translators, paradoxes and authorial sleight of hand. One is left uncertain as to the status of stories which are themselves a demonstration of uncertainty. Agneta Pleijel (b. 1940), earlier well known as a literary critic, made a name from the late 1970s onwards as a novelist, poet, and dramatist. Her novel *Vindspejare* ('He Who Observeth the Wind', 1987) makes several false starts, mirroring the nervousness of its female narrator, who discovers her literary voice as she discovers her subject-matter. The play *Summer Nights* (1984) is the story of three sisters returning to the summer house of their childhood and trying to reconcile their later lives with their earlier dreams.

Disillusion with political solutions is evident among the younger generation of Finnish writers, who describe the rootlessness and egotism of the 'yuppy' generation. Their descriptions of social disintegration and violence are presented as simple fact, without any moralizing. Among the more accomplished novelists are Annika Idström (b. 1947), Esa Sariola (b. 1951), and Rosa Liksom (b. 1958). Liksom's *One Night Stands* (1990) has been presented in English as 'post-punk writing': it consists of short prose accounts

of lives without stability or security or even any sense that such things are
desirable.

THEATRE

Theatre has flourished in Scandinavia in recent years. One spin-off from
political commitment was a determination to widen access to the theatre,
to bring plays to the people and to the regions, away from the élitist theatres of the capitals. In Denmark, Finland, Norway, and Sweden many groups
sprang up, often with left-wing affiliations, looking for contemporary, committed drama and interested in theatrical experiment.

Modern Swedish theatre owes a great debt to Ingmar Bergman (b. 1918),
who began work as a director and playwright in the 1940s. Although he is
much better known as a film director, he was instrumental in the revival of
post-war theatre, and still writes the occasional play. The most acclaimed
Swedish playwright of recent years is Lars Norén (b. 1944), who has been
performed in most theatres in Scandinavia, and in many abroad. The influence of Eugene O'Neill is evident in many of his plays about nuclear families, which are torn by strife but unable to break free, as in *Night is Mother
to the Day* (1982). *Munich–Athens* (1987), which had its première in London,
explores the tensions between a couple cooped up in a railway carriage,
who conceal their emotional needs beneath sparring and jealousy.

Pre-eminent among younger Swedish dramatists is Stig Larsson (b. 1955),
who relishes the role of *enfant terrible*. Many of his plays involve shocking
intrusions into domestic life, like *VD* ('MD', 1987), in which the Managing
Director of the title pays a friendly visit to an employee's flat and sets about
cynically seducing his girlfriend in front of him. *Red Light* (1991) consists of
a Beckett-like conversation at a pedestrian crossing, in which words often
seem to be a barrier rather than an aid to communication.

Regional theatres in Norway have fostered the talents of young writers
like Klaus Hagerup (b. 1946) and Edvard Hoem. In Hoem's *Good Night,
Europe* (1983) an ageing politician comes to terms with his own past failure,
and with the failure of Europe collectively to resist corruption and greed;
the gloom of the subject-matter is made bearable by lively staging, and the
action is intercut with cabaret songs in a style reminiscent of Brecht.

Older, more established playwrights who played to full houses in the
1970s and 1980s were Bjørg Vik, with her naturalist dramas of personal
relationships, and Peder Cappelen (1931–91), who in plays like *Whittenland*
(1981) moved as far away as possible from contemporary life and political

commentary, drawing instead on Norwegian folklore and legend to create a whimsical fable of the battle between creative warmth and sterile cold.

Cecilie Løveid is the most exciting dramatist in Norway today—though, like Hoem, her working relationship with the theatre has at times been stormy. Her radio play *Seagull Eaters* (1983), which won the Prix Italia, follows the fortunes of a working girl in wartime Bergen who has ambitions to be an actress, but meets with frustration and exploitation. Intertextuality is a feature of Løveid's work, and Kristine's struggles are commented on by extracts from Ibsen and Chekhov, as well as by Henriette Schønberg Erken, whose household hints are a mocking reminder of a woman's 'rightful' place. In *Dobbel nytelse* ('Double Delight', 1990), Provençal troubadour songs are combined with dance, mime, and slapstick to produce 'total theatre'.

Experimental theatre found conditions in Denmark particularly welcoming, and companies became more international in their outlook. Eugenio Barba's Odin group moved from Norway to Holstebro in Denmark in 1966, where it is still flourishing. This kind of ensemble, which relies on improvisation and mime, could to some extent be said to make the dramatist redundant; and the director's role has become correspondingly more pronounced. Nevertheless, alternative groups have fostered much new dramatic talent, and are more likely than established theatres to accept contemporary writing. Traditional theatres tend to play safe with the classics or imported box-office successes. Radio and television theatre has provided a wider audience for new dramatic writing.

Rifbjerg, Panduro, and Madsen are novelists who have all become successful dramatists. Madsen's *Nøgne masker* ('Naked Masks', 1987) borrows ideas from Freud and Pirandello, and recreates their personalities on stage, as they face each other in games of bluff and counter-bluff in which theatrical illusion becomes interwoven with a demonstration of the impossibility of knowing other people. Ulla Ryum (b. 1937), another of the 'strange story-tellers' of the 1960s, soon turned her hand to radio plays and since 1973 has concentrated on drama, including a cycle of five plays about Western civilization's accelerating rush towards self-annihilation by war. In *Krigen* ('War', 1975) timeless or mythical figures enact nightmarish parables in which those in whom love has been destroyed are used to 'sanitize' or destroy others whose messy human emotions have survived.

Theatrical activity has been lively in Finland since the 1960s, and has enjoyed considerable state support. The 1980s were a particularly energetic time, both architecturally and artistically: experimental stages were built and there was new emphasis on performing and directing, with directors like Jouko Turkka from the Helsinki State Theatre. Breakaway groups such as Finland's Folk Theatre came into being around collaborative ventures like *Pete Q* (1978), in which more than fifty people had a hand. Another joint venture, the Group Theatre, performed a trilogy of plays by Jussi Parviainen (b. 1955) which dealt with the topical theme of the tabloid press.

FURTHER READING

Brostrøm, Torben, *Denmarkings: Danish Literature Today* (Copenhagen, 1982).

Forsås-Scott, Helena (ed.), *Textual Liberation: European Feminist Writing in the Twentieth Century* (London, 1991).

Garton, Janet, *Norwegian Women's Writing 1850–1990* (London, 1993).

Lomas, Herbert (ed.), *Contemporary Finnish Poetry* (Newcastle upon Tyne, 1991).

Naess, Harald (ed.), *A History of Norwegian Literature* (Lincoln, Nebr., 1993).

Rossel, Sven (ed.), *A History of Danish Literature* (Lincoln, Nebr., 1992).

Scobbie, Irene (ed.), *Aspects of Modern Swedish Literature* (Norwich, 1988).

Zuck, Virpi (ed.), *Dictionary of Scandinavian Literature* (Westport, Conn., 1990).

23

SCOTLAND

KASIA BODDY

As the work of novelists such as Alasdair Gray (b. 1934), James Kelman (b. 1946), and A. L. Kennedy (b. 1965) finds ever-increasing acclaim, many are heralding another renaissance in Scottish writing; the first being that associated with such writers as Hugh MacDiarmid, Edwin Muir, and Lewis Grassic Gibbon in the 1920s and 1930s. While those writers largely drew on a threatened rural way of life which they felt contained the essence of Scottish identity, the writers whose work is acclaimed today tend to explore an urban Scotland.

Several explanations have been put forward for the current flowering of Scottish writing. The first is the simplest: that suddenly there are a lot of good writers around. This is true but it does not explain why so many writers have recently emerged. Again, the simplest explanation is probably right: that if one Scottish writer is successful doors open more readily to others. Familiarity with the fiction of Kelman and Gray made both publishers and public receptive to the work of Jeff Torrington (b. 1935), Janice Galloway (b. 1956), and Irvine Welsh (b. 1958). And the success of the novelists in turn brought many Scottish poets to the forefront.

Another explanation of the current vogue for (a certain type of) Scottish writing places it in the context of many years of Conservative government. Scotland has never voted Tory and is identified by the English Left as a stronghold of oppositional values. There is also a sense within Scotland that its very lack of political power encourages cultural creativity. Whatever the political implications of the current cultural scene, it is true that there has been an emphasis on a fiction of disaffection and nostalgia, largely coming from the industrially abandoned west of Scotland.

For some Scots the current emphasis on urban decline is as dangerously limiting as historical 'tartanry' or the 'kailyard' ever were. Liz Lochhead (b. 1947), for example, provides a version of 'Bagpipe Muzak, Glasgow 1990':

> Where once they used to fear and pity
> These days they glamorise and patronise our city—

Accentwise once they could hear bugger all
That was not low, glottal or guttural,
Now we've 'kudos' incident'ly
And the Patter's street-smart, strictly state-of-the-art,
And our oaths are user-friendly.

While the new urban writers are of great importance to contemporary
Scottish writing, both individually and as a collective phenomenon, a consideration of their work does not give a complete account of either its
current diversity or its historical context. More worryingly, to talk blissfully
of a new Scottish renaissance relies on concepts of nation and a national
literature that go largely unexamined. This is not the place even to begin
to approach the quagmire surrounding theories connecting nationality and
writing, but they are important to bear in mind when considering not only
what we read as 'Scottish literature', but how we read it.

There are many possible starting-points for a definition of what a national
literature might be. One is via subject-matter—that is, Scottish writing is
writing that takes Scotland as its subject, regardless of who writes it. This
is how the label 'Scottish writer' is most often applied—in much the same
way as the terms 'woman writer' or 'black writer' are used. (It is not how
'English writer' or 'male writer' are used.) If writers are only to be recognized as Scottish if they deal specifically and consciously with Scottish issues, two consequences ensue. First, many writers feel that in order to
succeed internationally they must not write of Scotland. Second, many who
choose not to write primarily about Scotland are told they have no right to
be considered Scottish. This prescriptive view can lead to the absurd conclusion that, say, Muriel Spark (b. 1918) is only a truly 'Scottish writer' in
The Prime of Miss Jean Brodie (1961), and parts of other works. Furthermore,
to talk of 'Scottishness' suggests some unified experience, but while politically many may strive for such unity, the reality of life in Scotland is very
diverse. Any claim to a national identity is always in tension with other
identities—local identities, and loyalties to class, race, gender, and generation.

The cultural diversity of Scotland does not just affect subject-matter,
however; there is also considerable diversity within literary forms. While
Islanders have a traditional affinity with Scandinavian myth and epic traditions (for example, George Mackay Brown's (b. 1921) novels and stories of
modern Orkney incorporate incidents and images from the Orkneyinga Saga),
the contemporary urban novel of central Scotland has more in common
with the 1940s Chicago 'existential' novel than anything closer to home.
Emma Tennant (b. 1937) and Angela Carter (1940–92) both argue that it is

their sense of Scottishness that allows them to escape the pervasive and parochial influence of the English novel and look further afield to the traditions of Europe and South America, as well as of Scotland.

An alternative definition of Scottish writing might include writers who, although born elsewhere, do their writing in Scotland. As Edwin Morgan (b. 1920) puts it, '"Scottishness" may be not more than a writer deciding to remain and work in Scotland, though wooed elsewhere; and despite my phrase "no more than" I regard this as being important.' Scottish writing would then include the Nigerian Kole Omotoso's (b. 1943) first novel, *The Edifice* (1971), which tells the love story of a Nigerian student and a Scots girl and is set predominantly in Edinburgh, and Wilson Harris's (b. 1921) *Black Marsden* (1972), which explores the cross-cultural links between Scotland and the Caribbean. Historical links between Scotland and Ireland are also very important, and many Irish writers based in Scotland have explored what is in many ways a parallel, if not shared, heritage. Bernard MacLaverty (b. 1942), for example, is claimed as both an Irish and a Scottish writer.

If 'foreigners' may be affected by their stay in Scotland, Scottish culture may also be affected by their presence. Arguably Scotland's most successful theatre in the last thirty years has been Glasgow's Citizens, which according to Morgan is 'alien and unScottish'. Although many complain of its emphasis on international rather than Scottish plays, that very internationalism has now become a part of Scottish theatre. Like other forms of Scottish writing, drama has found a way of breaking out of the English influence by looking further afield, particularly to the traditions of French, German, and Spanish theatre. An openness to international influences and ideas in general is one of the most encouraging and exciting things about contemporary Scottish writing.

In answer to what may seem loose definitions of Scottish writing, however, some might argue that being a Scottish writer is simply a matter of Scottish birth, that writers who have lived elsewhere for most of their lives and write of other places, but who were born in Scotland, should be considered primarily as Scottish writers. This may seem absurd, but it acknowledges the importance of origins in Scottish writing.

Childhood is an obvious starting-point for many writers, and the mentality of a child is something that many, very different, writers seem to want to cultivate for Scotland. For example, Walter Scott's often quoted verse 'O Caledonia! Stern and wild, Meet nurse for a poetic child!' provides more than simply the title of Elspeth Barker's (b. 1941) first novel, *O Caledonia* (1991). A vivid evocation of the birth of the (particularly Scottish) poetic imagination, it is set in a minutely rendered but wholly magical-seeming Aberdeenshire. The Scotland of childhood is seen very much as a place apart, far removed in its primitive cruelty not only from England, but from the tamed, mature cities of the Lowlands. Growing up means taming that magical Scottishness, and is therefore something to be resisted. If nation in Scotland always defines itself in terms of something lost—be it the Highland glens or the Clyde shipyards—then it is natural to equate that with one's own lost innocence and authenticity. 'Who are we,' asks Morgan, 'if we are not who we were?'

Works in which the search for identity is important inevitably pay attention to what Alexander Trocchi calls the 'odour of ancestors'. Parental influence intrudes particularly in the idealized working-class images of Trocchi, McIlvanney, and Kelman, where mothers are martyred saints while fathers inevitably give their sons 'their personal set of shackles' (McIlvanney's *Docherty*, 1975). There is, however, a counter-tradition of works, from Jessie Kesson's (1916–94) *The White Bird Passes* (1958) to Anne Smith's (b. 1944) *The Magic Glass* (1981), that seek to undermine the sentimental view of childhood. Perhaps the most powerfully de-familiarizing vision of all can be found in Bill Douglas's (1934–91) film *My Childhood* (1972), an unremittingly honest portrait of growing up in the bleak setting of a run-down mining town.

Also active is the romantic fantasy of being an orphan, for it contains the possibility of reinventing one's origins. For example, in Alasdair Gray's Victorian pastiche *Poor Things* (1992), a young woman is saved from drowning by being 'reinvented' with the brain of a child. Gray's motto, 'Work as if you live in the early days of a better nation', seems to suggest that Scotland, too, can shake off parental influence and start, innocently, again.

A belief in the value of self-improvement through education remains strong in Scottish culture, as is evident from any number of autobiographical accounts: for example, David Daiches's (b. 1912) *Two Worlds* (1987) or Ralph Glasser's (b. 1916) *Growing Up in the Gorbals* (1986). School, however, is also seen as a fall from childhood grace and anarchy: as the protagonist of William Boyd's (b. 1952) *The New Confessions* (1987) puts it, 'I was going away and nothing would ever be the same again.' But while George Friel (1910–76) writes of the failure of his idealistic teacher *Mr Alfred, M. A.* (1972) to educate the nastiness out of Glasgow life, there is also a persistent anxiety about teachers who are successful. Spark's Miss Jean Brodie is literally a Fascist who maintains, 'Give me a girl at an impressionable age and she is mine for life', while the protagonist of Kelman's *A Disaffection* (1989) fears that in being a teacher at all he is participating in what he sees as the

authoritarian control of the State, what A. L. Kennedy, in turn, characterizes as 'The Scottish Method (for the Perfection of Children)'. Tenet number
one, for example, decrees that 'guilt is good', while according to number
seven, 'joy is fleeting, sinful and the forerunner of despair'.

It is at school that Scottish children first experience a sense of division—
being forced to speak and write Standard English after a childhood spent
using some version of Scots. The protagonist of Barker's *O Caledonia*, on
first encountering English verse, finds its terms of reference often quite
alien to her Aberdeenshire experience: 'People in these parts did not use the
word "spring". They said "the end of winter" or "the beginning of summer"
or they used the month's name; winter ebbed into summer, there seemed
no transitional period, none of the joyous awakening so favoured by verse
and song.'

For Emma Tennant, the experience of linguistic division explains the
Scottish, and more particularly her own, attraction to the *doppelgänger* motif.
The classic work of the genre, James Hogg's tale of demonic possession *The
Private Memoirs and True Confessions of a Justified Sinner* (1824), forms the
basis of Tennant's feminist rereading *The Bad Sister* (1978), while Stevenson's
Dr Jekyll and Mr Hyde (1886) lies behind her 1989 novel *Two Women of
London*. Spark's Jean Brodie notably claims descent from Deacon Brodie,
the famous eighteenth-century burglar and notorious liver of a double life.

It is not only Scots sensitive to the pressure of England on their borders
and language who feel a sense of dual identity; less commented on are
those Scots of a mixed heritage. Spark, for example, Edinburgh's most
famous literary daughter, asserts that it was the experience of being Jewish
in that Presbyterian city 'that bred within me the conditions of exiledom',
and the principle of duality that informs her work. Trocchi writes of his
schoolyard unease with a foreign surname, and his father's rejection of the
work ethic in 'the land of the industrious Scot', while Jackie Kay (b. 1961)
examines the unresolved tensions involved in being an Afro-Scot:

> Whit is an Afro-Scot anyway? mibbe she can dance a reel and a salsa
> remember Fannie Lou Hamer and Robert Burns
> and still see Tam O'Shanter taken with the Cutty Sark
> —whit do you think of pair Meg's tail being pulled off like that?
> mibbe they wear kilts and wraps
> and know that Ymoja offered yams and fowl
> and Corra could prophesize.

If a Scottish childhood and education are widely considered to be powerfully affecting, and if Scottish writers are often nostalgic about that lost

childhood, the desire to leave it all behind, to stop having to think or talk of Scotland at all, is also prevalent. For Kathleen Jamie (b. 1962) leaving Scotland is equivalent to a 'clearance'—allowing the place to be poetically transformed. 'Stop thinking now, and put on your shoes,' begins her fine poetry sequence 'Karakoram Highway' (in *The Way We Live*, 1987), and a mood of intellectual liberation informs all her 'travel writing'. 'I | Found myself running away | From Scotland into the golden city,' writes W. S. Graham (1918–86), and many Scots have run to London in search of work and an easier life. Leaving Scotland has a similarly liberating effect for the protagonist of Bill Douglas's autobiographical trilogy, for it is as a soldier in Egypt that he encounters the Englishman who not only introduces whole worlds of literature, music, and film to him, but offers him another place he 'can call . . . home'.

Indeed, there is a long tradition of 'Scots made good' stories, a tradition which finds itself parodied in Alasdair Gray's mock morality tales *The Fall of Kevin Walker* (1985) and *McGrotty and Ludmilla, or The Habinger Report* (1990). The myth of the 'golden city' is further undermined by Irvine Welsh's caustic and funny fiction in which Hackney is revealed to be as parochial as Leith, while an Amsterdam housing scheme is indistinguishable from one in Edinburgh. Welsh's is a world, he ironically notes, of 'Eurotrash', of restlessly drifting characters for whom the idea of national loyalty is just one more irrelevance.

For many, however, the journey south means selling out, and it is usually only a temporary respite from Real Life. A. L. Kennedy's *Looking for the Possible Dance* (1993) begins with the protagonist's acknowledgement that 'this morning she will travel away from here. Probably, she will come back.' Her journey away from responsibility frames the novel, and it is finally rejected. In James Kelman's work the tension between staying and going is never really resolved. In a key scene in *A Disaffection* the protagonist plans to drive from Glasgow to England, and go on to France and Spain, but he only goes as far as Motherwell before turning back. In this context his decision is less an acceptance of local responsibility than a failure of nerve. In *How Late It Was, How Late* (1994) the protagonist finally does leave, first through his sudden blindness, which he experiences as a feeling 'of being somewhere else in the world' and his dreams of going to Luckenbach, Texas, to 'follow the outlaws', then in reality on a train. 'I'm thinking of heading,' he tells his son. Eventually he adds 'back to England', but the note of definiteness seems like an afterthought.

In many ways, however, leaving Scotland only increases the potency of its mythical influence. For example, two of the most acclaimed young poets

of the New Generation, Carol Ann Duffy (b. 1955) and John Burnside
(b. 1955), left Scotland as children, and this leaving forms a recurrent concern in the work of both. Duffy describes the fear of returning to find
'everything changed', while Burnside is ambivalent about an 'identity | to
be assumed like tartan'. Meanwhile, in Candia McWilliam's (b. 1955) novel
Debatable Land (1994), a journey from Tahiti to New Zealand is dominated
by memories of childhood in Edinburgh. Like Stevenson, her characters
find 'Scotland at the back end of the Pacific'.

Indeed, if we consider writers not themselves born in Scotland, but of
Scottish descent, we can find Scotland in all sorts of places. The Scots were
not only colonized, they were themselves great colonizers of other countries (if not always voluntarily). A major preoccupation in the work of the
Canadian writer Margaret Laurence (1926–87; see the Canadian chapter
earlier in this *Guide*), for example, is an uneasy inheritance of Calvinist
values and Celtic myth, while Alistair McLeod's (b. 1936) 'As Birds Bring
Forth the Sun' is the characteristic Cape Breton story of 'a family with a
Highland name who live beside the sea', speak Gaelic, and refer to Glasgow
and Toronto as being equally distant places. In Shena Mackay's (b. 1945)
Dunedin (1992) the conflicts of nineteenth-century Presbyterian exile in a
lushly evoked New Zealand carry on into the experiences of a contemporary New Zealander's exile in London; while for the Australian poet Les
Murray (b. 1938) Scotland is simply 'a place dad goes when he drinks rum'.
None of these writers deals simply with 'Scots in exile'; rather, what their
work examines is the clash of national identities and loyalties.

Exile can equally well be felt within one's homeland, and a persistent
preoccupation of much contemporary Scottish writing is the need to find
some escape from the realities of home. This escape often comes from the
romantic 'tartan' history of noble, defeated Jacobites—many more people
read the historical romances of Jean Plaidy (b.1906) and Dorothy Dunnett
(b. 1923) than read Alasdair Gray or James Kelman, while the John Buchan-
like adventure novels of Allan Massie (b. 1938) also have a devoted following.

The tendency to backward glances seems particularly strong in the theatre and in film. There are numerous tragedies and melodramas of Scottish
tartan history—plays about Robert Bruce, Wallace, Mary Queen of Scots—
equalled only by the numerous tragedies and melodramas concerning the
history of Clydeside. Then there are the 'kailyard' comforts of the 'wee
wifie', the 'lad o' pairts', and the 'wee big man', which continue to thrive
in the comic strips ('the Broons', 'oor Wullie') of the *Sunday Post* and in
Hollywood's version of Scotland (a recent example is *Mrs Doubtfire*, 1993),
a version to which Scotland itself often subscribes. The film-maker Bill

Forsyth's (b. 1947) *Local Hero* (1983) uses many of the traditional kailyard images of Scotland—wily communities, wily but innocent men, and fey women. Clyde-built plays, too, continue in the same vein, the most notable being *The Steamie* (1987) by Tony Roper, an affectionate tribute to a rosily remembered Glasgow community spirit.

Another form of 'exile' takes the form of an imagined life elsewhere, usually North America. When, for example, the protagonist of Gordon Williams's (b. 1934) *Walk Don't Walk* (1972) first arrives in the United States he is surprised to feel disoriented, for 'this was not a foreign country with strange foreign customs, this was America and he had lived around here for the better part of his life'. The America to which Scottish writers and their characters frequently escape is that of music and film, for, as Williams puts it, 'Life isn't like the movies, you know that? That's why the movies are so important.' William McIlvanney's meditative detective, Laidlaw, notes that 'the only available blueprint for a different kind of life' for the Glasgow poor comes from Hollywood—criminals chide each other, 'behave yerself. Ye've seen too many gangster pictures,' while the detective in turn scolds them, 'I didn't come in here to see a bad cowboy picture.' The characters in works as diverse as Iain Crichton Smith's *On the Island* (1979) and Roper's *The Steamie* translate their lives into the language of the 'Big Picture', while the film director Bill Douglas himself described the cinema as his 'real home . . . [his] happiest place . . . Up there was the best of all possible worlds.'

Irvine Welsh turns the longing on its head in a story, 'Where the Débris Meets the Sea', in which Hollywood stars dream of Leith removal men but despair of ever meeting them: ' "We'll nivir go tae fuckin Leith!" Kim [Basinger] said, in a tone of scornful dismissal. "Yous ur fuckin dreamin." "We might go one time!" said Kylie [Minogue], with just a hint of desperation in her voice. The others nodded in agreement. But in their heart of hearts, they knew that Kim was right.' (*The Acid House*, 1994)

The escapism that seems to be such a part of Scottish writing has its origins in the sense that there is not much to write about at home. The protagonist of Archie Hind's (b. 1928) *The Dear Green Place* (1966) tries to write a novel about his life but feels that 'all that background against which a novelist might set his scene, the aberrant attempts of human beings and societies to respond to circumstances, all that was bizarre, grotesque and extravagant in human life . . . All that was somehow missing from Scottish life . . . [where] there was only a null blot, a cessation of life, a dull absence.' Similarly the protagonist of Alan Sharp's (b. 1934) *A Green Tree in Gedde* (1965) compares the imaginative possibilities of Paris with those of Greenock:

Paris is quite a place, to look at as well as the people. I know it's because so much
has happened there and you know it has even though you don't know what it is.
In Greenock you know nothing has happened nor ever will happen, in the historical sense I mean, so you look at it differently or maybe don't look at all.

Being a writer in Scotland is further complicated by the fact that, as
Hind's protagonist notes, 'Ye cannae eat stories.' More recently, Gray notes:
'People in Scotland have a queer idea of the arts. They think you can be an
artist in your spare time, though nobody expects you to be a spare-time
dustman, engineer, lawyer or brain surgeon.' (*Lanark*, 1981)

If romanticized history thrives in the theatre and film, romance and
fantasy still flourish in the novel. Celtic mythology continues to provide an
imaginative source for writers such as Robin Jenkins (b. 1912), Sian Hayton
(b. 1944), and Margaret Elphistone (b. 1948). One of the distinctive features
of Scottish fantasy, however, is the tie it maintains with realism—as a recent collection of Scottish short stories puts it, the Devil and the giro carry
equal weight. The title of Sandy's treatise in *The Prime of Miss Jean Brodie*—
'The Transfiguration of the Commonplace'—in many ways sums up not
only Spark's method, but that of a range of writers, from Naomi Mitchison's
(b. 1897) historically precise but mythically infused novels to Iain Banks's
(b. 1954) fusion of hard-boiled realism and science fiction in *The Bridge*
(1986) and *The Crow Road* (1992).

The most renowned Scottish fabulist today, however, is undoubtedly
Alasdair Gray. For Gray acts of the imagination are more than simply escapes: they transform and illuminate the real. Following Joyce, and in direct
response to Sharp and Hind, he writes particularly of the need to *imagine*
the places one inhabits: 'Think of Florence, Paris, London, New York.
Nobody visiting them for the first time is a stranger because he's already
visited them in paintings, novels, history books and films. But if a city
hasn't been used by an artist, not even the inhabitants live there imaginatively.' In order for a city to exist imaginatively, however, the writer must
first come into possession of the appropriate skills, and *Lanark*, like *Ulysses*,
makes the struggle of the artist to depict his city central to the story of the
city itself.

Throughout Gray's work the individual is seen to be struggling against
various forms of physical and intellectual entrapment, represented not only
by the authority of school, Church, and the State, but also by the imaginative acts he hopes will liberate him. This unease with authority and institutions is shared by McIlvanney's boxers and detectives, Kelman's chancers
and bus-conductors, and Galloway's women on the edge of a nervous breakdown. There is a tendency, particularly in Kelman's and Galloway's work,

to give indiscriminately paranoid portraits of 'authority figures'—the DSS, the police, and doctors all seem to be in conspiracy.

Perhaps the classic outlaw figure is Jimmy Boyle (b. 1944), whose auto-biography of his early criminal and prison life, *A Sense of Freedom* (1977), was dramatized by Tom McGrath (b. 1940) as *The Hard Man* (1977), and also filmed under the original title (1981). On the other side of the fence, Detective Inspector Laidlaw fears his position of authority—'we're the shity urban machine humanised'—and is always aware of 'the sanctified network of legally entrenched social injustice towards which the crime I was investigating feebly gestured'. Criminals and police are engaged in the same fundamental battle for authentic existence: 'your only credentials were yourself.'

While *Laidlaw* (1977) and its successors employ the kind of detailed realism associated with the best American city crime fiction, Kelman's work rejects this, and indeed any other authorial interference (what he calls the novelist 'colonizing' the reader like a verbal imperialist). Instead, he dramatizes the search for an 'authentic' voice. *The Bus Conductor Hines* (1984) finds this in his monologues about 'this gray golden city', while Sammy in *How Late* dreams that 'one of these days he was gony write his own song, that would show the bastards'.

The most complete account of this creative quest comes in *A Disaffection*, where Patrick Doyle tries to reinvent himself as a contemporary equivalent of the Romantic poets he reads. Attempting to transform a set of plumbing pipes into musical instruments, he makes an important contrast between playing for yourself (which is selfish) and playing for others. He needs to find both a way of playing and an appreciative audience. He finds them in telling his brother's children the story of the pipes: 'It was as if these two pipes themselves were calling out to me to come on and play me come on and play me come on and play me, so I lifted one up and what I did I just, okay, blew into it, and out came this long and deep sound that made me think of scores and scores of years, and generations and generations and generations of people all down through the ages . . . It was really really beautiful weans and it made me think of magic.'

Despite Kelman's championing of the immediacy of performance and his fears of conceptualization, his work is in fact highly conceptual and self-consciously literary. He is at his best in descriptions of the controlling fetishes of his characters—their endless lists and rituals; and of the small pleasures and physical comforts that relieve their pain.

Kelman's intimate and detailed depictions of meals and baths, as well as his concern with finding an authentic voice, owe much to the work of

Alexander Trocchi. Trocchi's finest novel, *Cain's Book* (1963), in turn draws heavily on the techniques and the almost religious optimism of Henry Miller. Trocchi rejects the conventions of narrative—for 'there is no story to tell'—in favour of the 'art of digression', a 'mass of detail', and 'inventories'. He celebrates the power of the writer to be 'the agent of what is unremembered, rejected'. 'How', he asks, 'can a man not write? How can a man not paint? How can a man not sing?' Exuberance like Trocchi's, which Kelman rejects, has more recently informed Jeff Torrington's *Swing Hammer Swing!* (1992), which is a vivacious Joycean monologue of digressions, related and mimicked by a 'mercenary of the moment', and aspiring novelist, Thomas Clay.

If the work of Trocchi, Kelman, McIlvanney, and Torrington celebrates the authenticity of direct speech, it is also very 'literary', referring constantly, and often rather heavy-handedly, to their intellectual, predominantly existentialist, sources. Laidlaw, for example, keeps in his desk 'Kierkegaard, Camus and Unamuno, like caches of alcohol', while Thomas Clay's constant point of reference is 'JPS' (Sartre).

In these novels of troubled men, in which women feature only as idealized mothers or ruthless betrayers, Janice Galloway's fiction stands out for placing a solitary woman at the centre of the existential drama. Her highly praised first novel, *The Trick Is to Keep Breathing* (1989), is the disturbing first-person account of a woman's bereavement and depression after the death of her lover. But, as in McIlvanney's *Strange Loyalties* (1991), bereavement is the catalyst for an examination of the conditions of authentic existence and identity. Having 'lost the ease of being inside my own skin', Galloway's protagonist tries to follow the 'tricks' supplied by popular wisdom and the magazines she compulsively buys, but she constantly subverts her own intentions. Her final 'trick'—simply to keep breathing—is only tentatively hopeful. Similarly, the central dilemma of *Foreign Parts* (1994)—'fancying men and not liking them very much'—has no real resolution. Galloway's world, like Kelman's, is one of arbitrary disaster and encroaching authority, in which the individual's relationships with others are of little consolation.

Of the other writers whose work is usually considered as following in the wake of Kelman, Irvine Welsh is perhaps the most notable. His version of contemporary Scotland is, however, both bleaker and less despairing than theirs, revealing less self-pity and greater compassion. The fundamental difference maybe is Welsh's lack of self-consciousness and the fact that no single narrative voice is allowed to dominate. Both his novel *Trainspotting* (1993) and the stories of *The Acid House* experiment with form and voice, continually juxtaposing different points of view.

The potential of the short story to represent different voices and perspectives has also been used to advantage by established writers such as Elspeth Davie (b. 1919) and George Mackay Brown, and by a younger generation, including A. L. Kennedy in her fine *Night Geometry and the Garscadden Trains* (1990), and the less fine *Now That You're Back* (1994); Duncan MacLean (b. 1964) in *Bucket of Tongues* (1992); and Ali Smith in *Free Love and Other Stories* (1995). All suggest that the short-story collection's ability to play off different voices one against the other is often more effective than any single attempt at an authentic voice.

Traditionally, the debate about authenticity in Scottish writing has centred around language. For Edwin Muir, 'a homogenous language' was a 'prerequisite of an autonomous literature', while MacDiarmid's championing of Lowlands Scots (or 'Lallans') included the coining of new words. Today, however, Scottish writers emphasize the diversity of Scottish voices, acknowledging that there is no one way that people speak, and write, in Scotland, and no one way that they should do so. Scots is remarkably resilient, especially in poetry, but then so is Gaelic, and even within Scots English there are many variants. The urban street patter of Strathclyde (best known through the popular television character Rab C. Nesbitt) is very different from the rural dialect of Aberdeenshire. Furthermore, there is no standard orthography—most writers make up the spelling as they go along in order to create a precise sound.

The recognition of this linguistic plurality has not come easily, however. The double-edged sword of national pride and national self-doubt has meant that writers have felt either, like Muir, that English must be rejected outright, or that only standard English was suitable for Literature. For Archie Hind, Glasgow speech—'the gutter patois into which his tongue fell naturally when he was moved by strong feeling'—was a language more suitable 'for sneers and abuse and aggression' than for writing books.

According to Edwin Morgan, the fundamental difficulty for a writer in Scotland is 'to write naturally'. Too much pressure is placed on poets to conform to some programme. 'Obligations bark at him on all sides . . . there is so much he is asked to do.' By ignoring those 'obligations' and freely experimenting with a variety of poetic voices and styles (such as concrete poetry and Surrealism), Morgan was one of the first poets to achieve the natural voice he sought. His Glasgow poems in particular, in their detailed observation of both the sights and sounds of the city, created a sense of possibility for many Glasgow writers, novelists and dramatists as well as poets. Consider, for example, what is now a classroom classic, 'Good Friday':

Three o'clock. The bus lurches
round the sun. 'D's this go—
he flops beside me—'right along Bath Street?
—Oh tha's, tha's all right, see I've
got to get some Easter eggs for the kiddies.
I've had a wee drink, ye understand . . .

In the development of this Glasgow voice, the most important figure is
Tom Leonard (b. 1944). Like Morgan, he is a free and prolific experimenter,
exploring the possibilities of many poetic styles, as well as writing satires,
parodies, plays, criticism, and more besides. As the title of his *Intimate Voices*
(1984) suggests, Leonard is fascinated with the relationship of voice and
place, particularly in the political implications of different types of speech.
For example, his series 'Unrelated Incidents' attacks the claims of objectivity made by Standard English:

> this is thi
> six a clock
> news thi
> man said n
> thi reason
> a talk wia
> BBC accent
> iz coz yi
> widny wahnt
> mi ti talk
> aboot thi
> trooth wia
> voice lik
> wanna yoo
> scruff.

'Just because you speak in Glasgow dialect', he argues, 'doesn't mean you
can't be interested in Bartók.' So he presents all manner of things in Glaswegian—from the six o'clock news to debates on 'mehta' physics, religion,
linguistics, and the implications of minimalism ('a stul think yi huvty say
sumhm').

Another extremely influential figure has been Liz Lochhead. She, too,
admits the influence of American poetry—'Glaswegians tend to think they're
American'—and her best poetry has the relaxed tone and rhythm of contemporary American verse. Best known today for her monologues and
plays, Lochhead's poetry is also an art of impersonation, enabling her to

move from ironic social naturalism to political confrontation with simply a shift of tone, and a studied pause.

Within fiction 'the natural voice' has taken longer to establish itself. Alan Spence's (b. 1947) *Its Colours They Are Fine* (1977) was one of the first fictional works seriously to attempt to transcribe spoken Glaswegian and to explore its richness, but it still maintains a division between the Standard English of the third-person narrator and the reported Glasgow speech of the characters: 'He sipped at it, fingering the blackened, brittle toast. He pushed the plate aside and started to retreat. "Ah canny face the burnt offerin hen."' In his early work, Kelman tried to overcome this problem by limiting himself to a first-person narrative. Later, he went a step further and used Glasgow dialect for both first- and third-person narrative. Today, novels such as *Swing Hammer Swing!* and *Trainspotting* use these techniques as a matter of course.

The urban voice of central Scotland is not the only one that can be heard today. While the Gaelic novel has never really taken off, and Gaelic drama has failed to make a mark, Gaelic poetry flourishes in the work of Iain Crichton Smith (b. 1928), Derick Thomson (b. 1921), George Campbell Hay (1915–84), William Neill (b. 1922), and, above all, Sorley Maclean (b. 1911). Far from being inward-looking and nostalgic, Gaelic poetry is often the most 'international' of all Scottish verse. Crichton Smith's 'Shall Gaelic Die', for example, is less an elegy for a language that is being lost than a philosophical meditation on the relation between language and 'world', while younger Gaelic poets such as Anne Frater (b. 1967) and Meg Bateman (b. 1959) use Gaelic to express a political urgency about the current state of Scotland.

W. N. Herbert (b. 1961) and Robert Crawford (b. 1959), on the other hand, reject 'everyday speech' as a source of political poetry. Instead, their work seeks to explore and juxtapose many different 'languages', such as those of information science and formalist aesthetics, which they combine with a form of 'synthetic' or literary Scots in the tradition of MacDiarmid. They argue that the linguistic division central to the particularities of Scottish experience—Herbert's most recent collection is called *Forked Tongue* (1994)—makes it supremely representative of Post-Modern experience in general.

As aims to find a unified poetic voice splinter into polyphony, so does a similar aim within drama. Attempts to establish a National Theatre in Scotland, a theatre with its own distinctive style and voice reminiscent of Ireland's Abbey Theatre, have proved unsuccessful (so far). Instead, individual companies have emerged, each with its own style; some are short-lived but others, such as the Traverse, the Lyceum, and the Citizens, continue to flourish.

The Traverse Theatre, founded in 1963, consciously strives to promote new Scottish plays, its successes including Tom McGrath's *The Hard Man* and John Byrne's (b. 1940) *The Slab Boys* (1978), and more recently work by Chris Hannan, John Clifford, and John McKay. Byrne is perhaps best known for his television drama serial *Tutti Frutti* (1987), a playful examination of the national and gender stereotypes of popular culture. Scottish drama today is well represented indeed on television. The stereotypes may still be in place, but, as John Caughie says of the Laidlaw look-alike Taggart, at least 'he's our stereotype'.

The most exciting development in Scottish theatre in the 1970s and early 1980s was John McGrath's company 7:84 Scotland, a working-class theatre that sought to address the immediate concerns of its audience. Its first and most successful production, *The Cheviot, the Stag and the Black, Black Oil* (1973), attacks romantic images of Scotland, instead drawing parallels between the Highland Clearances of the last century and the contemporary rape of the land in search of oil. The play draws on a variety of forms, from Gaelic story-telling to music-hall patter, and each performance ends (where possible) with a ceilidh. At a time when Scottish nationalist confidence was high, *The Cheviot* struck a powerful note. Although the political agenda has since changed, 7:84's theatrical methods remain compelling and have inspired a whole generation of companies, including Wildcat, the Clyde Unity Company, and the ballad-based Theatre Alba.

While fictional representations of Scotland in theatre and film have been largely dominated by unremarkable historical illusions, Scotland's documentary tradition, dating back to the pioneering work of John Grierson in the 1930s, is highly respected. In 1961 *Seaward the Great Ships*, a visually powerful celebration of Clydeside, won an Oscar for the Best Short Film. Since then, documentaries have moved to television, but the Scottish presence is still strong. One director who began in documentaries was Bill Forsyth, whose Glasgow-based comedies (*That Sinking Feeling*, 1979, *Gregory's Girl*, 1980, *Comfort and Joy*, 1984) helped to re-establish the Scottish feature film industry. Often compared with the Ealing comedies in their emphasis on a specific locality and the gentleness of their humour, Forsyth's films have inspired many followers, notably Charles Gormley's *Living Apart Together* (1983) and *Heavenly Pursuits* (1986), Cary Parker's *The Girl in the Picture* (1986), and Michael Hofmann's *Restless Natives* (1985).

The supreme contemporary achievement in film is, however, Bill Douglas's autobiographical trilogy *My Childhood* (1972), *My Ain Folk* (1973), and

My Way Home (1978), which Philip French has predicted 'will come to be regarded not just as a milestone, but as one of the heroic achievements of the British cinema'. These are films that draw more on the techniques and moods of early Russian cinema than on anything particularly contemporary. Brief and austere monochrome images with little dialogue to relieve them creates film of formalized yet deeply felt pain. The scripts, published in *Bill Douglas: A Lanternist's Account* (1993), are well worth reading on their own account. Douglas went on to make *Comrades* (1987), the story of the Tolpuddle Martyrs, but died before he could make any other films. His unfilmed scripts include an adaptation of Hogg's *The Justified Sinner*.

FURTHER READING

Chapman, Malcolm, *The Gaelic Vision in Scottish Culture* (London, 1978).

Craig, Cairns (ed.), *The History of Scottish Literature*, iv: *The Twentieth Century* (Aberdeen, 1987).

Dick, Eddie (ed.), *From Limelight to Satellite: A Scottish Film Book* (London, 1990).

McGrath, John, *A Good Night Out. Popular Theatre: Audience, Class and Form* (London, 1981).

Malzahn, Manfred, *Aspects of Identity: The Contemporary Scottish Novel (1978–1981) as National Self-Expression* (Frankfurt, 1984).

Morgan, Edwin, *Crossing the Border: Essays on Scottish Literature* (Manchester, 1990).

Wallace, Gavin, and Stevenson, Randall (eds.), *The Scottish Novel since the Seventies* (Edinburgh, 1993).

24

SPAIN

ABIGAIL LEE SIX

In 1960 Spain was just beginning to emerge from the most isolated, oppressive, and economically lean years of General Franco's dictatorship. As the decade wore on, Spanish society gradually grew more open: tourism started to transform the country, bringing not only much-needed money but also the shock of a new contact with foreigners. The availability of books by Spanish writers in exile and non-Spanish writers considered subversive by the regime improved, too. In 1966 an important new law was passed: except in the theatre, there was no longer any need to submit work to the censors before publication. Censorship would only be *post facto*. This apparent improvement, however, masked a more insidious form of censorship that, according to one writer of the period, Juan Goytisolo, was already troubling him at the beginning of the decade: more than ever, writers were now going to have to be their own censors.

In fiction, the starting-point has to be *Time of Silence* (1962), the masterpiece of Luis Martín-Santos (1924–64). This novel marked both the end of the earlier vogue for social realism and the beginning of a new movement which has sometimes been called 'dialectical' realism. In this novel and others that followed it, Spanish society is still harshly criticized, being depicted as oppressive, pretentious, and superficial, as well as very unequal in economic terms. The style in which Martín-Santos and others write, however, is much more complex and demands an active effort on the reader's part in order to follow it—an effort which is richly rewarded. Some of the devices used in *Time of Silence* were to become hallmarks of the 1960s novel generally: stream-of-consciousness, a shifting between multiple narrators, irony, satire, black humour, and a virtuoso use of such rhetorical tricks as the repetition of a particular word or phrase. A good example of the book's style is the description of Ricarda, who lives in the shanty town outside Madrid where part of the action is set, and is the mother of a girl killed by an amateur abortionist, whom the protagonist had tried in vain to save:

Not to know anything. Not to know that the earth is round. Not to know that the
sun stands still, even though it appears to rise and set. Not to know that they [the
Holy Trinity] are three distinct Persons. Not to know what electric light is. Not to
know why stones fall earthwards. Not to know how to tell the time. Not to know
that the sperm and the ovum are two individual cells whose nuclei fuse. Not to
know anything. Not to know how to talk to people, not to know how to say: 'How
nice to see you', not to know how to say, 'Good morning to you, Doctor'. And
nevertheless, to have said: 'You did all you could'.

Among the older novelists still writing after 1960 were Gonzalo Torrente
Ballester (b. 1910), Alvaro Cunqueiro (1912–81), and Camilo José Cela
(b. 1916). Torrente Ballester had started his literary career back in 1943, but
received little critical recognition until he published his ninth novel, *The
Saga/Fugue of J. B.* (1973), a humorous, wide-ranging narrative which adopted
some of the new experimental techniques. *Fragmentos de apocalipsis* ('Fragments of Apocalypse', 1977) and *La isla de los jacintos cortados* ('The Island
of Cut Hyacinths', 1980) go even further in the direction of stylistic experiment, abandoning conventional plot-lines and characterization. Torrente
Ballester is an intellectual novelist, a satirist with a fascination for myth and
history, in whose novels fantasy and parody alternate with an underlying
realism.

Cunqueiro's literary career also began in the 1940s, although he, too, was
hardly noticed until much later. Often writing in Gallego (the language of
Galicia in north-west Spain), he has produced poetry and drama as well as
fiction. Of his novels written in Spanish, among the most notable are *Las
mocedades de Ulises* ('The Youthful Exploits of Ulysses', 1960) and *Un hombre
que se parecía a Orestes* ('A Man Who Looked Like Orestes', 1969). Even in
the social realist 1950s and beyond, he eschewed realism in favour of an
ironic form of fantasy: he likes reminding his readers that what they are
reading is not real life, that fiction is by definition fantastic. The structure
of Cunqueiro's novels tends to be episodic and this increases the scope
for playful—even capricious—variations in, for example, the narrative
perspective.

Cela is probably best known for two of his early novels, *The Family of
Pascual Duarte* (1942) and *The Hive* (1951). Of the books written after 1960, the
best are *Saint Camilo's Day, 1936* (1969), a complex stream-of-consciousness
novel set in the first days of the Spanish Civil War, and *Mazurca para dos
muertos* ('Mazurka for Two Dead Men', 1983) which looks back at the Civil
War from the new historical vantage-point afforded by the end of the Franco
regime. Most recently, *El asesinato del perdedor* ('The Murder of the Loser',
1994) is a novel based on the true story of a young man's suicide following
his conviction for a public display of affection towards his girlfriend.

Cela's *œuvre* as a whole is marked by his interest in the macabre and the grotesque, especially in respect of his major themes of sex and death, and by a very black sense of humour. Some readers find his tireless use of obscenity and his *machista* sexism both smutty and insulting; others see him as having set boldly out to challenge prevailing taboos. Cela is thus a controversial figure whose willingness to give offence and somewhat shady personal history—he fought on the Nationalist side during the civil war and served as a censor in the early years of Franco—have sometimes been allowed to overshadow his indubitable literary talent. In 1989 he was, surprisingly, awarded the Nobel Prize for literature.

Miguel Delibes (b. 1920) is a less controversial figure than Cela, but of equal stature as a writer. Among his best books are *Five Hours with Mario* (1966), a brilliant novel which tracks the thoughts of the newly widowed Carmen as she watches over her husband Mario's body for the duration of a night. The marriage, we learn, was a misalliance, but her complaints about Mario reveal the good qualities she failed to recognize in him, as well as his faults, and similarly, her representation of herself shows her up not only as narrow, bourgeois, and conventional in the worst sense, but also as a victim of her social milieu and cultural conditioning. *377 A, madera de héroe* ('377 A, Stuff of Heroes', 1987) is another novel about the Civil War written in the aftermath of Franco.

The most notable of the next, so-called 'Mid-Century' generation of novelists is Juan Goytisolo (b. 1931). He made his literary début in the 1950s, but the most important landmark in his literary career came in 1966, with the publication of *Marks of Identity*. This is the first in a trilogy of novels named after the protagonist, Álvaro Mendiola, a Barcelona bourgeois who goes to live in Paris. *Marks* and its sequels *Count Julian* (1970) and *Juan the Landless* (1975) record his growing alienation from his identity as a Spaniard, a Christian, a bourgeois, and a white man from a family with a slave-owning colonial past. While *Marks* does not venture too far from the conventional in terms of style, *Count Julian* is written in a magnificently delirious prose verging on poetry, which can best be appreciated by reading it aloud (Goytisolo's advice):

farewell, foul Stepmother, land of masters and slaves: farewell, black patent-leather tricorns and you, my people who tolerate them: may the sea of the Straits deliver me from your guardians: from their eyes that see everything, from their evil tongues that know everything: realizing once again, with calm resignation, that invective does not ease your pain: that the Stepmother is still there, lying in wait, motionless, ready to spring: that the invasion which will lay waste to everything has not yet taken place: flames, suffering, wars, deaths, desolation, evil deeds: patience, the hour will come . . .

Goytisolo's next novel was *Makbara* (1980), which he says was inspired by his reading of the great medieval Spanish poem *The Book of Good Love*, when sitting in a market square in Morocco, surrounded by a crowd of traders, story-tellers, acrobats, and passers-by. Two of Goytisolo's recurring preoccupations are developed particularly effectively in this novel: the figure of the social pariah, personified here in a hallucinatory depiction of an Arab being vilified on the streets of Paris; and the role of orality in literary creation. This second theme ties up with a new use of sexual imagery, since in *Makbara* oral sex becomes a metaphor for writing—heterosexual intercourse being once again ridiculed and shown as sterile in creative terms. In *Count Julian* images of homosexual rape stand for the delights of transgressive writing; in the less aggressive *Juan the Landless* Goytisolo prefers masturbation as the self-gratifying image of creativity, stressing its solitariness. In *Makbara*, he suggests that literary creation is an oral pleasure that can be mutually satisfying to both those who tell stories and those who hear them, as in the market square in Morocco.

Goytisolo has continued to write essays and has published two volumes of autobiography: *Forbidden Territory* (1985) and *Realms of Strife* (1986). He has also gone on writing fiction, notably *Las virtudes del pájaro solitario* ('The Virtues of the Solitary Bird', 1988), a novel that juxtaposes Christian and Sufi mysticism and which takes up the issue of 'contagion', both in the literary sense of the influence of one writer on another and in the medical sense, where it enables him to address issues like the reactions to AIDS. Like all of Goytisolo's mature novels, this is an audacious work, for it mixes together the writings of a Spanish saint—the mystical poet-monk St John of the Cross—with those of the Sufi Ibn Al Farid, thus assimilating the two ancient adversaries, the Catholic Church and Islam, whose enmity has been felt especially strongly in Spain, with its medieval history of occupation by the Moors.

Goytisolo's most recent novel, *La saga de los Marx* ('The Saga of the Marxes', 1994), has for its subject the demise of Communism in Eastern Europe. Karl Marx is here brought back to life in the present day and roams around attending Communist meetings in Paris, where no one recognizes him and he has difficulty understanding what the speakers are saying. He goes to an exhibition of Soviet art and is verbally abused by the figures represented in the paintings, the seemingly happy workers who, it transpires, are furious because they represent stereotypes that have nothing to do with real life in the Soviet Union. The novel powerfully exposes the way in which the principles of Communism were traduced by the Soviet regime, but at the same time Western capitalist society is likewise revealed as being both cruel and unpleasant.

Juan Benet (1927–93) was a novelist who did not make his literary début until quite late in life. Among his best work is a trilogy of novels: *Return to Región* (1967), *A Meditation* (1970), and *Un viaje de invierno* ('A Winter Journey', 1972). These are demanding and complex books, set in a dream-like, enigmatic region of rural Spain during and after the Civil War. Their tortured syntax and endless embedded clauses make for labyrinthine texts whose style conveys a world marked by similar characteristics. Benet also wrote short fiction, literary essays, and a cycle of novels called *Herrumbrosas lanzas* ('Rusty Lances', 1983–6).

Juan Marsé (b. 1933) is a prolific and versatile novelist who began writing as a social realist. *Últimas tardes con Teresa* ('Last Afternoons with Teresa', 1966) deals with the impregnability of the social barriers separating the Catalan upper class from the immigrant community of poor southern Spaniards in Barcelona. But as rich Teresa falls in love with poor Manolo, the novel also takes up the question of narrative perspective, subtly experimenting with each character's distorted image of the other. *The Fallen* (1973) is Marsé's masterpiece, however. Here, the aftermath of the Civil War is viewed through the distorting lens of a complex admixture of adults' memories and children's (often violent and voyeuristic) fantasies and semi-fantasies, inflected by images and stories from the cinema and half-understood adult conversations. The result is a very difficult text, where the reader's confusion reflects the confused world of the post-war years. *El amante bilingüe* ('The Bilingual Lover', 1991) and *El embrujo de Shanghai* ('Shanghai's Spell', 1993) are more accessible, highly accomplished recent novels by Marsé.

Juan Goytisolo's brother Luis (b. 1935) is also a novelist of standing. Apart from *Las afueras* ('The Outskirts', 1958), his best work has been written since 1960, most notably his major tetralogy *Antagonía* ('Antagony'), consisting of *Recuento* ('Recount', 1975), *Los verdes de mayo hasta el mar* ('The Greens of May down to the Sea', 1976), *La cólera de Aquiles* ('The Wrath of Achilles', 1979), and *Teoría del conocimiento* ('Theory of Knowledge', 1981). These appear to be part of a long-term project to confront and analyse his own past. *Recuento* is the previous life-story of the protagonist of the tetralogy, Raúl, at the end of which he becomes a writer. In *Los verdes* the events of Raúl's daily life merge with his writings, memories, and dreams. In *Aquiles* the focus shifts, since it is narrated by a former lover of Raúl's, who gives us her view of his world. The fourth and final volume, *Teoría del conocimiento*, takes in elements from the three previous volumes and restructures them, to form Raúl's conclusive perspective on his life.

Álvaro Pombo (b. 1939) is one of the best of a younger group of writers sometimes known as the 'Generation of 1968'—a reference to the student uprisings of that year by which they were allegedly influenced. *The Hero of the Big House* (1983) is a deceptively simple novel about a rich child in Santander and his relationship with a maiden aunt who lives at the top of the house. This turns from make-believe to blackmail and culminates in the aunt's suicide. The recent *Aparición del eterno femenino contado por S. M. del Rey* ('Appearance of the Eternal Feminine, as Told by His Majesty the King', 1993) stands out from Pombo's other work because of the importance it gives to the world outside the house where the action is centred. Humour is a striking feature of his writing, as is the interest he takes in children and their viewpoint, which often provides splendid material for satire.

Manuel Vázquez Montalbán (b. 1939) is a commercially very successful novelist of the same generation. He is most popular as the author of a series of crime novels which all feature the same detective, Pepe Carvalho. As well as being highly entertaining, the Carvalho novels criticize contemporary social, philosophical, and political values from a left-wing standpoint.

Of women writers of much the same generation and social background, one of the best is Carmen Martín Gaite (b. 1925). Of her novels, *Retahílas* ('Yarns', 1974) and *The Back Room* (1978) stand out as brilliant examples of her experimental technique, as well as building a vivid picture of life in the early post-war years in Spain. *The Back Room* especially demonstrates Martín Gaite's skill inasmuch as in this novel the process of writing forms part of the subject-matter: the story is that of a novelist who talks all night to an unidentified man who has called on her at home. As they converse, the typescript of what we realize is the novel we are reading mysteriously grows on the protagonist's desk. *Desde la ventana* ('From the Window', 1987) develops further Martín Gaite's abiding preoccupations with dialogue and the importance of the spoken word, as well as with women's position in Spanish society and with psychological exploration. Recently, *Nubosidad variable* ('Variable Cloud Cover', 1992) pursues these and other themes, as well as her concern with technique, this novel being structured around the metaphor of a broken mirror whose fragments must be pieced back together again.

Ana María Matute (b. 1926) is the other main woman writer of this generation, whose best work is to be found in a trilogy entitled *The Merchants* (1960–9). Her fiction is remarkable for the emotional deprivation from which her characters suffer.

Esther Tusquets (b. 1936) took the Spanish literary establishment by storm with a complex and compelling trilogy of novels: *El mismo mar de todos los veranos* ('The Same Sea as Every Summer', 1978), *Love Is a Solitary Game* (1979), and *Stranded* (1980). These mount a strong campaign against patriarchal values and consider such possible alternatives to sexual conformity as lesbianism, though without idealizing them. The novels' style is highly intellectual, sophisticated, and dense; and the books are memorable for her characters' profound sense of isolation, in spite of the many sexual relationships on which they embark.

Lourdes Ortiz (b. 1943) is an extremely versatile author, who has written everything from crime novels to historical novels, as well as erotic short stories. *Luz de la memoria* ('Light of memory', 1976) portrays the years of pointless opposition to Franco's dictatorial regime and of consequent disillusionment. *Picadura mortal* ('Deadly Jab', 1979) is a murder mystery solved by a woman detective cast in the cool, flippant mould of Raymond Chandler's Philip Marlowe. *Urraca* (1982; literally 'Magpie', but also the name of a tenth-century Spanish princess) is weightier, a novel which succeeds remarkably well in entering into the mind of a distant figure drawn from medieval history.

Rosa Montero (b. 1951) published her first novel, *Crónica del desamor* ('Chronicle of Lovelessness'), in 1979. *Te trataré como a una reina* ('I Shall Treat You Like a Queen', 1983) is perhaps her best novel to date, combining realism with eccentricity, humour with pathos, and displaying a decisive feminist angle on such issues as the demands made on women in order to meet a set ideal of physical beauty. *Temblor* ('Trembling', 1990), a feminist science-fiction novel, ingeniously explores a universe in which the male–female balance is reversed. Women are now the superior gender and wield the power in a society that is a strange admixture of a primitive, cave-dwelling matriarchy and a futuristic police state.

In the 1950s, many social realist writers used the short story to powerful effect in order to criticize contemporary society, and it is a genre that came back into vogue during the years of the transition to democracy in Spain after Franco's death. In these years, when the country was trying to catch up with the rest of Europe, culturally as well as politically, short stories provided a quick means by which new writers could make their mark.

Carmen Martín Gaite and Ana María Matute both published excellent collections in the 1960s. Later writers to practise this form with success include José María Merino (b. 1941), whose best stories tend to be self-referring, and to reflect on the making of fiction even as they make it. Antonio Muñoz Molina (b. 1956), well known as an author of detective novels, gives an ironical picture of provincial life in his collection *Las otras vidas* ('The Other Lives', 1988). Luis Mateo Díez (b. 1942) has also made a significant contribution: his most recent collection, *Los males menores* ('Lesser Evils', 1993), contains both short stories of the more traditional kind and thirty-six miniature stories, whose principal themes are human fragility, the paradoxes of the human condition, our secret yearnings, and the darker side of our nature. The perspective is first-person, and the tone humorous, nostalgic, often ironic.

In poetry, as in fiction, the tide turned in the 1960s against an earlier fashion for 'social' poetry, which had aimed to expose the defects of Franco's society in a language that was accessible to all. Instead, the creative process itself now became the focus, as poetry became personal and more intimate in style. A sparser, purer manner marks the poetry of the new decade, and irony and humour are introduced in order to veil, and thus to intensify, a sense of helplessness or melancholy.

A leader in the reaction against 'social' poetry was José Ángel Valente (b. 1929), at least once his first two collections, *A modo de esperanza* ('By Way of Hope', 1954) and *Poemas a Lázaro* ('Poems to Lazarus', 1960), were out of the way. Since then, he has worked towards what he calls the 'zero point' of an almost mystical purity of expression. Indeed, *Punto cero* was the title he gave in 1972 to a collection of all that he had published up until that date. With time, Valente's writing has become ever more introspective and hermetic, yet it remains both powerful and suggestive. Later collections include *Mandorla* (1982) and *Al dios de un lugar* ('To the God of a Place', 1989).

The standing of Jaime Gil de Biedma (1929–90) is second to none among contemporary poets in spite of the fact that he published comparatively little. Collections of 1959, 1966, and 1968 were later amalgamated into a single volume entitled *Las personas del verbo* ('The Persons of the Verb', 1975) and are characterized by a tone of calm irony, scepticism, and modesty.

A group of poets closely associated with the move away from 'social' poetry was that of the so-called Novísimos, a name originating in an anthology called *Nueve novísimos poetas españoles* ('Nine Ultra-New Spanish Poets', 1970). These nine poets—later joined by others—sought to return poetry to its aesthetic role, emphasizing the autonomy of poetic creation. Hallmarks of the new style are what amounts almost to an obsession with the theme of poetry itself—what it is or should try to be, the problems in creating it etc.—a luxuriant vocabulary, and a taste for both learned and popular references. Sometimes all this can give an impression of a fertile chaos or of collage; it also leads, inevitably, to a certain lack of accessibility.

Pere Gimferrer (b. 1945) is one of the best of the Novísimo poets. His first three collections were written in Spanish: *Arde el mar* ('The Sea is

Burning', 1966); *La muerte en Beverly Hills* ('Death in Beverly Hills', 1968), whose subject is the American cinema of the 1930s and 1940s; and *Extraña fruta* ('Strange Fruit', 1969), which again draws on Hollywood and on other aspects of popular culture such as comics, but also on classical material ranging from the story of Dido and Aeneas to the music of Bach. The combination of these diverse cultural references creates a startling montage effect. Gimferrer subsequently changed to writing in Catalan, although his own translations of his Catalan poems into Spanish are often included in anthologies.

Manuel Vázquez Montalbán is better known as a novelist but he has also written poetry, characterized by a sometimes bitter irony, and by his disenchantment with the world and with poetry itself, as in a poem from the collection *Pero el viajero que huye* ('But the Traveller Who Flees', 1991):

> Reality is an unstarted journey
> islands drifting waters frozen numb
> biting the axe of the cliffs
> waiting for the appointment with death.

Leopoldo María Panero (b. 1948) is another of the original Novísimos, but differs from them in certain significant respects. He does not employ the same luxuriant vocabulary and his concerns are hardly aesthetic. What his work expresses, rather, is the idea that poetic language has been mined to exhaustion, that nothing remains to be said. Panero's poetry has been thought by some to verge on madness, a description one might not want to agree with but which, nevertheless, gives an idea of the desperate tone to be found in his poetry. Of the same generation as the Novísimos, and displaying similar characteristics and preoccupations, are poets such as José Miguel Ullán (b. 1944), whose poetry tends to the experimental and surrealist, combining visual and typographical devices with purely verbal ones.

In the mid-1970s poetry changed direction again. New voices were heard and there was a return to a more straightforward type of romanticism, to a more emotional, or emotive, style, and to a use of classical metres. Antonio Carvajal (b. 1943) writes in a baroque style harking back to the seventeenth century in its virtuosity and refinement. *Extravagante jerarquía* ('Whimsical Hierarchy', 1983) is a collection of his work up until that time, though he has published more since. The neo-Romantic poetry of Antonio Colinas (b. 1946) is characterized by the importance he accords to the themes of nature, time, death, and beauty.

A striking number of the new poets who came to prominence in the 1980s were women. This was a decade marked more by a plurality of styles and approaches than by any monolithic view of what poetry should be like. The new poetry tended to be expressive and often humorous, with a liking for narrative and for describing the life of the city. Minimalism also took hold. In particular, the poetry of Jaime Siles (b. 1951) has evolved in this direction, in collections such as *Música de agua* ('Water Music', 1983) and *Columnae* (1987):

> Between what I give you and what I seek
> is the amount of what I find
>
>> The whole of you
>> from all of this
>> that I empty, empty
>> in the emptiness
> of a single glinting garden.
>
> ('Language')

Andrés Sánchez Robayna (b. 1952) started publishing poetry in the 1970s, but is better known for his collections of the 1980s, in particular *La roca* ('The Rock', 1984), which is a good example of his depersonalized, dispassionate style. Julia Castillo (b. 1956) is another minimalist poet, although also capable of being somewhat baroque at times, while Justo Navarro (b. 1953) uses traditional verse-forms to remarkable original effect.

Blanca Andreu (b. 1959) has revived a certain Surrealism in her poetry, most famously in a vibrant collection with the allusive title *De una niña de provincias que se vino a vivir en un Chagall* ('About a Girl from Out of Town Who Came to Live in a Chagall', 1981). In keeping with the surrealist tradition, Andreu makes use of sound-play in order to bring out the irrational aspects of language, and her methods have influenced several other younger Spanish poets.

Turning to the theatre, a first point worth making is that in Spain, the written, the performed, and the published do not always coincide: as well as published plays that have never been performed, there are plays that have been stage successes but remain unpublished.

The early post-war years were dominated in the commercial theatre by escapist comedies of bourgeois manners. By the 1950s, however, a greater realism was creeping in, thanks to the influence of what was then happening in both prose and poetry. This realist period lasted longer in the theatre than elsewhere, continuing all through the 1960s. There was by now, however, a lively underground movement, which coexisted with the less innovative commercial theatre.

The leading commercial playwright at the start of the 1960s was Antonio Buero Vallejo (b. 1916), who has been credited with starting the whole post-war drama movement with his first play, produced in 1949. The year 1960 saw the opening of *Las Meninas* ('The Maids of Honour'), inspired by the famous painting by Velázquez. Buero is famed for his use of a device known as 'immersion', whereby the audience is made to experience—rather than merely watch—what the characters on the stage are experiencing. In *The Concert at Saint Ovide* (1962) (another historical play, this time concerning blind musicians in pre-Revolutionary France), for example, the stage is plunged into darkness at one point, so as to give the audience (as well as one of the sighted characters) an experience akin to blindness. *The Sleep of Reason* (1970) is a play about Goya, in which the latter's deafness and madness are evoked by means of similar devices. Buero's most recent plays, such as *Diálogo secreto* ('Secret Dialogue', 1984) or *Lázaro en el laberinto* ('Lazarus in the Labyrinth', 1986), suggest that he may be past his best, but he remains one of the best loved and most important figures in Spanish post-war theatre, not least for having restored the reputation of the genre of tragedy.

Alfonso Sastre (b. 1926) is another key figure—though a more controversial one—associated above all with the theatre of protest in Franco's Spain. His deeply committed drama has its critics, who find that the intellectualism of his plays, and their transparent role as vehicles for protest, are to the detriment of their aesthetic qualities. Sastre's first plays were performed in the late 1940s and throughout the 1950s, but were often banned. His worst clashes with authority took place in the 1960s, though: what he wrote in many cases could be neither performed nor published and was circulated only in typescript. *En la red* ('In the Net', 1959) was performed in 1961 and *Oficio de tinieblas* ('Office of Darkness', 1962) in 1967, but this was the last of Sastre's plays to see the stage until *La sangre y la ceniza o MSV* ('Blood and Ash or MSV', these being the initials of the protagonist, 1965) was finally allowed to be produced after Franco's death, in 1976. Other plays of this period of censorship include: *La taberna fantástica* ('The Fantastic Tavern', 1966, first performed in 1984 and his biggest box-office success), *Ejercicios en terror* ('Exercises in Terror', 1970), *Askatasuna!* (1971), and *El camarada oscuro* ('The Dark Companion', 1972).

In his best work Sastre sustains a delicate balance between audience involvement and intellectual detachment. *Crónicas romanas*, written in 1968, first published in Italian in 1970, then in French in 1974, and in Spanish only in 1990, is a good example. The plot concerns the siege of the Iberian town of Numantia by the Romans, led by Scipio Aemilianus, in the year 134 BC, when the townsfolk showed enormous courage, holding out for sixteen

months and finally burning the town to the ground and committing mass
suicide. The play employs experimental techniques to fine effect, to break
down the conventional barrier between stage and auditorium: characters
are to be found emerging from the stalls, for example. Sastre also deliberately destroys the realist illusion by having speeches addressed straight to
the audience and by introducing such anachronisms as napalm, at the same
time as repeatedly reminding the audience that this is theatre, not reality.
The play is also an obvious commentary on imperialism and authoritarianism, and on those who have fallen victim to them in modern times, whether
the Vietnamese against the Americans or those Spaniards who suffered at
the hands of Franco during and after the Civil War.

Alfonso Paso (1926–78) is a prime example of a conformist playwright of
the late Franco years. He wrote nearly 200 plays, and, notwithstanding a
brief early period of association with fellow dramatists like Sastre, by the
1960s he had distanced himself from protest movements and preferred
commercial success. Politically anodyne though they may be, Paso's plays
are on the whole well wrought and entertaining.

Other commercial dramatists of the period include Lauro Olmo (b. 1922),
whose best-known play, La camisa ('The Shirt', written in 1960 but not
authorized for production until 1962), is an extremely successful and moving social drama, which exposes the plight of Spanish migrant workers. It
focuses on the typical case of a woman who feels forced to leave her husband and children in order to go and work as a maid in Germany. The style
is naturalistic, or documentary, but the structure and technique are deceptively simple. For example, Olmo creates a sense of simultaneity—to intensify his story's poignancy, or else simply to enhance its realism—by having
different scenes performed in different parts of the stage.

The underground theatre of the 1960s and the first half of the 1970s was
both fertile and innovative, as well as politically committed. José María
Bellido (b. 1922) is a good example of an underground playwright. He has
a cosmopolitan outlook and specializes in creating powerful dramatic symbols. He is one of the few underground writers who managed to have his
plays staged towards the end of the Franco years. José Ruibal (b. 1925)
began writing in the 1950s, but is best known for his play of 1968 The Man
and the Fly (first staged in Spain in 1977). Los mutantes ('The Mutants'),
written in the same year, is a good example of his allegorical manner. It has
only two characters, a man and a woman, living in a futuristic world. For
the man, technology is a marvellous improvement on the present, but the
woman feels desperately oppressed by all the material goods and machines
that crowd the couple's tiny home. The lack of understanding between the

sexes—the well-meaning man keeps bringing home more and more gadgets to cheer up the woman, when what she wants is air and sunlight—and the debatable benefits of modern conveniences and material wealth, are powerfully conveyed in this short but arresting play.

Antonio Gala (b. 1936), the most important of the new playwrights of the 1960s, has written plays which range from the lyrical to the realist. He has continued to write prolifically right through the 1980s and finally, in 1988, turned to musical comedy, with a smash hit, ¡Carmen, Carmen!.

The first play of Francisco Nieva (b. 1929) to be staged was *Es bueno no tener cabeza* ('It's Good not to Have a Head', 1971), and between then and 1975 he wrote numerous farces. He has also written what he calls 'furious theatre', a freer, more experimental type of play, which dispenses with such conventions as coherence of plot or character. His is a dramatic style recognized and admired by academics and critics, but undervalued by Spanish theatre-goers.

Fernando Arrabal (b. 1932), one of the most provocative and iconoclastic of contemporary dramatists (and also, less prominently, a novelist, painter, and film-maker), writes so-called 'panic theatre', a kind of Surrealism he inaugurated in 1962 in Paris, to where Arrabal had exiled himself. He practises a theatre of the absurd, arising from his perception of reality as incoherent and irrational, with a widespread use of abstraction and symbolism, sharp irony, and a tireless challenging of taboos and conventions. He is an example of a highly acclaimed underground playwright who exploded onto the Spanish stage after Franco's death, with plays like *The Car Cemetery*, which had been written in the 1950s but had to wait until 1977 to be put on in Spain. Unfortunately, the novelty of such demanding plays wore off rather fast, so that in 1990 *Róbame un billoncito* ('Just Pinch Me a Billion') never even reached the capital after its out-of-town run.

Plays with a historical setting were popular during the 1980s, when successes included works about Elizabeth I of England, Luther and Erasmus, and Isabella II of Castile. Probably the single most famous play of the decade—*Las bicicletas son para el verano* ('Bicycles are for the Summer', 1982), by Fernando Fernán Gómez (b. 1921)—is set during the Civil War but has a period feel to it reminiscent of the plays of Buero Vallejo. If it were not for the pervasive nostalgia, it would be indistinguishable from a piece written in the first half of the century. Fernán Gómez, a well-known actor, has written several more plays since, as well as essays and novels.

Women playwrights were virtually invisible in the Franco years and are scarce even now. The novelist Carmen Martín Gaite had a play called *A palo seco* ('By Oneself') produced in 1987, which takes the form of a monologue about loneliness. Concha Romero (b. 1945) carries the feminist torch in the theatre, writing plays that question the traditional passivity and obedience of women. María Manuela Reina (b. 1958), however, is better known, as the author of *Lutero o la libertad esclava* ('Luther or Liberty Enslaved', 1987), as well as several other plays. Her work is elegant in literary terms but it tends to perpetuate patriarchal values, by giving an excessive prominence to the male characters and allowing the female ones to remain as stereotypes.

FURTHER READING

Brown, Joan Lipman, *Women Writers of Contemporary Spain: Exiles in the Homeland* (Newark, NJ, 1991).

Edwards, Gwynne, *Dramatists in Perspective: Spanish Theatre in the Twentieth Century* (Cardiff, 1985).

Hart, Stephen M., *White Ink: Essays on Twentieth-Century Feminine Fiction in Spain and Latin America* (London, 1993).

Ilie, Paul, *Literature and Inner Exile: Authoritarian Spain, 1939–1975* (Baltimore, 1980).

Labanyi, Jo, *Myth and History in the Contemporary Spanish Novel* (Cambridge, 1989).

Ordóñez, Elizabeth J., *Voices of their Own: Contemporary Spanish Narrative by Women* (London, 1991).

Schneider, Marshall J., and Stern, Irwin (eds.), *Modern Spanish and Portuguese Literatures* (New York, 1988).

Schwartz, Ronald, *Spain's New Wave Novelists* (Metuchen, NJ, 1976).

Wright, Eleanor, *The Poetry of Protest under Franco* (London, 1986).

25

SPANISH AMERICA

MICHAEL WOOD

SPANISH American culture did not become sophisticated in the 1960s; it had been sophisticated for a long time before that. But it agreed to take its sophistication for granted, to let it loose as it were: it created an extensive literature which saw this sophistication as both precious and ordinary, to be deployed and enjoyed, not denied or exaggerated or apologized for.

This shift in attitude did not concern only the subcontinent's relation to Europe, but it often expressed itself through reflections on Europe, or on the changing meanings of the notion of 'Europe' in America. In a brilliant short story by the Guatemalan writer Augusto Monterroso (b. 1922), a Spanish monk captured by the Maya in the sixteenth century thinks of a trick which may save his life. He happens to remember that an eclipse of the sun is due, and says, 'If you kill me, I can make the sun go dark.' The Indians stare at him with some surprise, consult each other, and kill him. As the monk's blood drips onto the sacrificial stone, one of the Indians recites 'without any inflection in his voice, without haste, one by one, the endless number of dates on which solar and lunar eclipses occur, which the astronomers of the Maya community had predicted and noted in their codices without the invaluable help of Aristotle'.

This is a story not only about the monk's error and the Indians' mathematics; it is about the Indians' surprise at the Spaniard's assumptions about them. Modern Latin American culture is not made from the encounter between European conquerors and Indian conquered; there was no such encounter, only a take-over of one by the other. Nor is it made out of an idea of the superiority of indigenous peoples needing to be retrieved: the current condition of Indian communities makes a cruel mockery of all mythologies conceived along these lines. It is made out of whatever understanding has been gained over time of those old misunderstandings; out of a sense that all culture is plural and comparative, even the culture that thinks itself single.

Monterroso is also the inventor of what the Italian writer Italo Calvino called a new genre: the complete work composed of a single sentence. This is a genre with great possibilities but so far not many practitioners. Monterroso's example, which comes, like the story about the eclipse, from the marvellously titled *Obras completas (y otros cuentos)* ('Complete Works (and Other Tales)', 1959), is called 'The Dinosaur', and reads, *in toto*: 'When he (or she) woke up, the dinosaur was still there.' It would be brutal to bury this fine joke under interpretation, but it is important to see that it is all about assumptions, about what is not said or is not told. It is about the length of novels and the banality of suspense; about reading between the lines even when there is only one line; about sophistication and its (possible) discontents.

One of the greatest novels in Spanish of this century, *Hopscotch* (1963), by the Argentinian Julio Cortázar (1914–84), is about reading, and about falling between alternative worlds. Horacio Oliveira, a dishevelled Latin American intellectual living in exile in Paris, meets, loves, and loses La Maga, a strange young woman, also Latin American. Her child dies, and Oliveira is unable to cope either with his feelings or with his lack of access to them. Back in Buenos Aires, he hangs out with old friends, imagines reincarnations of La Maga, plays suicidal games.

'This book is many books,' Cortazar says in a 'table of instructions' concerning the way in which we might read it, 'but above all it is two books.' There is the book we read by turning the pages one after another in the normal way, and the other book we get by following Cortázar's instructions and interleaving later passages among the earlier ones. The game goes further than this, though, since the reader, once alerted to the existence of two books, can imagine any number of them, consisting of the same words in other arrangements. 'You are seeking the *mot juste*,' someone once said to Joyce. 'No,' Joyce said, 'I've got the words already. I'm looking for the right order.' *Hopscotch* is a book where the reader looks for the right order to read the words in—for one of any number of right orders. Cortázar's model here is the fiction of his compatriot Jorge Luis Borges (1899–1986), with its insistence on the possibility in narrative of presenting forking paths and thus alternative realities. In this novel, and in his short stories, Cortázar specializes in a sense, not of magic, but of conceptual possibility, of what it takes for the mind to move (and to fail to move) the world around. The game of hopscotch has the additional advantage that the space at the top of the playing area is called Heaven. Oliveira is much taken with the idea that in the game, and perhaps in life, heaven is on the same plane as the earth: you might get there just by kicking a stone and hopping after it.

Soon after its appearance, *Hopscotch* was identified as one of the major novels of the so-called 'Boom' in Spanish American literature. Other novels often seen as contributing to this phenomenon were *Three Trapped Tigers* (1965), by the Cuban Guillermo Cabrera Infante (b. 1929), *The Green House* (1966), by the Peruvian Mario Vargas Llosa (b. 1936), *Change of Skin* (1967), by the Mexican Carlos Fuentes (b. 1929), and *One Hundred Years of Solitude* (1967), by the Colombian Gabriel García Márquez (b. 1928). *The Obscene Bird of Night* (1970), by the Chilean novelist José Donoso (b. 1924), came out when the Boom seemed to be fading a little, but it is an ambitious complement to those earlier works. Indeed, in many ways it fulfils the promises they could not quite keep.

Was there a Boom? Certainly, a generation of writers came of age at much the same time, and produced a series of striking works. Some of these novelists (Vargas Llosa, Fuentes, García Márquez, Donoso) were at various times in regular communication with one another. With them, Spanish American fiction found a new confidence, a sense of its place in the world, and of what its sources of power were: strong local or family traditions of oral narrative; a set of political realities which were often already, without having to be arranged or refocused, operatic or farcical; a long tradition of dead-pan irony, and a remorseless commitment to jokes. The Cuban Revolution of 1959, when Fidel Castro came to power, caused a general infection of excitement. That excitement needed to find a cultural voice, or voices, and in the 1960s it did so. But these writers did not form a school; they had no programme. Those who had once been personally close went their separate ways, and the initial grouping now looks arbitrary.

Cortázar's career, for example, developed quite independently from that of the others, and the Cuban Alejo Carpentier (1904–80), frequently cited in the company of the novelists listed above, was a writer with a very marked individual style, subject-matter, and personal history. His *Explosion in a Cathedral* (1962) is a brilliant and profuse evocation of life in the Caribbean at the time of the French Revolution; and his *Reasons of State* (1974) is an exploration of the fading power of a Europe-loving Latin American dictator. These books are dense with detail, and very remote from any oral narrative tradition. They do, however, share with other novels of their time the sense of history as an often brutal farce, and it was Carpentier who coined the phrase *lo real maravilloso*, the 'marvellous real', which imperceptibly turned, for journalists and critics, into the supposedly defining Latin American characteristic of 'magic realism'.

This term in fact had another derivation—it was first used of a style of painting in the 1920s—but can now hardly be kept separate from its look-alike. It seems to be used in two or three rather different senses. One sense, which was Carpentier's own, and rather Eurocentric as it now appears, suggests that reality actually is marvellous in the Americas, being full of wonders unknown to Europeans or indeed to American city-dwellers. This 'magic realism' is thus a matter of geography and natural history, not of a literary mode, and an echo of this claim is to be heard in García Márquez's speech accepting the Nobel Prize for literature in 1982. Another version of the term has it that Latin Americans not only tell fantastic stories but also believe them; that they are superstitious and that superstition is therefore their reality; that there *are* ghosts and miracles if you believe in them. This view is meant to be sympathetic but can easily become very condescending. A third notion, overlapping partly with this, is that any story, including the most fantastic ones, can be told as if it were commonplace, and should surprise no one. This third 'magic realism' is a question, not of geography or comparative superstition, but of narrative technique: to practise 'magic realism' is to present the unlikely in a calmly realistic manner.

There is no real need to decide which of these alternative interpretations of the term is the most apt. What is clear is that in the 1960s Latin American fiction asserted the freedom of the story-teller, a traditional figure all but forgotten in modern European and North American fiction. The story-teller relays the community's sense of itself, which may require extremes of fantasy for its expression—or extreme mixtures of fantasy and a grimly fantastic reality. One or two European writers had done something similar—Günter Grass, for instance, in *The Tin Drum*, uses his narrator's madness (and sanity) as a screen for the perceived craziness of history—but it was with the Latin American fiction of the 1960s, and particularly with García Márquez's *One Hundred Years of Solitude*, that the full benefits of a retrieval of both probable and improbable stories (accompanied by a diminishing attention to what was now seen as narrowly rational) were recognized.

One Hundred Years of Solitude tells the unlikely tale of five generations of a single South American family. They inhabit an unnamed country whose history and geography much resemble those of (García Márquez's native) Colombia. They are visited by civil wars and by progress in many of its least manageable forms (bureaucracy, railways, cinema, North American investment), and they die out in an apocalyptic storm which destroys both their town and their story—except for what a young writer in Paris remembers or invents of it. The great power of this now very famous book lies in its mingling of the fabulous (magic carpets, a levitating priest, a man who suddenly spouts Latin without having learned a word of it) and the horrific (the massacre of more than three thousand protesters, who become historical ghosts because almost no one will admit they existed); and in its haunting sense of a potentially intelligible but always misunderstood history.

For Cabrera Infante, what is marvellous is memory, and both *Three Trapped Tigers* (the original Spanish title, *Tres Tristes Tigres*, is based on a tongue-twister) and *Infante's Inferno* (1979) are brilliant explorations of a lost and found world: the Havana of night-clubs and movies, and the arrival in the Cuban capital of a young man from the provinces. The supposedly defunct Infante (the Spanish title, *La Habana para un Infante difunto*, not only names Havana but also plays on the titles of two pieces of music by Ravel, *La Habanera* and *Pavane pour une infante difunte*) is very much alive in this writing, and a merciless adept of the pun: no verbal resemblance is too low for him, no excruciating gag too painful. Where many Latin American writers look to Faulkner and Hemingway as their models (García Márquez, more surprisingly, looks to Virginia Woolf), Cabrera Infante takes Joyce as his master, and has produced a body of work perhaps best seen as the implementation of several of the principles of *Finnegans Wake*, notably the idea that memory clings to words, that puns are a reminder of the verbal shadows and echoes, both wanted and unwanted, that surround the simplest statement.

In the work of Donoso, *The Obscene Bird of Night* and the equally impressive *A House in the Country* (1978), history becomes a malign carnival. For Vargas Llosa, particularly in the brooding *Conversation in the Cathedral* (1970) and the sweeping *The War of the End of the World* (1981), which recounts a historical rebellion in the backlands of Brazil in the last century, when religious fanaticism almost overcame all the forces of supposed reason and modernity opposed to it, history is a ruinous riddle, with its taunting, perennial question, Where did it all go wrong? Fuentes's *Terra Nostra* (1975) is a spectacular conflation of old and new history, gliding from contemporary Paris to the Spain of the time of the building of the Escorial Palace in the sixteenth century, and from there to the New World in the early days of its discovery by Europeans.

García Márquez, like Carpentier, and like the Paraguayan Augusto Roa Bastos (b. 1917), also wrote a dictator novel. Both his *Autumn of the Patriarch* (1975) and Roa Bastos's *I the Supreme* (1974) explore the fascination that dictators have repeatedly held for Latin American political culture. Younger novelists like the Argentinians Abel Posse (b. 1936) and Juan José Saer (b. 1937), and the Mexicans Angeles Mastretta (b. 1949) and Laura Esquivel (b. 1950), have been drawn even further into the labyrinths of history and memory. The moment of the so-called 'discovery' of the Americas frames both Posse's *The Dogs of Paradise* (1983) and Saer's *The Witness* (1988); while Mastretta's *Bolero* (1985) and Esquivel's *Like Water for Chocolate* (1989) explore the 'true romance' (and the true romance) of the Mexican Revolution and its aftermath.

García Márquez's long-awaited novel *Love in the Time of Cholera* (1985) turned out to be a romance, too, a sort of soap opera in which a near-geriatric couple wait for a whole lifetime to come together and consummate their love. The book's irony is so poker-faced one wonders whether it is irony at all; but García Márquez has understood better than anyone the intelligence of popular fiction, the way in which it animates what look like banalities. The novel is an invitation to see what genuine wit can do with threadbare romantic material. Towards the end, the woman finds herself wondering why she has never heard of any sexual conquests made by the man, and questions him about it. This is a mushy opportunity too good to be missed: he replies, 'It's because I remained a virgin for you.' This is not true, he has had hundreds of women; what is unusual is that no one has heard about it. The woman does not in fact believe him, but neither does she care. He rises to the sentimental occasion by talking like a bad novel; and she knows how to respond: 'She wouldn't have believed him anyway, even if it were true, because his love letters were made up of phrases like that one, that were effective not through their meaning but through their power of dazzlement. But she liked the spirit with which he said it.' This woman is not highly educated and not literary, but she knows when the literal meaning needs to be abandoned or ignored. She has escaped from the imprisonment of cliché because she has seen the work that clichés can do.

Something similar can be said about the apparently trapped characters in the remarkable novels of the Argentinian writer Manuel Puig (1934–90). Here, in *The Betrayal of Rita Hayworth* (1968), *Boquitas Pintadas* (1969), *The Buenos Aires Affair* (1973), *Kiss of the Spider Woman* (1976), people consume pulp fiction, comics, and old movies, and make their imaginative lives out of them. They find in them, not lessons or examples or literal information, but a store of possibilities of 'dazzlement'; and sometimes they are able to carry the dazzlement over into their lives. The implication is that possibility is a moral category; that a supposed escapism may be a way (may be the only way) of redeeming, of actually altering, a diminished reality.

Sometimes, however, as Puig makes clear, escapism just is escapism. But the question, for Puig as for Cortázar and Monterroso, is: What changes the mind? How can anger or righteousness, for example, be got to make way for the generosity that hides, cramped and embarrassed, in the same noisy place? Maybe nothing changes the mind, but Puig's novels offer persuasive accounts of affection growing in strange regions.

'There is true freedom on every one of her pages,' Cortázar said about the work of another Argentinian novelist, Luisa Valenzuela (b. 1938), even though she writes about the dark times her country has been through in the recent past. The *Lizard's Tail* (1985) is a satirical, quirky biography of an imaginary wizard, who closely resembles one of the weirdest and most powerful ministers of the government of Isabel Perón, the widow of the former President Juan Perón, who became President herself for a short time in the 1970s. This wizard is a 'man who might not even exist, a man who is like the personification of collective hysteria and its undefined fears: he makes me think of the Middle Ages.' But he makes people think of the Middle Ages only because they do not want to think of late twentieth-century Argentina. In the short stories of *Strange Things Happen Here* (1976) Valenzuela evokes the deaths and political 'disappearances' that have marked various dictatorial regimes in Argentina: to call these 'strange things' is to make horrors sound like mild topics of conversation. But that is, in part, how one learns to live with horrors.

Our life is quiet enough. Every once in a while a friend disappears, or a neighbour is killed, or one of our children's schoolmates—or even our own children—falls into a trap, but that isn't as apocalyptic as it seems; on the contrary, it's rhythmic and organic. The escalation of violence—one dead every twenty-four hours, every twenty-one, every eighteen, every twelve—ought not to worry us. More people die in other parts of the world, as that deputy said moments before he was shot. More, perhaps, but nowhere so close at hand as here.

Here one sees the pretence of calm cracking, in the simulation of quiet talk. What these people have lost is 'the luxury of being afraid': they are afraid, but afraid to admit even that. A little later in the same story, Valenzuela speaks of 'the luxury of writing a few stories', and quotes the titles of some that appear in this same collection. She is writing against death by preserving the liberty to register the things of this world and to imagine another world that is different, remote, redeemable. 'I want it to be known', she says, in what sounds like her own voice, 'that even though I'm a little naive and sometimes given to fantasy, not everything I've recorded is false. Certain things are true, the smell of incense, the sirens. It's also true that strange things are happening in the interior of the country and that I'd like to make common cause with them. It's true that we are—that I am—afraid.' The 'strange things' are now strange things occurring away from the city, as some kind of antidote to the strange things that have been happening there.

*

It is only mildly paradoxical to suggest that one of the most significant of contemporary Spanish American poets is a man who died in 1938. It is not that the Peruvian César Vallejo (b. 1893) had no reputation in his lifetime; just that he had nothing like the reputation he has had since. 'Everyone who used to Nerudize', as the Chilean poet Pablo Neruda wryly put it in 1969, 'started to Vallejoate (*vallejarse*)': there is a plaintive note to the joke because *vallejarse* sounds like the verb *alejarse*, meaning to go away or distance oneself.

Vallejo's intricate and lyrical *Trilce* (the title conflates the Spanish words *triste* and *dulce*, meaning 'sad' and 'sweet' or 'gentle') was published in 1922, the *annus mirabilis* of European modernism; his more direct and openly emotion-laden *Poemas humanos* between 1931 and 1937. Yet for the most gifted younger poets, like the Argentinian Juan Gelman (b. 1930) and the Nicaraguan Roque Dalton (1935–75), Vallejo continued as a coeval, a voice of inexhaustible protest, a writer of conscience who could combine pathos and irony, who saw the sorrows of Latin America as virtually permanent but without seeing them as natural. Vallejo was both a political and a private poet, dedicated above all to what he calls *querer*, a word which means both wanting and loving, an announcement of need, or what Vallejo himself called his own and the world's 'interhuman and parochial project'.

Pablo Neruda (1904–73), almost always paired with Vallejo as at once his poetic equal and stylistic opposite, had also completed important work before the 1960s—notably the three volumes of *Residencia en la tierra* ('Residence on Earth', 1931, 1935, 1947) and *Canto general* ('General Song', 1950), a book which includes as one of its sections the magisterial 'Heights of Macchu Picchu'. Neruda is one of the few twentieth-century poets in any language whose poems have repeatedly been turned into successful popular songs, and whose work is affectionately recited with the sort of familiarity the English wish they had with Shakespeare.

It is mainly his early work which is so widely diffused in Spain and Latin America—particularly the titles mentioned above and *Veinte poemas de amor y una canción desesperada* ('Twenty Love Poems and a Song of Despair', 1924). Yet Neruda died only in 1973, after the fall of Chile's Marxist President Salvador Allende; and he wrote major work in the 1960s, above all the five volumes of ob 'que and regret-free autobiographical verse he collected as *Memorial de Isla Negra* (1964) and the casual-seeming, valedictory poems of *Las manos del día* ('The Hands of the Day', 1968) and *Fin de mundo* ('World's End', 1969).

Neruda's gift was prodigious, but he was also a self-indulgent writer. He was a lifelong Communist, of the staunch and sentimental kind. This commitment produced some strong expressions of social passion, occasional patronizing of the unfortunate or the hard-pressed, and only one literary disaster: a rambling poem about Stalin called 'The Episode'. (Even those of us who do not think Stalin was in himself a refutation of socialism would want to be less casual than that.)

In his later work, Neruda likes to present himself as a child of nature, bookless, producing poems the way a tree produces leaves. There is of course nothing more bookish than such a pose, and Neruda is at his incomparable best when his lyrical ease is complicated a little by mischief or by intellect; when he places himself, for example, 'between yesterday and Valparaíso', or locates a curious mixture of nostalgia and rancour in 'the dirty streets of time'. 'What doesn't happen to one is what decides the silence.' He was born, he says, in a time and a place which had no history, only land, or earth:

> I arrived so early in this world
> that I chose an unfinished country
> where no one had heard of
> either Norwegians or tomatoes:
> the streets were empty
> as if the people had left
> who hadn't arrived yet,
> and I learned to read in books
> which no one had yet written:
> they hadn't founded the land
> where I set about being born.

This is the landscape of *One Hundred Years of Solitude*, mythical yet evoked in a tone which lightly mocks the myth. There is no such innocence, there never was; but the dream of it is part of what separates America from Europe. The wit in these lines involves both the mildly absurdist suggestion that the poet had a choice of birthplaces and the various dispensable items of which the country where he was born is innocent.

A darker but still superbly lyrical note is sounded in 'Paisajes' ('Landscapes'; both of these poems are from *Fin de mundo*):

> I want to see if sorrow grows,
> the flowers of uncertainty,
> the indecision of grief:
> I want to know the colour
> of the leaves of desertion.

Other contemporary poets of substance and range are the Uruguayan Sara de Ibáñez (b. 1910), the author of *La batalla* ('The Battle', 1967) and

Apocalipsis 20 (1970); and the tempestuous Nicaraguan Ernesto Cardenal (b. 1925), whose poems were collected in 1967. More important, however, are the Chilean Nicanor Parra (b. 1914) and the Argentinian Roberto Juarroz (b. 1925), the first because he dared to take rhetoric apart in a culture which has often loved rhetoric more than its life, the second because he is the author of the most sustained poetic achievement in modern Spanish America, apart from that of Octavio Paz (of whom more in a moment).

Parra wrote both poems and what he called 'antipoems', though even his 'poems' contain wonderful surprises, diving into different vocabularies and dictions. They may move, for example, from a literal invocation of onions to intimations of the metaphysical abyss as if these two things did not (should not) belong to different worlds. 'Think then', one poem says to a friend,

> Think then of these things for a moment,
> Of the little and nothing which will remain of us,
> If it seems right, think of the beyond,
> Because it is good to think
> And useful to believe we are thinking.

Between 1958 and the present, Juarroz has published twelve volumes of verse, each one called *Poesía vertical* ('Vertical Poetry'), and numbered. Within each volume the poems, too, are numbered, so producing a system rather like a philosophical treatise: 'Primera. 14', 'Novena. 34', 'Decima. 66', and so on. The poems are intensely lyrical, however. There are 'broken names' and 'acrobats of oblivion'; the 'infection' of a landscape by writing. 'Only much later,' Juarroz says in one poem, 'beyond the metaphors, | perhaps it will be possible | to look and to see?' And: 'We cannot bear the thought | that the shadow may be the origin of light.' Poetry is often Juarroz's theme as well as his practice; but it is a theme which engages closely with the world it wishes to refuse. 'Every poem is a vacillation of history,' 'Decima. 9' begins, and to cover history with poems is to place layer on historical layer. 'The poem is an action too,' Juarroz continues, and ends:

> The poem leaps outside of history
> like a hunting animal
> which unsettling the order of those layers
> puts another layer above them: the infinite.
>
> And then the hunting animal
> puts aside the still fossilized prey which is history
> and also sheathes its own claws,
> to run at last in the open air.

We see here again the fascination with history which informs so much of recent Latin American literature. The animal which is the poem sheathes its claws and runs free. But it has made history its prey, perhaps, because it has itself been so long and so painfully a prey to history.

The Mexican writer Octavio Paz (b. 1914) published a substantial collection of poems in 1960: *Libertad bajo palabra: Obra poética 1935–1958* ('Freedom under the Word: Collected Poems'). It included 'Piedra de sol' ('Sun Stone'), a harsh and demanding meditation on time and place, on history and the old Aztec calendar. Paz's later work is, if anything, even more impressive than the poetry he wrote when young. It includes delicate poems about India (to which country he went as Mexican Ambassador) and the human affections that he found there (*Ladera este* ('East Side', 1969)), bitter and bewildered poems about his return to Mexico in 1971, after an exile of some years (*Vuelta* ('Return', 1976)); a Wordsworthian long poem *Pasado en claro* ('A Draft of Shadows', 1975, 1977); and still more recent poems about language and memory and loss. 'At the time when the lights go out | who will wait for us | at the ashen frontier? | Buddha does not teach how to die: | he teaches that this life is an illusion.'

> We speak because we are
> mortal: words
> are not signs, they are years.
> When they say what
> the names we say say
> they say time: they say us.
> We are names of time.

Against these mortal gestures, these hauntings of language by time and consciousness ('I am the shadow cast by my words'), and against a political history he finds more and more desolate ('This century has few ideas, | all of them *idées fixes* and homicidal'), Paz offers a new version of an image which has pursued him since his early work: a hard Mexican light which knows neither pity nor prejudice, and which may stand for consciousness as it might be if it were not so ghost-ridden. Paz's 'light' is Juarroz's 'infinite', except that it does not involve any escape from time. On the contrary: time is what the light reveals.

> Light neither absolves nor condemns,
> it is neither just nor unjust,
> with its immaterial hands it raises
> the buildings of symmetry;

light leaves us through a corridor of reflections
and returns to itself:
it is a hand that invents itself,
an eye that is mirrored in its own inventions.

Light is time which thinks time.

A writer, Roland Barthes once suggested, is a person for whom language is
a problem. The implication is that anyone who has a problematical relation
to language is a writer, and that further determinations—novelist, poet,
critic—are merely technical or entirely trivial. Such a notion is largely irrelevant in a country like Britain, where there are no 'writers', only novelists,
poets, critics, and so on. In Latin America it makes very good sense, however: there, a writer is someone for whom the play of language is both an
opportunity and a custom, a 'form of life', to borrow Wittgenstein's phrase.

It is true that Octavio Paz has long been complaining about the absence
of genuinely *critical* criticism in Latin America; true, too, that contemporary
criticism now tends to the academic and the formalistic; and true, finally,
that Spanish American literature has always felt an anxiety about criticism,
which often expresses itself in the old charge that literary critics actually
fear creativity. In Monterroso's 'Obras completas' a distinguished but provincial scholar converts a talented poet into a biographer and editor, in
order that this young man may re-enact the scholar's own earlier fear and
failures. In Cortázar's memorable story 'El perseguidor' ('The Pursuer'),
which is based on the later years of Charlie Parker, a jazz critic prefers his
own (refuted) theories to the new style adopted by a creative musician.

Nevertheless, Spanish American writers do *write*, and they write all kinds
of things. Paz himself has written on the French artist Marcel Duchamp,
and on the anthropologist Claude Lévi-Strauss, on the film-maker Luis
Buñuel, and on Dostoevsky; he has published volumes about both old and
new poetry, and on Mexican and world politics. Fuentes and Donoso have
both written books on the new Latin American novel, and Fuentes has
written also on Cervantes, on Borges, and on contemporary politics. Vargas
Llosa has written a book on Flaubert and another on García Márquez.
Cabrera Infante is one of the most brilliant, and without doubt the funniest,
of contemporary film critics.

Among the individual works that fall under this barely classifiable head-
ing, two stand out: Paz's large-scale *Sor Juana: Las trampas de la fe* ('Sor Juana:
The Traps of Faith', 1982), a study of the seventeenth-century Mexican nun
Sor Juana, who was also one of the greatest poets of the Americas; and
Margo Glantz's (b. 1930) *Las genealogías* (1981), which is a witty and a

complicated evocation of the life of the Jewish community in Mexico, and of the echoes of Odessa and the Ukraine that are to be heard in it.

Paz's remarkable book is many things: a biography, a critical study, a recreation of an era, a meditation on Mexican history, a dialogue of poet with poet. In it he calls modern Mexicans 'a people without memory', but he is himself awkwardly caught between a desire to understand what is different about the colonial seventeenth century and a desire to make twentieth-century political points. 'Sor Juana,' he says, 'like each of us, is the expression and the negation of her time, its hero and its victim.' But she was a special victim, a gifted, learned woman forced to give up her books and her writing for the sake of a narrow and tormented religion. The trap or the trick ('trampa' means both) of faith is that she consented to this, or seemed to; and Paz is ready with his analogy. His Sor Juana becomes a sincere penitent in the same way as the victims of the Moscow show trials in the 1930s became self-confessed criminals; because they could not do otherwise, and because orthodoxy commands a queer sort of fidelity, even in its rebels: 'Orthodoxies are not satisfied with punishing dissent; they demand confessions, repentance, and retraction from the guilty. In these ceremonies of expiation, the faith of the accused is the surest ally of the prosecutors and inquisitors.' This must be right, but what was Sor Juana to do? She was not someone, as Paz thinks the Communists were, who had espoused one of her century's great false religions. She had the only religion she knew, or could know; the trap of faith was the world she lived in.

Glantz calls *Las genealogías* a 'book of stories', but adds a question mark. By this, she means that this book is not to be simply associated with the volumes of short fiction she has published, and also that she is herself wondering just what sort of book it is. 'I take my descent from Genesis,' Glantz writes, 'not out of pride but out of necessity.' Jews, she thinks, are 'minor people with a major sense of humour'. 'Jews are great ones for weeping, and Jewesses even more.' She records her parents' chaotic memories of the old country ('I can still remember Trotsky when he came through Odessa,' her father says) as well as their sense of the new (now old) life in Mexico City. The city is an important feature of the book, a busy but relaxed, cosmopolitan place; but so are the narrator's travels and returns, her present tense into which all these genealogical tales pour. She ends by contemplating the arrival of her fiftieth birthday 'with the same calm and exact astonishment and with the same startled and archaeological enthusiasm with which Napoleon contemplated the pyramids when he happened to be in Egypt'. 'Happened to be' is a particularly oblique phrase to use when one recalls that Napoleon was then engaged on a military campaign, and it spills over from the historical comparison into the life of the narrator and her family. It is one of the ways in which she acknowledges a tumultuous and often painful family history without letting history have the last laugh.

The finest example of the Spanish American writer as writer is, once again, Cortázar, who was always committed to the radical cause, in both culture and politics. In addition to his novels, short stories, and essays, he published writing in its purest, most liberated form: the notebook, not as confession or 'workshop' but as cultural conversation. *Último Round* ('Last Round', 1969) contains poems, essays, quotations, photographs, reportages, reflections: the sense of a writer living in his time, writing even when he is not 'writing'; never not writing. Even a later work of fiction like *A Certain Lucas* (1979) seems to avoid categorization. It is not exactly a disguised autobiography; more like the biography of a not entirely fictional *alter ego*. At a concert Lucas disappears under his seat, apparently looking for something as the pianist hammers away at Khachaturyan. 'Have you lost something?' asks the lady whose ankles he seems to be groping at. He was waiting for this. 'The music, madam,' he says. When he is coughing away in a hospital bed in Havana and learns of the death of Charlie Chaplin, Lucas knows that he himself will get better but feels less alive than he did:

When we are past fifty we begin to die gradually in the deaths of others. The great magicians, the shamans of our youth depart one after another. Sometimes we didn't think of them any more, they had remained behind in history; other voices, other rooms [in English in the text] claimed us . . . Then—we all have our beloved shades, our great intercessors—the day comes when the first of them horribly invades the newspapers and the radio.

Cortázar's *Cronopios y famas* (1962) are even less easily classifiable. These brief pieces are forms of fantasy which offer a typology of human creatures, applicable perhaps to most so-called civilized countries, perhaps just to Argentina, perhaps just to Buenos Aires. Or perhaps above all they apply to that Latin America of the mind mapped by the new literature, a place which intersects alarmingly with the historical world, and where most Latin Americans are living already in their imagination; a place where history is all too real but more like a fantasy than any history has a right to be.

The typology comprises three kinds of people: *famas*, *cronopios*, and *esperanzas*. *Famas* and *esperanzas* translate literally enough as 'fames' and 'hopes': fames are respectable and law-abiding, hopes scholarly and scientific. The *cronopios* on the other hand are chronically lazy and capricious, disruptive because they lack interest in any form of social order. It is hard to describe this typology without making it sound silly, and sometimes it is silly. At other times, however, it is both comic and haunting.

The following rough summary may give a sense both of its charm and of the extensive historical dangers it can rapidly conjure up. A *cronopio* is made Director-General of the national radio services, and decides that all broadcasts will be in Romanian, 'not a very popular language in Argentina'. News and advertisements are delivered in Romanian, even the tangos are sung in Romanian. The government orders the delinquent director to be shot, but unfortunately the firing squad is made up of other *cronopios*, who shoot at the crowd instead, killing six naval officers and a pharmacist. A firing squad of *famas* is next formed, the criminal *cronopio* is executed, and replaced as Director-General by 'a distinguished author of folksongs and an essay on grey matter'. Meanwhile, however, many *famas*, 'pessimists by nature', have taught themselves Romanian, and learned a little Romanian history. 'Romanian became the fashion, in spite of the government's anger, and the tomb of the *cronopio* was furtively visited by delegations who shed their tears and their correspondence cards, which were full of names known in Bucharest, city of philatelists and assassinations.' A city like many others.

FURTHER READING

Brotherston, Gordon, *The Emergence of the Latin American Novel* (Cambridge, 1977).

Donoso, José, *The Boom in Spanish American Literature: A Personal History*, trans. Gregory Kolovakos (New York, 1977).

Foster, D. W., *Cultural Diversity in Latin American Literature* (Albuquerque, 1994).

Franco, Jean, *An Introduction to Spanish-American Literature* (Cambridge, 1969).

Gallagher, D. P., *Modern Latin American Literature* (Oxford, 1973).

Kaminsky, Amy K., *Reading the Body Politic* (Minneapolis, 1993).

MacAdam, Alfred, *Textual Confrontations* (Chicago, 1987).

Martin, Gerald, *Journeys through the Labyrinth* (London, 1989).

Wilson, Jason, *An A to Z of Latin American Literature in English Translation* (London, 1989).

26

UNITED STATES

WENDY LESSER

CONTEMPORARY American literature might be said to have begun in 1965, with the serial publication of Truman Capote's (1924–84) *In Cold Blood* in the *New Yorker*. Capote's was not the first American work to mingle factual reportage with novelistic style: for that, one would have to go back to 1952, to Lillian Ross's (b. 1927) *Picture*, or even further, to the New York anecdotes and profiles written in the 1940s and 1950s by Joseph Mitchell (b. 1908; reissued in his collection *Up in the Old Hotel*, 1992). Nor does Capote's book mark the beginning of America's interest in murder as literary material: there was, after all, Edgar Allan Poe over a century earlier. And though *In Cold Blood* is a powerful and lasting work of literature, it is not necessarily the best work of its decade, or even the first remarkable book of that period. But it marks a watershed.

Rereading *In Cold Blood* thirty years later, one can see how it captures two Americas at once: the safe, childishly innocent, familial, small-town, Kansas-farmland world of the 1950s (the crime it chronicles took place in 1959), and the routinely violent, media-infested, cop-show-dominated, insecure, wryly ironic world of the present. No one now, perhaps, could get as worked up about the isolated and unexpectedly bloody deaths of a mere family of four as Capote got in 1965. Since then we have had Ted Bundy and Charles Manson, as well as the invention of the term 'serial killer'; we have had the 900 murder-suicides at Jonestown, instigated by the charismatic religious maniac Jim Jones; and we have had the fiery deaths, carried live on the nation's television sets, of the Symbionese Liberation Army's Los Angeles branch and the followers of David Koresh in Waco, Texas. But the America in which Capote wrote was not as innocent as he made it seem. By the time he published *In Cold Blood*, John F. Kennedy had already been assassinated and the Vietnam War had begun to appear on television. Truman Capote's shocked and violated America is a self-conscious manipulation, a fictional backward glance, and this, among other things, is what makes *In Cold Blood* a watershed, as well as by far the best book Capote was to write.

What Capote does is to play off the shaping influences of authorship against the inexplicable randomness of event. He gives us all the data we could ever want about the well-to-do Clutter household, murdered one November night by Richard Hickock and Perry Smith; and yet he withholds any final answers. The book is riddled with the kind of explicit foreshadowing that implies authorial omniscience: 'At the time not a soul in sleeping Holcomb heard them, the four shotgun blasts that, all told, ended six human lives,' Capote tells us on the third page of the first chapter, forecasting not only the deaths of the Clutters but the eventual execution of Hickock and Smith. Yet three-quarters of the way through the book, in a chapter tantalizingly called 'Answer', he gives us another perspective, conveying a Kansas detective's response to Perry's and Dick's initial confessions: 'But the confessions, though they answered questions of how and why, failed to satisfy his sense of meaningful design. The crime was a psychological accident, virtually an impersonal act; the victims might as well have been killed by lightning.' It is Capote's 'sense of meaningful design' which simultaneously shapes *In Cold Blood* and declares its own absence from the unfolding plot, giving the work both the rich yet fragmented texture of daily life and the haunting completeness of a novel.

This tension between journalism and fiction, between life as encountered and life as imagined, was to mark the succeeding three decades of American literature. And Capote's masterwork was to have other influences as well. With its divided sympathies, its concern for the criminals as well as the victims of their crime, *In Cold Blood* set a significant precedent. One might even say that, from the mid-1960s onwards, American literature became essentially the study of the criminal mentality ('criminal' here includes such violations as adultery and filial betrayal, ethnic disloyalty and personal ingratitude, narcissistic selfishness and untrammelled ambition, as well as the more prosecutable crimes of murder, assault, and theft).

The most deservedly famous sequel to Capote is Norman Mailer's (b. 1923) *The Executioner's Song*, published in 1979. Like *In Cold Blood*, Mailer's book is a 'true-life novel' that conveys, as if from an authorially omniscient perspective, the events surrounding Gary Gilmore's murders of two strangers, and his subsequent execution at the hands of a Utah firing squad. That Gilmore's was the first such death to follow a four-year Supreme-Court-imposed ban on capital punishment made this execution news; Mailer, in the manner of Capote, made it art. But whereas Capote's disinterested perspective was an elaborate disguise, an arras behind which he hid his own 'wretched, rash, intruding' journalistic self, Mailer's apparent detachment represented some version of the truth. He took over the Gilmore story only after Gary was dead, when others had already collected most of the data, and he therefore started with an above-it-all, distanced point of view. This alone would be enough to make *The Executioner's Song* unusual, for the main character in Mailer's non-fiction is almost always Mailer.

He had long been fascinated by the tensions Capote was drawing on— between factual history and imagined fiction, between detached perspective and intrusive author, between sympathy and condemnation, between innocence and guilt. Prior to *The Executioner's Song*, he had exercised these fascinations in *Armies of the Night* (1968), an account of the 1967 March on Washington, which was both the first major public protest against the Vietnam War and a mass-arrest media event. These two books of non-fiction (with the possible addition of *Advertisements for Myself*, 1959) are the ones that will ensure Mailer's continuing reputation as a great twentieth-century writer. His more conventional books, ranging from the Second World War novel *The Naked and the Dead* (1948) to *Harlot's Ghost* (1991)— a conspiracy novel linking the machinations of the CIA, the criminal activities of the Mafia, and the assassination of President Kennedy—have made him rich and famous in his own time; and even his bad novels (like *Ancient Evenings*, 1983, and *Tough Guys Don't Dance*, 1984) offer occasional rewards. But his fiction is often deeply flawed in ways that undercut its value, whereas the apparent flaws in Mailer's non-fiction—egotism, fragmentation, long-windedness, obsessiveness—turn out, in the end, to be narrative virtues.

In 1977, the year Gilmore died, a much smaller book by a less well-known writer accomplished many of the same ends as *The Executioner's Song* without the benefit of a historical prop. Denis Johnson's (b. 1949) first novel, *Angels*, must have been written the minute the ban on capital punishment was lifted in 1976, in a white heat of imagination. Yet Bill Houston and Jamie Mays, the two dirt-poor, drug-addled, ultimately destructive characters who fall in love and then fall apart in *Angels*, are at least as persuasive emotionally as Mailer's very real Gary Gilmore and Nicole Barrett. And while *The Executioner's Song* might, like *In Cold Blood*, occasionally be open to the charge of sentimentality, *Angels* consistently avoids it, even in a final sequence about Houston's execution. Partly this is because of Johnson's piercing, laconic, wryly hilarious style, which has flowered again repeatedly in his later novels—*Fiskadoro* (1985), *Stars at Noon* (1986), *Resuscitation of a Hanged Man* (1991)—and in his stories, collected in *Jesus' Son* (1992). Johnson's manner is to treat religious faith and other forms of transcendence with a touch of scepticism, but to remain serious about them nevertheless; in this respect he is like an American Graham Greene, continuing to argue for faith even in the face of faith's disappointments. None of the later works is as coherent or tightly woven as *Angels*, but all are the products of a brave, intelligent, prodigious talent.

Another small masterpiece that has remained inexplicably neglected is R. G. Vliet's (1929–84) final novel, *Scorpio Rising* (1985). Completed only days before its author died of cancer, *Scorpio Rising* consists of two tenuously linked plots: the late twentieth-century small-town Massachusetts life of an appealing, physically deformed narrator named Rudy Castleberry, and the early twentieth-century Texas family drama that perhaps engendered Rudy's problems. What makes Vliet's novel so remarkable is its treatment of the background story, which is simultaneously feverishly imagined and utterly tangible; it gives a home-grown Texas quality to material stolen wholesale from the Jacobean play *The Changeling*. To see this adultery-and-murder plot played out scene for scene in a twentieth-century American setting, and to see it *work*, is to understand something about the relatively unchanging nature of human character and behaviour.

After Capote, America began to develop a speciality in small-town murder novels. Another fine specimen came out in 1980: William Maxwell's (b. 1908) *So Long, See You Tomorrow*. This is less a murder novel, in fact, than a novel about memory, but one of the chief things Maxwell's narrator remembers is a murder that separated him forever from one of his only childhood friends. That it took place shortly after the narrator's mother died of influenza reinforces his sense of its importance. *So Long, See You Tomorrow*, like virtually all of Maxwell's delicately inflected, faintly sad fiction, is heavily autobiographical in content and sensibility. We come to care not just about the pathetically wounded child who is re-created through memory, but also about the older man—New-York-settled, dutifully psycho-analysed, artistic in his leanings and pursuits—who has never been able to escape that child's fate.

Maxwell's novel is unusual in that its violence is muted, its predominant tone one of languorous sorrow. (In this he resembles another master of the small-town memoir, Peter Taylor (b. 1917), whose *The Old Forest and Other Stories* (1985) was one of the best collections of the decade.) For the most part, contemporary American fiction about death and mortality has specialized in a tone of ominousness, of menace, of potential violence that may or may not be unleashed in the course of the work, but which can be powerfully sensed from the first few pages. Raymond Carver's (1938–88) short stories are classics in this mode; so are some of Tobias Wolff's (b. 1945) stories, especially those dealing with Vietnam veterans. Even quiet gems like Grace Paley's (b. 1922) 'Friends' (1985) and Amy Bloom's (b. 1953) 'Hyacinths' (1993) have death as a central, underlying presence. The notoriously prolific Joyce Carol Oates (b. 1938) has made a career out of introducing the threat of violence into both her stories and her novels—a threat that is almost always carried out. Practically all of Don De Lillo's (b. 1936) novels, from *White Noise* (1986)—a satirical novel in which the local university runs a Hitler Studies programme and whose subplot involves an ecological disaster—to *Libra* (1988), a Maileresque account of Lee Harvey Oswald's life and the Kennedy assassination, hinge on a preoccupation with violent death. And behind De Lillo stands the shadowy figure of Thomas Pynchon (b. 1937), whose novels are both more ambitious and more antic than those of his followers and imitators. From *V.* (1963) and *The Crying of Lot 49* (1966) to the enormously complicated *Gravity's Rainbow* (1973) and the relatively accessible *Vineland* (1990), Pynchon has traced both the craziness and the plausibility of the American obsession with death-dealing conspiracies.

Nor have far-flung expatriates escaped the national curse. Paul Bowles (b. 1910), long resident in Morocco and best known for *The Sheltering Sky* (1949), has published only one novel in the last three decades, *Up Above the World* (1966). In it, he manages to hint from the opening chapter that Vero, the main character, is a psychopathic murderer, though we do not actually get this suspicion confirmed until near the end. In the same vein, Bowles's *Collected Stories*, published to much-deserved acclaim in 1979, are filled with menacing characters and incidents. In his hands, the sense of menace is a moral instrument: he makes us acknowledge what frightens us, and thereby forces us to define for ourselves our own social, or moral, limits. Bowles himself would say that the social and the moral are one: he would not readily grant the difference between etiquette and ethics. Of the murderous Vero's opening non-appearance in *Up Above the World*, Bowles once wrote: 'One wonders fleetingly, I should think, what sort of son this is who can't manage to meet his mother who has come from England to see him.' This, he insists, is the first of many ' "hints" or subliminal suggestions' that Vero is a murderer.

Bowles's fellow expatriate Patricia Highsmith (1921–94), takes an opposite tack: her tales of murder aim for a kind of amorality. Ripley, her most famous character, is a well-to-do, self-made country gentleman—his adopted country, like Highsmith's, is France—who murders people when they happen to get in the way of his plans. The Ripley novels (the first came out in 1955; they appear together in a 1985 collection called *The Mysterious Mr Ripley*) usually begin with the intrusion into Ripley's life of some problematic figure, soon followed by the intruder's elimination; the bulk of each novel is then devoted to Ripley's cover-up of his crime. Tom Ripley is neither likeable nor dislikeable, neither appealing (in the manner of Mailer's Gary Gilmore or Capote's Perry Smith) nor distinctly off-putting (in the manner of Bowles's Vero). He is, if anything, chillingly admirable in his calculating execution of his own plots. As readers, we stick with Ripley because he tickles both our active intelligence and our latent sense of paranoia.

Paranoia, and its clever manipulation in fiction, are also central to the work of Rachel Ingalls (b. 1940), an American who lives in England. Her novellas and short stories are like Gothic tales written with a sceptical humour: something terrible has usually happened or is about to happen, but we watch it transpire as if from the outside, our horror muted by voyeuristic glee. Something similar—a kind of authorial coldness, a distance from people and events—characterizes the work of Paul Theroux (b. 1941), a former expatriate who returned to live in America early in the 1990s. When he is not writing travel books, Theroux focuses mainly on the dark side of human behaviour, from the bizarrely perverse (*Half Moon Street*, 1984) to the frankly murderous (*Chicago Loop*, 1990). Photography is a favourite medium of Theroux's; it plays a part in a number of his novels, and its capacity to freeze and silence its objects seems to express his own coolly distant take on reality. Only once in Theroux's career has he fully lived up to his enormous promise, and that is in *The Family Arsenal* (1976), a novel that pays homage to Conrad's *The Secret Agent* while simultaneously evoking the world of late twentieth-century terrorists. Like *In Cold Blood*, *The Family Arsenal* draws on an affinity between terrorism and novel-writing, one of which is trying to destroy 'meaningful design', the other to create it.

Terrorists and Novelists (1982) is, as it happens, the title of Diane Johnson's (b. 1934) best book, a collection of essays. Johnson is the author of, among other things, an engrossing mystery novel called *The Shadow Knows* (1974), a biography of the crime-writer Dashiell Hammett, and the screenplay for Stanley Kubrick's movie *The Shining*. She is evidently fascinated by the fictional treatment of murder. If it seems strange that her best book should be, not a novel, but a collection of essays, one should consider the American desire simultaneously to know and not to know; to pursue understanding through accumulation of facts and analysis, and then renounce the possibility of an explanation; to be authorially present in the work, but finally to escape through the back door. All of these tendencies are best practised in the essay form. America, through writers like Capote and Mailer, invented the twentieth-century version of the non-fiction novel; and it is no coincidence that some of our best novelists are even better essayists.

Gore Vidal (b. 1925), for one, has published many enjoyable novels, from the darkly comic *Myra Breckenridge* (1968) and *Duluth* (1983)—satires on, respectively, Hollywood and best-sellerdom—to the historically accurate *Burr* (1973) and *Lincoln* (1984). But his best and most characteristic work can be found in his essays, brought together in an enormous volume, *United States* (1993), which draws from earlier books such as *Matters of Fact and Fiction* (1977) and *The Second American Revolution* (1982), as well as from his previously uncollected journalism. Vidal is good on everything from politics to movies to neglected novelists; his sly humour is ever-present and never wasted; and though he has spent much of his later life in Italy, he is deeply, self-consciously, at times even grandiosely American. Which is not to say he is 'patriotic' in any simple-minded fashion—on the contrary, his Americanness has the self-critical bent one finds in the writing of Thoreau or Henry James.

Joan Didion (b. 1934) is another self-consciously American writer. Indeed, her most explicitly political novel, *Democracy* (1984), borrows the title of the only work of fiction by America's major nineteenth-century cultural historian, Henry Adams. It is probably Didion's most successful foray into fiction, but it is severely limited in terms of character development and emotional persuasiveness; her other novels are forgettable. Her essays, however, are not. In *Slouching toward Bethlehem* (1969), *The White Album* (1979), and (to a lesser extent) *After Henry* (1992), Didion helps to define the collective national character even as she attempts to define her own individual one. A Californian by birth and upbringing, she has made a career out of aimlessness and anomie. (In this she resembles the New Orleans novelist Walker Percy (1916–90), whose books *The Moviegoer* (1961) and *The Last Gentleman* (1966) were among the existentialist classics of the 1960s.) The only 'meaningful design', for her, exists at the level of language, out of which she forms flawless sentences, sentences that, in their tonal and rhythmic balance, are occasionally reminiscent of a master essayist like George Orwell. But where Orwell was essentially society-minded, Didion is self-enclosed and inward-facing. At her best, she gives us a quiveringly attuned sense of the surrounding culture's tenuous grasp on rationality and order; at her weakest, she renders phenomena as publicly disturbing as Latin American death squads through the filter of her own migraines.

A more outward-turning essayist is the *New Yorker* writer Janet Malcolm (b. 1934), who models her work on accomplished predecessors like Joseph Mitchell and A. J. Liebling (1904–63). Though Malcolm does not write fiction, her work is infused with a novelistic sensibility, gleaned from reading Henry James, Dickens, Dostoevsky, and Freud. In a series of book-length essays based on extensive research and reportage, she has covered such diverse topics as psychoanalysis (*In the Freud Archives*, 1983), crime reporting (*The Journalist and the Murderer*, 1990), and literary biography (*The Silent Woman*, 1994). In briefer essays she has also considered photography, art criticism, contemporary fiction, Lacanian analysis, anthropology, architecture, Victorian literature, and Czech politics. Like her colleague at the same magazine, Lawrence Weschler (b. 1952), who, in books like *The Passion of Poland* (1984), and *Shapinsky's Karma, Boggs's Bills* (1988), covers a similar range of topics, Malcolm has set a high standard for personally inflected, intensively researched critical journalism.

Essays are not Susan Sontag's (b. 1933) greatest love, but they are her greatest achievement. Ever since she burst onto the scene with *Against Interpretation* (1966), and then followed it up with collections like *Styles of Radical Will* (1969), *On Photography* (1977), and *Under the Sign of Saturn* (1980), Sontag has been a strikingly interesting, observant, and assertive cultural essayist. She has also produced two clever, moving books about disease, one focusing on the metaphors surrounding cancer and tuberculosis, the other on AIDS. But Sontag has always wished, most of all, to be a fiction writer. Her early novels are unsuccessful attempts at European modernist fiction (or perhaps successful attempts—who can tell with European modernist fiction?); only with *The Volcano Lover* (1992) did she finally produce a novel that is the equal of her non-fiction books. She did so by drawing on the same strengths—a passionate interest in history, a collector's love of the arcane, a richly intellectual voice—that also shape her essays.

Elizabeth Hardwick (b. 1916), a Kentucky-born, Boston-groomed, long-time resident of New York, is also both a novelist and an essayist, though in her case the line between the two genres is far less rigid than it is with either Sontag or Didion. Hardwick's intelligence, though pervasive and profound, is never as forthrightly aggressive as Sontag's; nor is her stance ever as private and idiosyncratic as Didion's. The voice in her essays is at once bemused and amused—above all, Hardwick has great wit—so that when she crosses over into fiction (as in her autobiographical novel, *Sleepless Nights*, 1979), the transition from authority to authorship is almost invisible. Her most lasting writing, however, may well be in her literary essays, collected in such volumes as *A View of my Own* (1962), *Seduction and Betrayal* (1974), and *Bartleby in Manhattan* (1983). In these, Hardwick's protean perspective allows her to get inside writers as disparate as Melville, Ibsen, and Virginia Woolf, enabling them to speak to us more clearly than they might have done on their own.

Cynthia Ozick (b. 1928) shares many of the good qualities of these other essayists: the wide-ranging literary background, the forceful intellect, the freedom from academic cant, the essentially urban sensibility, the concern with moral and political meaning. And she, too, is an extremely competent fiction writer, though novels like *The Cannibal Galaxy* (1983) and stories like 'The Shawl' (1989), powerful as they are, seem to suffer a little from their author's too-certain sense of their meanings. As an essayist, Ozick is deeply interesting, devastatingly truthful, and sometimes violently wrong-headed. When she writes about Henry James, for instance, she writes from the point of view of a lower-middle-class, brainy Jewish girl who renounced life for books because she wanted to *be* Henry James—a device that captures James's central artistic concerns perfectly. But when she writes about Salman Rushdie, and compares his persecution at the hands of the Ayatollah Khomeini to Israeli settlers being persecuted by Palestinian guerrillas, we have strayed into Cloud-cuckoo-land. Whether Ozick is tellingly eccentric or crazily mistaken seems to depend on how rigidly (or how politically) she feels gripped by her Jewish identity. As a moral-intellectual ladder which she can clamber up or down as needed, Judaism serves her well; but when she allows it to take precedence over everything else, dictating her responses to all worldly experience, it becomes a cage.

For most American-Jewish writers, Judaism is an ethnic identity rather than a religion. For the vast majority of them—from Isaac Bashevis Singer, Bernard Malamud, Saul Bellow, Harold Brodkey, and Philip Roth to Susan Sontag, Art Spiegelman, Tony Kushner, David Mamet, and Leonard Michaels—belief in God and in the observance of prescribed rituals takes second place (if any place at all) to more secular elements: Yiddish phrases, Jewish foods, certain intonations and gestures, a wry, self-mocking kind of humour, a love of reading, an admiration for high art, and an unshakeable conviction of the moral significance of human action. To embrace one's ethnic identity, for an American Jew, is to embrace all these things. But in the best ethnic writing—Asian, Hispanic, and African-American, as well as Jewish—the embrace is resisted, the affection for one's own kind being always mingled with a deep desire to flee them.

The work of Leonard Michaels (b. 1933), for instance, conveys a Lower-East-Side, Yiddish-inflected, nice-Jewish-boy sensibility that has been over-laid with numerous American incarnations: the street-smart teenager, the existentialist college student, the artsy beatnik figure, the cruel lover, the avid admirer of jazz, salsa, and merengue, the university professor of English literature. From the early stories collected in *Going Places* (1969) to the late novel *Sylvia* (1990), and the essay collection *To Feel These Things* (1993), Michaels is a man on the run. He may be running out of the ghetto, but he always has one eye cocked on what is behind him; he is an escape artist who is watching his back, a Jew addressing the goyim while none the less realizing how much he is still a Jew. The captivating rhythms of Michaels's prose would not have been possible without the Yiddish of his childhood home, but they are also shaped by the English of Byron or Wallace Stevens. His hybrid sensibility is at once highly idiosyncratic and deeply, typically American.

Bernard Malamud (1914–86), a prominent Jewish writer from an earlier generation, tends to stick closely to the immigrant experience in novels like *The Assistant* (1957), *The Fixer* (1966), and *Pictures of Fidelman* (1969). Malamud's work has often been viewed as the moral centre of Jewish writing by younger generations of American Jews, and this role carries with it heavy burdens (of geography, language, and tone as well as of ethnic 'representativeness') that limit his ability to soar. But even he feels impelled to escape at times—to the distinctly un-Jewish academic community in Oregon that provides the setting for *A New Life* (1961); to the *alter ego* realm of literary biography in *Dubin's Lives* (1979); to fantasy and magic in many of the stories and the final, fable-like novel, *God's Grace* (1982).

Another notable escape artist is Maxine Hong Kingston (b. 1940), who in *The Woman Warrior* (1976) describes a California-Chinese childhood in which all white people were labelled as 'ghosts'. The rebellious Maxine fled this world for a university education, a writer's bohemian existence, and marriage to a white man; from her family's point of view, this unbecomingly un-girlish behaviour made her into a ghost as well. But her memoir shows that this kind of rebellion against Chinese authority is itself a Chinese tradition. In a pendant work, *China Men* (1980), Kingston goes even further back in time, to the wave of Chinese immigration and the New York laundry-and-restaurant world that marked her father and grandfather's generations. Both books combine sympathy with ironic humour, as, in a richly expressive English, Kingston delves into a Chinese-American experience that had hitherto been closed to non-Chinese.

A similar delicate balance between Chinese and American identities can be felt in at least the first of Amy Tan's (b. 1952) hugely successful novels, *The Joy Luck Club* (1989). In a series of linked portraits, this portrays four very Americanized daughters and their much more traditionally Chinese mothers. The chapters concerning the mothers tend to be filled with eastern exotica, and are written in an English that rises to suit the milieu; in those concerning the daughters, Tan's English is much looser and slangier. The book pursues the Chinese-American culture clash two decades beyond Kingston, yet the astonishing thing is the extent to which the two cultures are still separated—in terms not just of language, but also of behaviour, morality, tradition, and expectation. Like Kingston, Tan goes back in her next novel, *The Kitchen God's Wife* (1991), to an earlier, more fully Chinese experience. In both cases, it is as if the emancipated daughter has had to work her way back to a hard-won cultural allegiance through her own revolt.

Emancipation from an immigrant past is not an issue for Louise Erdrich (b. 1954), a Native American writer (though part German-American, too) whose finest novel, *Love Medicine* (1985), stays on the reservation. If Erdrich herself has embraced the wider world, her fiction has not: its strength lies in its wilful immersion in the culture and sensibility of Chippewa Indians. Her subsequent novel *The Beet Queen* (1988) is beautifully written, as is *Love Medicine* (Erdrich is also a published poet, and this shows in her fiction), but it lacks the earlier work's intensity of focus, as it meanders in and out of the lives of its American Indian characters. Still less successful is *The Crown of Columbus* (1991), written in collaboration with her husband Michael Dorris (b. 1945), himself a masterful writer, particularly in *The Broken Cord* (1989), his deeply personal account of alcoholism among expectant mothers and its effect on Native American children.

One characteristic of American ethnic fiction is that it tends to merge autobiography and fiction. (This became evident as far back as Edward Dahlberg's (1900–77) *Because I Was Flesh* (1963) and James Baldwin's (1924–87) *Notes of a Native Son* (1955), two autobiographical books that virtually sang their laments in the cadences of biblical English.) Nowhere is this merging clearer than in Darryl Pinckney's (b. 1953) *High Cotton* (1992), a first novel that is also a factual tale of a young African-American, descended from three generations of college graduates, who rebels against his ethnic past and in doing so perhaps comes to understand it better. Pinckney's is a story that could not have happened prior to the 1960s Civil Rights movement. Real racial progress had first to be made before an individual member of the African-American race could, without violating his sense of ethnic identity, begin to pursue his own selfishly personal rather than broadly social version of progress. Both Pinckney's admirable prose style (heavily influenced by English writers, from Dickens to Conrad) and his narrative stance (cocky, disobedient, mocking, narcissistic) set up the crucial dilemma for a young black writer: he cannot with integrity leave his ethnic past behind, but he cannot get anywhere as a writer until he at least tries to do so. *High Cotton* is very aware of this problem, and very astute in dealing with it. Like that of Leonard Michaels or Maxine Hong Kingston, Pinckney's fiction deals with ethnicity in large part by rebelling against it.

Even more explicitly rebellious is Richard Rodriguez's (b. 1944) first book, *Hunger of Memory* (1981). Rodriguez's autobiography, which describes his childhood in a California barrio, his early experiences of negotiating between two languages, and his ultimate choice of English (he went on to get a Ph.D. in Renaissance English literature from Stanford), caused a great outcry when it was first published in 1981. Hispanic activists and advocates of bilingual education leapt on him for providing ammunition to the enemy—for arguing, in essence, that Spanish-speaking children should suppress their own language and acquire English. But to take Rodriguez's memoir as a piece of pedagogical advocacy is to misread its highly personal tone, its intensely pained sense of cultural and familial loss. *Hunger of Memory* begins with an artful reference to Caliban; Rodriguez himself is under no illusions about being part of Prospero's conquering race. In its descriptions of the separate worlds of school and home, this book goes beyond the confines of Hispanic-American experience, to address an experience of cultural conversion that is far more pervasive. The discovery that there are at least two ways of speaking, two ways of dealing with other people—the 'home' way and the 'outside' way—is one that children make all over the world, though perhaps they make it most intensely in immigrant families.

The universality (if that is not too discredited a word in modern critical parlance) of American ethnic literature has been recognized by no less an authority than the Nobel Prize Committee. Of the five Americans who have won Nobel Prizes for literature in recent decades, two—Saul Bellow and Toni Morrison—were squarely within the tradition of ethnic writing; the other three—Czeslaw Milosz, Isaac Bashevis Singer, and Joseph Brodsky—were immigrants still writing in their native, non-English tongues.

Like Mailer, Bowles, or Vidal, Saul Bellow (b. 1915) is a transitional figure between mid-century and contemporary American writing. Many of his best novels—*Dangling Man*, *The Adventures of Augie March*, *Seize the Day*, and *Henderson the Rain King*—appeared in the 1940s and 1950s; but the major works that have come out since then—*Herzog* (1964), *Mr Sammler's Planet* (1970), *Humboldt's Gift* (1975), *More Die of Heartbreak* (1987)—would have represented a pinnacle in anyone else's career. One gift Bellow has never lost is his ear for the odd combination of elegance and colloquialism. A sentence chosen almost at random reads: 'Fishl now was no longer the entrepreneur and seed-money man with me. He was changed altogether by the information I had brought him.' Here, street language like 'seed-money man' and the 'with me' construction (meaning 'to me', 'in my eyes', 'in our game together') contrasts with the grammatical formality of the past perfect 'I had brought' and the almost Yeatsian 'changed altogether'. But what makes the quotation vintage Bellow is the order of the first five words: 'Fishl now was no longer . . .' Standard English would have 'was now no

longer' or even just 'was no longer'. By introducing the strictly unnecessary 'now' and then emphasizing it through its unusual location, Bellow
not only gives a Yiddish inflection to this comment made by a Jew about
another Jew; he also reincarnates Fishl as the entirely new man being
described in this passage.

The planet does not really belong to Mr Sammler, of course; such claims
are always ironic in Bellow's works. (Henderson is hardly a king, or even
a prince, in the idiomatic sense; precisely what will not happen to Augie
March is any kind of adventure; *Seize the Day* is about someone who does
not seize it; and so on.) Bellow makes no obvious effort to create an Everyman, to write on universal themes. This is not to say that all his characters
are Jewish (Henderson and Herzog, among others, are WASPs), but that
they are all self-enclosed, limited, particular. Bellow has got into trouble
with women and with African-Americans because some of his characters
can be labelled as misogynist or racist. But to portray such characters is not
only Bellow's right, it is his special talent. And though he has angered critics
from a wide range of minorities (including Jews), he has also influenced and
inspired younger writers from all of these offended groups.

Toni Morrison (b. 1931) is something of an opposite case: an African-
American writer who has self-consciously striven to transcend the particular. Her early work—novels like *The Bluest Eye* (1970), *Sula* (1973), and *Song
of Solomon* (1977)—evoked black American life entirely from the inside. The
first two books are trial runs, but *Song of Solomon* is a perfect work of its
kind, with an unforgettable central character in the person of Milkman
Dead. Morrison, however, was not satisfied with such perfection; she wanted
a broader canvas, grander themes. So in *Beloved* (1987) she tackled nothing
less than the history of American slavery and the tragic killing of children
by parents.

Beloved is a major achievement and a powerful testament to Morrison's
talents, but it is a divided work, riven by two conflicting ambitions. On the
one hand, Morrison wants to make us weep with pity for the scarred backs
of horsewhipped slaves, the permanently separated families, the ruined lives;
on the other hand, she wants us to contemplate with all-knowing, steely
vision the evil of which humans are capable. But she cannot have it both
ways. She cannot be simultaneously both Dickens and Kafka, both Harriet
Beecher Stowe and Aeschylus. So the weepy parts of *Beloved* undercut the
steely parts, and vice versa. This does not ruin the novel, by any means (as
Randall Jarrell once said, a novel is a prose work of some length that has
something wrong with it), but it makes the double intention less effective
than either half of it would have been on its own.

Beyond ethnicity lies foreignness, and contemporary America contains a number of foreign-born writers who have seized on English as a second (or, in some cases, third) language and have enriched American literature with their 'alien' perspectives. Perhaps the most debated of them is Jerzy Kosinski (1933–91), a Polish-Jewish writer who, even before his death by suicide in 1991, had been virtually silenced by accusations that his novels were in fact ghost-written. Whether or not this was true (the charge was neither refuted nor definitively proven), one can still consider the body of work that his name is attached to as inherently valuable. *The Painted Bird* (1965), Kosinski's first novel, is a riveting account of his childhood (or *a* childhood) spent on the run from the Nazis. *Being There* (1971) is a mordantly witty fable about America's dependence on television. His other novels are of variable quality, though they are all interestingly bizarre.

A less instantly readable but possibly more enduring writer is Walter Abish (b. 1931), whose first language was German. In early works like the novel *Alphabetical Africa* (1974) and some short-story collections, he played with the usual (which is to say, tedious) strategies of intentionally off-putting experimentalism. But then, with the novel *How German Is It* (1980), he burst suddenly into full flower, finding a setting and characters—in present-day Germany—that for once matched his elusive style. The follow-up novel, *Eclipse Fever* (1993), is somewhat less good, perhaps because it lacks the suppressed intensity that an immigrant child of Austrian Jews can bring to bear only on a subject like modern Germany. *Eclipse Fever* is set in Mexico, an intriguing milieu for the reflective North American that Abish has become, but one that fails to give full scope to his compelling sense of literary displacement.

Another immigrant whose works have enriched American culture is Bharati Mukherjee (b. 1940), a Bengali who came to the United States by way of Canada. Mukherjee is known for her novels, but her best writing is in her short stories, which manifest a talent for cultural mimicry that verges on ventriloquism. In the collections *Darkness* (1985) and *The Middleman and Other Stories* (1988) we are allowed to inhabit, sequentially, a range of American types, from the status-conscious, recently arrived Indian housewife, through the thuggish Italian-American city boy, to the Midwestern suburbanite; and are permitted to discover the ways in which each person's world-view is both limited and fortified by a specific cultural inheritance. The multi-lingual, multi-ethnic Indian childhood that helped give Mukherjee her attentive ear is hinted at in her first novel, *The Tiger's Daughter* (1972), which—in its drily humorous treatment of serious subjects like family, marriage, and death—remains her most appealing full-length work.

An American who grew up speaking French but now writes without discernible accent is Luc Sante (b. 1954). Belgian by birth, Sante has thus far published only one proper book, a marvellous evocation of turn-of-the-century New York called *Low Life* (1991). This is history of an unusual sort: largely anecdotal, and with 'characters' who are more likely to be tramps, vaudeville actors, or bar-room *habitués* than important personages. Its language, while beautifully extravagant in places, is never wastefully 'literary'; every line, every description is apt and precise. Other than *Low Life*, Sante has produced to date only essays, including a series written to accompany police-morgue photographs in a strange little book called *Evidence* (1992). He promises to be a writer of the first rank.

The poet Thom Gunn (b. 1929), though he has lived in America for two-thirds of his life, still retains a British passport, referring to himself as an 'Anglo-American'. He seems to have drawn equally from both literatures, though his early books (*Fighting Terms*, 1954, *The Sense of Movement*, 1957, *My Sad Captains*, 1961) perhaps show more of Yeats, Hardy, and Ben Jonson, while his later poems (especially from *The Passages of Joy*, 1982, onwards) are more likely to reflect the influences of Americans like Walt Whitman, William Carlos Williams, and Robert Duncan (1919–88). Both traditions have come together powerfully in *The Man with Night Sweats* (1992), which considers (among many other things) the effect of AIDS on Gunn's circle. The whole range of Gunn's work, from early to late, can be appreciated in the *Collected Poems* (1994). He is also an accomplished essayist, as collections like *The Occasions of Poetry* (1982) and *Shelf Life* (1993) make clear. What distinguishes his poetry from that of even the best of his contemporaries, in America or elsewhere in the English-speaking world, is the presence in his poems of what can only be described as thought. Gunn does not write philosophical treatises in rhyme, nor does he make his own consciousness the centre of his verse; but there is a forward movement in each of his poems, a sense of considering, shaping, and presenting an idea, that is other than purely lyrical or purely narrative. Gunn's thinking is never pretentiously elevated or abstruse, but it is ever-present.

Gunn differs from many other American poets in his evasion or refusal of the confessional mode. This is not to say that he hides from us, for he writes directly about his homosexuality, his domestic life, his drug experiments, his friends' deaths, his love affair with San Francisco in particular and with cities in general. But the bits of personal information which accrue in the course of reading Gunn's poems are never handed over to us with the self-dramatizing, half-ashamed, begging-for-attention-and-forgiveness tone that marks the confessional poet.

Confession is at least as deeply rooted in the American psyche as criminality; the two, indeed, are obviously linked. Yet they may not be linked as neatly as the habitual solver of mysteries might wish. In this context, it is useful to recall Truman Capote's observation in *In Cold Blood* that 'the confessions, though they answered questions of how and why, failed to satisfy [the detective's] sense of meaningful design. The crime was a psychological accident.' The 'crimes' we hear about from American confessional poets tend to be those that are widely shared among the population: hating a parent, hating a lover, hating oneself. The mode of confession varies markedly, from the naked directness of Sharon Olds (b. 1942) to the filmy abstractions of John Ashbery (b. 1927). But in each case the confession follows the pattern noted by Capote: it offers a great many raw data but no conclusive answers. In fact, it is the necessarily frustrated search for the answer—for what Capote calls 'meaningful design'—that provides the occasion for the poem.

The master of this form was Robert Lowell (1917–77), a powerful poet whose influential books included *Life Studies* (1959), *For the Union Dead* (1964), and *Day by Day* (1977). Lowell was ruthless in his use of real-life material: *For Lizzie and Harriet* (1973) is composed largely of letters to (and, worse, from) his estranged wife and daughter; a masterpiece like 'Waking in the Blue' depends heavily on his experiences of being in hospital suffering from periodic manic-depression; and the titles of poems in his last book ('For John Berryman', 'Jean Stafford: A Letter', 'To Mother', 'For Sheridan', 'Caroline in Sickness') read like a catalogue of his closest personal relations. Mental illness is partly what caused Lowell to mine this lode so deeply, but it may also be what gave his best poetry its unmistakable tone, for there is a cold distance to Lowell's vision that saves the most frightening poems from pathos by making them rather inhuman.

Lowell's inheritors are a wide-ranging group, from the quietly contemplative Robert Hass (b. 1941) to the richly sensory Robert Pinsky (b. 1940) to the operatically intense Frank Bidart (b. 1939). Bidart's *In the Western Night* (1990) brings together four of his earlier books and some uncollected poems: it includes major poems like 'Ellen West' and 'The War of Vaslav Nijinsky', as well as notable shorter ones like 'The Sacrifice'. Bidart's central theme is guilt (even, or especially, guilt felt by the innocent); his most frequent technique is the dramatic monologue; and his primary pitch is a howl. (In this, as well as in the allusive title of his collected poems, he pays homage to Allen Ginsberg (b. 1926), whose revolutionary *Howl* appeared in 1956.) Like his contemporaries Hass and Pinsky—as well as a younger generation that includes Jim Powell (b. 1951), Brenda Hillman (b. 1941),

Mary Jo Salter (b. 1954), Michael Ryan (b. 1946), and Alan Shapiro (b. 1952) —Bidart grows, as a poet, out of a strange marriage between Robert Lowell and Elizabeth Bishop, whose excellent *Geography III* (her last book of new work, published in 1976) echoes through *In The Western Night*.

John Berryman (1914–72), who invented a figure named Henry to stand in for him in his *Dream Songs* (1969), has been another, less easily discernible influence on contemporary American poetry. There are shadows of his bleak humour and scathing self-examination in the long lines of C. K. Williams (b. 1936); August Kleinzahler (b. 1949) has picked up on Berryman's jazzy inflections and sardonic anecdotalism; his incantatory technique and talent for stark brevity can be found in the work of Louise Glück (b. 1943). And Philip Levine (b. 1928), whose personal, often memorial, frequently working-class poetry does not *sound* anything like Berryman, pays tribute to him as a teacher in one of the essays making up his autobiography *The Bread of Time* (1994).

Autobiography is another logical channel for confession, and contemporary Americans have done fine things in this form. Sometimes, as with Levine and Donald Hall (b. 1928), or earlier works by Eudora Welty (b. 1909), Mary McCarthy (1912–89), and Lillian Hellman (1907–84), the autobiography is a life-crowning gesture by a writer whose major achievements lie in the past, in fields such as poetry, fiction, or drama. But a peculiarly American vein of autobiography, worked by more and more writers nowadays, is one in which the memoir is its own occasion. The writer's fame accrues after the fact, is the result of the autobiography rather than its cause.

One of the most striking examples of this is Lars Eighner's (b. 1948) *Travels with Lizbeth* (1993). Eighner was not exactly unpublished before he wrote this best-selling book of memoirs, but his publications were mainly in the field of homosexual erotica. *Travels* is something different: an account of three homeless years spent living in parks, hitch-hiking between major cities, and scrounging food and clothing out of garbage cans with the aid of his faithful dog Lizbeth. Composed in a highly distinctive language that is part eighteenth-century man-of-letters (vocabulary, too, can be rescued from garbage cans), part refugee from the 'helping professions' (Eighner once worked in a mental hospital), and part eccentric American critic in the tradition of Thoreau, *Travels with Lizbeth* is both funny and touching. The fact that homelessness is an enormous problem in 1990s America has given Eighner's book some of its impact, but this cannot account for its literary virtues; on the contrary, Eighner has had to fight the mentality that sees homelessness purely as a social problem in order to produce this highly idiosyncratic work. Because it has been actually lived by its author, his story is more persuasive than most fictional renderings of similar material (even including William Kennedy's *Ironweed* (1983), one of the better novels about homeless characters). The book finally goes beyond its ostensible subject-matter and becomes its own justification. We read *Travels with Lizbeth* because we imagine Lars Eighner to be representative, but the point is that he represents no one but himself; and if a man who speaks in tones of such particularity cannot simply be lumped in with a category called 'the homeless', then perhaps the category itself needs to be questioned.

A writer whose first book was a volume of memoirs, and who was only in her twenties when she published it, is Natalie Kusz (b. 1962). *Road Song* (1990) is already the work of an accomplished writer. As with Eighner's, Kusz's memoir gains a great deal from having been written at the well-lit exit from a long, dark tunnel: we look back on the darkness she has travelled through, and marvel that she has achieved a safe arrival, however temporary. In Kusz's case, the terrible experience that made her a writer was a childhood accident: she was maimed at the age of 7 by vicious Alaskan sled-dogs, who left her flayed, one-eyed, and nearly dead. That this terrible story has been told in a voice of cheerful contemplativeness is one of its wonders. Another is Kusz's portrayal of the members of her family, particularly her mother and father, and of their pioneering life in the Alaskan wilderness in the 1970s. *Road Song* is an odd hybrid, a mixture of *Little House on the Prairie* and *Moby Dick*; it is warm and inspirational, yet shot through with a cold, deep strength and transcendent fear.

Another memoir that involves trials endured and (temporarily) survived is Paul Monette's (1945–95) *Borrowed Time* (1988), which is subtitled 'An AIDS Memoir'. Monette's was one of the earliest books to dwell in detail on the death from AIDS of a beloved companion. In its evocation of Roger Horwitz and his daily life with the author, the book becomes an *aide-mémoire* for Monette himself and for Roger's other friends, as well as an AIDS-memoir for the rest of us. Because we know the end before we start, *Borrowed Time* has something of the rich solemnity of a funeral mass; yet it does not lack suspense. At each stage, the discovery both men make is that, much to their surprise, life is still very much worth living in its reduced state; at each stage, they wish, fruitlessly and heart-rendingly, to halt the progress of the disease *there*—not for Roger to get better, but simply for him not to get any worse. If Monette's book is emblematic of a whole era, it is because he has taken great pains to make *Borrowed Time* movingly personal and specific.

Most American autobiographies derive from their Puritan antecedent,

the public confession, in which the central question to be asked and answered was 'How did I, a careless sinner, eventually come to God?' In the
modern secular version, the question is more 'How did I, the flake or fool
or general nogoodnik whose antics you are reading about, eventually become the skilled author whose work you hold in your hands?' As with the
religious question, the underlying implication is: How did I turn out so well
after all?

A diptych that fascinatingly and complicatedly plays out such questions
is the pair of autobiographies written by the Wolff brothers, Geoffrey
(b. 1937) and Tobias. Both are known mainly as fiction writers, but in 1979
Geoffrey published a memoir of his father called *The Duke of Deception*,
which was followed in 1989 by Tobias's memoir *This Boy's Life*. The curiosity in this is that the two boys were separated at a young age by their
parents' divorce, which awarded each brother to a different household; so
whereas the deceptive Duke (a con-man of the first order) takes centre
stage in Geoffrey's story, he is merely a shadowy figure in the wings in
Toby's. *This Boy's Life* focuses instead on their mother Rosemary; her
horrible second husband Dwight (a stepfather of truly Murdstonian pro-
portions); and the adolescent Toby, whose misbehaviour made him the
rebel-without-a-cause of his backwoods community in the Pacific North-
West. While Geoffrey was dining out with the New England aristocracy
and progressing from prep school to Princeton, Toby was running away
from home, stealing from the neighbours, and shooting things. The implicit
theme of *This Boy's Life* is that Tobias Wolff was always a great liar; he
leaves it to us to decide how much of this mendacity has got into his
autobiography. *The Duke of Deception*, on the other hand, restricts the lying
gene entirely to the trickster father. Geoffrey, the deceiver's son, appears
mainly as an innocent victim, even as an adult. The paradoxical result is
that whereas Geoffrey often seems to be putting something over on us
(or on himself), Tobias appears to be telling the naked truth—naked as
in a Degas painting, the way only art can make it.

The author as liar is one of the conceits at the heart of Harold Brodkey's
(b. 1930) most searing work. Officially, Brodkey writes fiction—his best
book, *Stories in an Almost Classical Mode* (1988), is a collection of three decades' work in short fiction, and he has also written two novels and an
earlier book of stories. But because his main character is often named 'Harold
Brodkey', and because the same biographical facts are reiterated obsessively
throughout, it is easy to see his work as autobiographical. The facts are
these: an adorable Jewish baby boy (Brodkey harps incessantly on his own
beauty as a child) is given away to relatives when he is 2 years old because

his saintly, loving mother is dying of cancer. The adoptive household, in St Louis, contains a distant but doting father, a vain, shrewish mother, and a monstrous older sister who enjoys torturing the adopted baby in her spare time. Eventually, during the boy's teens, the parents die or disappear—first the father, then the mother—usually as the result of a wasting illness, cancer or whatever ('or whatever' is a typical Brodkey locution). The boy, brilliant as well as beautiful, leaves for Harvard, where he carries on an active sex life and experiences spiritual revelations. Mostly the stories end there, and then the cycle starts over again. And over, and over. What Gertrude Stein was to sentence structure, Brodkey is to plot: the Great Repeater.

Yet the fact that Brodkey annoyingly proclaims himself to be a genius (as Stein did) does not mean he is not one. The title story of his major collection—and a few others like 'Ceil' and 'Largely an Oral History of my Mother'—will last as long as people read stories in English. What Brodkey has mastered is the ability to create both doubt and conviction in the reader's mind—to make us mistrust his narrative perspective at the same time as he persuades us that his is the most compellingly truthful rendering of events. This is no whimsical game of literary perspectives, no Post-Modern toying with notions of so-called 'truth', for the questions that Brodkey poses in his work all presume that reality matters. Was he loved as a child, or not? Did he behave badly or well, or was such a choice not open to him? Is confession restorative, or artfully pleasing, or merely embarrassing?

Working with background myths like those of Oedipus (the childhood scars) and the Christ Child (the saintly mother), Brodkey grandiosely portrays his personal history as a one-victim holocaust. Art Spiegelman (b. 1948), in contrast, is a writer who had no need to go to such lengths: the real Holocaust was his personal history, or at least that of his parents. Where Brodkey uses a heightened vocabulary and creates myths 'in an almost classical mode', Spiegelman moves in the opposite direction, down the literary scale to the comic book. *Maus* is the resulting achievement: a personal memoir that is also a history of the twentieth century, a strip cartoon (complete with speech balloons) that rises to the demands of barely articulable tragedy.

Issued in two separate volumes, *Maus I* (1986) and *Maus II* (1991), Spiegelman's masterpiece sounds like a joke in impossibly bad taste. A comic-book history of the Holocaust in which the Jews are portrayed as mice, the Nazis as cats, the Poles as pigs, and so on? But Spiegelman's weird technique turns out to be amazingly effective, and somehow more true to its subject-matter than a straight prose account would be. In creating his caricatures, he has borrowed from a long tradition—of morality tales told to children, of political cartooning, of American popular culture, and even of the Nazis' own anti-Semitic propaganda—and this feeling of connection to the past is partly what gives the cartoon images their depth. Intercut with the Second World War, and equally important to the narrative, are Spiegelman's encounters with his self-centred, difficult father, the Holocaust-survivor from whom he is trying to glean the story. The story of the Holocaust is also, indirectly, the story of Spiegelman's family life, for he lost an older brother he never knew in Poland, and eventually lost his mother, too, by suicide. That this horrific material can be treated at all in the context of a comic book is a wonder in itself; that it can be treated with tenderness, sly humour, irony, and dignity is cause for major gratitude.

The fruitful tension between Art Spiegelman and his father, and the historical account he has woven around it, are the patrimony he stole, Esau-like, from a resistant parent. A similar dynamic informs *Patrimony* (1991), Philip Roth's (b. 1933) finest book to date. In this particular snippet of autobiography (he has, less successfully, given us others), Roth describes the relationship between himself and his mildly complaining, proudly loving, classically Jewish father as the older man approaches death. The patrimony referred to in the title is, literally, shit: Philip's father, having fouled himself with disease-induced diarrhoea, begs his son not to tell anyone of his shame. Philip, at the time, agrees and dutifully cleans up the mess. Then, after the old man dies, he writes this book, giving all the details in his typical confessional (not to say blabbermouth) manner. The betrayal of confidence is not a mere sidelight to the story Roth is telling us about his father and himself; it *is* the story, as he very self-consciously realizes.

Betrayal of a similar sort is at the heart of all Roth's novels. Curiously, this is equally true of his worst novels (for instance, *Deception*, 1990) and his best (*Portnoy's Complaint*, 1969, *The Counterlife*, 1986, *Operation Shylock*, 1993). Whether he is betraying a woman, or his family, or a whole ethnic category (he tries, whenever possible, to do all three at once), Roth presents himself as manically guilty—fully aware of his own wrongdoing, but none the less revelling in it. His betrayal gives him something to write home about, a story to tell in exaggeratedly humorous form, a taunting joke in which he gets to play both perpetrator and victim. The process feels circular: he commits the betrayal in order to tell us about it, and he tells us about it in order to expiate the betrayal. In his best work, such as *Patrimony*, the circle is pulled even tighter by the fact that the telling *is* the betrayal.

A more toned-down version of betrayal (one is tempted to say: a much WASPier version) occurs in the novels of John Updike (b. 1932). The best of these are the Rabbit series, from *Rabbit Run* (1960) through *Rabbit Redux* (1971) and *Rabbit Is Rich* (1981) to the final (or so we were promised) *Rabbit at Rest* (1990). Appearing at intervals of a decade or so, these snapshots of Harry 'Rabbit' Angstrom's increasingly upper-middle-class life tell us something about the state of the nation at large. Updike does this mainly through his devastatingly accurate rendering of detail: initially trained as a visual artist, he has a deadly ability to shoot reality through the heart with a precisely turned descriptive phrase. (In this respect he is very much the inheritor of Vladimir Nabokov (1899–1977), whose writing life in English spanned the period from 1941 to 1969, and whose famous *Lolita* came out in 1955. Nabokov's only major works after 1960 were *Pale Fire* (1962), a hilarious send-up of academia, and *Ada* (1969), a book whose heroine's name was meant to evoke its central theme, ardour; but even with this relatively small output, Nabokov's effect on a later generation of American writers has been significant.)

Updike is in some ways what Orwell accused Salvador Dali of being, a genius only from the elbow down, for in portraying the larger, more ephemeral human qualities—love, or friendship, or familial affection—he often seems wide of the mark. These, however, are the topics he focuses on in most of his work. One might say that Updike's central subject is love, or at any rate sex: the two often, for him, seem to come to the same thing. But sex in Updike is not the vast, romantic, overpowering element it is in the work of D. H. Lawrence, say, or Henry Miller (1891–1980). In Updike's hands, it is almost always coldly clinical: detailed, but dead. He aspires to be our national expert on adultery (the crime, or sin, that most preoccupies his Puritan imagination), but he is actually better on greed, which is why *Rabbit Is Rich* may well be his best book.

Updike's writing often offends women, yet, ironically, women writers have proved to be his most successful followers, especially in the fictional territory of adultery. Laurie Colwin (1944–92), Elizabeth Tallent (b. 1954), and Jane Smiley (b. 1949) have all written repeatedly on the subject, and Tallent, at least, has made her debt to Updike explicit in a brief book of criticism. All three have learned from him the intensity of observed detail, the thrill of deception, the private language of lovers. And all three have superseded him in the degree of sympathy they are able to generate for their characters. Smiley, in particular, is a masterful writer at her best (her best includes the novellas *Age of Grief*, 1987, *Ordinary Love*, 1989, and *Good Will*, 1989): her portrayals of adulterous relationships in particular, and family relationships in general, move beyond the clinically observed into the passionately compelling.

Updike's other major follower is Nicholson Baker (b. 1957), whose book-length tribute to his mentor (an odd mixture of memoir and literary criticism called *U and I*, 1991) is one of his best works. His masterpiece is *The Mezzanine* (1988), which out-Updikes Updike in its treatment of quotidian detail. Here descriptive phrases grow to cover whole pages, with footnotes to boot; and Baker's serio-comic rendering of office life makes this slim volume better even than the Rabbit novels in its astute portrayal of white-collar boredom.

At the opposite extreme from Baker's word-conscious, almost plotless novels lie the swashbuckling white-collar thrillers of Scott Turow (b. 1949) and Tom Wolfe (b. 1930). Wolfe first made his reputation as a so-called New Journalist and produced several noteworthy books in that capacity; but he came, on the basis of a single fictional work, to fancy himself as a classic social novelist in the tradition of Dickens and Trollope. In reality, *Bonfire of the Vanities* (1988) is a hollow, carelessly written satire, fit only for rapid reading on aeroplanes. Scott Turow's popular thrillers are a cut above that, particularly the first one, *Presumed Innocent* (1987). He is a practising lawyer and knowledgeable about the wrongdoing that lawyers can get up to, which gives an extra kick to his murder mysteries. In Turow's world, the guardians of the legal system tend to be at least as guilty as the people they prosecute or defend.

America has yet to produce a really good socially-minded mystery writer of the order of Sweden's Maj Sjowall and Per Wahloo, or Britain's Derek Raymond—someone whose investigations into urban crime have wider political implications. The closest it has come so far is probably Ed McBain's (b. 1926) 87th Precinct series, or maybe Patricia Cornwell's (b. 1956) Virginia medical examiner novels. (No, on second thoughts, the closest it has come is the excellent television cop shows developed by Steven Bochco, such as *Hill Street Blues* and *N.Y.P.D. Blue*.) Occasionally, however, an American writer produces a serious, fictionally rich book about urban crime that happens also to function well as a mystery novel. Richard Price's (b. 1949) *Clockers* (1992) is one of these.

The technique of *Clockers* is very similar to that of non-fiction works like *In Cold Blood* or *The Executioner's Song*. Like Capote and Mailer, Price, a talented fiction writer, followed and interviewed real people whose lives impinged on the criminal underworld (detectives, murderers, big-time drug-dealers, small-time punks, residents of dilapidated housing projects, social service workers, etc.) and accumulated information about then. But then, rather than writing a documentary, 'non-fiction' novel, Price wrote a real one, with made-up characters who only faintly resembled their real-world counterparts and a plot entirely drawn from his own imagination. Though Price's previous work, which included several screenplays, showed skill, *Clockers* is leaps and bounds ahead of its predecessors. Its dual narrative, told alternately by a young black dope-dealer and a middle-aged white cop, is consistently gripping, and its picture of poor, urban New Jersey rings absolutely true (to the extent that such things can be judged by a mere amateur).

Where Price concerns himself with the highly visible, prosecutable, often violent crimes that characterize modern American life, William Gaddis (b. 1922) is interested in more intangible kinds of theft. His first novel, *The Recognitions* (1955), was about art forgery. *JR* (1975), which features an 11-year-old entrepreneur and a lot of deliciously rendered bureaucratese, focuses on the devious machinations of the Stock Exchange. And his latest book, *A Frolic of his Own* (1994), is located in the jungle of the American legal system, amidst suits for personal injury, trespass, copyright infringement, plagiarism, and other violations against the jurisprudential notion of the self. All of Gaddis's novels are somewhat difficult to read: the characters are composed almost entirely of dialogue, and of dialogue that is not signalled as such by quotation marks, but flows from and merges with the surrounding speech and occasional description. Stop concentrating for even a second while reading Gaddis, and you are lost. On the other hand, your concentration will be richly rewarded. Gaddis has a perfect ear for how Americans really speak, and the confusions his characters get themselves into are fertile ground for the cultivation of wild humour, scathing social satire, and a deep appreciation for the beauty of language.

American theatre has had a resurgence in the 1990s in the person of Tony Kushner (b. 1956). *Angels in America* (1992–3), Kushner's two-part 'Gay Fantasia on National Themes', is the most invigorating work of drama to come out of this country in at least a decade. The play treats many themes— love, betrayal, AIDS, marriage, politics, power; mostly power, especially in the form of Roy Cohn, an unforgettable character based on Senator Joseph McCarthy's real-life legal counsel. Kushner's Roy Cohn—a homophobic homosexual, an anti-Semitic Jew, a highly successful right-wing lawyer who eventually succumbs to AIDS—is remarkable because he is both hateful and entrancing. Cohn's appearances on stage are the dramatic high points of the play, especially in his encounters with the ghost of Ethel Rosenberg, the Communist martyr who, with her husband Julius, was convicted of espionage and executed in 1953. (The Rosenberg case has attracted other writers before—notably E. L. Doctorow (b. 1931) in *The Book of Daniel* (1971)—but Kushner's treatment of it is unusually imaginative.) Nothing is easy or settled in *Angels in America*; the play harps constantly on the individual case, the surprise, the exception. And though the dialogue has occasional moments of weakness, the play as a whole is richly literate.

Indeed, a number of recent American playwrights have been interested above all in language—not simply as a means for constructing a plot, nor even as an essential key to character, but as a melodic element in itself. Sam Shepard's (b. 1943) best work, including *True West* (1980) and *A Lie of the Mind* (1985), is filled with idiom, with consideration of what people sound like and convey, or fail to convey, when they use an American vernacular. Similar discoveries about the simultaneous meaning and meaninglessness of language can be found in the work of John Guare (b. 1938), Edward Albee (b. 1928), and David Rabe (b. 1940), one of whose plays has the suggestive title *Hurly Burly* (1984).

But perhaps the master of this form of theatre is David Mamet (b. 1947). Mamet has a string of good and successful plays to his credit, including *American Buffalo* (1977), *Glengarry Glen Ross* (1983), *Speed-the-Plow* (1988), and *The Water Engine* (1992)—this last a lovely fable performed in its finished version only on television. Usually they involve a bunch of men in a room—a bunch, in Mamet, can be just two—fighting over status or power. Sometimes a woman is the occasion for the fight, but more often it is a job, a sale, a piece of work. Mamet's self-consciously excessive machismo and obsessive repetitiveness may be sure to annoy a certain portion of the audience, but no one can fault his ear for the oddities of American speech. This comes through most clearly in the three movies he has written and directed—particularly the first one, *House of Games*, which draws on the language of the confidence game. To examine this film in detail (and every detail deserves examination: Mamet, in his films, is a perfectionist) would be to discover the ways in which the confidence game is itself the model for Mamet's idea of the theatre.

To end a discussion of the last thirty years of American writing by asserting that the essential piece of theatre is a film may seem perverse; but no more perverse than beginning by citing a work of non-fiction as the period's essential novel. Americans have always been interested in pushing out the frontiers and American literature, from beginning to end, has been colonizing the margins of the strictly literary. Asked for a prognostication, one might go so far as to guess that in a retrospective consideration of the next thirty years, film and possibly even television will turn out to occupy centre stage.

FURTHER READING

Bercovich, Sacvan, and Patell, Cyrus R. K. (eds.), *The Cambridge History of American Literature*, viii: *Poetry and Criticism since 1945* (Cambridge, 1996).
Bradbury, Malcolm, *The Modern American Novel* (new edn., Oxford, 1992).
Elliott, Emory (ed.), *The Columbia History of the American Novel* (New York, 1991).
Hilfer, Tony, *American Fiction since 1940* (Harlow, 1992).
Parini, Jay, and Millier, Brett C. (eds.), *The Columbia History of American Poetry* (New York, 1994).

27

WALES

NED THOMAS

To understand contemporary writing in Wales requires a complex cultural map. We have to deal with two languages that are used in varying degrees across the whole country. An outsider might think that what is written in the more generally accessible language of the two, English, offers a way into the hidden world of the Welsh language, but that is seldom the case. Many Welsh writers in English have little knowledge of Welsh history, language, or tradition; others are steeped in them, but even they cannot be regarded as simple interpreters of Welsh-language culture, for languages and literary traditions are themselves important shaping elements, irrespective of the way individuals may use them for their own literary purposes.

To this may be added the difficulty of defining a Welsh literature in English. Writing in Welsh defines itself by the medium used—a novel may be set in Prague or Italy and be no less Welsh in that sense; but what makes a novel written in English 'Welsh'? Usually the fact that it deals with Wales. But there are writers born in Wales, or living there, whose work makes no claim by its language or subject-matter to be Welsh, and who can easily be subsumed into English literature proper. And whereas for literature in Welsh there is a 'great tradition' that can be argued with and reacted against, the study of Welsh writing in English has a very precarious academic presence, which is another reason why the border between English and Anglo-Welsh writing is so fluid. For reasons of space as much as ideology, I shall here adopt a narrow definition, and concentrate on those writers and works in which identification with the Welsh context is strong.

WRITING IN WELSH

Those who began to publish in Welsh in the 1960s and 1970s did so in the shadow of the great generation of writers born around the turn of the century: of Saunders Lewis and Kate Roberts, R. Williams-Parry, D. J.

Williams, Waldo Wiliams, Euros Bowen, John Gwilym Jones, Thomas Parry-Williams, and Gwenallt. Many of these originated from a working-class culture that was monoglot Welsh, or very nearly so. But they were also among the first to have a higher education that made it possible for them to study the early and medieval literature of their country and to connect their own work with these earlier great periods of Welsh literature. Some were active politically in the Welsh Nationalist Party (later Plaid Cymru), and almost all became part of a wider nationalist movement, which by the 1970s had established a broad hegemony within Welsh-language culture.

The younger writers of the time inherited a standpoint and a rhetoric that were confirmed by the worsening demographic statistics for the Welsh language and the perceived retreat of the medium in which they worked. Saunders Lewis's 1962 radio lecture 'Tynged yr iaith' ('The Fate of the Language'), which foresaw the demise of Welsh early in the next century if revolutionary methods were not adopted, led to the founding of Cymdeithas yr iaith Gymraeg, or Welsh Language Society, whose direct-action campaigns were to secure the support of many writers and absorb their energies. This was a time of considerable political and social ferment, when the Welsh-speaking community summoned up its strength and won several important concessions which, if they do not guarantee the language's survival, at least give it a chance.

In the short term, this was not particularly productive for literature, though there were some memorable propagandistic texts. Islwyn Ffowc Elis's *Wythnos yng Nghymru fydd* ('A Year in the Wales of the Future', 1957) had set the scene for the protests of the 1960s with its frightening vision of what Wales could become if current trends continued. Singers such as Huw Jones and Dafydd Iwan, later to be important figures in the Welsh media, sang songs to their guitars that were by turns humorous, satirical, and passionate. Their role can be compared with that of singers in other European minorities, Catalan, Breton, or Basque, during roughly the same period. And in the pages of *Barn* ('Opinion'), a Welsh-language monthly, Alwyn D. Rees (1911–74) brought the sharpest of academic minds to the defence of the language in editorials whose intellectual power effectively erased the arguments put forward by the Welsh Office or the Lord Chancellor in London. At the time of the investiture of the Prince of Wales in 1969, the strict alliterative metres (*cynghanedd*) of Eisteddfod competitions emerged to achieve a wider political resonance in the savagely concise verses of Gerallt Lloyd Owen (b. 1944), where the servility of the Welsh is the poet's main target.

Material of this kind inevitably dates, and in retrospect work that was only indirectly relevant to the campaign or that ploughed its own furrow may turn out to have lasted better. *The Secret Room* (1975), the first of several historical novels by Marion Eames (b. 1921), dealt with the persecution of the Quakers in seventeenth-century Meirionnydd, but few of her readers at the time the book was first published can have failed to draw a parallel with those other criminals of conscience who in their own time and own small towns were being taken to court for what were termed 'Welsh-language offences'. Dafydd Rowlands's (b. 1931) novel *Mae Theomemphus yn hen* ('Theomemphus is Old', 1977) stood outside most of the conventions of the time in its individualistic concerns and its prose-poetry form. Meanwhile, the plays of Gwenlyn Parry (1932–91) combined a sure hold on his own region's Welsh demotic with the kind of philosophical questioning associated with the Theatre of the Absurd. Like Beckett, Gwenlyn Parry had emerged from a Protestant religious background whose questions would not go away, though he had lost faith in the answers.

In the 1960s and early 1970s, not many Welsh writers dealt with contemporary life in the realist mode. Among those who did, Eigra Lewis Roberts (b. 1939) particularly deserves attention. In novels, short stories, and plays, she looks honestly at the lives of the much-mythologized *gwerin* (ordinary folk), addressing such topics as wife-beating and abortion before it became generally acceptable to do so. Though less inward and profound, and less of a stylist than the great short-story writer Kate Roberts, she works on territory that Roberts opened up. This is true also of Jane Edwards (b. 1938) in her treatment of childhood and adolescence, and in her use of dialect. Kate Roberts certainly cast a long shadow, which women writers who came after her could find oppressive. Yet having a woman as one of the half-dozen undisputed great figures at the heart of Welsh twentieth-century literature gave women an important role model and a sense of self-confidence, particularly in relation to the writing of prose.

Among the poets, Bobi Jones (b. 1929) confirmed that it was possible to become an effective poet in one's second language—something that has happened more than once in Welsh literature and (in the reverse direction) in Anglo-Welsh literature. As critic and activist, Bobi Jones has made strong commitments, but his earlier and more successful poetry propagandizes in an indirect way. In it, the discovery of new experience—falling in love, the birth of a child—runs parallel with the discovery of a whole new world in Welsh, leading to a double sense of intoxication. His *Selected Poems*, translated into English by Joseph Clancy, appeared in 1987. Gwyn Thomas (b. 1936), like Bobi Jones an academic, has also won a wide reputation with poetry that has become increasingly accessible, having a delightful freshness of tone that verges sometimes on the *faux-naïf*.

Both these poets come, formally speaking, from the innovative end of the spectrum. Meanwhile, poetry in *cynghanedd* experienced a revival in the 1970s. The craft had been kept alive, on the one hand by groups of poets (invariably men) meeting locally and learning from each other, and on the other hand by those who came to *cynghanedd* through school and higher education. These two currents met in the annual competitions of the National Eisteddfod, where a farmer-poet such as Dic Jones (b. 1934), working with fairly conventional themes, is able to delight a wide audience with a skill mastered to the point of seeming effortless. In 1976 this tradition was given a new impetus when a society was founded which went on to establish the magazine *Barddas*, and in time its own publishing house. A younger generation was drawn into the society's activities, and membership today stands at over a thousand, which is remarkable in a language-community of half a million.

The movement was the creation of one man in particular, Alan Llwyd (b. 1948), perhaps the most accomplished living poet in Welsh, and an indefatigable publisher. As an editor, he took up a defensive position which cast those who disagreed with him into outer darkness. For a while it seemed as if subscribing to the formal tradition of *cynghanedd* also involved embracing traditional Christianity and forswearing various contemporary critical theories. The question was even asked whether women were biologically capable of *cynghanedd*! Fortunately, individuals proved more flexible than some of the ideology, and *cynghanedd* has survived, to be written by women and men. Indeed, not for the first time in modern Welsh literature, mastery of it has been carried over into non-traditional fields. Myrddin ap Dafydd (b. 1956), as well as achieving Eisteddfod triumphs in the strict metres, has found a wider audience by writing songs that draw on them.

The period immediately following 1979 is a watershed in both Welsh and Anglo-Welsh writing, though in rather different ways. The referendum held on St David's Day 1979 saw the comprehensive defeat of the Labour government's proposal for the devolution of power to a Welsh assembly. With the election of Mrs Thatcher two months later, and mass redundancies in the steel industry, Wales seemed to be reeling from a succession of blows; but when the government reneged on its manifesto pledge to establish a separate Welsh-language television channel, the level of outrage and protest reached unprecedented levels. The government thereupon performed a U-turn and honoured its pledge.

A Welsh-language media industry now came into being, creating as many as 3,000 skilled and relatively well-paid jobs. It became possible for a number of people to make a full-time living by writing in Welsh, scripting television dramas and soap operas. The status of Welsh improved considerably, and a degree of guilt was felt even that such success for the professional classes should have been won at a time when the rest of the Welsh economy was being devastated. In 1984–5 the miners' strike briefly revived the political radicalism of South Wales before it ended in defeat. Agriculture, the economic base of so many Welsh-speaking communities, was next to suffer.

Welsh literature as hitherto defined could no longer feel it was central to a national movement, nor to the social issues of the time. It had lost its innocence, come to doubt itself, become part of a modern pluralist world, and, at the same time, had discovered its own internal tensions and divisions. The signs were already there before 1979, but that year crystallized the change. In so far as cultural and political nationalism was challenged in English, this period seemed simply like a repeat of earlier hostilities between what was perceived as an urban, English-speaking, and a rural, Welsh-speaking, Wales. But in so far as the debate was now happening within Welsh, the culture was growing, and outgrowing some of its redundant myths. The urban–rural dichotomy no longer held water. Welsh was becoming weaker in the countryside and gaining strength in towns and suburbs, particularly in and around Cardiff.

The rhetoric of traditional nationalism was challenged by the left-wing republican (and later Communist) dramatist Gareth Meils (b. 1938) in a series of plays which hit their mark more cruelly than any outside attack could have done because he knew the nationalist phraseology he was satirizing only too well. His *Hunllef yng Nghymru fydd* ('Nightmare in Wales of the Future', 1990) was an ironic echo of the title of Islwyn Ffowc Elis's novel (see above). In that, the threat had been from outside; in Meils's play, a *comprador* Welsh establishment connives with international capital to create the nightmare.

The Welsh literary tradition was challenged, too, by proponents of critical theory of various kinds, and by feminism, which arrived late in Wales, among other reasons because the national and language struggles had previously claimed precedence. But most of all it was challenged by the changed reality. The Welsh blues of the singer and songwriter Steve Eaves (b. 1952) were no merely fashionable imitation of black America; their words and mood grew out of unemployment and dereliction on the Welsh-speaking council estates of Gwynedd, which the old tradition could not easily cope with.

One trend noticeable in writing of the 1980s and 1990s is the growing strength of the novel relative to poetry, which has traditionally been preeminent in Welsh. Within the Welsh novel the city comes into its own, reflecting the increasing pull of Cardiff for young Welsh-speakers who move to work in the various national institutions where in previous generations they might have gone to London and been lost to Wales. From Goronwy Jones's *Dyddiadur dyn dwad* ('Diary of an Outsider', 1978) and Siôn Eirian's *Bob yn y ddinas* ('Bob in the City', 1979) to Mihangel Morgan's *Dirgel ddyn* ('The Secret Person', 1993), life in the city offers possibilities very different from those of the rooted communities dear to so much Welsh literature: anonymity, picaresque adventure, sex, the contrast between Wales as you were taught to think of it in literature with the Wales you find all around you. However, these are urban novels in the rather special sense that they see the city through the eyes of those who have come from elsewhere, and who experience it, at least in part, as release. We still await the novels of the truly urban Welsh-speakers, those who have grown up in Welsh in the city and received their education in its Welsh schools.

More ambitious in their different ways are Robat Gruffydd's *Y Llosgi* ('The Burning', 1986) and William Owen Roberts's *Y Pla* (1987, later published in a somewhat different English version as *Pestilence*, 1991; a subsequent German translation acquired something of a cult following there). The hero of *Y Llosgi*, a language activist in his youth, works in public relations with the Welsh Development Council, selling Wales to foreign investors and negotiating European funding. What starts as a thriller, when the hero finds his car burnt out, turns into a quest for authenticity, for a definition of Wales that will ring true and not prove just another image for manipulation. Satirical and surreal scenes—in the 'Welsh Publishing Corporation' or in a Berlin transvestite club—remain within a realist framework. The hero finally re-centres his life around something he can believe in, but only by withdrawing to the local and particular from the complex world of power relations which the novel has succeeded in mapping.

Y Pla likewise has the merit of setting Wales in a wide context—that of fourteenth-century Europe at the time of the Great Plague. This is not the historical novel that readers had been used to in Welsh—an illuminated, distant world of national wholeness—but something much closer to Umberto Eco: a self-conscious fiction constructed in an energetic language that enacts a scene of perpetual change, a world where the weak go to the wall and poets hymn the powerful. There is a Marxist sense of history turning on its hinges like a door, to usher in a new age and a new confusion as wage labour takes over from serfdom; but this is Marxist historicism without the hope of an inevitable progression to an ultimate resolution. Therein, no doubt, lies the novel's contemporary resonance.

Protest literature still exists, but not in the old sense. As practised by Meg

Elis (b. 1950) or Angharad Tomos (b. 1958), it now concerns the experiences that come to the protester and the maturity that grows from those experiences. Imprisonment put many Welsh-language activists in contact with other young people, less socially privileged than themselves and suffering other kinds of injustice. If the writers were women, they often came out of prison more strongly feminist.

Angharad Tomos has been one of the Welsh Language Society's leading activists, imprisoned on several occasions for her part in direct-action language campaigns. The chief protagonist of *Yma o hyd* ('Still Here', 1985), a novel in diary form, not only records the detail of prison life but has time to wonder about the nature of those respectable supporters at home who hail her as a saviour of Welsh culture and yet will do absolutely nothing to make her action unnecessary. While she is in prison, she hears of the arrival of the nuclear warheads at Greenham Common, and feels an overwhelming sense of defeat.

Something of this same mixture of feminism with language activism and compassion for others can be found in the raw and tender poetry of Menna Elfyn (b. 1951), a selection of whose work can be found with English translation in *Eucalyptus* (1995). Her themes arise, not from ideology, but from the events of a woman's life in Wales—as when a miscarriage precipitates a sense of multiple loss; when her husband, also a language activist, is taken off to prison; or when the house next door becomes an English holiday home. If the personal has become increasingly political in her work, the political is always realized in very personal terms.

I have discussed writing in Welsh here largely in terms of cultural history, partly because of the difficulty for many readers of assessing the literature in question through translations, but also because the period in question lends itself to this treatment. It was not a time of outstanding individual figures but rather of interesting new trends. With writing in English, to which I now turn, the reverse is true.

WRITING IN ENGLISH

The poetry of the period is dominated by R. S. Thomas (b. 1913); Emyr Humphreys (b. 1919) occupies a central position in the novel. Raymond Williams (1921–88) made his name as a cultural critic without paying any attention to his Welsh origins; but his novels are profoundly concerned with the society that formed him.

Welsh writing in English in the immediate pre- and post-war years had been dominated by a talented school of writers who included Glyn Jones and Gwyn Thomas, Jack Jones, Lewis Jones, and Gwyn Jones. They issued from, and celebrated, the industrial culture of the mining valleys: a Welshness that had no difficulty in defining itself within the British framework as urban, proletarian, and articulate in a way that favoured word-play and eloquence. In this last respect, Dylan Thomas can be assimilated to the group.

R. S. Thomas was the antithesis of all this. At the stylistic level, throughout all his changes of theme, his method has been to pare language to the bone, a technique that reinforces his strategy of using rejection and negation to seek out and celebrate what is residually authentic. Born in the year after Dylan Thomas, his writing only began to reach a wider audience after Dylan's death in 1953, and he was still writing after the publication of his monumental *Collected Poems* (1993). Brought up in Holyhead and directed towards the Church by his mother, the young R. S. Thomas arrived in Manafon in upland Montgomeryshire with Romantic expectations. He finds, however, that the unrefined hill-people 'Affront, bewilder, yet compel my gaze', but their essential humanity communicates itself without words and saves him from triviality:

> You served me well, Prytherch.
> From all my questionings and doubts;
> From brief acceptance of the times'
> Deities; from ache of the mind
> Or body's tyranny, I turned,
> Often after a whole year,
> Often twice in the same day,
> To where you read in the slow book
> Of the farm, turning the field's pages
> So patiently, never tired
> Of the land's story.
>
> ('Servant')

At Manafon, Thomas learned Welsh, read history, made contact with the nationalist movement, tried without success to write poetry in Welsh, and came to see Wales as a ruin of its former self. Industry he perceives as an invasive Anglicizing force which finds ready collaborators within. Yet Wales survives as an ideal, a land beautiful enough to offer images of eternity. Nor does he ever entirely give up the hope that an alternative to modern industrial society might be created in Wales. Indeed, Thomas's anti-industrial views have been held long enough for them to begin nowadays to seem Green and modern.

Later, Thomas moved westwards and northwards to the far tip of the Llŷn peninsula, where his daily work and life were conducted largely in Welsh and he no longer felt the anxious need to define his Welshness in his poetry. In the 1980s and 1990s he became a public figure, speaking for CND or the Welsh Language Society, and refusing to condemn unequivocally the burning of holiday cottages by the radical Meibion Glyndŵr (Sons of Glendower).

His poetry in this period becomes more consistently religious in its preoccupations. His is an undogmatic religion which uses the language of science for the exploration of inner space. R. S. Thomas is capable of immense rejections, as when he dismisses the whole tradition of Western thought—'Plato, Aristotle, | —all those who furrowed the calmness | of their foreheads, are responsible | for the bomb'—but also of a breath-taking spiritual audacity:

> I am alone on the surface
> of a turning planet. What
>
> to do but, like Michaelangelo's
> Adam, put my hand
> out into unknown space,
> hoping for the reciprocating touch?
>
> ('Threshold')

Emyr Humphreys is a novelist who cannot be effectively quoted because structure, and the careful counterposing of different times and places, are fundamental to his books. An early novel, *A Toy Epic* (1958), for example, consists of the intercut voices of three boys, schoolfriends, who occupy different positions on the interrelated scales of language and social class. At the end of the novel it is clear that all three are headed in different directions and will inhabit different conceptual worlds within what is conventionally called Wales. Interestingly, the Welsh version of this novel, published as *Y Tri Llais* ('The Three Voices', 1958), adds an opening sequence in which the narrator, echoing the opening of an early eighteenth-century Welsh visionary poem, hears the voices of the three boys in a dream. This device seems to suggest that a continuity in the literary tradition does indeed hold Wales and its otherwise disintegrating society in a single perspective.

This, indeed, can be seen as Humphreys's general position—an organizing intelligence places itself in the continuous tradition of the Welsh language, and from that vantage-point uses English to make a meaningful shape out of the internal tensions and divisions of a society which has in large measure forgotten what it is to be a nation, and consoles itself with sentimental platitudes.

Humphreys's novels are set in the years between the First World War and the time of writing, often covering more than one generation's experience in the same novel. The scene moves between North and South Wales, and the characters include passionate young nationalists, Marxist materialists, pacifist idealists grown old in their powerlessness, and self-serving pragmatists. A deeply Protestant emphasis on individual conscience, on taking one's life seriously, runs alongside a sense of a mysterious Providence shaping the nation's history. *Outside the House of Baal* (1965) draws together most of Emyr Humphreys's great themes, which are carried through with varying success into his sequence of seven novels under the general title *The Land of the Living* (1971–91).

Border Country (1960), the first volume of Raymond Williams's trilogy, seems by its title to set a different agenda from that of Humphreys. Not only do the three books cross the territorial border into England, but they start off by investigating the border more as a metaphor for a threshold in experience between the worlds of custom, family, neighbourhood, on the one hand, and of education, reading, and ideas on the other. In the volume that made Williams's name, *Culture and Society* (1958), he attempted to reclaim large tracts of English working-class culture. Wales was ignored, so was imperialism, which was such a central element in British society in the nineteenth century. When taxed with this second omission in an interview, Williams interestingly ascribed it to a blindness deriving from his own still unexplored Welshness. That was an exploration he embarked on increasingly as he grew older.

Mathew Price, who in *Border Country* is a young historian visiting home during his father's last illness, has, by the time of *The Fight for Manod* (1979), become a respected older academic, hired as a consultant for a projected new city, to be built in his native region. He can bring the vital knowledge of the power centres outside Wales which may help the true inheritors of the local community to defend themselves. Seen in this light, *The Fight for Manod* is a coming home and a commitment, rather than a continuing celebration of the border country.

It is much harder to decide what is being said about history or about place in Raymond Williams's largest and unfinished project *People of the Black Mountains*, of which a first volume appeared in 1989, a second was published posthumously in 1990, and a third was projected but not written. By its structure, this immensely ambitious work posited an element of continuity running through the lives of the generations living in the Black Mountains of Gwent, from prehistoric times up until our own. At the very least the books must be thought to question conventional notions of nationhood, whether Welsh, English, or British.

In *The Fight for Manod*, and again in *Loyalties* (1985), characters from the English Left are treated with what at first sight appears to be a surprising animosity given Williams's own political positions. They lack charity in human relations and that broad humanism which Williams admires. This question is taken up most interestingly in the volume of interviews *Politics and Letters* (1979), where it becomes clear that Williams's socialism derives from the memory of a face-to-face community without deep internal divisions, threatened from outside but not breeding class hatreds within itself. Bearing this in mind, it might be possible to interpret his entire critical *œuvre* in the light of his Welshness.

In the 1960s and 1970s, a number of writers in English attached themselves to the Welsh-language movement. Some, like myself, were Welsh-speakers who adopted an interpretative role. The urge to put the case for the survival of Welsh to England and the world beyond lay behind my founding in 1970 of the cultural magazine *Planet* and my volume *The Welsh Extremist* (1971), the 'little red book' of the time. Others, starting out from English-speaking Wales, took up a nationalist position that gladly yielded pride of place to Welsh. Harri Webb (b. 1920) and John Tripp (1927–86) wrote a public poetry that reached a wide audience, entertaining but also provoking. Webb's targets were often English institutions in Wales or Welsh provinciality. His 'Synopsis of the Great Welsh Novel' in *The Green Desert* (1969) will always find a place in the anthologies. It is in fact a list of the stereotypes of Wales found in English and Anglo-Welsh literature, and concludes: 'One is not quite sure | whether it is fiction or not.' If Webb tended to use the blunderbuss rather than the rapier in his satire, in poems such as 'Dyffryn Woods' he also shows a lyric gift that dares to express feelings an unsophisticated audience could respond to.

John Tripp's was a more complex talent. A man of strong enthusiasms and loyalties, he was at his best when he mixed in some irony towards the causes he espoused. He was a good magazine poet, writing out of the drama of the times, and over-committed himself rhetorically on many occasions, even wishing away the medium in which he wrote. But he had a nice epigrammatic talent and a deep underlying humanity and sympathy for the poor and marginalized. This came to the fore in his last years, after the débâcle of 1979, and particularly in his long poem 'Life under Thatcher' (1985).

Gillian Clarke (b. 1937) is of a younger generation and in no obvious sense a political poet, yet she belongs with those writers who claim an ancestry in, and seek an affiliation with, Welsh-speaking Wales. Her earlier work (*The Sundial*, 1978) was sometimes attacked or patronized for its domestic and suburban settings, and her poem 'Blaencwrt' can be read as a townswoman's naïve country idyll; but it also contains a sense of a communal past. In Wales, 'the country' is where most of us came from, along family tracks that can still be reopened; progressively, Gillian Clarke has explored that family and community background. Her long radio poem 'Letter from a Far Country' in the volume of that same name (1982) starts as a feminist complaint at domestic drudgery, but this theme is held in increasingly complex tension with a wish to celebrate her grandmothers, their crafts, and their skills.

These years also saw the growing institutionalization of English-language literature in Wales. Roland Mathias (b. 1915) and Raymond Garlick (b. 1926), both poets and editors of the *Anglo-Welsh Review*, gave the study of Welsh literature in English its first academic legitimacy, and a toe-hold in the educational world. The foremost writers in Welsh opened the doors of their *Academi* to writers in English, who formed their own section. This development, like many others of the time, was due in large measure to the influence of Meic Stephens (b. 1938), himself a poet and founder of the magazine *Poetry Wales*, who became the first Literature Director of the Welsh Arts Council. Although this Anglo-Welsh literary world was small and lacked influence among the population at large (as compared with Welsh-language writers), a sense of nation-building prevailed in the cultural sphere.

The poem 'How to Write Anglo-Welsh Literature' (1976), by John Davies (b. 1944), is an early sign of a reaction setting in:

> First, apologize for not being able
> to speak Welsh. Go on: apologize.
> Being Anglo-anything is really tough;
> any gaps you can fill with sighs.

What this poem satirizes is the embracing of subaltern status by English-language writers in Wales and the tendency of nationalist poets to define themselves in terms of a sense of loss and therefore as incomplete. The poem had a special resonance after the referendum of 1979, which proved more of a cataclysm for English-speaking Welsh nationalism than for language nationalists. The label 'Anglo-Welsh' was now rejected in favour of 'Welsh writing in English', and R. S. Thomas fell out of favour with many younger writers, who resolved to be themselves without any preconceptions about their Welshness or lack of it. A number of individual writers were set free to explore a much wider range of experiences than had been usual among the Anglo-Welsh, but they came up against the old dilemma.

If Welsh writing in English does not in some way define itself as specifically Welsh, there may be no good reason to consider it as a body of work distinct from English literature proper.

The miners' strike of 1984–5, though it has up to now left little mark on literature, was a much more central experience to the community at large than it was in England. It revived a sense of the industrial culture of South Wales which the historian Dai Smith (b. 1945) celebrated in his *Wales! Wales?* (1984), and gave writers in English the possibility of attaching themselves to an alternative Welsh ideology. Dai Smith's thesis was that the rapid growth of the industrial areas, with their mixing of populations and the growth of political radicalism, had produced a culture that was discontinuous with the Welsh past: English in language, yet distinctively Welsh within a British identity. Though an oversimplification, this was perhaps a necessary reaction to the nationalist oversimplification that had gone before. As things have turned out, however, it was more celebration and elegy than an ideological launching pad. Mining has now virtually disappeared from Wales, creating a crisis of identity for those whose self-image was based on the industrial culture of the mining areas.

Faced with this crisis, another eloquent historian, Gwyn A. Williams (b. 1925), in *When Was Wales?* (1985), rewrote the history of his country to illustrate his thesis that Wales is a concept which the perennially marginalized Welsh nation constantly reinvents in order to survive, a notion not too far removed from that with which Emyr Humphreys sought to unify his account of Wales in *The Taliesin Tradition* (1983).

The travel writer, and commemorator of the British Raj, Jan Morris (b. 1926), who had already nailed her colours to the mast as a defender of the Welsh language, wrote a Post-Modern celebration of things Welsh in *The Matter of Wales* (1984), which did not find favour among professional historians; but once the idea of a nation reinventing itself is allowed, why should historians claim a special authority? A decade in which historians had claimed a central place not only by their ideas but by the quality of their writing closed with John Davies's *Hanes Cymru* (1990), later translated as *The History of Wales* (1993), the most comprehensive account yet of the country's history from prehistoric times to our own. This is a life's work predicated on the assumption that Wales, with all its complex internal variations and divisions, does indeed exist and is to be understood within the broadest comparative perspectives.

There are some literary figures who in different ways stand outside the map as I have drawn it. Dannie Abse (b. 1923) is usually discussed in an English context as a poet, but his autobiographical novels are firmly set in

Cardiff and are studied in Welsh schools. John Ormond (1923–90) stood aside from the politics of his time but earned a general respect for the craftsmanship of his poetry. Alun Richards (b. 1929) has lived by writing both novels and television scripts on a range of subjects, but continues to return to the subject-matter of Valleys life, updated and nicely ironized.

As we move into the 1990s, the map itself gets harder to draw. There are now bursaries and prizes for writers in Wales, a small presence for Anglo-Welsh literature in the schools and universities, and a few small publishers publishing in English; a contemporary national literature in English is harder than ever to posit, however. In a country which has seen half a million inmigrants in a decade, and where six months' residence qualifies you by Welsh Arts Council standards as a Welsh writer, it is not easy to find a pattern which relates the writing to a distinctive society or to show Welsh writers in English interacting with each other. Which is not to say that there are not a great many interesting individual talents.

Poetry is thriving in the sense that one could name a dozen Welsh poets writing in English who have three or four volumes to their credit and a recognizable voice, but if one asks about Welshness—and perhaps it is in bad taste by now to do so—that list would provide a wide range of attitudes, subject-matter, and even audiences. Most are published in Wales and a few in London. Within Wales, Robert Minhinnick (b. 1952) is among the best-known and most prolific. He has sought to live as a professional writer and never falls below a well-crafted competence. My own preference, however, is for the work of Christine Evans (b. 1943), a Yorkshirewoman of Welsh extraction who teaches English in a Welsh-speaking area and writes out of the complexity of that situation.

There has also been a minor renaissance in the novel in English, as in Welsh. Chris Meredith (b. 1954) has two remarkable if disparate works behind him. *Shifts* (1988), which drew on his background in the former steel-town of Ebbw Vale, was followed rather unexpectedly by *Griffri*, set in the Welsh Middle Ages, a time depicted as brutal, competitive, and analogous with the period in which the novel was written. In many ways it is convergent with *Y Pla*; indeed, there are signs of a more general convergence between those younger writers who have a knowledge of both languages and may even, as in the case of the playwright Ed Thomas (b. 1961), write in both.

Duncan Bush (b. 1946) has tried a number of literary forms, as if in search of the one that will allow him fully to express what he has to say. His novel *Glass Shot* (1991) investigates an obsessive killer's mind in a way that is all the more disturbing for the writer's strong identification with the

main character. It is set mainly in Cardiff, and in the time of the miners'
strike; but the strike figures as a curious sideshow to the main action—
which may be true to the times, and say something about the decay of a
communal consciousness usually perceived as being characteristically Welsh
in both literature and life.

FURTHER READING

Aaron, Jane, *et al.* (eds.), *Our Sisters' Land: The Changing Identities of Women in Wales*
(Cardiff, 1994).
Johnston, Dafydd, *The Literature of Wales: A Pocket Guide* (Cardiff, 1994).
Smith, Dai, *Wales! Wales!* (London, 1984).
Stephens, Meic (ed.), *The Oxford Companion to the Literature of Wales* (Oxford, 1986).
Thomas, M. Wynn, *Internal Difference: Literature in 20th-Century Wales* (Cardiff, 1992).
Thomas, Ned, *The Welsh Extremist: A Culture in Crisis* (London, 1971).

28

WEST INDIES

AL CREIGHTON

EVER since Caribbean literary criticism first established itself, in the 1960s and 1970s, language has been identified as the major issue in the region's literature, so that, even thirty years later, linguistic choices and appropriations, and syntactical variations, remain central to discussions of both form and content in Caribbean writing. A recent critical work on poetry, for example, ends with the statement:

Language is where this business begin for the poets of the West Indies. Language both rooted in the land and rising into song. Language that is their own as poets and as West Indians; so that when they write, each phrase go be soaked in salt; and when we read their poetry, its language go be the wind.

This is J. Edward Chamberlin (in *Come Back to Me my Language*, 1993), trying to demonstrate his thesis by writing the closing sentences of his book in an imitation Caribbean English, such as one is likely to find in some of the region's poetry, fiction, and drama.

Many Caribbean writers not only experiment with language, but also take it as one of their main themes. Chamberlin's comment gains strength because it is, among other things, an echo of a declaration by the Caribbean's most distinguished poet-dramatist Derek Walcott (b. 1930), in one of his earliest poems:

> I seek as climate seeks its style
> to write verse crisp as sand, cold
> as the curled wave, ordinary as a
> tumbler of island water
> ('Islands', 1962)

Walcott is a writer for whom the search has been successful. In his latest and most accomplished poem, *Omeros* (1990), he unobtrusively both illustrates and explains how he appropriates the classical heritage of Greek and Latin and applies it to the language of his native St Lucia. He explains/

translates the title of the work—Omeros being the Greek for Homer as
well as a metaphor for the English word 'home':

> and O was the conch-shell's invocation, *mere* was
> both mother and sea in our Antillean patois,
> *os*, a grey bone, and the white surf as it crashes
>
> And spreads its sibilant collar on a lace shore.
> Omeros was the crunch of dry leaves, and the washes
> that echoed from a cave-mouth when the tide has ebbed.

In other poems, such as 'The Schooner *Flight*' and 'The Spoiler's Return',
he explores more direct, orthodox Creole forms but also, in a technique
used by many other writers, gives Standard English a distinctive note by the
subtle intrusion of a Caribbean lexicon, syntax, and rhythm. In a deliberate
mingling of the Greek and Yoruba pantheons, for example, Walcott, as in
folk cosmology, turns an island hurricane into a vision of the gods having
a wild party:

> the abrupt shango drums
> made Neptune rock in the caves. Fête start! Erzulie
> rattling her ra-ra; Ogun, the blacksmith, feeling
> no pain; Dambala winding like a zandoli
>
> lizard, as their feet thudded on the ceiling,
> as the sea-god, drunk, lurched from wall to wall, saying:
> 'Mama, this music so loud, I going in seine'
> . . . what brings the gods close is this thunderous weather,
> where Ogun can fire one with his partner Zeus.

The colonial and linguistic history of the Caribbean naturally provides
much material for writers. Their use of it goes beyond mere exercises in
grammar or syntax because the various aspects of the cultural heritage, the
issues being discussed, and the dialect chosen to communicate them in
achieve a close symbiosis. Throughout his career Walcott has emphasized
that the Caribbean psyche is a product of the total colonial experience,
owing as much to Europe as to Africa and India. Because the Greek and
Latin classics have been at the root of secondary education, the poet is able
to give a plausible translation of the word 'Omeros' into the sound of a
conch-shell (important once as a means of communication in the islands).
The sea of course is the element crucial both to Homer's Greece and to the
Caribbean islands, while bone ('a grey bone') serves as the symbol of both
a structural foundation and an indestructible relic. And Walcott's language
shifts as easily into a Creolized rhythm as a people for whom it is normal

to have two languages, English and Creole, shift between a received European religion and a native Shango worship that has survived from Yoruba religion in Africa. He captures the thunderous rhythm of carnival music by reference to shango instrumentation and the appropriate gods from the two mythologies. Brotherhood between Zeus and Ogun comes about because they are both gods who control thunder; they 'fire one' together—this being a reference to having a drink together as well as to hurling thunderbolts.

Caribbean writing is not homogeneous; many elements in Walcott's writing are peculiar to him. Nevertheless, the distinctive character of Caribbean English, along with the question of its use, is a factor in every category of writing, including the critical and theoretical. It was identified as a problem in such early critical works as Louis James's *The Islands In Between* (1968) and Gerald Moore's *The Chosen Tongue* (1969). Both these critics are party to the consensus articulated by Edward Baugh that 'the pervasiveness of the agony over language . . . is a most acute indication of what is . . . an insufficiently acknowledged idea, that literature, all literature, is ultimately *about* language'. (The book from which this quotation comes, *Critics on Caribbean Literature* (1978), contains a good sample of critical writing in the Caribbean from the 1960s on.)

The 'agony over language' has been in evidence from the start in West Indian writing: it is 'where this business begin'. It is an issue even in the naming of the region. Caribbean history is largely clouded in myth prior to the arrival in 1492 of what the Anglo-West Indian essayist Sir John Squire aptly called 'Columbus's doom-burdened caravels'. The large body of water that extends between the archipelago and the American mainland is called the Caribbean Sea after the Caribs, one of the many Amerindian groups native to the region. The name 'West Indies', on the other hand, derives from Columbus's expectation that he was arriving in the East, so giving rise to the argument that to use it is somehow to perpetuate the admiral's mistake. Besides which, the settlement that began with Columbus led to colonialism and slavery, with all their negative connotations, together with the imposition of European languages.

'When they conquer you, you have to read their books' is how Derek Walcott puts it. Indigenous Amerindian languages retreated with those who spoke them into the interior of the mainland. Africans imported as slaves, unable to use their native languages, learned to develop Caribbean Creoles, which were also adopted by indentured East Indians. And, with language use, there went political power, education, social hierarchy, with their stratifications of race and class. The twentieth-century anglophone Caribbean thus inherited a structure in which Standard English was the language of officialdom and education, of the expatriate plantocracy and the middle class, while Creole was the first language of the unprivileged class of workers and peasants. This linguistic hierarchy corresponded to the racial one, since the upper classes were either white or mulatto, the lower classes Indian or black.

This basic social and linguistic structure was not radically changed by the strong nationalist movements which accelerated in the 1940s and led eventually to self-government. Its vestiges remained, indeed, even after independence, the liberalizing influence of socialist politics failing to break down entrenched attitudes towards language.

All the various aspects of this history have been treated in West Indian fiction, poetry, drama, and criticism, and in such works of commentary as V. S. Naipaul's (b. 1932, Trinidad) *The Middle Passage* (1962) or Jamaica Kincaid's (b. 1949, Antigua) *A Small Place*. Kincaid has herself criticized Naipaul, who has lived the whole of his adult life in England, for his pessimism in respect of his native region, but has none the less written about many of the same negative Caribbean attitudes: the new materialism, cultural imperialism, corruption, the pettiness of local society. More recently, Kincaid has satirized the 'neo-colonialism' brought about by the promotion of tourism to the islands.

Naipaul, meanwhile, in *Guerrillas* (1975), took up the question of the political violence that had occurred in his native Trinidad in the early 1970s, as well as a number of highly publicized murders committed by the self-styled Black Power activist Michael X. The book is an incisive and compassionate psychological examination of both the situation and the setting, and its English heroine is clearly based on the Englishwoman Gail Ann Benson, who was one of the victims of the murders.

Although his Caribbean background has remained the single most influential factor in Naipaul's writing, he had by this time moved away from the satirical novels about Trinidadian life on which his earlier career had been built (see the English chapter in this volume). In the 1960s he produced some of his outstanding, if also locally controversial, works of fiction, notably *A House for Mr Biswas* (1961) and *The Mimic Men* (1965). Taking also into account his works of non-fiction, *The Middle Passage* and *An Area of Darkness*, it could be said that Naipaul is in general sharply critical, cynical even, about the Caribbean, and also about India, the source of the region's large East Indian population, including his own ancestors. In *Guerrillas*, he extends his concern with left-wing political rebellion in Trinidad into a much wider context of economic inequality and the misuse of ideology by romantic and misguided middle-class intellectuals. Naipaul's attitude in this, as in later books in which he writes about similar situations in Africa (e.g. *A Bend in the River* (1979), a novel set in Idi Amin's Uganda), is that of the outsider, detached yet sympathetic also to the private *Angst* of his characters.

Naipaul's engagement with more global issues is one possible response to 'exile' in Britain. A rather different response has been that of the writer who is, after Naipaul, the most highly regarded of Caribbean novelists, Wilson Harris (b. 1921), who arrived in London from his native Guyana in 1959.

Many readers find Harris's books difficult, in part because of the philosophical preoccupations he pursues in them and in part because of a prose style that has before now been described as 'maverick' and which makes for obscurity. His first novel, *Palace of the Peacock* (1960), is set in the Guyanese hinterland, where Harris had himself spent seventeen years working as a government surveyor. It set the pattern for many of the books that were to follow and for poet Mark McWatt (b. 1946, Guyana). His first four novels, indeed, form a cycle—*The Guyana Quartet*—in which the same ideas and motifs are continued or extended from book to book. *Palace of the Peacock* is at once a Jungian-Freudian journey of self-discovery into the subconscious and, outwardly, a boat journey up river undertaken by a group of men aiming to relive earlier expeditions by European imperialists. Their voyage of plunder carries them to their deaths, but also to an experience of spiritual rebirth.

The theme of rebirth is extended in the second and third novels of the Quartet, *The Far Journey of Oudin* (1961) and *The Whole Armour* (1962). In the final volume, *The Secret Ladder* (1963), a surveyor involved in a project up country that threatens to upset the natural order finds himself confronting the virtual spirit of the rainforests. Others of Harris's novels are set outside Guyana—*Black Marsden* (1972) in Scotland, for instance; *Companions of the Day and Night* (1975) in Mexico; *Da Silva da Silva's Cultivated Wilderness* (1977) in London—but more recently he has returned to his native country for inspiration. The three books making up *The Carnival Trilogy* all have vaguely Guyanese settings, New Forest and Old New Forest, and return to the themes established right from the start. *Carnival* (1985), *The Infinite Rehearsal* (1987), and *The Four Banks of the River of Space* (1990) all involve Odyssean voyages through both time and space, in the course of which Harris interrogates the past as well as the future as he searches for solutions as to how the world may be saved from man-made disasters. And as if this theme were still not exhausted, he comes back to it yet once more in *Resurrection at Sorrow Hill* (1993), whose title indicates how central to Harris's work the notion of death and rebirth has been. Here, the Guyanese setting

is more specific than in the books of the *Trilogy*, as it is also in his latest
novel, *Jonestown* (1996) which is centred on the Jonestown massacre in
which some 900 followers of the American cult leader Jim Jones were
murdered or committed mass suicide on his orders.

Harris has been prolific also as a theorist and critic, concerning himself
especially with mythology, in both its classical European and Amerindian
forms. Some of his most important essays are collected in *The Womb of
Space: The Cross-Cultural Imagination* (1983). In fact, for all the use he has
made in his best-known novels of local settings and motifs, Harris's concerns as a writer have been consistently global.

As such, they far transcend the topicalities of the Caribbean, to which I
must now return. A very different response from that of a Naipaul to the
radical, Afrocentric political/cultural movements of the late 1960s and early
1970s was that of the novelist and playwright Earl Lovelace (b. 1935). He
supported them, and this had effects on the form of his writing. *The Dragon
Can't Dance* (1979), for example, is an interesting development on the old
traditions of 'yard' fiction. It is set among proletarian characters in a tenement
yard in Port-of-Spain at carnival time, the carnival providing a cathartic
outlet for the social pressures under which they are forced to live. The
protagonist finds himself involved in an unplanned armed insurrection, which
ends in confusion, just as the real-life insurrection of 1970 in Trinidad had.
Like other writers who have taken up the same theme, Lovelace sees a
dangerous irony in the way in which carnival play-acting can become mixed
up with the serious business of revolution.

In a later novel, *The Wine of Astonishment* (1984), Lovelace again displays
his concern with the popular political struggle and with liberation. Here, he
goes back in time to 1917, when the colonial government imposed a law
banning the traditional form of worship of the Spiritual Baptists, a law that
was not repealed until 1951. In the novel, the persecuted Baptists suffer not
only at the hands of the colonialists but also for their own errors, as Lovelace
examines the tragic loss of strong village traditions and values and their
replacement by the cheap values disseminated from a new American base
on the island. The story is narrated by one of the Baptist women in her own
language, revealing the biblical sensibility of a persecuted people who have
been made to drink 'the wine of astonishment'.

The effects of colonialism are nothing new, of course, as a literary theme
in the West Indies. They were apparent in the earliest efforts of native
writers, who tended to be imitative of the nineteenth-century British Romantics. These, however, were necessary beginnings, for as the critic Sylvia
Wynter has explained: 'to write at all was and is for the West Indian a
revolutionary act.' The non-Europeans in the Caribbean—with the excep-

tion of East Indians—came after all from oral cultures and took time to adapt to a literate one. It took time, too, for the process of decolonization to develop, away from the cultural orientation imposed by the educational system. There was only a slow acceptance of Creoles as literary languages.

There were, on the other hand, outstanding exceptions to the prevailing attitudes earlier in the century, in particular Claude McKay (1889–1948, Jamaica), whose *Songs of Jamaica* (1912) and *Constab Ballads* (1912) recorded the plight of local native peoples in their own Creole languages. There was also the Marxist writer C. L. R. James (1901–89, Trinidad), who contributed greatly to the rise of social realism in the 1920s and 1930s.

Neither McKay nor Una Marson (1905–65, Jamaica), nor novelists such as V. S. Reid (1913–87, Jamaica), was able to overcome certain awkwardnesses or inaccuracies in their Creole orthography and rhythm. The writer who eventually achieved this was the foremost Creole poet, Louise Bennett (b. 1919, Jamaica), whose acceptance as an establishment writer had to wait until the 1960s although her career dates back to the late 1930s. One important catalyst for this acceptance was an essay called 'On Reading Louise Bennett Seriously' (1967), written by Mervyn Morris (b. 1937, Jamaica), a progressive critic and poet with a keen sensitivity towards the Creole voice and the influence of the oral tradition on Caribbean writing. Bennett's poetic personae are for the most part unexceptional urban or rural folk who voice their concerns in their own language and take a pragmatic approach to the issue of their blackness, an approach that is anti-colonial but without subscribing to the extremism of the 'New Blacks' movement.

Like Dennis Scott (1939–1990, Jamaica, cf. *dreadwalk*), Morris himself is a good example of an important poet well known for working in Standard English but who occasionally adopts Creole personae and dialects, including a dialect strongly influenced by the 'dread talk' of the Rastafarians. This is evident as much in his early work as in the most recent (see *Examination Centre*, 1993), in poems, for example, such as 'Valley Prince' (1973, in a collection entitled *The Pond*), which is a tribute to Don Drummond, a tragic figure and folk hero who was a talented trombonist prone to fits of insanity; or 'Malefactor (Left)' and 'Malefactor (Right)' (from *On Holy Week*, 1976), which are dramatic, Jamaicanized accounts of the two thieves crucified with Jesus on Calvary.

Two other poets deserving mention are Edward Baugh (b. 1936, Jamaica) and the highly metaphysical Martin Carter (b. 1927, Guyana), both of whom are prominent among the 'committed' writers of the region. Baugh captures well the audience-conscious eloquence of the traditional rural 'speechifier', as well as the rum-induced tones of the oral 'performer' at cricket matches or the 'verandah talk' of middle-class academics. His *A Tale from the*

Rainforest (1988) has established him as one of the most skilful craftsmen in the Caribbean.

Carter was long active in revolutionary politics and after independence in Guyana became a government minister, but his concerns as a poet transcend the local political events that he uses as a springboard. It is above all themes of being and time, and the struggle for human dignity that preoccupy him in *Poems of Resistance* (1954), *Succession* (1977), and *Affinity* (1981), and he often expresses shock at events that betray 'the nature of our vileness', at the depravity and criminality that he sees as going against the natural order and as incriminating not just the perpetrators but entire communities.

In general, this sort of writing was a development of the 1970s, when writers were growing in confidence and could use oral traditions without apology, unconcerned whether or not they might be alienating a universal audience for their work. Morris has been influential in this development additionally as a critic and as an anthologist/editor. His critical introductions to Louise Bennett's *Selected Poems* (1983) and *Aunty Roachy Seh* (1993), which is a collection of topical prose commentaries spoken in Jamaican 'patwa' (patois) by a folk persona, or to a collection by the 'dub' poet Mikey Smith (1954–83)—'dub' is a popular, performance-oriented form of protest poetry—have been persuasive contributions to the incorporation of this kind of work into mainstream West Indian literature. The anthology that Morris edited with Gordon Rohlehr and Stewart Brown, *Voiceprint* (1989), is an excellent guide to the current forms of Caribbean verse and its loss of linguistic inhibitions; bearing out the judgement of Lloyd Brown that 'Increasingly, critics, as well as the writers themselves, have been emphasising the importance of these [oral] traditions, not merely as the source for the writers but also as significant art forms in their own right.' These traditions, incidentally, include those of calypso and reggae, both of which are now recognized as belonging to the literary mainstream.

The old dominance of Standard English was brought about of course by the existence both of an educated cultural élite at home in the West Indies and of a foreign market in Britain. The recognition of this has meant that the notion and experience of exile have been important themes in Caribbean writing. There has been a constant exodus of leading writers, mostly to Britain, where they found it easier to make a living from their writing. Foremost among those who have dealt with the theme of exile is George Lamming (b. 1927, Barbados). In his first book, *In the Castle of my Skin* (1953), he addressed the destructive aspects of the education he had received under colonialism, and the pressures that forced him into exile. These were the themes also of *The Emigrants* (1954) and *Water with Berries* (1971), in which the frustrating outcomes of exile, especially its artistic barrenness, are played out. In a work of non-fiction, *The Pleasures of Exile* (1960), Lamming complains about what he and others were forced to inherit from the colonial experience, though he also recognizes the gain to be had from their appropriation of the colonizers' language. In the past writers may have tried to avoid or distort native dialects in order not to deter a foreign readership, but nowadays Caliban feels quite happy about adopting Prospero's tongue, without having to feel guilty. As Lamming has written of the West Indian novel: 'the language in which these books are written is English—which, I must repeat—is a West Indian language.'

One of the advances made by the more interesting of contemporary fiction writers, as opposed to earlier generations, is the way they have chosen to handle what the critic Kenneth Ramchand has identified as 'the relationship between the language of narration (the language of the implied author) and the language of the fictional character'. For the earlier writers—except perhaps for Samuel Selvon (1923–94, Trinidad)—these two 'languages' were largely different, often necessitating a switch within the text from Standard English to Creole. V. S. Reid had been among the first to attempt to narrate a novel in Creole, as opposed to preserving dialect simply for the spoken dialogue. But his experiments remained rather clumsy, reminiscent in this of the uncertainties of such pioneers as McKay and Marson. Selvon, however, managed to create 'implied authors' whose language is the same as that of his characters (or who might on occasions actually be one of the characters). This is the case in *Lonely Londoners* (1956) and some of the stories in *Ways of Sunlight* (1957). A vital component of Selvon's work is humour, through which he brings out the comic side of the behaviour of West Indians in their home situation or of their plight under the conditions of migration to Britain. He chooses his language to suit his themes. His implied author does not exactly wear a calypso singer's mask or use the poetic form of the calypso, but he tells his story or 'ballad' in a similarly mischievous fashion to evoke a whole range of tones, from the satirical to the pathetic.

Selvon's narrators do not reproduce Trinidadian Creole as precisely as Naipaul, for example, has done when writing dialogue. Nevertheless, he can be said to have captured its authentic sound, rhythm, and vocabulary. In *Lonely Londoners*, for example, he is able to vary his linguistic registers to give us both the typical scandal-mongering of the calypso artist as well as the tragic undertones of unemployed West Indian exiles in London. He achieves the same when he is writing of conditions back home in Trinidadian society (even if he has been criticized for concentrating too much on local village life).

In his later novels, Moses Ascending (1975) and Moses Migrating (1983), which complete a trilogy following the career of his hero Moses that began in Lonely Londoners, Selvon's 'ballad'-style narrative plays a less significant role and the fiction is more mature. Through following the fortunes of Moses, the leader as it were of a lost people, Selvon carries his study of emigration further. Moses 'ascends' from living in a basement to occupying the attic of his own house in London in order to be able to accommodate some of his fellow West Indians, while at the same time achieving greater, if not almost saintly, heights in his role of 'saviour'. At the end of the trilogy Moses decides to return to the Caribbean, but he finds he is unable to settle in Trinidad and goes back to London, where, significantly, as if foreseeing the failure of his return 'home', he had not sold the house that he owns.

Such an episode makes this a good moment to turn to consider the group of British-based Caribbean writers who have come to prominence more recently and who form a sort of bridge between post-colonial and indigenous British writing. Some of these writers either grew up in England or have spent the greater part of their adult lives there. Their work is set variously in the Caribbean, in Britain, or back in colonial history, during the period of slavery, which enables them to reflect both on their Caribbean roots and on their confrontations with the problem of racism in contemporary Britain. The issues are ones of identity, 'otherness', and the sense of belonging.

The best of these writers are Caryl Phillips (b. 1958, St Kitts), a novelist and dramatist; Fred d'Aguiar (b. 1960, England), a poet and novelist; David Dabydeen (b. 1955, Guyana), a novelist and poet; Grace Nichols (b. 1950, Guyana), a poet and novelist; Jan Shinebourne Lau (Guyana), a novelist; Merle Collins (b. 1950, Grenada), a poet and fiction writer; and Joan Riley (Jamaica), novelist Beryl Gilroy (Guyana), and the foremost dub poet in Britain, Linton Kwesi Johnson (Jamaica). There are notable playwrights also: Mustapha Matura (b. 1939, Trinidad), Trish Cooke (Dominica), and Michael Abbensetts (Guyana). The concerns of these writers are those of a second or third generation of blacks in Britain. Identity and language are still issues for them but they treat their literary heritage somewhat differently. They are obliged to confront the problem of 'belonging', or that state of mind implied by the title of Joan Riley's novel The Unbelonging (1985). At the same time, they share the same confidence in respect of the linguistic register they choose to write in as their contemporaries at home in the West Indies.

Dabydeen is an especially interesting case. His two novels are set in England but return in certain sequences to his Caribbean roots and draw intertextually on Caribbean models, such as Naipaul or Wilson Harris. In Disappearance (1993), in a strongly post-colonial reversal of roles, a Guyanese engineer finds himself being sent to save the ancient coastline of an English county from erosion. Similarly, Dabydeen's poetic *Turner* (1994) takes the celebrated artist—whose works include a painting entitled simply *Slave Ship*—and casts him somewhat unkindly as a slave-trader, focusing on the terrible voyages endured by both Africans and Indians on their way to the Caribbean. The black diaspora and its contacts with Britain is a theme exploited very effectively also by Caryl Phillips in his novels *Cambridge* (1991) and *Crossing the River* (1993).

In recent years, writers in the Caribbean have gone beyond the achievements of such predecessors as Reid and Selvon in the exploration and literary use of Creole. Especially notable has been the work of Erna Brodber (b. 1940, Jamaica) and Olive Senior (b. 1941, Jamaica), in which the old tension between the language of the narrator and that of the characters has been dissolved. The problem of the 'language of the master', once so potent, has assumed a new, post-colonial dimension, especially among the most recent women writers. The 'master' is now the writer of Caribbean fiction him- or herself.

In *Jane and Louisa Will Soon Come Home* (1980) Brodber explores the emotional state of her female protagonist in a modern urban setting. It is a political setting in which the issues of rootedness and liberation matter. But the novel's sustaining force is the 'alternative' culture of the traditional rural community which writers such as Brodber acknowledge as their own background. This particular novel reflects a Jamaican society that is influenced by radical, left-wing politics as well as by a new black consciousness, pitted against a still entrenched bourgeois, neo-colonial establishment. This conflict, including the search for 'roots', was a major issue in the Caribbean during the 1970s, but writers like Brodber have concentrated on its psychological aspects, exploring the effects that social and political pressures can have on the consciousness of an individual.

For writers like these, true liberation from the colonial past and its heritage involves some identification at least with the genuineness of rural, oral, black traditions. And this goes deeper than any merely fashionable, proletarian 'rediscovery' of pan-African culture. They pay particularly close attention to the liberation of women.

Brodber's very innovative novel has been rightly described as celebrating 'aspects of the life of the small Jamaican country community as it focuses on the problems associated with the growing up of a girl child in the Caribbean'. Thanks to the book's structure, Brodber can bring us to experience both the turmoil of the urban community in which the girl finds herself and the source of the strength she needs if she is to combat its dangers—a strength she does not find, since she eventually goes mad. The girl is vulnerable and has to 'go inna Kumbla' to find the protection of her rural folk roots. Brodber makes ironic use of a song that is actually of English origin

> Jane and Louisa will soon come home
> They will soon come home
> They will soon come home . . .
> Into this beautiful garden

which was sung to accompany a ring-game played by Caribbean children. The song's suggestion of an idyllic innocence is juxtaposed with the process of growing up and with a sensitive awareness of the way in which girls in a rural community discover sexuality.

Where this novel's language is concerned, the shifts between Standard English and Jamaican Creole are managed very effectively. They may occur, for instance, when the narrator comments on the half-understood adult stories that the young girls gossip about: 'Uhhhmmm. That is that. If there is more, we a grow, we will see. And we allowed another mystery to seduce us.' Or they may occur when the narrator seeks to match the rhythm of a country dance (itself an appropriation of European square dancing):

He hug up that banjo with its white basin and sway her and drag his fingers back against the strings and you 'fraid to draw your breath as the old people stand up like buckram in a bottle, man holding woman round her waist like we never see in ordinary life. She looking up at him like she beautiful and slim and in the Viewmaster machine. Man leaning his head and looking down at his partner like he do that every day for the last century.

Brodber's fiction achieves a quality that is perfectly in harmony with the cultural process of 'creolization' or 'indigenization', as it has become known. Her post-colonial explorations continue in her second novel, *Myal* (1989), [whose sequel is *Louisianna* (1994)] which contrasts a colonial system of education with the more successful one of a similar rural setting. The heroine of the book is an academically gifted mulatto girl in a country village who is purged of the evil effects she has suffered from the irrelevant and culturally dangerous primary education she has received in a 'colonial' school. She then herself becomes the agent whereby similar malignant spirits are exorcized from her community, partly through the way in which she is able to identify subtly subversive messages in the apparently harmless textbooks printed in Britain for use in Caribbean schools.

Myal, from which the title of the novel derives, is a magical practice, of African origin, by which the harmful spells inflicted by the 'obeahman', or practitioner of the twin magic of obeah, are exorcized. Brodber uses these both as metaphors and as real social forces. The novel suggests that much has been inherited from the colonial past, and from neo-colonialism, which afflicts the Caribbean psyche like a malignant obeah, and which needs to be identified and flushed out. Significantly, however, not all the ills that Brodber believes should be purged are of European manufacture. Her concern is with the process of liberation, in which an African consciousness and the strong foundations of the traditional community often play a part. At the same time, that community needs to be liberated from certain indigenous elements. The novel's heroine is of mixed ancestry, and can thus embody both the colonial heritage and the sources of enlightenment, whether these are thought to come from within or from outside the indigenous tradition. Mixed race is, obviously, a demographic fact of importance in the West Indies and has been used as an artistic device or metaphor by other writers, including Olive Senior and Derek Walcott.

The strength of women as a major force in society has also been a strong theme as it happens of a leading male writer, Eddie Kamau Brathwaite (b. 1930, Barbados), who has been one of the dominant poets of the period and of the region, ever since the publication of what might be called his 'foundational' trilogy of verse collections, *Rights of Passage* (1967), *Masks* (1968), and *Islands* (1969), which were published together as *The Arrivants* (1970). These had a great influence on the growing number of Afrocentrists and radicals, in fostering the mood of anti-imperialism and the search for roots, as well as the rise of orality and dub poetry, in the early 1970s. The best of his work since then is perhaps to be found in his second trilogy: *Mother Poem* (1977), *Sun Poem* (1982), and *X-Self* (1987).

The Arrivants is one of the outstanding works of Caribbean literature. No one has written better than Brathwaite of the condition of blacks in the diaspora, starting with the devastating experience of slavery (the theme of *Rights of Passage*). He favours avant-garde verse-forms, whose lean, economical lineation can be reminiscent of the American poet E. E. Cummings, with words being broken up into syllables that come to bear an accentuated meaning. This is a form of poetry intended to represent the fractured mentality of a lost, leaderless, emigrant people, for whom even repatriation (*Masks*) could not represent journey's end until such time as they have been regrounded culturally and spiritually in their African roots. Only then would it be possible for them to be healed and to come to terms with the new experience of nationhood in the Caribbean (*Islands*).

In his second trilogy Brathwaite goes back to his own roots in Barbados: *Sun Poem*—the title involves a pun on the notion of 'Son-Poem'—is especially autobiographical. In formal terms he has moved in his later work even further in the Post-Modernist direction, especially in *X-Self*. In his influential critical and theoretical essays he has championed Creole as a 'nation language', as an attempt by its speakers to reclaim vestiges of their lost African languages.

Lorna Goodison (b. 1947) is another poet who has done much to assert the strength of women against an established social order dominated by men who are either predatory or indifferent to them. Her best work has appeared in *I Am Becoming my Mother* (1986) and *Selected Poems* (1992). In the first she fortifies her vision of women as a powerful psychological and material force in contemporary society by reflecting on the ancestral strength of her own mother. In addition to which, she identifies woman with the landscape, a device used earlier by Brathwaite in his *Mother Poem*, in which women's strength is contrasted with the failure of men, who are seen as broken victims of the region's history. Goodison, too, has been much influenced by oral tradition.

Another outstanding woman poet is Pamela Mordecai (b. 1942, Jamaica), who has taken a notably progressive approach to female sexuality as she celebrates the strengths of womanhood. In *Journey Poem* (1989) she calls for a new self-assertiveness with which women should challenge the established masculine order, too complacently accepted as that has been. Well equipped for 'all love's traffic', woman is equipped also to be a dominant moral and material force in society.

Autobiographical fiction, concentrating on the experience of growing up in the Caribbean, is a firmly established literary tradition there, found in older writers such as Lamming or Naipaul, as well as younger ones like Merle Hodge (b. 1944), in her *Crick Crack Monkey* (1970), Merle Collins, the author of *Angel* (1988), Grace Nichols, in *Whole of a Morning Sky* (1986), and Jan Shinebourne, in *Timepiece* (1986) and *The Last English Plantation* (1989). The work of writers like these—whose great West Indian predecessor was Jean Rhys (1895–1979, Dominica)—represents a development of the autobiographical tradition in the heightened attention they give to gender; although it should also be said that a male writer living in Britain like David Dabydeen, in *The Intended* (1991), has similarly extended the tradition, by describing his upbringing in London.

A writer to be singled out here is Jamaica Kincaid, who is among the very best women writers of the Caribbean. She has published two works of fiction, *At the Bottom of the River* (1983) and *Annie John* (1985), in which the idyllic memories of the Antigua of her childhood to be found in the first volume progressively disappear as one moves on to the second, at the end of which, indeed, the heroine Annie leaves Antigua to go and live in the

United States. The myth that controls the two narratives is explicitly that of a Paradise Lost, of a fall from a state of innocence.

The story of Annie's growing up in the island community is told in the first person. At the centre of it is an account of her mother as a girl, walking miles from the fields back to her home, carrying on her head a bunch of bananas in which, unbeknownst to her, a snake is lurking. As the novel progresses, Annie is gradually introduced to the deceitful ways of the grown-up world and rebels silently against her mother. Her mistrust increases when she discovers the sexual relation between her parents. Mother and daughter move steadily away from one another. Annie stands out against the prospect of marriage and channels her newly developing sexuality into lesbian relationships with her peers. It is as if her mother is guilty of the 'treachery' of introducing the serpent into a garden where love and harmony had once existed, and Annie's disenchantment eventually extends to the whole of her island society.

Another woman writer of accomplishment is Velma Pollard (b. 1937, Jamaica). Her best work is to be found in her novella *Karl* (1994). Its hero is an honest, very genuine man whose roots are among the country people but whose academic brilliance has meant that he has been educated in a foreign university and has graduated into the middle classes. He is unable, however, either to overcome or alternatively to join an unwholesome society, whose prejudices, snobbery, and hypocrisy are shared by his own wife; he escapes in the end into insanity. His madness is only one of the ironies that pervade the book, where sane rural values are juxtaposed with the literally maddening falsehoods of the city. Pollard is adept at conveying the different psychological viewpoints of her characters and the conversational style of the narration has the authentic rhythms of speech.

Like Pollard, Olive Senior also is a writer disturbed by what Caribbean society has become, both in her poetry (*Talking of Trees*, 1985, and *Gardening in the Tropics*, 1994), and in her collections of short stories: *Summer Lightning* (1986) and *Arrival of the Snake Woman* (1989). She confronts the unrest that exists in the urban subculture of Jamaica, which is controlled by poverty and by violence, and by the loss of traditional community values. She is keenly alive as well to issues of gender.

In many of her poems and her stories Senior is concerned, not with the urban situation but with rural communities that are themselves in need of enlightenment. In the title story of *Arrival of the Snake Woman*, long enough to count as a novella, she implies the need for a new social order, for a broadening of horizons and an escape from a retrograde age in a mountain village chained to a very static tradition. The 'liberator' of the village is an

Indian woman immigrant who first achieves independence for herself and then extends it to the village as a whole. The narrator of the novella is a man, who finds himself being influenced to bring about his own 'liberation'. There are ironies at work, however. The narrator is a failure because he gains an education and independence for himself without contributing anything to the village, which he comes to see as an insufficiently progressive place for him to live in. In addition to which, in bringing about order and commercial progress in the village, and opening it up to the outside world, the Indian 'liberator' erodes the old sense of camaraderie, which had been embodied in a form of primitive communism.

Senior maintains a balance between what she believes to be lacking and what she believes to be valuable in rural communities. In many of her stories of conflict between the old folk-consciousness and the new bourgeois society, she exposes the unhealthiness of the latter and celebrates the wisdom and solidarity of the former. The same preoccupations are present in her poetry. In 'Caribbean Basin Politics', for example, a poem of 1994, she reveals her distrust of modern regional politics and her respect for folk traditions, despite the potential for tragedy that they may contain:

> Marcelin and Anselm
> unseasoned young men
> went into the forest
> to cut the tree for
> their boat. It's funny
> how grudgingly that
> tree fell. Funny how
> each day it grew back
> again. They never could
> hollow it enough to
> make it float.
>
> Never send a boy to
> do a man's job, I say.
> They will not follow
> the old way.
>
> Feed the spirits before
> you feed the children.
> Before you make the first
> cut, you must pay.
>
> Some rules cannot
> be flouted. Some gods
> Will not uphold
> the unconverted.

Agué Lord of the Sea,
Watch over me.

Writing for the theatre in the West Indies has followed a broadly similar course to what has happened in both fiction and poetry. During the 1950s, in a first attempt to escape from the colonialist tradition, dramatists pioneered the so-called 'backyard' theatre, which focused on local, urban, working-class or folk situations, usually in the communal setting of a backyard, and exploiting them above all for humour. Errol Hill (b. 1921, Trinidad) was a leading playwright in this tradition (e.g. *The Ping Pong*, 1950), experimenting also with the use of steel bands, stick-fighting, and the African bongo. Hill has also been the most prominent historian of local theatre, as in his long essay 'The Emergence of a National Theatre in the West Indies', which appeared in the *Caribbean Quarterly* in 1972. More recently he has written that 'the search continues for a narrative theatrical form that captures the expressive qualities of Caribbean life', a judgement that underestimates what has been achieved by the increasingly confident and innovative West Indian playwrights since the 1960s.

Leading figures in this growth are Errol John (1923–88, Trinidad) and Douglas Archibald (1919–93, Trinidad), who brought new powers of analysis as well as pathos to stock Caribbean themes. Most influential of all, however, was Dennis Scott (1939–90, Jamaica), with his *An Echo in the Bone*, first performed in 1974. This was his response to the urgent call in the 1970s for a drama of 'relevance'. In it he uses the Jamaican folk tradition of the 'nine-night' wake, in which participants are possessed by the spirit of the dead, and links it with episodes from the history of slavery, in which the local people are 'possessed' by the spirit of their past. The play ends in a cathartic purging of the social ills inflicted by the past on the present. What is important, however, is the way in which Scott has integrated the indigenous material with various avant-garde theatrical techniques taken from the current practice of the international stage.

Similarly, in his *Old Story Time* (1979), Jamaica's leading playwright Trevor Rhone (b. 1940) shows black people successfully exorcizing the characteristic self-contempt and bitterness imposed on them by history. Rhone's basic, Brechtian technique is to employ a *conteur*, or story-teller, to entertain an audience on the stage who also become the chorus as well as actors in the drama. Others of Rhone's plays that have been very successful are *Two Can Play* (1982), in which he investigates through satire the effects of street violence, the economic crisis, and emigration; and *Smile Orange* (1971), a hilarious play about the tourist industry.

The escalating social crises of the 1970s led to a big demand for naturalistic theatre and produced such gifted new dramatists as David Edgecombe (b. 1952, Montserrat) and Harold Bascomb (b. 1951, Guyana). Edgecombe, whose work can best be read in *Heaven and Other Plays* (1992), remains largely in a mode of (often domestic) realism. Other important dramatists write in a poetic mode. These include Michael Gilkes (b. 1933, Guyana), whose *Couvade* (1974) is based on the Amerindian birth ritual of the 'couvade', in which the father takes to his bed and undergoes certain privations at the time when his child is born; the play advocates a kind of general healing of social ills to be achieved through the use of multi-ethnic traditions. A revised version of *Couvade*, published in 1993, along with a new play, *A Pleasant Career* (1991), concerned with the life and times of the Guyanese novelist Edgar Mittelholzer, have established Gilkes as one of the inheritors of Scott's form of theatre. Another member of this group is Alwin Bully (b. 1948, Dominica), whose *MacB* is an excellent example of avant-garde Caribbean theatre, adapted from *Macbeth*.

Derek Walcott has also been very active in the theatre, starting in the 1950s, when he wrote a series of plays set in the St Lucian countryside and seeking to bring out what he referred to as the tragic stature of the country-folk. Since 1970 his work for the theatre has reflected developing trends in the Caribbean and, like Scott's, is marked by formal innovation. Some of his plays represent a direct response to prevailing political moods, but without sharing the ideological (proletarian) standpoint of a work such as Scott's *Dog* (1977). *Dream on Monkey Mountain* (1970), for example, rejects the stagy Black Power ideology of the 'New Blacks' in favour of individualism, but is equally critical of the colonial mentality and self-contempt still to be found among black West Indians. It is a psychological drama in which the hero Makak overcomes his inferiority complex and rediscovers his identity through a dream in which, inspired by a white muse, he regains the mythical spiritual powers lost by Africans when they travelled to the Carib-bean as slaves.

To anger Walcott prefers compassion, including acceptance by blacks of the white Creoles, who also form a part of Trinidadian society—this is brought out in *The Last Carnival* (1987). In his musical *O Babylon* (1976) he shows his sympathy towards the Rastafarians, and *Pantomime* (1977) is an ironic, anti-colonialist work that draws its force from the myth of Robinson Crusoe, as the archetype of the white colonizer. Of his more recent work, particularly trenchant is *Beef, No Chicken* (1983), a farce in which he satirizes the shallowness of the new urban lifestyles which have done away with sound traditional values.

Walcott has also written a musical adaptation of Tirso de Molina's original Don Juan play *El burlador de Sevilla*, and an adaptation of the *Odyssey*.

Both were commissioned by the Royal Shakespeare Company and are good illustrations of the present state of Caribbean drama and of Walcott's own development as poet-dramatist. In *The Joker of Seville* (1978) he resituates the legendary Don Juan in the New World of the West Indies and in so doing makes telling comments on the history of transatlantic imperialism, as well as demonstrating the ease with which Tirso's social setting, language, and verse rhythms translate into those of the Caribbean. The phallic imagery appropriate to Don Juan is an important element as it happens in the macho tradition of the Caribbean *kalinda*, or lore of the champion stick-fighter. Walcott has also in this play drawn on the indigenous musical tradition of the *parang*, which is partly of Spanish origin.

He has taken fewer liberties in his adaptation of the *Odyssey*, but has still managed to produce a very Caribbean play in terms of language, characterization, and the geographical parallels between the Greek Mediterranean and the Caribbean islands, so exhibiting, as in his poetry, his lifelong concern for those islands' classical heritage. Yet, when Walcott calls 'come back to me | my language. | Come back', it is his native St Lucian patois that he is calling for:

> . . . z'aman
> sea almonds . . .
> cacao,
> grigri,
> solitaire,
> ciseau
> the scissor-bird

And similarly, Merle Collins, writing from her 'exile' in London, remembers that her native Grenada has its own heroes, history, and language:

> Kay sala se sa'w
> Esta es
> su casa
> This is
> your home!

FURTHER READING

Baugh, Edward (ed.), *Critics on Caribbean Literature* (London, 1978).

Benson, Eugene and L. W. Conolly (eds.), *Encyclopedia of Post-Colonial Literatures in English* (London, 1994).

Chamberlin, Edward J., *Come Back to Me, My Language* (Illinois, 1993).

James, Louis (ed.), *The Islands in Between* (London, 1968).

Lindfors, Bernth and Reinhard Sander (eds.), *Dictionary of Literary Biography, Vol. 125: C20th Caribbean and Black African Writers* (Detroit and London, 1993).

Ramchand, Kenneth, *The West Indian Novel and Its Background* (London, 1983).

Index

Translations of foreign titles are given in parentheses. Individual poems or parts of larger works are given in square brackets, after the title of the work in which they appear, if known.

A Very Short Introduction

CLASSICS

Mary Beard and John Henderson

This *Very Short Introduction* to Classics links a haunting temple on a lonely mountainside to the glory of ancient Greece and the grandeur of Rome, and to Classics within modern culture—from Jefferson and Byron to Asterix and Ben-Hur.

'This little book should be in the hands of every student, and every tourist to the lands of the ancient world . . . a splendid piece of work'
Peter Wiseman
Author of *Talking to Virgil*

'an eminently readable and useful guide to many of the modern debates enlivening the field . . . the most up-to-date and accessible introduction available'
Edith Hall
Author of *Inventing the Barbarian*

'lively and up-to-date . . . it shows classics as a living enterprise, not a warehouse of relics'
New Statesman and Society

'nobody could fail to be informed and entertained—the accent of the book is provocative and stimulating'
Times Literary Supplement

A Very Short Introduction

POLITICS

Kenneth Minogue

Since politics is both complex and controversial it is easy to miss the wood for the trees. In this Very Short Introduction Kenneth Minogue has brought the many dimensions of politics into a single focus: he discusses both the everyday grind of democracy and the attraction of grand ideals such as freedom and justice.

'Kenneth Minogue is a very lively stylist who does not distort difficult ideas.'
Maurice Cranston

'a dazzling but unpretentious display of great scholarship and humane reflection'
Professor Neil O'Sullivan, University of Hull

'Minogue is an admirable choice for showing us the nuts and bolts of the subject.'
Nicholas Lezard, *Guardian*

'This is a fascinating book which sketches, in a very short space, one view of the nature of politics . . . the reader is challenged, provoked and stimulated by Minogue's trenchant views.'
Talking Politics

A Very Short Introduction

ARCHAEOLOGY

Paul Bahn

'Archaeology starts, really, at the point when the first recognizable 'artefacts' appear—on current evidence, that was in East Africa about 2.5 million years ago—and stretches right up to the present day. What you threw in the garbage yesterday, no matter how useless, disgusting, or potentially embarrassing, has now become part of the recent archaeological record.'

This Very Short Introduction reflects the enduring popularity of archaeology—a subject which appeals as a pastime, career, and academic discipline, encompasses the whole globe, and surveys 2.5 million years. From deserts to jungles, from deep caves to mountain-tops, from pebble tools to satellite photographs, from excavation to abstract theory, archaeology interacts with nearly every other discipline in its attempts to reconstruct the past.

'very lively indeed and remarkably perceptive ... a quite brilliant and level-headed look at the curious world of archaeology'
Professor Barry Cunliffe,
University of Oxford

A Very Short Introduction

BUDDHISM

Damien Keown

'Karma can be either good or bad. Buddhists speak of good karma as "merit", and much effort is expended in acquiring it. Some picture it as a kind of spiritual capital—like money in a bank account—whereby credit is built up as the deposit on a heavenly rebirth.'

This Very Short Introduction introduces the reader both to the teachings of the Buddha and to the integration of Buddhism into daily life. What are the distinctive features of Buddhism? Who was the Buddha, and what are his teachings? How has Buddhist thought developed over the centuries, and how can contemporary dilemmas be faced from a Buddhist perspective?

'Damien Keown's book is a readable and wonderfully lucid introduction to one of mankind's most beautiful, profound, and compelling systems of wisdom. The rise of the East makes understanding and learning from Buddhism, a living doctrine, more urgent than ever before. Keown's impressive powers of explanation help us to come to terms with a vital contemporary reality.'
Bryan Appleyard

OXFORD

MORE OXFORD PAPERBACKS

This book is just one of nearly 1000 Oxford Paper-
backs currently in print. If you would like details of
other Oxford Paperbacks, including titles in the
World's Classics, Oxford Reference, Oxford
Books, OPUS, Past Masters, Oxford Authors, and
Oxford Shakespeare series, please write to:

UK and Europe: Oxford Paperbacks Publicity Man-
ager, Arts and Reference Publicity Department,
Oxford University Press, Walton Street, Oxford
OX2 6DP.

Customers in UK and Europe will find Oxford
Paperbacks available in all good bookshops. But in
case of difficulty please send orders to the Cash-
with-Order Department, Oxford University Press
Distribution Services, Saxon Way West, Corby,
Northants NN18 9ES. Tel: 01536 741519; Fax:
01536 746337. Please send a cheque for the total cost
of the books, plus £1.75 postage and packing for
orders under £20; £2.75 for orders over £20. Customers outside the UK should add 10% of the cost
of the books for postage and packing.

USA: Oxford Paperbacks Marketing Manager,
Oxford University Press, Inc., 200 Madison Avenue, New York, N.Y. 10016.

Canada: Trade Department, Oxford University
Press, 70 Wynford Drive, Don Mills, Ontario M3C
1J9.

Australia: Trade Marketing Manager, Oxford University Press, G.P.O. Box 2784Y, Melbourne 3001,
Victoria.

South Africa: Oxford University Press, P.O. Box
1141, Cape Town 8000.

ILLUSTRATED HISTORIES IN
OXFORD PAPERBACKS

THE OXFORD ILLUSTRATED HISTORY
OF ENGLISH LITERATURE

Edited by Pat Rogers

Britain possesses a literary heritage which is almost
unrivalled in the Western world. In this volume, the
richness, diversity, and continuity of that tradition
are explored by a group of Britain's foremost literary scholars.

Chapter by chapter the authors trace the history
of English literature, from its first stirrings in Anglo-
Saxon poetry to the present day. At its heart towers
the figure of Shakespeare, who is accorded a special
chapter to himself. Other major figures such as
Chaucer, Milton, Donne, Wordsworth, Dickens,
Eliot, and Auden are treated in depth, and the story
is brought up to date with discussion of living
authors such as Seamus Heaney and Edward Bond.

'[a] lovely volume . . . put in your thumb and pull
out plums' Michael Foot

'scholarly and enthusiastic people have written inspiring essays that induce an eagerness in their readers to return to the writers they admire' *Economist*

A Very Short Introduction

CLASSICS

Mary Beard and John Henderson

This *Very Short Introduction* to Classics links a haunting temple on a lonely mountainside to the glory of ancient Greece and the grandeur of Rome, and to Classics within modern culture—from Jefferson and Byron to Asterix and Ben-Hur.

'This little book should be in the hands of every student, and every tourist to the lands of the ancient world . . . a splendid piece of work'
Peter Wiseman
Author of *Talking to Virgil*

'an eminently readable and useful guide to many of the modern debates enlivening the field . . . the most up-to-date and accessible introduction available'
Edith Hall
Author of *Inventing the Barbarian*

'lively and up-to-date . . . it shows classics as a living enterprise, not a warehouse of relics'
New Statesman and Society

'nobody could fail to be informed and entertained—the accent of the book is provocative and stimulating'
Times Literary Supplement

A Very Short Introduction

POLITICS

Kenneth Minogue

Since politics is both complex and controversial it is easy to miss the wood for the trees. In this Very Short Introduction Kenneth Minogue has brought the many dimensions of politics into a single focus: he discusses both the everyday grind of democracy and the attraction of grand ideals such as freedom and justice.

'Kenneth Minogue is a very lively stylist who does not distort difficult ideas.'
Maurice Cranston

'a dazzling but unpretentious display of great scholarship and humane reflection'
Professor Neil O'Sullivan, University of Hull

'Minogue is an admirable choice for showing us the nuts and bolts of the subject.'
Nicholas Lezard, *Guardian*

'This is a fascinating book which sketches, in a very short space, one view of the nature of politics ... the reader is challenged, provoked and stimulated by Minogue's trenchant views.'
Talking Politics

A Very Short Introduction

ARCHAEOLOGY

Paul Bahn

'Archaeology starts, really, at the point when the first recognizable 'artefacts' appear—on current evidence, that was in East Africa about 2.5 million years ago—and stretches right up to the present day. What you threw in the garbage yesterday, no matter how useless, disgusting, or potentially embarrassing, has now become part of the recent archaeological record.'

This Very Short Introduction reflects the enduring popularity of archaeology—a subject which appeals as a pastime, career, and academic discipline, encompasses the whole globe, and surveys 2.5 million years. From deserts to jungles, from deep caves to mountain-tops, from pebble tools to satellite photographs, from excavation to abstract theory, archaeology interacts with nearly every other discipline in its attempts to reconstruct the past.

'very lively indeed and remarkably perceptive . . . a quite brilliant and level-headed look at the curious world of archaeology'
Professor Barry Cunliffe,
University of Oxford

A Very Short Introduction

BUDDHISM

Damien Keown

'Karma can be either good or bad. Buddhists speak of good karma as "merit", and much effort is expended in acquiring it. Some picture it as a kind of spiritual capital—like money in a bank account—whereby credit is built up as the deposit on a heavenly rebirth.'

This Very Short Introduction introduces the reader both to the teachings of the Buddha and to the integration of Buddhism into daily life. What are the distinctive features of Buddhism? Who was the Buddha, and what are his teachings? How has Buddhist thought developed over the centuries, and how can contemporary dilemmas be faced from a Buddhist perspective?

'Damien Keown's book is a readable and wonderfully lucid introduction to one of mankind's most beautiful, profound, and compelling systems of wisdom. The rise of the East makes understanding and learning from Buddhism, a living doctrine, more urgent than ever before. Keown's impressive powers of explanation help us to come to terms with a vital contemporary reality.'
Bryan Appleyard

A Very Short Introduction

JUDAISM

Norman Solomon

'Norman Solomon has achieved the near impossible with his enlightened very short introduction to Judaism. Since it is well known that Judaism is almost impossible to summarize, and that there are as many different opinions about Jewish matters as there are Jews, this is a small masterpiece in its success in representing various shades of Jewish opinion, often mutually contradictory. Solomon also manages to keep the reader engaged, never patronizes, assumes little knowledge but a keen mind, and takes us through Jewish life and history with such gusto that one feels enlivened, rather than exhausted, at the end.'
Rabbi Julia Neuberger

'This book will serve a very useful purpose indeed. I'll use it myself to discuss, to teach, agree with, and disagree with, in the Jewish manner!'
Rabbi Lionel Blue

'A magnificent achievement. Dr Solomon's treatment, fresh, very readable, witty and stimulating, will delight everyone interested in religion in the modern world.'
Dr Louis Jacobs, University of Lancaster

OPUS

TWENTIETH-CENTURY FRENCH PHILOSOPHY

Eric Matthews

This book gives a chronological survey of the works of the major French philosophers of the twentieth century.

Eric Matthews offers various explanations for the enduring importance of philosophy in French intellectual life and traces the developments which French philosophy has taken in the twentieth century from its roots in the thought of Descartes, with examinations of key figures such as Bergson, Sartre, Marcel, Merleau-Ponty, Foucault, and Derrida, and the recent French Feminists.

'*Twentieth-Century French Philosophy* is a clear, yet critical introduction to contemporary French Philosophy. . . . The undergraduate or other reader who comes to the area for the first time will gain a definite sense of an intellectual movement with its own questions and answers and its own rigour . . . not least of the book's virtues is its clarity.'
Garrett Barden
Author of *After Principles*